Managing Global Supply Chains

What are the key factors affecting global supply chains today and how can we manage them?

Starting from the concept that 'there is no point driving a Ferrari in a traffic jam', Ron Basu provides practical tools and techniques of good supply chain management to add value, deliver cost reduction and improve customer satisfaction.

This new edition specifically focuses on seven contemporary challenges that have affected global supply chain management. Recent disruptions to global supply chains created by Covid-19 and the Ukraine conflict have resulted in significant geographical shifts in supply and demand. High inflation and the cost of living crisis have, in turn, created problems for finely-tuned global supply chains. The economic and business environment has also become more demanding, due in part to political pressures including nationalism and Brexit: for example, supply chain pressures caused by Brexit have resulted in increased red tape. Other factors have had a gradual and positive effect, such as climate change initiatives, Industry 4.0 and the digital revolution. The issues that affect the performance of global supply chains are sometimes interrelated, but all of them really matter because businesses have become increasingly global. This book addresses these challenges and explores how to deal with them. In addition, there are new and updated chapters on lean and agile supply chains, e-business, emerging markets, sustainability and green issues, global supply chains for services and event management, retail management and major project management.

Managing Global Supply Chains is a practical and highly readable text with real-life examples and excellent coverage. It is an ideal companion for post-experience business students, learning professionals and anyone interested in supply chain management.

Ron Basu is Director of Performance Excellence Limited and a Visiting Executive Fellow at Henley Business School, University of Reading, UK. He is also a Visiting Professor at SKEMA Graduate School of Management, France.

Managing Global Supply Chains

Contemporary Global Challenges in Supply Chain Management

Third Edition

Ron Basu

Routledge
Taylor & Francis Group

LONDON AND NEW YORK

Third edition published 2023
by Routledge
4 Park Square, Milton Park, Abingdon, Oxon OX14 4RN

and by Routledge
605 Third Avenue, New York, NY 10158

Routledge is an imprint of the Taylor & Francis Group, an informa business

© 2023 Ron Basu

British Library Cataloguing-in-Publication Data
A catalogue record for this book is available from the British Library

First edition published by Routledge 2011
Second edition published by Routledge 2017

ISBN: 978-1-032-37676-9 (hbk)
ISBN: 978-1-032-37675-2 (pbk)
ISBN: 978-1-003-34135-2 (ebk)

DOI: 10.4324/9781003341352

Typeset in Bembo
by Deanta Global Publishing Services, Chennai, India

To the memory of my friend Nevan Wright

Contents

Acknowledgements

I acknowledge the knowledge and experience that I gained during my working life at Unilever and GlaxoSmithKline and also my teaching and research experience at Henley Business School, SKEMA Business School, Essex Business School and Kingston Business School.

Every effort has been made to credit the authors, publishers and websites of material used in this book. I apologise if inadvertently any sources remain unacknowledged and if known I shall be pleased to credit them in the next edition.

This book contains the outcome of teamwork with my co-author of the previous edition, Nevan Wright, and that is why I have used the word 'we' in the relevant sections of the text. Sadly, Nevan is no longer with us but his contributions remain in this edition.

I am grateful to two reviewers for their constructive comments on my proposal for this edition. I also thank Bill Jones for lively discussions related to Brexit.

My sincere thanks go to the staff of my publishers, especially to Andrew Harrison for getting this project off the ground.

Finally, the project could not have been completed without the encouragement and help of my family, especially my wife Moira, daughter Bonnie and son Robi.

About the author

Dr Ron Basu is Director of RB Consultants and a Visiting Fellow at Henley Business School, the University of Reading, UK. He was also a Visiting Professor at SKEMA Business School, France, Kingston University and Essex University. He specialises in operational excellence and supply chain management and has research interests in performance management and project management.

Previously, he held senior management roles in blue-chip companies like GSK, GlaxoWellcome and Unilever and led global initiatives and projects in Six Sigma, ERP/MRPII, Supply Chain Re-engineering and Total Productive Maintenance. Prior to this, he worked as a Management Consultant with A.T. Kearney.

He is the co-author of *Total Manufacturing Solutions*, *Quality Beyond Six Sigma*, *Total Operations Solutions* and *Total Supply Chain Management*, and the author of books with titles *Measuring e-Business Performance*, *Implementing Quality*, *Implementing Six Sigma and Lean*, *FIT SIGMA*, *Managing Project Supply Chains*, *Managing Quality in Projects*, *Managing Projects in Research and Development* and *Green Six Sigma*. He has authored a number of peer-reviewed papers in the operational excellence and project management fields. He is a regular presenter of papers in global seminars on project management, six sigma and manufacturing and supply chain topics.

After graduating in Manufacturing Engineering from UMIST, Manchester, Ron obtained an MSc in Operational Research from Strathclyde University, Glasgow. He has also completed a PhD at Reading University. He is a Fellow of the Institution of Mechanical Engineers, the Institute of Business Consultancy, the Association for Project Management and the Chartered Quality Institute. He is also the winner of the APM Project Management Award.

Ron lives with his wife Moira in Gerrards Cross, England, and has two children, Bonnie and Robi and four grandchildren.

Preface

Background

Supply chain management has become more global and, in particular, the service sector and major infrastructure projects are embedding both the challenges and opportunities of global supply chains. Since the publication of the first edition, the new challenges of global outsourcing, the growing impact of the service sector, emerging markets, the digital revolution (especially mobile technology) and green supply chains have matured and added more complexities. Since 2019, global supply chains have been experiencing additional challenges due to the impact of the Covid-19 pandemic, the war in Ukraine, de-globalisation by nationalism (e.g. Brexit) and the climate change crisis. The focus of supply chain management has also shifted from cost reduction to improved customer satisfaction, digitalisation, sustainability and connectivity.

This new edition, *Managing Global Supply Chains,* aims to retain or update the fundamentals of holistic approach and tools and processes of supply chain management presented in *Total Supply Chain Management* with in-depth analyses of the impact of contemporary challenges, such as the Covid-19 pandemic, Brexit and the war in Ukraine. Furthermore, the enhanced edition will add new chapters with more emphasis on managing new technology and sustainability, managing globalisation and managing project supply chains.

About this book

This book is aimed at a broad cross-section of readership, including:

- Logistics managers, procurement managers and production managers and planners dealing with day-to-day practical aspects of global supply chains.
- Project managers and leaders who aspire to make a difference in global infrastructure projects dealing with multinational and multi-tier suppliers.
- The members of professional bodies will find this book as a total approach to global supply chain management and managing major project topics that are underpinned by this book.
- Senior executives, both in government and infrastructure projects, will find that this book will give them a better understanding of basic concepts of global supply chain management strategy and sustain a strong competitive position.
- Professional management and training consultants will find a comprehensive approach to global supply chain management-related assignments and seminars.
- Management schools and academies and research associations will find this book valuable to fill the visible gap in the fundamentals of global supply chain management.

Application

The book allows for maximum flexibility for readers and users to apply it depending on their requirements and interests. The application areas of the book include:

Implementing global supply chain management

Organisations, whether services or manufacturing, private or public sectors, large, medium or small, should particularly benefit from the practical approaches to implementing the holistic processes of supply chain building blocks. The strategic planners and supply chain management task groups should acquire a copy of the book and gain a common understanding of the tools and techniques described in this book.

University and college courses

The book can be as a textbook or a reference book for advanced programmes in operations management and supply chain management in universities and business schools. The descriptive questions in each chapter and exercises in Chapter 18 and also the case studies with questions in Chapter 24 should give students the chance to practice and assess their level of understanding achieved from the relevant chapters. The tutors will have the opportunity of applying these case studies as part of their lecture materials and course contents.

Enhancing knowledge

The book contains both the strategic approach to managing global supply chains and detailed coverage of tools and techniques that underpin the planning and operations of supply chain management. The reader, whether a CEO, employee or student, should find the book as self-help in enhancing the knowledge and understanding of the challenges of managing global supply chains.

I hope you find this book both stimulating and exciting as I have found researching and writing it.

Ron Basu
Gerrards Cross, England

Part 1

Introduction

1 The role of the supply chain as a key value driver in the global market

Introduction

In this chapter, the basic concepts of supply chain management are explained. It has been shown that supply chains in some shape or form are required to deliver products and services. Since earliest recorded times, the trading of goods and materials between regions and states has resulted from the combined activities of many individuals, governments and the global community. The development of societies, cultures and history and mere chance led to specific characteristics of countries and regions. The differences in characteristics have become less distinct for a variety of reasons. Since 1945 there have been revolutionary changes in the modes of transport and logistics (containerisation, 100,000-ton bulk carriers now the norm, pipelines between and through nations, long-range air freight, freight consolidation), the means of production (robotics, automation, new materials that are lighter and stronger), communication (the world wide web, e-mail, e-business, social media), integration and the means to foster integration (Enterprise resources planning (ERP) systems and variants such as SAP, barcoding, RFID), free trade and the easing of economic blocs (European Union, free trade agreements between groups of nations such as the newly formed Trans-Pacific Partnership Arrangement, the emergence of the People's Republic of China as the second single biggest economy after the United States, the dissolution of the Soviet Union and the fall of the Berlin wall) and social conscience (the green movement, awareness of climate change, human rights and fair trade), all leading to a truly global market place.

Within every market, there are exchanges of goods and services, and for each transaction, there is a supplier and a customer and there are activities, facilities and processes linking the supplier to the customer. Supply chain management is the process of balancing these links to deliver the best value to the customer at minimum cost and effort for the supplier. Simplistically, each of us experiences and benefits from supply chains several times a day, for example, running your home, managing a manufacturing business, health services, hotels, banks, government, utilities, non-profit organisations, sports clubs, universities, entertainment, retail, professional services and so on.

Supply chains vary significantly in complexity and size, but the fundamental principles apply to all operations whether they be large or small, manufacturing or service, private or public. Supply chain management is not limited to big-name businesses such as Apple Inc, Walmart, Toyota or Royal Dutch Shell. It is for all businesses and operations, and the basic functions of forecasting, capacity management, staffing, inventory management, scheduling quality management and service are present no matter how small the operation.

DOI: 10.4324/9781003341352-2

Learning objectives

1. What is supply chain management?
2. Supply chain in manufacturing, services and non-profit organisations.
3. Logistics in Supply chain management.
4. New technology and the e-supply chain.
5. How do we deliver value in supply chains?
6. Contemporary global challenges in supply chain management.

What is supply chain management?

In a typical supply chain, raw materials are procured (some local and some imported) and items are produced at one or more factories, transported to warehouses for intermediate storage and then transported locally and internationally to retailers or customers. Production will require energy: gas, petrol and electricity, which will often be provided by global companies. Gone are the days of a country being self-sufficient by mining its own coal for steam-driven factories. In the UK, a new nuclear power station is to be built with the People's Republic of China taking a one-third stake in a French-led project. This is more than just providing the finance, China will be involved in the design and providing technological knowledge.

If you asked people involved in business to define the term supply chain, you would get many different answers. Each definition would reflect the nature of the business and the inputs and outputs produced. For some, the supply chain is related to purchasing and procurement, to others, it is warehousing, distribution and transportation. Yet, for others, it is a source of capital and labour.

Melnyk and Swink (2002) see the supply chain 'as a product cradle-to-grave concept, including all value-added activities required to plan, source, make and deliver products and services that meet customer needs'. This definition in a few short years appears to be very dated... very much last century!

Supply chain management (SCM), as defined in the APICS Dictionary by Blackstone (2013), is the 'design, planning, execution, control and monitoring of supply chain activities with the objective of creating net value, building a competitive infrastructure, leveraging worldwide logistics, synchronizing supply with demand and measuring performance globally'.

The global nature of a supply chain and the integration provided by information technology cannot be ignored. For example, in New Zealand, I had problems connecting my e-mail to a new laptop. I phoned a help desk and realised that the very pleasant and patient person I was talking to did not have a typical New Zealand accent. When asked, she happily informed me that she was in the Philippines. After about 20 minutes, my new Filipino friend said she could not solve our problem and connected me to a specialist. The specialist was a man with a very different accent. He took over and talked me through the steps to be taken to solve the problem which took less than five minutes. I asked where he was, he said California and proved it by telling me to have a nice day.

To be cost effective across the whole global supply chain requires a system-wide approach to optimisation. In short, supply chain management must consider every organisation and facility and every step involved in making the product and the costs involved in doing so.

The objective is to make the entire chain efficient and not just one element. The final objective is to deliver at the end of the supply chain a product or service to the satisfaction of the end user.

To be cost effective across the whole global supply chain, a system-wide approach to optimisation is required.

The supply chain in manufacturing

Supply chain management in a manufacturing and supply organisation considers demand, supply and inventory needs for each item of production and in particular looks at how inventory flows through the system to achieve output to the customer's specification on time and at least cost. With supply chain management, customer service is increased through the reduction of lead times and the product is always exactly as specified and always delivered on time. In Chapter 23, we describe this as the delivery of a 'perfect order'. Costs are reduced through the elimination of any activity that does not add value and the reduction of inventories of material and associated holding and handling costs.

Activities and measures based on customer requirements, as explained in Chapter 4, are very important in improving business performance. But externally driven customer-based measures have to be matched by measures of what the company can do (feasibility, capacity, know-how and resources) to consistently meet customer expectations. A high standard of customer performance derives from planning, processes and actions integrated across the whole organisation.

Supply chain management focuses on the critical measures of all elements of the supply chain. Externally, the measures include the suppliers at one end and the customer at the other end of the supply process. These externals, the supplier and the customer, are matched with the internal requirements of the manufacturing process. The focus is two-fold; to satisfy customer needs and keep costs to a minimum.

In reality, the elements of supply chain management are not new — we all have been managing parts of the supply chain for years (e.g. buying, planning, scheduling, stock control, warehousing, logistics, distribution) without realising the significance of the whole chain concept. Likewise, the cost of the various elements of supply and distribution has been long recognised. 'In 50 years between 1870 and 1920 the cost of distributing necessities and luxuries has nearly trebled, while production costs have gone down by one fifth — what we are saving in production we are losing in distribution' (Ralph Barsodi, 1929).

It is relatively new to view the supply chain as a process — a single integrated flow across all the functions of the business. Traditionally, activities within a supply chain were seen as separate and with specialist functions such as purchasing, planning, scheduling, manufacturing and distribution. With supply chain management, the flow of materials and information across traditional functional boundaries is seen as a single process. These flows are depicted in a simplified model in Figure 1.1.

In the past, information flow was the domain of the commercial division while the conversion process of materials flow was a manufacturing or technical division responsibility. With an integrated supply chain approach, the responsibility for all elements of supply is now with operations management or supply chain management. In many businesses, the integrated approach is being extended to include all suppliers (including 'upstream' first-, second- and third-tier suppliers) through the manufacturing process and 'downstream' to each level of customer (including distributors, wholesalers and retailers out to the end user or consumer). This is known as the extended supply chain.

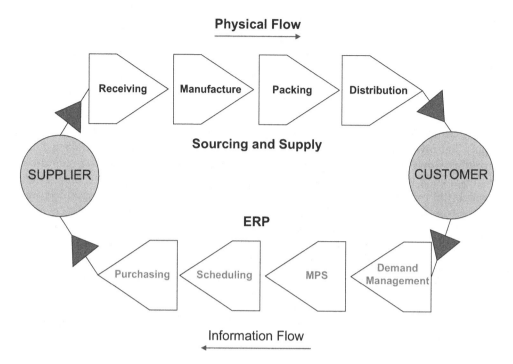

Figure 1.1 Supply chain management

The supply chain in services

Thanks to the ease of travel, the media and 'worldwide web' customers have never been more informed than they are today. Customers know what they want and know what can be done; they understand the concept of world-class and continuous improvement. This is especially true in service industries. As a result of the heightened expectations of customers, operations managers in service sectors have been forced to focus their attention on managing the complete value-adding system using the principles of supply chain management.

But how can service industries apply supply chain management? The supply chain of a service organisation contains suppliers, products or services and customers and their demand for products and service level agreements. Service inventory can be in the form of information databases, stocks of consumables (as with the hotdog stand), stationery items (including brochures and promotional material), energy and other infrastructure suppliers and subcontractors (including facility managers, travel agents, caterers, accountants, lawyers and advertising agencies).

Swank (2003) described a successful application of supply chain management and lean production principles in a typical insurance service company in the United States, Jefferson Pilot Financial (JPF). JPF believed that the processing of their almost tangible 'service product' was comparable to a car assembly process. Swank explains as follows:

> Like an automobile on the assembly line, an insurance policy goes through a series of processes, from initial application to underwriting or risk assessment to policy

issuance. With each step value is added to the work in progress – just as a car gets doors or a coat of paint.

The supply chain in not-for-profit organisations

The good practices of supply chain management can be adapted to provide major practical benefits to not-for-profit organisations, such as charity organisations, in meeting their objectives. International disasters have a huge impact on the world's population, increasing the need for aid organisations to improve their logistics capability and capacity. Perhaps the biggest impact of supply chain management in not-for-profit organisations is responding to unpredictable demands through quick response supply and distribution.

Since 2005, humanitarian organisations have become more adept at using supply chain optimisation. Lessons were learnt from the Hurricane Katrina disaster in New Orleans. Waller (2005) said that he was not surprised that Walmart, the world's largest retailer, beat the Federal Emergency Management Agency (FEMA) and the Red Cross to areas devastated by the hurricane. He found that Walmart delivered supplies quickly and efficiently because that's what it does every day. Walmart is the master of supply chain management and the company's expertise in this area worked well during a natural disaster. How Walmart was able to do this is further explained in Chapter 10.

An example of the application of global supply chain management in a not-for-profit organisation is the National Health Service in the UK (see the case study).

CASE STUDY: DHL AND THE NHS

The NHS in the UK was spending £15 billion annually on the procurement of goods and services. It was determined that there was enormous potential for NHS organisations to save money through effective purchasing. As a result, the NHS Purchasing and Supply Agency (PASA) was established in 2000 as a part of the government's modernisation of NHS procurement activities to act as a strategic adviser to the NHS on all supply issues. The primary goal of PASA was to improve the performance of the NHS purchasing and supply system and to become the centre of expertise, knowledge and excellence in purchasing and supply matters of the NHS for the benefit of patients and the public.

Some of the achievements of PASA included:

- Savings for the NHS totalling £580 million over the three-year period of April 2000–2003.
- Implemented pilot supply 'confederations' as recommended in the May 2002 policy document 'Modernising Supply in the NHS' to develop a middle tier between national (PASA) and local (individual NHS trust) level purchasing.
- Produced an eCommerce strategy for the NHS through the development of an eProcurement toolkit to provide a framework to help NHS trusts and confederations understand the benefits of eProcurement and plan its implementation in a structured way.
- Developed a national set of purchasing and supply performance management measures to better assess the performance of NHS trusts with respect to supply

chain activities through benchmarking analysis and strategic assessment of trust and confederation spending.

Source: National Health Service, UK (2004)

Laudable though these achievements were, there is always room for improvement. In 2006, the NHS entered into a joint venture with DHL and the PASA was phased out. DHL is a German-owned logistics company and was initially charged with handling an annual NHS spend of US$5 billion with a target of US$1 billion over ten years. In 2015, the contract was extended by two years to 2018 with a further targeted savings of US$300 million. DHL provides end-to-end purchasing and logistics working with the NHS supply chain service.

What about logistics management?

Is there a difference between 'logistics' and 'supply chain' management? In 2004, the Council of Logistics Management recognising that logistics management is part of the supply chain process changed its name to the Council of Supply Chain Management Professionals. Prior to the change of name, they defined logistics management as follows:

The process of planning, implementing and controlling the efficient, cost effective flow and storage of raw materials, in-process inventory, finished goods, and related information from point of origin to point of consumption for the purpose of conforming to customer requirements.

The new definition is as follows:

Supply chain management encompasses the planning and management of all activities involved in sourcing and procurement, conversion, and all logistics management activities. Importantly, it also includes coordination and collaboration with channel partners, which can be suppliers, intermediaries, third party service providers, and customers. In essence, supply chain management integrates supply and demand management within and across companies.

Council of Supply Chain Management Professionals (2015)

If we consider these definitions, we see they are very similar to the APICS Dictionary definition we gave earlier and can conclude that for our purposes in a manufacturing and supply organisation, logistics and supply chain management are synonymous. If one is inclined to separate the physical movement of logistics in a service organisation, we can see that there is but a fine border between logistics and supply chain management in the service sector.

Taylor (1997) divided supply chain management into:

*   Logistics and supply chain strategy.
*   Purchasing and supplies management.
*   Manufacturing logistics.
*   Distribution planning and strategy.
*   Warehouse planning and operations management.
*   Inventory management.
*   Transport management.
*   International logistics and international market entry strategies.

Taylor's definition infers that 'Logistics' is a subset of 'SCM'. Each subtopic contributes to the performance of the overall supply chain process and, as a consequence, to improved stakeholder satisfaction.

What are inbound and outbound logistics?

The flow of information and physical goods from both customers and suppliers to the business or the conversion centre (e.g. a factory or a warehouse or an office) is termed inbound logistics. Likewise, the flow of information or goods or service from the conversion centre to the customer constitutes outbound logistics. To put it more simply, inbound logistics relate to demand and procurement while outbound logistics relate to supply and service.

Figures 1.2 and 1.3 show examples of inbound and outbound logistics in a food factory.

Demand and supply planning capabilities enable companies to balance inbound and outbound logistics and thus maximise return on assets and ensure a profitable match of supply and demand. Inbound and outbound logistics are also described, as upstream and downstream processes. For example, Christopher (1992) defines supply chain management as the management of upstream and downstream relationships with suppliers and customers to deliver superior customer value at less cost to the supply chain as a whole.

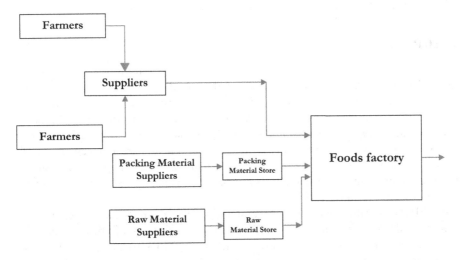

Figure 1.2 Inbound logistics

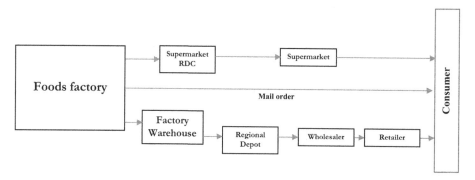

Figure 1.3 Outbound logistics

New technology and the e-supply chain

As shown in Figure 1.1, the traditional supply chain was concerned with a linear flow of information and products/services from customers to suppliers through various stages of processes, while the information flow was the domain of the commercial division and the conversion process of materials flow was a manufacturing or technical division responsibility. During the 1990s, the concept of total supply chain management shifted the responsibility for all elements of supply to operations management or supply chain management.

According to Basu (2002), the Internet-enabled integrated supply chain or e-supply chain has extended the linear flow of the supply chain to an Ecosystem or a supply web (see Figure 1.4). It now includes all suppliers and customers to the end user or consumer suppliers' customers and customers' suppliers and so on. The front runners of this collaborative business model were Dell and Toyota, who aimed to source materials and produce products in response to customer demand with the objective of minimising both factory inventory and dealer inventory. This collaborative approach enables these companies to manage relationships between customers, suppliers and multidisciplinary company functions with a sharing of transparent information and knowledge exchange.

What is ERP?

The business objective is to convert customer demand by optimising the utilisation of resources to deliver effective customer service applies to all organisations regardless of whether they are in manufacturing or service sectors. Enterprise resources planning (ERP) systems provide a single up-to-date database incorporating manufacturing, finance and human resource applications extended to include tracking of orders and inwards goods, work in progress and delivery of finished goods. The system is accessible to all departments for planning and execution of supply chain activities. Thus, ERP systems integrate (or attempt to integrate) all data and processes of an organisation into a single unified system to achieve integration.

The term ERP originally implied systems designed to plan the utilisation of enterprise-wide resources. Although the acronym ERP originated in the manufacturing environment as a successor to manufacturing resources planning (MRPII), today's use of the term ERP systems has a much broader scope. ERP systems typically attempt to cover all basic

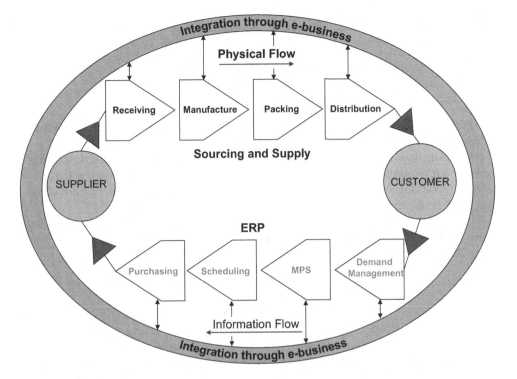

Figure 1.4 e-Supply chain or e-web

functions of an organisation, regardless of the organisation's business or charter. Businesses, not-for-profit organisations, governments and other large entities utilise ERP systems.

How do you balance the voice of customer and voice of business in supply chain management?

In any business or operation, a manager has to find a balance between two conflicting objectives of demand from customers and supply from operations. The voice of customer (VOC) is articulated as customer service. Customer service is the primary objective of supply chain management. However, customer service has to be sustainable and balanced with efficient use of resources. The secondary objective of supply chain management is to reduce costs and make effective use of resources. For simplicity, three key parameters of customer service are considered. These are specification, cost (or price) and timing. The customer expects the goods or service to be delivered according to acceptable standards, affordable and to arrive on time. The relative importance of specification, cost and time could change depending on the market condition, competition and the desirability of demand. The second objective, to efficiently utilise resources to meet customer service requirements is the voice of business (VOB). Given infinite resources, any system can provide adequate customer service, but many companies have gone out of business in spite of possessing satisfied customers (Wild, 2003; Basu, 2004). To provide a sustained and sustainable level of customer service efficiently, the use of resources is essential. A starting point for balancing VOC and VOB is resource utilisation and customer service

Table 1.1 Operations objectives chart

	Resource utilisation			Customer service		
	Machines	Materials	Labour	Specification	Cost	Time
Operation						

(RU/CS) analysis, which aims to determine gaps between what is desired and what is feasible (Basu, 2004)

RU/CS analysis is a simple tool to establish the relative importance of the key parameters of both resource utilisation and customer service and to identify their conflicts.

Wild (2003) suggests the starting point of the RU/CS analysis is the operations objectives chart as shown in Table 1.1.

The relative importance of the key parameters for RU (i.e. machines, materials and labour) and CS (i.e. specification, cost and time) can be given a rating of one, two or three (three being the most important).

Consider a mail order company where customers are expecting good value for money and do not mind receiving goods from catalogues within a reasonable delivery time. The operation manager has focused on the utilisation of their own resources to minimise operational costs.

Figure 1.5 shows the ratings of objectives, the actual performance and highlights the misalignment. It is evident that further examination is required for timing and material.

As shown in Figure 1.6, there is a conflict between cost and materials and further attention or a change of policy is required to resolve this conflict.

	Machinery/Space	People	Materials
Utilisation Objectives	3	3	1
Actual Utilisation	3	3	2
Alignment	✔	✔	✚

1=low, 2=medium, 3=high

	Specification	Cost	Timing
Customer Service Objectives	1	3	2
Actual Level of Service	2	3	1
Alignment	✚	✔	✚

✔ Good

✚ Issues to look at

Figure 1.5 The balance of objectives: mail order company

	Machinery/Space	People	Materials
3 High Relative Importance	3	3	1

	Specification	Cost	Timing
1 Low Relative Importance	1	3	2

	Machinery/Space	People	Materials
Specification			
Cost			✚
Timing			

Figure 1.6 RU/CS conflicts in a mail order company

When we study the apparently conflicting objectives of RU and CS, we realise that they have one thing in common, which is cost and price. If we can reduce the cost of production of goods or services down by improving resource utilisation, then we are in a better position to reduce the price to the customer.

RU/CS analysis does not provide solutions to the conflicts but identifies broad areas for attention. It is also important to note that the relative priorities of RU and CS can vary within the same business depending on the product and customer. To find solutions, the supply chain manager will seek other tools, techniques and processes of supply chain management that we shall explain in later chapters. One such process is ERP.

How do you deliver value in supply chain management?

The delivery of goods and services of expected standards on time at the 'best in class' cost is creating value for money for customers and thus adding value to the business. An effective supply chain management team can deliver value through a value stream approach or a total supply chain management approach.

The value stream approach transcends the traditional manner of departmentalising stages of the business process. The value stream highlights the importance of the operations manager being involved in all aspects of the process, from suppliers right through to the customer and, if possible, the customer's customer. The 'old' approach was that one department or function would be responsible for purchasing goods and services, and another for planning. Scheduling of activities was often a separate function, as was warehousing and distribution, and operations were just one step in the whole process of providing services. With the value stream approach, functional boundaries are ignored, and in many organisations, it is now accepted that the operations manager has to control the total process from purchasing input goods and services to the final stage of satisfying the customer. Marketing, accounting, human resources and other support functions do not show up on the value stream as such, but operations managers must be vitally interested and involved in these internal functions of the organisation.

If we include all business activities from research and development to sales and services, then supply chains can be called value chains. The economy has become more integrated by unbundling financial services into discrete tasks that can be accomplished online from different locations of the world.

The value stream approach in the supply chain aligns well with Porter's value chain as shown in Figure 1.7. The idea of the value chain is based on the process view of

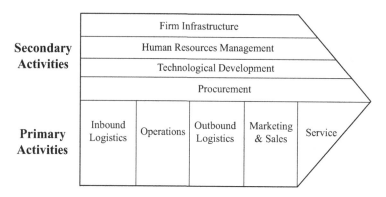

Figure 1.7 Porter's value chain

organisations, the idea of seeing a manufacturing (or service) organisation as a system, made up of subsystems each with inputs, transformation processes and outputs. How value chain activities are carried out determines costs and affects profits.

Most organisations engage in hundreds, even thousands, of activities in the process of converting inputs to outputs. These activities can be classified generally as either primary or support activities that all businesses must undertake in some form.

According to Porter (1985), the primary activities are:

1. *Inbound logistics* involve relationships with suppliers and include all the activities required to receive, store and disseminate inputs.
2. *Operations* are all the activities required to transform inputs into outputs (products and services).
3. *Outbound logistics* include all the activities required to collect, store and distribute the output.
4. *Marketing and sales* activities inform buyers about products and services, induce buyers to purchase them and facilitate their purchase.
5. *Service* includes all the activities required to keep the product or service working effectively for the buyer after it is sold and delivered.

Secondary activities are:

1. *Procurement* is the acquisition of inputs, or resources, for the firm.
2. *Human resource management* consists of all activities involved in recruiting, hiring, training, developing, compensating and (if necessary) dismissing or laying off personnel.
3. *Technological development* pertains to the equipment, hardware, software, procedures and technical knowledge brought to bear in the firm's transformation of inputs into outputs.
4. *Infrastructure* serves the company's needs and ties its various parts together. It consists of functions or departments such as accounting, legal, finance, planning, public affairs, government relations, quality assurance and general management.

The success of a supply chain could be synonymous with the success of the value stream approach or the total supply chain approach underpinned by the interaction between three key groups of players, viz. customers, external suppliers and the departments involved with the primary and secondary activities of the organisation.

The customer is the central focus of any organisation. Churchill once said that war is too important to be left to the generals, and the same can be said of marketing. Marketing is too important to be left to the marketing department. Everyone in an organisation should be vitally interested in marketing the organisation. Nonetheless, it is the function of the marketing department to *know* what the customer wants and what the competition is doing or is likely to do. Marketing specifies the product and its attributes. Attributes may range from the essential down to the desirable and perhaps include extras that the customer does not even know they want. As well as defining the product or service to be offered, marketing has to establish the price, forecast demand, have a say in how the product or service will be distributed or delivered and be responsible for promotion with the aim of stimulating demand. Marketing also has to sell the product/service internally within the organisation to the operations and other functions of the organisation. Marketing is the link between the market and customers and operations.

In some organisations, suppliers are treated with distrust, and the business strategy adopted is to shop around and get the best deal on each occasion. In these types of organisations, information is not shared with suppliers. When orders are placed, the supplier is not told what the purpose of the order is, and thus are not in a position to advise, even if they were so inclined, of alternative products or new technology. With this approach, little loyalty is shown to any supplier and the supplier is almost treated as an adversary. The value stream approach is to treat key suppliers of goods and services as part of the team and share information and seek advice. Key suppliers are those that are important to the smooth operation of the system. In some cases, the supplier can become involved in the day-to-day operations of the organisation and might also be expected to advise and assist in product development. Cost no longer becomes the key issue. Instead of price alone, suppliers will be judged on their loyalty and ability to deliver goods and services to the required standard and on time. Suppliers can also become part of the information-gathering arm of the organisation; often suppliers have a different perspective on what the competition is up to (changes in buying patterns, timetables, new packaging, use of new materials and so on). Suppliers are also in a good position to offer technical advice regarding new technology and alternative materials.

Communication between departments (especially marketing, operations and logistics) within an organisation has to be two-way and be aimed to help rather than as a means of apportioning blame or criticising. With traditional hierarchical organisations, a bunker or silo mentality can develop whereby each function is walled off from the other, and any suggestion, no matter how helpful, is taken as a threat or challenge. World-class organisations are noted by the manner in which the figurative brick walls that separate functions have been broken down, and teamwork exists between all functions to achieve the common goal. This requires that everyone in the organisation knows what the goals and objectives are and that the culture is conducive to the enthusiastic pursuit of the goals for the common good of the whole, rather than for the specific interests of one department. Information is open to all and there are no secrets.

Contemporary global challenges in supply chain management

The past four years have exposed major vulnerabilities in the global supply chain. For many companies, the pressure from the Covid-19 pandemic stretched logistics to their limits, revealing inefficiencies and areas for improvement. These existing weaknesses are being compounded by new supply chain challenges and changing market conditions. Here are seven of the most important emerging challenges for global supply chains.

1. *Impact of Covid-19*. Since the outbreak of Covid-19 in China at the end of 2019, more than 210 countries and territories have reported the outbreak and as of 9 May 2022, over 521 million people were infected, resulting in at least 6.3 million deaths (Statistica, 2022). The threats of the global pandemic aroused worldwide concern for the immediate damage to global supply chains. The short-term impact is a human resources bottleneck.

2. *Economic nationalism*. Economic nationalism and political populism are interrelated. A recent example of this in the United States is the election of Donald Trump, running his campaign around the 'America first' slogan and blocking southern immigration. Indeed, it was seen that Trump's victory through such assured and bold moves has sparked populism in other nations. Brexit in the UK is also an example of political populism. Political populism encourages de-globalisation.

3. *Impact of Brexit in the UK*. Following a referendum in 2016, the UK left the European Union on 31 December 2020: out of its political and legal structures, its single market and its customs union. This is popularly known as the Brexit deal. The impact of Brexit on the global supply chain is also significant. Brexit made the shortages hitting the UK economy worse compared with the rest of the world the government's spending watchdog has said.

4. *Impact of Ukraine conflict*. Global supply chains were once again being tested by the so-called 'special military operations' in Ukraine by Russia in February 2022. The impact was almost immediate on the supply of foods and fossil fuels. Europe exposed its vulnerabilities in its over-dependence on natural gas and crude oil from Russia and key agricultural commodities from Russia and Ukraine.

5. *Impact of climate change*. What is beyond dispute is that the Earth's temperature is rising, and even growth of 2°C would melt the ice sheets of the polar regions, resulting in a sea level increase of many metres. The pressure of climate change on businesses and global supply chains has become more dominant since the final outcome of the Glasgow Climate Pact document at the COP26 conference in November 2021.

6. *Impact of Industry 4.0*. Industry 4.0 is the transition of the fourth industrial revolution in industry. The first industrial revolution started through steam power and then evolved to the second with mass production and assembly lines using electricity. Then came the third revolution with the adoption of computers and automation. Now we are in the fourth revolution in industry (Industry 4.0) powered by big data, cloud computing, blockchain, IoT, AI and machine learning.

7. *Impact of the digital revolution*. As part of Industry 4.0, global supply chains are benefiting from a digital revolution. The most significant application in supply chain management has been demand forecasting. In the ERP systems of supply chains (such as SAP), the blockchain feature allows users of cloud platforms (such as SaaS) to extend and build applications with blockchain technology and unlock new functionalities into the blockchain ecosystem. Big data and analytics use data and quantitative methods in the supply chain to improve decision making for all activities across the supply chain.

The impact of contemporary challenges is discussed in more detail in Chapter 4 and also covered throughout this book where appropriate.

Summary

The primary purpose of this introductory chapter was to provide an overview of supply chain management principles and indicate how an effective supply chain management process adds value to all types of businesses, whether in manufacturing or service sectors, or public and not-for-profit organisations. It also aims to initiate the understanding of some core concepts of the book including 'it is people, not processes or technology, that makes things happen'. It is critical to have data sharing and interaction between all stakeholders in the total supply chain using a value stream 'total global supply chain' approach.

Of all the contemporary challenges on global supply chains, the digital revolution has had a positive impact that can be utilised to combat and mitigate other challenges.

Discussion questions

1. Simchi-Levi et al. (2003) use the word integration in their definition of the supply chain. What do you understand this to mean?
2. How would you define supply chain management? Is it a concept, process or combination of processes? What are the key objectives of supply chain management?
3. Explain how the role and importance of supply chain management have changed with the additional challenges and opportunities of globalisation. Is global supply chain management different from traditional supply chain management?
4. It is often considered that integrated logistics management is synonymous with supply chain management. Discuss.
5. What are the similarities and differences between the supply chain management processes in manufacturing and services? Is supply chain management appropriate for a non-profit organisation?
6. Explain the key components of Porter's value chain. Discuss how a value chain differs from a supply chain.
7. If each component of a supply chain from the farmer sowing seeds to the retailer selling bread is efficient, will the whole supply chain be efficient?
8. Of the seven contemporary challenges, which ones can be converted into opportunities for global supply chains?

Exercise

1. Consider yourself a customer of a fast food restaurant such as McDonald's. Following the example of RU/CS analysis in this chapter, address the following exercise.

Briefly describe the 'operation'.

Develop an IPO (input, process, output) diagram.

What are the present objectives (RU/CS) for the chosen operation? Highlight the relative importance on a scale of 1–3 (3 as the most important). Identify the conflict between the components of RU and CS

2 Why global supply chain management is also total supply chain management

Introduction

In Chapter 1, we established the key role of supply chain management in the global market and how it is critical to have interaction between stakeholders in the total supply chain. In this chapter, we intend to expand further on why the total supply chain approach is vital in managing global supply chains. Globalisation has created not only great opportunities for global supply chains but also has introduced a high level of complexity and risks. If we cannot work in harmony at the same flow rate, and only achieving a high-performance level in a manufacturing site, then this is akin to driving a high-performance Ferrari in a traffic jam.

In the 1960s and 1970s, the manufacturing and supply strategy of multinational companies focused on vertical integration. One of the earliest, largest and most famous examples of vertical integration was the Carnegie Steel Company. In the 1890s, the company expanded to have a controlling interest beyond the mills where the steel was manufactured to include the mines from where the iron ore was extracted, the coal mines that supplied the coal, the barges and ships that transported the iron ore, the railroads that transported the coal to the factory, the coke ovens where the coal was coked and so on. One hundred years on vertical integration was still in vogue, for example, in the 1980s, Unilever, originally a soap manufacturer, had grown to own businesses and investments in forests, timber milling and refining, paper manufacture, board and plastics manufacture, chemicals, fast-moving consumer products manufacture and packaging, marketing and advertising, computer services, distribution warehouses, shipping and retail outlets. Vertical integration of a supply chain was not always successful.

In the 1980s (and subsequently), large organisations started to concentrate on their 'core business' and rather than vertically integrate began divesting non-core arms of the business. The gradual privatisation of the public sector also helped to create many supporting service industries. At the beginning of the 21st century, we are witnessing the explosion of outsourcing and the emergence of competent but lower-cost manufacturing in Eastern Europe, China and other states in Southeast Asia, India and South America (in particular Brazil). It is now recognised that in the global marketplace a systems supply/value chain approach has to be taken that embraces service and manufacturing as a whole. This chapter describes a total supply chain management concept and the analysis of the supply chain process. Management of the activities making up a supply chain is described in later chapters.

DOI: 10.4324/9781003341352-3

Learning objectives

Learning objectives for this chapter are as follows:

1. Trend towards services.
2. Shift from enterprise to network.
3. Increased complexity of processes.
4. Why total supply chain management?
5. Value chain and value stream.

Trend towards services

In the UK, statistics show that 78% of the workforce is engaged in service industries (www.statistics.gov.uk), and in the United States, 80% are employed in service industries (www.census/gov/). Although a shift back to manufacturing has been identified (Basu and Wright, 1997), it is obvious that a greater percentage of the workforce of developed nations will continue to be employed in service activities. There are two reasons for this:

1. Continual advances in technology mean that manufacturing is considerably less labour intensive than previously. Automation, robotics, advanced information technology, new materials and improved work methods all have led to the reduction of manual labour.
2. For larger organisations, manufacturing has become internationalised. For example, a company (such as Nike) might outsource its manufacturing to overseas contractors or allied companies and concentrate on design, marketing and distribution itself.

Additionally, organisations can no longer regard themselves as being purely in manufacturing and hope to survive. The market first and foremost now takes for granted the reliability of the product and expects good service.

Market expectations of the level of quality are driven by perceptions of what technology is promising and what the competition is offering. Organisations now operate in a global market where national barriers, tariffs and customs duties no longer provide protection for a home market. Any manufacturer, even if the focus has been on supplying a local market, is in reality competing on the world stage. Competition is no longer limited to other local organisations, and the fiercest competition in the home market will be from goods and even services produced overseas or provided by overseas organisations. For example, a bus service in New Zealand is owned and operated by the Scottish company 'Stagecoach' based 20,000 km away. And McDonald's for over 30 years has competed and indeed set the benchmark for fast food providers all around the world.

This overseas involvement in a home market means that manufacturers (and service providers) can no longer make products just to suit their engineering strengths but must now be aware of what the market wants and what global competition is offering. In manufacturing, what the competition is offering, apart from well-engineered products, is service in the form of delivery on time, marketing advice, training, installation, project management or whatever else is required to provide a total service as well as a reliable product.

Never before has the customer been better travelled, more informed and had higher expectations. Many of these expectations began with the quality movement of the 1980s where it was trumpeted that the customer was king, and these expectations have been kept alive by continuously improved product and services, global advertising, and for the last decade, the World Wide Web.

If they are honest with themselves, most organisations realise that their products actually differ very little from those of their competitors, and any technological improvement is soon copied, thus, the difference – the 'competitive edge' – comes from service.

There are many examples of successful application of supply chain management principles in the service sector which accounts for over 80% of the economy in advanced countries. The success of American Express is one such example.

CASE EXAMPLE: AMERICAN EXPRESS' SUCCESS IN GLOBAL SUPPLY CHAIN MANAGEMENT

As a global organisation, American Express is arguably a leader in the service sector, benefiting from the successful implementation of total supply chain principles. For example, American Express has introduced two new corporate purchasing services as part of its S2S (Source-to-Settle) product suite. Both S2S Catalog Pro and S2S Contract Audit Recovery are intended to help companies optimise performance, realise savings and minimise non-compliance within their supply chains. Contract Audit and Recovery, in particular, is an analytic service that provides best practices to help companies achieve negotiated contract savings and recover money lost through non-compliance. Following an analysis of contracts, billing data and business processes allow for the development of an action plan by the audit and recovery team, who can also advise on best practices for addressing future contract situations. Catalog Pro is an online service that integrates with a company's existing procurement software to enhance business-to-consumer (B2C) features. The product improves the ability of employees to order from preferred suppliers and secure negotiated rates. Catalog Pro was originally a B2C application that was acquired by American Express, which added business-to-business functionality.

As a recognition of its supply chain success, American Express has been successfully recertified for the Corporate Certification Standard. Maggie Willis, Vice President of International Global Supply Management at American Express, said the process provided the company with an opportunity to reassess its policies to ensure that American Express remains at the forefront of best business practices.

Service separated from production operations

If no serious operation can ignore market demands for service and world-class quality, why bother to try and separate manufacturing from service in the study of operations management? Indeed, for a manufacturing organisation aspiring to world-class status, we would most emphatically agree that the management of such organisations must concern themselves with service and quality if they are to compete on the world stage.

But managers in service industries such as health, retail, distribution, education, travel, real estate, consultation, brokering, law, accounting, administration of central and local government and transportation of goods or people – where no direct manufacturing is involved, or where the manufacturing is light and simple (such as in a restaurant) – do not have to know much about manufacturing. Naturally, all the above industries are reliant on manufacturers to varying degrees for the equipment they use, or in the case of a retailer for the goods they sell, but the physical heavy work of making the goods is not their concern. The analogy is that of a driver of a car: one can be a very good driver without knowing much about what happens under the bonnet. In some cars, a knowledge of when to change gears, and understanding the danger of overheating due to a lack of oil or water will be an advantage, but in other models, the car will even 'tell' the driver when tyre pressure is low, it will turn the headlights on and off depending on light conditions and the driver does not need to worry about gear changing. Likewise, a retail salesperson of washing machines does not need a detailed knowledge of high-tech mass production line balancing. For the salesperson, some knowledge of lead times for deliveries, operating instructions and the capacity of the washing machine will be sufficient as a basis for good service to the customer.

Thus, there can be a separation of operations management into two broad streams: the management of production including service and the management of operations in service industries where only some rudimentary knowledge (if any) of manufacturing is required. But irrespective of whether a manager is involved primarily in production or service, a total system approach is needed based on the supply or value chain philosophy.

For organisations involved directly in production and manufacturing, management needs to be well-versed in strategies, tactics and methodologies of production operations management and also has to be aware of what constitutes service and quality from the customer's point of view. A total operations approach to providing a quality product coupled with the service required is essential.

Managers of service industries will benefit from some basic knowledge of production systems and methodologies.

The shift from enterprise to network

A little more than a decade ago, companies were urged to attain 'world-class' performance within the enterprise. Departments within a company were striving for islands of excellence, and then with a succession of operational excellence initiatives (e.g. TQM, BPR, MRPII and Six Sigma), the fences between departmental turfs were gradually demolished. The organisations started to become customer focused and established performance metrics in all areas of the business (e.g. 'Balanced Scorecard') began to emerge. However, it is fair to say that both the business model and the performance metrics were site-centric or at most were confined within the company or enterprise. Today, with web-based technologies now accelerating the collaborative supply chain, it is becoming imperative to rethink the selection and implementation of external metrics. This shift is not only in measurement criteria but also in the mindset of business practices. This shift has made organisations think globally. Collaboration requires a capacity to work in association, sometimes, with the 'enemy' and does not achieve business success at the competitor's expense. To maximise the advantages of collaboration, the buy-in and commitment of employees to the new mindset are essential. The following are a few reasons for this fundamental shift from a site-centric linear supply chain to a collaborative network or web of supply:

1. Demands for flexibility of partnerships. In today's marketplace, consumers have a degree of choice and a greater ability to make a comparison. As a result, their expectations are rising and their needs constantly changing. Value in this environment is a

moving target. Organisations must be flexible to be able to adapt to these changes. It is very difficult for a single organisation to possess all the capabilities required to keep up. Organisations now look for suppliers who can provide the skills and capabilities needed as and when they require them. A firm can easily form partnerships with appropriately skilled suppliers to last as long as the need exists. As demand changes so can partnership arrangements.

2. Advances in technology. The merging of information and communications technologies has supported the growth in supply chain partnerships. These technologies have enabled extensive connectivity. Today's computer networks, open systems standards and the Internet have enabled people working in different areas of the supply chain to maintain constant contact. Since information transactions have become so easy, there is less of a need to restrict operations to within traditional organisational boundaries. The new capabilities of e-supply chains offer the ability for supply chain partners to share information in real time. This enables the partnering firms to hold lower inventories and incur fewer transaction costs. These lower costs can in turn be passed on to the customer in the form of lower prices and better value, or alternatively retained as increased profit!

3. Collaborative networks. Companies have now recognised that great improvements in value can be attained by coordinating the efforts of partners along the supply chain. When firms focus only on their internal operations, they are making decisions in isolation and as a result, this can lead to the overall performance of the supply chain deteriorating. As we will see later, firms that work together and share their plans and other information are actually able to improve the overall supply chain performance to their mutual benefit.

4. Recognition of core competencies. Recently, there has been a shift away from focusing on markets and products towards considering what the organisation's capabilities are. A focus on core competencies allows a firm to concentrate on those few skills and areas of knowledge that make the organisation distinct and competitive. These competencies are what provide the firm with its competitive advantage. Recognising what processes they are best at allows the firm to concentrate on these processes. This has led to firms rationalising what they do and the emergence of supply chains where each of the partnering organisations focuses on what they individually do best.

5. Growth in outsourcing. The dynamic growth in the large emerging economies, especially China and India, particularly of manufacturing, supply and service capabilities, has provided opportunities for new outsourcing partners. When a specific process moves from a competitive advantage to a commodity, and/or when a supplier's operation performance is superior to the organisation's performance, outsourcing must be considered. A well-documented example of business process outsourcing (MCA, 2002) is the Coca-Cola Corporation. For over 100 years, Coca-Cola has been producing syrup, but the actual production of Coca-Cola is the responsibility of its global network of business partners. A recent study by IBM (IBM, 2006) demonstrates that companies engaged in information technology (IT) outsourcing realise improved financial health and performance in comparison with their sector peers.

Increased complexity of processes

The processes in the supply chain are becoming more and more complex both in terms of the variety of products and the variability of operations. In a preferred condition, a high

Figure 2.1 The bullwhip effect

volume and low variety of products and a low variation in manufacturing processes will deliver products at a lower cost in comparison with a situation with low volume, high variety and high variation. An increase in customer contacts and choices has led to the need for complex supply chains with many variables.

The impact of this increased complexity is challenging the stability of supply chains. This challenge is compounded by the multiple stages and stakeholders in the supply chain from the demand point to the source of supply. The variability in demand increases as it moves along the supply chain away from the retail consumer. Small changes in consumer demand can result in large variations in orders placed upstream. This variation can oscillate further in larger swings as each stakeholder in the supply chain attempts to solve the problem from its own point of view. This phenomenon is often cited as 'the bullwhip effect' (see Figure 2.1) and has been experienced in most industries following linear supply chain principles, which results in increased costs to organisations and poorer service to customers. The bullwhip effect is discussed in greater detail in Chapter 15.

Contemporary challenges such as the Covid-19 pandemic, the bottleneck of human resources by Brexit and the shortage of food and energy supply caused by the Ukraine conflict are contributing to the increased complexity of global supply chains. However, the trend towards digitalisation and environmental sustainability is also helping to find solutions to the complexity of processes.

CASE EXAMPLE: COLLABORATIVE FORECASTING

This case example involves three individual companies representing a brand owner (manufacturer), a first-tier supplier and a second-tier supplier. The target is to build a lean and transparent business model in a three-entity demand chain.

Figure 2.2 Collaborative forecasting model

In the traditional process, the purchase order is the key impulse for the supplier, whereas in this model, the key input is the rolling forecast. The challenges of the implementation come from forecasting capabilities, openness and trust. The utilisation of modern information and communication technology (ICT) technology also creates both challenges and advantages.

A selected starting point for this example is that the collaborative forecasting model exists already between two parties and this model is extended one step further. In a two-entity chain, the forecast of the customer affects the supplier. In this example where the second-tier supplier is included, the initial forecast is if the brand owner affects another step higher in the upstream. Furthermore, the planning process of the first-tier supplier, where the manufacturer's forecast is processed into a raw material forecast for the second-tier supplier, plays a key role. A general description of the model is shown in Figure 2.2.

The production processes in all three parties involved are different – it varies from process industry to manufacturing. The process industry is capital intensive, and the profitability depends more on capacity utilisation. In manufacturing, the production cycles are shorter, and the working capital tied to the process has a higher impact on profitability. Hence, the key drivers for effective planning in each party are not the same.

As the collaborative forecasting between the manufacturer and the first-tier supplier is already in place, the key metric between them is treated as best practice when defining the targets for the second-tier supplier with the first-tier supplier.

The new business model reduces the inventory levels and increases the inventory turnover in the second-tier supplier/first-tier supplier part of the demand chain. Other expected benefits are fewer out-of-stock situations, fewer non-optimal transports, better planning and better production efficiency at the second-tier supplier and increased customer satisfaction.

In order to sustain these results, a thorough commitment based on trust is expected from each partner. In practice, it also means implementing new ICT tools to share data and monitor the supply chain

Adapted from: Lukka and Viskari (2004).

Supplier partnership

Reviewing the impact of new technologies on supply chains provides an interesting development of partnering with suppliers. In the past, many manufacturers regarded their suppliers with some suspicion, almost as adversaries. Little loyalty was shown to the suppliers and consequently the supplier was never certain as to their future relationship with an organisation. Often, the purchasing or procurement department would see their role as securing the best deal possible from a supplier. The huge growth in outsourcing and more importantly the online access to information by Internet have changed that. Companies have realised that achieving world-class excellence in their own sites is not enough. It is important to raise the standards of suppliers as well as learn from them by working in partnership. The tightly controlled service level agreements are being replaced by joint service agreements with a free exchange of data and knowledge. However, the success of the benefits will depend on mutual trust, a highly developed commercial relationship and an efficient system of data exchange. In order to improve the effectiveness of data exchange, companies are sharing with their suppliers (and customers) common systems such as European Article Numbering (EAN) standards, Electronic Data Interchange (EDI) and web-based extranets. For example, EDI enables companies to communicate with each other. Purchase orders to suppliers can be eliminated by using customers' order schedules. And by EDI and extranets, the supplier can be authorised to link directly into the manufacturer's MRP II or enterprise resource planning (ERP) system. The emergence of the Internet protocol has helped interaction between powerful supply chain systems such as i2, Manugistics, Ariba, Oracle and SAP/R3.

Why total supply chain management

Our analysis of the key factors and new developments in global supply chain management clearly indicates that focusing on the conventional practices of supply chain management within the organisation, such as forecasting, capacity planning, inventory management, scheduling and distribution management, may achieve operational excellence within the confines of an individual business organisation but will offer only a partial solution to optimising customer service. As indicated earlier, it can be compared with sitting in a high-performance motor car in a traffic jam, the sound system and air conditioning might be state of the art but the overall travel experience is not great. Likewise, what is the point of having a perfect stainless steel link in a rusty chain? Unless the whole process is efficient, the individual unit cannot achieve its potential.

It is therefore vital for any organisation, being more and more dependent on both local and global outside resources and information, to work in harmony with all stakeholders of the supply chain including customers and suppliers. We need a holistic value stream approach to the supply chain or a total supply chain management approach.

In 'Total Manufacturing Solutions' (Basu and Wright, 1997), we defined total manufacturing to include all the interactions between the conversion process inside a 'factory' with all other business processes including marketing, research and development, supply chain management, financial and information management and human resource management – also with external factors such as environmental concerns, customer care and competition. The method of analysis, which in effect determined strengths, weaknesses and gaps in performance, was developed around 200 questions designed for self-benchmarking against world-class standards. The structure of the benchmarking was to measure the performance of the business against 20 defined areas of the business that were described as foundation stones. There were ten questions for each foundation stone. The aim is to get the right balance of foundation stones to support the pillars of the business. Over a period of eight years, we refined the six pillars and the 20 foundation stones of *Total Manufacturing Solutions* to give a greater emphasis on service and relationships with suppliers and customers. Partnering and alliances were also included in a new model that we named 'Total Operations Solutions'. In total operations solutions (Basu and Wright,

2005), we continued to provide a process of self-assessment to systematically measure all aspects of an organisation, be it manufacturing or service. This includes both internal functions and external relationships. We showed how the concepts of Six Sigma as further developed in 'Quality Beyond Six Sigma' (Basu and Wright, 2003) can be used without too much fuss to determine strengths and weaknesses. *Quality Beyond Six Sigma* is written around 'Fit Sigma'. Fit Sigma was developed by Ron Basu to build on strengths and to understand where weaknesses are so that corrective action can be taken to gain a competitive advantage.

Building upon the experience of the holistic models for total manufacturing solutions and total operations solutions, we have now developed a model for total supply chain management comprising six building blocks:

- Customer focus and demand.
- Resources and capacity management.
- Procurement and supplier focus.
- Inventory management.
- Operations management.
- Distribution management.

These building blocks are integrated by three cross-functional processes:

- Sales and operations planning.
- Systems and procedures.
- Performance management.

Value chain and value stream mapping

In Chapter 1, we discussed Porter's value chain (see Figure 1.7). The value chain of a product from research & development (R&D) to service is shown in Figure 2.3.

The value chain starts with R&D, the outcome of which is new product development creating the specifications for the product. The next stage is the commercialisation of the product when marketing creates demand by advertising the attractive features of the product. Operations and supply transform the product specifications into marketable products. Sales and distribution then deliver the product to customers. After sales, customer service then follows to respond to subsequent customer requests. Secondary activities such as finance, information technology and human resources support complement the auxiliary activities of the value chain.

The terms 'value stream' and 'value chain' are often used interchangeably, but there is a difference between them. As discussed earlier, the value chain is a high-level model of how businesses receive raw materials as input, add value to the raw materials through various processes and sell finished products to customers. The value chain categorises the

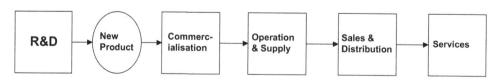

Figure 2.3 Value chain for a typical product

generic value-adding activities of an organisation. A value stream is an end-to-end collection of activities that creates a result for a 'customer', who may be the ultimate customer or an internal 'end user' of the value stream. The value stream has a clear goal, that is, to satisfy the customer. The term value stream refers to an end-to-end set of activities.

The importance of the total supply chain approach can be evaluated by value stream mapping (VSM) (Basu, 2004: p. 118). VSM is a visual illustration of all activities required to bring a product through the main flow, from raw material to the stage of reaching the customer. According to Womack and Jones (1998), the initial objective of creating VSM is to identify every action required to make a specific product.

CASE EXAMPLE: THE VALUE STREAM OF A COLA CAN

The following example is adapted from Womack and Jones (1998: pp. 38–43).

Consider a cardboard case containing eight cans of cola chosen at random in the beverage aisle at a Tesco store.

Figure 2.4 shows a value stream map of cola, from the mining of bauxite (the source of aluminium of the cans) to the user's home. Bauxite ore is mined in Australia and then transferred in trucks to a nearby chemical reduction mill to produce powdery alumina. Bulk alumina is then shipped by boat to Norway with cheap hydroelectric power for smelting. The molten aluminium is cast into ingots that are then shipped by trucks, boats and trucks to Germany. The ingot is heated to 500°C and then passed through successive rollers to reduce the thickness from one metre to three millimetres and stored as coils. The coils are then transferred by trucks to a cold rolling mill where the aluminium sheets are reduced from three millimetres to a thickness of 0.3 millimetres suitable for can making. The thin coils are then shipped to a can maker's warehouse in the UK. Cans are manufactured and then stored. From the can maker's warehouse, the cans are then transferred to the bottler's warehouse in pallets. They are then de-palletised and loaded into the can filling line where they are washed and filled with cola. At the end of the filling line, cans are then unitised

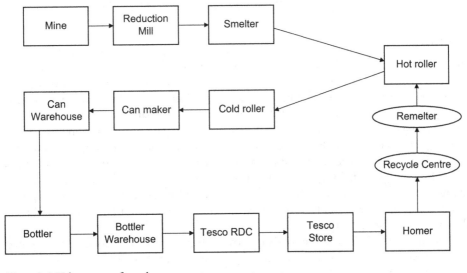

Figure 2.4 Value stream for cola cans

Table 2.1 Quantitative data of Coca-Cola cans

	Incoming storage	Process time	Finished storage	Process rate	Cumulative days
Mine	0	20 min	2 weeks	1000 t/hr	319
Reduction mill	2 weeks	30 min	2 weeks	–	305
Smelter	3 months	2 hr	2 weeks	–	277
Hot rolling mill	2 weeks	1 min	4 weeks	10 ft/min	173
Cold rolling mill	2 weeks	<1 min	4 weeks	2100 ft/min	131
Can maker	2 weeks	1 min	4 weeks	2000/min	89
Bottler	4 days	1 min	5 weeks	1500 min	47
Tesco RDC	0	0	3 days	–	8
Tesco store	0	0	2 days	–	5
Home storage	3 days	5 min	–	–	3
Total	5 months	3 hr	6 months	–	319

in stretch wrappers and stored in the warehouse on pallets. They are then transported on trucks to Tesco's regional distribution centres around the UK and then distributed to Tesco's supermarkets. When cola is taken home, it is typically stored again and chilled and finally consumed. Empty cans are then recycled to reintroduce them into the production process at the smelting stage.

The quantitative data related to the activities in the value stream are summarised in Table 2.1.

It is evident from the details in Table 2.1 that value-added activities take only three hours compared with the total time (319 days) from the mine to the recycling bin. This proportion is surprisingly small when one considers the alarmingly lengthy overall duration of the process.

We believe that the example of the value stream for a carton of cola firmly establishes the need for a total supply chain management approach. It is important to note that most of the 40,000 other items in a typical supermarket would produce similar results. The impact of the value stream or total supply chain approach in the service sector is not as dramatic as FMCG (fast-moving consumer goods) but highly significant all the same.

Summary

The key issues of supply chains as discussed in this chapter emphasise a need for a total supply chain management approach. With the expansion of outsourcing and Internet-driven e-supply chains, it is essential that key players and stakeholders understand the importance of the accuracy and transparency of data for collaborative management for mutual benefits. Improved forecast accuracy and the real-time exchange of data not only reduce the 'bullwhip effect' but also reduce processing costs, inventory levels and improves customer service. We also discussed the trend towards the service-based economy and the importance of total supply chain management in the service sector. The building blocks of the supply chain underpinned by the total supply chain management approach as explained further in this book will assist in the improved understanding and management of a collaborative global supply chain.

Contemporary challenges such as the Covid-19 pandemic, de-globalisation by populism, climate change initiatives and the digital revolution have caused both additional constraints and new opportunities for global supply chains.

Discussion questions

1. It has been said that in the global market the competitive edge comes from service. What do you understand by the term service? How is service determined and measured in your organisation in terms of your immediate customers and your immediate suppliers?

2. Explain why in the global economy the greater percentage of the workforce of developed nations will continue to be employed in service activities.

3. Island of Excellence was a term widely used some ten years ago. Why is this an outdated concept?

4. In the case example for American Express discuss how the introduction of the S2S (Source-to-Settle) product suite helped to improve service in organisations' global supply chain performance.

5. What are the major reasons for this fundamental shift from a site-centric linear supply chain to a collaborative network of global supply chains? Discuss the collaborative forecasting model and its advantages. Why do we need a total supply chain management approach in managing global supply chains?

6. Explain with illustrative examples value chain and value stream mapping.

3 Understanding total supply chain management and its building blocks

Introduction

In Chapter 2 we discussed, in the context of global supply chains, the need for a total supply chain management approach and introduced the concepts of building blocks. The importance of each building block is explained in this chapter. No block stands alone, each is a component of the whole. In combination, the blocks show activities, stages and processes of the extended supply chain. The sequence of processes creates a flow between different stages to fulfil a customer's need for a product or service. The processes of making things happen within a supply chain can be viewed as a sequence of progressive cycles (e.g. planning cycle) or the nature of the response to a customer order (e.g. push or pull). There are debates between supporters of a make-to-order policy or a make-to-forecast policy as if one policy is better than the other regardless of customers, demand patterns, products or organisations.

Learning objectives

Learning objectives for this chapter are as follows:

1. What are the process views of a supply chain?
2. What are the building blocks of a supply chain?
3. Are all the building blocks suited to all organisations?

What are the process views of a supply chain?

Chopra and Meindl (2016) describe the two views – cycle view and push/pull view – as follows:

1. Cycle view. The processes in a supply chain consist of a series of cycles, each performed at the interface between two successive stages.
2. Push/pull view. Pull processes are initiated by a customer order and push processes are initiated and performed on the forecast of customer orders.

Cycle view

The cycle view of a supply chain consists of several stages of process cycles and forms the components of manufacturing resource planning (MRPII) or enterprise resource planning (ERP) systems and are shown in a simplified form as three process cycles in Figure 3.1. These cycles are discussed in more detail in Part 2 (Chapters 5–10).

DOI: 10.4324/9781003341352-4

Figure 3.1 Simplified process cycles in a supply chain

The demand cycle is the cycle of time covering from when a customer buys or orders from a retailer or wholesaler. The demand cycle can also be based on the forecast of demand. If the retailer holds the product in stock, then the demand cycle will comprise order request, order fulfilment and order receiving. However, if the product is not readily available, then the customer order request will form a part of a demand forecast that also includes predicted demand, market intelligence and promotion of the product.

The planning and procurement cycle covers short-term and longer-term requirements. The demand for the product and its components (bill of materials) is compared with the inventory and capacity and the replenishment requirements are planned. Planners will decide what to buy and what to make. This make-or-buy decision process also applies to a service organisation leading to either in-house or outsourced services.

The supply cycle typically occurs with a production schedule if the product is to be manufactured, or a purchase schedule if the product is to be procured from an external supplier. Once finished, goods are manufactured or received and the next stage of the supply cycle is direct delivery to customers or storage in the warehouse and subsequent distribution to customers.

Push/pull view

A push process conforms to a conventional supply chain management system going through typical stages in sequence. As shown in Figure 3.2, orders arrive at or after the demand cycle but always before the planning and procurement cycle and the process is activated by a forecast or demand plan. Both raw and packaging materials are stored

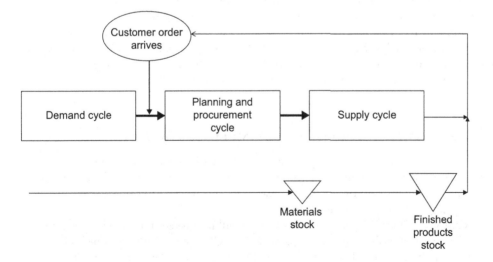

Figure 3.2 Push process in a supply chain

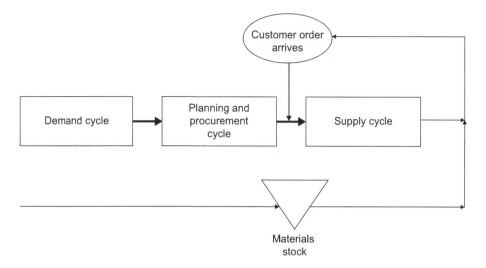

Figure 3.3 Pull process in a supply chain

before production and products are manufactured to stock. Order fulfilment is achieved from the inventory of finished products.

A pull process is activated in response to a confirmed order from a customer. This includes make-to-order or a just-in-time (JIT) manufacturing process. As shown in Figure 3.3, in a pull process, the supplier does not stock finished products but holds a higher quantity of semi-finished materials and often has a higher supply capacity so that order fulfilment can be achieved rapidly. The orders arrive at or after the planning cycle as if bypassing a few steps of the traditional ERP process.

A pull process is also associated with Kanban and lean thinking or lean manufacturing, which are covered in more detail in Chapter 14. In essence, lean manufacturing requires materials to arrive at each stage of production when required and no buffer stocks of inwards or outwards stocks of materials are held. The lean approach is also referred to as just-in-time or JIT. Pull processes control the flow of resources in the production process by replacing only what has been consumed. Production schedules are based on actual demand and consumption rather than forecasts. With lean manufacturing, there is no room for errors in specification, production or late delivery.

CASE EXAMPLE: A PULL SYSTEM IMPLEMENTATION

A heating and ventilation company in Canada employs 250 people and supplies products to new homes and for property renovation. The declining Canadian dollar was increasing costs and competition was getting tougher. Customers were more demanding and margins were eroding.

Customer requirements were met by scheduling production based on a forecast using a materials requirement planning (MRP) system. Although the finished goods warehouse was full and storage was becoming a problem, on-time deliveries to customers were under 80%. Lead time was three weeks from quote to shipment to the customer. Part of the warehouse was set aside for returned goods (for when a unit or units were returned because they did not meet customer specifications).

Led by their manufacturing team, the company started an improvement strategy based on lean principles and shared it with all the employees including administration office staff. All employees were then trained in the principles of lean and they started to change by thinking about the improvement strategy. The key initiative was to convert from a scheduling system based on sales forecast to a 'pull system' (Kanban) based on customer demand.

The results were remarkable. For example:

- Lead time was reduced from three weeks to two days.
- On-time delivery was increased to 96.5%.
- Stocks of finished goods were reduced by 60%.
- The return area was converted into R&D where new products were developed to fill the released warehouse capacity.
- Daily production meetings were reduced from 1.5 hours to half an hour.
- Employees were more involved and empowered.

Despite the dollar continuing to decline and customers becoming more demanding, margins started to improve.

Kanban literally means card. Originally developed by Toyota in the 1980s, a Kanban was usually a printed card in a transparent plastic cover that contained details of specific information such as part number and quantity. It is a means of pulling parts and products through the manufacturing or logistics sequence as needed 'just in time'. Most Kanban systems are now computerised.

What are the building blocks of a supply chain?

From the pull system used in the Canadian company, one might be tempted to believe that forecasting and making to stock is inefficient and old fashioned. Further, in the well-documented model of Dell Direct (see Basu and Wright, 2005: pp. 334–337), where the traditional retail channels are bypassed through the manufacturer selling and delivering directly to the customer, it might be considered that wholesalers, distributors and retailers are redundant. These are good examples but are isolated approaches to suit particular circumstances and products. Some products are best processed in batches and stocked in bulk, for example, food processing and cool stores. In the course of this book, we aim to establish the appropriateness of each model in the context of a big-picture approach.

It is therefore important that a 'total supply chain management approach' is applied and all the building blocks of the supply chain are examined. The synergy that results from the benefits contributed by all elements as a whole far exceeds the aggregate of benefits achieved for individual elements. The integrated approach is truly more than the sum of its elements. If one concentrates exclusively on isolated areas, a false impression may be inevitable and inappropriate action taken.

This maxim can be illustrated by the Indian folk tale of four blind men who were confronted with a new phenomenon, an elephant! The first man, by touching its ear, thought that the elephant was a fan. A second was hit by the elephant's tail and concluded that it was a whip. The third man bumped into a leg and thought it was a column, while the fourth, on holding the trunk, decided that it was an oversized hose. Each man, on the evidence he had, came to a logical conclusion, but all had made an erroneous judgment by failing to deduce that the total object was an elephant. As with all feedback devices where a basic message is given, inferences and decisions may be drawn from isolated data that will be false and misleading.

A story in the business context will further underline the limitation of tackling only a part of a total problem. The technical director of a multinational company, having been to a conference, decided that line performance improvement must be the best thing in manufacturing. So he organised his technical team, called in experts from the corporate headquarters and set up a line efficiency exercise. The team did an excellent job on two production lines by systematically eliminating all machine-related downtime problems (with the aid of video recording analysis). As a result, the production efficiency of the lines increased by 20%. However, it soon transpired that the product for one of the lines was going to be discontinued, and the other line, despite its excellent standard of reliability and efficiency, encountered a severe long-term shortage of materials due to planning and procurement problems. Therefore, in isolation, the line efficiency programs did not improve the overall business performance.

As we mentioned in Chapter 2, our model for total supply chain management comprises six building block configurations:

- Customer focus and demand.
- Resources and capacity management.
- Procurement and supplier focus.
- Inventory management.
- Operations Management.
- Distribution management.

And three cross-functional integrating processes:

- Systems and procedures.
- Sales and operations planning.
- Performance management.

This model is illustrated in Figure 3.4. The composition of building blocks by supply chain configuration and supply chain integration is shown in Figure 3.5. Each of the supply chain configurations will be covered in more detail in Part 2 and the integrating processes in Part 3.

Customer focus and demand

Customers are both at the start and the end of the supply chain. A customer is the one who is paying for the goods or services or is most affected by the outcome of the process. In a supply chain, a customer could be a consumer, wholesaler, distributor or retailer. The demand for a product or service is created by customers.

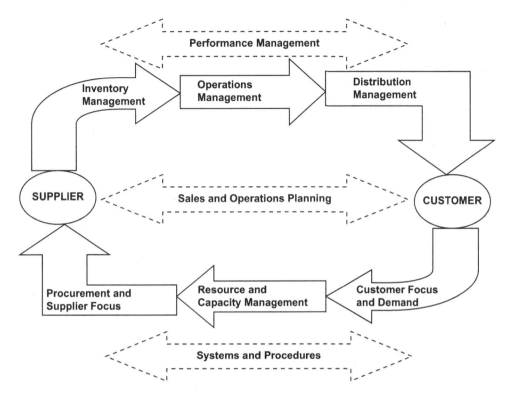

Figure 3.4 Total supply chain building blocks

TOTAL SUPPLY CHAIN BUILDING BLOCKS	
SUPPLY CHAIN CONFIGARATION	**SUPPLY CHAIN INTEGRATION**
• Customer focus and demand • Resource and capacity management • Procurement and supplier focus • Inventory management • Operations management • Distribution management	• Systems and procedures • Sales and operations planning • Performance management

Figure 3.5 Total supply chain building blocks composition

The basis of all supply chain planning and decisions is underpinned by the forecast of future demand. A supply chain process cannot exist without the knowledge and planning for the future. All push processes are executed in anticipation of customer demand and all pull processes are carried out in response to customer demand. It is a misconception that a demand forecast is not required in a pull or just-in-time process. Without a forecast of future demand in a pull system, a manager cannot plan the capacity and have the resources required to respond to a customer order. For a traditional push process, a manager plans the level of production and capacity based on the forecast of future demand. Even in a service industry, where the demand is not discrete, business planning will be unsatisfactory without an estimate of future demand. In a not-for-profit organisation, demand is unpredictable, but it has customers and a core budget based on a demand forecast.

In all instances of a supply chain, the first step is to forecast what the customer demand will be in the future. It is important to note that is not possible to produce a perfect forecast as there are so many variables affecting a future demand, such as past demand, promotion and advertising of the product, market share, state of the economy, price discounts, competition and new product introduction. Peter Drucker once said. 'the best way to predict the future is to create it'. There are also some recognised characteristics of forecasts, for example, there will always be a forecast error, longer-term forecasts are less accurate than short-term forecasts and aggregate forecasts are usually more accurate than individual forecasts.

This building block of customer focus and demand including forecasting methods is covered in more detail in Chapter 5.

Resource and capacity management

A primary objective of supply chain management is to optimise supply capacity to fulfil demand in time. In the real world, resources are not infinite. Satisfying customers on time can be crucial. An increase in capacity, be it machines and equipment, warehouse space, transport, stocks of input materials and finished products, and, of course, people are expensive. Therefore, a supply chain manager must make decisions regarding capacity levels and buffer them to meet the variation in demand either by adjusting capacity or producing to hold output stocks of goods. An organisation may provide excess capacity to satisfy demands for peak periods or set an upper limit of the capacity based on the average demand and balance the cost of holding excess inventory on one hand or losing sales on the other.

There are a few options for capacity optimisation open to a manager and there are proven processes to assist him or her. One such process is aggregate planning where an organisation determines levels of capacity, production and inventory over a planning horizon to maximise the profit. The optimisation can be attempted either in theory by a mathematical model (e.g. linear programming) or in practice by a cross-functional continuous review process (e.g. sales and operational planning). Our preferred and practical option is sales and operations planning (S&OP), which is covered in Chapter 22.

Another proven process is ERP, which has evolved from MRP and MRPII. ERP is closely linked with S&OP and comprises a series of sequential processes by using a single set of databases, viz, demand planning, rough cut capacity planning, master operations scheduling, materials requirement planning, detail capacity planning, purchase scheduling and production scheduling. Number crunching is done using a computer system such as SAP R/3. The success of ERP depends on the structured review process by planners, managers and users.

This building block of resource and capacity management including ERP is covered in more detail in Chapter 6.

Procurement and supplier focus

The optimisation of internal capacity can be supplemented by buying in external capacity and resources. As Reid and Sanders (2002: p. 56) indicate:

> make or buy is a type of backward integration decision, where the company decides whether to purchase certain materials or tasks or perform the operation itself. Often this is called outsourcing. Many companies routinely out-source certain services, such as janitorial services, repair, security, payroll, or records management.

For the supply chain, procurement of external capacity and resources could include packaging materials, part-built assemblies, contracting out utilities and maintenance, hiring contract or casual labour, selecting approved suppliers and outsourcing. An example of part-built assemblies is where an American car typically consists of 25,000 components to be assembled on the manufacturing line, while a Japanese car of a similar class might only consist of 12,000.

In a typical manufacturing organisation, the cost of bought-in resources accounts for 60–90% of the cost of goods sold (COGS). Thus, a powerful way to improve shareholder returns is to address the reduction of purchasing costs. Proper purchasing and supply management can give a network of suppliers capable of delivering service quality beating competitors and at the same time securing cost reductions over time. In a market-driven competitive world, businesses are continuously seeking new suppliers and partners, including outsourcing.

The Internet has provided new challenges and potential solutions and has enabled extensive connectivity. As Wright and Race (2004) say:

> today's computer networks, open systems standards and the internet enable people to working in different areas of the supply chain to maintain constant contact. Since information transactions have become so easy, there is less of a need to restrict operations within the traditional organizational boundaries. These new capabilities offer the ability for supply chain partners to share information in real time. This enables the partnering firms to hold lower inventories and incur fewer transaction costs. These lower costs can be passed onto the customer in the form of lower prices and better value. Or, alternatively retained as increased profits. Companies have now recognized that great improvements in value can be attained by co-ordinating the efforts along the supply chain. When firms focus only on their internal operations they are making decisions in isolation and as a result this can lead to the overall performance of the supply chain deteriorating. (p. 210)

In short, firms that collaborate and share plans and information are able to improve the overall supply chain performance to their mutual benefit.

The development of a professional service industry has also in recent years increased considerably; however, as observed by Mitchell (1998), purchasing teams appear to have made less effort to reduce costs by outsourcing services. Nonetheless, the importance of service level agreements and supplier partnerships is growing in the global supply chain. A survey by Wade (2003) showed that 31% of total procurement cost is for bought-in services.

The selection of appropriate or preferred suppliers should involve alternative and complementary attributes between the suppliers and the receiving organisation. Slack et al. (2012) suggest four basic capabilities to make sensible trade-offs, viz:

* Technical capability – the product or service knowledge to deliver sustainable quality.
* Operations capability – the process knowledge to ensure effective supply.
* Financial capability – the financial strength to fund the business.
* Managerial capability – the management talent to develop future business.

It is important to raise the standards of suppliers as well as learn from them by working in partnership. Tightly controlled service level agreements are being replaced by joint service agreements with a free exchange of data and knowledge. Success will depend on mutual trust, a highly developed commercial relationship and an efficient system of data exchange.

This building block of procurement and supplier focus including outsourcing is covered in more detail in Chapter 7.

Inventory management

The purpose of inventories or stocks is to buffer against variations in demand and supply. Inventories usually reside in three stages of a process, viz. input stocks (e.g. raw and packaging materials), process stocks (e.g. semi-finished products) and output stocks (e.g. finished products). Wild (2003) introduced the concept of consumed and non-consumed stocks. Consumed items (e.g. materials or products) are used by the process or customers and must be replenished in shorter cycles. Non-consumed items (e.g. capital equipment and labour) are repeatedly used by the process needing repair and maintenance and are replaced in longer intervals.

Inventories could be allocated either by design or can accumulate as a result of poor planning and scheduling. Generally, inventory is viewed as having a negative impact on business incurring costs of capital (interest paid or interest foregone), handling, insurance, increased risk of damage and theft, storage space and obsolescence. On the other hand, a lack of inventory leads to lost production in the factory and lost sales at the end of the supply chain. Holding inventory of materials and finished products can be seen as insurance against the uncertainty of supply and to overcome unforeseen variations in demand.

Inventory management is a good indicator of the effectiveness of supply chain management. It is relatively easy to achieve higher levels of customer service by accumulating excessive stocks. It will also obscure short-term operational problems, however, this is a costly and risky option in terms of cash flow. Obsolete inventory, be it for changes in technology, fashion or in foodstuffs past the use-by date has little salvage value. It is vital to optimise the inventory level.

In optimising inventory levels, two types of stocks are considered: cycle stock and safety stock. Cycle stock depends on costs associated with ordering, transportation, quantity discount, lead times from suppliers and customer demand. Safety stock is the buffer against the variation of demand during the lead time and depends on forecast accuracy, reliability of suppliers and customer service level.

In service industries, operations managers might have a nonchalant attitude towards inventories but not so the accountants. Differences between services and physical goods are addressed both from operations and marketing. Among the differences identified within marketing and operations literature are intangibility, heterogeneity, inseparability and perishability (Grönroos 2000). It is perceived that services are one-offs and cannot be stored. There are of course consumed stocks (e.g. stationery) in service industries for conventional inventory management. However, in the service sector, more emphasis should be focused on managing non-consumed stock (viz. database and skilled people).

This building block of inventory management is covered in more detail in Chapter 8.

Operations management

In a supply chain, operations management is the building block that makes things happen. This is where plans are executed in factories and facilities to produce goods or services for customers. Operations management is the activity of managing resources and processes that produce goods and services. Input resources (viz. information, materials and utilities) are transformed by three converting components (viz. people, process and technology) into desired outputs. Along with distribution management, operations management accounts for the physical flow of the supply chain. Most texts on operations management give scant coverage of supply chain management.

Operations exist in all types of supply chains whether it is for delivering a product or a service. A popular perception of an operation is where physical activities or transformations are involved, for example, manufacturing. If you think that you do not have an operation if you are in sales and marketing, or banking or insurance, or health service or charity organisations, you are incorrect. You will always have an operation as long as you use resources to produce products, services or a mixture of both. In other words, if you have input, process and output, you have an operation. During the 1960s and earlier, operations management was exclusively the domain of manufacturing industries. Since the 1970s, operations management is used in both manufacturing and service sectors, and it also implies a service operation can be decoupled as repetitive and non-repetitive operations and manufacturing principles and techniques can be applied to repetitive service operations. More recently the term operations and process management has been used to cover all parts of the organisation. In this book, operations management will include all types or parts of organisations.

This building block of operations management will be covered in detail in Chapter 9.

Distribution management

There is no doubt that supply chain order fulfilment is the Achilles' heel of the e-business economy. At the end of every e-commerce, online trading and virtual supply chain there is a factory, a warehouse and a transport. The Internet has elevated the performance of information accessibility, currency transactions and data accuracy, but the real effectiveness of supply chains from the source to the customer cannot be achieved without the physical efficiency of the supply chain. Web-based software and e-marketplaces are increasing the alternatives available to e-supply chain managers in all operations including the service industry. More opportunities may also mean more options and complexity. Therefore, it is vital that a process is in place to ensure the performance of the e-supply chain for both virtual and physical activities.

Many organisations outsource distribution activities to third parties and do not employ in-house expertise to manage distribution which directly affects customer service. If there is a failure in order fulfilment whether it is due to quality, quantity or time or even the attitude of the distributor then the organisation, not the distributor, bears the consequence. The problems of returned goods or reverse logistics are becoming a growing concern in supply chain management.

This building block distribution management addresses this challenge under two headings:

- Physical distribution.
- Strategic alliances.

In the same way that enterprise resource planning is concerned with information flow, suppliers and inbound logistics, distribution management is likewise concerned with materials flow, customers and outbound logistics.

With the management of distribution, which is the physical transportation of goods from the factory to the customer, invariably some stock is held to buffer the variability of demand and supply lead times. The focus on outbound logistics is to balance customer service level against cost. The cost of distribution is not just transportation costs but also includes warehousing including special requirements such as refrigeration, insurance and financing of stock, and stock slippage (deterioration, damage, pilfering and obsolescence). The more stock that is held the greater the cost of storage and the greater the chances of losses.

The main components of distribution management are:

- Distribution strategy.
- Warehouse operations.
- Stock management.
- Transport planning.

As regards strategic alliances, in order to achieve an integrated supply chain, the various players need to work together. The four most important types of distribution management strategic alliances are third-party logistics (3PL), retailer–supplier partnerships (RSP), distributor integration (DI) and customer relationship management (CRM).

This building block of distribution management is covered in more detail in Chapter 10.

Systems and procedures

Systems and procedures are essential components to integrate the building block configurations of the total supply chain. There are three major categories of systems and procedures:

- External regulatory and internal quality standards.
- Financial and accounting procedures.
- Information and communication technology.

The activities of a supply chain are affected by both national and international regulatory requirements on packaging, storage, pallets, vehicles, working hours, tariffs and many other issues. In addition, an organisation maintains its own quality standards and service level agreements with suppliers and partners.

Another important issue is improving the financial performance of the company. Under pressure to participate in fashionable improvement activities, or to become involved with the newest business wisdom, management may lose sight of the real issue – improving profitability. In response to pressures from stakeholders, there is a risk of overemphasis on short-term financial performance. Consequently, this myopic approach results in over-investment in short-term fixers and underinvestment in longer-term development plans. There is a need for a balanced approach.

The Internet, now taken for granted, has seen the use of technologies to create electronic communication networks within and between organisations and individuals. The implementation of ERP, websites, e-commerce, electronic data interchange and e-mail systems have allowed individuals within organisations, and business to business and business to customer, to communicate freely together and share data in 'real time'. Information technology (IT) has now grown into information and communication technology (ICT). In this ICT domain, we consider two broad areas:

- Information technology and systems.
- e–Business.

There is a visible absence of a dedicated chapter on systems and procedures in the published books on supply chain management. This building block of systems and procedures is covered in more detail in Chapter 21.

Sales and operations planning

S&OP is a cross-functional management review process to integrate the activities of the total supply chain. The classical concept of sales and operations planning is rooted in the MRPII process. In the basic S&OP, the company operating plan (comprising sales forecast, production plan, inventory plan and shipments) is updated on a regular monthly basis by the senior management of a manufacturing organisation. The virtues, application and training of the S&OP have been promoted by Oliver Wight Associates (see Ling and Goddard, 1988) since the early 1970s.

In recent years, the pace of change in technology and marketplace dynamics has been so rapid that the traditional methodology of monitoring the actual performance against predetermined budgets set at the beginning of the year is generally no longer valid. It is fundamental that businesses are managed on current conditions and up-to-date assumptions. There is also a vital need to establish an effective communication link, both horizontally across functional divisions and vertically across the management hierarchy to share common data and decision processes. Thus, S&OP has moved beyond the operations planning at the aggregate level to a multi-functional senior management review process. The traditional S&OP is a senior management review process of establishing the operational plan and other key activities of the business to best satisfy the current levels of sales forecasts according to the delivery capacity of the business.

Ling and Goddard (1988, p 113) summarised a 'capsule description of the process':

> It starts with the sales and marketing departments comparing actual demand to the sales plan, assessing the marketplace potential and projecting future demand. The updated demand plan is then communicated to the manufacturing, engineering and finance departments, which offer to support it. Any difficulties in

supporting the sales plan are worked out…with a formal meeting chaired by the general manager.

This building block of S&OP is covered in more detail in Chapter 22.

Performance management

Performance management acts both as a driving force of improvement and a fact-based integrating agent to support the planning, operations and review processes. The foundation of performance management is rooted in quality management principles supported by key performance indicators.

There are many different definitions and dimensions of quality to be found in books and academic literature. Basu (2004) defines quality with three dimensions – design quality (specification), process quality (conformance) and organisation quality (sustainability). When an organisation develops and defines its quality strategy, it is important to share a common definition of quality and each department within a company can work towards a common objective. The product quality should contain defined attributes of both numeric specifications and perceived dimensions. The process quality, whether it relates to manufacturing or service operations, should also contain some defined criteria of acceptable service level so that the conformity of the output can be validated against these criteria. Perhaps the most important determinant of how we perceive sustainable quality is the functional and holistic role we fulfil within the organisation. It is only when an organisation begins to change its approach to a holistic culture emphasising a single set of numbers based on transparent measurement with senior management commitment that the 'organisation quality' germinates.

A good reference line of key performance indicators of a supply chain is the 'balanced scorecard' by Kaplan and Norton (1996). Kaplan and Norton argue that 'a valuation of intangible assets and company capabilities would be especially helpful since, for information age companies, these assets are more critical to success than traditional physical and tangible assets'. The balanced scorecard retains traditional financial measures, customer services and resource utilisation (internal business process) and includes additional measures for learning (people) and growth (innovation). This approach complements measures of past performance with drivers for future development.

Performance of the supply chain is covered in detail in Chapter 23

Are all building blocks suited to all organisations?

Although the objectives of supply chain management, that is, to balance the demand and supply for the right product or service on time and at an affordable price, remain the same for all businesses, it is also true that supply chains serving different markets should be managed in different ways. Both Fisher (1997) and Christopher (2000) have drawn the distinction between 'lean supply chain' and 'agile supply chain'. Agility should not be confused with lean or leanness. Lean is about doing more with less, often with minimum inventory with an emphasis on efficiency. Key characteristics of an agile supply chain include responsiveness and flexibility.

As shown in Figure 3.6, the approaches for an agile or lean supply chain are determined by volume and variety/variability. An agile supply chain responds quickly to changes in demand whether caused by a low volume for high variety products or unpredictability

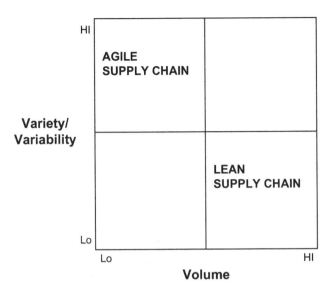

Figure 3.6 Lean and agile supply chains

of demand. A lean supply chain works very efficiently when the volume is high and variability is low. The occasions for a pure agile or pure lean supply chain are likely to be infrequent. It is a popular perception, though not always validated, that functional or commodity products need a lean supply chain and innovative and new products require agile supply chain management. As Christopher (2000) points out, there will often be situations for a 'hybrid strategy' where a combination of the two may be appropriate.

Our building blocks of the total supply chain will apply to both lean and agile supply chains, but their end objectives require different ways of using the building blocks. In a lean supply chain, the emphasis will be on accurate demand and capacity planning, keeping the inventory low and running the plant efficiently. In an agile supply chain, the emphasis will be on high service levels by responding rapidly to end customers. This will require flexibility in process and plant capacity and a higher inventory, usually of semi-finished products, nearer the demand point.

The supply chain in the service sector will also need all the building blocks of the total supply chain, although they should be used and managed differently depending on services. For example, in an insurance service industry, the approach to inventory management would be different to that in an automobile manufacturing business. In the service sector, the variation in demand is buffered by managing 'non-consumed' stock (such as people and a database), while in the manufacturing sector, the emphasis is on consumed stock (such as materials).

Summary

In this chapter, we have explained the characteristics and roles of supply chain building blocks in total supply chain management. The building blocks consist of nine components out of which six components are for supply chain configuration (e.g. customer focus and demand management, resource and capacity management, procurement and supplier focus, inventory management, operations management and distribution management) and three components are for supply chain integration (e.g. systems and procedures, sales and operations planning and performance management). These building blocks will be applicable, to a varying degree, to all types and strategies of supply chains whether they are primarily pull or push processes, whether agile or lean supply chains or whether in they are in manufacturing or the service sector.

All the building blocks in total supply chain management need to be regularly updated with the impact of seven contemporary challenges. The changes will be more significant in three cross-functional integrating processes, namely, systems and procedures, sales and operations planning and performance management. These changes will be covered in more detail in relevant chapters.

Discussion questions

1. Explain the difference in the materials planning process for a push system and a pull system. Which system is more in line with a conventional MRPII system and why?
2. Is Kanban a push or pull system? Explain how Kanban works with an example.
3. What are the building blocks of total supply chain management? Which blocks relate to 'information flow' and 'materials flow'?
4. Why do we also need building blocks for cross-functional integrating processes? What are these building blocks?
5. Procurement outsourcing is not always understood or used. What are the pros and cons of procurement outsourcing? For example, it is said that when you outsource you are giving away a profit opportunity to the outsourcing organisation.

4 Contemporary global challenges in supply chain management

Introduction

Four big issues of global supply chain management became particularly apparent in 2021. First, and probably the most obvious to many of us, was the disruptions in global supply chains created by the Covid-19 pandemic and the subsequent series of lockdowns and restrictions. This has resulted in significant geographical shifts in supply and demand, which in turn has created problems for finely tuned global supply chains. Second, the economic and business environment became more challenging by nationalistic pressure on de-globalisation. For example, in the UK and the rest of Europe, supply chain pressures were caused by Brexit as a result of increases in red tape and cross-border checks. This all matters because business has become increasingly globalised in recent years. Third, the impact of climate change on supply chain activities was beginning to be more widely understood since Glasgow's COP26 in November. Fourth, the direct impact of the invasion in Ukraine from March 2022 has created an acute shortage of food grains and restrictions on the supply of oil and gas stoking inflation and the cost of living crisis.

There are three other disruptive factors that have been gradually affecting the performance, both positive and negative, of global supply chains. These are economic and political nationalism, Industry 4.0 and the digital revolution. Hence, we have seven contemporary challenges, some of them being interrelated, on global supply chains. This chapter addresses these challenges and explores how to deal with them.

Learning objectives

Learning objectives for this chapter are:

1. Impact of the Covid-19 pandemic.
2. Impact of Brexit.
3. Impact of climate change.
4. Impact of the Ukraine conflict.
5. Impact of nationalism.
6. Impact of Industry 4.0.
7. Impact of digital transformation.

Impact of the Covid-19 pandemic

Since the outbreak of Covid-19 in China at the end of 2019, more than 210 countries and territories have reported the outbreak, and as of 9 May 2022, over 521 million people had

DOI: 10.4324/9781003341352-5

infections resulting in at least 6.3 million deaths (Statistica, 2022). The threats of the global pandemic aroused worldwide concern for the immediate damage to global supply chains.

A range of precautionary measures to curb the spread of Covid-19 was adopted by all governments. These included travel restrictions, shutdowns of factories, shops and entertainment and also the virtual confinement of all inhabitants. These restrictions led to a short supply of labour, raw materials and finished products. Shelves of supermarkets were left bare. As a result, global supply chains also faced delays, inventory shortages and tightening controls on logistical systems. Also, there was a complete inability to predict when this pandemic would be contained.

Covid-19 not only disrupted local supply chains, but it profoundly affected global supply chains at all stages, from the supply sources to the final customers. The disruptions in global supply chains happened in all sectors. However, on the customer side, demands relevant to the prevention of Covid-19 (e.g. masks) were rising. Disrupted commodities had a variable impact on global supply chains as explained in the following sections.

Foods. Food supply chains, from seeds to dry products such as rice and wheat, as well as fresh food, such as meat, vegetables and fruits, are mainly affected by three aspects: farming, conversion and transportation. Almost all the stages of food production, such as seeding, processing, packing and delivery, are labour-intensive. Lack of farmers, production workers and truckers, cancelled flights, time-consuming inspections and quarantine in customs hampered the delivery of fresh foods.

Medical products. Chinese manufacturers are estimated to account for 40% of all active pharmaceutical ingredients (API) used worldwide and consequently medical supply was badly affected. The global shortage of personal protective equipment (PPE), particularly of medical masks, respirators, protective gear, footwear, gowns and goggles severely affected the containment of the virus.

Automotive products. The global output for the automotive industry is expected to drop by 13%. Car manufacturers across the world had to shut down their plants worldwide due to a shortage of labour and supply of parts. 'Working from home' rules may support some service industries but cannot run an automotive plant.

High-tech products. The high-tech industry covering products such as smartphones, virtual reality headsets and other tech accessories had their supply chains tangled by shortages of various parts. For instance, Apple had to postpone deliveries of its new products to the market due to the shutdown of Foxconn plants in China

Industrial products. The pandemic affected many industrial products too. For example, high gas prices in Europe led to the temporary closure of a few fertiliser plants, which suddenly led to the shortage of carbon dioxide, its key by-product

International logistics. The logistics sector suffered from a lack of workers throughout all the stages of the supply chain. For example, a shortage of HGV drivers paralysed the supply of petrol and diesel in the UK. The shutdown of commercial aviation severely limited air cargo capacities making it harder to move vital supplies such as medical equipment to fight the outbreak around the world. Over 30% of container capacity was removed from the market due to blank sailings. The International Civil Aviation Organization claimed that the number of seats offered by airlines was reduced by around 60% in 2020 (Xu et al., 2020).

Retail activities. With COVID-19 dominating the headlines, panic behaviour prompted people to do forward buying for basic products such as toilet paper and non-perishables (e.g. dry goods). Sales of basic consumer goods increased by up to 53% in the early stages of the outbreak in the United States. Online sales grew by 46% in 2020 – its strongest growth for more than a decade.

Entertainment and hospitality. In 2020, the global pandemic impacted theatrical and home/mobile entertainment, as movie theatres and production studios temporarily closed. Pubs, restaurants and holidays were also badly affected due to lockdowns.

In 2021, vaccines for Covid-19 became widely available in wealthier countries such as the UK, but many parts of the world struggled to access vaccines. With the rollout of vaccines, economies began to reopen and consumer demand began to return to pre-pandemic patterns and global production struggled to meet it. The legal restrictions of Covid-19 began to be lifted during the first quarter of 2022 and most of the world population was adapting to live with Covid-19. Unfortunately, as of April 2022, China imposed draconian measures (zero-Covid policy), trapping most of Shanghai's inhabitants at home for weeks as the country combated its worst outbreak since the pandemic began. However, the World Health Organisation warned that China's zero-Covid policy was not sustainable. Then came the war between Ukraine and Russia.

The move to outsourcing reduces costs but increases risk. The risk is caused by longer transport connections. It is further enhanced by an increased concentration of production in China and supply from Russia. We can never eliminate supply chain risk and increasing geopolitical uncertainty inevitably increases those risks. Modern supply chains are driven by efficiency, and they work extraordinarily well when demand is predictable but are just not designed for a global pandemic.

We may have to live through the shortages and make ad-hoc adjustments to supply chains. The current crisis will put further pressure on companies to bring production closer to home and innovate to keep costs low, for example, through further digitalisation and automation. We will also see a drive towards more sustainable production.

Impact of Brexit

Following a referendum in 2016, the UK left the European Union on 31 December 2020, out of its political and legal structures, single market and customs union. This is popularly known as the Brexit deal. There has been some pride among nationalists in 'taking back control', but the impact of the deal is negative for the British economy. Trade economists consistently warned that the benefits of free trade agreements with other countries were being oversold by the government The Northern Ireland Protocol also caused significant political problems. Brexit also created 'red tape' at ports and the UK stopped selling many products to smaller EU countries.

> The extent of economic damage from Brexit has been made clear by the Office for Budget Responsibility, which predicts that leaving the EU will reduce our long-term GDP by around 4%, compared to a fall of around 1.5% that will be caused by the pandemic.
>
> (*The Guardian*, 25 December 2021)

The think tank UK in a Changing Europe (UKICE, 2022) said trade barriers introduced after leaving the EU had led to a 6% increase in UK food prices between December 2019 and September 2021. Food prices increased further in 2022 partly due to Brexit. By making trade with Europe difficult and costly, it has so far added to the economic travails of the UK.

The impact of Brexit on the global supply chain is also significant. Brexit made the shortages hitting the UK economy worse compared with the rest of the world, the government's spending watchdog has said. UK ministers repeatedly blamed a 'global crisis' for empty shelves and depleted petrol stations across the country – confusing international observers who are not facing similar problems at home.

In a recent article, Harris (2022) concluded that in ten areas, Brexit has severely damaged the economy and lifestyle of the UK. These ten areas are:

1. *Labour shortages* extend from transport to pubs to hospitals and care homes.
2. British *food growers* cannot find seasonal workers and crops are lying in fields.
3. Brexit is also terrible for *food imports* despite import controls on EU food products being postponed for the fourth time.
4. *British exports* to the rest of Europe have fallen by 14%, partly by Covid and mostly due to excessive paperwork.
5. The Port of Dover declared a 'critical incident' on 22 July 2022 as droves of people trying to go to the continent caused *six-hour queues* as a result of post-Brexit passport controls.
6. While the EU's *GDP per head* has grown 8.5% since Brexit, the UK's figure is only 3.8%, and the UK is also behind other G7 nations in its recovery from the pandemic.
7. The UK has the highest *inflation* of any country in G7, higher than France, Italy and Germany. In addition to the impact of the war in Ukraine, since the departure from the EU, the pound has weakened, adding to the price of imported energy.
8. Brexit has drastically changed UK *universities*; since Brexit, there has been a 40% drop in EU students coming to the UK and Horizon Europe (£80 billion research fund) is in doubt.
9. In the over-promised *fishing industry*, 'it is quicker to sell products to China than to France' due to the massive burden of paperwork for the EU.
10. For the arts, and *music in particular*, Brexit demands rules and fees, and as a result, British musicians playing EU festivals have fallen by 45%.

The EU is the UK's largest business partner, accounting for 49% of all British goods exports to the EU and 55% of imports from the EU. The rise of emerging economies is also radically reshaping global trade flows: emerging markets' share of global consumption has risen by roughly 50% over the past decade. Brexit is here to stay, and it is time to stop waiting for the uncertainty about Brexit to disperse. UK businesses must embrace the new realities of world trade. Here are some ideas:

- UK companies need to make the most of digital technology to optimise their supply chain management processes.
- Both the government and businesses need to respond more rapidly to the changing environment of green technology.
- UK exporters need to prioritise speed to market and proximity to customers.
- Retain business partnerships with the EU and expand trade relationships in emerging markets.

Impact of climate change

'Climate change' as a scientific term may well sound quite tame and vernacular, and possibly does not convey a sufficient sense of urgency. The term 'global warming' has also been used as another phrase for the same thing, but by contrast, this expression clearly

Table 4.1 Greenhouse gases

Greenhouse gases	Percentages
Carbon dioxide	82
Methane	10
Nitrous oxide	6
Others	2

Source: US EPA (2019).

imparts an unambiguous message concerning the imminent danger posed to humans and other living objects on earth. I have to admit that in the context of discussions regarding our future well-being I do prefer the term 'global warming'. However as 'climate change' is the official term being used by the United Nations (e.g. UNFCCC: United Nations Framework Convention on Climate Change and IPCC: Intergovernmental Panel on Climate Change), I shall also use this phrase primarily to express the impact of global warming.

The world is producing 51 gigatonnes or 51 billion tonnes of greenhouse gases every year. These greenhouse gases include carbon dioxide (CO_2), methane (CH_4), nitrous oxide (N_2O), water vapour (H_2O) and ozone (O_3) as shown in Table 4.1.

Carbon dioxide has been found to be the most important greenhouse gas related to global warming. It constitutes 82% of all greenhouse gases and stays in the atmosphere for a long time. Recent studies have shown that 75% of carbon will not disappear for hundreds to thousands of years while the other 25% will stay with us forever. Methane causes many times more warming, molecule for molecule, than carbon dioxide when it reaches the atmosphere, but methane does not stay in the atmosphere as long as carbon dioxide does.

If we look at a supply chain in another way, it is made of how we grow and procure things (land and agriculture), how we make things and provide services (industry) and how we get around (transport). Global supply chains will include agriculture, land and industry and in total accounts for 45% of greenhouse gas emissions. The pressure of climate change on global supply chains and industries has been more significant and transparent since the UN COP26 summit in Glasgow. The event was held during the first two weeks of November 2021 in order to thrash out a deal to curb global warming and accelerate the shift to cleaner economies. Nearly 40,000 people participated in the two-week summit, which ended in overtime on Saturday 13 November with leaders signing up to the Glasgow Climate Pact after frantic last-minute talks. The spirit of change was there and clearly discernible. This was strengthened by the final outcome of the Glasgow Climate Pact document.

Key pledges of the Pact

- Pledges were made by 140 countries to reach net-zero emissions by 2050. This target includes the reduction/elimination of 90% of current global greenhouse gas emissions.
- More than 100 countries, including Brazil, vowed to reverse deforestation by 2030.
- Over 40 countries have undertaken to move away from fossil fuel subsidies and the use of coal; 190 countries, including China and India, pledged to 'phase down' coal.

- India promised to draw half of its energy requirement from renewable sources by 2030 and to achieve net-zero emissions by 2070.
- China committed to achieving net-zero emissions by 2060.
- The governments of 24 developed countries and a group of major car manufacturers committed to 'work towards all sales of new cars and vans being zero emission globally by 2040'. However, it should be noted that major car manufacturing nations including the United States, Germany, China, Japan and South Korea did not join this pledge.

The Pact includes a doubling of money for adaptation by 2025, by comparison with 2019 levels, but the US$100 billion target is likely only to be met by 2023.

Impact of the Ukraine conflict

When global economies were beginning to recover from the severe impact of the Covid-19 pandemic, global supply chains were once again being tested by the so-called 'special military operations' in Ukraine by Russia in February 2022. The impact was almost immediate on the supply of foods and fossil fuels. Europe exposed its vulnerabilities in its over-dependence on natural gas and crude oil from Russia and key agricultural commodities from Russia and Ukraine.

According to the Food and Agriculture Organization (FAO), Russia and Ukraine account for more than 25% of the world's supply of wheat, more than 60% of global sunflower oil and 30% of global barley (FAO, 2022). As a result, consumers experienced a huge increase in prices at supermarkets and petrol stations. Energy bills also went up. In the UK, 27% of households had to choose between 'heating and eating'. Inflation reached a 40-year high to nearly 10%.

There were also medium-term impacts on the agriculture and industry sectors. Russia is also a major global exporter of fertilisers, which meant that any supply shortages could impact crop yields globally. Russia is a major source of many critical minerals including 30% of palladium, 13% of titanium and 11% of nickel (Kilpatrick, 2022). Russia is also a major source of neon, used for etching circuits on silicon wafers causing a shortage in microchip supplies.

The Ukraine conflict caused sanctions on Russian banks and the assets of oligarchs and Russian leaders. The exodus of major multinationals from Russia, including BP, Apple, Netflix, American Express and McDonald's, contributed to the economic shift of de-globalisation.

So what type of mitigating actions can be taken by both governments and industries? There is no 'silver bullet', but here are some ideas to lessen the impact of the Ukraine conflict on global supply chains:

- Governments should try to provide some short-term financial support to affected households, especially to pay energy bills.
- Industries should make sure that the proper risk management tools are in place in the extended supplier network and in relation to the supply and inflationary pressures on key commodities.
- Both governments and industries should have immediate plans for alternative sources of supply for key commodities such as oil, gas, wheat, sunflower oil and fertilisers.

- Industries should seriously consider 'on-shoring' and 'friend-shoring' of supply wherever justifiable. 'On-shoring' will bring supply chains nearer and 'friend-shoring' will aim to swap risky foreign suppliers with close allies.
- It would be useful to challenge the minimum inventory policy and review the 'safety stock' of commodities from risky foreign suppliers.
- Supply chains are rapidly becoming digital. State-sponsored and organised attacks have reinforced the critical need for cybersecurity for digital systems.

Impact of nationalism

George Orwell distinguished between patriotism and nationalism. 'Patriotism is the love of your country. Nationalism is a "them and us" ideology. You find enemies where they don't exist, you build your case around resentments and there is always the other' (Orwell, 2018).

Economic nationalism is built on Orwell's version of nationalism. It is an ideology that favours state interventions and opposes open market mechanisms. These interventions are usually affected by the imposition of tariffs and other restrictions on the movement of labour, goods and capital. The core belief of economic nationalism is that the economy should serve nationalist goals (Helleiner, 2021). Economic nationalists oppose globalisation, favour protectionism and advocate for self-sufficiency.

Economic nationalism and political populism are interrelated. A recent example of this in the United States was the election of Donald Trump, running his campaign around the 'America first' slogan and blocking southern immigration. Indeed, it was seen that Trump's victory through such assured and bold moves has sparked populism in other nations. Brexit in the UK is also an example of political populism. However, research by Foster et al. (2017) indicated that the recent rise in populism in the United States and Europe had a negative effect on global supply chains. In spite of initial support, citizens' trust in their government's representative democracy weakened. President Trump did not get re-elected in 2020 and President Macron was re-elected in France by beating a populist candidate Marine Le Pen. The implications of a populist government suggest that it can be avoided, and also the countries reliant on democracy do not indicate a possibility for a change.

A recent survey (Cunnane, 2018) indicated that 66% of manufacturers would change their supply chains in order to tackle economic nationalism. In addition, 50% of respondents say economic nationalist policies will increase operational costs, and 45% were considering alternative suppliers. Economic nationalism is recognised as one of the most severe challenges facing manufacturing supply chains the survey finds. When asked to choose their biggest global concerns, respondents place economic nationalism (46%) second only to taxes and duties (50%).

In the UK, the world's sixth largest economy, 64% of respondents are most worried about economic nationalism, namely Brexit – but their concern is not limited to that one region. As a result of Brexit, 45% of respondents globally are likely to change their supply chain design. This figure increases to 53% in the UK, 54% in France, 56% in Germany and 51% in North America.

In addition to protectionism, one major outcome of economic nationalism or populism is trade wars between bigger trading groups. President Trump's love of tariffs and trade wars with China in 2017 accelerated the protectionist trends. In retaliation, Beijing excluded US internet giants and increasingly looked towards self-sufficiency in key technologies. It was estimated that the tariffs imposed an additional burden of between 500 million to 1 billion US dollars on these countries (Mao et al., 2020). The threat of the unilateral discontinuation of the 'Northern Ireland protocol' by the UK Government in 2022 had the potential of a trade war with the European Union.

Nationalists oppose globalisation and argue that globalisation may have made rich people in wealthy economies richer and also both the rich and poor people in emerging economies richer, but globalisation has made poor people in rich countries poorer.

Impact of Industry 4.0

Industry 4.0 is the transition of the fourth industrial revolution in industry. The first industrial revolution started through steam power and then evolved to the second with mass production and assembly lines using electricity. Then came the third revolution with the adoption of computers and automation. Now we are in the fourth revolution in industry (Industry 4.0) powered by big data, cloud computing, blockchain, the Internet of Things (IoT), artificial intelligence (AI) and machine learning.

Industry 4.0 creates a disruption and requires companies to rethink the way they design their supply chain. These disruptive technologies also created Supply Chain 4.0 with the application of the IoT, the use of AI and System as a Service (SaaS), and the application of blockchain and advanced analytics of big data in supply chain management. Digitisation brings about a Supply Chain 4.0 that will be faster, more granular with individualised products, more accurate and above all more efficient. The potential impact of Supply Chain 4.0 in the next five years is huge. Alicke et al. (2016) predict that up to 30% lower operational costs and a reduction of 75% in lost sales while decreasing inventories by up to 75% are expected. These are big numbers and indicate the potential of the digital revolution in supply chain management or digital supply chains.

The application and impact of new disruptive technologies in supply chain management processes are interrelated. Table 4.2 shows a summary of the application of Industry 4.0 in supply chains.

Supply chains will change radically over the next five to ten years, with different industries implementing Supply Chain 4.0 at varying speeds. Companies that get there first will gain a competitive advantage in the race to Industry 4.0 and will be able to influence technical standards for their particular industry.

Raji and Rossi (2019) presented a conceptual model to provide a decision tool for practitioners at identifying potential Industry 4.0 technologies for strategic lean and agile supply chain strategies. It is important to point out that the model is yet to be tested and provokes some future research agendas.

Impact of digital transformation

Digital transformation is the outcome of the digital revolution of Industry 4.0 as described earlier. Digital transformation actually means exactly what it says. It is about transforming supply chains through the use of digital technologies into more effective versions of businesses. We have already transformed the way global supply chains work through effective applications of new digital systems offered by IoT, AI, blockchain, big data analytics, cloud computing and 3D printing. As the impact of digital transformation is positive and sustainable in global supply chains, new digital systems are described in more detail in this chapter and also in Chapter 13.

Table 4.2 Industry 4.0 applications in supply chains

Technology	Key features	Application areas	Potential improvement
Big data analytics	Big data analytics is the use of advanced analytic techniques against very large, diverse data sets. Cloud computing, AI and IoT process data complexity through sources of big data analytics.	Can deliver real-time insight and speed-of-thought queries across the entire supply chain.	Can drive significant operational efficiencies by providing visibility.
Cloud computing	Cloud computing can be thought of as utility computing. It is the on-demand availability of computer system resources without direct active management by the user.	Primarily SaaS applications in ERP.	Significant savings in ERP systems licence and maintenance.
Machine learning	Machine learning allows software applications to become more accurate at predicting outcomes without being explicitly programmed to do so. Machine-learning algorithms use historical data. It is seen as part of AI.	As part of AI applications in demand planning, procurement, inventory management and customer service.	Significant improvement in data accuracy to improve supply chain performance.
Artificial intelligence	AI is a wide-ranging branch of computer science concerned with building smart machines capable of performing tasks that typically require human intelligence. AI is powered by machine-learning algorithms.	Similar to machine learning.	Similar to machine learning.
Internet of Things	IoT refers to the number of physical and sensory devices around the world that are now connected to the internet, all collecting and sharing data.	Performance and quality monitoring in manufacturing and services; storage conditions; shipments by using GPS.	Enables businesses to integrate their IoT networks smoothly with other supply chain IT systems.
Blockchain	Blockchain is a digital system of recording transactions across many computers via cryptography.	In the ERP systems of supply chains (such as SAP), blockchain technology can ensure that the information is only visible to users with the appropriate cryptographic key. Access to data security is more important in SaaS applications.	The data is protected between supply chain partners.
3D printing	3D printing is the construction of a three-dimensional object or a prototype from a CAD model or a digital 3D model.	Product design and the production of components.	As a toolless process with real-time capability, it reduces complexity and inventory and enhances customer interaction.

Internet of Things

The use of smart technologies in machines and processes is allowing information to be generated and analysed, improving supply chain capabilities. One such smart technology is IoT. The Internet of Things describes the network of physical objects connecting and exchanging data with other devices and systems over the Internet. It works like in Figure 4.1.

- *Sensors.* Smart sensors (such as RFID) are attached to objects to collect, send and act on data they acquire from their environments.
- *Network.* Wired and wireless networks obtain data from sensors and connect it to the internet.
- *Analysis.* Data collected from smart sensors are either sent to the 'cloud' to be analysed or analysed locally.
- *Intelligence.* These devices communicate with related devices and act on the information they get from one another to produce actionable insights.
- *Decision making.* Insights derived from IoT assist in the decision making of individuals and machines.

The devices do most of the work without human intervention. However, people can also interact with the devices, for instance, to set them up, give them instructions or access the data.

A 'thing' in the IoT can be a person with a heart monitor implant, a farm animal with a biochip, a machine on the shop floor or a car that has a built-in sensor to alert the driver when tire pressure is low.

Increasingly, organisations in a variety of industries are using IoT to operate more efficiently, better understand customers to deliver enhanced customer service, improve decision making and increase the value of the business. When applied to supply chains, IoT can help businesses source more sustainable products. Information collected and exchanged from sensors can explain how the product was made, from where inputs were sourced, how they were manufactured and how they were consumed. In addition, these sensors can store and provide information to consumers about how these products should be disposed.

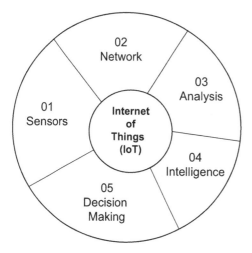

Figure 4.1 Internet of Things process cycle

IoT technology has been applied to smart homes including security devices and home appliances that can be controlled by smartphones. IoT can also be used in service industries and healthcare systems. There are, however, some concerns regarding IoT, especially in the areas of security and privacy.

AI in supply chain management

We know that AI and machine learning are inextricably linked. AI refers to the science of training machines to perform human tasks. Where AI is the broader science, machine learning refers to the specific subset of AI that trains a machine how to learn. Once a machine-learning algorithm understands all the available data, it is able to apply that knowledge to new sets of data, thus increasing accuracy and performance.

AI powered by machine learning is being used to identify patterns and influential factors in supply chain data with algorithms and constraint-based modelling. This data–rich modelling empowers warehouse managers to make much more informed decisions about inventory stocking by using AI-powered software (e.g. *NETSUITE*). Warehouse managers also have access to data on inventory levels in real time, including detailed information about all stock items. AI-powered route optimisation platforms and GPS tools powered by AI like *Orion* create the most efficient routes. A logistics leader like UPS uses Orion.

The most significant application of AI in supply chain management has been in demand forecasting. According to MGI (2017), demand forecasting tools powered by AI can reduce forecast accuracy by 30 to 50% in supply chain networks leading to a 65% reduction in lost sales due to inventory out–of–stock situations and lower warehousing costs. In traditional forecasting models, such as moving average, and exponential smoothing methods only historical data is considered. These are getting outdated. The main strength of AI is the use of machine-learning algorithms. With the help of external data and modern machine-learning algorithms, supply chain networks can outperform networks managed more manually or by conventional forecasting software. For new products that lack historical data, machine-learning forecasting tools can identify and use the datasets of similar prior products as a substitute to make predictions. Modern AI-powered demand forecasting tools include *FutureMargin*, *amoCRM*, Capsule and *COLIBRI*. As an example, the partnership of *FutureMargin* (supplied by Algopine of Slovakia) and its customers resulted in improvements in average order fulfilment time by 14%.

Demand planning is a critical activity in the sales and operations planning (S&OP) process. Therefore, the application of AI is extended to S&OP. The objective of S&OP is to obtain alignment from all actors in the company, ensuring that operations mobilises its resources to supply what the business needs to meet its customer service and financial goals. A fundamental pillar of the S&P process is the notion of 'one set of numbers', which means that operations and finance are working off a shared understanding of the forward plan based on the same set of numbers. A successful AI-generated demand plan would also have to be linked to the 'one set of numbers' principle. However, AI may also cause the reluctance of some managers to using AI applications that seem like a 'black box' to them. This 'black box' problem is likely to be a tangible hurdle for successful AI deployments. This does not preclude the use of AI for demand planning and logistics application, but it does suggest that AI in S&OP should be considered, especially for companies that achieved very high S&OP maturity.

Cremer and Kasparov (2021) estimate that AI could add approximately US$15.7 trillion to the global economy by 2030. However, this estimate is not supported by evidence, and we should contain our expectations from AI in the medium term. Furthermore, a major limitation of AI is that relies on having access to data. The quality of the data directly determines the quality of the output. Nonetheless, the potential benefits of AI in supply chains are far-reaching.

Blockchain in supply chain management

Blockchain is a digital system of recording transactions across many computers via cryptography that makes it impossible to change the information retroactively. It is best known for its role in cryptocurrency systems such as bitcoin. However, blockchain technology is now having wider applications in industries including supply chain management.

This is how blockchain works. When a transaction is requested, it is broadcast to a network of nodes. The transaction is validated and unified with other transactions as a block of data by using known algorithms. The new block is added to the blockchain via cryptography in a transparent but unalterable way. The transaction is now complete.

Global supply chains operate sequentially in two paths, one physical and one digital. Both paths need to be monitored and measured and used to drive the next level of the process. Blockchain technology can ensure that the information is only visible to users with the appropriate cryptographic key. The data is protected between supply chain partners.

In the enterprise resource planning (ERP) systems of supply chains (such as SAP), the blockchain feature allows users of cloud platforms (such as SaaS) to extend and build applications with blockchain technology and unlocks new functionalities in the blockchain ecosystem.

Big data analytics in supply chain management

The term 'Big Data' refers to piles of data that are meaningless unless you have the power to analyse them. Everyone has a limited vertical view of data sitting in their own silo. The advantage of big data is that it lets you get a 360-degree view of information in both vertical and horizontal planes and right across your organisation. Data from discrete silos are brought together by a single data lake in web services (such as AWS or Amazon Web Services), now commonly known as cloud computing.

A typical flow of big data analytics is shown in Figure 4.2 where unprocessed information from multiple sources is extracted into a daily batch of raw evidence. This data is then cleansed and brought into a data lake using cloud computing. The data is then transformed and queried by a set of web services tools (e.g. Apache) and then personised and visualised by using Tableau.

Big data and analytics use data and quantitative methods in supply chains to improve decision making for all activities across the supply chain. The dataset for analysis is extended beyond the traditional internal data held on enterprise resource planning (ERP) and supply chain management (SCM) systems. Here are some applications of big data analytics.

In operations planning, retailers can use expanded data sources to improve planning processes and their demand-sensing capabilities. For example, Amazon has patented an 'anticipatory shipping' approach, in which orders are packaged and pushed into the delivery network before customers have actually ordered them. In manufacturing, big data and analytics can already help improve manufacturing. For example, energy-intensive production runs can be scheduled to take advantage of fluctuating electricity prices. Big data sources and analytical techniques are also creating new opportunities in warehousing.

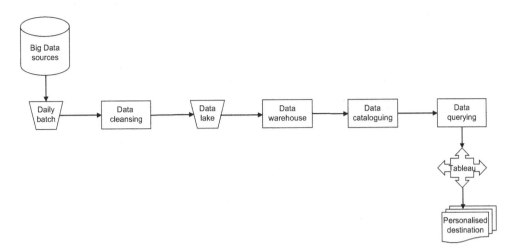

Figure 4.2 A typical flow of big data analytics

A leading forklift provider is looking into how the forklift truck can act as a big data hub that collects all sorts of data in real time to be integrated with ERP and warehouse management system (WMS) data. Truck companies are already using fuel consumption analytics to improve driving efficiency.

As these examples show, big data is already helping leading organisations transform the performance of their supply chains. However, most companies appear to lack a structured process to explore, evaluate and capture big data opportunities in their supply chains (Alicke et al., 2016).

Cloud computing in supply chain management

Cloud computing is the delivery of all types of computing services over the Internet ('the cloud') to offer faster, cheaper and more flexible digital resources. These resources include servers, storage, databases, networking, software, analytics and intelligence.

Often people interchange the term Cloud Computing with SaaS (System as a Service). Both are closely related but these terms mean different things. Cloud computing (often simply referred to as 'the cloud') is a broad term that encompasses various models used to deliver computing services through the Internet as a utility. SaaS is the best-known model in the cloud. There are other models such as Platform as a Service (PaaS) and Infrastructure as a Service (IaaS).

The SaaS version of ERP has been the most effective and popular application of the cloud in supply chain operations. It offers scalability, immediacy, flexibility, reliability and above all cost-effectiveness. For example, if an organisation wishes to install a full-fledged ERP system (such as SAP R3), it will not only require procuring the system at a high cost, but it will also need to build and maintain the infrastructure and employ personnel to operate it. The implementation period will also be longer. However, with a SaaS application, there is no upfront capital required for the software and you do not have to worry about building and maintaining the infrastructure. Instead, the software is available via a web browser and the SaaS provider, in exchange for your subscription fee, handles all the heavy lifting. SaaS applications are particularly attractive to small and medium enterprises (SMEs).

Although cloud technology has been around for almost 20 years, supply chain professionals have been relatively slow in its implementation. The situation is now starting to change, with recent reports (Gartner, 2021) estimating that the value of cloud-based supply chain management solutions could exceed US$11 billion by 2023.

Three-dimensional printing technology in supply chain management

Three-dimensional (3D) printing (also known as additive manufacturing) is also part of the digital revolution in manufacturing and supply chain management. It leads to disruptive innovations that create a global impact on the logistics of industries and the supply chain. The main impact of this technology is to fabricate and customise the products in real time and be closer to the expectations of customers around the world. It has great benefits over supply chain management by means of a reduction in inventory, shipping costs and capital expenditures on factories and warehouses. These benefits provide the potential for a transformation of global supply chain management.

SGS Maine Pointe (2022) suggests that 3D printing can provide competitive advantages in many areas, which are shown in the following sections.

Decentralise production. The portable nature of the technology enables businesses to take production to low-cost countries in favour of more local assembly hubs. Companies will also have the capability to produce components closer to home rather than relying on imports. This is especially important during times of geopolitical tensions, for example, during the Ukraine war or a trade war.

Faster product customisation. As a toolless process with a real-time capability, 3D printing technology provides freedom to respond rapidly to clients' specific requirements and enhance customer interaction. This will result in more agile supply chains that can rapidly adapt to changes in the market with a greater client involvement in the entire design and production process.

Reduce complexity. Three-dimensional printing technology has the ability to consolidate the number of components and processes required for manufacturing. This will have a significant impact on global supply chains, decreasing complexities, reducing lead times and improving time-to-market.

Reduce inventory. This technology takes 'just-in-time' manufacturing to a new level. As 'on demand and on time' production becomes the norm, the need to transport physical goods across countries and continents will reduce. Combined with the lower number of stock keeping units (SKUs) required for production, this will have a major impact on the supply chain inventory.

Green supply chain. Three-dimensional printing is a 'greener', more energy-efficient and cost-efficient production method. It creates almost zero waste, lowers the risk of overproduction and excess inventory and reduces the carbon footprint.

Summary

The overall impact of seven contemporary challenges on global supply chains as experienced in 2022 is restraining the global economy. High inflation and the supply of food and energy are affecting the cost of living of many households.

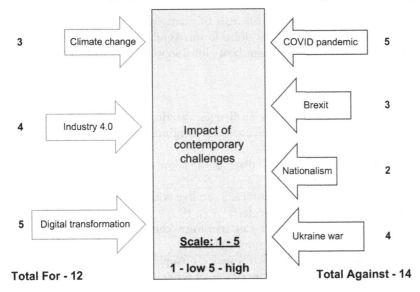

Figure 4.3 Force field analysis for contemporary challenges

However, all challenges should not be detrimental to global supply chains. As shown in the force field analysis diagram in Figure 4.3, three challenges (e.g. climate change, Industry 4.0 and digital transformation) with appropriate actions can be converted into opportunities.

Climate change initiatives and new tools (e.g. the tools and approach of Green Six Sigma; Basu, 2022) supported by the determination of governments and industries can be a catalyst for the implementation of sustainable green supply chains. With the application of Industry 4.0, major industries can bolster the productivity of goods supply, contributing to the growth of the global economy. Supply chains are rapidly becoming digital, underpinned by the advanced systems of digital transformation.

The opposing challenges (e.g. Covid-19 pandemic, Brexit, nationalism and war in Ukraine) are stronger at the moment and hence the performance of global supply chains is affected, causing bottlenecks at ports and airports, a shortage of grain and higher energy prices. However, it is realistic to expect that the restrictions of Covid-19 will gradually reduce and the war in Ukraine will soon cease to be manageable. The global economy will adjust to the impact of Brexit and nationalism with some movement towards 'on-shoring' production. A recent survey by Alicke et al. (2002) shows that companies have made significant progress in mitigating current supply chain challenges such as Ukraine war disruption and the worldwide shortage of supplies. Over the past year, many companies have implemented dual or multiple sourcing strategies for critical materials and moving from global to regional networks. Supply chain digitisation efforts are also entering a new phase. And despite progress over the past 12 months, many companies are still facing challenges of acute labour shortages and skyrocketing energy prices.

Unless there are other major disruptions, subject to the duration of the war in Ukraine, say from 2024, we should move towards environmentally sustainable global supply chains powered by digital transformation and climate change initiatives.

In order to combat the opposing challenges of managing global supply chains, it is vital that global leaders should convene a global forum (similar to G7, G20 and the Davos Economic Summit) with the primary agenda of global supply chain challenges.

Discussion questions

1. What are the seven contemporary challenges affecting the performance of global supply chains? Discuss which challenges will continue to influence global supply chain operations.
2. Discuss with the help of a force field diagram the negative and positive impacts of the seven contemporary challenges.
3. Explain how UK and European businesses can live with the impact of Brexit. How does Brexit affect outsourcing strategies?
4. Discuss how innovative initiatives can transform climate change challenges into opportunities for sustainable green supply chains.
5. Explain with examples how the performance of supply chain building blocks can benefit from the application of advanced digital systems.

Part 2

Building blocks of global supply chains

5 Customer focus and demand management

Introduction

Customer focus and demand are the first of our six building blocks for supply chain management. In Chapter 3, we said that customers create demand. Marketing and sales personnel and advertising agents might argue that through advertising and promotion they create demand. It is true that marketing will create interest and might initially generate some sales. But no matter how clever or entertaining advertising and other forms of promotion might be, unless the product is wanted or needed by the customer, demand will soon evaporate. A customer could be a consumer (end user), retailer, wholesaler or distributor but ultimately the demand for a product or service is determined by the end user. An example of promotion creating interest can be seen in two West End shows opening on the same night in London. Although both might have similar-sized casts with well-known 'stars' and have the same type of promotion, one will run for several months, and one will close after a few weeks. Whether a show is successful or not will be determined by the number of people who buy tickets for the show, in other words, customer demand, based on reports of critics and word of mouth. Why one was a success and the other a flop will be due to customer perception of the show, not on the quality or amount of promotion. Indeed, the flagging show is likely to have more spent on advertising than the successful show. The same applies to any product or service, advertising and other forms of promotion can arouse initial interest but if the product does not closely meet customer expectations, marketing alone cannot sustain demand. Our rule of thumb is that unless a product or service meets 80% of customer needs, the customer will be lost. Why only 80%? Should we not be aiming for 100%? The answer is yes, but it might not be economically feasible for us to exactly meet every customer's needs or expectations, even if we knew exactly what they wanted. As a customer, if we always received service and products meeting 80% of what we wanted, taking into account the price, most of us would be reasonably satisfied. Organisations know this, and instinctively strive to give important customers service at a greater level than they do to less important customers, and the less important customers either through necessity or lethargy accept the rules of the game providing the service or attributes of the product do not fall too far below what they want. Airlines do not hide the fact that first class and business class passengers get priority at check-in, better service and food in flight and even better choice of movies than economy class passengers. In reality, the reason people travel business class is for more legroom and to be able to sleep on long-haul flights, rather than for the quality of the food or the choice of wine. When was the last time that you checked the menu before buying an airline ticket? Economy class passengers, all of whom would prefer to travel business class,

DOI: 10.4324/9781003341352-7

trade service to reduce their cost, and although the economy class passenger will have limited expectations if their perception of the service is poor, they will, often without complaining, simply go to another airline for their next journey even if it means paying a little more. Business class and first class passengers even more so. The lesson here is that customers do not always bother to complain or give you a reason, they just fade away.

This chapter considers how to get closer to the customer to determine what they really want and how to keep customers. In particular, the concept of customer relationship management (CRM) is explained. We begin with a short section on the need to estimate demand and conclude with a short introduction of techniques for forecasting. As explained in Chapter 3, without some form of forecast of demand, management will have difficulty in establishing what the capacity of the operation is and what it should be and what resources to invest in.

Learning objectives

Learning objectives for this chapter are:

1. Customer focus.
2. Customer relationship management.
3. PESTLE analysis.
4. Demand forecasting techniques.

Customer focus

Our first rule is that a world-class organisation aims not to just make sales but to build relationships. Customers are at each stage of the supply chain and each wants to receive materials that meet their needs in terms of specification, timing and at a reasonable cost. This is often known as right thing, right time, right price. Each component of the supply chain, from manufacturer or processor to distributor through wholesalers to retailers and ultimately to the end user, aims to minimise the cost of stockholding. They are not so worried if their supplier has to hold excess stock if this enables them to minimise their own stockholding. For the supply chain as a whole, the ideal for each component is to hold no stock and have reliable suppliers who provide goods and service on time. For each downstream customer to receive such a service, each upstream component, unless they in turn are getting dramatically perfect service from their upstream supplier, must hold stocks of all the stock-keeping units. If a stock of every stock-keeping unit is held, the cost of storage, handling and funding (interest on capital invested) will be high. In the United States, the number of grocery stock-keeping units available in average supermarkets is 47,000, and some hold 100,000. Imagine the cost for any store manager who aimed never to have a stock out.

> Once upon a time, there was a tube of toothpaste. It was called Crest or Colgate or maybe Pepsodent. You chose your brand and went on your way. Today their spawn and competitors occupy entire shelves. Do you pick a product formulated to freshen breath, control tartar, combat plaque or attack gingivitis? Do you have sensitive teeth, sensitive gums or sensitive enamel? And that's just the tip of the iceberg. We know because those are just some of the 27 varieties of Crest we recently bought at a single supermarket (for Colgate, we found a mere 25).
>
> (www.consumerreports.org, 2016)

The cost of stock holding as detailed in Chapter 7 includes interest, insurance, storage space, materials handling, damage, theft, obsolescence, past used-by date, fashion changes and of course the wages of staff involved in handling, counting, checking and raising orders. Thus, what the customer would like and what an organisation can economically provide has to be a trade-off between great service with high stock holding, huge variety, small deliveries and high transportation costs, or a mixture of lower stockholding and transportation cost with diminished customer service, reduced choice, longer lead times and inflexibility.

It should also be noted that at each level of the supply chain there will be additional and different needs. Downstream from the retailer, the end user will not only expect the basics (goods meet specification, available when required), but they will also appreciate after-sales service and the opportunity to return goods. At the retail level of the supply chain, retailers will expect the basics (goods meet specification, available when required) plus they will appreciate sharing the risk of stock holding such as provided by a vendor-managed inventory system. Sharing of risk, such as using a vendor-managed inventory (VMI) system is explained in more detail in Chapter 15.

Determining what the customer wants means more than asking them to fill out satisfaction questionnaires or taking them out for a cup of coffee.

Customer relationship management

Remember the aim is to build relationships not just to sell commodities.

CRM is a relatively new term. CRM did not begin to be covered in marketing textbooks until 2002, but, in effect, the concept was well-known for decades before this. In essence, it is a proactive approach to understanding who your customer is and their strengths and weaknesses, as well as their direct needs with your organisation. It is the move from transaction to interaction by companies managing business relationships from a single platform.

The accountants' approach to CRM is for information to be gathered to determine which customers are profitable and which are not. Often overlooked is how much is given away in discounts, transportation costs and entertainment of 'important' customers. Basu and Wright (2005) relate that in one organisation, the top 5% of customers accounted for 40% of the sales, and because of their perceived importance, were able to negotiate volume discounts and special delivery agreements. When these benefits were examined, it was found that whereas the balance of customers was providing the company with a true 40% gross profit margin on sales, the top 5% were only providing a gross margin of 10%. Thus, overall, the gross margin for the company was reduced to 28%. This had not been apparent as the annual accounts had shown discounts and transport costs as general expenses and not as costs of sales. From a marketing point of view, CRM is used to identify the needs of customers, demographics and market segmentation, and to promote customer loyalty. From a supply/operational aspect, CRM provides information on past demand, trends and seasonal patterns. In short, from history, CRM indicates when periods of heavy demand are likely to occur.

The CRM system requires information to be gathered and stored on a database for each customer, and for the database to be readily accessible across the whole organisation. Thus, each function will be using and making decisions based on common data. The database will have records of what each customer is buying and when (seasonality of demand). For retail customers, such information can be gathered through loyalty cards (see Chapter 14). Information collected can show individually or for a group of customers what they are buying and when and if sales to a particular customer, or group of customers, are profitable. Direct marketing information is gathered through sales staff from call reports, quotes and orders lost. And, of course, the customer should directly be canvassed as to what they want from their supplier. In some circumstances, important customers can be involved in research and development for new products. Other information for the CRM database can be gathered, without the customer's awareness that a database is being built, from customer annual reports, media statements and comments by analysts in the business sections of the day-to-day news media and from business and trade journals. For large (important) customers, this would include tracking the share price.

The CRM database system allows information to be retrieved quickly and is invaluable in forecasting demand and the seasonality of demand. It also helps if the customer can be enlisted in providing early advice as to what their own budgets and forecast of demand are likely to be. If a supplier can get close to a customer, and if there is mutual trust, the customer and supplier can jointly plan for forecasted demand. A component halfway up the supply chain, such as a distributor, should be working closely in the guise of being a customer with their major suppliers in much the same manner as they are working with their major customers. It is not enough to know the strengths and weaknesses of your direct customers, a supplier should have market intelligence for the end user, and in the CRM file for each customer, information regarding their customers should also be gathered. Macro and micro approaches are needed.

Not one-sided.

CRM if properly applied allows us to know our customers and know their market. The aim is to get close to the customer to build a long-term and interactive relationship. Interactive means gathering information should not be one-sided! We need to share information with our customers. Long-term partnerships take time to build and require trust and respect. A full trusting partnership would include sharing technical information and market intelligence. Instead of the old, almost adversarial, approach with customers driving a hard bargain and with suppliers hiding material prices and labour costs and adding on hidden margins where they could, benefits can be gained for both supplier and customer through jointly working to reduce costs and improve relations.

PESTLE analysis

In forecasting, knowing your direct customer and your direct supplier is a good beginning, but in the global market, knowing the origins of their suppliers and understanding external factors as normally covered in the PESTLE analysis used in strategy planning is also important. PESTLE stands for the political, economic, societal, technological, legal and environmental aspects that could impact on a global organisation. Each of these aspects can be examined as a threat and as an opportunity.

Political, legal and societal factors. Laws and regulations might seem to be tiresome limitations, but they do provide protection and a measure of stability. For our own home market, we will know what is legally acceptable, hours and conditions of employment, health and safety issues, taxation and regulatory requirements. When operating overseas, it is wise to understand that what is acceptable in one country may not be acceptable in another. With overseas trading partners, stability of government has to be taken into account when importing or exporting. At home, it is necessary to understand the policies of the government of the day and the major opposition parties.

Economic factors include the state of the economy in general including interest, unemployment, inflation and foreign exchange rates and likely movements.

Socio-cultural includes the movement towards triple bottom line accounting (people, profit and planet) for reporting on social issues, traditional economic and financial results and environmental and sustainability bottom lines. The impact on the supply chain of pressure from the environmental green movement with their concerns, real or imagined (such as global warming), is given in chapter 16.

Technological changes. In the supply chain, technology plays an important part. It is true to say that the supply chain of today would not function without information technology to provide point of sale, electronic data interfaces, electronic funds transfer, manufacturing resource planning, enterprise resource planning and, of course, the focus of this chapter, CRM. The e-supply chain is fully explored in Chapter 13.

Technology includes more than information technology, it includes handling and stacking equipment, packing material, storage, tracking with RFID and barcoding. In manufacturing, it includes computer-aided design, automation and robotics. All these areas are touched on in elements of Chapters 5, 7, 8, 9 and 10.

Competition. Competition is not normally shown in a PESTLE but it is very important. Competition is where your customers can go! Identifying and understanding the competition, what they are doing and what they are threatening to do is essential. However, it is dangerous to overreact, what the competition says it can do, or will do, may not be quite the same as what actually happens. In essence, the very least an organisation can do is to meet the service level provided by the competition and recognise that your performance is judged against customers' perceptions of world-class standards and, rather unfairly, customers will be swayed by hyperbolic claims of the competition. The following questions are designed to help an organisation understand the threats and weaknesses of the competition. These questions are adapted from Basu and Wright (2005).

1. How well do you know the true market size and share for your product/service?
2. Who are your three main competitors?
3. How good is your knowledge of the strengths and weaknesses of your top three competitors?
4. How well do know and compare the service level your competition provides?
5. Do you actively monitor your competitor's acquisitions, expansion and divestments?
6. Do you know the capacity of your competitors' manufacturing and distribution centres?
7. Do you regularly benchmark your performance against the competition?
8. Do you have a dashboard of key performance indicators for your supply chain?

Performance measures in supply chain management can include return on assets employed, stock turn, on-time delivery, transportation costs and other costs and measures as explained in Chapter 23.

Demand forecasting techniques

The three approaches for forecasting are:

* Qualitative
* Quantitative (mathematical or time series approach)
* Causal

In reality, all three approaches are interlinked and should be taken into account when determining a forecasted demand figure. Invariably, all forecasts will also have an element of subjectivity associated with them.

Qualitative forecasting

Qualitative forecasting uses judgement, experience and existing past and present data. However, if forecasting on past results and based on current conditions was easy, the bookmakers would soon be out of business and the weather forecast would always be right! Relying on past information alone to forecast the future is like driving a car forward by looking back through the rearview mirror.

The best-known methods of qualitative forecasting are:

* Expert opinion (including scenario planning and the Delphi method).
* Market surveys.
* Life cycle analysis

Expert opinion

Individuals or groups can undertake this method. If we think about it, managers use expert opinion all the time as they plan and make decisions every day. Scenario planning consists of creating hypothetical circumstances that may happen in the future and then formulating solutions to each scenario. Trend analysis and understanding causal factors are essential to good scenario planning (Getz, 2005).

Imagination is required, as the event manager should then determine the impacts on forecasts using these different scenarios.

As explained in Tum, Norton and Wright (2005), another method of using expert opinion is the Delphi model. Delphi is named after the city in ancient Greece that was the site of the most famous and powerful oracle in the temple of Apollo, noted for giving ambiguous answers. The approach was that if the supplicant asked the right question, they got the right answer. A priestess spoke the oracular messages while in a frenzied trance and sitting on a golden tripod. A priest would interpret these sounds to the supplicant usually in verse. People seeking help would bring gifts to the oracle, and the shrine became very wealthy. Nowadays, the Delphi method is considered by many to be the most successful of the qualitative methods, although it could hardly be considered useful if it were ambiguous. It is time-consuming and costly and is best used by large organisations. The method uses a set of questions to a group of managers or 'experts' who, working without collusion, give their individual opinions. A coordinator then tabulates the opinions, and if individual results differ significantly, then the results are fed back anonymously to the panel with a further set of questions. The process is repeated until a consensus is reached. Questions and feedback generally continue for four rounds, with the questions becoming more specific with each round. The benefit of the method is that a group opinion can be achieved without the team meeting. This overcomes one of the weaknesses of a face-to-face group meeting, where it is possible for members to be swayed by a dominant member, or perhaps an 'expert' member may be embarrassed to back down from a publicly stated opinion.

Market surveys

Market surveys are generally not used to forecast demand for capacity management. They are best used to determine why a product or service is not performing as well as expected.

Market surveys collect data from a sample of customers and potential customers, analyse their views and make inferences about the market at large. Wright and Race (2004) advise that surveys can be carried out by telephone, personal interview, surface mail or email. Market surveys use two approaches: structured and unstructured. With the structured approach, the survey uses a formal list of questions. The unstructured approach enables the interviewer to probe and perhaps guide the respondent. The survey enables the manager to learn why people did not buy and gives the potential for attracting new segments in the future. Framing questions is an art, and when the questions are completed, they should be tested to check ambiguity and relevance. The key is to establish from the outset exactly what information is wanted, and then to design questions that will give the required information. Questions that are not relevant to the issue are a waste of time and money. A weaker form of market survey includes group interviewing or focus groups. With the focus group approach, six to ten people are invited from a market target group to a meeting. The conditions are relaxed with refreshments and so on, and after the interviewer has set the scene, it is hoped that group dynamics will bring out actual feelings and thoughts. At the same time, the interviewer attempts to keep the discussion focused on the subject of the research. The concern with this approach is that too much can be read into the opinions of a small and possibly non-random sample. Holding several focus group meetings on the same subject and then pooling the results can to some extent overcome this problem.

Life cycle analysis

It is generally accepted that products and services have a time-based life cycle. The stages of the life cycle are development, launch, growth, maturity and decline. In preparation for the launch stage, it will be necessary to have stocks of product at each level of the supply chain to make the launch a success, and likewise for the growth stage where there might be a rapid growth in demand. Once a product reaches the maturity stage, the demand will be relatively stable. For most types of products, life cycles are readily predictable, and the rate of growth/decline will not be unexpected. Experienced marketing managers can often, with some degree of accuracy, forecast how long a product will stay in each stage of the life cycle. In the fashion industry, in particular, the demand will be seasonal, and for each new season, products will be manufactured and stocked in the previous season. In Chapter 15, the example is given of a chain of retailers having to order 11 months in advance.

Quantitative

Time series forecasting

Time series forecasting uses mathematical analysis of past demand trends to forecast future demand. However, the accuracy of a forecast will not be known until after the event, and this is usually monitored by the deviation of the actual result from the forecast result. Short-term forecasting involves taking historical data on demand patterns from a few past periods and projecting these patterns into the future. The simplest method is to take the last period's actual demand and use it for the next period(s) forecast, this method gives a quick response to a trend; if the trend is upwards, then the forecast will be upwards but may lag behind. If, however, there are marked annual fluctuations, with this method, following a buoyant year, the forecast will be higher demand. An example of forecasting using seasonal trends is given in Table 5.1.

Table 5.1 Forecasting with seasonal trends

Period	Forecast demand (based on last period)	Actual demand	Deviation
1	No prior data	20	
2	20	22	−2
3	22	23	−1
4 (winter)	23	18	+5
5 (spring)	18	24	−6

Table 5.2 Past average

Period	Forecast	Actual	Deviation (forecast to actual)
1	–	20	–
2	20	22	−2
3	21	24	−3
4	22	23	−1
5	22	13	+ 9
6	20	9	+11
7	18	8	+10
8	17	6	+11

Table 5.3 Three-period average forecast

Period	Forecast	Actual		Deviation (forecast to actual)
1	–	20		–
2	–	22		–
3	–	24	66/3 = 22	–
4	22	23	69/3 = 23	−1
5	23	13	60/3 = 20	+10
6	20	9	45/3 = 15	+11
7	15	8	30/3 = 10	+7
8	10	16	33/3 = 11	−6
		Total absolute deviation		35
		Mean absolute deviation 35/5 =		7
		Deviation spread = +11 to −6		17

This method gives a quick response to a trend; if the trend is upwards then the forecast will be upwards but lag behind. If, however, there are marked seasonal fluctuations then this method would, following low winter sales, forecast low spring sales, although it is well known that for this product, spring sales will always be higher than winter demand. In the above example, based on actual results, the forecast for period five (spring) is 18, although history shows that spring sales are always about 33% above winter demand.

Forecasting by past average

This method is to average all of the past results (see Table 5.2).

A refinement is to take a moving average. In Table 5.3, the last three periods are averaged. This method provides a response to trends and also dampens fluctuations. Although there are still significant variations shown in Table 5.3, the forecasts for periods seven and eight are more accurate than those shown in Table 5.2.

Total absolute deviation (TAD) is the sum of all the deviations ignoring plus or minus signs. Mean absolute deviation is the average of the deviations. In this example, there are five forecasts and five deviations (actual to forecast). The sum of all the deviations ignoring plus or minus is 35. Plus or minus is ignored as it is just as serious to over forecast as it is to under forecast demand. In this example, after the first forecast, which was reasonably accurate, the variations are significant. For example, for period six, the forecast is 122% of actual demand. Although using averages of past actuals 'dampens' rapid responses when there are fluctuations, the method is slow to respond when there is a definite trend, either up or down.

The number of periods used for averaging is a matter of judgement. If there are definite cycles, the number of periods in the cycle can be used to determine the number of periods used for averaging.

Seasonal adjustments

Where there are distinct seasonal trends, then the forecast can be further refined by adjusting for seasonality.

In Table 5.4, we can see that on average the first three quarters each year have accounted for 82% of the total demand for the year. Therefore, based on the previous year's history, the actual first three quarters demand $30 + 55 + 60 = 145$, which we can assume will be 82% of the full year. Thus $145/0.82 = 176.8$ for the full year of 2016, thus quarter four of 2016 will be 31.8. This can be checked for trends. Each year, the total demand has increased from 2012 to 2013 by 17%, 2013 to 2014 by 16%, 2014 to 2015 by 9% and 2015 to 2016, if we accept that our forecast is 176.8, will be 8%. However, is 176.8 a reasonable forecast? Although 176.8 is an exact figure, we must always remember that a forecast is only a forecast and that it will seldom be correct. We should therefore forecast either 180 or 175, never 176.8. In deciding on 180 or 175, we would need to take into account market trends and indicators, economic trends and indicators such as unemployment rates, interest rates, currency fluctuations, the political situation and of course what the competition is doing or threatening to do.

We now have a forecast for the next 12 months (four quarters), which is seasonally adjusted, and has allowed for growth based on the past trend. Naturally, as each new 'actual' comes to hand we recalculate our moving forecast. The main weakness of using past averages is that equal weight is given to each of the historical figures used, and it is also necessary to have, or to build up, a history of information to test against and forecast from.

In general, there are two frequently used models for time series forecasting:

* Moving averages.
* Exponential smoothing.

Table 5.4 Seasonal adjustment

Year	2012	2013	2014	2015	2016
Qtr one	15 (14%)	22 (17%)	25 (17%)	28 (17%)	30
Qtr two	35 (32%)	40 (31%)	45 (30%)	52 (32%)	55
Qtr three	40 (36%)	45 (35%)	50 (33%)	54 (33%)	60
Qtr four	20 (18%)	22 (17%)	30 (20%)	30 (18%)	?
Full year	110	129	150	164	?

The moving averaging model, as shown in the example in Table 5.3, uses the average of the past period data in a time series to forecast future activities. In another simple example, it assumes the sales of the last four months of a mobile handset are 10,000, 12,000, 11,500 and 13,000. Then, using a four-month moving average, the forecast for the fifth month would the average of the past four months: (10,000 + 12,000 + 11,500 + 13,000)/4 or 11,625.

Exponential smoothing is similar to the moving average methods, but it eliminates some of the calculations. The model uses a smoothing factor (less than one) to forecast the next period of activity. The mathematical formula is:

$$F_{n+1} = aA_n + (1 - a)F_n$$

where:

F_{n+1} is the forecast for the next period
F_n is the forecast for the current period
a is the smoothing factor
A_n is the actual data for the current period

Causal

Causal forecasting is when an event (such as sales) is caused by some other event. For example, the demand for small cars increases with the increase in the petrol price. In forecasting, it is easy to get caught up with the method of calculating and to overlook the purpose. The purpose is to get the best possible forecast of what might happen in the future. Past results must be examined to understand why fluctuations in past demand occurred. For example, what was the state of the economy, noting key indicators such as interest rates, inflation rates, currency exchange rates, employment rates and factors such as the entrance of new competitors, new technology and materials, fashion trends and marketing drives. Knowing the past causes for changes in demand is important when making forecasts for the future. Although the information used has a quantitative source, the application and usage of the data rely on a qualitative interpretation.

Common sense

Finally, the common-sense approach with forecasted figures is to test by asking, are these figures sensible, what happened before and what is likely to happen in the future? This approach shows the link between the use of quantitative data and a qualitative approach, and uses the experience, knowledge and expertise of the management team. The common-sense approach with forecasted figures is to test them by asking 'Are these figures sensible, what happened before and what is likely to happen in the future?' Once the future demand forecast has been agreed upon, then we must determine the future capacity of the organisation and anticipate what changes might be needed to meet the level of forecasted demand. This might mean having to consider adding new plant and equipment, increasing human resources, finding new suppliers, increasing warehouse space and so on.

More examples of types of forecasting

As we have discussed earlier, there are basically two approaches to forecasting. Qualitative methods are based on past experience and quantitative methods are based on numeric data.

Quantitative methods are often described in two parts such as time series method and causal models. However, the success of a forecast depends on regular reviews by key stakeholders based on both experience, best judgement and available quantitative data. Here are some examples of types of forecasts and how they are applied to achieve acceptable outcomes.

EXAMPLES: QUALITATIVE FORECAST

History shows that it is unlikely that England will win the next Football World Cup. This does not prove that they won't!

Last quarter (spring) the demand was twice that of the previous (winter) quarter. Further examination might show that the trend for the last few years that demand in the spring quarter has always been double that of the previous quarter (winter). However, the circumstances existing each previous spring might have influenced the results. For one year, demand might have been high due to a new product launch, another year the high demand was due to a successful TV promotion, and on another occasion, a major competitor might have failed and we got the business by default. The figures cannot stand alone but need to be supported by information as to the circumstances at the time.

EXAMPLE: LIFE CYCLE ANALYSIS

The product life cycle curve of develop, launch, growth, maturity and decline is shown in Figure 5.1. It is generally accepted that products have a life cycle that is time based. At the launch stage demand is low, the growth stage shows a rapid demand increase and relatively stable demand at the maturity stage. Most product life cycles are predictable, and for a product such as petrol, the life cycle has extended over many decades, but for some fast-moving consumer goods and fashion items, the rate of growth/decline can be dramatic. Some consumables only reach the decline stage if there is a dramatic change in technology. An example is the replacement of

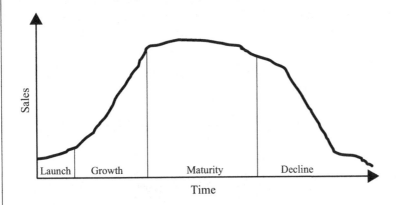

Figure 5.1 The product life cycle

canned vegetables such as peas by frozen vegetables. However, once the decline has steadied there is still a demand (easily forecast) for canned vegetables. Managers who have a history of experiencing the introduction of new products can be expected to forecast with a reasonable measure of accuracy how long a fashion will take to pass through each stage of its life cycle. Where there is an obvious life cycle capacity, decisions can be made such as ordering and holding materials during the growth stage in anticipation of a high demand in the growth stage.

EXAMPLE: TIME SERIES FORECASTING

Forecasting by time series employs analysis of past demand and trends of demand to anticipate future demand. Any forecast or method of forecast can be tested for past accuracy. Accuracy is usually monitored by the deviation of the actual result from the forecast result.

Short-term forecasting considers historical data patterns (of demand) from past periods and projects these patterns into a forecast. Thus, if last period demand was 50,000, the forecast for the next period would be 50,000. If, for each period, the trend is upwards, then the forecast will follow the trend but always lag behind (see Table 5.5).

The method gives a quick response to a trend, depending on the length of time of each period. If the trend is upwards, then the forecast will be upwards but lagging behind – the total absolute deviation in the above example – this indicates that having a higher forecast than actual is as serious as having a lower than actual forecast. In the calculation of total absolute deviation, the symbols for plus or minus are ignored. The mean absolute deviation in Table 5.1 is the average deviation of forecast from actual and in this case the forecast on average is ±-6000 wrong on each occasion. If the forecast is too high, it is likely that too much resource will be provided, and if too low, there will not be sufficient resources to satisfy demand. If the periods shown above are daily forecasts, and the resource is not perishable, the damage in poor forecasting might not be great. If, however, each period represents a year, the damage done could be serious. If the industry is seasonal then this method would, following a buoyant autumn, forecast high winter sales, when in fact past

Table 5.5 Absolute deviation spread

Period	Forecast	Actual	Deviation
1	45,000	50,000	+5000
2	50,000	55,000	+5000
3	55,000	45,000	−10,000
4	45,000	40,000	−5000
5	40,000	45,000	+5000
Total absolute deviation			30,000
Mean absolute deviation			6000
Deviation spread (from −10,000 to +5000)			15,000

Table 5.6 Seasonal variation

$,000,000	2004	2005	2006	2007	2008
Quarter one	20 (11%)	22 (11%)	21 (15%)	26 (11%)	31
Quarter two	40 (22%)	45 (22.5%)	18 (13%)	52 (22%)	62
Quarter three	40 (22%)	44 (22%)	28 (20%)	52 (22%)	?
Quarter four	80 (45%)	89 (44.5%)	75 (52%)	105 (45%)	?
TOTAL	180	200	142	235	?

history shows that winter sales will always be lower than autumn sales. This is better illustrated in Table 5.6.

In Table 5.6, it can be seen that apart from 2006, there is a very obvious seasonal trend. Quarter one is 11% of the total demand for a year, quarter two, 22%, quarter three, 22%, and the fourth quarter is on average 45%. Obviously, something went terribly wrong in 2006. As we are now only in the first half of 2008, it should be easy to find the reason for the 2006 aberration. It could simply be due to the product life cycle and that the competition was able to steal a march on us with an updated product, and it wasn't until the end of the year that our new product came on line. Or if we were in an overseas market, there might have been a natural disaster such as a tsunami or earthquake in 2006 that disrupted our supply lines. Once we understand what went wrong in 2006, we can with some confidence predict that the first two quarters of sales will be 33% of the full year and thus the full-year forecast will be 281.8. We would never forecast 281.8, as this suggests an exactitude that could not happen. Thus, we would either say 280, or if the economy was buoyant, we would say 285, but never 281.8!

Factors affecting forecast errors

Forecasting is a multi-function review process and marketing should own the responsibility for agreed forecast data. There are many factors affecting the accuracy of a forecast and marketing is involved in most of them. The key factors are:

Internal organisation factors

- Historical sales performance of the product.
- Product marketing and promotion.
- Introduction of a new product.

Macroeconomic factors

- Interest rates, exchange rates and inflation.
- Political climate and government regulations.
- Employment rate and industrial relations.

Market intelligence factors

- Competitors' performance and strategy.
- Market share and market saturation.
- Reputation for quality.

CASE EXAMPLE: VOLKSWAGEN 2015

In 2015, Volkswagen (VW) launched a major marketing campaign in the United States claiming low emissions for their diesel engine cars. The low level that they claimed was a major selling point.

In September 2015, the US Environmental Protection Agency (EPA) uncovered that Volkswagen had been using a modification to software (known as a defeat device) to falsify the emission levels of nitrogen oxide pollutants to give a reading below the emission level permitted in the United States. In fact, it was found that the actual emission level was an incredible 40 times higher than the permitted level of 482,000. By December 2015, VW admitted that about 11 million cars worldwide, including 8 million in Europe, had been fitted with the 'defeat device'.

In 2016, VW had to recall millions of cars with an estimated cost of €6.7 billion. In the United States, on top of the cost of the recall, the EPA has the power to levy a fine for each vehicle that breaches their standards, this cost is estimated at about $US18 billion. By the end of 2015, the shares in VW had fallen by a third and sales were down 20% in the UK and 25% in the United States.

Forecasting to two decimal places means little in cases such as the VW scandal or when there is a major economic downturn such as the sudden global financial crisis of 2008 or there is a natural major disaster such as the earthquake and tsunami in Japan in 2011, which resulted in 16,000 deaths.

Summary

Customers create demand. Demand forecasting plays a number of key roles in effective supply chain management. Any forecasting error will affect all subsequent processes of the total supply chain management. At the most basic level, forecasting provides the basis for essential business activities, including financial planning and risk assessment. Demand forecasting is also the starting point for numerous processes in the supply chain that deals with raw material planning and purchasing. At those stages, businesses can draw upon estimates of consumer demand to optimise their inventory levels. Without proper forecasting, businesses run the risk of creating a costly surplus of product or materials.

As indicated in Chapter 4, the most significant application of AI in supply chain management has been in demand forecasting. It has been proven that demand forecasting tools powered by AI can reduce forecast accuracy by 30 to 50% in supply chain networks, leading to a 65% reduction in lost sales due to inventory out-of-stock situations and lower warehousing costs.

We conclude this chapter with questions derived from Basu and Wright (2005) designed to enable an organisation to understand their customers and their customers' needs.

1. How well do you know the relative importance of your main customers?
2. Is your CRM database up-to-date and is it readily accessible to all key members of your organisation?
3. How often do you conduct market research on trade and customer needs to the end user?
4. How well are customer complaints handled and recorded?
5. How is customer satisfaction measured (on-time delivery, accuracy of delivery, lead time, order fill, after-sales service)?
6. How close is your link with internal functions of marketing, planning and operations?
7. How close are your links and sharing of information with other components, upstream and downstream in the supply chain?
8. Are staff other than sales and marketing encouraged to meet with customers?
9. How well are you aware of the opportunities and constraints of emerging markets such as Indonesia and Brazil?
10. How closely is your operations manager involved with customers to achieve a good understanding of customers' needs?

A world-class organisation in the global marketplace has to know their customers and know what they want. Keeping customers relies on building relationships not just selling commodities. There are plenty of competitors who can and will sell to your customers. Without customers, any organisation, profit or non-profit, will not survive. It has to be understood that for any commercial organisation, profit is necessary for survival. The level of customer service provided must be affordable and sustainable. The overriding objective has to be to build long-term relationships, built on trust and integrity.

Discussion questions

1. Briefly describe the main characteristics and importance of forecasts in the supply chain management of any business.
2. Discuss the three approaches of forecasting methods. In which type of business would you consider applying Delphi methods?
3. Describe the process of CRM. Explain how CRM can help to generate customer demand and facilitate the tracking of orders.
4. As a supply chain manager, explain how you would forecast the demand of a product group that displays seasonal demand.
5. Discuss the internal and external factors that influence forecast errors. Suggest how these factors should be addressed to improve forecast accuracy.
6. In the case example of Volkswagen, when the emission scandal of 2015 created a heavy downturn in demand, suggest a forecast strategy for the next five years.
7. In demand planning, which of the following three factors would you consider most important:
   - Historical demand data.

- Forecasting software.
- Regular demand planning meetings with key stakeholders.

8. Which department has the ultimate responsibility for forecast accuracy?
9. Explain with examples how AI can demand forecasting accuracy.

(NB. For exercises on demand planning, please refer to Chapter 18.)

6 Resource and capacity management

Introduction

This chapter shows why resource and capacity management is an important building block in supply chain planning and management. We begin by explaining what effective capacity is as opposed to theoretical capacity. The objective of capacity management is to meet demand, and thus we show that the effective capacity for a complete supply chain is how many units could be supplied in a specific time period, such as a daily basis, to end users if required. The supply chain consists of many stages from preparing the ground and sowing the seed to the final consumer, and from seed to mouth might take 12 months or longer. Unless you are a supermarket group such as Tesco or Sainsbury's, it would be rare for any one player to be able to control the complete supply chain; therefore, it is more practical to consider how each component can manage its part of the supply chain while working closely with immediate supply and customer partners. Thus, we include in this chapter considerations of how any one component of the supply chain can at their level manage various aspects of resource and capacity management.

Learning objectives

Learning objectives for this chapter are:

1. Capacity forecasting and planning.
2. Materials and manufacturing requirement planning.
3. Production scheduling.
4. Enterprise resource planning.
5. Capacity adjustment to meet demand.
6. Demand manipulation.

Capacity forecasting and planning

Wild (2003) says, 'Capacity management is concerned with the matching of the capacity of the operating system and the demand placed on that system'. Capacity is the output that a plant, an operation or a process, can deliver in a defined unit of time. For example, the capacity of a bottling plant can be expressed as tonnes per year, litres per shift or bottles per hour.

The basic formula for calculating capacity is:

Capacity = Output Rate × Duration × Efficiency

DOI: 10.4324/9781003341352-8

There are a number of ways the magnitude of capacity can be described, of which theoretical capacity and effective capacity are more commonly used.

Theoretical capacity

In supply chain management, capacity refers to the amount of inventory that can be held in the supply chain. The aggregate capacity is the sum of the total inventory that could be held simultaneously at each stage. In theory, this total is the capacity of the entire chain. However, a supply chain does not stand still, as material is constantly moving into factories and food processing plants, being transported by road, rail, sea and air, sometimes in large amounts (for example, a 100,000-tonne oil tanker or other bulk carriers), and through successive stages out to the end user.

Effective capacity

The effective capacity can be defined as the amount of material or product available at *each* upstream stage of the supply chain. Beginning with the end user, how much could the upstream supplier provide at any given time to customers and so on up through the various tiers of the chain? Some texts measure capacity in the supply chain based on the capacity of warehouses, in the sense of how much can physically be stored. While storage space might be a concern if you are the manager or owner of a warehouse, the effective capacity is how much can pass through your warehouse in a given period, rather than how much you can physically store. Movement through the warehouse will be limited by the speed and reliability of inward supply and by the availability of outward transport. The objective of good warehouse management is not to have huge amounts of material, but to have a high rate of throughput. Dangers and costs of large stocks of slow-moving stock at any stage of the supply chain are:

Cost of premises.
Cost of capital (interest on cash tied up in stock holding).
Handling costs.
Insurance.
Damage and deterioration of materials.
Stock shrinkage, due to miscoding and theft.
Loss due to obsolescence, fashion changes and passed used-by dates.

Thus, effective capacity is measured in terms of throughput for each stage of the supply chain. At the end of the supply chain, effective capacity is the amount of finished product that can be supplied to end users on a daily basis. For example, in the military, capacity could be measured by the number of rounds of ammunition or the number of ration packs that could be supplied daily to the front line. Capacity is not the number that is supplied, but the number that *could* be supplied if required.

Effective capacity is also described as delivered capacity.

The minimum factors on which capacity depends, as shown by the above formula, are the specification of the output, the duration over which the output is required and the efficiency of the plant (also known as 'capacity leakage'). However, two other major factors determine capacity planning and these are demand forecast and product mix.

Demand forecast

Planning to match demand and capacity begins with the forecasting of what the demand is likely to be. Capacity decisions are based on forecasts of demand at several different levels. Long-range capacity planning needs forecasts to be made several years ahead and includes facility planning. Short- and medium-term forecasts span two to three years, and generally are used to determine people requirements, leasing of premises, machines and equipment and product details. In the more immediate short term, forecasts are used to plan, order and schedule resources on a monthly, weekly and daily basis. The shorter the time frame, the more precise the forecast must be.

As discussed in Chapter 4, in long-term forecasting, past experience and trends will be factored into the calculations. Considering the past numbers alone is not sufficient, as the numbers will merely reflect a variety of circumstances that influenced or determined the outcome. Establishing circumstances or events that shaped past demand will not be easy as it cannot be certain that all the facts will be remembered or that they will occur again in the same way. The danger for statisticians and forecasters relying on the past is not knowing the circumstances and relying on the numbers. Obviously, for some industries and products, seasonal trends might well provide a reasonably accurate forecast.

In the short term, if orders are made in advance, market trends are apparent and all components of the supply chain are sharing information, actual demand should be readily known. In Chapters 2 and 15, we discuss the bullwhip effect that refers to poor information sharing resulting in panic ordering and overreaction with wildly fluctuating demand. Assuming that the bullwhip effect can be mitigated, and this is discussed in Chapter 15, knowing what the actual demand will be a week, a month or even three months in advance gives little scope to substantially adjust capacity. Machinery cannot be added overnight, it takes time to recruit and train new staff, additional warehouse space takes time to find and fit out and often transport has to be booked well in advance. Short-term adjustment of capacity is often more reactive than proactive.

As discussed in Chapter 5, there are three ways of looking at forecasts: the qualitative approach, the mathematical or time series approach and the causal approach. In reality, all three are interlinked and should be taken into account when determining a forecasted demand figure.

Supply chain management is distinguished by its role in providing a strategic and integrated function at all levels of logistics, including suppliers. Ideally, the supplier becomes part of the team and is involved in the planning process, not only for scheduling deliveries when required but in the design stage for new products. The business objective to convert customer demand by optimising the utilisation of resources to deliver effective customer service applies to all organisations regardless of whether they are in manufacturing or service sectors.

Product mix

How much a plant can deliver depends on the mix of the product it is required to produce. For example, consider a bottling plant has the following output rates and share of demand forecast:

2-litre bottle	250 bottles per minute (500 litres per minute)	20% of demand forecast
1-litre bottle	200 bottles per minute (200 litres per minute |)	50% of demand forecast
0.5-litre bottle	150 bottles per minute (75 litres per minute)	30% of demand forecast

With this product mix, the weighted average output rate is $500 \times 0.2 + 200 \times 0.5 + 75 \times 0.3$ or 222.5 litres per minute. This is often described as aggregated output rate for the given product mix. This example ignores the duration of the production run and efficiency for each type of bottle, but it is a good approximation to illustrate the effect of pack sizes in a product mix. Longer-term and medium-term capacity planning is usually concerned with estimating capacity levels in aggregated terms rather than calculating the detailed capacity of individual pack sizes.

Duration or time deployed

The level of capacity is obviously determined by the duration of the running time of the plant or operation. Duration is the defined unit of time such as the number of hours or the shift pattern for the plant or how long the operation is planned to operate. For example, during peak period warm and sunny months, an ice cream plant is planned to operate in three shifts, while in a normal period, the plant may be running in a single shift. The duration of planned operational hours is also determined by the demand forecast for the product.

Efficiency

The theoretical capacity of a plant or operation is not achievable in practice. Some reasons for not achieving the theoretical capacity are predictable, such as unavailable time due to holidays and weekends, scheduled maintenance activities and routine changeover and set-up activities. Other stoppages – such as shortage of materials or labour, plant breakdown and quality problems of packaging materials – are not easily predictable. All these stoppages reduce capacity and are sometimes called 'capacity leakage'. When these stoppages are high, the efficiency of the plant or operation is low.

Overall equipment effectiveness (OEE) is a popular measure of assessing efficiency and is an index of measuring the delivered performance of a plant or equipment based on good output. The method of monitoring OEE is devised in such a way that it highlights the losses and deficiencies incurred during the operation of the plant and identifies the opportunities for improvement.

OEE is defined in the following formula:

$$\text{OEE \%} = \frac{\text{Actual Good Output}}{\text{Specified Output}} \times 100$$

Where Specified Output = specified speed $\times$ operation time

Application

The application of OEE has been extensive, especially when driven by total productive maintenance (TPM) programmes, to critical plant and equipment. It can be applied to single equipment, a packing line, a production plant or processes. In order to appreciate the usefulness of OEE, it is important to understand equipment time analysis as shown in Figure 6.1.

Total Time defines the maximum time within a reporting period, such as 52 weeks a year, 24 hours a day, 8760 hours a year.

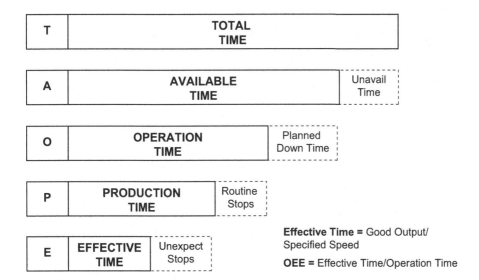

Figure 6.1 Equipment time analysis

Available Time is the time during which the machine or equipment could be operated within the limits of national or local statutes, regulations or conventions.

Operation Time is the time during which the machine or equipment is planned to run for production purposes. The operational time is normally the shift hours.

Production Time is the maximum time during which the machine or equipment could be expected to be operated productively after adjusting the operation time for routine stoppages such as changeover and meal breaks.

Effective Time is the time needed to produce a 'good output delivered' if the machine or equipment is working at its Specified Speed for a defined period. It includes no allowances for interruptions or any other time losses.

It is important to note that Effective Time is not recorded, it is calculated from the Specified Speed as

$$\text{Effective Time} = \text{Good Output/Specified Speed}$$

Where Specified Speed is the optimum speed of a machine or equipment for a particular product without any allowances for loss of efficiency. It is expressed as quantity per unit such as tonnes per hour, bottles per minute, cases per hour or litres per minute. In addition to OEE, two other indices are commonly used as shown below:

$$\text{Production Efficiency}\left(\%\right) = \frac{\text{Effective Time}\left(\text{E}\right)}{\text{Production Time}\left(\text{P}\right)} \times 100$$

$$\text{Operational Utilisation}\left(\%\right) = \frac{\text{Operation Time}\left(\text{O}\right)}{\text{Total Time}\left(\text{T}\right)} \, 100$$

Figure 6.2 Soap production line

A properly designed and administered OEE scheme offers a broad range of benefits and a comprehensive manufacturing performance system. Some of its key benefits are as follows:

- It provides information for shortening lead time and changeover time and a foundation for SMED (single minute exchange of dies).
- It provides essential and reliable data for capacity planning and scheduling.
- It identifies the 'six big losses' of TPM, leading to a sustainable improvement of plant reliability.
- It provides information for improving asset utilisation and thus reduced capital and depreciation costs in the longer term.

As shown in the example (Figure 6.2) of a soap packaging line, the specified speed is 150 tablets per minute, that is, this constitutes the speed of the wrapper (which is the slowest piece of equipment).

Consider the production data of a toilet soap packing line where the control station (slowest equipment) governing the specified speed is an ACMA 711 wrapping machine.

Week number	31
Operation time	128 hours
Specified speed	150 tablets per minute
Good output	4232 cases
Routine stoppages	11 hours 30 minutes
Unexpected stoppages	27 hours 15 minutes

Given that each case contains 144 tablets,

Good Output = 4232 × 144 = 609,408 tablets

$$\text{Effective Time} = \frac{Good\ Output}{Specified\ Speed} = \frac{609,408}{150 \times 60} = 67.71\ \text{hours}$$

Production Time = Operation Time − Routine Stoppages

= 128 − 11.5 = 116.5 hours

Total Time = 7 × 24 = 168 hours

$$\text{OEE} = \frac{Effective\ Time}{Production\ Time} = \frac{67.71}{128} = 0.53 = 53\%$$

$$\text{Production Efficiency} = \frac{\textit{Effective Time}}{} = \frac{67.71}{116.5} = 58\%$$

$$\text{Operation Utilisation} = \frac{\textit{Operation Time}}{\textit{Total Time}} = \frac{128}{168} = 76\%$$

It is important to note that the Effective Time was calculated and not derived from the recorded stoppages. The success of an OEE scheme depends heavily on the rigour of continuous training. It is important that each operator, supervisor and manager of a production department receives a half-day training programme covering the definitions, purpose and application of the OEE scheme. The training is continuous because of the turnover of staff. Senior management should also benefit from a one-hour awareness session. The principles of OEE are conceptually simple but detail rich. The main strength of this tool is that it highlights the areas of deficiency for improvement and the key results cannot be manipulated. The specified time is calculated from tangible 'good output', Operation Time is well-established shift hours and Total Time is absolute.

Material requirement and resource planning

In most manufacturing companies, the focus is on a reliable flow of inward materials. This is achieved through a materials requirements plan for inbound logistics to achieve an appropriate balance of stock and satisfy demand.

Materials requirement planning (MRP) is the set of techniques that use bills of material, inventory on hand and on order data, and the production schedule or plan to calculate quantities and timing of materials. Such a plan is incomplete if it does not take into account whether manufacturing resources (e.g. plant, people, energy, space) will be available at the desired time.

Manufacturing resource planning (MRPII) arose from an appreciation of the need to time and phase materials with resource availability to achieve a given output date. Manufacturing resource planning is an integrated computer-based system. A computer-based approach is essential due to the amount of data required. Various software systems are available, each based on the same principles. MRPII is depicted in Figure 6.3.

With manufacturing resource planning, the planning process arises from the innovation of new products and the strategic marketing plan. Starting with this information, a business plan is constructed to determine and communicate estimates of the sales volume of each product range. The business plan should be developed at least once a year and during the year periodic updates will be required.

From the business plan, an operations plan is formulated that covers the materials and other resources needed to translate the business plan into reality. It follows that to keep the operations plan in line with updates to the business plan, regular communication is required between the various functions involved. This updating process is best achieved by face-to-face meetings that we recommend should take place at least once a month and always with all parties present at one time. There is a very real danger of misunderstandings and ambiguities if meetings are not face-to-face and if all concerned are not present at the same time. Meetings need not be long drawn-out affairs. From experience, we believe that any planning meeting that takes longer than an hour is wasting time. The key managers at these meetings will be from sales, operations and planning. The issues

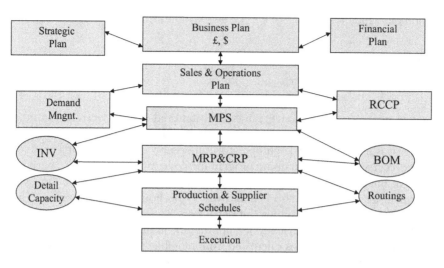

Figure 6.3 MRPII: Manufacturing resource planning

that will be agreed upon will include time and availability of resources, and conflicting requirements and priorities will be resolved. Above all, demand is the crucial issue, and as future demand can never be certain, there should be a formal mechanism of forecasting using the best combination of historical models, past results from promotions, data from customers and market intelligence. Likewise, the inventory data system has to be up to date and accurate with details of raw materials on hand, goods on order, lead times and finished goods on hand.

Only with up-to-date information, and with the continuous review and management of information, can an organisation hope to achieve a balance of resources and stocks of inventory to meet planned service levels. The master planning and production scheduling process, therefore, has to be continuously monitored and updated to ensure that this occurs.

CASE EXAMPLE: MRPII SYSTEM IMPLEMENTATION

BM is a bus body manufacturer in South Africa within a subsector of the automotive industry. The majority of buses manufactured worldwide are made up of two distinctly separate elements, the first being the chassis, and the second, being the bus body. Chassis selling prices to the market are fixed and differentiation in the finished product price is determined by the bus body price.

BM was experiencing an operational crisis caused by a phase of exceptional fast growth that changed its manufacturing from a 'Jobbing' environment to one of 'batch production/manufacturing'. BM's main activity prior to 2011 was building a lot of small quantity one-off bus bodies for a dispersed market, this changed in 2011 when the government implemented the Preferential Procurement Policy Framework Act. This put BM in a unique position where it was one of only three body builders in South Africa. BM furthermore started supplying buses in complete knock down (CKD) format in Kenya for assembly only.

As a manufacturing company, BM did not utilise any form of MRP or MRPII systems to plan, schedule or execute any of its stock management or manufacturing activities. The old system in use for manufacturing was informal, causing poor planning and a loss of sales and market share.

A research study in 2015 (Lombard, 2015) provided clear evidence that there are close interrelationships between MRPII/ERP and supply chain performance and recommended an MRPII system with improved business processes and data accuracy underpinned by a companywide training programme

In 2015, BM started the implementation of a functional MRPII system with the assistance of a consulting firm and began to integrate all the departments into working with the same set of data. This led BM to a better position to address poor planning and a loss of sales problems. The implementation of an effective MRPII system as a manufacturing strategy in one of the largest bus body manufacturers in the world to effectively manage materials, capital, technologies, labour, equipment and other manufacturing resources is expected to lead to the following benefits:

- Significant inventory reduction.
- Dynamic production planning.
- Cycle times reduction.
- High market responsiveness.
- Reconciling of planned schedules.
- Meeting promised delivery dates.

Source: Adapted from Lombard (2015)

Production scheduling

The master production plan or master schedule is at the heart of MRP, where both the timing and quantity of orders are determined by offsetting from the current stock the demand during the lead time to meet the master production plan.

As shown in Figure 6.4, the concepts of MRP underpinned by the master plan can also be extended to the distribution channel to allow integrated scheduling throughout the supply chain. The approach of distribution requirements planning (DRP) is compatible with MRP as used in the factory.

The next stage is to follow a rough cut capacity planning process to assess to what extent the capacity of manufacturing facilities could meet the master schedule. The feedback loop at this level tests the master plan against problem areas such as known bottlenecks and other critical resource areas. Often, as this is a short- to medium-term approach, action has to be taken to make the best use of existing resources rather than to add extra long-term resources. The company should decide which alternative to follow if the existing resources are not adequate, for example, review the schedule, increase resources, work extra shifts, delay maintenance, outsource to third parties and so on. With computer systems, it is relatively straightforward to simulate using 'what if' scenarios to evaluate alternative courses of action.

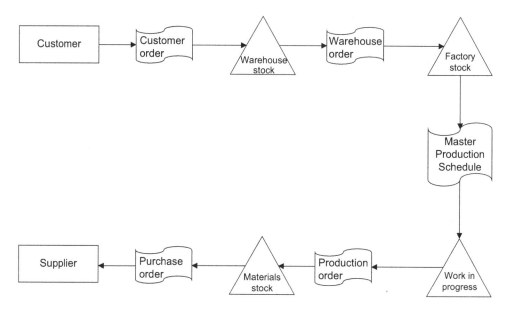

Figure 6.4 Order flow in MRPII

Having established that the resources are sufficient, or having adjusted the plan to fit the resources, then the next step is the detailed material requirements planning and the detailed capacity requirements planning for day-to-day operations. This stage includes the production of detailed bills of materials for each product or batch of products. With the revised master schedule for each product and each stock-keeping unit (SKU) and bills of material for each SKU, the materials required for each item of raw materials (RM) and packaging materials (PM) are then matched with the current inventory levels to derive the additional procurement requirements. The requirements are modified, if required, after comparing with the detailed capacity planning process.

The execution of the planning process then commences with the final production scheduling and purchasing (supply planning) processes.

We have outlined a generic description of the manufacturing resource planning process. There are, of course, variations – more significantly between batch production processes and continuous production processes and between so-called 'push' or 'pull' demand systems. With the 'push' system, stocks of materials and finished goods are used to ensure maximum plant capacity utilisation by having level production. The 'pull' system is driven by customer orders and just–in–time principles that can result in some underutilisation of capacity. It is said that just–in–time requires greater flexibility and reliability of plants plus a multi-skilled workforce. In its simplistic form, just–in–time is reactive (demand pull), whereas MRPII can be described as proactive. MRPII looks forward and determines what will be needed to achieve the desired output date. Internally, MRPII is a push system; inventory is driven through the process by the schedule. Thus, customer requirements are linked to the resources and materials necessary to precisely meet a just–in–time delivery date. From a customer's point of view, it could be argued that as long as the goods arrive on time and meet the specifications, the system used by the manufacturer is irrelevant!

To be effective, MRPII has to be an integrated computerised system and should be online and accessible to all interested parties. It follows therefore that data has to be kept up to date on the system. For example, if engineering changes are made to the design of a product, the MRPII database has to be updated otherwise the bill of materials for procurement purposes will not be in line with the new design. It is clear that MRPII can't be effective unless a 'single set of numbers' is used by all functions (i.e. marketing/sales, finance, manufacturing, human resources and information technology) of the organisation or enterprise. This has led to the migration of MRPII to enterprise resource planning (ERP).

Enterprise resources planning

ERP replaces the old standalone computer systems for finance, manufacturing, HR and distribution and replaces them with a single integrated software system divided into software modules that approximately represent the old standalone systems. The growing market of ERP systems is dominated by SAP R/3, followed by Oracle, PeopleSoft, Baan, JD Edwards and MfgPro. It is fundamental to note that if you simply install the software without rationalising the processes or changing the way people do their jobs, you may not see any value at all.

ERP in service enterprises

There are five major factors why companies undertake ERP systems:

* Integrate financial information.
* Integrate customer order information and demand plan.
* Standardise and speed up supply processes.
* Reduce inventory.
* Standardise HR information.

It is true that ERP is basically a second-generation MRPII system that is predominantly in manufacturing organisations. However, if we consider the above five reasons from the standpoint of a service organisation, we see that all factors, arguably with the exception of 'reduce inventory', are applicable to justify an ERP system. More importantly, if you consider the ERP process rather than the software, it is evident that the interaction between all functions with a 'single set of numbers' is equally important for an effective service enterprise.

As indicated in Chapter 4, the SaaS version of ERP has been the most effective and popular application of the cloud in supply chain operations. It offers scalability, immediacy, flexibility, reliability and above all cost-effectiveness. For example, if an organisation wishes to install a full-fledged ERP system (such as SAP R3), it will not only require procuring the system at a high cost, but it will also need to build and maintain the infrastructure and employ personnel to operate it. The implementation period will also be longer. However, with a SaaS application, there is no upfront capital required for the software and you don't have to worry about building and maintaining the infrastructure. Instead, the software is available via a web browser and the SaaS provider, in exchange for your subscription fee, handles all the heavy lifting. SaaS applications are particularly attractive to small and medium enterprises (SMEs).

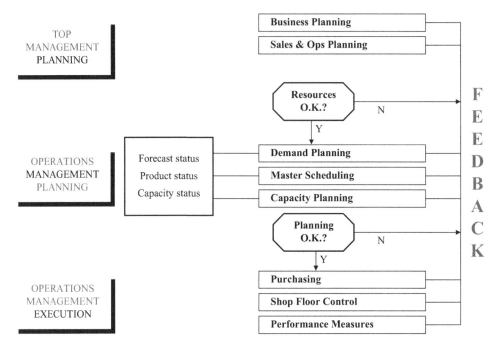

Figure 6.5 Operations resource planning

The second and third factors of applying ERP relate to resource planning. Every service company has customers, demands, in-house resources and suppliers, and therefore, requires resource planning to deliver effective customer service. We call this operations resource planning (ORP) as illustrated in Figure 6.5.

Operations resource planning

It is evident from Figure 6.5 that although ORP is not as detailed as MRPII, the key steps of the process are similar. From the business plan, a sales and operations plan that covers key products and resources is needed to deliver the business plan. The monthly sales and operations planning meeting by senior managers approves the master operations plan. The operations team will review the product portfolio, supplier status and the capacity of the resources and ensure that purchase orders are raised to procure appropriate resources or services from suppliers. If the capacity of the resources is adequate, then an internal control document for the customer order is processed. But a partnership with customers and suppliers can and will achieve very obvious benefits to all. A partnership with suppliers and a partnership with customers are the beginnings of a radical change in supply chain management. As a result, the service provider, the supplier and the customer achieve benefits in:

- Lower operating costs.
- Improved service level.
- Greater certainty of a continued relationship.

The boundaries between companies will blur as they view themselves as part of an eco-system, supply chain or value chain.

Hasso Platner, co-founder and vice chairman, SAP

Capacity adjustment

There are two approaches to managing capacity: one is to adjust capacity, and the other is to manipulate demand. Generally, organisations will seek to match capacity and demand using both approaches.

The first step is to know what your effective capacity is and what is the constraint that limits the throughput of your operation. The constraint could seemingly be a lack of space, lack of handling equipment, lack of people or lack of reliable supply. Once the constraint that limits your capacity to serve your customers is identified then corrective action can be taken. However, what at first might be seen as a constraint might in fact be disguising a lack of planning and vision. For example, lack of space might not be the basic issue. If a warehouse is running out of space to hold materials/finished goods, the issue might be overstocking and lack of planning. Indeed, all of the possible constraints listed above – lack of space, lack of handling equipment, lack of people and lack of reliable supply – could well be eliminated by coordinated planning within the organisation and by working closely with suppliers and customers.

Basu and Wright (2005) provide a set of questions that will help to identify where the true constraints are. The questions in Table 6.1 are a sample taken from 200 questions designed to enable an organisation to reach world-class standards.

Once demand is known or forecast, and once the constraints are identified, resources might have to be added or perhaps reduced to meet the expected demand. If demand changes, capacity will need to be adjusted to meet the new demand. If there is insufficient capacity, customers must either wait for delivery, or if they are not prepared to wait, they will be lost. If there is too much capacity, then resources will be underutilised, and stock

Table 6.1 Sample of self-assessment questions

	Poor				*Excellent*
1 How effective is your master scheduling process to ensure sufficient resources (materials, stocks of finished goods, people) to support the sales plan and expected demand?	0.1	0.2	0.3	0.4	0.5
2. How good is your capacity planning? Do you use a rough cut capacity plan to develop a detailed capacity requirement plan?	0.1	0.2	0.3	0.4	0.5
3. How well is your purchase scheduling managed? What controls are there in place?	0.1	0.2	0.3	0.4	0.5
4. How well do you pursue a make-to-order policy with an emphasis on material velocity (stock turn)? (Large stocks of raw materials, work in progress and finished goods = 0.1; just-in-time philosophy with little or no buffer stock = 0.5.)	0.1	0.2	0.3	0.4	0.5
5. How effective are your business processes supported by an ERP system (e.g. SAP R/3)?	0.1	0.2	0.3	0.4	0.5
6. How good is your integrated point-of-sale system?	0.1	0.2	0.3	0.4	0.5
7. How effective is the inclusion of key suppliers in the planning process?	0.1	0.2	0.3	0.4	0.5
8. How effective have you been in the sharing of common coding and databases facilitated by Internet or electronic data interchange (EDI) with suppliers and customers?	0.1	0.2	0.3	0.4	0.5

holding with all the attendant costs will increase. For many organisations, underutilisation of resources and holding of buffer and reserve stock might be considered more profitable than the loss of customers.

Where there is a change in demand, the two basic strategies are as follows:

* Strategy one: Variation or adjustment of capacity.
* Strategy two: Elimination/reduction of the need to adjust capacity.

Strategy 1: Variation or adjustment of capacity

This strategy has a short-term approach and a longer-term approach.

In the short term, capacity can to some extent be adjusted. Overtime/double shifts can be worked, unskilled people can be employed to make better use of trained people, people can be re-deployed, jobs or deliveries can be prioritised and supply and production expedited, subassemblies can be subcontracted and non-essential maintenance delayed.

In the longer term, facilities, machines and equipment and people can be added. Production can be made in advance and stockpiled. Adding extra people will not immediately add to effective capacity. All organisations rely heavily on people, and a strong corporate culture with the goodwill of people will, in the short term, ease the burden of increases in demand. Likewise, the longer people are with the organisation, their ability to respond positively will increase, as will their experience. This is referred to as the learning curve. On the other hand, the addition of a new piece of machinery or equipment once it has been set up will immediately add to the effective capacity

In the previous paragraph, we have considered adding to capacity in the face of growing demand. But when demand is falling, it is often difficult to sell or dispose of capital assets such as buildings, machines, equipment and vehicles. Generally, the disposal of assets will not realise book value. Often, an expensive piece of equipment will be valuable when demand is high, but if demand is low, it might only have scrap value if sold. Thus, when considering adding new capital assets, it is important to understand the effect of demand and product life cycles. Sadly, reducing the number of people is the quickest way of reducing unwanted capacity. Again, before new people are added, it is important to be sure that the demand will continue at the current or expected level. Adding new people takes time to recruit and train, and intellectual capital once lost is hard to recover.

Strategy 2: Elimination/reduction of the need to adjust

If the objective is never to keep the customer waiting, then it follows that there must always be a sufficient amount of all the required resources available at any given time.

It is more likely, however, that it will not always be possible to have sufficient capacity to meet every demand. Therefore, it has to be accepted that there will always be surplus resources in the system, which, in a supply chain, generally relates to buffer stocks of materials or finished goods and the holding of reserve stocks. Thus, the capacity of every constraining resource will be set above the expected/forecasted demand level

On the other hand, if the policy is not to adjust capacity even when demand exceeds capacity, it has to be accepted that from time to time customers will have to wait for delivery. The danger is if customers have to wait too long that the organisation will get a reputation for poor service and customers will be lost to the system.

Strategy 2, elimination/reduction of the need to adjust capacity has several substrategies that we have labelled 2a, 2b, 2bi and 2bii. Also, see Wright and Race (2004) and Wild (2003).

2a: Surplus capacity of key resources held.

2b: Sufficient capacity to meet normal demand, but:

    2bi: It is accepted that customers might have to wait, and it is likely that some customers will be lost.

    2bii: Stocks of materials/finished goods are held to meet changes in demand.

Manipulation of demand

With this approach, demand is manipulated to match the available capacity. Recognised ways of demand manipulation are advertising campaigns, special promotions, discounts, two-for-one deals and so on. The travel industry is adept at demand manipulation with high, shoulder and low season fares and tariffs. Where demand exceeds capacity, prices are raised or customers might be allowed or even encouraged to go elsewhere.

If demand is known in advance and is stable, the operations manager's job is to plan and make the best use of resour

ces to meet the demand. In Chapter 2, the bullwhip effect was introduced, and Chapter 15 shows how early sharing of information can reduce major and misleading demand fluctuations. Minor fluctuations cause only minor problems. Where demand cannot be accurately predicted, although the aim has not changed, operations management problems can become extremely complex.

Summary

Resource and capacity management is all about planning. Planning is not possible without information. Resource and capacity planning begins with knowing what our effective capacity is. Effective capacity is the amount of material or product that can be delivered in a given period of time to customers. Having the capacity to meet customer demand requires advanced knowledge of what the demand will be. This chapter began with the need to forecast demand and moved to the planning of resources to meet demand. The chapter concluded with strategies for capacity management and also considered how demand might be manipulated. Chapter 15 deals with the sharing of information flowing up through the supply chain, beginning at point of sale. An early supply of information allows a quicker response to demand fluctuations and reduces the bullwhip effect introduced in Chapter 2.

Resource and capacity management is also benefiting from the advanced systems offered by digital transformation such as cloud computing and artificial intelligence. Longer-term demand and capacity planning (RCCP) should take into account the impact of contemporary challenges such as the supply of critical materials and resources.

Discussion questions

1. Explain effective capacity or delivered capacity. What is the formula for calculating effective capacity by taking into account three key factors?
2. What is OEE? Illustrate with an example of how OEE is calculated for a production line.
3. What is MRPII? How does MRPII relate to ERP?
4. What is rough cut capacity planning (RCCP)? Explain at what stage RCCP is applied and for which items RCCP is considered. How would you take into account the impact of contemporary challenges in RCCP?
5. What are the two basic capacity management strategies? Explain with examples the application of each strategy and how they can be applied together.

7 Procurement, purchasing and supplier focus

Introduction

Global supply chains have created more opportunities to source products while developing and implementing long-term supplier relationship strategies. Working with international suppliers also provides the platform to bring the latest technology to national organisations engaged in delivering both manufacturing and service products. In a global framework, there are also more challenges in collaborating with suppliers while building and maintaining strong partnerships. The balancing of these opportunities and challenges through purchasing strategies and processes is critical and we aim to address these in this chapter.

Procurement and supplier focus is the third building block of supply chain management. Procurement includes:

* Purchasing raw materials and packaging.
* Hiring contract or casual labour and professional services.
* Selecting approved or dedicated suppliers.
* Outsourcing.

Learning objectives

Learning objectives for this chapter are:

1. Buyer–supplier relationship.
2. Procurement processes.
3. Purchasing ethics and environmental issues.
4. Make or buy decisions.
5. Outsourcing strategy.
6. e-Procurement.
7. Procurement schedule.

Buyer–supplier relationship

The Industrial Marketing and Purchasing Group (IMP) in the 1970s developed a dynamic model of buyer-supplier relationships in industrial markets (the interaction model) and illustrated its applicability through comparative studies of buyer-supplier relationships within and across a number of European countries (France, Germany, Italy, Sweden, the

DOI: 10.4324/9781003341352-9

UK). The main conclusion of these pan-European studies was that buying and selling in industrial markets could not be understood as a series of discrete and serially independent transactions. Instead, transactions could only be examined as episodes in often long-standing and complex relationships between the buying and selling organisation (IMP, 2007).

Procurement or buying is the act of purchasing. Within an organisation, the purchasing or procurement department is often seen as a less than glamorous department that buys things as cheaply as possible to meet specifications set by more glamorous and important departments such as marketing and operations. However, as Porter found, purchasing is a key activity in determining the competitive advantage of an organisation (Porter, 1985). Lysons and Farrington (2006) rather simplistically say the purchasing process consists of a chain of processes. The chain consists of:

Receive requisition,
> Solicit quotations,
>> Vendor selection,
>>> Negotiate with suppliers,
>>>> Place order,
>>>>> Receive supplies,
>>>>>> Make payment.

Setting specifications, inspection and quality assurance are all included in the overall process.

We contend, as does the IMP Group, that purchasing is more than looking for the right product at the right price and at the right time. We say that a world-class company will be aiming to build alliances and long-term relationships with key suppliers. Ideally, key suppliers to an organisation will be involved in the design and development of new products and services. They will be able to provide advice on new technology and methods, suggest alternative materials, observe and report market trends, and in short, they will become an additional source of market intelligence. Gone are the days when we simply placed an order on a supplier and the supplier was not told what or how the product was going to be used. The point being, if the supplier knew to what purpose the materials ordered were going to be used, they could well provide suggestions of alternative products and technical advice. It could be argued that organisations are not purchasing materials but looking for solutions. Lou Gerstner recognised this when he became CEO of IBM in 1993. Up until then, IBM developed and built computers. Gerstner came out with a new mission statement that said in effect that IBM would lead the world in the development of information technology and would provide *solutions* for their customers. The mission statement is largely unchanged and reads

> At IBM, we strive to lead in the invention, development and manufacture of the industry's most advanced information technologies, including computer systems, software, storage systems and microelectronics.
> We translate these advanced technologies into value for our customers through our professional solutions, services and consulting businesses worldwide.

The big change in 1993 was that IBM moved from selling technology to getting alongside customers, understanding their needs and developing a solution customised to those needs. For the sales staff of IBM, this required a major change in thinking, from selling a box not fully knowing what the customer was going to use it for, to understanding the customer's business and finding a solution to the customer's needs. As Gerstner (2002) said, this required a major change in culture.

Since 2003, IBM has not had an official mission but has relied on a staff-generated set of values: 'IBMers value; dedication to every client's success, innovation that matters – for our company and for the world, and trust and personal responsibility in all relationships'.

An example of how IBM works to find solutions for customers is given in the case example reported by IBM Global Services (April 2004)

CASE EXAMPLE: IBM GLOBAL SERVICES

Toyota teams with IBM to drive system performance

To handle significant growth in product volume and variety while maintaining service levels, Toyota looked to IBM Business Consulting Services to help improve its inventory position.

Business need

A process-focused organisation, Toyota continually seeks to implement key business practices that will help the company enhance performance and customer service at the lowest cost.

Key challenges

Toyota was experiencing significant growth both in product volume and in the variety of products required to meet customers' needs. Company IT staff faced challenges in integrating new components with the interconnected legacy systems to make system improvements. Old code had been edited frequently over the years and was inconsistently documented, and as a result, could be deciphered only by select IT team members. To respond to dealer needs, Toyota required a resilient supply chain management solution to help ensure delivery of the right part to the right dealer at the right time. The solution had to enable Toyota to perform the correct calculations to accurately predict inventory levels for more than 100,000 service parts and more than one million part/location combinations.

Solution

IBM business consulting services

Believing that custom development to improve legacy system performance was too expensive and time-consuming, Toyota selected software from i2 Technologies. IBM business consulting services provided extensive i2 Technologies implementation experience and skills to develop a state-of-the-art enterprise architecture and infrastructure strategy that included capabilities for performance measurement, data warehousing, demand forecasting, service parts planning and business process and organisational design change.

IBM worked with Toyota associates and i2 to develop an integrated solution that connected Toyota's legacy systems to i2 software to facilitate service parts planning across the Toyota service parts supply chain. Toyota uses i2 Demand Planner for core business forecasting and i2 Service Parts Planner for slow-moving spare parts forecasting, inventory optimisation and replenishment planning. A data warehouse enables users to access both i2 and legacy system information via drill-down, self-directed activities or a series of reports.

Results

Through improved demand and order forecasting, and better calculation of safety stock requirements, Toyota has reduced over US$46 million in inventory as a result of the implementation. The IBM and i2 solution has enabled the division to eliminate less-critical work, thereby improving efficiency. Better inventory planning also has helped Toyota boost its customer fill rate, limiting rush orders and reducing airfreight expenses.

Thus, purchasing is more than simply buying a product. Nonetheless, the basic objective of purchasing is to have available the correct materials in manufacture or processing or product in warehousing and retailing when required and to ensure continuity of supply. Therefore, in true operations management parlance, the basic objectives are the right thing (meeting specifications) at the right time and at the right price.

For key products, these objectives can best be met by developing partnerships with suppliers, and for suppliers, as shown in the IBM case study, to be proactive in forming relationships with customers.

Procurement processes

Once a requisition or order has been received by the purchasing department, the customary approach is to check the order or the bill of materials for accuracy and for conformance to the specification and to check records to determine if this is a repeat purchase or a new requirement. For everyday consumables, if it is a repeat buy and there have been no problems in the past (the supplier provided the product to specification on time and the price is competitive), a repeat order will be placed. If the order is for a new product, or if there were problems in the past that can't be resolved, then the following steps will be taken.

1. Possible suppliers will be identified. Identification of suppliers includes gaining intelligence on their reputation and financial stability. There is no point in dealing with an organisation that might not be in business in the next few months. Ideally, we will be aiming to build up a long-term relationship.
2. Seek quotations. Provide to a short list of suppliers the details of specifications, quantities and dates. At this stage, it might not be wise to be too forthcoming as to the purpose of the purchase. We don't want to be providing too much information in the marketplace that could help our competitors.

3. Quotations will be received and a decision made as to who our first preference is.
4. Negotiations entered into. At this stage, we can provide more detail as to what the product will be used for and seek advice from the supplier. If the product is going to be repeatedly used and ordered and/or is an important item such as a new piece of expensive equipment, and we are seeking a long-term relationship, the cementing of a relationship can be more important than a contract written in legalese.
5. Ongoing re-orders. For fast-moving consumer goods, such as in supermarkets, ideally, re-orders will be automatically triggered at the point of sale once stock levels drop to a predetermined level. For details of barcoding and point-of-sale re-ordering systems (e-procurement) see Chapter 14.
6. Ordering. Each order will have an order number. The importance of order numbers is explained in the following section of this chapter.

Receipt, inspection, quality assurance

When goods are received, they should be immediately booked into the inventory system and married to the order number. No material or product should ever be issued until it has been booked in. Failure to do so will lead to confusion and inaccuracy in the stock records. In lean or just-in-time operations, materials are delivered as required directly to the production line. In a cross-docking operation, materials will arrive at one side of the warehouse and be broken down and sorted into despatch lots for forwarding. For details on cross-docking, see Chapter 14. In other operations, materials will be received in bulk and stored in warehouses. No matter how received, an order has to be booked in and subsequently when despatched or issued must be booked out.

The traditional way of ensuring quality and quantity was to inspect and count goods as received. If suppliers are trusted then only a sample check should be necessary, and in a just-in-time system, the test will be as the product goes into production, either a component fits or it doesn't!

Quality inspection and quality control

Quality inspection and control rely on supervision to make sure that no mistakes are made. The most basic approach to quality is an inspection on receipt of materials. The next recommended stage is following inwards goods inspection and the detection of problems to work with the supplier in a non-confrontational way to investigate and find the causes of problems and jointly take actions to prevent errors from reoccurring.

Quality assurance

Quality assurance includes the setting of standards with documentation and also includes the documentation of the method of checking against specified standards. Quality assurance can also include third-party approval from a recognised authority, such as ISO. With quality assurance, inspection and control are still the basic approaches, but in addition, one would also expect a comprehensive quality manual jointly agreed by the supplier and the purchaser, perhaps including the use of statistical process control and the use of sampling techniques for random checking and the overall auditing of quality systems.

Quality inspection, control and assurance are aimed at achieving an agreed consistent level of quality, first by testing and inspection, then by rigid conformance to standards and procedures, and finally by efforts to eliminate causes of errors so that the defined accepted level will be achieved. As Wright and Race (2004) says:

> this is a cold and often sterile approach to quality. It implies that once a sufficient level of quality has been achieved, then, apart from maintaining that level which in itself might be hard work, little more need be done.

Where a genuine alliance/partnership has been forged between the buyer and supplier, both will continuously be working together to improve the product and the service.

Purchasing ethics and environmental issues

The golden rule of doing unto others as you would have them do unto you is for most people an easily understood code of ethics. Likewise, in the medical profession, the easily understood Hippocratic oath was for over 2000 years seen as being sufficient (the modern version removes references to Greek deities and allows for abortion, which was written in 1964). However, in today's changing environment and with conflicting requirements, it has been found by many organisations and professional bodies such as lawyers and accountants that a more detailed code is required. Likewise, increasingly commercial organisations feel it necessary to have a code of ethics and some also have a specific code of ethics for purchasing management. The Purchasing Management Association of Canada is an example of a detailed code and it states the following.

Values

Members will operate and conduct their decisions and actions based on the following **values**:

1. **Honesty/integrity**
   Maintaining an unimpeachable standard of integrity in all their business relationships both inside and outside the organisations in which they are employed.
2. **Professionalism**
   Fostering the highest standards of professional competence amongst those for whom they are responsible.
3. **Responsible management**
   Optimising the use of resources for which they are responsible so as to provide the maximum benefit to their employers.
4. **Serving the public interest**
   Not using their authority of office for personal benefit, rejecting and denouncing any business practice that is improper.
5. **Conformity to the laws**
   In terms of:
   A. The laws of the country in which they practice,
   B. The Institute's or Corporation's Rules and Regulations,
   C. Contractual obligations.

Norms of ethical behaviour

1. To consider first, the interest of one's organisation in all transactions and to carry out and believe in its established policies.
2. To be receptive to competent counsel from one's colleagues and be guided by such counsel without impairing the responsibility of one's office.
3. To buy without prejudice, seeking to obtain the maximum value for each dollar of expenditure.
4. To strive for increased knowledge of the materials and processes of manufacture, and to establish practical procedures for the performance of one's responsibilities.
5. To participate in professional development programs so that one's purchasing knowledge and performance are enhanced.
6. To subscribe to and work for honesty in buying and selling and to denounce all forms of improper business practice.
7. To accord a prompt and courteous reception to all who call on a legitimate business mission.
8. To abide by and to encourage others to practice the Professional Code of Ethics of the Purchasing Management Association of Canada and its affiliated Institutes and Corporation.
9. To counsel and assist fellow purchasers in the performance of their duties.
10. To cooperate with all organisations and individuals engaged in activities which enhance the development and standing of purchasing and materials management.

CASE EXAMPLE: PURCHASING ETHICS

In the United States in the 1980s, Jim Locklear was known as a first-rate buyer of houseware products. In 1987, he joined J C Penny with a significant salary cut. As a buyer, Locklear controlled the spending of millions of dollars a year and also sold crucial information, such as the amount of competitors' bids, to suppliers. Over the years, he supplemented his salary with as much as US$1.5 million in bribes and kickbacks. After a little over a year at J C Penny, a cutlery supplier of the firm blew the whistle. However, the firm was unable to establish any substantial proof of bribery. Locklear enjoyed the trust of management by dint of his sparkling performance as the sale of tabletop merchandise at J C Penny nearly doubled during Locklear's tenure.

In July 1992, an anonymous letter informed a Penney official of a special relationship between Locklear and Charles Briggs, a Dallas manufacturers' representative, from whom Locklear later admitted to taking US$200,000 in bribes. Penney subsequently launched a second investigation and uncovered Locklear's front companies. As a result, he was fired by J C Penny and after a trial by federal authorities, he was prosecuted. Locklear faced up to five years in prison and a maximum fine of twice his financial gain.

Adapted from Waller (2002: p. 497)

Rules of conduct

In applying these rules of conduct, members should follow guidance set out below:

A. Declaration of interest

Any personal interest which may impinge or might reasonably be deemed by others to impinge on a member's impartiality in any matter relevant to his or her duties should be immediately declared to his or her employer.

B. Confidentiality and accuracy of information

The confidentiality of information received in the course of duty must be respected and should not be used for personal gain; information given in the course of duty should be true and fair and not designed to mislead.

C. Competition

While considering the advantages to the member's employer of maintaining a continuing relationship with a supplier, any arrangement which might prevent the effective operation of fair competition should be avoided.

D. Business gifts and hospitality

To preserve the image and integrity of the member, employer and the profession, business gifts other than items of small intrinsic value should not be accepted. Reasonable hospitality is an accepted courtesy of a business relationship. The frequency and nature of gifts or hospitality accepted should not be allowed whereby the recipient might be or might be deemed by others to have been influenced in making a business decision as a consequence of accepting such hospitality or gifts.

E. Discrimination and harassment

No member shall knowingly participate in acts of discrimination or harassment towards any person that he or she has business relations with.

F. Environmental Issues

Members shall recognise their responsibility to environmental issues consistent with their corporate goals or missions.

However well thought out a code might be, it cannot cover every eventuality. For example, under Values, they say 'Optimizing the use of resources for which they are responsible so as to provide the maximum benefit to their employers'. Their 'Norms', clauses 1 and 3, reinforces the need to put the employer's interests ahead of all else in gaining the maximum value for each dollar. The final section on Environmental Issues could well be in conflict with such an approach. Likewise, gaining the maximum value for each dollar, in the short term, might not be in the best interests of building up a long-term relationship with a supplier.

The more detailed a code, the easier it will be for a member to find a way around the code to fit a particular set of circumstances. The best any individual can do is to understand the spirit of the code and to do their best to act as they would have others do unto them.

Having said this, sadly not all people are honest, or even if in the past they have been honest, they can still be tempted. Thus, there will always be a need for checks and balances.

Fraud

Every organisation has to be mindful of the possibility of purchasing fraud. The ingredients of fraud are intent, capability and opportunity. Fraud is not the same as making an error. Errors are mistakes and are not intended to happen, fraud is intentional and will include deception. Errors should be found by normal checks and audits. With fraud, the perpetrator or perpetrators will do their best to hide what they are doing. Fraud in purchasing often includes collusion. But what is fraud? Does a supplier who offers a free holiday to secure an order commit fraud? If the holiday is advertised widely, for example, an advertisement that says all purchasers of a particular model of a car this month will have a free weekend at a holiday resort is legitimate for the advertiser, but if our purchasing manager takes advantage of this offer when a cheaper car of another make was available, would this constitute fraud? It doesn't take much thought to see that the purchasing manager was putting his own interest ahead of the company, and has acted unethically, however, this would not constitute fraud. Fraud is more devious and is often hard to detect. Much fraud is only detected by outside information including disgruntled junior staff reporting on their managers, or by ex-wives, and in many cases, discarded mistresses.

Some signs of possible fraud are as follows:

Employees not taking holidays.
Overstocking, over ordering from one supplier.
Stock shortages at stock take.
Sudden affluence of an employee.
Falling profit margins.
Missing files and documentation.

The best protection against fraud is to have a culture of trust and integrity supported by internal and external audits. No code of ethics is going to prevent large-scale fraud. A code of ethics can help people to understand the difference between a business (free) lunch and a bribe.

Environmental purchasing

Environmental purchasing is the most important step in the war against global warming and pollution. Sustainability and accountability for waste and pollution cannot be ignored. At the very least, organisations need to be aware of environmental issues and make their concerns and needs known to their suppliers. This will begin with management establishing a policy, and communicating the policy internally and to their key suppliers. Although the United States has not signed the Kyoto Protocol, nonetheless, Americans as a whole are very conscious of environmental issues and several state governments have published environmental purchasing codes. For example, in Minnesota, the purchasing ordinance states:

> From copy paper to cleaners, automotive fluids to printing services, every product purchased can have an impact on human health and the environment. To reduce the quantity and toxicity of waste in Minnesota, state law requires state agencies and other public entities to purchase recycled, repairable, and durable goods.

Tools and resources are provided to incorporate environmental considerations into standard purchasing practices (www.pca.state.mn.us, 2007). For further details about the green supply chain, see Chapter 16.

Make or buy decisions

The fundamental objective of a sourcing strategy is to determine where to make or buy a product or service and why. The sourcing strategies for both manufacturing and service organisations are discussed separately, although there are many obvious common features between them. The sourcing strategy goes hand in hand with supply chain management.

Manufacturing

There has been considerable hyperbole regarding world-class manufacturing (WCM) and many articles and books have been written on the subject. There have been many interpretations of WCM. Some people associate WCM with working practices influenced by Japan's 'quality movement'. Others understand WCM to be manufacturing at the highest level of performance.

We define WCM as the term applied to organisations that achieve dominance in their segment of the global market and who sustain this dominance against world-class competition. Up until about 1990, manufacturing strategy tended to focus on the local area, for example, for manufacturers in the UK, the concern was the domestic market and the near neighbours of Europe. The emphasis has now moved to the determination of either a global strategy or regional strategy, not only for marketing but for sourcing.

Sourcing includes materials and labour and also includes the basic decision of whether to make or buy. The globalisation of manufacturing began with sourcing and a search for low labour costs. Manufacturing was transferred from the Western nations and Japan through the establishment of manufacturing facilities in Asia, the Indian subcontinent and Latin America. However, it soon transpired that once overseas investment is made in a country, the cost of labour creeps up. Additionally, as other overseas companies with similar products follow the lead (and move to a country where labour is cheaper), the initial competitive edge of cheap labour gained by the 'pioneer' company becomes a diminished advantage. There have been significant changes in the global marketplace, demanding a sound sourcing strategy for the manufacturing company as the changes accelerate. These changes include newly industrialised countries (the 'little dragons', now not so little, such as South Korea, Taiwan and Malaysia) and the big dragon of The People's Republic of China who all have acquired world-class manufacturing (WCM) capabilities in the last 20 years. Investors wishing to set up manufacturing in these countries will find labour is not as cheap in real terms as it was even five years ago. But more importantly, these countries are now, without a doubt, competitors of world-class standing. India is also on the cusp of becoming a WCM, and further down the line, Pakistan and Indonesia show WCM potential. Other regions that are emerging as WCM contenders include South America and South Africa.

The gradual elimination of tariff barriers and the regional pacts for 'common markets' (e.g. Mercosur, NAFTA, Andina, EU, CER) are encouraging competition from regionally based groupings of countries. The 'new' markets of what was the East European Communist bloc have provided new opportunities in the global market. Additionally, manufacturers in this region are close to achieving the status of WCM.

Improved logistics and electronic communication systems are assisting the implementation of sourcing strategies. The growing similarity of what people want to buy across the world is encouraging global product/process development and marketing. Investment costs for innovation and new technology are becoming too expensive to concentrate in one local market.

A sound sourcing strategy for a manufacturing company will be a requirement for future survival. Catching up with the manufacturing performance of the competitors is not enough. The sourcing strategy of the company must move in step with the corporate strategy and reflect the marketing strategy and innovation programmes of the company. The sourcing strategy should be dynamic in a relentless pursuit of value to customers in a changing marketplace. As Hamel and Prahalad (1994) accurately forecast over 20 years ago, 'the market a company dominates today is likely to change substantially over the next ten years. There is no such thing as "sustaining" leadership, it must be regenerated again and again'. In order to develop a sourcing strategy for manufacturing, it is necessary to have a formal strategic planning process. The process should be flexible and simple to follow, and it should be incorporated with other corporate planning processes. Our strategic planning process for sourcing for manufacturing can be found in 'total operations solutions' (Basu and Wright, 2005) and consists of these eight steps.

Step 1: Project brief

The process is best carried through by setting up a project team of about ten people and defining the brief of the project. The project team should consist of a project director (e.g. head of manufacturing), manufacturing staff (e.g. industrial engineer, plant engineer, manufacturing manager, quality manager), logistics staff (e.g. planning manager, distribution manager), marketing staff (e.g. brand managers) and commercial staff (e.g. accountant, purchasing management and human resources staff).

When preparing the project brief, it is useful to have those documents that cover current company activities such as capital investment, annual operating plans and long-term plans. In addition, any other relevant reports (such as information on competition, marketplace, economy and government regulations) of the countries covering the scope of the strategy will help with this activity. The project brief should clearly state the scope, time scale, deliverables and resources required for the project.

Step 2: Operational mission and objectives

The manufacturing mission defines the aim of manufacturing in the corporate strategy or the business plan. The mission statement must fit the capabilities of the manufacturing function. Unless the mission is feasible, it will be no more than mere words or rhetoric. Usually, the mission statement is described in broad terms as illustrated by the following example: 'The manufacturing mission is to achieve the lowest unit manufacturing cost relative to competition without sacrificing high standards of quality, service and flexibility to the customer'.

This mission statement has a priority on low cost. Alternative priorities could include one or more of the following: quality, customer service, rapid introduction of product, visible presence in emerging markets, combating a dominant competitor and so on. The point to note is that the mission has to be sufficiently specific for a clear objective or objectives to be readily distinguished.

Manufacturing objectives consist of performance measures that the company's manufacturing must achieve as part of the annual operating plan. Achievement of the objectives will result in the achievement of the mission.

Step 3: Strategic factors

The understanding and analysis of strategic factors can determine the success of a sourcing strategy. Strategic factors relate to the longer-term implication of both external and internal factors to project manufacturing into the future. These factors are competition, customer preferences, technology, environment, economic conditions and statutory regulations. To develop a sourcing strategy for manufacturing to gain a competitive advantage, a detailed competitive position analysis will be necessary. This analysis determines how the strengths and weaknesses of the company's manufacturing position relate to major competitors (both current and potential competitors). The dimensions for this analysis can be cost, quality, dependability, flexibility and innovation. Following this analysis, the company should be able to identify any gaps in manufacturing competence and establish priorities for a future strategy so as to gain a competitive advantage. It is critical to determine what should be made and whether to make or buy. Such decisions depend on the long-term volumes of the product and the level of technology required. To identify the preliminary grouping of the sourcing of products. The project brief may be reviewed and restated after the analysis of all strategic factors.

Step 4: Data collection and data analysis

Once the revised project brief has been finalised, the next stage is the collection and analysis of data. Although the need for data will vary, the following areas will need to be considered:

- General information and internal information of the company regarding annual plans, long-term plans, R&D and marketing.
- External information regarding competition, economic and political factors of countries involved, social and cultural aspects and environmental (green) issues.
- Product information:
    - Future, ten-year sales forecast by products.
    - Past, five-year sales history.
- Plant information:
    - Present capacity of own plants.
    - Investment plan to increase capacity.
    - Present levels of efficiency.
    - Other manufacturing alliances, e.g. subcontractor capabilities.
- Stock information
    - Stock policy of materials and finished products.
    - Warehousing area (space and capacity) and method of storage.
    - Method of distribution to customers.
- Personnel information:
    - Projection of people availability and skills.
    - Industrial relations of manufacturing sites.
    - Amenities required.
- Cost information:
    - Manufacturing costs of products by site.
    - Distribution cost elements.
    - Cost of warehouse building per square metre.
    - Cost of office building per square metre.
    - Cost of an employee per year (total cost, i.e. wages, benefits and training).

The purpose of this stage is to calculate the capacity of the plant and services for the projected volume and estimate the space required for each activity for each manufacturing site. It is normally sufficient to carry out these analyses for the current year, at the mid-stage and at the completion of the plan or when a significant event (e.g. the manufacture of a new product) occurs. The utilisation of assets as determined at this stage should help to establish what to manufacture and where, and the profitability of each site.

Step 5: Strategic options

Strategic options determine how sourcing or own manufacturing is going to meet the objectives of the mission. It is useful to reiterate that the objectives refer to performance measures (such as cost, flexibility, quality, etc.) and strategy refers to how these objectives will be achieved. Strategic options are normally expressed in a number of sourcing scenarios. These are derived from the understanding of the competitive strengths and weaknesses from the foregoing stages. As a general rule, there should not be more than eight scenarios. Eight scenarios are manageable and enable adequate attention to be given to each scenario. A critical analysis of each scenario is then carried out against the criteria of manufacturing objectives and strategic factors. Two or three scenarios are then short-listed for quantitative evaluation.

Step 6: Options evaluation

The aim of this stage is to evaluate two or three main options in order to select the best strategy for the future. The analysis should take advantage of simulation modelling tools to select a strategy by optimising the total operating cost. Costs only need to be broad estimates for the evaluation of options.

The strategy should then be further tested by comparing the investment costs of alternative development plans with quantitative tools such as discounted cash flow (DCF) analysis.

Step 7: Implementation plan

The success of a sourcing strategy for manufacturing will depend on how effectively the changes have been implemented. There should be a structured implementation plan describing the phasing, responsibility, costs and obstacles that have to be overcome.

The strategy itself should not have major changes every year or there will be little chance of maintaining the strategic goal. Tactics should be continually adjusted to meet changing circumstances.

Step 8: Review

As stated previously, there is a need for regular evaluation and a review of progress to implement the strategy. In addition to the regular review, the entire strategy should be formally reviewed on an annual basis.

Service sector

In the service sector, sourcing strategy buzzwords such as 'outsourcing', 'off-shoring' and 'in-sourcing' have gained currency. Outsourcing is the collaboration with a partner to manage a part of your business. An example is IBM supplying and managing on-site the information and technology function for Toyota. There are distinct categories of outsourcing in the service sector:

- Information technology outsourcing (e.g. programming).
- Business process outsourcing (e.g. handling all administration).
- Managed services (e.g. call centres).

Outsourcing strategy

A well-documented example of business process outsourcing, albeit in manufacturing, is provided by the Coca-Cola Corporation. For over 100 years, Coca-Cola has been producing syrup and marketing bottled products. The actual production and bottling of the product (to Coca-Cola's strict standards) is done locally by its global network of business partners. A huge explosion in outsourcing can be attributed to the concept of 'core competence' popularised by Hamel and Prahalad (1994). The principle is fundamentally simple. For example, by analysing and understanding Porter's 'value chain' (1985), an organisation can focus on the elements that are core to its business and outsource others while maintaining strategic control. Examples of successful outsourcing companies include Dell and CISCO. Dell Computers Company has focused on its key activity as sales and outsourced non-core functions such as logistics and maintenance. CISCO has identified design and network solutions as its core activity and outsourced the manufacturing of infrastructure components.

Rationale of outsourcing

Outsourcing strategy is also discussed in Chapter 19. A particular advantage of outsourcing is cash flow, flexibility and releasing key management resources, but other benefits include external expertise and cost savings. There are several external factors driving the growth of outsourcing:

- With the rapid change in the technology landscape, especially in information and communication technology (ICT); external vendors are often in a position to provide more effective solutions support with new technology.
- Globalisation is a strong catalyst in outsourcing by enhancing transparency in financial reporting, having a wider choice of suppliers and more competition.

Outsourcers offering service level guarantees have a powerful proposition.

Basu's outsourcing matrix

Basu's model (Basu, 2004, p. 270), as shown in Figure 7.1, provides a useful framework in make or buy decisions. The model shown uses the core strength (technology and/or patent life) as the x axis and product volume as the y axis. The sourcing strategy is determined according to the location of products on the grid.

1. High technology/high volume. These products are suitable for own manufacturing. It will be appropriate to invest to retain the core strength.

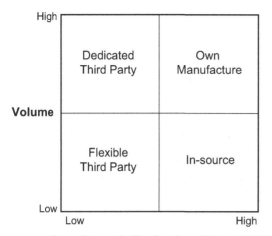

Figure 7.1 Basu's outsourcing matrix

2. High technology/low volume. When the volume is low, the preferred strategy is to 'in-source'. This means that either the global manufacture of a product is centralised at a single site or the capacity of high technology is utilised by gaining orders from outside companies.

3. Low technology/high volume. After a period, the technological advantage of a product reduces and it becomes a mere commodity. If the volume is high then a supply partnership can be considered with a dedicated third-party supplier.

4. Low technology/low volume. If demand is low and there is more than one supplier available, long-term supplier agreements/partnerships are not important.

Decision logic of outsourcing by Slack et al.

Slack et al. (2012) provide a decision logic of outsourcing that can be applied to both manufacturing and service operations. As shown in Figure 7.2, if an operation has long-term strategic importance, it should not be outsourced. Similarly, if the company has specialised skills or knowledge for the operation or a higher potential for performance improvement, it is unlikely to outsource it. It would be unwise to give away such capability. The

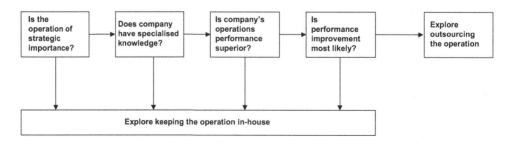

Figure 7.2 Decision logic of outsourcing by Slack et al.

company should consider operations of low-skill operations of less strategic advantage for outsourcing.

The outsourcing decision logic of Slack et al. is alignment with Basu's outsourcing matrix.

Off-shoring

Off-shoring is a form of outsourced managed services where skilled labour is cheaper. Cost savings are primary benefits. Other benefits include time zone differences enabling 24-hour services and access to more willing well-qualified workers to tackle boring jobs. An example is call centres located in India serving callers (customers) in the UK. There are some risks of off-shoring. These include:

- Services going down because of telecommunication problems and inadequate training.
- Data and physical security are in potential danger.
- Excessive foreign travel.

The ways to minimise these risks include minimising foreign travel, keeping your software code and using a third-party broker.

In-sourcing or on-shoring

In-sourcing or on-shoring is domestic outsourcing. It involves the transfer of your company's operation within your own country. In-sourcing also means centralising multiple, distributed operations into a semi-autonomous unit. This is managed separately and accountable to the business, like an outsourcer, but remains under the organisation's control. Contemporary challenges will likely encourage more on-shoring decisions.

The advantages of in-sourcing include:

- The business maintains strategic control.
- It reduces logistics costs and carbon footprints.
- It avoids third-party margins and tariffs.
- It reduces the risk of global disruptions.

Service level agreements and joint service partnerships

In a service level agreement (SLA), all three words carry equal importance. The document should define what services are to be delivered and the levels of performance expected. It is also an agreement between the customer and the supplier and not a unilateral declaration. For simple functions like catering, fixed-price contracts by SLAs are easy to implement. However, they are highly limiting and inappropriate for strategic partnerships. The agreements (also known as joint service partnerships) should include:

- Shared gains or structured incentives based on added value beyond core services.
- Shared risks.
- Best practices, training and cost-effectiveness initiatives are freely shared.
- Forecast data and planning processes are shared.

CASE EXAMPLE: THE GLOBAL PROCUREMENT OF IKEA

Swedish home furnishing giant IKEA, founded by Ingvar Kamprad in Sweden in 1943, is a remarkable success story. The first IKEA store was opened in Älmhult, Sweden, in 1958. The first store outside Sweden was established in Norway in 1963 and the first store outside Scandinavia was established in Switzerland in 1973. Over a few decades, IKEA has persistently grown its turnover by around 10–15% annually. At present, IKEA offers a range of around 12,000 products that are all principally the same in IKEA stores around the world.

A key component in the low-cost strategy at IKEA has been to own only a small proportion of the means of production and to depend on a global procurement strategy. Therefore, the products that are sold in IKEA stores, including signature products like the BILLY bookshelf, the PAX wardrobe, the LACK table and the SULTAN bed are to a very large extent sourced from a global network of suppliers.

In 2012, it was revealed by Ernst and Young that IKEA had used political prisoners in East Germany to keep costs and prices down. It was reported that many of the IKEA suppliers in China, Vietnam, India, Nepal and Pakistan were using low-wage workers including child labour. Presumably as a reaction to such adverse publicity, in 2009, IKEA signed up to a new Global Social Compliance Programme in an attempt to take a more collaborative approach to ethical sourcing. Their head of supply chain and procurement compliance also announced:

> We're looking to do more on the local sourcing side of things, it makes more sense from both a business and environmental perspective. For example, for our stores in North America we're looking to areas such as Mexico as much as possible.

After Ernst and Young revealed that IKEA had previously used political prisoners in East Germany to keep costs and prices down, IKEA made a public apology. Also in 2012, IKEA announced their decision to cease cooperation with many Chinese OEMs as they did not comply with IKEA requirements relating to working hours and conditions.

In the mid-1990s, IKEA had more than 2000 suppliers, but by 2012, its supply base had been reduced to 1026 suppliers in 53 countries despite increasing sales volumes. The initial development of a supplier network outside the Nordic countries and later in Eastern Europe was in fact a reaction to a ban on suppliers to IKEA by the Swedish furniture trade organisation. The establishment of supplier relationships in Poland and later in other parts of Eastern Europe enabled IKEA to sustain and develop its strong position as a low-cost alternative in the market for home furnishing. Almost two-thirds of its products (64%) were sourced from European countries; the largest single supply market was China with a 22% share of the supply, and the second largest supply market was Poland with a 16% share.

Without close collaboration with suppliers, the balancing act between stock costs and avoiding the risk of stock-outs would not have been possible. With its dominant leadership in the home furnishing market, a cornerstone of this strategy is the ownership of product rights, allowing IKEA to switch suppliers when necessary. In addition, IKEA seems to concentrate on as few supply markets as possible

Source: Adapted from IKEA web pages,
The New York Times, 16 November 2012

e-Procurement

The influence of the Internet on the supply chain and electronic transfer of information and funds is detailed in Chapters 12 and 14.

The key aspect is that the internet enables systems to communicate across organisational boundaries. The various e-procurement models are as follows:

- EDI networks. Providing communication between a few trading partners (buyers and sellers).
- B2E. Allowing the transfer of information within an organisation between departments and employees. For example, templates of documents, automated approvals for routine requisitions and standardisation of procedures.
- B2B. A website where businesses 'meet' to buy and sell.
- A closed exchange open only to members. An example is Covisint's B2B platform that enables enterprises and industries to get trusted information across business-to-partner, business-to-customer and business-to-enterprise, while connecting more than 212,000 business partners and customers (www.covisint.com, April 2016).
- A public exchange sometimes referred to as a portal allows almost anyone to enter and trade online.
- B2C. An email address or webpage that allows customers to buy online, for example, airline bookings and e-tickets.

Other expressions used in e-procurement are e-catalogues, e-auctions and reverse auctions.

e-Catalogues. These provide online and up-to-date lists, photographs, video clips of products, specifications, prices and so on. Amazon is a good example.

e-Auctions. Here a seller can display a product online and buyers can make bids until a price is reached and a sale agreed. The bids might be public or sealed. With sealed bids, the various buyers are in fact tendering as they cannot see what the other bids are.

Reverse auctions. Here the buyer advises the product and quantity they want, and suppliers complete online by offering lower prices. In a reverse auction, it would not be regarded as ethical for the buyer to lodge proxy bids.

Procurement schedule

Finally, we should also emphasise the importance of a procurement schedule to monitor the effectiveness of procurement and purchasing processes. A procurement schedule helps to decide what to buy, when and from what sources. It is useful in both managing global supply chains and major projects considering ethical and green considerations.

The procurement schedule is a key piece of the database used to monitor the progress of purchase orders while reviewing them in conjunction with the construction schedule. The construction schedule for each work package is documented in bar charts and, where appropriate, is supported by a network diagram. The procurement schedule should be considered after reviewing the network diagram and bar chart of the construction schedule.

The procurement schedule for each work package is documented in a spreadsheet and a bar chart. Sometimes the schedule is also presented as a network diagram. A master

Table 7.1 An example of a master production schedule

Contract number	Description	Vendor	Work packages	Date of contract	Expected date of completion	Lead time
	Design	A	1, 2, 3, 4, 5	February 2009	March 2010	13 months
	Enabling works	B	8, 9, 10, 20	August 2009	December 2010	17 months
	Tunnels, portals and shafts	C	11, 12, 13, 14	December 2009	March 2013	52 months
	Stations	C	15, 16	March 2010	July 2012	29 months
	Systems	D	6, 7	June 2011	March 2014	34 months
	Logistics	B	21, 22, 23	March 2010	June 2011	16 months
	Rolling stocks and depots	C	17, 18, 19	December 2010	September 2013	34 months

procurement schedule at a high level of procurement contracts is developed and compared regularly with the master construction schedule. Table 7.1 shows a simple and hypothetical example of a master procurement schedule.

It is emphasised that Table 7.1 is shown at a high level, but the more detailed schedule for each work package contains further items of information in the spreadsheet, including purchase order reference, category of work, the actual start date of the contract, the total value of the order, value per annum and responsibility.

The master procurement schedule is also supported by a bar chart as shown in Figure 7.3. If any construction activities are delayed due to late procurement, the network diagram of the total project is reviewed to see if the knock-on effect delays any other activities. It is important to identify the procurement items that have a long lead time, especially if they are on the critical path and have any special logistic requirements.

Summary

In this chapter, we began with a discussion as to why procurement and supplier focus are important building blocks of supply chain management. The advantages of developing

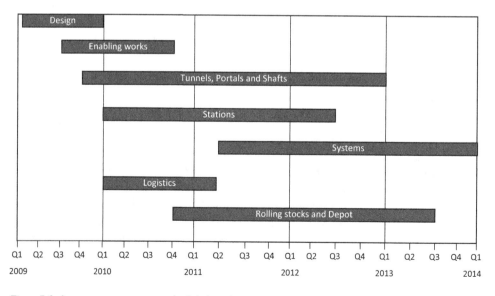

Figure 7.3 A master procurement schedule bar chart

long-term relationships with key suppliers were explained. It was shown that cost is only one aspect. When selecting suppliers, reliability and delivering to specification on time and to the right quantity are key issues. Ethical and green issues are also important considerations. The advantages of outsourcing and issues to consider when deciding whether to make or buy were also explained. Other issues covered were ethics, fraud and e-procurement.

Discussion questions

1. What are the key components of procurement management? Explain why the challenges and opportunities of global supply chains have enhanced the importance of procurement management.
2. With reference to the case example in this chapter, describe how the implementation of i2 software helped Toyota to improve supply chain performance including the global purchasing operation.
3. What are the key steps that should be followed in the purchasing process of a global organisation? How would you ensure the cost, quality, time and risk of a large purchasing order?
4. Discuss the need for purchasing ethics and fraud control. Describe the guidelines of purchasing ethics and the code recommended by the Purchasing Management Association of Canada.
5. In a multinational manufacturing organisation, what are the key challenges and opportunities of a make or buy decision? With reference to the guidelines provided in this chapter, outline the eight steps of developing and implementing an outsourcing strategy.
6. In the service sector, describe the key factors and services influencing a decision for outsourcing. What is the difference between outsourcing and off-shoring? Comment on how outsourcing of services may affect customer service.
7. What are the decision criteria for applying an SLA (service level agreement) or a partnership agreement in a procurement contract?
8. Explain how the e-procurement process has transformed the purchasing function.

8   Inventory management

Introduction

In this chapter, we discuss the role of inventory or stock in supply chain management. Both the theoretical and practical aspects of inventory management will be addressed.

Stocks of materials (inventories) are kept as a buffer against variations in demand and to overcome uncertain supply. This buffer can be regarded as safety stock. Inventory is held along the supply chain in various warehouses, factories (work in process) and retail store shelves. Holding stocks of materials can add a minimum of 15% to 40% to costs per year. Holding costs include storage space, energy costs including heating and refrigeration, stock slippage and insurance, handling costs and obsolescence (past use-by date). Therefore, careful management of stock levels makes good business sense.

Learning objectives

Learning objectives for this chapter are:

1. Location of inventory.
2. Inventory costs.
3. Consumed and non-consumed inventory.
4. Inventory management tools.
5. Performance measures.

Location of inventory

As explained in Chapter 3, stocks of materials are usually held in three stages of a process, viz. input stocks (e.g. raw and packaging materials), process stocks (e.g. semi-finished products) and output stocks (e.g. finished products). Within each stage there can be a number of stock locations each holding base stock. The 'base' stock is the amount of inventory essential to meet normal or planned demand. It is also likely that there will be buffers of safety stock at each location. Buffer stock is held to meet above-average demand and overcome the uncertainty of delivery lead times. The more stock locations there are the greater amount of total stock held in the system. Consider a supply chain that has one factory, two warehouses and three distributors each holding base stock and buffer stock and compare it with a situation where the factory distributes directly to retailers. It does not take much imagination to see that the greater number of stages in the supply chain, the greater amount of base and buffer stock held. The ramifications of the number and location of distribution points and warehouses are considered more fully in Chapter 10.

DOI: 10.4324/9781003341352-10

Inventory costs

Inventory costs comprise holding costs, risk costs and storage costs.

Holding costs

Inventories can accumulate as a result of poor planning and scheduling or by design. Generally, inventory is viewed as a negative impact on business as it incurs costs of capital (interest paid or interest foregone), storage space, insurance, increased risk of damage and theft, handling and obsolescence.

Risk costs include:

- Fashion changes (style, colour, texture).
- Past 'use-by date' for foods.
- Deterioration.
- Obsolescence due to new technology or model changes that make existing models outdated.
- Damage.
- Pilfering/theft.

Storage costs include:

- Buildings.
- Racking.
- Special storage such as refrigeration or secure storage of dangerous goods.
- Handling costs (specialised equipment, wages etc.).

Finance costs include:

- Interest on money invested in stocks of materials (either the organisation has had to borrow money to pay for the stock held or the money 'invested' in the stock could have been used elsewhere in the organisation).
- Insurance.

Most of the costs above require no explanation, as it is readily apparent that old stock, whether it is old technology or simply no longer fashionable, is hard to sell, and in some cases, scrap value will not even cover the original cost. On the other hand, a lack of inventory leads to lost production in the factory and lost sales at the end of the supply chain. Holding inventory of materials and finished products therefore can be seen as an insurance against the uncertainty of supply and to overcome unforeseen variations in demand.

Inventory management is a good indicator of the effectiveness of supply chain management. It is relatively easy to achieve higher levels of customer service by accumulating excessive stocks. It will also obscure short-term operational problems. But this is a costly and risky option in terms of cash flow. Obsolete inventory, be it for changes in technology, fashion or in foodstuffs past the use-by date has little salvage value. It is vital to optimise the inventory level.

Consumed and non-consumed inventory

Wild (2003) introduced the concept of consumed and non-consumed stocks. Consumed items (e.g. materials or products) are used by the process or customers and must be replenished in shorter cycles. Non-consumed items (e.g. capital equipment and labour) are repeatedly used by the process needing repair and maintenance and are replaced in longer intervals. This chapter considers the inventory of stocks to be consumed at the next level of production or inventory held to meet the demand of (i.e. supplied to) the next stage of the supply chain. Wild refers to this as single-stage inventory.

In service industries, operations managers might have a nonchalant attitude towards inventories but not so the accountants. Differences between services and physical goods are addressed both from operations and marketing. Among the differences identified within marketing and operations literature are intangibility, heterogeneity, inseparability and perishability (Grönroos, 2000). It is perceived that services are one-offs and cannot be stored. There are of course consumed stocks (e.g. stationery, brochures, catalogues) in service industries that require inventory management. However, in the service sector, more emphasis should be focused on managing non-consumed stock (viz. database and skilled people).

Inventory management tools

In traditional inventory management there are two basic approaches: the pull approach and the push approach. In a pull system, as shown in Figure 8.1, a warehouse is viewed as independent of the supply chain and inventory is replenished with order sizes based on a predetermined stock level for each warehouse. The stock management model for the pull system is normally geared to establish ROL (re-order level) and ROQ (re-order quantity).

That is, when the stock drops to a certain level, a re-order is triggered of a predetermined amount. The re-order quantity takes into account past demands and the lead times for a re-order to be satisfied. The aim is to have as small an amount of inventory as possible on hand at any one time, and the re-order quantity should likewise be as small as

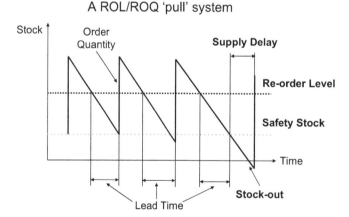

Figure 8.1 A basic ROL/ROQ model

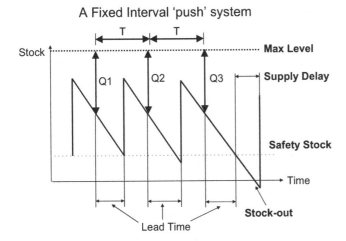

Figure 8.2 A basic fixed interval model

possible. However, in some processes, such as a batch system, there will be a minimum amount that can be produced and in other cases there can be economies of scale that will determine the optimal size of an order. The push method is used when economies of scale in procurement outweigh the benefits of minimum inventory levels as achieved in the pull method (see Figure 8.2).

That is, the warehouse does not decide the quantity of the order but will receive deliveries as determined to meet the production schedule. Normally, a fixed interval review model with a forecast demand for manufacturing planning is used in a push system.

With the support of information technology, businesses are moving towards a virtual inventory system with a single stock concept that can be held anywhere in the system, be it on order with the supplier, in production or at the point of sale. This is the concept of virtual inventory management (VIM) or electronic inventory. Thus, instead of considering stocks of raw materials, work in progress at the various stages of production and finished goods in warehouses each as separate stocks of inventory, purely because of their physical location, inventory is now considered as being part of one single stock.

Economic order quantities

The economic order quantity (EOQ) system is a push system that can be used when there is an advantage in buying in bulk rather than making several small purchases. The EOQ system calculates a re-order amount using a formula known as EOQ – economic order quantity. The EOQ assumes that:

- Demand is known and is constant.
- Deliveries when received are to specification, are the right quantity and are made on time.
- There is no slippage of stock due to theft or damage and what the computer shows as being in stock is physically present.

The formula for EOQ is

Q = The square root of 2 DO/PH

where:

Q = The re-order quantity

D = The annual demand (in units)

O = Cost of raising an order

P = Price per unit

H = Holding cost

EXAMPLE: ECONOMIC ORDER QUANTITY

Demand 60,000 units per annum

Order cost 100 pounds per order raised

Price per unit 75 pounds

Holding cost 12% pa.

Thus, $2 \times 60,000 \times 100 = 12,000,000$

Divided by $75 \times 0.12 = 9$

$12,000,000/9 = 1,333,333.33$

The square root of 1,333,333.33 is 1154.

However, the supplier might only supply in packages of 100, thus each order would be for 1200 rather than the odd amount of 1154. As the total demand is 60,000 per annum, there will be 50 deliveries (orders) required a year.

Cost of ordering

The cost of ordering might not seem to be a big cost (old-fashioned order form, an envelope and a stamp). However, consider the savings made when the British Stock Exchange implemented an electronic share transfer system in the mid-1990s. Prior to this, share transfer cost 30 pounds per transaction, once share transfers were made online or 'paperless', the cost was reduced to 30 pence per transfer. Many organisations have made savings of a similar magnitude by adopting an online purchasing system. For example, in the supermarket, barcoding at the checkout can trigger an automatic online re-order when the stock of a particular item drops to a preset level. This will save on staff numbers that in a manual system would be required to physically count stock, calculate forecasted usage, raise order forms and so on.

Calculation of safety stock

Safety stock is the buffer inventory to cover the variation of demand and supply during lead lime. There are many uncertainties of demand and supply, for example, customers may increase an order, machinery might break down or a supplier might be unable to deliver on time due to transport problems.

There are key parameters affecting the calculation of safety stock:

- Forecast accuracy.
- Lead time.
- Service level.

EXAMPLE: RE-ORDER LEVEL WITH SAFETY STOCK

Consider the given data for a garden centre selling sacks of fertiliser:

* Average demand 10 sacks per day
* Service level required 95%
* Lead time 15 days
* Standard deviation of daily demand 3 (for a normal distribution)

Determine safety stock and re-order level

For 95% service level safety stock = 1.64 × standard deviation of demand during lead time

Standard deviation of demand during lead time

$= $ Square root of (15×3^2)

$= 11.6$

Safety stock $= 1.64 \times 11.6 = 19$

Re-order level = Average demand during lead time + safety stock

$= 10 \times 15 + 19 = 169$ sacks

EOQ and lean production

It might be considered that the lean or just-in-time approach where items are purchased to arrive just when required is not compatible with the bulk ordering approach of an EOQ system. This is true when ordering most components in a just-in-time system. Nonetheless, some items will be consumed in such quantities that buying one item at a time would not be sensible, for example, the purchase of one metre of cable when dozens of metres are used daily.

Vendor managed inventory

The use of third-party logistics (3PL) to take over some, or all, of a company's logistics responsibilities has become common. Third-party logistics is simply the use of an outside company to perform all or part of the firm's materials management and product distribution function. By using a 3PL provider, there is no need for the client to own, manage and staff warehouses, fleets of trucks and other means of transport. Using a 3PL provider saves in capital investment and is of particular benefit when there is variation in the need for warehousing transport and other facilities. Third-party logistics also provides flexibility and can provide a wide variety of services. The downside can be a loss of control and the need to commit to long-term contracts. The client also tends to lose physical interaction with their clients.

As customer satisfaction becomes more imperative and margins get tighter, it makes sense to create cooperative efforts between suppliers and retailers in order to leverage the knowledge of both parties. The types of retailer–supplier partnerships can be viewed on a continuum. At one end is information sharing. At the other is vendor managed inventory (VMI), where the vendor (supplier) completely manages and owns the inventory until the retailer sells it. In a simple quick response strategy, suppliers receive point-of-sale (POS) data from retailers and use this information to synchronise their production and inventory activities based on actual sales demand at retail. Retailers can still prepare individual orders, but the POS data is used by the supplier to improve delivery performance and hence reduce supply variability. Generally, for fast-moving consumer goods, a continuous replenishment strategy will be used, sometimes called rapid replenishment, whereby suppliers receive data transmitted directly from POS and use this data to prepare shipments at agreed intervals to maintain a sufficient level of inventory.

With a VMI system, the supplier decides on the appropriate inventory levels of each product and the appropriate policies to maintain these levels. The goal of many VMI programmes is to eliminate the need for the retailer to oversee specific orders for replenishment. The ultimate is for the supplier to manage the inventory and only receive payment for it once it has been sold by the retailer; in essence, the retailer is providing an outlet for the supplier!

Distributor integration

The use of information technology enables several distributors to be integrated and share a common database. This enables inventory held by one distributor to be available to the other distributors in the network. Distributor integration (DI) can be used to address both inventory-related and service-related issues and share expertise and technical knowledge. In terms of inventory, DI can be used to create a large pool of inventory across the entire distributor network, thus lowering total inventory costs while raising customer service levels. Similarly, DI can be used to meet a customer's specific needs by directing those requests to the distributor best suited to address them.

Balance date/stocktakes, or 'Where did the stock go?'

Wright (2012) considers the problems that occur when a physical stock-take does not tally with computer records. Generally, physical stock will be less than the stock record.

> The only true way of knowing what is really on hand is to physically count it. The problem at balance date is that when the auditors count the stock and compare it to stock records generally there will be a shortage. Stock discrepancies only occur for a limited number of reasons:
>
> 1. The stock was never received (short deliveries or over-invoiced).
> 2. The stock was sold but the sale was not recorded.
> 3. Stock has been stolen.
> 4. Stock has been damaged or disposed of but disposal has not been recorded.
> 5. Stock has been miscoded on receipt or when sold (e.g. 200 hoses booked in, but actually 200 hose-clips received).
> 6. The stock was sold before it was booked in.
> 7. Stock has been 'borrowed' (in the sale representative's van for display/demonstration purposes).
>
> (Wright, 2012: p. 189)

The generally accepted methods for maintaining the integrity of stock records are as follows:

1. Stock orders entered into the computer system.
2. Stock booked into the system when received. The system will compare and verify what was ordered is the same as what is received.

3. The system will not allow stock to be sold before it is booked in.
4. Sales must be entered through the system.
5. The system triggers payment advice. Payment is not triggered by suppliers' invoices. In this manner, you will only pay for what was ordered and actually received.
6. It is advisable to have weekly, fortnightly or monthly rolling stocktakes on a portion of the inventory. 'This should overcome the drama of an annual stock-take, and should also reduce your audit account' (Wright, 2012: p. 189).

The above system relies on a standard computerised system.

With an integrated supply chain approach, heavy reliance is placed on the information technology system. Thus, if goods are barcoded as they pass over the sensor at the point of sale, the customer's statement is updated, a delivery docket and invoice are raised, stock records of the retailer are updated, sales figures and margins are calculated and recorded and a re-order is triggered. If suppliers are linked into the system, the supplier will also be automatically notified of a replacement re-order.

ABC analysis

ABC analysis is an adaptation of Pareto analysis. Wilfredo Pareto was a 19th-century economist who determined that 80% of the wealth was held by 20% of the population. This axiom can be adapted to most circumstances, for example, 80% of car accidents are caused by 20% of the drivers (young men between the ages of 17 and 25). In inventory management using the Pareto approach, the assumption is that 20% of the items held will account for 80% of the value of materials on hand. A further refinement is ABC analysis. Using the ABC approach, inventory will be categorised as high value, medium value and low value. The high-value 'A' items will require the greatest control, the 'B' items will require lesser attention and the low-value 'C' items (nuts and bolts) will require minimal control. A breakdown of ABC items might look something like that shown in Table 8.1.

ABC analysis facilitates cyclical rolling stock takes whereby a series of 'mini' stocktakes are made during the year. For example, all 'A' class items might be counted weekly, and a percentage of 'B' items might also be counted on a weekly basis.

Performance measures

Chapter 23 is our measurement chapter, but as each chapter is designed to stand alone, inventory measurements are discussed here. Performance measures are needed to drive continuous improvement. If we don't know have a means of measurement, we will not know our level of performance. And if we don't have measurements, how can we know if we have improved, in terms of client satisfaction, stock outs and stock turns? Measurement is also necessary to set directions and targets for the future. The criteria for performance measures should cover a balanced approach for all key parameters of the supply chain and should provide operational measures rather than purely financial measures.

Table 8.1 ABC analysis of inventory

	A class items	B class items	C class items
Number held	11%	29%	60% of total
Value	54%	41%	5% of value

Measures should be simple, easy to define and easy to monitor. In determining what should be measured, it is useful to get away from standard accounting measures. Supply chain management requirements are different from those of accountants. In determining our own measurements, we should ask:

- What should be measured and why?
- What is the benefit of this measure and how does it help us to achieve our goal?

Once we decide what should be measured, then we can determine how it should be measured. Measurements are only of any use if they are fed down to the workers and if the workers understand what the measurements mean. Ideally, if a worker receives a measurement, the worker should be encouraged to become involved in finding ways to improve the system so as to achieve improved results. Measurements should never be used as a means of levelling blame on one department or to criticise any one individual. Measurements should be aimed at finding where problems occur so that action can be taken to prevent future mistakes. After all, no one section or department works alone; we are all in this together. If the company goes down, we all go down!

Without upsetting the accountants, we believe that no measurement is sacrosanct and each measurement should be challenged. A measurement that does not help to improve the system is an unnecessary cost. Figure 8.3 shows basic measurements needed in inventory management.

Stock turn

'Stock turn' is the ratio of the total sales (or throughput of a product) and the actual stock at any time, both being expressed in either money or volume. The objective is to maximise the stock turn (i.e. minimise average stock level) but also to maintain stock availability. Stock availability (the percentage of demand that can be met from available stock) is another measure of performance; availability can also be measured by the number or percentage of orders satisfied within a given target time frame.

The unit of stock turn is a number or ratio. It is also a common practice to express stock profile in terms of equivalent weeks or days of stock. For example, if the cost of goods sold (raw materials plus direct labour and other manufacturing costs but not overheads) is £25,000, and the amount of stock of finished goods on hand totals £5000, then the number of days of finished goods equals 73 days (5000/25,000 × 365 × 73). That is, on past performance, it is going to take two and half months to sell all the finished goods we have on hand. Assuming that we have already paid the suppliers and have paid

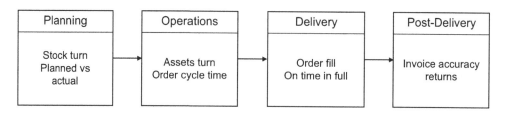

Figure 8.3 Inventory measurements

our workers' wages and the other costs of production, this shows that our inventory of finished goods is putting pressure on our cash flow. The same types of calculations can be made for stocks of raw materials and work in progress.

Case example

One company we visited was proud of the fact that in their high street stores they only ever had seven days of retail stock (own product) on hand. Their re-order system to their central warehouse was online and re-orders were delivered within 24 hours. The warehouse of finished goods held six months' stock, and the stockpile of raw materials for production amounted to seven months' supply. Assuming suppliers were paid within one month of supply, this meant that this company was waiting 13 months and seven days to recover the cost outlaid for stock! Not really anything to be proud of when looked at in this fashion.

The share of stock by primary materials (i.e. raw materials and packaging materials), work in progress and finished products varies according to the products and method of manufacturing as illustrated in Figure 8.4.

'Planned versus actual' (also known as planning efficiency) is a simple measure of whether the plan is being achieved. This measure can be for any period, i.e. this month we planned to produce 80,000 units, but our actual production was 70,000 units. Therefore, we were 87.5% efficient. This measure is of little use if we cannot trace back to why production was short of the plan, not to criticise, but with a view of correcting the system so that we will be more efficient in future. It is more meaningful if efficiency is expressed for each product or SKU rather than for total volume. Sometimes this measurement will be more hard-hitting if it is expressed in lost sales.

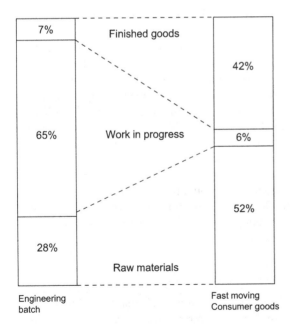

Figure 8.4 Stock profile as a percentage of total stock

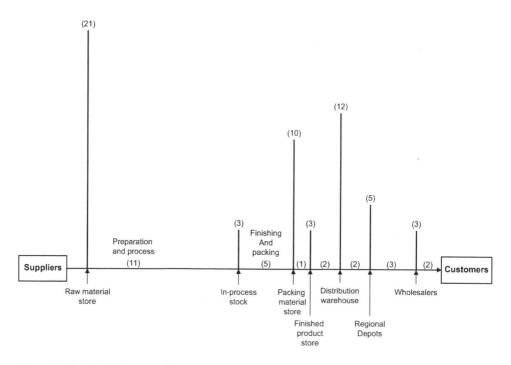

Figure 8.5 Stock pipeline map of an FMCG product

Planned vs actual

Figure 8.5 shows a 'pipeline map' of a fast-moving consumer good (FMCG). It is a common practice to express both the planned and actual production of each week in graphs
and calculate planning efficiency figures for the week and cumulative year to date. But
all this effort is only of any use if the information, however expressed, leads to corrective action being taken. Too many measures too often will only serve to confuse the real
issues. Scott and Westbrook (1991) introduced the concept of a pipeline map to present a
snapshot of the total stock in a supply chain. In Figure 8.5 the supply chain of an FMCG
product is mapped by a series of horizontal lines representing the average time spent in
major processes between stock-holding points, and a series of vertical lines showing in
the same scale (e.g. days) the average stock cover at each point. Pipeline volume is the
sum of both the horizontal and vertical lines and represents the time needed to 'flush' the
inventory in the supply chain at an average rate of throughput.

Pipeline mapping is a useful tool to understand the planning performance of a supply
chain, in particular inventory management, but additional analytical techniques should be
used to identify the key areas of improvement.

Cycle times

'Asset turn' is the ratio of total sales and fixed assets. It is important that the value of fixed
assets is updated by taking into account the depreciation rate for the type of asset according to a defined accounting policy of the company. Assets utilisation (time-based) is more

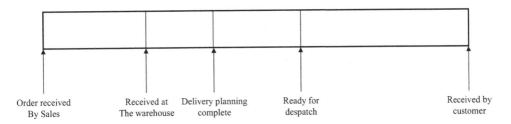

Figure 8.6 Order cycle times

relevant to all manufacturing performance. However, the measure of assets turn (value-based) provides an indication of investment in the supply chain. In the short to medium term this measurement is of little use as the investment in the assets has already been made and the measurement is against a past decision. In biblical terms, the sins of the fathers are being visited on the next generation.

'Order cycle time' (also known as lead time) is the elapsed time from the placement of an order by the customer to the receiving of delivery (see Figure 8.6). It is important to state standards to suit customer requirements and analyse the total cycle time into relevant components. Lynch and Cross (1991) claim that only 5% of cycle time is devoted to adding value. In many cases, 95% of production is waiting time between processes or material held in stock and this measure excludes raw materials in stock and finished goods in the warehouse!

'Order fill' is the percentage of first-time satisfied orders. From the customer's point of view, this is probably the most important measurement. The order is the correct quantity and quality. The next most important measure as far as the customer is concerned is if the delivery is on time! 'On-time delivery' can be expressed as a percentage of full orders delivered on or before the due date as agreed with the customer.

Summary

This chapter has considered the importance of having sufficient stock on hand so as not to delay production or keep the customer waiting longer than is acceptable. However, holding stock is a cost. A balance has to be found between achieving the objective of customer satisfaction and the objective of a reasonable return on assets employed. Stocks of inventory are a major asset in manufacturing and retailing and in the intermediate stages of distributing and warehousing. This chapter has covered several approaches to inventory management within the supply chain.

More advanced techniques of inventory management are also covered in Chapter 18.

Discussion questions

1. Explain why inventory management is important in optimising cost and customer service in supply chain management. What are the key data rata requirements in inventory management?
2. Describe the principle of re-order level (ROL)/re-order quantity (ROQ) and fixed interval systems of inventory management. In what circumstances is the use of these types of systems appropriate?

3. What is economic order quantity (EOQ)? Express EOQ as a formula. When the interest rate goes up, will EOQ go up or down?
4. What is vendor management inventory (VMI)? Explain how VMI help the performance of retail customer service.
5. What is the role of safety stock in inventory management? Describe the three key factors determining the level of safety stock.

   (NB – For exercises on inventory management, please refer to Chapter 18.)

9 Operations management

Introduction

Within an organisation, operations management is the function that interacts with and delivers products and services to customers. Operations management is not limited to the manufacture of products. Everyone, no matter what their role, is an operations manager. We all use resources, and we all have a mission to employ these resources as efficiently as possible for the benefit of the organisation for which we work. Efficient operations management is crucial to the success of any organisation. For supply chain management, operations management is where, with factories and facilities, plans are converted into reality to produce goods and services. Input resources basically consist of information, materials and utilities. They are transformed into desired outputs by the three converting components of people, process and technology. In addition to the conversion of inputs into outputs, operations management is responsible for the physical flow of the supply chain. This includes the upstream flow of input resources and the downstream flow (distribution) of outputs.

The input–process–output model shown in Figure 9.1 is the cornerstone of operations management and can be found in most operations management texts. The modern approach to operations management is to consider operations as a process and a whole systems approach is taken.

Learning objectives

Learning objectives for this chapter are:

1. Manufacturing operations.
2. Service operations.
3. Resources.
4. Systems structure.
5. Operations analysis.
6. Operations improvement.

Manufacturing operations

Operation management applies to both manufacturing and service operations. In manufacturing operations, customer interaction is not essential. For example, cars can be manufactured, food can be harvested and processed, hamburgers can be made and houses can be built, all without customer input. Although it might be desirable that the customer has

DOI: 10.4324/9781003341352-11

Inputs => PROCESS => Output

Figure 9.1 The IPO model

input into the design and the specifications of the product (be it a car, a hamburger, or a house), customer input is not essential. In a 'bespoke' operation, the desired policy is to make only to order, that is, manufacture will not begin until an order has been received. The limitation of not beginning until an order has been received is self-imposed and can be overridden. For example, a house builder might prefer not to begin building unless a client has signed a contract, nonetheless, the builder can change his strategy and build a house without having a client (in the belief that the house will be sold before it is completed or soon after completion).

Service operations

The distinguishing features of service operations are that service cannot be provided without customer input and that ownership does not change. Service includes transportation of goods and people. Transportation can only take place if there are goods to move or passengers to carry. At the end of transportation, ownership has not changed, when you travel on a bus or aircraft you, the passenger, do not own or get to take the seat with you when you disembark! In other service operations, such as a consultant providing advice without the customer, the service cannot be provided and again there is no change of ownership. A more mundane example is a hairdresser, without customers, hair cannot be cut! Further examples are a freight train – it can travel from one city to the next, but if it carries no freight, it has not carried out its function. The same applies to a bus service, the bus can leave the depot and travel around the planned route and finally return to the depot, but unless it has carried a passenger, its function has not been fulfilled. The function is to carry passengers not to simply drive in circles without passengers.

> A service organization exists to interact with customers and to satisfy customers' service requirements. For any service to be provided, there has to be a customer. Without a customer, and interaction between customer and the service organization, the objective of providing service cannot exist.
>
> (Wright, 2012: p. 4)

The amount of interaction between the customer and the service-providing organisation depends on the type of service offered. For example, a computer consultant will have high 'face-to-face' interaction with the customer, whereas service provided over the Internet such as a currency exchange conversion calculation will have no face-to-face interaction. Irrespective of the level of 'face-to-face' interaction, without customer input, service cannot be provided. However, this does not mean that the customer always has to be present when the service is being provided. For example, when a vehicle is due for a routine service, once delivered to the garage, the driver does not have to be present, but unless the vehicle is available, the service cannot be provided. With all of the above, resources are held waiting for the input of a customer before an output can be provided. Without the customer, there cannot be an output. In manufacturing operations, the major difference is that eventually ownership will change and end the product will end up in the hands of the end user.

Resources

Resources in operations management include:

- *Materials.* Materials include the goods that are consumed by the system, goods that are transformed by the system and finished goods held for sale. Utilities such as fuel, water electricity and gas are also materials. Conversion or transformation refers to changing the shape, form or combination of materials to produce an output. For example, by assembling 12,000 components sourced from a variety of suppliers a car is 'manufactured'.
- *Machines/equipment.* These include plant, fittings, tools, vehicles and storage facilities available to the operating system.
- *Information systems.* This covers the flow of information within the organisation, and externally from and to suppliers, customers and other stakeholders. Electronic systems are important communication conduits, but they are not the only means of communication in an information system. An information system includes all means of communication, for example, speech, newsletters, manuals, brochures, radio and television.
- *People.* People not only means the number of people employed in the operating system but also includes the knowledge and skill levels of the people. People also includes the pervading culture of an organisation including intangibles of dependability, attitude and shared values.
- *Real estate.* This includes owned, leased or rented offices, warehouses, factories, display areas, yards, parking spaces, etc.

All of the above represent either a capital investment or an ongoing expense to the organisation. Tangible inputs are physical and can be seen and touched, and the amount or rate of use can be measured in quantifiable terms. Intangible inputs are difficult to quantify. They cannot be seen or touched and include knowledge (intellectual capital) culture and values.

Money is not a resource. Money is used to buy resources (people, machines, buildings, etc. are the resources).

Likewise, time is not a resource. Time, like money, is used to measure the efficient use of resources or performance (for example, on-time delivery, lead time, idle time, down time).

With today's technology, information is abundant, indeed, there can be an overload of information – how many emails did you receive today and how many were actually of use? The concern of the operations manager is to know what information is required and in being able to interpret and use information for the benefit of the organisation.

To summarise, in a service organisation, customers and resources are brought together to provide a service output. For manufacturing, input resources are transformed to provide an output, and the customer draws from the system, that is, the product is made and the customer buys the finished good. With a service operation, output cannot be stocked and the service cannot begin without customer input.

Systems structures

Wild (2003) developed a set of system structures to illustrate the flow of inputs through to outputs in various systems. In considering systems structures, Wild uses the following symbols:

O = the transformation process of combining resources including utilities to add value.
V = 'stock' of input resources and output stocks, or the 'queue' of customers waiting to enter the system.
➔ = the flow of resources through the system.
C = the customer. Note, the customer does not have to be external to the organisation but may be an internal customer. The 'internal customer' is the next person, or department, in the process.

Overall, there are three basic service or transport structures (Figures 9.2–9.4) and four basic manufacturing or supply structures. Most organisations will consist of a combination of systems.

Service and/or transport structures

In this structure, the strategy is always to have sufficient of all resources on hand so that the customer never has to wait to enter the system. Service is provided directly to the customer from a stock of resources.

> The stock of resource could be the bus moving from stop to stop, an accident ward waiting for patients, a fire brigade waiting for a call-out, a restaurant waiting for diners, an accountant waiting for customers, or a betting shop waiting for punters. In this structure, the customer does not normally wait: the resources do).
>
> (Wright and Race, 2004)

V

C

Examples:
a. Call centre waiting for customers.
b. Ambulance or fire service.

Figure 9.2 Customer does not wait

(Resources) ➔

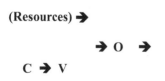

Examples:
a. Customers waiting in line (queue) for service (e.g. supermarket checkout).
b. Customers make an appointment to see a specialist for advice (e.g. lawyer, doctor, hair stylist).

Figure 9.3 Customer queue

C ➜ V

➜ O ➜

C ➜ V

Examples:
a. Empty containers in Western seaports in the United States waiting for freight, and at the same time, container shortages in Eastern sea ports in Asia.
b. Taxi cabs waiting for fares at the airport, and at the same, time passengers frustrated as there are no taxis available at downtown hotels.

Figure 9.4 Idle key resource and customer queue

This structure is aimed at the efficient use of resources and customers are expected to wait to enter the system. The objective is for customers to wait and the key resource is kept fully employed. For example, a business school has resources of lecture rooms and other facilities that are relatively fixed and cannot be used 24 hours a day. The key resource is the lecturers. Students do not determine when the lectures will be and need to enrol before the semester begins. Lecturers are scheduled for classes (and other duties) and are not paid to have idle time. In some cases, such as high-profile lawyers and other professionals, we would be surprised if we did not have to make an appointment for a consultation. Thus, the consultant's time is not wasted waiting for clients and clients are conditioned to make an appointment.

This structure implies inefficiency as neither objective of customer service nor efficient use of resources is being achieved.

It might be asked why a service system could not be balanced so that there are no idle key resources and no customer queue. The answer is that if customers are never kept waiting there MUST be spare resources, or if resources are to be fully utilised with no idle time, there MUST be a store of customers. Occasionally, a balanced system might exist, but this will be by chance and last for a short period of time (Figure 9.5).

Manufacturing and/or supply structures

For the factory manager, this structure is easy to manage. It enables batch and/or level production, and the manufacturing line can be balanced by building to output stock. The downside is that it is expensive in stock holding costs. In the fashion industry and other areas where technology changes, or is likely to change (e.g. electronic goods such as cell phones), there is a danger of the manufacturing organisation being left with goods no longer in fashion or obsolete (Figure 9.6).

V ➜ O ➜ V ➜ C

Examples:
a. Manufacture from a stock of input materials and hold a stock of finished goods. The customer draws from the system, for example, the Ford Motor Company.
b. Manufacture drawing from own warehouse of materials and stockpile for expected future demand, for example, women's shoes manufactured in winter months for release in spring.

Figure 9.5 From stock to stock

V ➔ O ➔ C

Examples

a. Make-to-order, such as the manufacture of a high-voltage transformer. High-voltage transformers are high-capital items and are made to customer specifications. It is possible to build a high-voltage transformer without a customer order, but few manufacturers would do so due to the specialised nature of each transformer. Likewise, few shipyards would build a cruise liner without a contract from a customer.

b. Retail or supply from the warehouse. Goods are stocked and the customer draws from the system. Unlike service structures, ownership changes hands.

Figure 9.6 Input stock, nil output stock

➔ O ➔ V ➔ C

Examples:

a. Food processing. Once the food is harvested, it goes straight into production. If not processed straight after harvesting, it would deteriorate.

b. Oil drilling. Once the oil begins to flow, it is held in storage tanks.

c. In a manufacturing operation, this structure would apply where materials are ordered just as required and a stock of finished goods is held.

Figure 9.7 Nil input stock, stock of finished goods

➔ O ➔ C

Examples:

a. A small house building firm. Materials are ordered as required and once finished the client takes possession (ownership changes)

b. Just-in-time or lean production as pioneered by the Japanese.

Figure 9.8 Just-in-time model

This structure covers holding an input stock of materials, drawing from this stock for manufacturing/processing and direct supply to the customer with no output stocks held. This structure also applies to a retail operation, supply from a warehouse to a customer or the next component of the supply chain where stocks of finished goods are held and the customer is supplied from stock (Figure 9.7).

This structure applies where it is either not feasible to hold input stocks or it is not desirable to hold input stocks. The customer is supplied from an output stock (Figure 9.8).

The Toyota just-in-time approach often referred to as the Toyota Production System is well explained by Womack et al. (1990) and Berggren (1993). The objective is to have no stock of finished cars. The theory is that the purchaser will visit a showroom and be able to see a car indicative of the type of product that Toyota makes. There will not be a wide range of vehicles to inspect; instead, the purchaser will be shown on a computer screen the various models available and a list of optional specifications. The purchaser will then select, by keying into the computer, the basic car model and required details such as size of engine, type of transmission, colour scheme, type of upholstery, sound system and so on, but all chosen from a given list. This information will be electronically transmitted to the factory and the suppliers of the factory. Within 72 hours, the car will be delivered to the purchaser. The benefits include the customer getting what they want. But, in fact, the customer is now more than just a customer – the customer is now very much part of the manufacturing process. In effect, by keying in their requirements, the customer initiates the whole process, raises the raw materials order for the factory and updates the production schedule. From Toyota's point of view, there is a further substantial benefit. Presumably, the purchaser will pay on delivery, so there will be no cash flow problems (within a 72-hour period, it is unlikely that Toyota will have paid for the materials or for the direct labour). As Taiichi Ohno (1998) of Toyota said, we are 'Looking at the time line from the moment the customer gives us an order to the point where we receive the cash. And we are reducing the time line by removing the non-value wastes'. Obviously, a system such as this does not, and cannot, make allowances for mistakes. It relies on good planning by management, quality designed into the product, well-trained workers who are empowered to work as a team, suppliers who are trusted to supply when required and who are also part of the team, an integrated computer system and the elimination of 'non-value wastes'. We challenge you to ring any car dealer, other than for a Japanese brand, and ask how long it would take for a car meeting your various requirements to be delivered. Unless you pick a stock vehicle, and the colour you want is in stock, you are likely to be told that you will have to wait more than 72 hours and more like 72 days!

Combined structures

Although seven basic service system structures are shown in the figures, in reality, most service organisations will employ a combination of structures, for example, a freight consolidator and forwarder. The customer does not have to wait to enter the system but arranges for a part container load of goods to be left with the consolidator for forwarding. The structure for the complete operation is as per Figure 9.9. Note that this is a transport service operation and ownership does not pass to the freight consolidator.

The freight consolidator and forwarder's policy is to only ship fully loaded containers. The second stage of the operation is out of sight of the customer(s) and is the loading (consolidating) of the container. As this is a separate operation, it can be shown as a back room 'factory'-type activity (see Figure 9.10). This represents a container being loaded from a stock of goods (waiting to be loaded), culminating in delivery to the destination.

Figure 9.11 shows the two structures in sequence.

A further example is the small building firm. The owner of a block of land seeks information from the builder as to what can be built within the parameters of local regulations. The builder has a book of house designs that can be altered to some degree to meet the client's needs. Eventually, both parties agree but as the builder is currently working on

V

➜ O ➜

C

Figure 9.9 Overall operation freight forwarder

V ➜ O ➜ C

Figure 9.10 Backroom activity

V

→ O → V → O → C

C

Figure 9.11 Combined structure: freight forwarder

(Builder) →

→ Oi → Vii → Oii →

C → Vi

Figure 9.12 Combined structure: small builder

→ V → Oi → V → Oii → C

Figure 9.13 Preparation in advance of demand

another house, the client might have to wait six weeks before construction can begin. Once the house is completed, ownership of the house passes to the client. This combined structure is shown in Figure 9.12

Vi = Customer makes an appointment to see the builder
Oi = Consultancy
Vii = Builder has a 'stock' of work waiting to be started
Oii = House constructed

Another situation is where the 'back room' activity takes place before the customer enters the system. An example is the breaking down of a bulk consignment by a distributor into small lots in anticipation of small orders from downstream retailers. This is shown in Figure 9.13, the first operation is the breaking down and storage of the inward shipment, and the second operation is supplying a retailer from stock.

Operations analysis

In order to identify opportunities for operations improvement, four tools for operations analysis have been selected. These are:

- Supplier Input Process Output Customer (SIPOC) diagram.
- Five Vs.
- Operations performance objectives.
- Process mapping.

SIPOC diagram

SIPOC is a high-level map of a process to view how a company goes about satisfying a particular customer requirement in the overall supply chain. SIPOC stands for the following:

Supplier. The person or company that provides the input to the process (e.g. raw materials, labour, machinery or information). The supplier may be both external and internal to the company.

Input. The materials, labour, machinery or information required for the process.

Process. The internal steps necessary to transform the input to output.

Output. The product (both goods and services) being delivered to the customer.

Customer. The receiver of the product. The customer could be the next step of the process or a person or organisation.

A SIPOC diagram is usually applied during the data collection of an operation to define the problem and the logistics of the operation. SIPOC not only shows the inter-relationships of the elements in a supply chain but also provides an overview of the operation with more information than the Input Process Output (IPO) diagram.

Figure 9.14 shows a SIPOC diagram for a company that leases equipment (adapted from Basu, 2009).

Five Vs

Slack et al. (2012) also refer to the input–process–output model but add four 'Vs' of processes to analyse processes. Their four Vs of processes are 'volume, variety, variation and visibility' to which we have added a fifth, 'velocity'.

Volume. Processes with a high regular demand will have a high degree of repetition. In operations management, this means that tasks are repeated frequently and it makes sense to train staff to specialise in a limited number of tasks. Tasks become systemised and

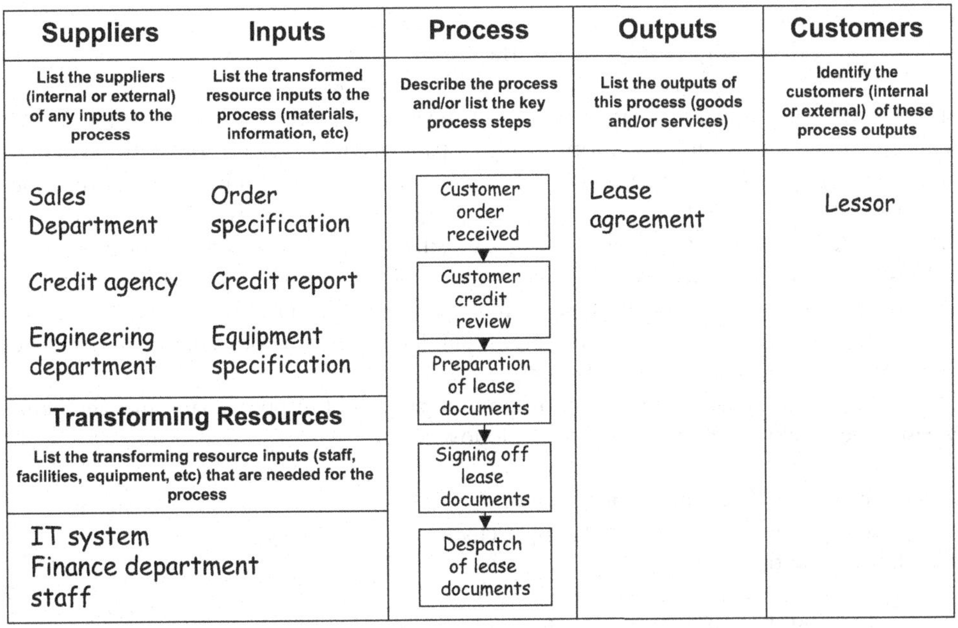

Suppliers	Inputs	Process	Outputs	Customers
List the suppliers (internal or external) of any inputs to the process	List the transformed resource inputs to the process (materials, information, etc)	Describe the process and/or list the key process steps	List the outputs of this process (goods and/or services)	Identify the customers (internal or external) of these process outputs
Sales Department	Order specification	Customer order received	Lease agreement	Lessor
Credit agency	Credit report	Customer credit review		
Engineering department	Equipment specification	Preparation of lease documents		
Transforming Resources		Signing off lease documents		
List the transforming resource inputs (staff, facilities, equipment, etc) that are needed for the process				
IT system Finance department staff		Despatch of lease documents		

Figure 9.14 SIPOC Process Diagram

repeated. Henry Ford back in 1913 is reputed to have said give me a stupid person and in 24 hours I can make that person a specialist – a specialist in a very limited and repetitive operation. With high-volume processes, the opportunity to mechanise and automate and/or use robots is obvious. In the supply chain, if components can be standardised and common parts used in the manufacture of different models then ordering in bulk at regular intervals will be possible. The margin for manufacturing errors by the supplier will be minimised and unit costs will reduce. Low volume demand on the other hand is not likely to make high throughput technology cost-effective. The same applies to transportation costs. Full containers reduce the cost per unit. Parcel post, where one item is sent by courier, will obviously increase the unit cost.

Variety. The greater the variety, the more stock has to be held, and the amount held will multiply with the number of stocking points within the supply chain. As Slack et al. (2012), p 21 say, 'A high level of variety may also imply a relatively wide range of inputs to the process and the additional complexity of matching customer requirements to appropriate products or services'. So, high-variety processes are invariably more complex and costly than low-variety ones.

Variation. Under this heading, Slack et al. (2012), p 21 say that 'processes are easier to manage when they only have to cope with predictably constant demand. Resources can be geared to a level that is just capable of meeting demand' (Stack et al., 2012: p. 21). In short, all activities can be planned in advance. This applies to ordering materials to arrive 'just-in-time' and for outputs to be completed to meet demand dates just-in-time without the need to hold input or output stocks. By contrast, when demand is unpredictable, buffer stocks will need to be held to cover sudden changes in demand. This applies especially in the fashion industry, for example, women's footwear. The range will be designed months in advance of the next season, but until the new season's pre-orders are received from retailers, and then subsequently once the season is underway and repeat orders flow in, knowing what amount and which materials to hold will be difficult. Lower variety eases the stock holding pain, but if variety is too low, sales will be lost.

Visibility in the supply chain relates to the exposure of the process. In Chapter 16, we introduce the 'bullwhip' effect, which occurs when each component of the supply chain only receives one-way information from the next downstream component. The result is an escalating and wildly fluctuating demand pattern known as the bullwhip effect. If information is shared, that is, if visible, the intensity of the bullwhip effect can to some extent be softened. The front office is usually highly visible, that is, in materials movement acceptance of goods for consolidation, but the consolidation and transportation are not visible to the customer. Visibility can be increased for goods in transit by the use of barcoding or RFID tags to track the movement of materials. In general, processes that are directly in contact with the customer (e.g. retail) should have more visibility than those that are carried out in an office or factory.

Velocity. Velocity, or time, is an important aspect of supply chain management. Measurements of time performance are as follows:

- Time taken to fulfil orders (lead time).
- Time taken at each stage of the supply chain.
- Delivery on time.
- Age of stock (used by dates).
- Numbers of days of stock on hand.
- Stock turn.

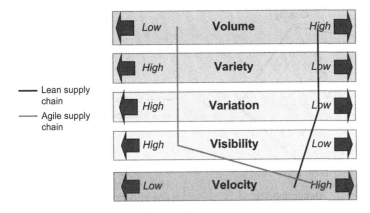

Lean supply chain

Agile supply chain

Figure 9.15 Five Vs diagram

A process related to lean and agile supply chains (see Chapter 14) should increase its velocity.

The Supply Chain Council (www.supply-chain.org/) recommends a metrics system for performance covering the four areas of customer satisfaction/quality, time, cost and assets. They provide a range of measures for each category and also provide benchmarking for their members. A sample measure is supply chain response time (SCRT).

This represents the measure of time taken to recognise and react to changes in demand. For the Supply Chain Council, perfect order fulfilment only occurs when all orders are delivered in the quantities required, on the agreed delivery date, the documentation is complete and correct and the goods are received in perfect condition and meet the specifications.

Figure 9.15 illustrates the profiles of lean supply chains and agile supply chains in a five Vs diagram

Operations performance objectives (QSDFCE)

There are five key aspects of operations performance that affect customer satisfaction and consequently operational effectiveness. These are:

Quality. Doing things right and providing 'fit for purpose' services.
Speed. Doing things fast and minimising the lead time of delivery.
Dependability. Doing things regularly on time and keeping delivery promises.
Flexibility. Adapting the operation's activities to meet customers' changing requirements.
Cost. Doing things cheaply or at a competitive price and providing 'value for money' for the customer.
Ethics. Following corporate social responsibility and a sustainable process.

Figure 9.16 illustrates in a polar chart the performance objectives as perceived by the customer and supplier when five is most important and one is least important.

Of the above six aspects, arguably quality, speed and cost are considered the most important by customers. Different operations will have different views of each of the performance objectives. The relative priority of performance objectives also differs between

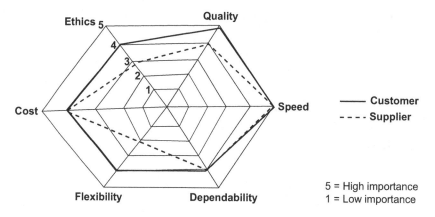

Figure 9.16 Operations performance objectives

product and services. For example, a customer seeking a Prada product will emphasise quality while a customer for an ASDA product will look for value for money.

Process mapping

Process mapping is a tool to represent a process by a diagram containing a series of linked tasks or activities that produce an output. At its most basic level, it describes processes or activities within an operation related to each other. There are many broadly similar process mapping tools but in general these tools have some common features, including:

- They identify the sequence of different activities within the operation.
- They identify activities related to people, materials or information.
- They help to pinpoint fail points and non–value–added activities.

Different symbols are often used to represent different types of activities. These symbols are borrowed from a classical industrial engineering 'flow process chart' or 'flow charting' from information technology. They can be arranged in order, either in series or in parallel (known as 'swim lanes') to describe an operation.

   Figure 9.17 illustrates an example of process mapping.

Operations improvement

There are many tools and techniques to improve the performance of an operation (Basu, 2009). The improvement initiative may apply to a process, department, infrastructure facilities or an organisation both in the manufacturing and service sectors. We have selected the tools as described previously in different stages of the improvement initiative. As a guide, we recommend the use of these tools as follows:

Define stage: systems structure and SIPOC.
Measure stage: operations performance objectives (QSDFCE).
Analyse stage: five Vs and process mapping.

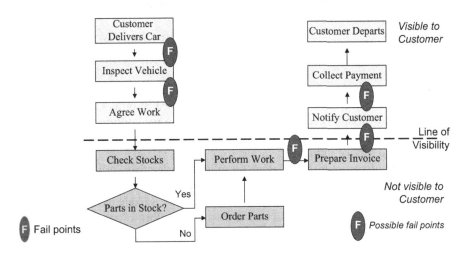

Figure 9.17 Operations performance objectives

Case example: J&J sales operation in Ireland

Johnson & Johnson is the fastest-growing top-ten pharmaceutical company globally.

The Irish consumer business had a turnover of US$64.6 million in 2015, of which the pharmacy channel contributed US$38.8 million. The Irish division operated with two field sales teams that covered 1200 out of the 1800 pharmacies in Ireland.

In 2015, the field sales teams were servicing pharmacies with an outdated ordering system that focused on order-taking. There were two challenges within the ordering process:

1. The delivery timescale to the customer was too long.
2. The added value capability in calls was limited due to the lack of engagement with the customer.

The analysis of the sales order process by using SIPOC clearly demonstrated that the sales teams were predominantly taking their orders and completing tasks on paper and then inputting them into a system. A review of performance objectives, based on interviews with customers and internal stakeholders, revealed that high importance was given to quality, speed and ethics, and cost and flexibility had a lower priority. The dependability of delivery was also low.

Process mapping reflected the barriers that prevented streamlined flow, which were waiting time, transport, process inefficiencies, inventory and wasted motions. At an overall level, customers were not satisfied with a three- to five-day delivery time lagging between the placement of order and delivery.

The recommendations included a new order-taking process with direct input from customers with an overarching vision to transform their sales teams into business development. This was underpinned by a Customer Relationships Management system that was considered best in class and processes using industry-leading tools to win customers. Process verification was also introduced as an opportunity for the nominated sales team members to gain an understanding of the proposed CRM system, and more importantly, to feedback to the database that would add value to their customer base.

Source: http://www.janssen.ie.

Infrastructure facilities.

What are infrastructure facilities? They include factories, offices, equipment and hardware, conversion technology and third-party suppliers/service resources. Infrastructure facilities do not include people, procedures and systems. Here we consider the challenge of selecting the most appropriate infrastructure facilities and whether this challenge differs for manufacturing and service industries.

The challenges of infrastructure facilities are far more complex than cash flow management, and the parameters are not of the short-term nature of labour and software. The outcome of an investment decision for a manufacturing facility is likely to last for 10–100 years. Likewise, it normally takes several years of disciplined effort to transform an existing weak service unit into a strong unit.

Manufacturing sector

Skinner (1969) described manufacturing facilities as either a corporate millstone or a competitive weapon depending on the strategy applied and pursued. As Wheelwright and Hayes (1985) observed in a manufacturing business, a number of interrelated functions (such as marketing, innovation, engineering, purchasing, manufacturing and distribution) work towards a common objective of satisfying the customers and at the same time ensuring an attractive return on investment for shareholders.

Of these, the manufacturing function shares the organisation's assets and people. Wheelwright and Hayes' four stages in the strategic role of manufacturing are as follows:

Stage 1. Minimise manufacturing's negative potential: 'internally neutral'.
Manufacturing is kept flexible and reactive.
Stage 2. Achieve parity with competitors: 'externally neutral'. Capital investment is the primary means of catching up with the competition.
Stage 3. Provide credible support to the business strategy: 'internally supportive'.
Longer-term manufacturing developments and trends addressed systematically.
Stage 4. Pursue a manufacturing-based competitive advantage: 'externally supportive'.
Long-range programmes pursued in order to acquire capabilities in advance of needs.

In a typical fast-moving consumer goods (FMCG) manufacturing business:

- 98% of the products sold are either own-manufactured or co-produced.
- 90% of the assets of the company are for manufacturing.
- 75% of the people work in manufacturing.
- People or 'human ware'.

It is not enough just to formulate and pursue an 'up front' manufacturing strategy, no matter how good the strategy is. To maintain a competitive advantage, it is essential to support the strategic planning of facilities with the ongoing monitoring of performance and with continuous improvement programmes. The management of manufacturing facilities should be dynamic with the relentless pursuit of the elimination of unnecessary

Table 9.1 Categories of services

	Direct service	*Isolated service*
Small scale	Professional service (e.g. doctor, hairdresser)	Service shop (e.g. garage, tailor)
Large scale	Mass service (e.g. university, supermarket)	Service factory (e.g. banks, post offices)

Adapted from Schmenner (1993).

non-value-adding expense, and always with the objective of adding value for customers. Competitive advantage once achieved through a strategy such as investment in new facilities will require hard work if the advantage is to be retained.

Service sector

A service business is one where the perceived value of the offering to the customer is determined by the service rendered than the product offered.

This intimacy of a customer in a service function has led to the perception that service cannot be stored and has to be produced and consumed simultaneously. Of course, there are some services that have to be produced at the delivery point, such as emergency medical treatment. However, in a higher proportion of services, the activities that can be isolated from the interaction of the customer are uncoupled from the organisation. The isolated operations can be managed using similar methods as those used in manufacturing operations. Examples of these types of services include tailors, banks and hotels. Whether it is a small-scale or a large-scale operation, all services can be grouped as direct services or isolated services as shown in Table 9.1.

The strategic and operational considerations related to infrastructure facilities for isolated services are likely to be similar to those for manufacturing operations. For direct service, it can also be argued that manufacturing principles can be selectively applied, for example, with fast food service often like pre-setting the work outside the machine running cycle in a mass production packing line.

Social sustainability

Most of the research work concerning sustainability has focused on the environmental dimensions and less attention has been paid to the social aspects of sustainability across the supply chain from the operational perspective. Social sustainability is about identifying and managing business impacts, both positive and negative, on people. The quality of a company's relationships with its stakeholders may unlock new markets and help retain business partners.

The first six of the UN global principles focus on this social dimension of corporate sustainability, of which human rights are the cornerstone. As well as covering groups of rights, social sustainability encompasses education and health.

At a minimum, we expect businesses to undertake due diligence to avoid harming human rights and address any adverse impacts on human rights that may be related to their activities. In addition, multi-national organisations managing global supply chains should ensure the following:

- The establishment of organisation quality in quality standards (see Basu, 2012).
- The implementation of corporate social responsibility as a form of business self-regulation by engaging in or supporting ethically oriented business practices. The

practices should include ethical procurements (see Chapter 7) and fair trading (see Chapter 16).

• The practising of corporate governance is the system of rules and processes by which a business is directed and controlled. Business objectives should aim to balance the interests of a company's many stakeholders such as shareholders, senior management executives, customers, suppliers, financiers, the government and the community.

Directly or indirectly, social sustainability affects workers in the supply chain, which, in turn, affects the sustainable performance of global supply chains.

Hutchins et al. (2008) developed a framework for implementing a global supply chain sustainability strategy – which includes social sustainability – and recommend that this framework should be a component of the ERP system.

Summary

This chapter has explained the importance of operations management in the context of supply chain management. The traditional operations management input–process–output model was introduced and extended to include system structures. The five Vs of volume, variety, variation, visibility and velocity were explained and how these 'Vs' can be managed to add value (yet another 'v') for the supply chain. Additional tools such as SIPOC, QSDFCE trade-off and process mapping can help to define and analyse an operational problem leading to a solution. The chapter concluded with a section on infrastructure facilities. There are many books, including 'Total Operations Solutions' by Basu and Wright (2004), dealing with detailed processes in operations management. Our primary objective of this chapter is to set the critical role of operations management as a building block in the physical flow of the total supply chain. The processes of operations management described in this chapter are applicable to global supply chains.

Discussion questions

1. Identify seven basic types of operating systems structures and give examples of each system making simplifying assumptions. What are the key factors influencing a systems structure?
2. Explain the IPO model in a typical manufacturing operation. What are the transforming and transformed resources in a manufacturing operation?
3. Explain with examples the five Vs model. What is the role of velocity in the five Vs model?
4. How do you differentiate between a service operation and a manufacturing operation? Illustrate with examples.
5. What are the categories of services? Describe with an example of how some aspects of a service operation can be isolated and analysed like a manufacturing operation.
6. How would you ensure the principles of social sustainability for a sustainable performance of operations management?

10 Distribution management

Introduction

The physical movement and delivery of goods and services to customers is a key objective of supply chain management. The three key aspects of customer service are specification, price and timing. Specification and timing are often measured by the metric, 'on time in full' and are the direct result of distribution management. Distribution management is closely linked with the 'customer intimacy' model of Treacy and Weisma (1993) but many organisations outsource distribution management to third-party hauliers, thus reducing the frequency of direct customer contact.

Web-based software and e-marketplaces have increased opportunities available to e-supply chain managers in all operations, including the service industry.

Information technology and the internet have improved the access to information, enabled currency transactions and improved data accuracy. However, the real effectiveness of supply chain management is the physical movement of materials from source to customer. Important components for e-commerce, online trading and virtual supply chains are factories, warehouses and transport.

It is vital that a physical distribution process is in place to ensure the performance of the e-supply chain for both virtual and physical activities, but it is well recognised that supply chain order fulfilment is the Achilles' heel of the e-business economy.

Learning objectives

Learning objectives for this chapter are:

1. Physical distribution.
   * Distribution strategy.
   * Warehouse operations.
   * Stock management.
   * Transport planning.
2. Strategic alliance.
   * Third-party logistics (3PL).
   * Retailer–supplier partnership (RSP).
   * Distribution integration (DI).
   * Customer relationship management (CRM).
3. Non-profit organisations.

DOI: 10.4324/9781003341352-12

Physical distribution

In the same way that enterprise resource planning is concerned with information flow, suppliers and inbound logistics, distribution management is likewise concerned with materials flow, customers and outbound logistics. Inbound logistics is characterised by demand variability, and outbound logistics is characterised by variable service levels.

With the management of distribution, that is, the physical transportation of goods from the factory through the various components of the supply chain to the customer, invariably some stock will be held in the system to buffer the variability of demand and to make allowance for vagaries in supply lead times. The focus on outbound logistics is to balance customer service level against cost. The cost of distribution is not just transportation costs but also includes warehousing including special requirements such as refrigeration, insurance and financing of stock and stock slippage (deterioration, damage, pilfering and obsolescence). The more the stock held, the greater the cost of storage and the greater the chance of losses.

The main components of distribution management are as follows:

* Distribution strategy.
* Warehouse operations.
* Stock management.
* Transport planning.

Distribution strategy

A company in a consumer-focused business must have a defined distribution strategy. The first criterion of distribution strategy is to decide whether the management of activities should be by the company or by a third party. With assets (buildings, equipment and transport vehicles), the strategy can go three ways:

Own the assets or some of the assets.
Lease or rent assets.
Contract (outsource).

Some of the various strategy mixes are shown in Table 10.1. Note there are 64 possible combinations, for example, own premises, leased premises, own management of premises, third-party management of premises, own transport, leased transport, third-party supplied and managed transport and so on. Table 10.1 shows 24 of the most likely combinations.

Table 10.1 Distribution strategy combinations

	Warehousing		Transport	
	Building	Operation	Trunking	Delivery
Strategy A	Own	Own	Own	Own
Strategy B	Rent	Own	Leased	Own
Strategy C	Rent	Own	Third party	Third party
Strategy D	Own	Own	Third party	Third party
Strategy E	Rent	Third party	Third party	Third party
Strategy F	Rent	Own	Own	Own
Strategy G	Own	Own	Third party	Own

There are some obvious advantages of distribution management by a third party, for example, the distribution expertise of third-party companies, the avoidance of capital outlay and underutilised equipment. It has become a popular practice with many original equipment manufacturers organisations (OEMs) to outsource warehousing and transport to third-party companies. However, as the delivery of the finished products is closest to the customer on the supply chain, there could be some degree of risk if the management of outbound logistics is totally left to third parties. Global retailers (e.g. Zara, Walmart) invest in their own distribution capability to retain a competitive advantage in customer service as the case example on Walmart distribution strategy illustrates.

CASE EXAMPLE: WALMART'S DISTRIBUTION STRATEGY

Walmart is unarguably the largest and leading retailer in the global retail industry with net sales of US$482.2 billion in the financial year ending 2015. It serves nearly 250 million customers every week, managing and operating over 1050 retail stores across the world in over 26 countries.

However, the most important yet interesting fact about Walmart is defined as its supply chain and distribution strategy, which is also considered the industry benchmark. The company also claims that the primary reason behind its fast-paced growth, continuous financial success and diversified product, market and customer portfolio is its distribution strategy, which is further supported by logistics and operations. Walmart has established highly automated and centralised distribution units that operate around the clock for 365 days a year. In order to ensure that customers in each of its targeted regions are served effectively, the company has established multiple distribution centres in every regional zone. For instance, in the case of the United States, over 45 distribution units have been established, which are dedicated to importing goods from around the world and ensuring each of the stores is managed with the demanded products. These 45 regional distribution units are further supported by over 150 distribution centres that are in direct contact with retail units across the region. It is also important to understand each of the distribution centres caters for the needs of 75 to 100 retail stores. Furthermore, each of its distribution centres has high-tech and modernised systems to move hundreds of thousands of cases each day. In addition, each distribution centre caters for 90 to 100 stores on average that are strategically located with an aim to provide rapid responses to the connected retail stores.

Taking the global distribution context into consideration, it is observed that the company in total has established 158 distribution centres, which are claimed to be the key to organisational success.

Its logistics activities are performed with the help of more than 6450 tractors and over 54,000 trailers that are operated by more than 7000 drivers. Since distribution activities involve logistics too, the company ensures that each of its drivers is not only qualified but also experienced. The strict company's policy can be noted from the fact that it only hires drivers who have driven a minimum of 300,000 accident-free miles. The company achieved an 80% improvement in the efficiency of its truck fleet since 2005,

Source: Adapted from Walmart (2015).

A distribution strategy is significantly influenced by economic factors, channels of distribution and their location and location of service centres and warehouses. Shorter channels are ideal, especially for perishable items, services requiring closeness to customers and urgent products. An intermediary in the channels of distribution can reduce distribution costs where the sources of supply are not in abundance, there are numerous destinations or transportation is difficult or expensive. The choice of location is usually driven by cost objectives for warehouses and manufacturing facilities and by revenue objectives for service-type operations. With the impact of the Internet, the distance of a service centre to the customer has become less important.

Channels of distribution

It is important for a manufacturer of fast-moving consumer goods (FMCGs) that the distribution strategy should consider the opportunities for both present and future business through an appropriate mix of the channels of distribution. Examples are:

Factory to:
 distributor,
 wholesaler,
 supermarket,
 direct to end user (e.g. Dell).

The distribution strategy should also include the company policy of exclusive agents or stockists and direct mail or online orders to end users. Figure 10.1 illustrates an example of the channels of distribution in a typical FMCG business. The selection of a strategy may be influenced by the cost of distribution, and it should be tempered by the business judgement of customer service and future opportunities.

 The channels of distribution are also determined by the stages required to deliver products or services depending on the type of business. An organisation exercises more control or influence on the service for a single-stage channel, that is, delivering products or services directly to the customer. If, however, more stages exist with intermediaries between the organisation and the customer, then each party may have some influence over such decisions as stock holding, service levels and market cover. Table 10.2 shows typical examples of stages in distribution channels in different kinds of organisations.

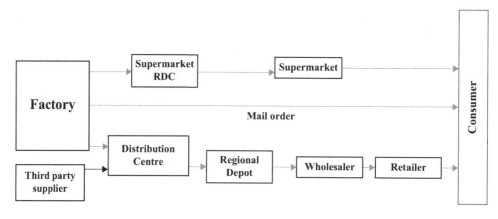

Figure 10.1 Channels of distribution

Table 10.2 Stages of distribution channels

Original equipment manufacturer	No. of stages	Intermediaries
Manufacturing sector		
Civil engineering	1 (direct)	
Foods manufacture	2	Supermarket
Car manufacturer	4	Overseas agent
		Distributor
		Retailer
Service sector		
Original supplier	No. of stages	Intermediaries
Hairdresser	1 (direct)	
B2C Internet sale	2	Transporter
Hospital	2	Doctor
Charter airline	3	Holiday
Company		Travel agent

Facilities location

Another important aspect of the distribution strategy is the location of distribution ware-houses. The location, design and operations of distribution warehouses are all vital ingre-dients of a supply chain – not only for cost optimisation but also for the quality and safety standards of products and for improving customer service by a faster turnaround at the warehouse. There are computer simulation models available for determining the size and location of a distribution centre, but local body planning regulations, the proximity of a highway and a big demand centre very often will be the prime determinants of the location.

The location of a warehouse can be influenced by many factors both objective and sub-jective. The factors that generally affect the selection of a warehouse site can be grouped into three sets of factors:

- Cost factors.
- Revenue factors.
- Local factors.

The cost factors have three main components – variable cost, fixed cost and inventory cost. The variable cost of a warehouse operation includes the costs of labour, material and utilities. The accessibility to labour and materials will affect the variable cost. The fixed costs are associ-ated with the provision and maintenance of facilities and the cost of security services. When the number of facilities is reduced, there is a saving in the fixed cost. If we, for example, cen-tralise the inventory of a number of warehouses to a single location, the base stock will remain the same, but the safety stock will reduce according to the following equation:

$$S_n = S_1(n) / \sqrt{n}$$

Where S_n = sum of safety stocks for n locations
S_1 = safety sock for one location
N = number of locations

The location of a retail outlet or service centre has traditionally, and for obvious reasons, been determined by the proximity to customers, or expected growth of the population (and future customers) in the region. The opening of a warehouse, such as Ikea, in the proximity of a town has been known to increase the revenue in that town. With the impact of e-commerce, traditional 'bricks and mortar' locations are now to some extent challenged by 'clicks and mortar', nonetheless, large new superstores and shopping malls continue to open and prosper.

The local factors influencing the selection of a location include management preferences, congeniality of the district, local infrastructure and transport networks, industrial relations and availability of trained labour. There are often incentives or investment grants available to encourage organisations to establish facilities in areas designated for regeneration or industrial development.

CASE EXAMPLE: WAREHOUSE LOCATION

The brief. After the merger between Fosroc★ and Expandite in England, the joint operation had main warehousing facilities in the neighbouring towns of Tamworth and Greenford, with a smaller warehouse at St Helens. As a result of a logistics structure review, the client decided to rationalise the warehousing facilities by centralising and consolidating all finished goods in a single facility on their production site in Tamworth. It was agreed that the best approach to producing a building, which would efficiently meet their requirements, was to design the facility 'from the inside out'.

The approach. Due to the sensitive nature and possible closure of warehousing, it was important to keep the study confidential. The project started with a feasibility study of various configuration options. As the client had available land to build the new warehouse, a study into the location was not needed and this meant that we could start calculating the required size immediately. The stock was analysed and activity data from the three warehousing locations was used to work out the site size needed in conjunction with the proposed layouts. After the decision on the favoured design had been made, the option was developed to the level where the scheme could be put-out to a design and build organisation for tendering. During this stage, detailed analysis was produced of the proposed floor space, equipment requirements and pallet racking locations. Another aspect of the project was the production of staffing requirements together with a staff structure diagram.

The result. The floor space was reduced from the three combined units of 80,000 sq. ft to 50,000 sq. ft in the new single distribution centre by removing duplication of stock and improving operating techniques. Also reduced were staffing levels by 30 and other costs.

Trade counters with minimal stock holdings at the old sites were retained but the major storage facilities were closed. Due to its central location, the new warehouse provides consistent, accurate delivery throughout the mainland UK within three to four working days from receipt of order.

★Fosroc Expandite is one of the largest manufacturers of construction and civil engineering products in the world.

Source: Supply Chain Planning UK Ltd (2007).

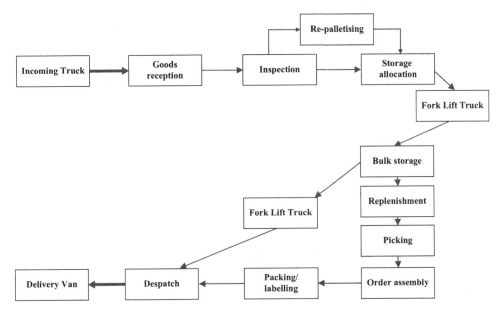

Figure 10.2 Warehouse operations

Warehouse operation

The operations of a distribution warehouse in general can be represented by Figure 10.2. There are good opportunities for re-engineering the warehouse functions when the total process from reception to despatch is critically examined.

The design issues of a warehouse include:

1. Storage systems:
   Block stock
   Back-to-back racking
   Double deep racking
   Narrow aisle racking
   Drive-through racking
   Mobile racking
2. Handling systems:
   Counterbalanced trucks
   Reach trucks
   Turret trucks
   Stacker cranes
   Automated guided vehicles
   Overhead cranes
3. Product quality:
   Ambience
   Chilled store (e.g. margarine)
   Cold store (e.g. ice cream)

4. Safety and control systems:
    Detection systems
    Sprinkles and fire hydrants
    Warehouse management system software

In view of the above inter-related design issues, there should be a structured approach for designing a warehouse. We suggest the following steps:

1. Calculate pallet positions by taking into account:
    *   Annual volume
    *   Stock policy (amount of safety stock)
    *   Units or kg per pallet
    *   Variability of stock-keeping units (SKUs; peak, growth)
    *   Lead times from suppliers
2. Evaluate functional options of storage and handling systems.
3. Establish quality requirements (e.g. chilled).
4. Establish systems and infrastructure.
5. Select the location of the warehouse.
6. Estimate budget costs (±20% accuracy).
7. Evaluate financial and risk options including own or rent.

EXAMPLE: PALLET CALCULATION

The calculation of pallet positions is illustrated by the following worked-out example

*   Given data
    *   Annual demand: 12,000 tonnes
    *   Load per pallet: 400 kg
    *   Stock turn: 13
    *   Weekly peak: 1.2 × average
    *   SKUs: 4 (same weight)
*   Calculation
    *   Weekly demand = 12000/52 = 230.8 tonnes
    *   Pallets for 4 weeks = (230.8x4)/0.4 = 2308
    *   Allowing 20% for peak and 85% pallet utilisation, pallet positions = (2308 x 1.2)/0.85 = 3258 pallets

---

The following case example illustrates an outline design process of the physical requirements of a warehouse in response to an invitation to tender.

CASE EXAMPLE: WAREHOUSE DESIGN

Background. Zigafroos Consolidated Industries (ZCI) is the UK's leading importer of high-quality consumer electrical goods for the independent retailer. The current storage centre in Edgware, London, is at the end of the lease period and is not considered adequate for future operations. The company is also considering offering the operation of the storage centre to a third-party logistics partner. You are therefore invited to tender for the sourcing, design and operation of a new dedicated storage centre. The tender will be a two-stage process, with the first stage concentrating on defining the physical requirement for the new facility.

The operation. ZCI purchases products from multiple overseas sources. Stock is delivered to the storage centre in 20 or 40 ft sea van containers and is generally loose loaded. Stock is stored pending orders and picked for a network of independent regional wholesalers. Currently, there are 25 wholesalers covering all of the UK. Stock availability is declared to wholesalers electronically and orders are passed to ZCI weekly. Stock picking is at the individual carton level and orders are built up for delivery to wholesalers on multi-SKU pallets. The manufacturer arranges transportation into the UK, customs and port clearance and transport to the warehouse are subcontracted by ZCI as is delivery to the wholesalers. ZCI is planning on 5% growth year on year.

Given data. In addition to the above information, ZCI has provided the results of an internal study to estimate the peak pallet holding for 2002. The calculation is shown in a spreadsheet that contains the following summary data for 2002:

* Annual sales: 217,390 boxes
* Product groups: 49
* SKUs: 1839
* Peak stockholding: 8385 pallets★

★Euro pallets: 800 mm × 1000 mm.

Next steps. Based on these submissions, the Zigafroos board will shortlist prospective partners and issue a comprehensive request for proposals.

Please deliver your proposal to our Edgware offices for the attention of Mr Harry Zoogorilla.

Exercise

Provide your recommendation on size and configuration for the new Zigafroos Storage Centre. Address the following issues:

1. Size of warehouse required: design for five years of growth.
   * Maximum pallet positions for design.
   * Approximate area for the chosen storage method.★★

2. Outline layout.
   * Pallet and shelving configurations.
   * Picking and despatch area.

3. Recommended mechanical handling equipment.

Provide the rationale for your choice of design and equipment and an indication of your company's experience with this type of operation.

**As a rough guide for estimating the approximate area for given pallet positions you may use the data in Table A.

Table A

Approximate area (sq. m) requirement per 100 pallets.

Pallet dimension: 1200 mm × 1000 mm.

	2 high	3 high	4 high	5 high
Wide aisle	138	92	69	46
Narrow aisle	117	78	59	47

Note: If six or higher is required, then the area needed can be prorated.

SAMPLE SOLUTIONS

Answer to Question 1

Compound growth for 5 years @ 5% = 27.6%

Peak stockholding after 5 years = 1.276 × 8385

$$= 10,701 \text{ pallets}$$

Assuming a five-high narrow aisle, approximate storage area:

= 10701 × 47/100

= 5034 sq. m

Answer to Question 2

The outline layout will depend on the configuration of the space available. Assuming a greenfield site, a configuration could be:

Width of the warehouse: 100 m

Span between columns (bay): 17 m

Storage space = 3 bays

$$= 3 \times 17 \times 100$$

$$= 5100 \text{ sq. m}$$

Picking and despatch area = 2 bays

$$= 2 \times 17 \times 100$$

$$= 3400 \text{ sq. m}$$

Total warehouse area = 8500 sq. m

Answer to Question 3

For a narrow aisle five-high warehouse recommended mechanical handling equipment:

Storage and retrieval: Reach trucks

Despatch area: Counterbalanced forklift trucks

Picking area: Hand pallet trucks

Stock management

As indicated earlier in Chapter 7, stocks are kept as a buffer along the supply chain in various warehouses, factories (work in process) and retail store shelves. These inventories can cost between a minimum of 15% and 40% of their value per year (storage space, handling costs, energy costs including heating and refrigeration, stock slippage and insurance). Therefore, careful management of stock levels makes good business sense.

In traditional stock management, there are two basic approaches (see Chapter 7), namely, the pull approach and the push approach. In a pull system, a warehouse is viewed as independent of the supply chain and inventory is replenished with order sizes based on a predetermined stock level for each warehouse. The stock management model for the pull system is normally geared to establish re-order level (ROL) and re-order quantity (ROQ). That is, when the stock drops to a certain level, a re-order is triggered of a predetermined amount. The re-order quantity takes into account past demands and the lead times for a re-order to be satisfied. The aim is to have as small amount of inventory as possible on hand at any one time, and the re-order quantity should likewise be as small as possible. However, in some processes, such as a batch system, there will be a minimum amount that can be produced, and in other cases, there can be economies of scale that will determine the optimal size of an order. The push method is used when economies of scale in procurement outweigh the benefits of minimum inventory levels as achieved in the pull method. The warehouse does not decide the quantity of the order but will receive a delivery as determined by the production schedule. Normally, a fixed interval review model with a forecast demand for manufacturing planning is used in a push system.

With the support of information technology, businesses are moving towards a virtual inventory system with a single stock concept that can be held anywhere in the system, be it on order with the supplier, in production or at the point of sale (POS). This is the concept of virtual inventory management (VIM) or electronic inventory. Thus, instead of considering stocks of raw materials, work in progress at the various stages of production and finished goods in warehouses each as separate stocks of inventory, purely because of their physical location, inventory is now considered as being part of one single stock.

The movement and management of inventory in a warehouse are further enhanced by the application of advanced technology such as warehouse management systems (WMS) and radio frequency identification (RFID).

The evolution of WMS is very similar to that of many other software solutions. Even though WMS continues to gain added functionality, the initial core functionality of a WMS has not really changed. The primary purpose of a WMS is to control the movement and storage of materials within an operation and process the associated transactions. Directed picking, directed replenishment and directed put away are the key to WMS. The key functionality of a WMS must include:

- A flexible location system.
- User-defined parameters to direct warehouse tasks by using live documents.
- Built-in levels of integration with data collection devices or an established ERP system.

Automatic identification

Barcodes are used to track the progress of products through a supply chain. In warehouses, barcodes can keep track of products in terms of identifying storage locations and types of items. However, coded products can be scanned only one by one and a barcode cannot identify the product itself. These disadvantages of barcodes can be mitigated by the use of automatic identification such as RFID.

RFID is an automatic identification method, relying on storing and remotely retrieving data using devices called RFID tags. An RFID tag is an object that can be attached to or incorporated into a product, pack or pallet in a warehouse for the purpose of identification using radio waves. They may not ever completely replace barcodes, due in part to their higher cost, but with the advantage of more than one independent data source on the same object, the application of RFID is likely to grow in supply chain management.

CASE EXAMPLE: THE FDA TRACKS DRUGS SUPPLY

The US Food and Drug Administration (FDA) announced in February 2004 new steps to strengthen protection against the problem of counterfeit drugs in the supply chain. The agency's Counterfeit Drug Task Force recommended RFID tags to track drugs from the source to the point of sale.

The Prescription Drug Marketing Act of 1987 requires a drug distributor to provide documentation of drug products throughout the distribution system. This chain of custody of medicines is also known as 'pedigree' regulation. The Task Force outlined the new measure in a report to safeguard the drug supply with the use of electronic track and trace technology such as RFID. This would create an electronic pedigree for tracking the movement of drugs through the supply chain. This report recommends that drug manufacturers and distributors continue to work towards that goal and that their implementation of RFID technology is used first on products that are most susceptible to counterfeiting.

In order to ensure the appropriate usage of RFID technology, the recommendations from the Task Force also include:

*   Consumer education about RFID and the labelling of RFID-tagged products.
*   When RFID-tagged drugs are dispensed to consumers, there should be the protection of consumer privacy to prevent unauthorised information stored in RFID tags.

Dr L M Crawford, Acting FDA Commissioner, said:

> We intend to work with industry and standard-setting organizations to explore the feasibility of allowing the FDA to access relevant electronic pedigree information, as that information would greatly improve our ability to minimize exposure of consumers to counterfeit drugs by facilitating rapid criminal investigations of illicit transactions. The FDA also applauded the initiatives announced by the pharmaceutical companies Pfizer, GlaxoSmithKline and Purdue Pharma.
>
> Source: FDA (2004).

Transport planning

Transport planning is a key decision area of distribution management. Transportation is a non-value-added item to the cost of the product and absorbs, in general, the biggest share

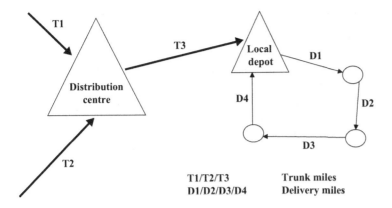

Figure 10.3 Distribution routes

of the logistics cost. Students often argue that unless a product is in the right place it is of little value and thus transportation does add value. Not so! The concept of adding value relates to the transformation process, that is, the conversion of inputs of raw materials, labour and machinery into a finished product. Storage, inspection and transportation all add cost but do not add value. Some of these costs will be unavoidable; materials have to be moved, goods have to be distributed, but storage, handling and movement only add to the cost, and not to the value of the product.

The main factors in transport decisions are (see Figure 10.3):

Transport mode selection.
Trucking routing.
Delivery planning.

There are various means of transportation such as railway, river, canal, coastal shipping and pipelines for products such as oil. In some countries, for some products, air transport might prove to be the most viable option. Generally, however, because of dependability, flexibility, speed and door-to-door service, road transport has proved to be the best option. For the UK, the Channel Tunnel has added to the convenience of road transport to and from Europe.

There are significant opportunities in optimising the selection of hauliers or types of trucks. In order to take advantage of the competitiveness and the up-to-date development of vehicles, companies are building partnerships with hauliers.

After the selection of the mode, the planning of trunking or primary transport for single-drop repetitive journeys between known or well-known locations (e.g. factory to warehouse), is relatively straightforward. However, the routing and scheduling of delivery vehicles to customers is extremely variable and therefore require more systematic planning. There are computer-based procedures to optimise delivery to customers. The objective is not to minimise the total mileage but to maximise the utilisation of vehicle time (delivery window) and space (by volume or weight) and ensuring customer service.

CASE EXAMPLE: FRESH FOODS: CHRISTIAN SALVESEN

Christian Salvesen is a major logistics business specialising in the strategic management of outsourced supply chains.

A key task of Christian Salvesen is defined in its mission statement as: 'To meet customer service requirements consistently and reliably through a mutually cost effective supply chain'. This usually takes some time to achieve, not because it is either complex or controversial, but because the supply chain can mean different things to different people. Furthermore, although the objectives are unanimous, the way in which each organisation achieves them through their respective supply chains is different.

According to the logistics director, 'It is these two elements – customer service and resource efficiency – that drive any supply chain'.

Let us examine Christian Salvesen's experience in implementing these principles in the area of the supply of fresh foods through Evesham chilled depot. Here is a product group whose availability is measured in hours. Meticulous planning and coordination are required for customer demand in rigid 'delivery windows' and plans have to cope with the most unpredictable element of a supply chain – Mother Nature.

Evesham is a chilled depot of approximately 20,000 sq. ft situated in the Vale of Evesham in Worcestershire, which is one of the major produce growing areas in the UK. It has a staffing level of 94 and nearly half of them are qualified reefer vehicle drivers. It is a stockless depot for cross-docking operation under temperature-controlled conditions. The main function of the depot is to act as a consolidator of suppliers' produce and chilled products received from various parts of the country for subsequent onward despatch to the majority of the UK and Irish regional distribution centres. It is a stockless depot for cross-docking operations.

Operating on a 24-hour/seven-day-a-week (24/7) basis, Evesham is a critical link in the fresh food temperature-controlled supply chain and allows the quickest possible route from field to plate, thus preserving both product quality and maximum shelf life. The depot has an operating revenue budget of £7.6m from which it generates a return on investment (ROI) of 21% and a profit margin of 10%.

The depot is subject to seasonality due to the nature of its core volume product but continues to develop its year-round chill business.

The majority of its profits, however, are derived during the summer months of the produce season. Volumes peak during August at a throughput of 7600 pallets per week, with a peak day activity of 1600 (21%) pallets.

Regular daily collections are made from suppliers/packers during the day and returned to the depot during the afternoon/evening. Product is off-loaded into a cross-dock/straight through chilled warehouse facility where it is sorted for onward delivery destination and despatched anytime from 16.00 hours until 01.30 that night.

Orders from the major retailers would have been received into Evesham between the hours of 11.00 and 17.00 that day. A typical example of the complexity of the physical operation is for suppliers such as Flamingo/Wealmore, which are based in the northwest of London.

10.00: Vehicle leaves Evesham to collect clean empty trays from Corby for delivery to Flamingo.

16.00: Arrives at Flamingo, off-loads trays and reloads half the vehicle with product for that day's retail orders.

17.00: Arrives at Wealmore to collect the balance of load for that day's retail orders.

20.30: Arrives back at Evesham to off-load product into the chill warehouse where it is sorted into delivery destinations for Ireland and Scotland.

Tesco – Dublin/Belfast/Livingston
Safeway – Bellshill
Asda – Grangemouth
Somerfield – Pitreavie
(Irish product would leave asap.)

23.00: Vehicle leaves for Salvesen depot at Ormskirk in Lancashire.

01.30: Arrives at Ormsmirk where further product is put on.

(Ormskirk is a produce-growing area) and the trailer is then taken to Scotland by an Ormskirk driver, with the Evesham driver returning with another trailer (may be loaded) to Evesham.

07.30: Arrives at first of Scottish delivery points.

On completion of deliveries, the vehicle would go into the Salvesen operation at Camerons Wood (Livingston, Scotland) to confirm all activities onto the Salvesen 'Track and Trace' Sharp system (confirms visibility of delivery to the customer). The vehicle may then reload with produce or soft fruits collected earlier by Camerons Wood from Scottish growers, returning via the Ormskirk changeover link into Evesham for consolidation and onward delivery to the retail redistribution centres (RDCs).

The transport fleet at Evesham comprises 34 owned tractors supported by 53 temperature-controlled trailers including 40 hired trailers. In addition to ten tractor/trailers based at Ormskirk, the operation has the flexibility to 'buy in' extra resources from other depots in the Salvesen temperature-controlled network. The hired tractors are made up of both long-term rental contracts and short-term casual hire to meet the variable demand and seasonality in a changing market.

Currently, Salvesen covers the following retailer RDC profiles for fresh foods:

Tesco   11
Safeway   8
Somerfield   7
Asda   8
CWS   2
M&S   3

The service level agreements with retailers include that delivery should be made within the limit of the delivery window. Any significant variation in delivery time is subject to penalty. There is no buffer stock because a short shelf life of such a perishable product group does not allow for it. There are also other challenges, such as forecasting the effect of weather or promotions. The supply chain cannot afford any shortage of refrigerated trucks of appropriate capacity when needed. Even if we achieve 100% availability on all products, it may count for nothing if the absenteeism of drivers is out of control.

Exercise

1. What are the customer service and resource utilisation objectives at Evesham?
2. What are the demand planning and supply planning problems at Evesham? Outline a strategy to deal with these problems.

Sample solution

The customer service objective at Evesham is to provide fresh food products on time in full to RDCs according to their delivery windows. The most important criterion is timing. The compromise is cost. However, the reefer supply is now moving from a specialist business to a commodity business and thus the cost should be competitive. Thus, cost is of medium importance. The specification is also of medium importance. Students may argue that as the customer expects all deliveries in the right quantity at a controlled temperature, the specification should be of high importance, but the quality of product is the primary responsibility of the farmer.

The resource utilisation objective is maximising the utilisation of resources owned by the company – people (drivers) and facilities (own vehicles). Facilities refer to those owned by the depot. The materials are not owned by the depot and stock control is not an issue. As the products are handled at controlled temperatures, the importance of materials is medium.

The capacity management strategy should be to provide an efficient adjustment of capacity.

As output stocks are not feasible, an efficient adjustment of reefer vehicle capacity has been provided. The depot provided own and contract vehicles (34 tractors and 53 trailers) to cover the average throughput (e.g. 1100 pallets per day @ 20 pallets per trailer, 55 trailers). In addition, ten tractor/trailers from Ormskirk are available to adjust for variation and seasonality.

Of the 94 staff, nearly half of them are qualified drivers. Therefore, some extra capacity for drivers is planned to cover both variations and absenteeism.

Because of the agreed delivery window, the principle of 'backward scheduling' is applied. A route scheduling optimisation programme is available to provide recommended schedules, based on which final adjustments are made by the route planner.

In order to improve the exchange of information, the company has installed electronic data exchange (EDI) systems with some supermarkets.

Source: Christian Salvesen, UK (2002).

Strategic alliances

In order to achieve an integrated supply chain, the various players need to work together. The four most important types of distribution management strategic alliances are 3PL, RSP, DI and CRM.

Third-party logistics

The use of a third party to take over some or all of a company's logistics responsibilities is becoming more prevalent; 3PL is simply the use of an outside company to perform all or part of the firm's materials management and product distribution function. The relationships of 3PL are typically more complex than traditional logistics supplier relationships. Modern 3PL arrangements involve long-term commitments and often multiple functions or process management. As organisations focus on their core competencies, they are looking for other specialist organisations to partner with.

Retailer–supplier partnerships

As customer satisfaction becomes more imperative and margins get tighter, it makes sense to create cooperative efforts between suppliers and retailers in order to leverage the knowledge of both parties. The types of retailer–supplier partnerships can be viewed on a continuum. At one end is information sharing. On the other is a consignment scheme of vendor-managed inventory (VMI), where the vendor completely manages and owns the inventory until the retailer sells it.

In a simple quick response strategy, suppliers receive POS data from retailers and use this information to synchronise their production and inventory activities with actual sales at the retailers. In this strategy, the retailer still prepares individual orders, but the POS data is used by the supplier to improve delivery performance and hence reduce supply variability.

In a continuous replenishment strategy, sometimes called rapid replenishment, vendors receive POS data and use this data to prepare shipments at previously agreed intervals to maintain specific levels of inventory.

In a VMI system, the supplier decides on the appropriate inventory levels of each product and the appropriate policies to maintain these levels. The goal of many VMI programmes is to eliminate the need for the retailer to oversee specific orders for replenishment. The ultimate goal is for the supplier to manage the inventory and only receive payment for it once it has been sold by the retailer, in essence, the retailer is providing an outlet for the supplier!

Distributor integration

Modern information technology has enabled this strategy in which distributors are integrated so that expertise and inventory located at one distributor are available to the others. DI can be used to address both inventory-related and service-related issues. In terms of inventory, DI can be used to create a large pool of inventory across the entire distributor network, thus lowering total inventory costs while raising customer service levels. Similarly, DI can be used to meet the customer's specific needs by directing those requests to the distributor best suited to address them.

The influence of the Internet on the economy in general and business practice in particular has been tremendous. The direct business model employed by industry giants such as Dell and Amazon enables customers to order products over the Internet and thus allows these companies to sell their products without relying on third-party distributors apart from those providing the physical delivery service.

Similarly, the Internet and the emerging e-business models have produced expectations that many supply chain problems will be resolved merely by using these new technology and business models. While it has promised so much, in reality, the expectations have not been achieved. In many cases, the downfall of some of the highest-profile internet businesses has been attributed to their logistics strategies.

While the success of the business-to-customer concept has not yet been eventuated, the use of the Internet for business-to-business integration has more likelihood of success. Integration of supply chain players is made possible with the use of the Internet and the associated technologies.

Reviewing the impact of the new technologies on the supply chain provides an interesting development. The Internet and the evolving supply chain strategies have seen a shift in transportation and order fulfilment strategies away from case and bulk shipments to single-item and smaller-size shipments and from shipping to a small number of stores to serving highly geographically dispersed customers. This shift has seen the importance of partnerships with parcel and LTL (less than truckload) industries. It has also increased the importance and complexity of reverse logistics, that of handling the significant numbers of product returns. Thus, one of the big winners in the new developments is the parcel industry. Indeed, one of the important advantages of the parcel industry is the existence of an excellent information infrastructure that enables real-time tracking. Those players in this industry who work to modify their own systems in order to integrate them with their customers' supply chains are likely to be successful.

As businesses come to understand the role of the Internet, we will see new models of business evolving. As yet, what those models will be is unsure, but one thing is for certain, the Internet will have an impact on how supply chains of the future will be managed.

Customer relationship management

The recent growth in the availability of CRM systems has led to the access of data that can be used to improve overall supply chain performance. The objective of CRM is to develop a customer-centred organisation that ensures every opportunity is used to delight customers, foster customer loyalty and build long-term relationships that are mutually beneficial. The ultimate goal is to ensure that each individual customer's current and future wants and needs can be satisfied. What this involves is the capture of individual customer transaction details, and from this historical data, developing a picture of what that customer needs and purchasing habits are.

CRM's relevance to overall supply chain management lies in the need to integrate such systems with the management of the supply side. The information gathered by CRM systems can be used to improve the overall performance of the complete supply chain. As the need for supply chain transparency increases, businesses are looking for ways to improve the efficiency of supply. This has led to the development of the concept of total demand chain management

The partnership with customers is the mirror of working with suppliers with the role reversed. Ideally, the relationship will be that the customer involves the manufacturer in the market research phase so that together the best product can be designed to meet the end consumers' needs. Likewise, the customer through EDI or Extranet can input directly into the ERP system. Improved internal relationships within the business between manufacturing and logistics staff interfacing directly with customers should achieve a more precise specification of customer needs and sharing data (e.g. EDI or business-to-customer (B2C) web).

Thus, it is useful to carry out an ABC analysis (Pareto chart) to identify the top customers as shown in Figure 10.4. The Pareto theory is that 20% of the customers will account for roughly 80% of the business. ABC analysis takes this a step further by dividing customers into three groupings as shown in Figure 10.4. Normally, the division will be

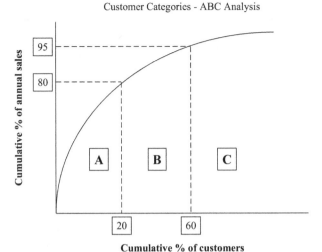

Figure 10.4 ABC analysis of customers

the top 5%, the next 15% and the balance of customers –80%. In this example, the analysis has been further broken down so that it can be seen that the top five customers account for 84% of the sales, and overall just 3% of the customers account for 80% of the sales.

Another challenge of working with customers is to identify the true profitability of all customers and then improve the profitability of key customers. Figure 10.5 illustrates that a 'tail' of unprofitable customers actually reduces the total profit contributions.

In one organisation we encountered, the top 5% of the customers accounted for 40% of the sales, and because of their importance to the company, they had been able to negotiate volume discounts and special delivery arrangements. When these benefits were examined and costed out, it was found that whereas the balance of the customers was providing the company with a true 40% gross profit margin on sales, these top 5% were only providing the company with a margin of 10%. Thus, overall, the gross margin on all

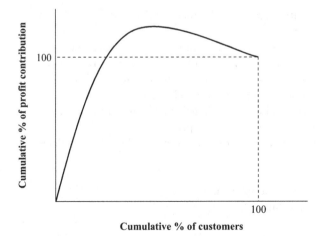

Figure 10.5 Customer profitability

sales for the company was reduced to 28% whereas the budget had allowed for 40%. This had not been apparent as the discounts had been shown in the accounts as an overhead expense and the extra transport costs had also been included as an overhead cost. There were also other reasons why the drop in true margin was not obvious.

In order to assess the true profitability of customers it is necessary to move away from the average allocation of cost (e.g. cost per tonne) and conventional cost accounting. Logistics managers are now working towards what is known as 'activity-based costing' (ABC) where cost is allocated according to the level of activity that consumes the resources. For example, the order picking cost of an order will vary according to its work content depending on whether the order is in full pallets or small units, the number of lines or SKUs or whether it requires additional packaging.

Summary

It is generally accepted that unless you are in the distribution business, you should seriously consider outsourcing your distribution to a third-party specialist. It is reasonable to expect that a specialist distribution company is likely to provide a more cost-effective service for a supplier. However, being cost-effective is not the same as being service-effective and it is arguable if a third-party company is likely to have full customer satisfaction. When a distribution company is delivering goods on behalf of a group of suppliers, it is fair to assume that the distributor will not offer any extra service beyond what is specified in service level agreements. Therefore, order fulfilment and customer relationship management will be affected by outsourced distribution policy.

In this chapter, we have described the fundamentals of distribution strategy, warehouse operations, stock management, transport planning and customer relationships management to encourage a better understanding of distribution management. With this backdrop, a manager will hopefully be better equipped to manage their own distribution operations or monitor the distribution activities of third-party distributors. The knowledge of distribution management principles as a building block of total supply chain management also highlights its key role in delivering goods and services to the customer.

Discussion questions

1. What are the three ways distribution assets can be managed? Discuss the advantages and disadvantages of each option.
2. In the case example of Walmart, describe how Walmart both achieved savings and improved customer service by owning both warehousing and transport networks.
3. Explain with examples how the total safety stock in a multi-site warehousing network can be reduced by reducing the number of warehouses.
4. What are the key factors to be considered in designing a warehouse? Discuss the seven steps to be considered in a warehouse design project.
5. Which of the following would be your key consideration for scheduling vehicles for local delivery:
   - Minimise mileage.
   - Maximise volume utilisation of the vehicle.
   - Maximise vehicle time utilisation.

   Explain the rationale of your answer.
6. Discuss the advantages and disadvantages of 3PL.

7. A distributor learnt that a major supplier of its products is considering going direct to consumers. What advantages of channel management can it offer to the supplier that the supplier cannot offer?

Exercise

Given the following data for an ambient storage warehouse:
- Annual demand: 12,000 tonnes
- Load per pallet: 400 kg
- Stock turn: 13
- Weekly maximum peak: 1.4 × average
- SKUs: 4 (same load per pallet)

Calculate the pallet positions required allowing 20% average peak and 85% utilisation of pallets.

Part 3

New demands and trends

11 Service industries, event operations and non-profit organisations

Introduction

Operations require materials just as any other organisation does, but their needs and way of working merit special consideration. In service industries, the output is intangible, and performance will largely be measured in qualitative terms, for example, the value of advice with friendly empathetic service. Each service delivery will be to some extent unique. In service industries, demand is often erratic and the duration of each interaction can vary. For example, a doctor in general practice might schedule ten minutes per consultation, but by the end of the day, patients will be waiting up to an hour for their appointment due to the doctor needing longer time than planned with some patients and the late arrival of others. In events operations, each event can be planned and resources scheduled in advance with some degree of certainty. Each event is unique. If an event consists of more than one performance, each performance, no matter how skilled the participants, will be unique, and once the event is over, it can never be exactly repeated and in many cases not at all. For example, if the television and video recording equipment fails during a cup final (be it cricket, football, rugby or darts), there is no chance of a repeat. The actual performance of the actors in an event can sometimes be measured, for example, 15 young Chinese women breaking the world record for the number of people on a bicycle, but for many events, performance measurement is subjective, for example, can Kiri Te Kanawa still hit the high notes? In non-profit operations such as relief for flood or earthquake victims, organisations exist and contingency plans might exist, however, when and where the disaster will occur cannot be known. The performance of the relief organisation will be hard to judge, although lives might have been saved, could more have been done? And how much of the money donated is spent on administration or wasted and what percentage actually gets to the victims?

All of the above types of operations have several things in common: each occurrence will be unique and performance to a large extent will be judged in qualitative terms and judgement can well be uninformed and emotional. In a pure supply or manufacturing operation, performance can be measured in quantitative terms, for example, how many delivered, specification met, delivery on time and cost. This chapter considers the special requirements of service, event and non-profit organisations and shows how the application of supply chain management principles will improve efficiency and effectiveness.

DOI: 10.4324/9781003341352-14

Learning objectives

This chapter considers the special supply chain requirements for the following:

Service industries.
Event management.
Non-profit (humanitarian) organisations.

Service industries

In the UK, 81% of the workforce are engaged in service industries (in 1948, the percentage was 44%; Statistica, 2022b).

It is also evident from Figure 11.1 that the service sector contributes a major share of the economy in advanced countries. It is also important to note a service organisation, like a bank, airline or legal business, has customers, suppliers, demand forecast and supply chains.

In Chapter 9, we distinguished service and transport from manufacturing and supply operations with the use of system structures. We repeated Wright and Race (2004) who say that 'A service organization exists to interact with customers and to satisfy customers' service requirements. For any service to be provided there has to be a customer' (p. 4). Without the input of the customer, the service cannot be provided. From the client's point of view, where in some service industries such as law and accounting where time charged is calculated in six-minute blocks (ten units per hour), the cost of the service is not cheap. Customers are becoming price-conscious and thus service industries across the board are under pressure to reduce costs and at the same time provide an accurate and fast service.

Before the service provider can provide a service, they will need a supply of resources. The acquisition of tangible resources such as office space, computer/information system,

COUNTRY	AGRICULTURE	MANUFACTURING	SERVICE
Australia	4	26	70
Brazil	6	28	66
Canada	2	26	72
China	10	47	43
France	2	19	79
Germany	1	28	71
India	19	26	55
Italy	2	25	73
Japan	1	25	74
Russia	4	38	58
Singapore	0	28	72
UK	1	22	78
USA	2	22	77

Figure 11.1 Percentage of GDP by sector

electricity and water, stationery, forms and brochures and so on are generally not a big issue and any problems associated with the acquisition of these basic and direct requirements will be the same for any type of organisation and need not be discussed further. Service industries rely on the intellectual capital of their people. Wages will be the biggest direct cost. Service industries in turn will require services. A big area, and often neglected, for savings in service industries is the purchase of indirect goods and services. When a service organisation has several offices, some distance from each other, spending escalates, and suppliers of services to the offices become passive and complacent. For the remote office, it seems to be cumbersome to be expected to be continually applying for approval for routine purchases, and generally, it will not be obvious as to who is responsible for what. Further, when mergers and takeovers occur, there is a reluctance to impose rules and regulations from the 'head' office for day-to-day expenses and there will be little commonality in how expenses are controlled at each remote office.

Costs can be reduced. There is no reason why service industries and clients of service industries cannot adopt supply chain management and supplier relationship management to reduce costs. One of the big savings can be made by formalising service purchasing.

Service spend by non-service companies

Fearon and Bales (1995), also cited in Lyson and Farrington (2006), found from a study of 116 large American companies that 54% of total purchasing was for services. According to the Center for Advanced Purchasing Studies (CAPS), the spend for services in some organisations is as high as '86% of the total purchasing spend' (also see Knowledge Storm, 2006). Fearon and Bales (1995) in their study also found that 70% of services purchasing is made by staff not in the purchasing department. In other words, staff went direct to their preferred service providers and less than 30% of the expenditure was handled by purchasing staff. One of the largest and not well-controlled expenditures is in travel and entertainment. Travel might in many cases require advance approval, but the actual amount spent is not well monitored or queried. It is reported that Delta Airlines by analysing service spend was able to leverage discounts with suppliers. They had several hubs each doing their own purchasing, by centralising purchasing in 2002, over a three-month period, they were able to save US$11 million on the cost of hotel rooms for staff (a saving of US$44 million per annum).

The reasons why staff bypass the purchasing department are fairly obvious:

1. They think they have better expertise than the purchasing department, know what they want and cannot be bothered with following procedures and form filling.
2. They have a personal relationship with the supplier and prefer to communicate directly rather than through an intermediary.

The dangers of allowing staff, no matter how well-intentioned and honest they may be, to do their own thing are obvious. A study by Denali Consulting found that when cost savings are pursued, savings on services ranged from 10% to 29% compared with an average of 5% to 17% for other commodities or materials (Stratford and Tiura, 2003).

Once an organisation realises how much is being spent on services, then the next step is to determine:

What and why.
Where and why.

When and why then.

Who and why that person.

The objective being to determine 'How'. How being to agree on the most efficient and cost-effective system. It goes without saying that the new system has to be monitored to be kept in place. It is too much of a temptation for staff in a hurry to try and bypass the system.

The use of information and communication technology (ICT) is now the norm when considering the 'How' of efficiency.

According to a report by yStats.com, released in February 2016, Europe is one of the largest B2C e-commerce markets worldwide. This region is home to two of the five highest-ranking countries globally in terms of online retail sales. These two markets, the UK and Germany, accounted for nearly half of the region's B2C e-commerce sales and had some of the highest online shopper penetration rates in the region in 2015. France was Europe's third-leading country in B2C e-commerce sales, likewise benefiting from a high double-digit online shopper penetration rate. Due to these markets being in advanced stages of development, their sales growth rates are predicted to be more moderate compared with the rapid growth of emerging B2C e-commerce markets such as Turkey and Poland.

Some common characteristics emerge in the various online retail markets across Europe, including the increasing importance of mobile and cross-border shopping, yStats .com's report reveals. For example, in Italy, e-commerce's share of total online retail sales is projected to more than double through 2017, and in Russia, China-based cross-border shopping websites are gaining popularity each year. Another market trait shared by many countries in Europe is the leadership of clothing as the product category purchased by the highest share of online shoppers in 2015.

The competition landscape in European B2C e-commerce features both international and local companies. Amazon has remained one of the market leaders in terms of sales and website visits in the region's major countries for the past several years. Due to the popularity of the clothing category, online fashion retailers, such as Germany-based Zalando and Bonprix, UK-based Asos and Russia-based Wildberries, have also kept high ranks in their markets of operation. Overall, the report by yStats.com shows that competition remains intense as some of the European B2C e-commerce markets mature, while others continue to grow rapidly.

CASE EXAMPLE: BARE ESCENTUALS

The California-based cosmetics company Bare Escentuals' (BE) Omni-Channel Distribution Centre serves large wholesalers such as Macy's, Sephora Ulta and more than 1000 spa salons, 230 company-owned boutiques and direct consumers through its website, infomercials and catalogues. It services this multitude of channels from a single 400,000 sq. ft distribution centre in Ohio. Prior to 2007, before they launched their website, they operated from several distribution centres in different locations, each with a differing capacity to service the various channels. Bringing the fulfilment for all channels into one facility enabled Bare Escentuals to save costs and vastly improve getting the right product to the right place at the right time. Full-case wholesale orders are picked by workers on forklifts using hand-held RF devices, whereas direct-to-consumer orders are batch-picked 20 orders at a time direct to shipping cartons by voice-directed pickers. Retail store replenishment and spa salon orders are picked using pick to light technology.

In 2010, Shiseido acquired Bare Escentuals and has taken advantage of the service structure built by BE, thus creating a shared services model for all of the Shiseido brands.

Michael Thompson, BE's vice president of operations, cites how during Cyber Monday when e-commerce business was processing three times the normal number of orders, he was able to quickly leverage workers from other channels. 'E-commerce customers want their orders immediately. With a consolidated multi-channel facility, we can support demand peaks quickly and internally, achieving that critical speed to customers'. Source: Plunkett (2007).

Outsourcing

Purchasing departments, if not accustomed to buying services, almost certainly will need to develop new skills. A study by CAPS (2003) found that 75% of the respondents (from purchasing departments) found it was more difficult to manage (and buy) services than to buy/manage goods. If an organisation does not have the right purchasing staff, outsourcing specialist purchasing should be considered.

It is becoming increasingly cost-effective for organisations to outsource service provision. For example, in 1999, Harley-Davidson outsourced its entire indirect spend to three suppliers, who either provide the service required or who in turn arrange services from other suppliers. The savings in 2000 amounted to a reported US$4 million.

Service providers can be grouped under the following headings:

* Professional
* Personnel
* Property
* Support

A recent report by the UK consultancy Johnson Controls, in partnership with PeopleWise, found an increasing trend towards outsourcing, integrating and globalising services with the objective for organisations to drive down costs, create efficiencies and improve service delivery. According to their survey, 87% of the 118 respondents currently outsource facilities management and the strong expectation is that there will be growth in the number of outsourcing in the range of service activities; 80% of the organisations surveyed purchase from a single provider who uses specialist knowledge to integrate service delivery, procurement and service delivery management. The largest facility management company is ISS, a Danish Group that began operations in 1901. It has 510,000 employees and operates in over 75 countries, with services in specialist divisions for cleaning, office support, call centres, property, catering, healthcare and home care services.

It can be argued that any organisation, large or small, will find it more efficient, effective and cheaper to subcontract to specialist organisations and concentrate on their core business. Whereas once large organisations such as hospitals and military bases would have their own support services of kitchen and laundry and do their own cleaning, all of these activities are now subcontracted. Likewise, for a small or medium enterprise, having its own in-house lawyer or other professional specialist would not be warranted.

Public sector and government organisations are engaged in initiatives to improve the performance of their service supply chain and reaching out to the experience of global service providers such as UPS, FedEx, DHL and TNT. The national institution of the NHS in the UK, which is known to be an icon of self-contained healthcare services, has formed an outsourcing service supply chain partnership with DHL Logistics.

CASE EXAMPLE: DHL SERVICE SUPPLY CHAIN FOR THE NHS

In 2006, DHL Logistics won a ten-year deal to manage £22 billion of the UK Department of Health's annual procurement spending. Under the agreement, DHL was to run a division called NHS Supply Chain on behalf of the NHS Business Services Authority and be responsible for delivering all procurement and logistics services across an initial 500,000 products to support 600 hospitals and other health-care providers in England. NHS Supply Chain was to have its own management team and be governed by a board dedicated to managing the performance of the operations. The range of products managed by NHS Supply Chain encompasses a range of goods including supplier and maintenance contracts, food, bed linen, office equipment, stationery, cleaning products, patient clothing, medical and surgical equipment, dressings and provisions. The UK Department of Health believes the arrangement will allow public health authorities more resources for patient care and continue to manage their cost base.

DHL has committed to return £1 billion in savings over the contract period back to the UK National Health Service. John Allan, Chief Executive of DHL's Logistics division, said, 'The contract will ensure that NHS Trusts get access to a wide range of high quality, innovative products that will be selected by having extensive dialogue and testing procedures with clinicians'. However, the contract was not without controversy. Savings achieved were not as transparent or as great as planned, but nonetheless, no matter how they were calculated, they were substantial, and the NHS announced in August 2015 that the contract would be extended until September 2018 with further saving targets for the next two years of £150 million.

Supply chain management in banking

Banking and financial services account for 9.5% of the GDP of the UK and have benefited from integrated methods of payment and management of the cash supply chain.

Automated teller machines (ATMs) and other technologies make cash easily available to customers. For retail banks, however, the cost and complexity of operating these technologies continue to rise across the entire cash supply chain from holding, counting

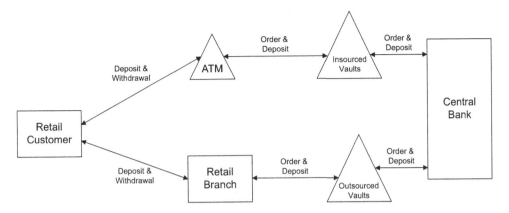

Figure 11.2 Cash supply chain in banking

and validating cash to processing, transporting and protecting it. Figure 11.2 illustrates the supply chain of cash movement between the central bank and customers.

With this cash supply chain in mind, banks can adopt a fresh perspective by comparing how leading consumer business (CB) organisations efficiently move goods through their supply chains as shown in Figure 11.3.

By thinking of cash as goods, retail banks can apply proven CB strategies to reduce excess inventory, lower handling and processing costs, improve operating efficiency and optimise their network of ATMs. Figure 11.4 illustrates how banks may manage their

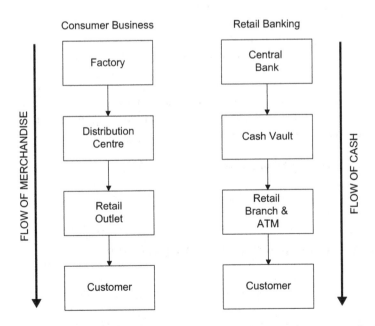

Figure 11.3 Comparison of the banking supply chain with the consumer business supply chain

	Consumer Business	Retail Banking
Inventory reduction	5 – 15%	Yes
Logistics cost reduction	2 – 5%	Yes
Margin from lost sales	20 – 30%	Partial
Obsolete inventory	20 – 30%	No

Figure 11.4 Potential savings in the banking supply chain

cash supply chain more effectively and improve productivity and better position themselves to compete in the marketplace.

Event management supply chain

The events industry includes festivals, meetings, conferences, exhibitions, ports and a range of other events. With the growth of government regulation and corporate involvement in events including sponsorship, the event environment has become increasingly complex. Event managers are required to understand the needs of their direct customers and the final customers and to satisfy several stakeholders. The number of suppliers including performers can be complex. And in some cases, the event manager will have no direct control but will be held responsible if things go wrong.

The following section is derived, with amendments, from Tum, Norton and Wright (2005).

Resources and specialisations used for each event are diverse and can be sourced from many different suppliers. Some of the resources may be under the events manager's direct control, and others may be subcontracted or outsourced to agreed specialists – for example, lighting and sound contractors, caterers, musicians and pyrotechnic companies.

The event supply chain is shown in Figure 11.5.

SUPPLIER →

SUPPLIER → EVENT MANAGER ←→ CLIENT ←→ CUSTOMER

SUPPLIER →

Figure 11.5 Event supply chain

Managing this chain will normally involve dealing directly with purchasing and supply and inventory management. The feedback that flows backwards is essential because it allows the event manager to see how well received the products, supplies and services were, and whether there should be any changes in the future.

The flow of resources should be managed from its very origins right up to the point where the customer experiences the event. For example, the event manager needs to know the health and safety procedures for a visiting Chinese circus company, including a firework display to coincide with Chinese New Year, at a local football ground booked through an agent. Although the agent will have covered many of the details, the event manager will still need to be assured about the suitability of the performance, how it will match the needs of the audience and how it can be coordinated with all the other activities into a whole event.

For an event, there can be many different supply chains through which the varied resources flow. They all have to be managed and coordinated into one event, which is delivered at the moment it is experienced.

Supply chain management is a holistic approach that stretches forward across the event manager's own organisation to the client and customers (see Figure 11.5), and backwards through the many different suppliers and to their suppliers. By having this holistic approach and integration across company boundaries, there can be substantial benefits for all stakeholders. It should be viewed as a chain, and any break in that chain will have an adverse effect on the client. The aim is to develop an integrated supply chain to achieve those critical success factors judged by the customers and required by the client and other stakeholders including local regulatory authorities. Unlike most other industries, the project that the event manager is responsible for cannot fail. It must happen on time, and there is no chance of a repeat. For example, a one night concert cannot be repeated if the hall has been double booked. If, on the night, ten minutes after the start, the lighting system or sound system fails for a rock concert, the event manager will not be able to arrange another supplier

Basic objectives of purchasing

Like any other manager, event managers are responsible for providing events at the right cost, at the right time, to the right specification and quality, and for the right duration. These requirements are made even more challenging when many of the resources are arranged through third and fourth parties. As for any operation, the event manager will be under pressure to keep costs down.

Often within an event company, there is not a specific purchasing officer, and many of the staff may create buyer/supply relationships with different companies. Some products may be bought outright and owned by the organisation, and others will be used for only one event. In the case of some of the purchase agreements, for example, the caterers or security service, it is the whole service and system that is purchased and the contracted company will bring their own resources and staff. To be successful, these relationships and the method of purchasing or leasing must be managed effectively since they all provide vital supply chains throughout the operation.

In arranging contracts, the events manager must always take time to check legal implications and assess what can go wrong and what the implications will be. Risk management is crucial.

The companies from whom products and services are purchased should not be just seen as suppliers but should be considered as customers. They are customers in the way they are approached for quotations. All businesses are customers for some other business. Every operation and part of an operation should be seen as a network, linking together customers' customers and suppliers' suppliers. In the event industry, many of the suppliers are specialists and have their own marketplace and rules and regulations that have to be conformed to. This includes health and safety, government agencies, international companies and international customers and many other organisations. The event manager needs to be able to stand back and see the myriad of operations and contracts, working together to deliver the event, as a whole and integrated network of supply chains.

Slack and Lewis (2002) point out that there are qualitative issues to understand:

1. How does an operation relate to other players in its network?
2. What knowledge of its supply network does it have? Is it close and intimate?
3. Does its supply network have an intimate and close understanding of its own operations, and ultimately, its customers' needs and objectives?

Single-sourcing or multi-sourcing of suppliers?

The event manager should question the number of suppliers with whom the organisation is involved. Does one supplier provide a 'one-stop shop' where many of the resources required can be purchased, or are there a great many suppliers providing a range of different services for the same event? If the latter is the case, then there are consequently more supply chains to be managed. Often in events management, many brief relationships will be made and there will not be time to develop loyalty, trust and understanding of each other's needs. In reality, depending on the type of event, a combination of the two policies would be used.

For example, if you produce classical concerts nationwide, you could use a UK-wide sound and lighting company that produces bespoke requirements for each event, including design and set building, but you would most likely use a local caterer and security company. Silver (2004) recommends that all projects or purchases should be put out to three bids every time to ensure competitive pricing. On the other hand, Tum et al. (2005) argue that a company that is assured of continued business with an organisation will provide competitive prices. It avoids quotation and administrative costs and will know which staff and resources are necessary for the provision of the service. This close relationship might be jeopardised if frequent competitive tendering is undertaken. However, complacency within this special relationship must not be allowed to propagate and lead to decreased customer satisfaction or overpricing.

Some event companies prefer to complete everything in-house – both important and non-important activities. This style of company is known as being vertically integrated, that is, it creates and supplies all the necessary resources and services from within its own resources. An example of a vertically integrated company is a circus owner who owns the circus animals; has the artists on the payroll; owns the big top, other tents, caravans and transporters; employs his own costume-makers, scene designers and constructors; has a supply of memorabilia for sale; runs a refreshment booth; and does his own promotion.

At the other end of the scale, some event companies do nothing in-house and buy in all of their requirements. This style of company is referred to as being virtual. An example of a virtual company is a promoter who arranges the tour of an overseas ballet troupe, hires the theatres, arranges accommodation for the artists, hires the orchestra and so on, and uses an advertising agency for promotion. In essence, the promoter owns nothing and works from a rented office. However, the event manager in this case cannot subcontract the risk or the responsibility!

Vertically integrated organisations

Making a choice to buy out a supplier or to make/provide those products and services in-house is known as backwards integration. In the event industry that might entail buying out a lighting specialist or a catering company or making all the props for themed evenings in-house rather than using an external company. This may be worthwhile if that specialism is being used a great deal within all events, and if the cost of acquisition and integration into the company would create savings and increase a better provision of what is needed. Other advantages include preventing competitors from gaining control of key suppliers.

Forward integration is when an organisation buys out or actively completes the work done by a customer. In the event industry, an example might be a lighting or catering company which, instead of always waiting for an event company to come to them to ask for a quotation to supply certain goods and services for an event, proactively seeks out customers and puts on the event itself.

As covered in Chapter 13, the Internet and e-mail provide quicker responses and access to information. The Internet also opens up a greater choice of providers.

The integrated flow of materials and services through and from the operation is a prerequisite for achieving high-quality, rapid and low-cost provision for clients. Therefore, managing the supply chain is a major concern and of major importance for event organisations, where a high proportion of their products and services often come from different suppliers or different parts of the organisation.

In delivering this well-managed supply chain, the aim of the event company should be to diminish obstacles between functions and departments within the organisation, minimise activities undertaken and improve the links between departments so that there is no unnecessary repetition. External to the organisation, the event manager should look to improve communication and relationships with suppliers.

O'Toole and Mikolaitis (2002) see the contract as central to the correct procedure for project planning and implementation. Much is written about contracts in engineering, building and software industries, and event managers can take advantage of lessons learned from successes and failures in these other industries in their use of project management. Each contract specifies who will do what, when and how. It can contain many details or be a simple letter of agreement or purchase order.

Decision points in purchasing for an event organisation

Although each event is unique, the following nine-stage purchasing chain of decisions is provided as a checklist to enable the event manager to assist in planning. Stage 9 is important as it enables the event manager and future event managers to benefit from past experience.

1. When it is initially considered that an event should go ahead, there is a need for a range of products and services. There should be detailed discussion regarding how these might best be procured – in-house or from an external company.
2. The next stage is to create a clear specification of what is required.
3. Some organisations may have a list of preferred suppliers. This provides useful contacts regarding reliable companies who are known to deliver as per specification of quality and who also respect and value working with the event manager's organisation.
4. Suppliers should be approached for a price and an overview of what they could provide. Can the exact specification be provided? Is there flexibility of provision?
5. When the quotations are returned, it is important that they are examined fairly and checked to see that what is being offered is as per specification.
6. The price and quality and reliability may be compared against in-house provision where that is possible. If you buy on price alone, you will get what you pay for. Cheap can be expensive!
7. When the event manager is satisfied that the goods and services are as required in all respects, including competitive price and appropriate provision, then an agreement can be made with the supplier. This may be called a purchase order, but in reality, what happens is that a contractual relationship is formed between the event manager and the supplier. A contract is said to exist when something is offered and accepted in writing or verbally with witnesses. Its purpose and provisions must be legal, and the different parties should be capable of entering into the agreement. The standard contract elements, according to Catherwood and Van Kirk (1992), are:
   * Specification of the agreeing parties.
   * Purpose of the contract.
   * Duration of the contract.
   * Terms.
   * Signatures.
   * Witnesses and date signed.
8. The goods and services should be delivered as expected. In many instances within the events industry, the actual delivery and consumption will be simultaneous.

For example, a rock band delivers its services at the moment it is playing for the audience.

9. The final stage is a review. Did the purchased product or service deliver as expected and required? The review will inform the next set of decisions about a similar service/product. Reviewing after the event, when successes and problems are still fresh in the mind, is essential. Consider and note what went right, what went wrong and what would we do differently next time. It is advisable to record contact names and addresses on file for future reference. Each event should be better managed than the last one. There is always room for improvement. Event managers should ask staff and subcontractors what they think could be done better, and their opinions should be taken seriously.

Customer relationship management

Customer relationship management (CRM) software now exists to capture data to improve overall supply chain performance (also see Chapter 23). The objective of CRM is to develop a customer-centred organisation that ensures every opportunity is taken to delight the customers, foster customer loyalty and build long-term relationships that are mutually beneficial. The ultimate gain is to ensure that each customer's current and future wants and needs are satisfied. This involves recording details of each time we work with a customer and developing a picture from this information of what the customer liked and did not like in our past dealings. Although software exists to capture these data, for smaller operations such information can easily be recorded as notes on the customer's file.

Non-profit (humanitarian) organisations

Unlike event management, natural disasters do not keep to a timetable. Nonetheless, as a disaster will require quick response delivery of materials and services, an efficient supply chain would seem to be important. From a study of the literature and media reports, it has been found that the general perception is that money is not spent wisely, and overall performance of relief agencies be they government-funded or private is generally not as efficient as it could be or should be.

From a survey of 54 organisations, Oliver (2006) found the following when non-profit organisations were compared with commercial organisations:

1. Have fewer regular meetings with key suppliers, do not easily engage in collaborative product development, have little direct IT interface and seldom have a designated body responsible for coordination.
2. Have less trust in their supply partners, but ironically were less likely to monitor the performance of their suppliers. Where there is some distrust, the implication is that suppliers should be checked. He also quoted Kupila (2003), who believes that suppliers to humanitarian agencies were less approachable and proactive. Kupila also observed that donors to charities do not fully trust front-line agencies.
3. Have less control over their logistics network, with inbound and outbound logistics comparatively less efficient. Oliver found that humanitarian organisations have less power within the supply chain. He contends that cooperation in a supply chain can be achieved through power or by a strong drive to meet common goals and that generally both these factors were missing. He also found that single-sourcing was not prevalent and in his opinion, and from our experience, single-sourcing leads to tighter control and a better understanding of common goals. Oliver found that weakness in power and control leads to deficiencies in the management of incoming goods and services and insufficient cost information and control.
4. Supply chain professionals in humanitarian organisations are undervalued and are less likely to be encouraged to develop and be involved in key decisions.
5. Charities do not use IT effectively in the supply chain. This hampers performance in knowledge sharing, demand planning, collaboration and performance monitoring. End-to-end costs are not always clearly known.
6. Performance is not well assessed and therefore continuous improvement suffers.

CASE EXAMPLE: WALMART

Referring to the Hurricane Katrina disaster in New Orleans, Waller (2005) was not surprised that Walmart responded quicker and was more effective in providing what was required than the Federal Emergency Management Agency and the Red Cross. As he said, Walmart was only doing what it does every day. It has mastered supply chain management and the company's expertise worked well during the disaster.

Worthen (2005) provides an insight as to how Walmart was able to perform so well. 'The hurricanes that flattened the Gulf Coast in August and September tested corporate logistics and supply chain operations, as companies struggled to move relief supplies and inventory to and from the region before and after each storm'. Walmart trucks were distributing aid to Katrina's victims days before federal relief arrived. One lesson from these storms is that having procedures for communicating quickly about what needs to be done is as essential for companies as having integrated inventory and logistics systems.

> Wal-Mart, for example, was able to move food, water, generators and other goods to areas hit by hurricanes Katrina and Rita following each storm because it has an emergency operations center that is staffed every day around the clock by decision-makers who have access to all of the company's systems. Under normal circumstances, a six- to 10-person staff at the center responds to everyday emergencies, such as a fire in a store or a shooting outside one. When disasters such as hurricanes threaten, the staff is joined by senior representatives from each of the companies functional teams. The center is equipped with hurricane-tracking software, and on Aug. 24, days before Katrina made landfall, company managers were already planning their response.
>
> Worthen (2005)

The emergency response team works in a large, open room that is designed with efficient communication in mind. For the record, during the first two and a half weeks following Katrina, Walmart shipped 2500 containers to the region. Walmart also set up satellite links for its stores that lost phone or Internet service so that they could stay connected to headquarters.

Worthen reported that Starbucks was also able to get aid to hurricane-ravaged areas quickly:

> When the company got a request from the American Red Cross to donate coffee, managers at headquarters contacted the company's distributors to discuss how they could help. Starbucks determined that it could donate 30,000 pounds of coffee, 235,000 bottles of water and 44,000 pastries without affecting supplies to its retail stores.
>
> Adapted from Waller (2005) and Worthen (2005)

Summary

The economies of most advanced countries are heavily dependent on service industries and today's progressive business leaders are dramatically reshaping their enterprises and extending their reach through partners, resellers and e-commerce. This chapter has looked at the special circumstances that face managers of service industries, events and non-profit humanitarian organisations.

In service industries, it is found that service spend is less controlled than for direct goods and materials, and that in service industries, the expenditure on services is a comparatively large and generally not well-controlled expense. The same applies to all other types of organisations, the spend on services is not treated as seriously as the expenditure on goods and materials. Centralising all purchasing of services under the control of the purchasing department is one approach. The other is to outsource the purchasing of specialist services. The example given was Harley-Davidson, which saved US$4 million per annum by subcontracting service spend to three suppliers.

With events management, it was shown that there is seldom a second chance. Once an event has been staged, it cannot be recaptured. Thus, event managers have to get it right first time. The various methods of supply chain management practised by events managers were considered, including subcontracting. Although each event is unique, a nine-stage purchasing chain of decisions was provided as a checklist to enable the event manager to get it right first time and benefit from experience.

For non-profit humanitarian organisations, it was found that greater adoption of supply chain management principles will improve performance. A major issue is the need to have agreements with suppliers and procedures for communication in place before any disaster occurs. Unlike event management, the timing of a natural disaster cannot be known, but as shown in the Walmart case study, it is possible to have resources in place and on standby to meet emergencies when they occur.

Discussion questions

1. Explain why supply chain management in the service sector is vital for advanced global economies.
2. Describe how the DHL service supply chain is benefiting the NHS in the UK.
3. Illustrate with the example of the supply of cash to ATMs and retail banking branches how the banking sector can benefit from following the supply chain management of consumer businesses in the manufacturing sector.
4. Describe the common features of the supply chain management of event management with traditional supply chain management in the manufacturing sector.
5. Discuss how the supply chain management of a non-profit organisation can benefit from the efficient professional services of a profit organisation. Describe how the agile response of Walmart helped the victims of Hurricane Katrina in New Orleans in 2005.
6. Describe a supply chain management approach in managing a major event like an international book fair. Explain the nine-stage purchasing chain of decisions in event management.
7. Discuss the role of applying the traditional supply chain approach of manufacturing industries to a service industry such as hotel management. Explain how you would adapt the processes of supply chain building blocks in such a service environment.

8. Describe the key features of the market-based 'transactional' relationship and the longer-term 'partnership' relationship with suppliers. 'It is unlikely that any service business will benefit from engaging exclusively in one type of supplier relationship': discuss this in the context of a hospital services supply chain.
9. What are the common and uncommon supply chain management practices between profit and non-profit organisations? What are your recommendations in applying the supply chain management expertise of the profit sector to relief organisations responding to major natural or political disasters?

12 Supply chains in emerging markets

Introduction

The Observer, a Sunday paper in the UK, on 22 October 2006, wrote:

EMPIRE STRIKES BACK: INDIA FORGES NEW STEEL ALLIANCE. It is a dramatic illustration of the shift in the balance of power from West to East: a £5 billion bid for Corus, formerly British Steel, by Tata, an industrial conglomerate that has aspirations to turn itself into an Asian version of America's General Electric.

Founded by Jamsedji Tata in the 1860s, initially with a textile mill in Bombay (Mumbai), today, it is India's largest company with a controlling interest in 96 companies. In 2000, the Tata group became the first Indian company to gain a major international brand when it acquired the UK company Tetley Tea. Tata is one of the world's lowest-cost producers of steel, while Tata Chemicals is one of Asia's largest manufacturers of soda ash. Titan is one of the world's top six manufacturer brands in the watch sector and Tata Motors is among the top six commercial vehicle manufacturers in the world. Besides being the largest software services provider in India, it is also India's largest international long-distance telecom and internet services provider. The dynamics of the global supply chain in the steel sector with the dominance of China have affected Tata's steel strategy in the UK, and at the time of writing, Tata is in the process of selling steel plants in the UK.

Tata is not the only organisation from the emerging market that is making the world sit up and notice. Khanna and Palepu (2006) cite a list of companies from emerging economies that are competing in the global market, for instance, Brazil's AmBev (which in 2004 merged with Belgium's Interbrew to form InBev); Chile's S.A.C.I. Falabella; China's Baosteel, Galanz, Haier and Lenovo groups and Huawei Technologies; India's Dr Reddy's Laboratories, Infosys, NIIT, Ranbaxy, Satyam, Mahindra & Mahindra and Wipro; Israel's Teva Pharmaceuticals; Mexico's Cemex; the Philippines' Jollibee Foods and Ayala groups; Turkey's Koc and Dogus groups; and South Africa's SAB Miller and, of course, Korea's Hyundai is now the fourth largest car producer in the world.

The multinationals from North America, Western Europe, Japan and Korea appear to have near-unbeatable advantages over companies from emerging economies, such as well-established brand names, large R&D infrastructure, proven management systems, advanced technologies and access to a vast fund of both financial and intellectual capital. However, after a closer analysis, it is evident that the newly industrialised countries can benefit from the experience of advanced economies and adapt best practices to their local advantage. Historically Japan and later Korea did just this in the 20th century. It is

DOI: 10.4324/9781003341352-15

like the saying, 'an early bird catches the worm but the second mouse gets the cheese'. Furthermore, companies in emerging markets can count on their supply chain partners to make and deliver products cheaper and can work better around the local bureaucratic processes. We shall analyse these factors in this chapter.

Learning objectives

Learning objectives for this chapter are:

1. Emerging economies.
2. Supply chains in India.
3. Supply chains in China.
4. Supply chains in Latin America.
5. Supply chains in Russia.

Emerging economies

China is the fastest-growing market on the planet. Since the start of liberalisation in 1979, the country's GDP is growing at 9.3% annually – three times faster than the United States. With a combined population of 2.5 billion, China and India have the most consumers in the world. Besides China and India, over the past two decades, waves of liberalisation have swept aside protectionist barriers in developing countries in other regions such as Latin America (Mexico, Brazil, Chile and Argentina), Southeast Asia (Malaysia, Thailand, the Philippines and Indonesia), Eastern Europe (Poland, Czech Republic and Hungary) and Africa/Middle East (Turkey, Israel, South Africa and Egypt). As these nations adapted themselves and interface with the global economy, multinational corporations from the advanced economies of North America, Western Europe, Australasia, North Korea and Singapore expanded their outsourcing and supply chain network.

The most impressive growth in the last decade was in four of the biggest emerging economies: Brazil, Russia, India and China. This prompted Jim O'Neill of Goldman Sachs, an investment bank, to coin the acronym BRIC in 2001. These economies have grown in different ways and for different reasons. But their size marked them out as special. On purchasing-power terms, they were the only US$1 trillion economies outside the OECD countries. Today, they are four of the largest ten national economies in the world.

The remarkable growth of emerging markets in general and the BRICs in particular transformed the global economy in many ways. Commodity prices soared and the cost of manufacturing and labour sank. Global poverty rates also appear to have tumbled. A growing and vastly more accessible pool of labour in emerging economies played a part in both wage stagnation and rising income inequality in rich ones. It can be argued that emerging economies have fuelled the acceleration in globalisation where both the rich and poor in emerging economies have benefited while only the rich in old rich economies have prospered. The shift towards emerging economies will continue. But growth rates in all the BRICs (especially in Russia and Brazil) have dropped. The nature of their growth is in the process of changing too, and its new mode will have fewer direct effects on the rest of the world. The likelihood of growth in other emerging economies labelled MINT (comprising Mexico, Indonesia Nigeria and Turkey) in the near future comparable to that of the BRICs in the recent past is low. They do not have the potential for catch-up the BRICs had in the 2000s. The BRICs' growth has changed the rest of the world economy in ways that will dampen the disruptive effects of any similar surge in the future.

The MINT countries or more generally the 'Next 11' or N11 cannot have an impact on the same scale as that of the BRICs. The first reason is that these economies are smaller. The N11 has a population of just over 1.3 billion, which is less than half that of the BRICs. The second is that the N11 is relatively richer now than the BRICs were back in the early stage of growth, so starting from a higher base does not give the same scope for dramatic growth. 'The most dramatic, and disruptive, period of emerging-market growth the world has ever seen is coming to its close' (*The Economist*, 27 July 2013). Future growth rates in emerging economies could be relatively low but they will still grow and their impact on globalisation and global supply chains remains highly significant. Nonetheless, the BRICs will continue to be the dominant emerging economies. Therefore, with the above backdrop, we aim to explore supply chains in BRIC countries.

In this chapter, we focus on supply chain issues in four regions of emerging markets:

* India
* China
* Latin America
* Russia

Supply chains in India

Economics experts and various studies envisage India and China dominating the world during the 21st century. For over a century, the United States has been the largest economy in the world, but major developments have taken place in the world economy leading to the shift of focus from the United States, the rich countries of Europe and the Eastern dragons of Japan and Korea to the two Asian giants – India and China. Experts predict that by 2035, India is likely to be a larger growth driver than the six largest countries in the EU, although its impact will be a little over half that of the United States. India is now the fifth-largest economy in terms of purchasing power. We forecast that India will overtake Japan and become the third major economic power within the next ten years. The visible success factors are the liberalisation of a 1.2 billion consumer market, a good higher education policy supplemented by European and American training and English-speaking communication and management systems and a growing middle class with disposable income to provide a vibrant home market. The growth in the Indian economy can be attributed to domestic savings, which is around 31% of GDP (in the United States the comparable figure is less than 17%).

India is however still a country of visible contrasts. The sophisticated nuclear science technology in research centres contrasts with bullock carts in rural areas. Indeed, in Bangalore (population 6.2 million), regarded as the IT centre of India, bullock carts can still be seen. In the past few years, cities in India have undergone tremendous infrastructure up-grading but rural India has not seen the same improvement. Universities are producing millions of English-speaking graduates in science, medicine and engineering, yet in the realms of health and primary education and other human development indicators, India's performance has been far from satisfactory, showing a wide range of regional inequalities with urban areas getting most of the benefits. Although the Indian Railway network employs a vast army of employees with moderate effectiveness, the infrastructure of road networks and port handling facilities has a long way to go.

In spite of the above challenges, economic growth in India in the early 21st century has been remarkable. The growth in the Indian industrial sector in 2014/2015 remained healthy. The Index of Industrial Production (IIP) continues to grow at an average of 6.43% from 1994 until 2015. The major element of the buoyancy in the industrial growth was the manufacturing sector with 80% in the index of industrial production. The service sector accounts for more than half of India's gross domestic products. The growth rate of India's service exports in 2015 was just below China's 10.9% (*Hindu News*, 23 February 2015). The reason for a high growth rate in the service sector in India is the liberalisation of regulatory frameworks and a high demand for low-cost information technology, business process outsourcing (BPO) and call centre services. According to NASSCOM (February 2016), India's IT market reached a turnover of US$147 billion in 2015. The IT sector employs 3.1 million people, and 'provides employment in adjacent sectors such as hospitality, security services' (NASSCOM, February 2016). The BPO and call centre sectors were growing at 60–70% annually and their turnover in 2004/2005 reached US$5.8 billion. In recent years, business has been lost to the Philippines (where BPO in 2016 will generate US$25 billion for the Philippines), and although growth in India has slowed to below 6%, the turnover in 2014/2015 had grown to US$22 billion.

In congruence with the diverse infrastructure, level of technology and economic development, the supply chain and logistics models in India are also diverse. For example, the auto industry follows a traditional model of the West and Japan for a predominantly urban and growingly affluent middle-class market. At the other end of the scale, fresh food supply is limited to regional markets. Manufacturers of fast-moving consumer goods, such as Hindustan Lever, deploy a hybrid of urban and rural logistics by empowering regional wholesalers for stocking and distributing branded products to rural customers. Multinational retailers, such as McDonald's restaurant chain, are gradually applying the available local infrastructure to the best of their advantage. The following case examples illustrate the application of appropriate supply chain models in India.

CASE EXAMPLE: THE AUTO COMPONENTS SUPPLY CHAIN IN INDIA

The most highly developed supply chain in India is that of the automobile industry, and over the past decade, Indian companies have begun to play a major role in its extension. The liberalisation of local equity and regulatory control encouraged the arrival of a wave of international car makers as joint ventures with local partners.

A link-up with Suzuki, forming the Suzuki-Maruti company (now Maruti Udyog) led to early success. The once dominant Hindustan Motors, whose 'Ambassador' model had been India's biggest-selling car in a controlled market for decades, lost market share to the new Suzuki-Maruti model in the open market. Suzuki-Maruti went on to capture over 60% of passenger car sales by 2002, as shown in Table 12.1.

Table 12.1 Car makers in India in 2002

Maruti Udyog Ltd	62%
Hyundai Motor India Ltd	17%
Tata Engineering and Locomotive Co. Ltd	12%
Hindustan Motors Ltd	4%
Others	5%

The development of the auto industry supply chain in India proceeded rapidly at the level of car makers and their first-tier suppliers. Here, current standards are close to world-class standards and it has led to exports of components and subassemblies to overseas car makers. Furthermore, domestic car makers like Mahindra and Mahindra can outsource more effectively, achieving cost reductions while maintaining quality levels. Another strategic choice in a low-wage environment is the use of highly qualified employees for shop floor operations. For example, one car seat maker employs only science graduates for all production line operations. The car producers interact closely with low-technology components such as car seats and exhausts.

The main weakness of the supply chain lies in the fact that in spite of the effective collaboration between car makers and first-tier suppliers, international best practices are not permeating down to the second- or third-tier suppliers.

Source: J Sutton, London School of Economics (2004).

CASE EXAMPLE: SEAFOOD SUPPLY CHAIN IN INDIA

The sustainability of fish stocks is a global concern. According to the Food and Agriculture Organisation (2002), about 47% of the main fishing stocks are over-exploited and are very close to their sustainable limits. Several measures are being adopted at national and international levels, including India, to promote sustainable fisheries. With an annual fish production of approximately six million tonnes in 2003, India ranks fourth in global fish production. The seafood world market has doubled in the last decade, reaching approximately US$50 billion and India's share of exports to the world seafood market is nearly 3%. Chennai, Kerala, Mumbai and Visakhapatnam are the four biggest seafood exporting ports in India, accounting for about two-thirds of total seafood exports.

Most exports are in the form of frozen fish and more than 60% of India's seafood exports to southeast Asia are re-exported after processing. Fish is a depleting commodity and regulations on excess fishing have made supply conditions more irregular. In India, state governments are responsible for the development and sustainability of the fishery sector, but due to their inability to form a cartel (similar to the oil cartel), seafood exporters are unable to charge higher prices in spite of the rising costs of fuel and maintenance. Fishing efforts are largely (about 90%) confined to the inshore waters within a depth range of up to 70 meters.

There are generally two types of fish-landing centres. There are natural ports that are normally beach landings and constructed ports. Each has distinct infrastructure problems.

The seafood supply chain in India, in general, comprises fisherman to commission agent to supplier (pre-processor) to the exporter.

The average share of the final export price is typically as follows:

Fisherman	25%
Commission agent	15%
Supplier	20%
Exporter	40%

Transaction costs between the fisherman and commission agent are borne by the agent and those between the agent and the supplier are borne by the supplier. However, those between the supplier and exporter are borne by the supplier.

The fisherman sells his catch to the commission agent, who is the link between the fisherman and the supplier. The commission agent is useful because he deals with less literate fishermen as well as organised suppliers. The supplier has trucks to transport to his facility where stocks are cleaned and graded based on size and quality. The exporter is the price setter and the most sophisticated end of the supply chain. Issues such as HACCP (hazard analysis and critical control point) first emerge at the exporter's end. The rest of the downstream supply chain is vaguely aware or completely unaware of export–import and safety issues. Fishermen are the most disorganised group in the supply chain. They are spread across the country, practice different fishing methods and operate on a different scale but they are the most affected stakeholder of government regulations of fishing bans and conservations.

Although the seafood supply chain is organised and well connected with adequate clusters and sophisticated exporters, fishermen and bottom-of-the-chain workers are not trained in fish hygiene, safety and handling methods and are not adequately rewarded. Beach landing ports and most constructed ports are also inadequately equipped.

Source: P. Kulkarni (2005).

CASE EXAMPLE: MCDONALD'S INDIA SUPPLY CHAIN

McDonald's Corporation [USA] opened its doors in India in October 1996. McDonald's in India is a 50–50 joint venture partnership between two Indian businessmen. Amit Jatia's company Hardcastle Restaurants Pvt Ltd owns and operates McDonald's restaurants in western India. While Connaught Plaza Restaurants Pvt Ltd headed by Vikram Bakshi owns and operates the northern operations. Restaurants opened in Mumbai, Delhi, Pune, Ahmedabad, Vadodara, Ludhiana, Jaipur, Faridabad, Doraha, Manesar, Bangalore and Gurgaon and more are in the pipeline.

McDonald's India has developed a special menu with vegetarian selections to suit Indian tastes and preferences. McDonald's does not offer any beef or pork items in India. The company established what is known as a 'cold supply chain'. The term cold chain describes the network for the procurement, warehousing, transportation and retailing of food products under controlled temperatures. McDonald's restaurant store products to be used on a daily basis within a temperature range of $-18°C$ to $4°C$. About 52% of our food products need to be stored under these conditions before they are used.

All suppliers adhere to Indian government regulations on food, health and hygiene while continuously maintaining McDonald's recognised standards. As the ingredients move from farms to processing plants to the restaurant, McDonald's Quality Inspection Programme (QIP) carries out quality checks and HACCP at over 20 different points in the 'cold chain' system. Setting up the cold chain has also enabled the company to cut down on operational wastage.

The relationship between McDonald's and its Indian suppliers is mutually beneficial. As McDonald's expands in India, the supplier gets the opportunity to expand its business, have access to the latest in food technology, have exposure to advanced agricultural practices and have the ability to grow or export.

There are many cases of local suppliers operating out of small towns who have benefited from their association with McDonald's India. For example, the implementation of advanced agricultural practices has enabled Trikaya to successfully grow speciality crops like iceberg lettuce, special herbs and many oriental vegetables. Vista Processed Foods Pvt Ltd is a joint venture with OSI Industries Inc., USA, McDonald's India Pvt Ltd and Vista Processed Foods Pvt Ltd and produces a range of frozen chicken and vegetable foods. Dynamix has brought immense benefits to farmers in Baramati, Maharashtra, by setting up a network of milk collection centres equipped with bulk coolers. Amrit Food, an ISO 9000 company, manufactures widely popular brands: Gagan Milk and Nandan Ghee at its factory in Ghaziabad, Uttar Pradesh. An integral part of the Radhakrishna Group, Foodland specialises in handling large volumes, providing the entire range of services including procurement, quality inspection, storage, inventory management, deliveries, data collection, recording and reporting.

Source: www.mcdonaldsindia.com (2007).

CASE EXAMPLE: RURAL SUPPLY CHAIN AT HINDUSTAN LEVER LIMITED

By 2005, Hindustan Lever Limited (HLL), a subsidiary of Unilever Group, was one of India's largest fast-moving consumer goods companies with market leadership in home and personal care products and one of its seven biggest exporters. HLL operated over 100 manufacturing facilities across the country, together with several third-party manufacturing arrangements.

HLL's potential distribution outreach in India was 3800 towns and 627,000 villages. However, of the total number of villages, the existing distribution network only reached 300,000. HLL's dilemma was how to extend it into the remaining villages in inaccessible rural areas.

HLL already had one of the widest and most efficient distribution networks for consumer products in India; in fact, this was recognised as one of its key strengths. HLL's products were distributed through a network of about 7500 'redistribution stockists' (RS), who sold to shops in urban areas and villages with more than 2000 people that could be reached by vehicle. Its supply chain was supported by a satellite-based communication system, the first of its kind in the fast-moving consumer goods industry. This sophisticated network with its voice and data communication facilities linked more than 200 locations all over the country, including the head office, branch offices, factories, depots and the key 'redistribution stockists'. This was a tried and tested model.

However, HLL wanted to penetrate these local communities even further and work deep within the villages. A profound knowledge of Indian rural communities would give HLL an unbeatable market advantage. However, the only solution for many Indians below the poverty line was to borrow from a moneylender at extortionate rates. A solution had been found to counteract the power of the moneylender in rural Indian areas. The successful Grameen Bank initiative, launched in Bangladesh in 1976, had more than proved that commercial banking for the poor without collateral was not a pipe dream and was awarded the Nobel Peace Prize in 2006.

HLL's growth strategy was to ask 'self-help groups' (SHGs) to operate as 'rural direct-to-home' teams of saleswomen, who would accomplish several tasks by raising awareness and educating people about HLL products as well as selling the products directly within their communities. The idea was for the women to not only act as salespeople, but also as veritable brand promoters, often physically demonstrating products, such as shampoo, by offering hair washes at religious festivals and local village markets (*haat*) or by performing hand-washing experiments.

A pilot initiative was set up in the Nalgonda district of Andhra Pradesh in November 2000, with 50 SHGs in 50 villages and the participation of 1000 to 2000 inhabitants. Once fine-tuned, the model would be scaled upwards to cover more than 150,000 villages in India. This HLL-SHG business partnership initiative was called 'Project Shakti', meaning 'strength' or 'power'. By the beginning of 2002, the project team had already reached the entire Nalgonda district and exceeded 400 villages with no signs of the momentum slowing down (refer to Figure 12.1 for an illustration of HLL's rural distribution model).

NB. Hindustan Lever has been renamed Hindustan Unilever.

Source: Amann and Ionescu-Sommer, Henley Business School (2006).

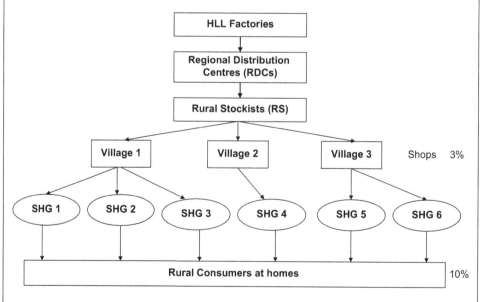

Figure 12.1 Rural supply chain model of HLL

Supply chains in China

For three years (2003–2005), China accounted for one-third of global economic growth (measured at purchasing-power parity), twice as much as the United States. In 2005, China became the world's fourth-largest economy replacing the UK. In 2006, China's official GDP growth rate surged to 10%. In 2015, China was recognised as the world's second-largest economy. It is predicted (Lieberthal 2003) that for the next ten years, and probably considerably longer, multinationals should be the biggest winners as China's economy becomes increasingly open.

In 2015, the growth rate was 6.9%, which was their slowest in 25 years. For any other country, a growth rate of almost 7% would be seen as a triumph (*Wall Street Journal*, January 2016). In addition to its phenomenal and sustained growth, China offers a powerful combination of a low-cost labour force, a large pool of skilled personnel, tax incentives to attract investment and infrastructure sufficient to support efficient manufacturing operations and exports. In total, China's labour force exceeds 800 million, almost twice that of the United States, EU and Japan combined. Like its export base, China's home market is also growing spectacularly. For example, six million mobile phone subscribers are signing up every month. Comparable growth is also seen in the use of computers, motor cars and retail stores.

China also has major challenges. Coal-fired power stations and emissions from cars and industrial and domestic facilities are causes of serious concern for the environment of the planet. A lack of management expertise plus a culture of a centralised economy is also a major constraint on the competitiveness of Chinese companies. However, after three decades of joint ventures and management training, Chinese managers are developing skills in critical multi-functional management tasks. China's transportation, distribution and retail infrastructures are rapidly being developed. Furthermore, provincial governments impose taxes on goods that are not manufactured in the region. Zeng and Williamson (2007) commenting on the backdrop described above of economic growth and local strengths and weaknesses, identified four groups of Chinese companies tackling global markets. China's 'national champions' (such as Haier Group, Huawei Technologies, Legend Group and Wanxiang Group) are using their advantages as domestic leaders to build global brands (see Haier Group case example). The second group is the country's dedicated exporters (such as Galanz, China International Marine Containers and BYD Battery) who are entering export markets on the strength of large economies of scale. Another group, 'competitive networks' (such as Wenzhou, Chenghai and Shenzhen) is expanding by bringing together small, specialised companies that operate closely in provinces. And finally, 'technology upstarts' (such as Dangdang.com, Innova Superconductor and Datang Microelectronics) are using innovations developed by China's government-owned research institutes to enter emerging sectors of new technology (see Dangdang case example).

CASE EXAMPLE: SUPPLY CHAIN OF HAIER GROUP IN THE UNITED STATES

Haier Group in China is a leading manufacturer of consumer durables with an annual turnover of about US$9 billion. By the early 1990s, the company had battled Whirlpool, Electrolux, Siemens and Matsushita to become the leader in China's market for home appliances. The group is now leads with 250 types of refrigerators, air conditioners, dishwashers and ovens, and in the United States alone, its market share is about 50%.

When it entered the US market in 1994, it focussed on selling only compact refrigerators (smaller than 180 litres) for hotel rooms and student bedsits. In 1997, Haier entered the market for wine coolers and captured 60% of that specialised segment by 2002. The company set up a manufacturing facility in Camden, South Carolina, to bypass the non-tariff barriers imposed by the United States on imports of appliances. Haier formed partnerships with nine of the ten largest retail chains in the United States to carry and sell its products.

By 2014, the Haier brand had the world's largest market share in white goods, and in January 2016, acquired the US company General Electric's appliance division (for US$5.4 billion), which will give it a chance to grow in the US market where previously it only had about 1% of the market.

Haier customers did not demand ground-breaking innovation or state-of-the-art technologies; they only wanted reliable and value-for-money products to meet their needs. The success of Haier in the US market demonstrated that Chinese companies are not only the suppliers of outsourced manufacturing facilities with cheap labour, but they are also now global competitors in advanced economies.

Developed from Zeng and Williamson (2007).

CASE EXAMPLE: E-SUPPLY CHAIN IN CHINA: DANGDANG.COM

By 2003, Dangdang.com (Dangdang) was rated as one of the most successful online bookstores in China. It featured almost 90% of the books published in China. Dangdong was launched in November 1999 by Peggy Yu, an MBA graduate from New York, and Li Guoging, a Chinese entrepreneur, and recorded sales worth China Yuan Renminbi (CNY) 1 million in the first two months. In a year's time, Dangdang was ranked as the number one online bookstore in China.

After studying the model of Amazon, Li Guoqing and Peggy Yu, realised that the website owed its success largely to its vast database of titles. It took the couple almost two years to make a comprehensive database of 200,000 book titles published in China. Ironically, in 2004, they turned down an offer from Amazon, which then invested in their major Chinese rival Joyo.

In November 1999, they launched the Dangdang website. Dangdang was chosen as a name because it could be easily pronounced, remembered and typed. Dangdang is derived from the Chinese adjective xiangdangdang, meaning resounding and worthy.

Within one year of its launch in 2000, Dangdang was ranked first among China's five major online bookstores by a significant margin in a survey conducted by the local industry publication, Computer Business Information. The most popular books on Dangdang.com are on computers, English language learning, science and tourism.

In April 2000, Softbank China Venture Capital (SCVC) and IDG invested US$22 million in Dangdang. This was to be used to strengthen Dangdang's logistics. Dangdang planned to build a 10,000 sq. m storage facility in Beijing and expand its delivery system to 40 major cities in China. It also had plans of getting listed on the US Nasdaq stock market by the end of 2000. But following the crash in tech stocks, it postponed its plans indefinitely. Subsequently, in 2006, Dangdang was able to attract substantial venture finance from the United States to fund the development needed.

Prior to the launch of Dangdang, online bookstores such as bookmall.com, cp1897 .com and 8848.net were already operational. The success of Dangdang inspired the opening of a few more online bookstores. While Dangdang was considered the most competitive in terms of price and variety of products; Joyo.com (Joyo) offered more popular products, bol.com (Bolchina) had the biggest advertising budget and store .sohu.com (Store.sohu) had a good brand name and heavy traffic.

In October 2002, Joyo, Bolchina, Dangdang and Store.sohu were engaged in a price war. All these websites sold books and audio video products online. The list price of the Chinese version of 'The Lord of the Rings' trilogy was CNY 62.6 per set whereas the websites were selling it at 40% below list price for CNY 45. Similarly, another bestseller, 'Harry Potter', was also sold on websites at heavy discounts. These players were mainly aiming for market share and were willing to sacrifice profits to acquire this.

By 2015, Dangdang's product range had expanded to include household merchandise, cosmetics, home appliances, books, audio and clothing, including children's clothing.

Today, Dangdang has over 10 million new registered customers per year and more than 100,000 sales are made daily. It is estimated 30 million people browse products per month and monthly revenue is US$20 million. In short, Dangdang sells over 200,000 book titles and 10,000 types of software and audio products (90% of China's mainland sales of software and audio).

Derived from www.chinatechnews.com (April 2007).

The potential of setting up joint ventures and expanding businesses for multinationals is tremendous. However, the risk of operating a supply chain needs to be analysed in a hard-nosed way. These risks could include the politics of the World Trade Organisation, implementation, oversupply and possible deflation, the structure of political power and political stability and currency exchange fluctuations. Lieberthal and Lieberthal (2003) recommend a five-stage strategy for Western multinationals to consider business expansions in China:

- Focus attention on properly nesting your China strategy into the organisation as a whole.
- Tailor strategies to both national and local governments and markets.
- Adopt a 'show me' attitude towards the purported advantages of forming a joint venture.
- Recognise and take steps to minimise the particular risks of operating in the Chinese environment.
- Avoid irrational exuberance in responding to the opportunities that China presents.

Supply chains in Latin America

Latin American countries have a current total population of over 626 million. The economy of Latin America gained momentum in the early years of the 21st century, bolstered initially by robust global demand and strong commodity prices. This was followed from 2000 by a brisk pickup in household consumption and business investment. However, according to the International Monetary Fund (April 2015), growth in Latin America and the Caribbean dropped below 1% and only a modest recovery is expected during 2016.

Considering the region's history of macroeconomic and political instability, growth, no matter how small, is good news. Only Peru and Chile show evidence of modest growth. The economic development of Latin America has notional 'common market' agreements such as Mercosur (the Southern Common Market), and NAFTA (North American Free Trade Agreement).

Mercosur was created by Argentina, Brazil, Paraguay and Uruguay in March 1991 with the signing of the Treaty of Asuncion, subsequently amended in 1994 by the treaty of Ouro Preto. Mercosur was originally set up with the ambitious goal of creating a common market/customs union between the participating countries on the basis of various forms of economic cooperation that had been taking place between Argentina and Brazil since 1986. Bolivia, Chile, Colombia, Ecuador and Peru currently have associate member status. Venezuela became a full member in 2006. The organisation has a South and Central America integration vocation (Paraguay was suspended in 2012 but re-instated in 2013).

In January 1994, Canada, the United States and Mexico launched the North American Free Trade Agreement (NAFTA) and formed the world's largest free trade area. The Agreement has brought economic growth and rising standards of living for people in all three countries. In addition, NAFTA has established a strong foundation for future growth and has set a valuable example of the benefits of trade liberalisation.

Clearly, Latin America still faces significant challenges, perhaps the most pressing of which is how to step up the pace of economic growth while maintaining stability. Throughout Latin America, unemployment and poverty remain unacceptably high, and severe income disparities persist. The primitive transport and logistics infrastructures in the remote interiors of especially Brazil, Bolivia and Colombia are encouraging population overspill into urban slums around megacities such as Mexico City, Sao Paulo, Rio de Janeiro, Buenos Aires and Bogota. The current uncertain economic environment in North America and generally in the world provides a backdrop that limits action that can be taken to ease these vulnerabilities.

Nonetheless, some Latin American companies have become world-class businesses by capitalising on their links with multinational companies like Proctor and Gamble, Unilever and global car and drugs manufacturers. Multinationals also utilised both people skills and markets of Latin American countries to consolidate their global earnings, systems and business practices. In this regard, local companies in China and India have been more successful in blunting the multinationals' edge. However, there are limited examples of local companies (such as AmBev and Bunge in Brazil and Cemex in Mexico) that have judiciously adapted to the special characteristics of local customers, suppliers and infrastructure The following three case examples illustrate some of the developments of supply chain management in Latin America.

CASE EXAMPLE: DATA WAREHOUSE SYSTEM
IN UNILEVER LATIN AMERICA

Unilever Latin America, the fast-moving consumer goods conglomerate, was facing the challenge of tracking business performance in a single data warehouse in 34 companies, 19 countries and currencies, thousands of users, three languages and operating over five time zones. The organisation had multiple ERP and CRM systems from various vendors, as well as 34 custom-built data warehouses, adding up to about 150 separate information systems and coding structures.

Each country had its own way of classifying information. Supply chain, ERP and CRM systems, for example, had different ways of classifying products and customers from country to country. 'Companies and countries have different cultures, different ways to run the business', noted Monica Parisi, information architecture manager at Unilever Latin America in San Paolo, Brazil.

Faced with a constantly changing marketplace where acquisitions and consolidations abound, Unilever Latin America believed there had to be an easier way to track regional information and improve business performance. So it initiated a dynamic information warehouse system to help harmonise processes and information through a project called Sinfonia, the Portuguese word for symphony.

Sinfonia is replacing all of Unilever Latin America's local ERP systems for finance, supply chain and order-to-cash processes. For this to work, Unilever needed to extract data from a wide variety of systems, including SAP, Siebel, Manugistics, PeopleSoft and legacy applications. In addition, the solution had to be adaptable to rapid and dramatic business changes.

Unilever Latin America has successfully implemented Sinfonia in Argentina, Paraguay, Uruguay, Chile and Brazil. 'That represents more than 50% of the revenue or sales of the total region', according to Parisi. The organisation is halfway to reaching its goal of implementing Sinfonia across the entire region.

The implementation thus far supports more than 2000 business users. Unilever Latin America expects that the final project will support more than 4000 users with about 12 million records loaded per day.

Sinfonia delivers an aggregated view of data across Unilever Latin America at high speed throughout constant business changes such as acquisitions and market consolidation.

That was the most significant challenge the organisation had to conquer: harmonisation across companies and countries. The overall architecture presented another challenge because Unilever Latin America had limited experience with very large databases. It brought in a team of consultants from Accenture, NetPartners and Kalido to help put Sinfonia in place.

Unilever Latin America's vision is to deliver the right information at the right time to the right people. Sinfonia is helping that vision become reality through daily monitoring of the extended supply chain. The organisation can dynamically generate information to track and manage the full supply chain from production to delivery.

What used to take the organisation a couple of weeks to determine performance information across the entire region can now be done immediately, online, even as Unilever Latin America, its suppliers or its customers are changing.

Unilever Latin America intends to grow Sinfonia and incorporate supply chain, finance and human resource processes into the mix. Eventually, the data warehouse will feed a regional balanced scorecard application as an executive information system and assist in strategic business planning. This will happen by enabling existing data to be viewed according to possible future hierarchies.

If given the opportunity to redo the project, Unilever Latin America would use internal people that could learn and stay with the development team, Parisi notes. The organisation began developing the system with third parties and consultants.

Source: Unilever (2004).

CASE EXAMPLE: BRISTOL MYERS SQUIBB SUPPLIER PARTNERSHIP IN MEXICO

Bristol Myers Squibb in Mexico has adopted supplier management as part of its Sustainability 2010 goals. In July 2006, the San Angel facility organised an event to recognise those suppliers to Bristol Myers Squibb and other companies who participated in Phase I of the eco-efficiency program 'Competitive Chains'. Phase I was held from October 2005 to April 2006 and resulted in the identification of more than US$1 million in cost savings. Written recognition was presented to the suppliers by the Ministry of Environment. Phase II of the program was launched in July 2006, with the participation of suppliers to Bristol Myers Squibb and other companies.

The company has developed an environmental, health and safety (EHS) questionnaire that may be sent to most third-party manufacturers and to a contractor or supplier if they fall into one of the following categories:

*   Sole source.
*   Manufacturer of a strategic material.
*   Manufacturer of a material to Bristol Myers Squibb's specifications.
*   Referenced in a New Drug Application submitted to the US Food and Drug Administration.

Based on the results of the questionnaire, a site evaluation is conducted. The evaluation team will make recommendations and then develop and track an action plan for the contractor.

Source: Bristol Myers Squibb website (www.bms.com) (2006).

CASE EXAMPLE: OILSEED SUPPLY CHAIN IN BRAZIL

Founded in 1818 in Amsterdam, Bunge is a leading agribusiness and food company with integrated operations that circle the globe, stretching from the farm field to the retail shelf. Bunge in Brazil is the largest producer of oilseeds in the world. The company has created a supply chain that links Brazil's farmers to customers all over the world.

The trading departments of the company track the supply and demand of oilseeds and decide when to buy oilseeds, when and where to crush them and when and where to transport oil products to customers. Bunge charters about 100 ships and leases warehouses and oil mills all over the world. The flexible infrastructure allows the company to respond quickly to changes in customer requirements and also to cope with logistics problems. The company feeds supply and demand data to Brazil's farmers along with technical advice so that the farmers can plant the right kind of oilseeds. Bunge's sales grew by 235% between 1997 and 2004, from US$7.4 billion to US$25 billion.

Source: Khanna and Palepu (2006).

Supply chains in Russia

The supply chain management challenges in Russia can be illustrated by the 'Four Forces Globalization Framework', developed by Kouvelis and Niederhoff (2007). It is applied to describe the position of Russia in the global economy. The framework classifies the major factors and driving forces behind the globalisation process into four main types of force: global market forces, technology forces, global cost forces and political or macroeconomic forces.

The global market forces in Russia, according to Kouvelis and Niederhoff (2007), are characterised by three main themes:

- Demand growth.
- Changing competitive priorities in product markets.
- Openness towards international trade.

Following the liberalisation of the market after the collapse of the Soviet Union (so-called Glasnost and Perestroika), Russia's market growth can be explained by its GDP growth, which peaked at 8.1% in 2007. However, since 2014, sales dropped significantly as a result of the global financial crisis of 2008, the sanctions resulting from disputes with Ukraine, and more significantly, the drastic drop in oil prices. The economy contracted almost 8% after crude prices plunged to US$34 a barrel from US$147.

With the improvement of communication and transportation technology, customers all around the world have direct access to the latest products and technologies. This trend is noticed in Russia as well. Concerning R&D centres, especially high technology companies like Siemens, Intel, Nokia, Microsoft, Airbus and so on are present in the Russian market. Russia exported US$325 billion in 2007. Major export commodities are mineral fuels, mineral oils and products of their distillation, iron and steel, wood and articles of wood. However, in spite of the dramatic fall in the rouble exchange rate, Russian exports declined by 9% in 2014.

Technological forces have influenced global and especially Russian operations strategies. Three aspects are important here: technology knowledge, technology sharing and R&D facilities.

In 2008, Russia ranked third in the world for the number of scientists and technicians per capita. At this moment, a Master of Business Administration (MBA) boom is occurring in Russia. In 1999, the first business school that offered an MBA programme was founded, since then, more than 60 schools opened their doors for MBA training and around 5000 students graduate each year. Russia is still a major player in space exploration with a leading role in managing the engineering and technology of the International Space Station.

The US–Russian aerospace joint venture is also an example of technology sharing.

The availability of low-cost, high-quality engineers in Russia has been a major factor contributing to the location of R&D facilities there. Intel, Alcatel, IBM, HP and many others have been setting up R&D centres in Russia. In total, already over 4500 centres have been established. However, there are some negative factors, including the underdeveloped regulation of intellectual property (IP), the outflow of researchers and the obsolescence of their research equipment.

Multinationals have always expanded to countries with a comparative cost advantage in various inputs to the production process. With the rapid evolvement of technology, the accent has, however, shifted from direct labour costs to factors such as transportation, telecommunications and supplier infrastructure and government regulations. The Russian government has founded approximately 20 Special Economic Zones (SEZs) to stimulate the development of particular regions and industries. However, the benefits offered are not sufficient to attract investors. Russia's poor reputation on human rights and administrative inertia downplay the advantages offered by the zones. This is compounded by the political tension with Ukraine, the EU and the United States and the recession caused by the drop in oil prices. Therefore, it is not surprising to note that foreign firms are a rarity in the zones. Russia still has great potential to be a big player in the global supply chain.

CASE EXAMPLE: UKRAINE'S SUPPLY CHAIN DURING ITS CONFLICT WITH RUSSIA

Demonstrations by pro-Russian and anti-government groups took place in major cities across the eastern and southern regions of Ukraine from February 2014. During the first stage of the unrest, Crimea was annexed by the Russian Federation after a crisis in the region and an internationally criticised referendum. A ceasefire deal was struck on 12 February 2015 in Minsk by the leaders of Germany, France, Ukraine and Russia, but it is fragile. Protests in Donetsk and Luhansk continued during 2015 and escalated into a separatist insurgence. This conflict caused supply sanctions on Russia and created political and economic instability in Ukraine.

Although Ukraine is not a major oil producer, it is the key 'middle-man country' in Russian energy export. More than 70% of Russia's oil and gas flows to Europe through pipelines in Ukraine. On the metal front, for example, Boeing buys nearly a third of its titanium for its planes from Russia.

With these constraints and challenges, supply chain practitioners in Ukraine have responded several innovative actions, including the following:

- A procurement and supply chain 'war room' has been set up in Kyiv to closely follow and monitor supply chain activities in the region. This includes understanding the impact of potential military activity and supply sanctions on forecast demand and supply availability.

- The supply risk of commodities in the eastern region in particular is assessed and regularly updated. The assessment of products from major providers such as Redilinc, HICX and Sourcemap has helped organisations to visualise the impact of supply chain risks.
- Direct sourcing from local manufacturers and suppliers has been encouraged. Solutions from local manufacturers such as Directwork, Fullstep and Pool4Tool have the speed of local procurement.
- Options to mitigate the volatility of commodity supply have been evaluated with government support. This included the hedging options supported by technology providers such as Eka, Brady and Triple Point

Adapted from Williams (2014).

According to the World Bank (2022), the war in Ukraine in 2022 and sanctions on Russia damaged economies around the globe. Russia's economy plunged into a deep recession with output projected to contract by over 11% in 2022.

The economy in Europe and Central Asia was forecast to shrink by 4.1% in 2022, as the economic shocks from the war compounded the ongoing impacts of the Covid-19 pandemic.

Ukraine's economy is expected to shrink by an estimated 45.1% in 2022, although the magnitude of the contraction will depend on the duration and intensity of the war.

Summary

In this chapter, we have discussed the shift of products and service supply in the global market due to the emergence of stronger so-called second- and third-world economies. The supply strategy of established multinationals of the West and Japan and Korea has been remodelled by enhanced outsourcing to emerging markets and, at the same time, big organisations, particularly from China and India, have extended their supply base as global players. Organisations in Latin America and Eastern Europe are less dominant in the global market, but their local economies and infrastructure are benefiting from the expansion activities of multinationals. The changing role of Russia in the current economic and political climate has been reviewed. Russia will continue to be an emerging force in the global supply chain.

Both local organisations and multinationals are capitalising and adapting to the specific opportunities and challenges of emerging markets. These include the availability of both low-cost semi-skilled and highly skilled labour, expanding consumer demands, especially in China and India, developing transport and logistics infrastructure, the importance of execution and governance according to local regulations and market structures in developing countries. Khanna and Palepu (2006) suggest that the 'four-tiered' structure (see Figure 12.2) of markets in emerging economies helps local companies counter their multinational rivals.

At the apex of this pyramid structure is the 'global' tier where global customers want products of global quality with global features and are willing to pay global prices for them.

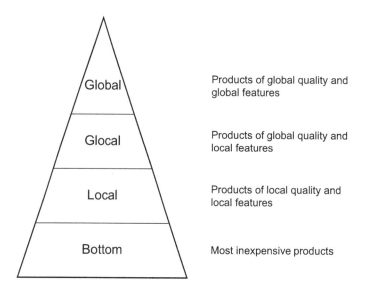

Figure 12.2 The four-tiered structure of emerging markets

The second tier is the 'glocal' segment where products are of global quality but with local features and prices are cheaper than those offered by developed countries. The customers in the third or 'local' tier are happy with products of local quality and at local prices. The 'bottom' tier of the market consists of consumers who can only afford to buy the most inexpensive products. The markets for talent and capital in developing countries are also roughly structured along the same 'four-tier' hierarchy. Multinationals typically compete in the 'global' tier, while smart local companies that dominate the 'local' and 'bottom' tiers move into the 'glocal' tier. However, some multinational corporations with a robust local representation (e.g. Hindustan Unilever in India) are also attempting to compete in lower tiers.

The contemporary challenges of nationalism, Brexit and the war in Ukraine have raised serious questions on globalisation and emerging markets in risk countries like Russia and China. It is likely that industries are seriously considering 'on-shoring' and 'friendly shoring' of supply wherever justifiable. 'On-shoring' will bring supply chains nearer and 'friendly shoring' will aim to swap risky foreign suppliers with close allies. However, it is important to note that whatever the challenges with globalisation, the tools and processes of global chain management underpinned by digital transformation can deliver more effective customer services.

Discussion questions

1. The most impressive growth in the last decade was in four of the biggest emerging economies: Brazil, Russia, India and China (BRIC). What are the new emerging countries (e.g. MINT)? Discuss the effect of new emerging countries on global supply chains.
2. With reference to two case examples of India in this chapter (viz. auto supply and seafoods), what is the difference in the role of second- and third-tier suppliers?
3. What are the specific changes McDonald's fast foods chain had to make for the Indian market?

4. Discuss the advantages of Unilever's strategy of 'self-help groups' to penetrate supply chains in rural India.
5. With the support of the Dangdang case example, discuss how quickly e-supply chains are developing in China.
6. Discuss how the present downturn in the Brazilian economy and other countries in Latin America (e.g. Mexico, Chile, Peru) may benefit global supply chains.
7. What are the current constraints causing a severe downturn in the Russian economy? Discuss a strategy for future growth in Russian GDP, albeit theoretical for political reasons.
8. Discuss, with appropriate examples, the new growth opportunities and supply chain challenges in the emerging markets of;
    • China
    • India
    • Latin America
9. In the HLL case study of rural supply chains, should HLL enter the informal sector in this way?

    What are the threats and opportunities of such a step?

    Should HLL roll out this business model?

    If the company rolls out this model, what do you think is needed in order to ensure success?
10. In 1997, Haier Group from China entered the market for wine coolers in the United States and captured 60% of that specialised segment by 2002. What was their strategy and why was it a success? Should Haier roll out this strategy for marketing larger refrigerators in the United States?

13 Digital revolution and e-supply chains

Introduction

There is no doubt that at the beginning of the 21st century, supply chain order fulfilment was the Achilles' heel of the e-business economy. At the beginning of every e-commerce, online trading and virtual supply chain there is a factory, a warehouse and transport. The Internet has elevated the performance of information accessibility, currency transactions and data accuracy, but the real effectiveness of a supply chain from the source to the customer could not be achieved without the efficient physical movement of goods and materials through the supply chain. Web-based software and e-marketplaces have increased the alternatives available to e-supply chain managers in all types of operations including service industries. More opportunities mean more options and complexity. Therefore, it is vital that a process is in place to monitor the performance of e-supply chains for both virtual and physical activities. A balanced scorecard approach to performance management is expected to ensure the sustainability of an e-business when it becomes a stable operation after the project stage.

Supply chain management of the 20th century with the maturing of the digital revolution is now e-Supply Chain Management of the 21st century.

Learning objectives

Learning objectives for this chapter are:

1. The digital revolution.
2. Digital hierarchy for e-supply chains.
3. e-Supply chain frameworks.
4. e-Supply chain processes.
5. e-Supply chain options.
6. e-Supply chain applications.
7. e-Supply chain learning points.

The digital revolution

The overall impact of the digital revolution on global supply chains was addressed in Chapter 4. In this chapter, we explore further how the e-supply chain has benefited from digital technology to transform the processes of supply chain management. The essence of the digital revolution was most succinctly captured by Negroponte (1995), who strongly associated the digital revolution with a shift away from an 'atom-based economy', and

DOI: 10.4324/9781003341352-16

towards one focused on the creation, manipulation, communication and storage of electronic binary digits or 'bits'. The 'atoms to bits' or 'analogue to digital' process of economic transformation highlighted by Negroponte unquestionably remains both a popular and powerful concept. For a decade or more, many forms of media production and distribution may have been heavily 'going digital', with e-banking, e-business, e-supply chains and personal digital communication also becoming mainstream. The 'First Digital Revolution' of the 1980s and 1990s is now coming to a close, and the 21st century heralds the dawn of a far more radical 'Second Digital Revolution' (Barnatt, 2001; UK Government Office of Science, 2014).

The two major technological developments that have catapulted digital technology to a customer-focused new generation of applications are cloud computing and Web 2.0 solutions.

Cloud computing is Internet-based computing that provides shared processing resources and data to computers and other devices on demand. It is a model for enabling ubiquitous, on-demand access to a shared pool of computing resources (e.g. networks, servers, storage, applications and services). It relies on sharing of resources to achieve economies of scale similar to a utility like the electricity grid over a network.

If Netscape was the standard bearer for Web 1.0, Google is most certainly the standard bearer for Web 2.0. A Web 2.0 site may allow users to interact and collaborate with each other in a social media dialogue in contrast to Web 1.0 sites where people were limited to the passive viewing of content. Examples of Web 2.0 include wikis, blogs, folksonomies, mashups, podcasting, hosted services and social networking sites.

Technology is rapidly changing the landscape of most consumer-orientated businesses in a fundamental way. Consumer buying habits and demand patterns are being significantly affected by high Internet penetration, ubiquitous access to information, rapidly growing social networks and the availability of smartphones and mobile devices.

With the present digital platform, digital supply chains can have the capability for extensive information availability and superior collaboration that result in improved reliability, agility and effectiveness (Capgemini, 2011).

In order to facilitate communications between software used by internal supply chain partners, multinational companies have tried hard, but generally unsuccessfully, to standardise computer systems. The emergence of the Internet protocol has helped the interaction between powerful supply chain systems such as i2, Manugistics, Ariba, Oracle and SAP/R3 to name a few. The rigour and problems related to the validation process still remain. Despite the complexity and regulatory requirements, or perhaps because of it, the healthcare industry remains a huge untapped market for e-supply chains. A recent study carried out in the United States by the Efficient Healthcare Consumer Response (EHCR) consortium showed that the healthcare industry could reduce its overall supply chain costs by over US$11 billion (48% of the current process cost) through the efficient application of collaborative e-supply chains.

Peter Drucker once said, 'Alliances are where the real growth is'. In the market-driven competitive world, businesses are continuously seeking new strategies and business models to excel. They strive to update the process and metrics used to measure and improve performance. The Internet is providing companies with both new challenges and potential solutions: the power of the Internet is revolutionising business culture. An area of significant impact is the collaborative supply chain.

The idea of a collaborative economy is not entirely new. Over the last 30 years, strategic collaborations and global sourcing have become familiar business strategies. Even during the 1970s and 1980s, multinational companies were setting up manufacturing sites to meet local demand and satisfy regulatory requirements. In terms of industrial relations, it was considered a high-risk strategy to focus on sourcing from a small number of sites. However, with gradual de-regulation and the improved manufacturing capabilities of developing markets, the strategy of global sourcing and third-party supply began to advance forwards. Perhaps the biggest transformation in the collaborative economy has been enabled by the Internet and improved reliability information systems. The visibility of real-time information, round-the-clock online trading and the gradual shift in power from suppliers to customers have accelerated this transformation.

CASE EXAMPLE: INTEL'S SMALL-STEP STRATEGY TO MOBILE TECHNOLOGY

Intel is the leading semiconductor chip maker in the world. At Intel, there is no lack of a sense of urgency; the company knows mobile technology is upending its market. The company has failed multiple times to become an important provider of mobile processors, including turning down the opportunity to provide chips for the original iPhone. Intel's culture has long been built around maintaining market dominance through intense internal competition. Now, Intel believes it needs a more collaborative culture to help it gain an edge in mobile processors. To start this cultural change, Intel's top 25 executives gathered for a strategy discussion. First, the group had to agree on the overall vision: the need for cultural change in order for Intel to compete effectively in the emerging mobile market. Then it had to create ways to bring people together. That would mean breaking down barriers to communication that existed in the company's culture of rivalry.

Among the steps Intel took to improve communications were adding 220 video conferencing rooms, electronic white boarding and search functions to its SharePoint implementation. All company employees are now on an internal social network. Intel has also set up teams based on accounts, not internal departments. Intel is taking small, concrete steps towards changing its culture, rather than massive, risky leaps. The small-step strategy is one many companies could adopt when trying to transform. As one survey respondent said, 'The kind of transformation being adopted does not give much leeway for failure and the cost to the organization's reputation and brand is great. A thoughtful and piloted approach needs to be adopted'. Small steps do not mean companies lack urgency.

Intel's competitive culture had to change to be successful in the future. In 2011, Intel introduced the first Pentium mobile processor and then Medfield – a processor for tablets and smartphones. Google's Android 2.3 uses Intel's Atom microprocessor.

Adapted from Fitzgerald et al. (2013).

Digital hierarchy for supply chains

One of the most common problems faced in the digital transformation journey is the temptation to implement digital initiatives in silos or through a technology-centric approach

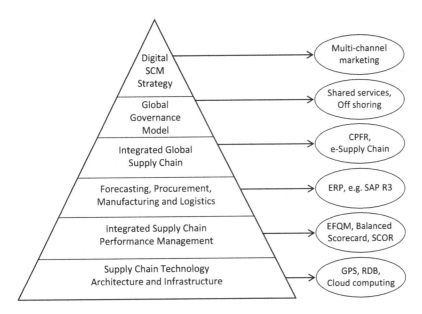

Figure 13.1 A digital hierarchy of e-supply chains

(Capgemini, 2011). The same holistic approach is applicable to the digital framework and hierarchy of supply chain solutions. Regardless of the scope of digital applications in any supply chain management environment, we suggest five transformation dimensions to be considered for the hierarchy of digital supply chain transformation as shown in Figure 13.1. The model in Figure 13.1 follows the principle of 'Anthony's Triangle' where the hierarchy of strategic, tactical and operational decisions are considered.

It is important that a digital supply chain strategy be an integral part of the overall corporate strategy of a company. This will avoid the competition for resources and also align supply chain solutions to related corporate initiatives such as multi–channel marketing. The identification of business benefits also requires top management inputs regarding currently perceived industry best practices.

The next dimension is a digital governance model that supports a flexible approach to the global opportunities of the supply chain. In order to realise the full potential of being a global organisation, companies must take a closer look into the internal alignment of procedures, service level agreements and transfer pricing schemes. This approach enables the sharing of data by cloud computing with outsourced and offshoring activities.

While the global governance model allows flexible data sharing, the global supply chain model is integrated with key suppliers and customers. For instance, demand forecasting and supply network planning require the integration of information and processes across big retailers (like Walmart, Tesco and Carrefour) and regional units. With the support of integrating systems like i2 and the Manugistics Collaborative Planning, Forecasting and Replenishment (CPFR) model, a holistic approach is taken to supply chain management that combines the intelligence of multiple trading partners in planning and fulfilling customer demand. If this is systematically done, it unlocks the hidden synergies in manufacturing and logistics networks alike.

It is important to integrate the different supply chain functions such as product development, procurement, production, maintenance and logistics across locations through an enterprise resource planning (ERP) system. An ERP system (such as SAP R3) is arguably the core digital supply chain engine in order to minimise 'waste' or non-value added activities such as double entry of data, the reconciliation of information from different sources or the correction of customer invoices. The main aim is to design end-to-end processes that give employees all the information they need for straight-through processing

The next dimension of the digital supply chain framework is integrated supply chain performance measurement based on the principles of balanced scorecard and supported by a data warehouse.

The digital supply chain framework is underpinned by the technology architecture. It is the design logic for business processes and IT infrastructure and reflects the integration and standardisation requirements of the organisation's operating model. Though many technology requirements may already be in place, the challenge is to select and implement digital technologies and integrated platforms that employ reusable and exchangeable components with minimal investment in time and effort. Using Web 2.0 technologies, every order or transaction can be traced in a digital operating model. Tagging technologies such as barcodes or RFID provide real-time data feeds for physical movements.

e-Supply chain management is a new dimension derived from the traditional supply chain management concept and developed as a result of the digital revolution.

Organisations need to design end-to-end processes in the e-supply chain that give employees all the information needed for straight-through processing of supply chain functions. The following section explores this new dimension and the opportunity of re-engineering the organisations' business processes towards stakeholders' cooperation enabled by the Internet.

e-Supply chain framework

As indicated in Chapter 1, the Internet-enabled integrated supply chain or e-supply chain has extended the linear flow of the supply chain to an ecosystem or a supply web (see Figure 1.4). It now includes all suppliers and customers to the end user or consumer suppliers' customers and customers' suppliers and so on. e-Supply chains and more broadly e-businesses have enhanced supply chain efficiency and effectiveness by sharing real-time information regarding forecasts, inventory, order status and other key information between partners. The process of e-supply chains is going through a rapid change through both technology and application. We will cover some of these opportunities and challenges under the following headings:

- e-Supply chain enabling technology
- e-Supply chain processes
- e-Supply chain options
- e-Supply chain applications (case examples)
- e-Supply chain learning points

e-Supply chain enabling technology

Adapting from Kulkarni (2001), we define three key components in the implementation of an e-supply chain:

1. Implementation of an ERP or enterprise resource planning (such as SAP R/3 and PeopleSoft) software in an organisation.
2. Adoption of collaborative planning and scheduling with critical suppliers and customers allowing effective sharing of forecasts and order status. This is also known as collaborative planning forecasting and replenishment (CPFR) and is supported by so-called global supply chain software (such as i2 and Manugistics).
3. Electronic linking of customer and supplier data using Internet technologies. This allows virtual communication between customers and suppliers anytime, anywhere.

The complex web and infrastructure of e-supply chains will be discussed in more detail in Chapter 20. Such complex elements are usually in the domain of an ICT (information and communication technology) specialist. In this section, we cover some basic technology enablers that are accessible to traditional users and stakeholders of supply chain management. These are electronic data exchange (EDI), Intranets, Extranets and B2B portals.

Electronic data exchange

EDI is computer-to-computer direct transfer of business data through electronic media between organisations and partners. It enables real-time information exchange between locations far apart and allows a significant reduction in lead time with accuracy of shared data. EDI is still the data format used by the vast majority of electronic commerce transactions in the world.

Intranets

Intranet is an Internet-linked network inside an organisation secured behind its 'firewalls'. Intranets help to share documents between employees only, with given password-controlled access, regardless of their geographic locations. Most companies have Intranet-based websites for internal use.

Extranets

According to Smith (2001), Extranets combine the privacy and security of Intranets with the global reach of the Internet, allowing access to external partners, suppliers and customers to a controlled section of the enterprise network, such as the ERP system.

CASE EXAMPLE: EXTRANET

Adaptec Inc is a US$1 billion microchip manufacturer supplying critical components to electronic equipment makers. The company, with its headquarters based in California, outsources the manufacturing tasks and concentrates on product research and development.

Before the introduction of the Extranet, Adaptec required 15 weeks to deliver products to customers. Some competitors were known to deliver similar chips within eight weeks. The longer delivery time was mainly caused by the need to coordinate design activities between the head office in California and the three manufacturing sites in Japan, Hong Kong and Taiwan. After the introduction of Extranet links between partners supported by enterprise-level supply chain integration software, communication with manufacturers in different zones became straightforward. Adaptec can send chip design diagrams and changes over the Extranet, enabling the manufacturer to prepare for product changes and new designs and lead times reduced below four weeks.

Source: PSG Institute of Management, Coimbatore, India (http://psgim.ac.in/).

Business-to-business (B2B) portals

With the Internet, it is easy for buyers and suppliers to meet, buy and sell across cyber marketplaces and collaborate more quickly than the traditional way. These are also known as B2B (business-to-business) and are classified under net marketplaces and private marketplaces. Net marketplaces are independently owned portals that bring numerous suppliers and buyers to cyberspace in a real-time environment. They could be either industry-orientated vertical marketplaces (e.g. metalsite.com) or product or service-orientated horizontal marketplaces (e.g. tradeout.com). A private marketplace is a trading hub in which membership is closed or by invitation or subscription only.

e-Supply chain processes

e-Supply chain processes conform broadly to the building blocks of a traditional supply chain plus a fundamental component, which is visibility. Visibility of information across the supply chain allows supply chain partners to automate some of their internal processes. For example, if a manufacturer knows the inventory level of the retailer, then the replenishment process can be automated by vendor-managed inventory (VMI) policy. This type of workflow automation within the supply chain forms the second characteristic of e-supply chain processes. Finally, a formal process of collaborative planning is required to harness greater efficiency and effectiveness from visibility and workflow automation. Figure 13.2 shows a framework of e-supply chain processes to complement the traditional supply chain building blocks.

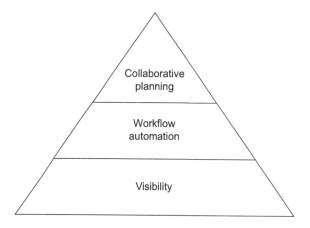

Figure 13.2 A framework of e-supply chain processes

Communication technologies such as the Internet and Web 2.0, information technology tools such as XML, Java and so on and information systems such as ERP have made the flow and accessibility of information seamless, visible and in real time. It is now possible to instantly trace an order placed with a retailer to the database of the original equipment manufacturer (OEM) and the intermediate suppliers can plan their activities to meet the requirements of the specific order.

The second characteristic of workflow automation uses automation tools to integrate the commonly occurring interactions between the stakeholders and companies of a supply chain. Some of the commonly deployed workflow automation applications include available to promise, VMI, electronic procurement and dynamic pricing. By harnessing the visibility within the supply chain and the automation applications, current ERP systems (such as SAP/R3) and supply chain management (SCM) systems (such as Manugistics) are enabling workflow automation requirements.

The core information system in supply chain management is ERP, which has been dominated by SAP R/3 since the mid-1990s. SAP R/3 is the former name of the ERP software produced by the German corporation SAP AG. The current successor software to SAP R/3 is known as SAP ERP. The latest version (SAP ERP 6.0) was made available in 2006. It is an enterprise-wide information system designed to coordinate all the resources, information and activities needed to complete business processes as shown in Figure 13.3.

As shown in Figure 13.3, core business processes including materials management, sales and distribution, production planning and quality management are provided by SAP R3 and, in addition, specific industry solutions modules can be added as required by customers. With the power of cloud computing and its hybrid SaaS (software as a service), the application SAP has become accessible to small and medium enterprises (SMEs) as illustrated in the case example of Oxford Bookstore in Chapter 19.

In spite of the great opportunities provided by supply chain visibility and workflow automation, the true potential of e-supply chains can only be realised when they are supported by an executive decision-making process that optimises the automated flow of materials based on the information available. This executive decision process of

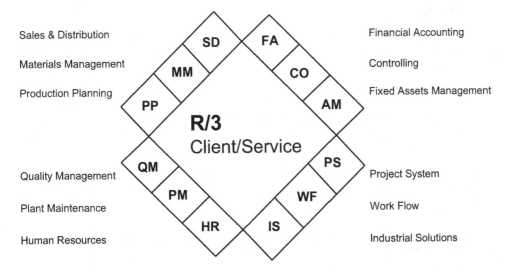

Figure 13.3 SAP R3 modules

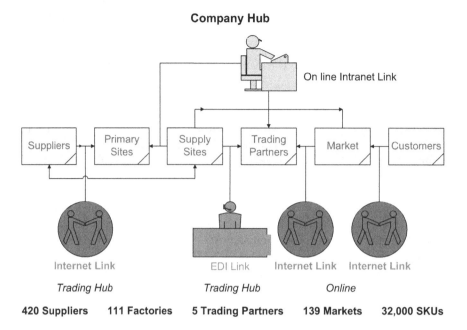

Company Hub

Figure 13.4 e-Supply chain network of a pharmaceutical company

collaborative planning can only be effective through a real-time communication network via connected intranet, extranet and B2B portals (or trading hubs) with a sales and operations planning process. Figure 13.4 show the e-supply chain communication network of a pharmaceutical company. The sales and operations planning process (S&OP) is described in Chapter 22. It is important that the key suppliers and partners are included in the S&OP meetings of the OEM.

e-Supply chain options

e-Supply chains are rapidly making inroads in all types of organisations and sooner or later most major players in supply chain management will voluntarily or involuntarily adopt e-supply chain management. It is a competitive advantage when all systems and infrastructure work as one and are not treated as just a substitute for the telephone. The fact is if you do not rapidly adapt to e-supply chains, you are likely to be left behind with the traditional ways of information exchange and your service will not be cost-effective and will be outmoded by new standards of performance. Table 13.1 shows the impact of the Internet on the cost per transaction in a bank.

Table 13.1 Transaction costs in banking

Channel	Cost per transaction (US$)
Branch	1.07
Telephone	0.54
Automated teller machine	0.27
Internet	0.01

Source: Booz, Allen and Hamilton (July 2006).

There is also the influence of big multinational companies that have implemented e-business networks with their suppliers and partners. According to Donavan (2004), a CEO of a large US conglomerate, 'all of our suppliers will supply us on [the] Internet or they won't do business with us'. There is little doubt that heavy emphasis and investment of resources have been deployed by larger organisations to implement sophisticated e-supply chains. Suppliers, regardless of size, should have received the message that the e-supply chain has arrived and is here to stay.

However, it is important to note that just throwing more software at the problem is not the answer to the core issues of supply chain management. Although software and web-based networks are needed, it is also necessary to define the process information flow at the right time and ensure accurate data in systems. Good supply chain managers know that information should be passed only to those who need to know and use it in the form they need to have it. The ambition and expectation of many so-called 'dot-com' companies ended in failure in the late 1990s, mainly because of not spending enough time on up-front strategy development. Basu and Wright (2004) expressed a cautionary note for all types of change management. 'Major, panic driven changes can destroy a company. A poorly planned change is worse than no change'.

In view of the above opportunities and challenges of the Internet-driven ICT revolution, we recommend that the following considerations should be included during the development of an e-supply chain strategy in any organisation:

1. It is evident that an e-supply chain strategy will be mostly driven and financed by large multisite and multinational companies. Only partial benefits will be achieved if the e-supply chain initiatives of larger companies focus solely on their own operations and sites and do not include key suppliers. Proactive policy should be in place in larger organisations to involve and train key partners in the development and implementation of an e-supply chain network.

2. Smaller organisations and suppliers should incorporate in their business strategy how to keep abreast with ICT technologies affecting their supply chains. It is important to cooperate fully with OEMs and larger customers in their e-supply chain programmes. Often relatively smaller companies may develop specialisation and expertise in specific operations or outsourced services (e.g. IT support) and they contribute a key link to the e-supply chain strategy.

3. Spending more time at the front end of e-strategy development for improving order-to-delivery cycles and supply chain management will pay dividends. The challenging aspect is to think through an e-supply chain strategy, network and appropriate infrastructure that will improve your performance ahead of your competitors. It is essential to design an appropriate roadmap and do it right first time.

4. The e-supply chain network and infrastructure should emphasise workflow automation and at the same time should accommodate some degree of flexibility to interface with non-automated suppliers. This consideration of system flexibility could be of particular importance for conducting business with emerging markets such as China and India.

5. It is paramount that before embarking on an e-supply chain programme, companies understand their supply chain priorities and the structure of Internet-enabled linkages with key suppliers and partners. The real benefits of an e-supply chain and the cost of implementing and maintaining it must be properly evaluated before taking a big leap into the e-supply chain.

The Traditional Supply Chain: Starts with Assets core competencies

The Customer-centric Supply Chain: Starts with Customers

Figure 13.5 Customer centricity in supply chains

6. It must be emphasised that the success of the systems in an e-supply chain will depend on the robustness and lean or agile characteristics of basic processes and the velocity of flow. Therefore, the re-engineering of the key business processes in the supply chain before the implementation of systems should be an essential part of an e-supply chain strategy.

7. Having understood the fundamentals of e-supply chains, it is also necessary to understand the emerging trends in supply chains that will impact the nature of future e-supply chains and consequently the e-supply chain strategy. Such trends include customer-centric supply chains (see Figure 13.5) and the outsourcing of supply chain activities. The customer-centric supply chain is basically a 'pull system' and is also branded as a demand-driven supply chain. Companies such as FedEx, UPS, DHL, TNT and InSite offer professional logistics and supply chain services customised to the user requirements. The trend of outsourcing logistics to third-party service providers (known as 3PLs) is fast gathering momentum. Outsourcing a major logistics contract is a strategic business decision and should also be part of an e-supply chain strategy.

e-Supply chain applications

Organisations today are faced with an incredible number of choices of web-based procurement applications, forward and reverse online auctions, vertical and horizontal marketplaces, global supply networking, collaborative planning and forecasting applications, electronic catalogues and so on. These and other applications comprise the e-supply chain applications that are in various stages of development today. Many companies are focused on buy-side order management applications (i.e. Ariba, Frictionless, CommerceOne) as the end-all solution to conducting business in the Internet economy. These buy-side procurement applications can help companies reduce costs by directing more spend to strategic suppliers enforcing standard product selections and reducing transaction costs and cycle times. However, the e-supply chain universe is much more than buy-side procurement applications. It is generally perceived that the e-business revolution is taking place mainly in the new environment created by a later generation of young 'dot-com' entrepreneurs. This is, of course, a partial view of e-commerce. The real changes are also happening quietly within 'traditional' or 'old economy' companies. This is a fast-changing area but one in which corporate stories of success and failure are beginning to emerge.

We have, therefore, chosen one case example of a small enterprise promoting e-procurement and three case examples to illustrate the application of e-supply chains in established businesses and to show that solutions are not only in buy-side procurement applications.

CASE EXAMPLE: E-LABSHOP FROM BIOTECH ANALYTICS UK

Biotech Analytics offers a biotech-dedicated portal that provides online resources for the biotechnology sector. Founded in 1997, Biotech Analytics is a member of the Bio-Industry Association, UK. Its services include the provision of FSA-regulated independent financial research and analysis of all UK biotechnology companies for investors.

Using Izodia In Trade business-to-business trading community software, Biotech Analytics has developed a customised online marketplace called e-labSHOP. It is designed to offer purchasers and suppliers of laboratory products a single resource that simplifies and streamlines the product search and ordering process. E-labSHOP integrates with suppliers' existing sales processes and purchasers can thus browse, order or transact via a single order point that is customised to their organisation's authorisation protocols.

Currently, Biotech Analytics is operating an e-labSHOP pilot. The participants include Teklab (ML) Limited, Scientific Systems Design Inc., Campsec Limited and a large government scientific research institution. Once live, e-labSHOP will make available online a broad range of biotech consumable products and services, and by using e-labSHOP biotechnology companies, research institutes and universities will be able to buy goods and services online.

The potential financial benefits for the users include:

1. For scientists:
   • Elimination of purchasing paper chains.
   • Electronic authorisation process.
   • Saving time by viewing catalogue information from multiple suppliers.
   • Reduction in errors.

2. For purchasing organisations:
   • Improved efficiency in the purchasing process.
   • Online internal accounts maintenance.
   • Multiple site organisations can collate purchasing power by aggregate orders.

3. For suppliers:
   • Receive aggregated orders and minimise administration costs for small orders.
   • Expand geographically without increasing the sales force.
   • Reduction in incoming erroneous orders.

4. For Biotech Analytics:
   • Licence fee from subscribers.

- Increase customer base.
- Market products to a highly specific scientific audience.

A business case for the Wolfson Institute

The application e-labSHOP at the Wolfson Institute is a good example of an e-procurement solution for scientists. With reasonable assumptions, and from the current data, it may be possible to justify a business case based on the productivity improvements. The Wolfson Institute for Biomedical Research was founded in 1995 as part of University College London. It is funded by many sources – the Wellcome Trust, MRC and industries. By 2002, the staff level reached about 250 and it has teaching facilities for 1200 medical students.

Current data:

Income	£10 million p.a.
External orders	360 p.a.
Number of lines	1090
Average value of order	£350
Error rate	13.5%
Transaction fee (e-lab)	5% of order value

Assumptions:

Loaded scientist cost	£50,000 p.a. = £25 per hour
Time to prepare and authorise an order	75 minutes
Time to order electronically	15 minutes
Document cost per order	£5
Error rate in e-procurement	3.5%

Calculations:

Average cost of a manual order: $25 \times 75/60 + 5 = £36.25$
Average cost of an electronic order: $25 \times 15/60 = £6.25$
Average saving per order: £30
Saving in ordering cost per year: $30 \times 360 = £10,800$ p.a.
Saving due to 10% reduction in error: $0.1 \times 360 \times 36.25 = £1305$ p.a.
Transaction charges @5%: $0.05 \times 350 \times 360 = (£6300)$ p.a.
Net savings per year: £5805 p.a.

Naturally, the costs and savings of an e-procurement initiative will vary according to the size and complexity of operations and the assumptions made to calculate them. In a large pharmaceutical organisation, the company may wish to develop their own e-procurement solution. The investment could include the software cost (£50,000+) and the implementation cost associated with the customisation of the software. In such an initiative, a traditional ROI approach is appropriate. However, for smaller organisations such as WIBR, it appears sensible to use systems such as e-labSHOP where functionalities have been tried, validated and implemented. Each organisation will avoid the investment cost and see their purchasing solution customised for them.

Source: Basu (2002).

CASE EXAMPLE: SAINSBURY'S E-SUPPLY CHAIN

The company

Sainsbury's opened its first grocery store in 1869 in London's West End. The business has grown to encompass over 400 'supermarket' stores, generating a turnover of over £12 billion. In a low-margin, fiercely competitive consumer market, Sainsbury's is still aiming for growth with a strategy of bringing the best products and excellent service to an increasing number of consumers. However, the company's market leadership has been threatened by the dominance of Tesco and the muscle of Walmart following their acquisition of Asda.

Drivers for the e-supply chain

The quality and perception of customer service is the key driver for the success or failure of a retail business. The visible aspects of customer service are demonstrated by the quality or freshness of produce sold, the choice available (for instance, vegetarian or organic choices) and, to a certain extent, the cost of items. The visible customer can only be as good as the invisible supply chain that supports it. The effectiveness of this supply chain is determined by the speed of response and availability of products. A further consideration is the cost of supporting the supply chain, including the stock holding rate.

During the 1990s, Sainsbury's adapted three detailed initiatives to improve the effectiveness of the supply chain:

- Centralisation of the supply chain.
- Centralisation of logistics management.
- Value chain initiative.

Sainsbury's wanted to apply a 'just-in-time' (JIT) supply chain enabling a continuous flow of products as and when the stores needed them. Under the old process, products were passed from group to group requiring several stops and this reduced responsiveness. There was a lack of ownership for the causes of delays, creating further difficulties. Following the centralisation of the supply chain under logistics management, half of the group focused on business processes and the other half was devoted to the development of IT systems.

The second initiative to satisfy the consumer is based on what is known as efficient consumer response (ECR). This aims to provide the retail consumer with the best quality service through collaborative supply chain operations. It relies on both the retailer's (viz. Sainsbury's) and the supplier's (e.g. Unilever) supply chain. Thus, the sharing of information between the systems of different partners within that chain is essential. ECR has been a philosophy put into practice within the retail market in Europe since the mid-1990s and Sainsbury's has embraced it. ECR encourages retailers and suppliers to share common data on promotion, demand planning and inventory levels. When this information sharing is feasible, significant savings can be made by optimising the order size and stock levels while at the same time improving the availability of products.

The value chain initiative (VCI) is an extension of the type of information sharing practised in ECR. It aims to improve end-to-end supply chain efficiencies from the sourcing of raw materials to the delivery of finished products to the consumer's hands. The goal of VCI is to link systems applications in a number of supply chain industries (e.g. distribution, import/export, warehousing) and share dynamic business information between new and existing trading partners. Sainsbury's is a proactive partner of VCI.

The above initiatives could not be effectively supported by traditional communication methods. 'We needed to look at further IT solutions that would enable the communication process to be effective', says John Rowe, Director of Logistics at Sainsbury's.

The e-supply chain solution

After evaluating several off-the-shelf applications, the IT team at Sainsbury's concluded that a business-to-business e-commerce system would have the potential to meet their requirements. They chose a solution called the 'EQOS Collaborator'.

The EQOS Collaborator was developed using Microsoft (MS) technology tools that allowed companies to publish information that could be viewed easily and downloaded into 'legacy' systems and back. The majority of companies, including Sainsbury's, standardised on Microsoft technology. The wide range of MS tools and available skills in the market was also an important factor.

The system was built on a Microsoft Windows NT server platform, by a Microsoft Internet Information Server and browsed by Microsoft Internet Explorer. The database is a Microsoft SQL server, but the information can be integrated into other legacy databases. The main program for displaying further applications is EQOS Administrator, which has been developed by using Microsoft Visual Basic and e-commerce functionality.

The EQOS Collaborator solution allows companies in the total value chain to automate and share-business information on a real-time basis among customers, suppliers, distributors and retailers.

Business benefits

The Internet-based information sharing and collaborations system (EQOS Collaborator) went live for Sainsbury's in 1998 and so far has demonstrated some significant business benefits.

A tangible advantage was achieved in the area of the forecasting of promotional uplift. The real-time information in the system exposed the fact that in some cases, suppliers had different expectations, but the data was visible before the start of the promotion and allowed Sainsbury's to go back to suppliers to agree revised dates and estimates.

The project enhanced the partnership with key suppliers. For example, Nestlé agreed to participate in the web-based collaboration system and invested heavily to ensure interfaces with their legacy systems. The EQOS collaborator enabled the realisation of an opportunity to synchronise dynamic supply chain information between suppliers and customers.

Another hidden plus point is the ability to pass on consumer comments to suppliers in an efficient manner. Previously, paperwork was complex and feedback was slow. Significantly, the EQOS system is now available to Sainsbury's suppliers for free.

'Sainsbury's has taken an important lead in shaping the way in and its suppliers can jointly benefit from developing collaborative information systems', comments Mike Quinn, Director of EQOS Systems Ltd.

EQOS is looking to build the Microsoft Commercial Internet Pipeline (CIP) technology into the solution. The CIP would enable a standard method of sharing any type of business-critical data using the Internet, e-mail or third-party virtual added networks (VANs). This solution would allow all 4000 of Sainsbury's suppliers to strive towards the ECR principles of integrated supply and demand.

Source: Basu (2002).

CASE EXAMPLE: GLAXOWELLCOME E-SUPPLY CHAIN

Long before the merger with SmithKline Beecham, GlaxoWellcome embarked upon their global supply chain project in 1996 and the use of e-business within the supply chain was in its infancy then. Following the integration between Glaxo and Wellcome, it was evident that the dominance of cash cows such as Zantac and Zovirax would soon be over. In the new level playing field environment, the supply chain network of GlaxoWellcome (GW) would have to deliver cost, speed, order fulfilment and reliability advantages to the company and its stakeholders including suppliers, trading partners, wholesalers and internal customers.

The worldwide manufacturing and supply division of the company set up a number of mutually complementary initiatives. Two such projects were most significant for the supply chain performance:

- Global Supply Chain supported by Manugistics software.
- International MRPII Programme supported by BPCS software.

The prime objective of the Global Supply Chain (GSC) was to enable forecasting, stock replenishment and visibility of real-time data among supply, sites trading partners and market sites. The International MRPII Programme (IMP) focused on ensuring S&OP and order fulfilment of individual sites.

The Global Supply Chain network of GlaxoWellcome comprised:

- Five primary sites (four in the UK and one in Singapore) for the manufacture of active ingredients.

- Ten FDA-approved secondary manufacturing sites in the United States and Europe.
- Two trading partners (Adecsa and Lapsa).
- Forty-one local supply and marketing sites.

At the early stage of the project, the trading partners were linked by EDI with the supply sites and most GW Sites were connected by e-mail. The global demand was aggregated and processed at the centre and simulations by Manugistics projected the stock status and replenishment requirements for all supply sites. With the progress of the programme, BPCS was replaced by SAP/R3 for FDA-approved sites and the ERP databases of local sites were interfaced with the Manugistics database. The global S&OP process enabled a regular review of demand, supply and inventory, and a stable process was established. The importance of internal market sites reaffirmed the B2B environment of the GW supply chain network. The company embarked upon web-enabled data exchange with key suppliers and smaller markets where the implementation of Manugistics and SAP/R3 was still a long way from reality. The process of an e-supply chain started to work in GW and the company began the measurement of key performance measures.

The initiative that underpinned the e-supply chain project was the development of a balanced scorecard on a data warehouse management system. The GW sites could access the data warehouse with appropriate password control and compare the site performance with other sites for a range of metrics related to customers, suppliers, quality, factory, cost, growth and innovation.

Source: Basu (2002).

CASE EXAMPLE: E-SUPPLY CHAIN AT HERMES ABRASIVES

Background

Hermes Schleifmittel (HS) GmbH is a leading manufacturer of abrasives, founded in 1927 with headquarters in Hamburg. Products include coated abrasives as well as bonded abrasives such as vitrified and resin-bonded products using aluminium oxide. Customers are from the metal working industry, the automotive industry and the glass manufacturing industry. Hermes abrasives tools are also used to produce aesthetically attractive surfaces and precision functional parts in ski industries. Registered and protected trademarks are Hermes, Hermesit, Sapphire Blue and webrax.

Problem

The market for HS is not of growth. The company was facing fresh logistical challenges with regard to an order processing system. The new opportunities in globalisation and e-businesses made it necessary for the company to re-engineer traditional supply chain strategy and structures. Within the framework of the global production network, a series of subsidiary units came within the scope of the new structure. There were already numerous internal customer–supplier relationships between individual sites without taking into account the external suppliers and customers. The complexity of an order event is characterised by the multi-level nature of the value chain as shown in Table 13.1.

Level of order processing	Order handling
Local order	The directly assigned site is the production site
Single-level composite order	The next assigned site is the production site
Two-level composite order	The next but one assigned site is the production site

Solution

HS defined the concept of the 'fractal company' as the creation of company units on the basis of the holistic and seamless view of the organisation. The core point of the change was to link sales and distribution to the production factories directly, without a production planning unit. The formal production planning unit became a strategic production planning responsible primarily for the definition of production sites and inter–company scheduling. The change was enabled by an ERP (SAP R/3) to form a holistic solution for the e-supply chain as shown in Figure 13.6.

The e-supply chain of the company comprised broadly five interlinked processes: source process, sell process, make process, deliver process and plan process.

Source process. Sourcing and acquisition were decentralised, that is, production units were responsible for all e-procurement activities.

Sell process. e-Commerce application was directly linked to the company's business information system and automatically performed by SAP R/3, the ERP system.

Make process. Orders were navigated automatically through all production sites following order allocation criteria shown in Table 13.1. Online displays of order status were also available for tracking orders.

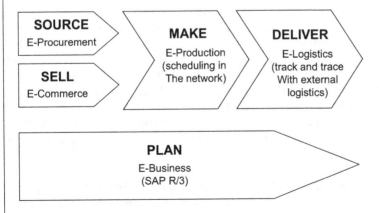

Figure 13.6 Hermes Abrasives e-supply chain

Delivery process. Customers and distributors had facilities to track orders via the Internet.

Plan process. The above four processes were underpinned by a plan process driven by SAP R/3. All network servers including SAP servers were operated initially under Windows NT, which were then updated to Windows XP. A total of 500 users worked on the e-supply chain network in European companies.

Results

The e-supply chain solution offered the company many intangible benefits including redesigning the business processes and better collaboration and trust between stakeholders and satisfied customers. A sample exercise two years after the start of the project also demonstrated some quantifiable benefits including:

- Increase productivity   +4%
- Delivery service within 24 hours   up to 98%
- Reduction in lead time   −40%
- Reduction in despatch complaints   −60%

Source: www.hermesabrasives.com/.

e-Supply chain learning points

The initial optimism that first e-movers would rapidly establish 'new economy' brands has proved unfounded. Nonetheless, the recent and chequered history of e-businesses has provided sufficient learning experience and data to develop a strategy for e-business.

Strategy for e-business

- *Continuous review.* Reviewing the impact of e-business in transforming business land-scapes, we conclude that we need to keep a close track of its progress and use the old rule of 'measurement is the driver'. Technology is changing rapidly, and we do not have any one-stop solution providers. It is equally important to manage technology, processes and people's culture. This must be borne in mind when developing models for measuring e-business initiatives and processes.
- *Weaker links.* Relative late-comers to e-business have not 'missed the bus', but they must take advantage of this powerful enabling technology. Smaller companies may not be enthusiastic to join the e-supply chain of larger organisations, perceiving that the benefits of automation may accrue to larger business partners and not to smaller companies. Appropriate tools for measurement are needed to optimise this open opportunity and bigger players should be proactive in sharing the cost of implementation.

Growth in e-business. e-Commerce will be a growth area, with Gartner predicting that while its pace will accelerate rapidly, it may be five to ten years before expectations are realised. While the initial hype that B2C e-business will replace traditional sales has been dispelled, it is true that e-business will enhance rather than replace existing revenue-generating activities. In the United States, this has been achieved by product-focused websites.

- *Electronic global network.* Internet-enabling technology has made it possible to link up with both suppliers and customers who did not already share ERP and SCM systems. The e-supply chain will become an acceptable process in both manufacturing and service industries, and ICT managers will be able to take advantage of the collaborative supply chain.
- *Knowledge sharing.* Traditional knowledge management will continue to support both Internet- and Intranet-based e-learning, and indeed all industries are investing in e-Knowledge Management Initiative. With the inclusion of e-Human Resources, Enterprise Directory and the Intranet, this combined B2E channel will form the largest segment of e-business in which e-supply chains will also be inclusive.
- *Future trends.* The share of wireless internet users is also set to rise, and interest in the adoption of this new technology is high in most industries. However, the technology is challenging and limited, and the telecommunications industry faces an additional problem currently in the difficulty of raising capital. The security of data, which is an area of major concern when a company considers joining an e-supply chain, will continue to be an area of detailed attention. New security measures like 'encryption' will emerge to protect data so that members of e-supply chains can only have access to data that is relevant to them.

Summary

In this chapter, we have described the impact of Internet-driven global information and communication systems in enhancing the management of supply chain processes. The Internet should be viewed as being complementary to traditional ways of competing in business. The e-supply chain as part of e-business is a vital, durable and enduring technology essential for transforming business and business efficiency, a powerful enabling tool that can be harnessed and utilised in almost any business. We have also suggested strategies, preferably led by larger organisations, on how to take advantage of new technology in the expansion of globalised markets and emerging sources. These strategies should be assessed in light of the learning points from the recent and chequered history of e-businesses.

> Ubiquitous information availability is at the core of digital supply chains. With the right organizational design and governance, they can enable superior collaboration and communication across digital platforms resulting in improved reliability, agility and effectiveness. This performance difference will force organizations with traditional supply chains to adapt to the new digital realities or run the risk of falling behind competition.
>
> (Capgemini, 2011).

It is to be noted, as we have emphasised in S&OP in Chapter 17, the technology, systems and processes of e-supply chains (such as CPFR) cannot be effective without human involvement and management and the support of a proven review process such as S&OP.

Discussion questions

1. Discuss how the digital revolution, especially with the impact of Web 2.0 and cloud computing technology, is transforming the best practices of global supply chains.
2. Explain with a diagram the levels of 'digital hierarchy' in e-supply chains. Discuss how the understanding of 'digital hierarchy' can help the strategies and governance of global supply chain management.
3. What are the key components of an e-supply chain framework? Discuss how an ERP system (e.g. SAP R/3) can improve the performance of e-supply chain processes.
4. With reference to case examples in this chapter, what are the success factors for implementing an e-supply chain in a global organisation? What are the learning points from the case examples?
5. Discuss the cost benefits of digital transformation in a global supply chain organisation.

14 Lean and agile supply chains

Introduction

With real-time access to the Internet and search engines like Google, as well as increased global competition, customers have more power than ever before. They demand innovative product features, greater speed, more product variety, dependable performance and quality at a best-in-class and competitive price. Furthermore, today's discerning consumers expect the fulfilment of demand almost instantly. The risk attached to traditional forecast-driven lengthy supply lines has become untenable for consumer products. In this chapter, we discuss how to take up this challenge through a lean and/or agile supply chain. As we discussed in Chapter 3, a distinction is often drawn between the philosophy of leanness and agility. Like the perennial business phrase 'quality', with both 'leanness' and 'agility', there appear to be differing opinions as to what is meant or intended.

In their 'pure' form, three models of supply chain can be identified: traditional, lean and agile.

Traditional supply chains are known for:

The protection of the market and aims for leadership.
Forecast driven.
A higher emphasis on customer service than cost.
Inventory held to buffer fluctuations in demand and lead times.

Lean supply chain characteristics are:

Integration upstream with suppliers.
Integration downstream with customers.
High emphasis on efficiency.
Aims for minimum stock holding.
Suitable for high volume low variety products.

Agile characteristics are noted for flexibility and speed in coping with innovative products and unpredictable demand.

Suitable for low volume high variety products.
Rapid response to market demand.

DOI: 10.4324/9781003341352-17

With the additional challenges of globalisation and competitiveness, global organisations are now more focused towards lean and agile supply chain principles. Although many supply chains will be a hybrid of models, it is important to understand the differences and applications of each model, and application whether pure or hybrid. The traditional supply chain model has been covered in various chapters of this book; this chapter will primarily cover lean and agile models.

Learning objectives

Learning objectives for this chapter are:

1. The origin of lean.
2. The tools of a lean supply chain.
3. The characteristics of a lean supply chain.
4. The characteristics of an agile supply chain.
5. The strategy of a lean and agile supply chain.

The origin of lean

As with all facets of the quality movement, the origin of lean enterprises is in manufacturing. Lean enterprise philosophy, and make no mistake, lean is more than a system it is a philosophy that began with Japanese automobile manufacturing in the 1960s and was popularised by Womack, Jones and Roos (1990) in 'The Machine that Changed the World' (1990). 'The Machine that Changed the World' is essentially the story of the Toyota way of manufacturing automobiles. Up until then, the manufacturing of automobiles had changed very little since Henry Ford in 1913 adapted the conveyor belt for manufacturing cars. Prior to Henry Ford's assembly line, the automobile had been a luxury item handmade by a group of workers in a stationary workplace. Ford's conveyor belt (the assembly line) approach was for production to take place on a moving belt with each worker doing a small, specialised task. Ford believed that if each step of production was broken down to the smallest element that 'the stupidest man could become a specialist in two days'. With this moving conveyor belt approach, Ford was able to produce 250,000 cars a year, which sold at US$500 each. The car from being a luxury item that only the rich could afford now became in effect a consumer item within the reach of most families. The downside was the minute division of labour and the cyclical nature of the work, and the inexorable pace of the moving conveyor belt. Workers lost a sense of the purpose of what they were doing, they could not see that they were building cars, they saw a repetitive mindless task such as putting bolts on a component as it moved past them.

> The assembly line is no place to work, I can tell you. There is nothing more discouraging than having a barrel beside you with 10,000 bolts in it and using them all up. Then you get another 10,000 bolts and you know that every one of those bolts has to be picked up and put in exactly the same place as the last 10,000 bolts.
>
> (Walker and Guest, 1952)

Chrysler and General Motors and other manufacturers soon adopted the assembly line approach, but whereas Ford only had one model (the model 'T'), the others began offering several models in the 1920s. Ford had to follow suit and to do so had to cease production for seven months while new models were rushed into production. The assembly line approach was still used and models were made in batches. Changing a model required set-up time for a change of dies and so on. Work at each stage of production was still broken down to the lowest level, workers were not expected to think and there was a heavy reliance on inspection and testing to maintain a standard of finished product. The next major change in car manufacturing is credited to Ohno Taiichi of Toyota. Ohno Taiichi, after visiting US car manufacturers in the 1960s, returned to Japan and developed a new method of manufacturing, which became known as lean production.

Womack and Jones (1998) introduced the five principles of lean thinking based on the Toyota Production System. The first principle, known as 'Value', indicates what creates value from the customer's point of view. The second principle, 'The Value Stream', is to determine the necessary steps to design, order and produce the product through the whole value stream eliminating non-value added activities. The third principle is 'Flow' to ensure that all actions that create value flow without any interruptions. The next is 'Pull', which requires the production process pulled by the end customer. The fifth principle is 'Perfection' to optimise the maximum value by continuously removing waste. Lean manufacturing is seen as the endless pursuit of eliminating waste or 'muda'. Liker (2004) in 'The Toyota Way' shows 14 principles, including the five principles of Womack and Jones (1998).

Lean manufacturing, sometimes referred to as Toyotaism or the Toyota Production System, is that materials flow 'like water' from the supplier through the production process onto the customer with little if any stock of raw materials or components in warehouses, no buffer stocks of materials and part-finished goods between stages of the manufacturing process and no output stock of finished goods. This 'just-in-time' (JIT) approach requires that materials arrive from dedicated suppliers on the factory floor at the right stage of production just when required, and when the production process is completed, it is shipped directly to the customer. With no spare or safety stock in the system, there is no room for error. Scheduling of activities and resources has to be exact, communication with suppliers must be precise, suppliers have to be reliable and able to perform to exacting timetables, materials have to arrive on time and meet specifications, machines have to be maintained so that there is no downtime, operators cannot make mistakes, there is no allowance for scrap or rework and finally the finished product has to be delivered on time to customers. This is often implemented by circulating cards or Kanban between a workstation and the downstream buffer. The workstation must have a card before it can start an operation. It can pick raw materials out of its upstream (or input) buffer, perform the operation, attach the card to the finished part and put it into the downstream (or output) buffer. The card is circulated back to the upstream to signal the next upstream workstation to do the next cycle. The number of cards circulating determines the total buffer size. Kanban control ensures that parts are made only in response to a demand.

This 'just-in-time' approach generally precludes large batch production; instead, items are made in 'batches' of one. This means that operators have to be flexible, the system has to be flexible and 'single minute exchange of dies' (SMED) becomes the norm. A lean approach reduces the number of supervisors and quality inspectors. The operators are trained to know the production standards required and are authorised to take corrective action, in short, they become their own inspectors/supervisors. The principles of total productive maintenance (TPM) and 5Ss are followed and, as a result, the equipment becomes more reliable and the operator develops 'ownership' towards the equipment.

Another important aspect of the Toyota approach was to expand the work done at each stage of production. For example, a team of workers will be responsible for a stage of production or 'Work Cell' on the moving assembly line, such as installing the transmission or installing the seats. Each team is responsible for its part of the assembly and might be able to make minor changes to procedures within the confines of a time limit (the time allowed on the moving line for production to move from one stage to the next) and within the limits of the specified standards (for example, the team can change the order of assembly at their workstation but would not have the authority to add extra nuts). Quality standards are assured with the application of Zero Quality Control or Quality at Source before the actual production and Poka Yoke (mistake proofing) during a production process.

A visitor to a lean manufacturer will be struck by the lack of materials; there is no warehouse, no stocks of materials between workstations and no stocks of finished goods. At first glance, this suggests that lean is an inventory system. But lean is not just an inventory system, Lean also means the elimination of 'muda'. Muda is a Japanese word, which means waste, with waste being defined as any human activity that absorbs resources but creates no value. Thus, the philosophy of lean is the elimination of non-value-adding activities. The rough rule is the elimination of any activity that does not add value to the final product, and the taking of action so that the non-value activity never again occurs.

Before anything can be eliminated it first has to be identified. The Toyota approach to identifying areas of waste is to classify waste into seven 'mudas'.

The seven 'mudas' are as follows:

* Excess production
* Waiting
* Movement or transportation
* Unnecessary motion
* Non-essential process
* Inventory
* Defects

The 'seven mudas' are basically an extension and refinement of the components of industrial process charts comprising operation, transport, inspection, delay and storage. The approach is to identify waste, find the cause, eliminate the cause, make improvements and standardise (until further improvements are found).

The tools of lean supply chains

The original Toyota model of lean manufacturing, from which various hybrids were developed, comprised eight tools and approaches:

1. TPM
2. 5Ss: These represent a set of Japanese words for excellent housekeeping (Sein – Sort, Seiton – Set in place, Seiso – Shine, Seiketso – Standardise, and Sitsuke – Sustain)
3. JIT
4. SMED
5. Jidoka or Zero Quality Control
6. Production

7. Kanban
8. Poka Yoke

The methodology of lean thinking and lean supply chain has moved on since Toyota's lean manufacturing model and embraced additional tools and approaches. We have, therefore, included two more:

9. Value stream and process mapping
10. Lean Sigma and FIT SIGMA

There are many other tools and techniques that can be found in 'Implementing Six Sigma and Lean' (Basu, 2011).

GLOSSARY OF LEAN TOOLS

A brief description of frequently used tools and approaches in lean supply chains is given below. For further details please see:

- 'Implementing Quality' (Basu, 2004)
- 'Quality Beyond Six Sigma' (Basu and Wright, 2003)

TPM. In TPM, operators are enlisted in the design, selection, correction and maintenance of equipment so that every machine or process is always able to perform its required tasks without interrupting or slowing down defect-free production.

Five Ss. The five rules of good housekeeping: sort, set in place, shine, standardise and sustain.

JIT is an inventory strategy implemented to improve the return on investment of a business by reducing in-process inventory and its associated costs.

SMED. Operator techniques pioneered by Shigeo Shingo, a Japanese industrial engineer, that result in changeovers of production machinery in less than ten minutes.

Zero Quality Control (Jidoka). The transfer of human intelligence to automated machinery so that machines are able to stop, start, load and unload automatically, detect when a defective part has been produced, stop themselves and signal for help. This means operators are freed up to do value-adding work. (The practitioners of the Japanese martial art Judo are called Judoka. Six Sigma also adopted terms like Black Belt and Green Belt from Japanese martial arts.)

Production work cells. At Toyota, the work done at each stage of production was expanded, so that a team of workers is responsible for a stage of production and has the power to be able to make minor changes to procedures within the confines of a time limit and standards. The autonomy of operators is in direct contrast to Ford's production line drones. Lending power to the workers, so they could take corrective action, meant that there was less need for inspectors to stop mistakes.

Kanban. Kanban cards ensure that parts are only made in response to demand – each workstation must have a card before it can start an operation.

Mistake proofing (Poka Yoke). A procedure that prevents defects or malfunction during manufacture by, for example, eliminating choices that lead to incorrect actions; stopping a process if an error is made; prevent machine damage.

Value stream and process mapping. Process mapping is a tool to represent a process by a diagram containing a series of linked tasks or activities that produce an output. Value stream mapping is a high-level process mapping to show the total operation or business and identify 'mudas'.

Takt Time is the pace of production needed to meet customer demand. It is the average rate at which customers buy products and hence the rate at which products should be manufactured. It is expressed in time units – one every so many minutes or so many minutes between completions.

$$\text{Takt Time} = \frac{\text{Available Work Time}}{\text{Customer Demand}}$$

Lean Sigma and FIT SIGMA. Lean Sigma incorporates the principles of JIT and now relates to the supply chain from supplier and supplier's supplier, through the process to the customer and the customer's customer. FIT SIGMA incorporates all the advantages and tools of total quality management (TQM), Six Sigma and Lean Sigma. The aim is to get an organisation healthy (fit) by using appropriate tools for the size and nature of the business (fitness for purpose) and to sustain a level of fitness.

The characteristics of lean supply chains

The characteristics and tenets of a lean supply chain are derived from the principles of TPS and the methodology of Lean Sigma. Womack and Jones (1998) proposed five lean principles based on TPS, viz. value, value stream, flow, pull and perfection. However, the application of lean principles has moved with time and the experience of organisations in both manufacturing and service sectors. Until recently, supply chains were understood primarily in terms of planning demand forecasts, upstream collaboration with suppliers and planning and scheduling resources. Emphasis perhaps is shifted to provide what the customers want at a best-in-class cost. Cost reduction is often the key driver for lean, but it is also about speed of delivery and quality of products and service. The competition for gaining and retaining customers and market share is between supply chains rather than other functions of companies. A supply chain, therefore, has to be lean with four inter-related key characteristics or objectives that are the updated five principles of TPS with customer service as the given value of supply chain management:

1. Elimination of waste.
2. Smooth operation flow.
3. High level of efficiency.
4. Quality assurance.

Elimination of waste

The lean methodology as laid out by Womack and Jones (1998) is sharply focused on the identification and elimination of 'mudas' or waste and their first two principles (i.e. Value and Value Stream) are centred around the elimination of waste. Their motto has been, 'banish waste and create wealth in your organisation'. It starts with value stream mapping to identify value and then identifying waste with process mapping of valued processes and then systematically eliminating them. This emphasis on waste elimination has probably made lean synonymous with the absence of waste. Waste reduction is often a good place to start in the overall effort to create a lean supply chain because it can often be done with little or no capital investment.

One popular area of waste in processes is excess inventory. Many organisations started to measure their 'leanness' only in terms of inventory performance. Inventory reduction attempts to reduce inventory through such practices as enterprise resource planning, JIT and modern approaches to supply chain management have led to lower inventory levels, but there is still plenty of room for improvement. In fact, most manufacturers carry at least 25% more inventory than they have to. The techniques of inventory management and reduction have been covered in Chapter 8. This inventory-centred approach seems to be encouraged by 'Leanness Studies' by Schonberger (2003). In these annual study reports, Schonberger measured the trends in inventory turnover (annual cost of goods divided by the value of inventory) and then graded and ranked the companies according to inventory performance. This approach is a good indicator of the inventory policy of a company but it does not necessarily reflect the business performance of the company. For example, the inventory policy of an FMCG (fast-moving consumer goods) company is different from that of a pharmaceutical company. Inventory is only one of the seven 'mudas'.

Cycle time or lead time reduction is another target area of waste reduction. Cycle time is the time required to complete a given process. The cycle time required to process a customer order might start with the customer's phone call and end with the order being shipped. The overall process is made up of many subprocesses such as order entry, assembly, inspection, packaging and shipping. Cycle time reduction is identifying and implementing more efficient ways of completing the operation. Reducing cycle time requires eliminating or reducing non-value-added activity. Examples of non-value-added activity in which cycle time can be reduced or eliminated include repair due to defects, machine set-up, inspection, waiting for approval, test and schedule delays. There are a few formal and publicised methodologies for cycle time reduction including quick response manufacturing (QRM: Suri, 1998) and SMED (Shingo, 1988). QRM is underpinned by two key principles. First, plan to operate at 80% or even 70% capacity of critical resources. Second, measure the reduction of lead times and make this the main performance measure. These principles are supported by material requirements planning (MRP) plans for production-oriented cells and continuous training. The SMED method involves the reduction of production changeover by extensive work study of the changeover process and identifying the 'in-process' and 'out-of-process' activities and then systematically improving the planning, tooling and operations of the changeover process (see Figure 14.1). Shingo believes in looking for simple solutions rather than relying on technology. With due respect to the success of the SMED method, it is fair to point out that the basic principles are fundamentally the application of classical industrial engineering or work study.

The reduction of cycle time has become an important feature of lean thinking beyond manufacturing industries where approaches other than QRM and SMED are applied. In service industries such as call centres, there has extensive application of value analysis around process mapping charts. The flow production technique (Ballard, 2001) is applied in reducing cycle time in the construction of repetitive residential homes. The technique comprises: (1) overlap activities within their phase of the work, (2) reduce activity

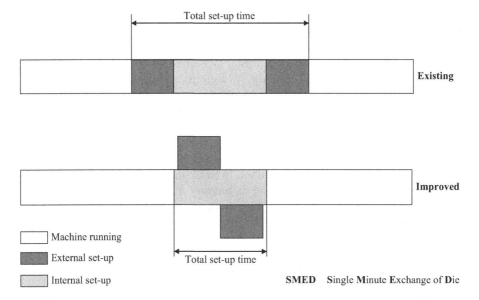

Figure 14.1 Set-up time reduction

durations through cycle time studies and (3) reduce work–in–process through the development of multiskilled workers. Cycle time reduction is also an important area of Lean Sigma projects as illustrated by the following case example.

CASE EXAMPLE: CYCLE TIME REDUCTION

Platinum catalyst is used for the production of an active pharmaceutical ingredient (API) in an Eastern European pharmaceutical company (henceforth referred to as 'company'). Used catalyst is sent back to the supplier who recovers platinum and uses it for the production of fresh catalysts. During that cycle, a certain quantity of catalyst evanesces, and a new quantity has to be purchased periodically to maintain the required levels of inventory. The catalyst is expensive because of the platinum and the related cost of capital for the required catalyst inventory is significant. A task team led by a Six Sigma Black Belt was formed to reduce the cycle time of procuring the platinum catalyst.

Catalyst inventory required for normal production of the API depends on catalyst consumption in production and catalyst regeneration cycle time. The time required for the cycle of regeneration of the catalyst (platinum recovery and new catalyst production) was about three months. During that period, it was necessary to have enough catalyst in possession for normal production. Since significant improvements in the production of the API were already achieved in reducing catalyst consumption, the scope of the project included only activities related to the reduction of regeneration cycle time.

For the monitored period, the mean regeneration times depending on the supplier varied between 77 days and 69 days (year 2003), and during year 2004, values were marginally better than the year before. During year 2004, significantly better results were also achieved for the transport time and the average transport time of five days ± two days was acceptable.

Transport time had relatively less influence on overall cycle time. It was important to minimise mistake opportunities during transport. This was assured by proper planning (sales, production, purchasing and distribution), regular communication (all interested parties) and using only reliable and proven carriers and forwarders. In addition, all transport details were carefully specified and agreed upon, transport of the catalyst always had high priority (because of the high value of shipment) and the company always had proper information about shipment status during the transport.

The biggest influence on overall cycle time was the regeneration of the catalyst. This was clearly the supplier's responsibility, and the company could not directly influence that process. The regeneration time specified in the contract between the company and each supplier was ten weeks for one major supplier and 11 weeks for another for year 2004.

After brainstorming, the team identified only two possible solutions:

* Ask each approved supplier to prepare an offer for year 2005 with a maximum regeneration time of eight weeks.
* Find and develop a new supplier for the catalyst who can fulfil the request.

Although the company developed four new suppliers for the platinum catalyst, only two of them were reliable and another two could not achieve the required quality each time. Another problem was that the specification for the catalyst was quite general and earlier analysis could not properly represent the regulated quality of the catalyst. Consequently, the development of approved new suppliers took a long time. The minimum regeneration time achieved in the past was eight weeks and six days, and because of that, the team decided to ask each of the qualified suppliers to regenerate the catalyst within eight weeks and the team prepared a negotiation strategy for that.

To test suppliers' ability to fulfil new requirements, the company asked each supplier to deliver their next shipments of regenerated catalyst by the end of year 2004 within nine weeks instead of 11 (including transport). One of the approved suppliers answered positively but asked for some adjustments in the packaging of spent catalyst that did not require additional cost. That allowed the company not to buy a new quantity of 1000 kg of fresh platinum catalyst and generated a saving of US$20,000 in the last three months of the year 2004.

Negotiations with key suppliers for the platinum catalyst finished successfully and resulted in new contracts where the maximum regeneration time was eight weeks. A new contract with one of them was signed in February 2005, and with another one on March 2005.

The new contract with the supplier was a powerful tool for sustaining new agreed platinum catalyst regeneration performance and performance in year 2005 was better than promised. All involved in platinum catalyst handling were educated on the standard operating procedure.

With these improvements, cycle time was reduced by 30% and the inventory of the catalyst was reduced from 7728 kg to 4500 kg. The overall annual savings related to the avoidance of the cost of capital needed for buying a new quantity of catalyst was US$408,615 per annum.

Smooth operational flow

The well-publicised JIT approach is a key driver of the lean supply chain and, as we indicated earlier, it requires materials and products to flow 'like water' from the supplier through the production process onto the customer. The capacity bottlenecks are eliminated, the process times of workstations are balanced and there are little buffer inventories between operations. Smooth operation flow requires the application of appropriate approaches. Three of the most frequently applied approaches are:

* Cellular manufacturing
* Kanban pull system
* Theory of constraints

In the cellular manufacturing concept, the traditional batch production area is transformed into flow line layouts so that ideally a single piece flows through the line at any time. In practice, an optimum batch size is calculated starting with the most critical work centres and the largest inventory carrying costs. Action is taken for improvement at the work centres and methods that have the greatest impact on the throughput, customer satisfaction, operating cost and inventory carrying charges. Good management consists of avoiding a wide variety of products. The cellular manufacturing concept is most appropriate when demand is predictable and products have low variety and high volume.

The Toyota Motor Company of Japan pioneered the Kanban technique in the 1980s. As part of lean manufacturing concepts, Kanban was promoted as one of the primary tools of JIT concepts by both Tauchi Ohno (1988) and Shingo (1988). Inspired by this technique, American supermarkets in particular replenished shelves as they were emptied and thus reduced the number of storage spaces and inventory levels. With a varying degree of success outside Japan, Kanban has been applied to maintain an orderly flow of goods, materials and information throughout the entire operation.

Kanban literally means 'card'. It is usually a printed card in a transparent plastic cover that contains specific information regarding part number and quantity. It is a means of pulling parts and products through the manufacturing or logistics sequence as needed. It is therefore sometimes referred to as the 'pull system'. The variants of the Kanban system utilise other markers such as light, electronic signals, voice commands or even hand signals.

Following the Japanese examples, Kanban is accepted as a way of maximising continuous flow and efficiency by reducing both cost and inventory.

The key components of a Kanban system are:

* Kanban cards.
* Standard containers or bins.

- Workstations, usually a machine or a worktable.
- Input and output areas.

The input and output areas exist side by side for each workstation on the shop floor. The Kanban cards are attached to standard containers. These cards are used to withdraw additional parts from the preceding workstation to replace the ones that are used. When a full container reaches the last downstream workstation, the card is switched to an empty container. This empty container and the card are then sent to the first workstation, signalling that more parts are needed for its operation.

A Kanban system may use either a single card or a two cards (move and production) system. The dual card system works well in a high up-time process for simpler products with well-trained operators. A single card system is more appropriate in a batch process with a higher changeover time and has the advantage of being simpler to operate. The single card system is also known as 'Withdrawal Kanban' and the dual card system is sometimes called 'Production Kanban'.

The system has been modified in many applications and in some facilities, although it is known as a Kanban system, the card itself does not exist. In some cases, the empty position on the input or output areas is sufficient to indicate that the next container is needed.

CASE EXAMPLE: KANBAN PULL SYSTEM

The following example is based on the experience of Level Industrial, the Brazilian subsidiary of Unilever in Sao Paulo.

Lever Industrial was engaged in the batch production of industrial detergents comprising nearly 300 stock-keeping units, which varied from a 500 kg draw to a 200 g bottle. After carrying out a Pareto analysis, the team selected three fast-moving products for a pilot Kanban system. These products in total accounted for 18% of output.

The company adopted a simple single card Kanban system for each product consisting of five stages as shown in Figure 14.2.

Both the planning board and the scheduling board contain three cards each as a buffer between the variability of production cycle time and the availability of materials.

When the card arrives from the despatch (Stage 5), it is kept on the planning board and planning for the product starts. When the planning board is full of three cards, the third card is passed to the scheduling board and production scheduling is ensured. Similarly, when the scheduling board is full, the third card is transferred to the pallet at Production Station 1 and actual production begins.

When the pallet in Stage 3 (Production 1) is full, the card then moves to the next station (Production 2) in Stage 4, and then on to despatch in Stage 5. After the goods are despatched, the card returns to the planning board and the next cycle begins.

The pilot exercise was successful. It achieved an improvement in customer service, which rose from 84% to an excellent 98% and inventory was also reduced. The Kanban system was extended to nine additional key products. The manual system

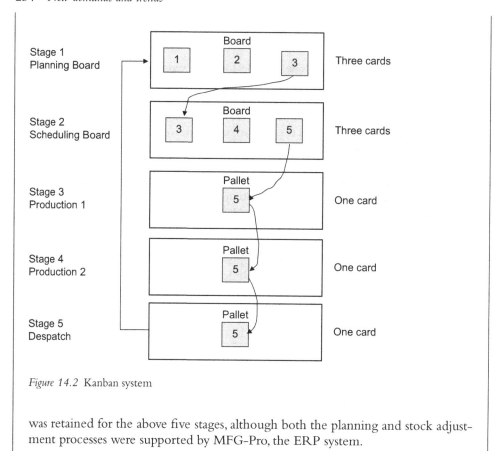

Figure 14.2 Kanban system

was retained for the above five stages, although both the planning and stock adjustment processes were supported by MFG-Pro, the ERP system.

The theory of constraints (TOC) is a management philosophy developed by Goldratt (1992). It enables the managers of a system to achieve more of the goal that the system is designed to produce. The concept of the objective is not new. However, in service operations where it is often difficult to quantify the capacity constraint, TOC could be very useful. For companies that employ skilled workers and for many service organisations the constraint is often the time of one or a few key employees. The key steps in this process are:

1. *Identify.* The first step in applying TOC is to identify the constraining or bottleneck factor.
2. *Exploit.* Determine the throughput per unit of the constraining factor.
3. *Subordinate.* Prevent the resources needed from waiting in a queue at a non-constrained resource.
4. *Elevate.* If still cannot produce enough products to produce demand, find ways to increase capacity.
5. Go back to Step 1.

Implementation of TOC, although simple in principle, is often difficult because it may require a complete change in the way a company operates. For example, TOC requires a shift from cost-based decision making to decision making based on continuous improvement.

The smooth operation flow of materials and products are further enhanced by Lean Sigma methodology where the variances within processes and between workstations are minimised by the statistical techniques of statistical process control (see Basu, 2009: pp. 159–165).

High level of efficiency

The more popular concepts of lean operations tend to be the concepts of muda, flow and the pull system. A preliminary analysis of all these methods, as we have described earlier, however, highlights the fact that all assume sufficient machine availability exists as a prerequisite. In our experience, for many companies attempting a lean transformation, this assumption is not true. Machine availability depends on maximising the machine's up-time by eliminating the root causes of downtime. The ratio of up-time and planned operation time is the efficiency of the operation. Therefore, in order to make lean concepts work, it is vital that the pre-condition of running the operations at a high level of efficiency should be met. The old approach of measuring labour efficiency (e.g. the ratio of standard hours and hours worked) has now shifted to the efficiency of the efficiency of the control or bottleneck workstation.

There are many methodologies and tools of ensuring a high level of efficiency in a lean supply chain. We are going to describe one such methodology (viz. TPM) and two such tools (e.g. overall equipment effectiveness (OEE) and 5Ss).

TPM is a proven Japanese approach to maximising overall equipment effectiveness and utilisation and relies on attention to detail in all aspects of manufacturing. TPM includes the operators looking after their own maintenance and thus encourages empowerment. The use of the word 'maintenance' in the title is misleading. Total productive maintenance includes more than maintenance, it addresses all aspects of manufacturing. The two primary goals of TPM are to develop optimal conditions for the factory through a self-help people/machine system culture and improve the overall quality of the workplace. It involves every employee in the factory. Implementation requires several years, and success relies on sustained management commitment. TPM is promoted throughout the world by the Japan Institute of Plant Maintenance (JIPM).

TPM is the manufacturing arm of TQM and is based on five key principles:

1. The improvement of manufacturing efficiency by the elimination of six big losses.
2. The establishment of a system of autonomous maintenance by operators working in small groups.
3. An effective planned maintenance system by expert engineers.
4. A training system for increasing the skill and knowledge level of all permanent employees.
5. A system of maintenance prevention where engineers work closely with suppliers to specify and design equipment that requires less maintenance.

TPM requires the manufacturing team to improve asset utilisation and manufacturing costs through the systematic study and elimination of the major obstacles to efficiency. In TPM, these are called the 'six big losses' and are attributed to (i) breakdown, (ii) set-up and adjustment, (iii) minor stoppages, (iv) reduced speed, (v) quality defects and (vi) start-up and shut-down.

The process of autonomous maintenance is to encourage operators to care for their equipment by performing daily checks, cleaning, lubrication, adjustments, size changes, simple repairs and the early detection of abnormalities. It is a step-by-step approach to bring the equipment at least to its original condition.

Some managers may hold the belief that in TPM 'you do not need experienced craftsmen or engineers and all maintenance is done by operators'. This is not true. The implementation of a maintenance policy with appropriate infrastructure is fundamental to planned maintenance. Planned maintenance is the foundation stone of TPM. However, if the skill and education levels of operators are high, then a good proportion of planned maintenance activities should be executed by operators after proper training. Cleaning, lubrication and minor adjustments together with an ability to recognise when a machine is not functioning correctly should be the minimum required of operators.

For TPM to succeed, a structural training programme must be undertaken in parallel with the stages of TPM implementation. In addition, 'one point lessons' can be used to fill in a specific knowledge gap. This uses a chart that is displayed at the workplace and describes a single piece of equipment and its setting or repair method.

While great progress can be made in reducing breakdowns with autonomous maintenance and planned maintenance, 'zero breakdowns' can only be achieved by the specification of parts and equipment that are designed to give full functionality and not to fail. All engineers and designers of the user company should work concurrently with the suppliers of equipment to achieve a system of maintenance prevention.

Although there is a special emphasis on input by different employees to different aspects of TPM (e.g. 'six big losses' for middle management, 'autonomous maintenance' for operators, 'planned maintenance' for middle management, 'maintenance prevention' for senior management), TPM involves all employees and total involvement is ensured by establishing TPM work groups or committees. Figure 14.3 illustrates an example of a TPM organisation.

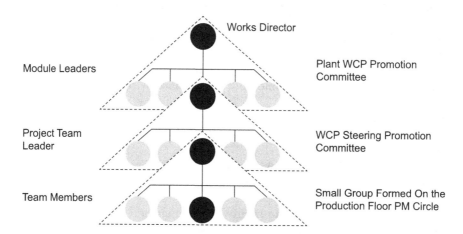

Figure 14.3 TPM organisation

To summarise, TPM is a factory-wide continuous improvement programme with particular emphasis on changing the culture of the shop floor through improved attitudes and skills. TPM progress is measured by the stages of autonomous maintenance completed, and visible progress is also seen in the higher reliability of equipment, reduction of waste and improvements in safety statistics.

CASE EXAMPLE: TOTAL PRODUCTIVE MAINTENANCE AT NIPPON LEVER, JAPAN

Background

The Utsunomiya plant in Japan was commissioned in 1991 on a greenfield site by Nippon Lever to manufacture household detergent products and plastic bottles for liquid detergents. The factory was experiencing 'teething' problems primarily due to the poor reliability and lack of local support for the imported equipment. Many of the employees were new to factory work.

To improve this situation, the company used the help of JIPM, an organisation working on TPM with over 800 companies in Japan. TPM has been widely used in Japan, having been developed to support lean/JIT and TQM. It was considered to be appropriate for the Utsunomiya plant. TPM focuses on machine performance and concentrates on operator training and teamwork.

Approach

A TPM programme was launched at the Utsunomiya plant in July 1992 with the objective of zero losses:

* Zero stoppages.
* Zero quality defects.
* Zero waste in materials and manpower.

Strong organisational support was provided by the Nippon Lever management in terms of:

* A top management steering team to facilitate implementation by removing obstacles.
* A manager to work full time supporting the programme.
* One shift per week set aside for TPM work.
* Training for managers, leaders and operators involving JIPM video training material.

The programme launch was initiated at a 'kick-off' ceremony in the presence of the whole Nippon Lever Board and managers from other company and suppliers' sites.

Implementation

The initial thrust of the programme was the implementation of 'autonomous maintenance' following JIPM's seven steps:

1. Initial clean-up.
2. Elimination of contamination.
3. Standard setting for operators.
4. Skill development for inspection.
5. Autonomous inspection.
6. Orderliness and tidiness.
7. All-out autonomous working.

To implement the seven steps, 'model machines' (those giving the biggest problems) were chosen. This approach helps to develop operators' knowledge of a machine and ensures that work on the model can be used as the standard for work on other machines. It also helps motivation in that if the worst machine moves to the highest efficiency, this sets the tone for the rest of the process.

The improvements to the machines were made using Kaizen methodology (small incremental improvements) and were carried out by groups of operators under their own guidance. Two means of support were given to operators – a Kaizen budget per line so that small repairs and capital expenses could be agreed upon without delay and the external JIPM facilitator provided encouragement and experience to workgroups.

Results and learning points

By the end of 1993, substantial benefits were achieved within a year at the Utsunomiya plant including:

- A £2.8 million reduction in operating costs.
- Reduced need for expensive third-party bottles.
- Production efficiency increased from 54% to 64% for high-speed soap lines and from 63% to 80% for liquid filling lines.
- A team of trained, motivated and empowered operators capable of carrying out running maintenance.

The success of the programme at the Utsunomiya plant led to the introduction of TPM to other two factories of Nippon Liver (Shimizu and Sagamihara). Over the next few years, the corporate groups of Unilever encouraged all sites outside Japan to implement TPM with remarkable successes achieved, particularly in factories in Indonesia, Brazil, Chile, the UK and Germany.

Tools and techniques used

OEE, 5Ss, Five Why, Kaizen, SMED.

Source: Leading Manufacturing Practices, Unilever Research and Engineering Division (1994).

OEE is an index of measuring the delivered performance of a plant or equipment based on good output.

The method of monitoring OEE is devised in such a way that it highlights the losses and deficiencies incurred during the operation of the plant and identifies the opportunities for improvement.

There are many ways to calculate OEE (see Shirose, 1992 and Hartman, 1991). In this section, we describe the methodology of OEE that was developed and applied by Ron Basu in both Unilever[1] and GlaxoWellcome.[2]

OEE is defined by the following formula:

$$OEE\ \% = \frac{Actual\ Good\ Output}{Specified\ Output} \times 100$$

where Specified Output = Specified Speed × Operation Time

The application of OEE has been extensive, especially when driven by TPM programmes to critical plants and equipment. It can be applied to a single piece of equipment, a packing line, a production plant or processes. In order to appreciate the usefulness of OEE, it is important to understand equipment time analysis as shown in Figure 14.4 and described below.

Total Time defines the maximum time within a reporting period, such as 52 weeks a year, 24 hours a day, and 8760 hours in a year.

Available Time is the time during which the machine or equipment could be operated within the limits of national or local statutes, regulations or conventions.

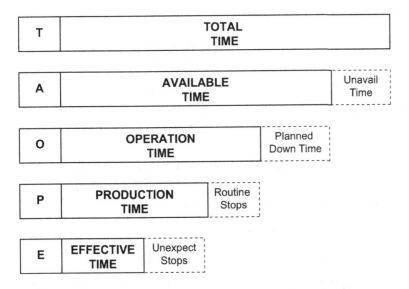

Figure 14.4 Equipment time analysis

Operation Time is the time during which the machine or equipment is planned to run for production purposes. The operational time is normally the shift hours.

Production Time is the maximum time during which the machine or equipment could be expected to be operated productively after adjusting the operation time for routine stoppages such as changeover and meal breaks.

Effective Time is the time needed to produce a 'good output delivered' if the machine or equipment is working at its Specified Speed for a defined period. It includes no allowances for interruptions or any other time losses.

It is important to note that Effective Time is not recorded, it is calculated from the Specified Speed as

Effective Time = Good Output/Specified Speed

where Specified Speed is the optimum speed of a machine or equipment for a particular product without any allowances for loss of efficiency. It is expressed as quantity per unit such as tonnes per hour, bottles per minute, cases per hour or litres per minute.

In addition to OEE, two other indices are commonly used as shown below:

$$\text{Production Efficiency}\,(\%) = \frac{\text{Effective Time}\,(E)}{\text{Production Time}\,(P)} \times 100$$

$$\text{Operational Utilisation}\,(\%) = \frac{\text{Operation Time}\,(O)}{\text{Total Time}\,(T)} \times 100$$

A properly designed and administered OEE scheme offers a broad range of benefits and a comprehensive manufacturing performance system. Some of its key benefits are as follows:

- It provides information for shortening lead time and changeover time and a foundation for SMED.
- It provides essential and reliable data for capacity planning and scheduling.
- It identifies the 'six big losses' of TPM, leading to a sustainable improvement of plant reliability.
- It provides information for improving asset utilisation and thus reduced capital and depreciation costs in the longer term

---

CASE EXAMPLE: OEE OF ACMA SOAP WRAPPING MACHINE

Consider the production data of a toilet soap packing line where the control station governing the specified speed is an ACMA 711 wrapping machine.

Week number:	31
Operation Time:	128 hours
Specified Speed:	150 tablets per minute
Good Output:	4232 cases
Routine Stoppages:	11 hours 30 minutes
Unexpected Stoppages:	27 hours 15 minutes

Given that each case contains 144 tablets:

Good Output $= 4232 \times 144 = 609,408$ tablets

$$\text{Effective Time} = \frac{Good\ Output}{Specified\ Speed} = \frac{609,408}{150 \times 60} = 67.71 \text{ hours}$$

Production Time = Operation Time − Routine Stoppages

$$= 128 - 11.5 = 116.5 \text{ hours}$$

Total Time $= 7 \times 24 = 168$ hours

$$\text{OEE} = \frac{Effective\ Time}{duction\ Time} = \frac{67.71}{128} = 0.53 = 53\%$$

$$\text{Production Efficiency} = \frac{Effective\ Time}{duction\ Time} = \frac{67.71}{116.5} = 58\%$$

$$\text{Operation Utilisation} = \frac{Operation\ Time}{Total\ Time} = \frac{128}{168} = 76\%$$

It is important to note that the Effective Time was calculated and not derived from the recorded stoppages. There will be an amount of unrecorded time (also known as Time Adjustment) as, in the example, given by:

$$\text{Unrecorded Time} = (\text{Production Time} - \text{Unexpected Stoppages}) - \text{Effective Time}$$

$$= (116.5 \quad 27.25) - 67.71$$

$$= 21.54 \text{ hours}$$

Five S is a tool for improving the housekeeping of an operation, developed in Japan, where the 5Ss represent five Japanese words all beginning with 's':

- Seiri (organisation). Separate what is essential from what is not.
- Seiton (neatness). Sort and arrange the required items in an orderly manner and in a clearly marked space.
- Seiso (cleaning). Keep the workstation and the surrounding area clean and tidy.
- Seiketson (standardisation). Clean the equipment according to laid down standards.
- Shitsuke (discipline). Follow the established procedure.

In order to retain the name 'Five S', a number of English language versions have evolved. These include:

- Seiri: sort
- Seitor: set in order/stabilise
- Seiso: shine
- Seiketsu: standardise
- Shitsuki: sustain

The Five S method is a structured sequential programme to improve workplace organisation and standardisation. Five S improves the safety, efficiency and orderliness of the process and establishes a sense of ownership within the team.

Five S is used in organisations engaged in Lean Sigma, JIT, TPM and TQM. This principle is widely applicable not just for the shop floor, but for the office too. As an additional bonus, there are benefits to be found in environmental and safety factors due to the resulting reduced clutter. Quality is improved by better organisation and productivity is increased due to the decreased time spent searching for the right tool or material at the workstation. Consider the basic principle of a parent tidying a small child's room that is overflowing with clutter and sorting together various types of toys. The end product should be a neater, warmer, brighter and more civilised play environment that will encourage the child to utilise all toys and equipment more productively because all relevant pieces are together, space is enhanced and mess is reduced.

It is useful to note that the quality gurus of Japan like numbered lists, for example, the Seven Mudas, the Five Whys and the Five Ss. However, the exact number of Ss is less important than observing the simple doctrine of achieving the elimination of waste.

As the Five S programme focuses on attaining visual order and visual control, it is also a key component of visual factory management. As Five S is primarily a visual process, a good example of promoting its message would be to display pictures of a workplace with photographs showing both 'before' and 'after' depictions of the implementation of Five S.

CASE EXAMPLE: FIVE S AT NORTHROP GRUMMAN INC. USA

Northrop Grumman Corporation is a global defence company headquartered in Los Angeles that provides technologically advanced products, services and solutions in systems integration, defence electronics, advanced aircraft and space technology.

Northrop Grumman first deployed Five S on a part delivery process. The work area assembled a variety of components into a single product.

Before Five S, the area was not well organised, and the process was inefficient. With Five S implementations, the area saw a huge 93% reduction in the space employees travel to complete tasks as well as a 42% reduction in the overall floor space and a 20% improvement in operational efficiency.

The system has become a one-piece flow operation between assembly and mechanics, enabling everyone involved to know what the station has and what it needs.

Source: Skinner (2001).

Quality assurance

Womack and Jones (1998) propose perfection as the fifth lean principle, and according to this, a lean manufacturer sets his/her targets for perfection in an incremental (Kaizen) path. The idea of TQM is to systematically and continuously remove the root causes of poor quality from the production processes so that the organisation as a whole and its products are moving towards perfection. This relentless pursuit of the perfect is a key attitude of an organisation that is 'going for lean'.

The incremental path to total quality management progressively moves from earlier stages of quality control and quality assurance. Quality assurance focuses on the prevention of failures or defects in a process by analysing the root causes and sustaining the improved process by documenting the standard operating procedure and continuous training. TQM is quality assurance of all processes across the organisation involving everyone from the top manager to a trainee. Therefore, the central driver towards perfection is quality assurance.

This drive for quality assurance has now been extended beyond TQM to Six Sigma with additional rigour in training deployment (e.g. Black Belts and Green Belts), the methodology of DMAIC (e.g. define, measure, analyse, improve and control) and measurement (both variances and savings). The principles of Six Sigma are embedded in the path towards perfection in a lean supply chain and Six Sigma has now moved to Lean Sigma and FIT SIGMA. Basu and Wright (2003) explain that the predictable Six Sigma precisions combined with the speed and agility of lean produces definitive solutions for better, faster and cheaper business processes. Through the systematic identification and eradication of non-value-added activities, optimum value flow is achieved, cycle times are reduced and defects are eliminated. The dramatic bottom-line results and extensive training deployment of Six Sigma and Lean Sigma must be sustained with additional features for securing the longer-term competitive advantage of a company.

CASE EXAMPLE: LEAN SUPPLY CHAIN AT SEAGATE, USA

Background

Seagate Technology is the world's largest manufacturer of disc drives and HDD recording media. With its headquarters in Scotts Valley, California, the company employs 62,000 people and its turnover in 2000 exceeded US$7 billion. The business operates in a market environment of short product life cycles and quick ramp-up to high volume. The data storage market is growing by 10–20% per year and the technology content doubles every 12 months. Volume products remain in production for only six to nine months.

Approach

In 1998, Seagate's senior executive team was concerned that business performance was not on par with expectations and capabilities. The quality group was charged with recommending a new model or system with which to run the business. The Six Sigma methodology was selected and launched in 1998 to bring common tools, processes, language and statistical methodologies to Seagate as a means to design and develop robust products and processes. Six Sigma helps Seagate make data-based decisions that maximise customer and shareholder value, thus improving quality and customer satisfaction while providing bottom-line savings.

Six Sigma was one of the three key activities seen as essential for Seagate's continuing prosperity. The other two were:

- Supply chain – how to respond to demand changes promptly, execute commitments and provide flexibility to customers.
- Core teams – how to manage product development from research to volume manufacture.

Implementation

Seagate Springtown (which is part of Seagate Recording) started a supply chain project to improve materials management and develop a strategic vendor relationship. The fabrication plan at Springtown introduced the lean manufacturing philosophy that recognises WASTE as the primary driver of cycle time and product cost. Very soon, a change had taken place at Springtown and lean manufacturing was wholly integrated with the supply chain initiative.

The corporate office at Scotts Valley was rolling out a global Six Sigma deployment programme. The Springtown site followed the Six Sigma training programme and implemented a number of tools and techniques including the process map, sampling plan, cause and effect analysis and control plans, which identified a 'hidden factory'. The less visible defects of this 'hidden factory' included:

- Repeated measurements (in and out).
- Repeated chains (post and pre).
- Transits between manufacturing areas.
- Process steps conducted in 'non-standard operating conditions'.
- High rework on a process.

Results and learning points

The Six Sigma methodology proved a key enabler for supply chain /lean manufacturing and the integrated programme achieved improved process capability and quality as shown by:

- Increased throughput by 31%.
- Significant impact on capital expenditure due to increased efficiency of:
- Existing equipment.
- Lower work-in-progress.
- An 80% pass rate on qualifications for vacuum tools (previously 40%).

The main learning points from the Six Sigma programme at Seagate Technology were as follows:

1. Companies using Six Sigma need to learn how to use metrics to manage – to make appropriate decisions on a holistic basis, avoiding sub-optimisation. This task of integration with the whole of the company's business process is the key.

2. Set aggressive goals – don't make them too easy.
3. Develop a system for tracking 'soft savings'.
4. Develop a common language and encourage its use on a widespread basis early in the programme.
5. Embed the business process within the organisation by training all functions – use Green Belt, Black Belt and customised programmes as appropriate.

Source: Basu (2009: p. 277)

The Toyota Production System is frequently modelled as a house with two pillars. One pillar represents JIT, and the other pillar is the concept of jidoka. Jidoka is 'automation with a human touch'. This is usually illustrated with an example of a machine that will detect a problem and stop production automatically rather than continue to run and produce bad output. The jidoka principle contributes to the achievement of both high efficiency and sustainable quality assurance.

The JIT principle was first used by Sakichi Toyoda at the beginning of the 20th century when he invented a loom that stopped when the thread broke. Jidoka comprises a four-step process that engages when abnormalities occur.

1. Detect the abnormality.
2. Stop.
3. Fix or correct the immediate condition.
4. Investigate the root cause and install a countermeasure.

The first two steps can be mechanised or automated. The Poka Yoke method also allows a process to detect a problem and stop. Ultimately, it is about transferring human intelligence to machines to eradicate the problem.

The characteristics of an agile supply chain

Christopher (2000) defines agility as achieving a rapid response on a global scale to constantly changing markets. The rapid response needs to cover changes in demand for both volume and variety. A third dimension is lead times and how long it takes to replenish the goods in order to satisfy demand.

Agility is achieved by flexibility and in order to achieve flexibility, standard platforms are postponed and components and modules are final assembled when the demand for volume and variety are known. The standardised components and modules enable the minimum stock keeping of finished products while at the same time the late assembly makes mass customisation possible with short lead times. Buffer capacity is maintained in order to satisfy the fluctuation of demand. The above-described agile set-up demands that the full global supply chain is involved. The subassembly of components into modules can be done in a low-cost environment, whereas the final assembly will often be done close to demand in order to localise the product. Christopher suggests four characteristics of a truly agile supply chain: (1) market sensitive and capable of reading and responding to real demand; (2) virtual – information based rather than inventory based; (3) process integration ensuring collaborative working between buyers and suppliers; and (4) network committed to closer and responsive relationships with customers.

Fisher (1997) offers a similar view on agile and a responsive supply chain based on predictable demand versus unpredictable, but also with the product component of functional versus innovative products. Functional products are like staples that can be bought at grocers and petrol stations to satisfy basic needs and have a predictable demand with a long lifecycle and low profit margin. Innovative products on the other hand are like state-of-the-art MP4 players or fashion clothes having a short lifecycle, with higher profit margins but with very unpredictable demand. These distinctions are exemplified as the product life cycle for functional products is typically more than two years, but for innovative products, it can be from three months to one year. The margin of error for forecasting functional products is in the 10% range, but for innovative products, it varies from 40% to 100%. Based on the short lifecycle and the unpredictable demand and forecasting, innovative products need an agile supply chain. An agile supply chain is achieved by buffer capacity and buffer stocks.

Fischer further argues that it is critical that the right supply chain strategy is chosen in order to match the demand and the product so that innovative products with a high margin are channelled through a responsive supply chain. The cost of the buffers in capacity and inventory will be offset by a higher margin and the lower number of goods needed to be sold. The agile supply chain is achieved, according to Fischer, by adopting four rules: (1) accept that uncertainty is inherent in innovative products; (2) reduce uncertainty by finding data that can support better forecasting; (3) avoid uncertainty by cutting lead times, increasing flexibility to produce to order or move manufacturing closer to demand; and (4) hedge against uncertainty with buffer inventory and excess capacity.

Yusuf et al. (2003) claim that there are four pivotal objectives of agile manufacturing as part of an agile supply chain. These objectives are (1) customer enrichment ahead of competitors, (2) achieving mass customisation at the cost of mass production, mastering change, (3) mastering change and uncertainty through routinely adaptable structures and (4) leveraging the impact of people across enterprises through information technology. This list clearly shows that enhanced responsiveness is a major capability of an agile supply chain.

In congruence with our research and experience, we summarise that in order to achieve the responsiveness required for innovative products, an agile supply chain should contain the following key characteristics:

1. Flexibility
2. Market sensitivity
3. A virtual network
4. Postponement
5. Selected lean supply chain principles

Flexibility is a key characteristic of an agile supply chain. Flexibility in manufacturing is the ability to respond quickly to the variations of manufacturing requirements in product volume, product variety and the supply chain. The variability in volume is demonstrated by product launching, seasonal demand, substitution and promotional activities. The changes in variety relate to the increased number of stock-keeping units (SKUs) in new products, distributors' own brands (DOB) and so on. The variations in the supply chain result from the variability of lead times of both suppliers and customers, increased service level, change in order size and so on. There were instances of failures during the 1980s where companies invested in sophisticated flexible manufacturing systems (FMS) in pursuit of flexibility. At the other end of the scale, all the attention was given to organisational flexibility (e.g. cultural and skills integration between craftsmen and operators), producing limited success. By recognising a closer link between agile processes, there is a huge interest in the service sector in how to optimise the benefits of agile processes for a faster response to customer demand. In order to improve flexibility in a supply chain, it is crucial to reduce complexity in product specifications to maximise mass customisation, reduce complexity in processes by standardising them and enhance organisation flexibility through multi-skilling and seamless working practices.

Market sensitivity means that the supply chain is capable of responding to real demand. This requires demand planning not to be driven by periodically adjusted annual forecasts but by actual customer requirements. The scheduling of operations will be reverse scheduling based on customer orders rather than forward scheduling based on forecasts. In addition to actual customer order, the use of information technology and efficient consumer response (ECR) and customer relationship management (CRM) systems should be utilised to capture data directly from point of sales and consumer buying habits. The growth in 'loyalty cards' and 'store cards' is also another source of consumer data to enhance the management of market sensitivity.

The use of the Internet and information technology has enabled the real-time sharing of data between customers, buyers, suppliers, planners, manufacturers and distributors in a virtual network. The visibility of demand and collaborative planning forecasting and replenishment (CPFR) systems (see Chapter 13) in a virtual network are important tools to respond to the real needs of customers in a global market. The concept of competitive advantage through world-class manufacturing in individual sites has now shifted to network excellence. The supply chain where a group of partners can be linked together in a virtual network and communicate online and on time is a vital characteristic of agility.

Postponement is based on the principle that semi-finished products and components are kept in generic form and the final assembly or customisation does not take place until the final customer or market requirements are known. The principle of postponement is an essential characteristic of an agile supply chain. The rapid response tailored to the customer needs is also helped by the buffer capacity of key workstations. The point in the supply chain where the semi-finished products are stocked is also known as the 'de-coupling' point. This point should be as close to the marketplace as possible in the downstream of the supply chain. In addition to responding quickly to specific customer demand, the concept of postponement offers some operational, economic and marketing advantages. As the inventory is kept at a generic level, there are fewer SKUs and this makes easier forecasting and less inventory in total. As the inventory is kept at an earlier stage, stock value is also likely to be less than the value of finished product inventory. A higher level of variety can be offered at a lower cost and marketing can promote apparent exclusivity to customers by 'mass customisation'.

An agile supply chain also shares some lean supply chain principles or characteristics. The enhanced responsiveness of an agile supply chain is in addition to the high level of efficiency, quality assurance and smooth operation flow which are the key characteristics of a lean supply chain. An agile supply chain also focuses on the elimination of waste or mudas as in a lean process but with a different strategy for buffer capacity and inventory required for postponement. However, a pure lean strategy can be applied up to the de-coupling point and then an agile strategy can be applied beyond that point. It should be possible to achieve volume-oriented economies of scale-up to the de-coupling point. This is similar to a service operation (e.g. a bank) where the repetitive activities are isolated or de-coupled and carried out in the back office with lean thinking while responsive customer service is provided at the front end.

The strategy of a lean and agile supply chain

The above analysis and our experience strengthen the suitability of a pure agile supply chain for innovative products with unpredictable demand patterns with a high profit margin and high variety requiring many changes and shorter lead times. A pure lean supply chain, on the other hand, is suitable for high volume functional products with a lower margin and variety requiring a few changes. A lean supply chain may also compromise a longer lead time for a lower cost.

A survey by Yusuf et al. (2003), which was carried out by questionnaire to 600 manufacturing companies, showed that only a few companies adopted agile supply chain practices, but many companies embraced long-term collaboration with suppliers and customers, which was conceptualised as a lean supply chain practice.

Christopher (2000) comments, 'There will be occasions when a pure agile or a lean might be appropriate for a supply chain. However, there will often be situations where a combination of the two may be appropriate, i.e., a hybrid strategy'.

Naylor et al. (1999) agree that both agile and lean can be combined in the same supply chain and calls it 'Leagile'.

In the business world, it is more likely that companies have a mixed portfolio of products and services. It is also likely many high volume manufacturers or service providers experience short-term or seasonal demand for novelty products (e.g. chocolate eggs at Easter and t-shirts for the Olympics). There will be some high volume products where demand is stable and more predictable and there will be products with sporadic demands seeking an agile response. Therefore, it is not important to follow either lean or agile supply chain strategies. However, it is important to recognise that a supply chain can be lean for part of the time, agile for part of the time and both lean and agile (hybrid) for part of the time.

CASE EXAMPLE: LEAN AND AGILE H&M

Hennes & Mauritz (H&M) is a Swedish company, engaged in the design, production and retailing of clothing items and accessories. They are famous for their concept of cheap and chic clothes. H&M was established in 1947 by Erling Persson. The first store was opened in Vasteras and was called Hennes, which means 'hers' in Swedish. The company started by selling only women's clothes, and in 1968, the company bought Mauritz Widforss, a hunting and men's clothing store located in Stockholm. The company changed its name to Hennes and Mauritz and later abbreviated it to H&M. H&M now operates some 1700 retail shops in 30 countries with its largest markets in Germany, the UK, Norway and Sweden. H&M has increased its revenues by 12.5% each year on average since 2003 and sales revenue reached US$24 billion in 2015.

The company outsources its manufacturing in Asia, Africa and Europe. About 30% of its merchandise is produced in China. H&M does not have any factories of its own and operates 22 production offices, ten are in Europe, ten are in Asia and one each in Central America and Africa. H&M has contracts with approximately 750 suppliers, most of them are located in Bangladesh, China and Turkey. They all manufacture H&M's products. The production offices ensure that the buyer places their order with the right supplier, that the goods are produced at the right price and with good quality.

H&M's method of production is customer-driven. The company plans its work on research and prediction of emerging trends. H&M uses traditional research means and innovative ideas such as street trends. At H&M, lead times vary from two to three weeks up to six months, depending on the nature of the goods. In recent years, H&M has reduced the average lead time by 20% thanks to developments in the buying process. This activity is led by central staff and national offices that are responsible for detecting new trends. H&M imposes strict terms on its suppliers in terms of price, time to deliver, quality and location. Time is not a sufficient factor for working with H&M, suppliers have to be able to give samples of new products within 24 hours. H&M opted for a supply chain with two levels. The first supply chain is mainly concerned with cost efficiency – it is the lean model. It means that the manufacturers are located in Asia to optimise the cost of the products mainly thanks to low wages. This first loop is characterised by large order volumes, long transportation distances and slow lead times. The rapid reaction loop is used to adjust the offer with the demand. It is a quick response system to be close to fashion trends. This agile supply chain ensures the possibility to have new garments in less than two weeks. Fabrics are mainly based in Europe to reduce transport time. This system requires a strong logistic department, which employs 3200 people in H&M. The central warehouse is located in Hamburg, Germany. From there, the clothes are distributed to regional warehouses around Europe, each country has a warehouse adapted to country specificities (fashion, weather, habits, etc.). The rest of the world is covered by 13 smaller warehouses. While stock management is primarily handled within the H&M organisation, transport is contracted to third parties. Goods are inspected and allocated in a store or the regional warehouse called the 'Call off warehouse'. The role of the warehouse is to dispatch items to stores according to selling trends.

Fashion retailing is characterised by volatile markets, short product lifecycles and high product variety. Similar to Zara, Benetton and New Look, H&M is based on a hybrid supply chain that mixes agile supply chains for unpredictable demand and adjustment, and lean supply chains for predictable demand.

Summary

Changing customer and technological requirements, volatile markets and global sourcing have created fresh challenges to supply chain management and the traditional forecast-driven longer and slower logistic pipelines are becoming non-competitive and therefore unsustainable. In this chapter, we have discussed how to respond to this challenge with a lean and agile supply chain. We have developed the key characteristics of a lean supply chain as elimination of waste, smooth operation flow, high level of efficiency and quality

	LEAN	**AGILE**
OBJECTIVES	• Low cost • High utilisation • Minimum stock	• Fast response • Buffer capacity • Deployed stock
PROCESS CHARACTERISTICS	• Elimination of waste • Smooth operation flow • High level of efficiency • Quality assurance	• Flexibility • Market sensitivity • A virtual network • Postponement • Selected lean supply chain principles
PRODUCT CHARACTERISTICS	• Functional products • Low variety • Low margin	• Innovative products • High variety • High margin

Figure 14.5 Lean and agile characteristics

assurance. We have differentiated the characteristics of an agile supply chain as flexibility, market sensitivity, a virtual network, postponement and selected lean supply chain principles. We have also given guidelines to apply appropriate strategies for lean and agile supply chains. The supply chain objectives and characteristics of lean and agile supply chains are summarised in Figure 14.5.

We accept that lean is typically for high volume, low variety products and agile is for usually low volume and innovative high variety products. However, a valid question is 'is it either, or, or both'? On some occasions, either an agile or a lean strategy might be appropriate for a supply chain. However, many companies will probably face situations where a hybrid strategy is a better fit. In global supply chains, a lean and agile strategy is not an option, but a necessity.

Discussion questions

1. What are the characteristics of a lean supply chain and an agile supply chain? Comment on their similarities and differences.
2. Discuss how the evolution of lean thinking is influenced by the Toyota Production System.
3. Discuss seven 'Mudas'. How do they compare with the components of the classical industrial engineering flow process chart?
4. What are the key tools and processes of implementing lean>
5. What is Kanban? Discuss which type of operation Kanban can be most effective.

6. What are the key requirements of a successful TPM? Describe with a case example how global supply chains can benefit from the application of TPM.
7. Explain the principle of JIT. Comment on the role of JIT in a lean supply chain.
8. The supply chain of which type of product is more suitable for agile? Explain the principle of postponement in the agile supply chain.
9. Describe how the principles of both lean and agile ('Leagile') can be combined in managing global supply chains. Support your argument with the case example of H&M.

Notes

1 In Unilever Plc, the methodology was known as PAMCO (plant and machine control).
2 In GlaxoWellcome, it was called CAPRO (capacity analysis of production).

15 Retail supply chains

Introduction

We believe all our readers will be familiar with how barcoding is used at the checkout counter in supermarkets. Most customers realise that computer systems are triggered by swiping barcoded goods over a reader that links sales to stock records and subsequently raises re-orders based on stock levels. We also understand that computer-generated orders make allowances for stock already on order but not yet received, adjust for seasonality, allow for promotions and take into account stock on hand but nearing the use-by date. Such systems are also meant to calculate stock turn and profit margin by line item and can indicate the customer profile for a particular store. For example, the products being purchased in a particular store could suggest that most of the customers in that store's location have young families, one pet animal, buy lower-priced wine and will be susceptible to promoted 'specials' that are targeted to their profile. When combined with a loyalty card, where customers gain points for each purchase with a reward once a certain amount has been spent, the computer system could 'know' more about the purchasing habits of a household than will be known by the customer themself. How many of us know how much bread and milk we buy a week or how much we spend on fruit a week?

Learning objectives

Learning objectives for this chapter are:

1. Theoretical 'ideal' model.
2. Cross-docking model.
3. Supply chain speed.
4. Supply chain forces.
5. Strategic alliance.
6. Retail pricing.
7. Advances in technology.
8. Online retailing.

The theoretical 'ideal' model

For the following described model, barcoding and barcode readers are essential in the retail supply chain. In the not-too-distant future, barcoding will be replaced by radio frequency identification tags (RFID). The major difference is that RFID readers can recognise and record transactions without the goods having to be removed from the shopping trolley. Operationally, the process and benefits are essentially the same.

DOI: 10.4324/9781003341352-18

Point of receipt of goods

When goods are received, barcode scanning results in:

Receipt of goods tallied, and stock balances updated.
Received goods married to an order number, and the balance of outstanding orders updated and highlighted.
Highlights delivery shortfalls.
Enables outstanding orders to be followed up.
Amount owing to suppliers – accounts payable – updated.

Point of sale

When sold, barcoding at the point of sale adds up the cost of all the items the customer has picked and does not rely on the arithmetic ability of the checkout clerk. The customer generally will present, swipe or wave a bank debit or credit card, and sometimes a loyalty card. Irrespective of whether a debit or a credit card and/or loyalty card is used, the result from the retailer's point of view is the same. Exchange of funds at point of sale (EFPOS) transfers money from the customer's bank and directly into the retailer's bank account (less a bank fee) at the time of the sale. No money needs to physically change hands. The checkout clerk does not have to possess arithmetic skills and is absolved from having to add up, calculate change or for being blamed for entering the wrong prices. Once the barcode is read into the system, the computer does it all.

The barcode action at the point of sale reduces the potential for human error between the customer and the checkout clerk, but even more importantly updates stock records.

Stock-keeping records

The point of sale barcode action automatically:

Adjusts (reduces) the stock balance.
Triggers a re-order on the supplier once a re-order level is reached.
Updates the general ledger for sales and margins.
Calculates daily, weekly, monthly and year-to-date actual results of sales and revenue and compares to budget.
Upgrades the sales and revenue forecasts.
Produces exception reports for management on slow-moving/high-moving items.
Calculates stock turn for each line item.
Calculates the margin (profit) per line item.
Updates customer profile details for marketing.
Updates the bank account balance.

Re-order system

The re-order system will require a calculation taking into account stock turn, lead times, seasonality and a reserve level to determine a re-order level. It is important in the grocery industry not to hold too much stock not only because of the financial cost of holding stock and limited shelf space, but also the perishability of food items (used-by dates). It is also important not to run out of stock. The calculation of a re-order point is important. Barcoding updates information on average lead times and average demand and adjusts for seasonal ups and downs.

Flow of information

A point-of-sale system that is integrated with suppliers will enable information to be transmitted directly to the suppliers and further up the supply chain. Apart from the saving in clerical work of repetitive entering, and checking data and correcting errors, the electronic exchange of data as described earlier enables fast and accurate sharing of information. If organisations can have faith in the system and trust each other, major suppliers (factories and distributors) will be responsible for the replenishment of their products based on the information received directly, electronically, from the retail point of sale. The responsibility for the smooth flow of goods is transferred to the supplier. In effect, the supplier can manage the sales and marketing of their products in the retail stores. The major benefits of the direct sharing of information are that key suppliers can react quicker, delivery is quicker, inventory of materials is reduced and product is fresher.

Cross-docking model

With the cross-docking process, pioneered by Walmart, orders are transmitted directly to the factory distribution centre or to the distributor (for example for imported goods). The distributor (factory or distribution centre) aggregates the demand from all the retail stores and goods will be shipped in bulk to a regional cross-docking facility. At the cross-docking facility, picking slips for each retail store will have been received and made up of the various items required per store. Once the trucks arrive from the distributors, they are unloaded into the cross-docking warehouse. Within no more than 48 hours, the goods received from the various distributors will have been sorted to match the picking slips, packed and loaded onto trucks at the other side of the cross-docking facility for delivery to retail stores in the region.

Figure 15.1 depicts a point-of-sale integrated system and shows cross-docking.

Reality

The above describes what could happen.

The reality is that although the technology has been available for years, not all supermarkets or other fast-moving consumer goods retailers actually make use of the technology to the extent portrayed above and manual entry of data and repetitive entries at each level of the supply chain are made.

Typically, shelves are manually checked, orders are raised by hand and are sent, generally by email, to the regional warehouses rather than directly to the distributors. The regional warehouses manually load orders received from retailers into a computer system. The computer system aggregates orders that are emailed to the distributors. As stock-outs in retail are unacceptable, to avoid late deliveries, regional warehouses find it prudent, indeed necessary, to carry buffer stock in anticipation of orders and to order more than actual demand in anticipation based on past seasonal demand and late delivery from suppliers further up the supply chain.

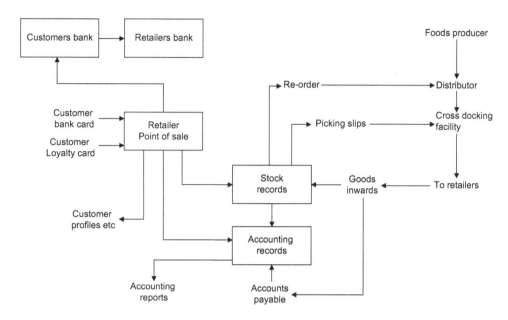

Figure 15.1 Integrated point-of-sale system

Once an order is received from the regional warehouse, the distributors in turn manually load the aggregated demands into their computer systems and place orders further up the supply chain. At this level, they are physically remote by some distance from individual retail points of sale and do not know what the actual end-user demand is. They are working from the demand placed on them by the regional warehouses and have added a buffer to their orders. The distributors therefore in turn will add their own buffer to their orders.

Back at the regional warehouse when inward goods are received, they will be entered into the computer to update the regional warehouse stock records. Most systems will not allow goods to be despatched until they have been receipted into the computer system. Picking slips are generated by the regional warehouse computer. In a parody of the cross-docking process, goods are received in one side of the warehouse and despatched from the opposite side. When received, after being entered into the computer, goods are stored in racks. When the picking slips for each retail store are printed, they show the packer the order in which to collect and accumulate the various items required by each retail store. The computer will calculate and show the shortest route around the warehouse to pick the required bundle of goods. By using a barcoding wand, the packer will record what has been packed and the regional warehouse stock records will be updated. Goods are loaded onto pallets for delivery to retailers at the other side of the warehouse. As each delivery truck will be delivering to several stores, the delivery route will be planned to reduce the distance travelled. The order in which pallets are loaded onto the delivery trucks will take into account the order in which they will be delivered.

The above process, with data being re-keyed (with added opportunities for human error) into respective computer systems is shown in Figure 15.2. It is not hard to find non-value-adding activities in this approach. Compare this with the true cross-docking process shown in Figure 15.3. The more entries required, the more chance there is of errors and delays.

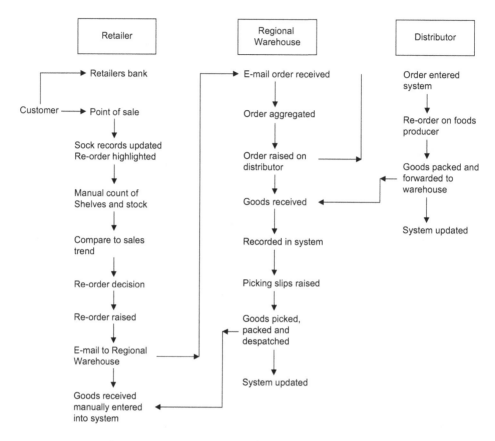

Figure 15.2 Non-value-added activities in three separate systems

The automated integrated system shown in Figure 15.3 requires trust in the system and trust in each member of the supply chain. Having trust in the system is one thing, being practical is another. An often-quoted example of where an organisation reacted to computer-generated information is Volvo and its green cars. In the mid-1990s, Swedish car maker Volvo found itself with too many green cars in the middle of the year. The marketing department was tasked with moving the green cars. They did a great job, but the problem was that the supply chain planning department hadn't been notified of the promotion of the green cars and it appeared that there was an increasing demand for green cars! As sales increased, production stepped up to match demand. The end result was Volvo was left with a huge inventory of green cars at the end of the year. Having trust in other members of the supply chain is also difficult to achieve. The lesson is, don't rely entirely on the system, human judgement might be needed to override the system to compensate for sudden changes in demand or in the economy in general.

Supply chain speed

The amount of information available to retailers about point of sale, buying patterns, customers' tastes, seasonal fluctuations and lead times is enormous. But we have all

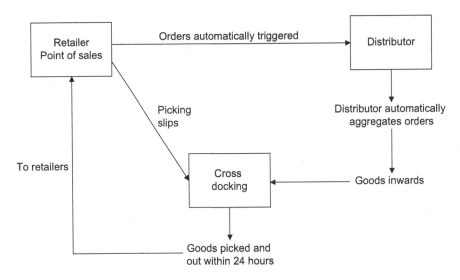

Figure 15.3 Cross-docking system

experienced going to a store to find that it doesn't have the item we want. And what retailer, especially in the fashion industry, has not been caught with huge stocks that have to be cleared at below cost at the end of the season? It would seem obvious that retailers at the beginning of a 'season', once early sales figures are known, would update their sales forecasts and order accordingly and thus reduce the likelihood of selling out of 'hot' products and/or being caught with large stocks of unpopular items at the end of the season. However, in many cases, especially in the apparel industry, retailers can't change their pre-season sales orders as the lead time is such that orders have to be 'fixed' before the season begins. Some fashion apparel retailers have to order 11 months in advance for products with product lifecycles of only three months.

CASE EXAMPLE: ZARA

One manufacturer has found a way to overcome the lead time problems to be able to quickly respond to fashion. Zara, which is based in Spain, has 176 stores in 86 countries. In 2015, it was reported that Zara had annual sales of US$13.6 billion. Over 450 million items of clothing are made annually for their own stores. Zara produces fashionable and trend-setting clothing to meet the market using a tightly controlled and integrated just-in-time system. To a large extent, they own the supply chain and pride themselves on speed to market or as they put it 'fast fashion'. It is claimed that within two weeks of new 'creations' first appearing on the 'catwalk', garments are on sale in the retail stores.

Not only is Zara famed for its ability to deliver new clothes to the stores quickly, but it also delivers in small batches. The re-order process is inflexible, but this inflexibility results in flexibility and quick responses. Twice a week at set times, store managers place orders and twice a week on a given day, new garments are received at the retail stores. Thus, store managers know that they do not have to hold large amounts of speculative items. New stock will be delivered to meet changing and fickle customer taste so the need for end-of-season sales is minimised.

Zara keeps most of the production in-house and 85% of production capacity is held for in-season adjustments. This in-house approach gives agility with a quick response to market trends and with the launch of a variety of new fashion items on a continuing basis. Indeed, 50% of its clothes are produced during a season, rather than in advance of a season. Instead of summer clothes being produced six months in advance in winter as is the industry norm, new summer fashions are being introduced and supplied during the season with only 14 days from prototype to on the shelves.

Zara has not transferred production offshore to get cheap labour but designs, sources, cuts and sews in facilities close to its Spanish headquarters. Although labour cost is higher, the turnaround time and control of quality are well above average for the industry. The ability to replenish stores quickly and to be stocking what is selling means that Zara achieves 85% of the full price for the sales of its clothing whereas the industry benchmark is less than 70%.

The seven steps to Zara's success are as follows:

1. Centralised information sharing for retailers and suppliers, using EDI and point-of-sale data.
2. Quick response replenishment, with small batch production.
3. Centralised design and product development.
4. Controlled scheduling, stores order twice a week and shipments are prepared and shipped out within 24 hours.
5. In-house production, not outsourced, provides flexibility.
6. Automated production and warehousing, constantly under review and updated.
7. Inflexible to provide flexibility processes must be strictly adhered to.

Information drawn from Zara website: www.supplychainopz.com and www.trade-gecko.com.

Accuracy of information

The underlying assumption with the barcoded 'ideal' model is that information is accurate. Stock or inventory shrink is a term used for the discrepancy between what the records show as being the balance and what is actually physically on hand. This is a loss that goes straight to the bottom line! The problems are many, but according to a survey in the United States by National Retail Security (2010), employee theft accounts for 44% of shrinkage, shoplifting for 33% and vendor fraud accounts for the balance.

Human error is most likely to occur when entries are hand-keyed rather than barcode read. Other examples are when an item is returned because it is the wrong size, and it is replaced by the salesperson without scanning the return and the replacement product, although the prices could be different. Irrespective of price, the stock records for both 'small' and 'large' sizes will be wrong. In the grocery trade, the checkout clerk will often scan one item several times rather than scanning six similar items. For example, six packs of different flavoured yoghurt, only one will be scanned perhaps six times at the same price although each flavour might have a different price. Fisher, Raman and McClelland (2000) report that one supermarket chain consistently recorded sales of medium ripe tomatoes to be 25% higher than the actual amount of medium ripe tomatoes delivered to the stores, 'if it's red and soft it's a medium tomato at checkout although the actual tomato might be a higher priced vine ripened' (p. 121). Other problems are the recording of inward goods, for example, the number of items per container could be entered as 20 in the re-order system when the delivery pack only contains 12. Unreported breakages, damaged goods and goods past the use-by date account for much of the balance of shrinkage.

Supply chain forces

> The dynamic nature of the supply chain is evident in both the changing nature of the structure of the supply chain and is also evident in the day-to-day activities of members at each level. In a typical supply chain, each member creates disturbances, either independently or in response to actions taken elsewhere within the supply chain. These disturbances frequently create a chain reaction.
>
> (Wright, 2012: p. 200)

This latter phenomenon is often demonstrated in a management simulation known as 'the beer game'. The beer game has its origins in a role-playing exercise for a simple production and distribution system developed by MIT in the 1960s. Variations of the game have been used in business schools around the world for over 40 years, in particular, in MBA programs. Simchi-Levi et al. (2003), as have others, developed a computer-based simulation game to enable students to explore issues associated with supply chain dynamics. The original beer game consists of a basic supply chain of a single retailer, drawing on a single wholesaler, who in turn draws on a single distributor, who in turn is supplied from a single brewery with unlimited raw materials that supplies the distributor. There is no limit to the amount of stock each member of the supply chain can keep. The constraints are that there is a lead time for delivery and a fixed order delay time for each re-order and delivery step in the chain.

In the original game, each of the players manages one of the supply chain companies. Each 'week', the lecturer in the role of the end user customer gives the 'retailers' a demand order, and the retailer fills that order if possible and calculates an order for the wholesaler. If the order cannot be totally fulfilled, a 'back order' is recorded. Each of the other two members of the supply chain, wholesaler and distributor, also observe the demand, satisfy the demand if possible and/or record a backorder and place an order, or in the case of the factory, schedules production. The person running the game (the lecturer) after a few 'weeks' feeds in a change to demand and the whole supply chain has to react to this change. The lead time and delivery time constraints cause a delay in the system. As a result, the players tend to over-order especially when backorders exist. Due to these disturbances, the supply chain as a whole appears to have dramatic up-and-down demand changes. These changes are magnified at each successive stage of the supply chain. Thus, inventory and backorder levels vary markedly from week to week. At the end of the simulation, players blame the other players for causing the situation.

The game is also described in great detail in Senge (1990). As Wright (2012) says, there is no real beer in the beer game, and it does not promote drinking, although it does lead to some interesting behaviour among participants. What is interesting about the beer game is that it has been played so many times, yet the patterns of behaviour generated in the game are remarkably similar. The beer game introduces the players to the phenomenon known as the 'bullwhip effect'. In practice, this phenomenon is observed in all forms of the supply chain but especially in retail supply chains.

The bullwhip effect

As Melnyk and Swink (2002) describe, the bullwhip effect occurs when a small disturbance generated by a customer produces successively larger disturbances at each upstream stage in the supply chain. Bullwhip effects are of great concern because they incite excessive expediting (moving certain orders ahead of others), increased levels of inventory, uneven levels of capacity utilisation (where plants go from being idle to working overtime), and ultimately, increased holding costs for stocks of goods.

Simchi-Levi et al. (2003) give the following illustrative example. Proctor and Gamble (P&G) in examining the demand for Pampers disposable nappies noticed an interesting phenomenon. As expected, retail sales of the product were fairly uniform; there is no particular day or month in which demand is significantly higher or lower than any other. However, it was noticed that distributors' orders placed to the factory fluctuated much more than retail sales. In addition, P&G's orders to its suppliers fluctuated even more.

Why does this effect occur? In the absence of information, suppliers are likely to overreact to changes in order sizes, whether upwards or downwards. The amplification of variations through the stages of the supply chain results in the bullwhip effect.

Wright (2012) explains that the main factors contributing to the increase in variability in the supply chain are as follows:

1. *Demand forecasting.* Traditional inventory management techniques, practised independently at each level in the supply chain, lead to the bullwhip effect. Forecasting is typically used to estimate average demand and demand variability. These are used to determine the re-order point and safety stock levels. The more variable the demand, the higher the safety stock level and hence this can lead to changing the order quantifies and increasing variability.
2. *Lead time.* Increase in variability is magnified with increases in lead time. With longer lead times, a small change in the estimate of demand variability implies a significant change in safety stock and thus re-order quantities, therefore, leading to an increase in variability.
3. *Batch ordering.* If the retailer uses batch ordering, the wholesaler will observe a large order followed by several periods of no orders, followed by another large order. Thus, the wholesaler sees a distorted and highly variable pattern of orders. Also, requirements to ship full truck loads can lead to the same order pattern. Similarly, end-of-season sales quotas or incentives can also result in unusually large orders being placed on a periodic basis.
4. *Price fluctuation.* If prices fluctuate, retailers often attempt to stock up when prices are lower. This is accentuated by the prevailing practice in many industries of offering promotions and discounts at certain times of the year.
5. *Inflated orders.* During shortages or periods of allocations, retailers will inflate their orders to ensure that they will receive supply proportional to the amount ordered. When the period of shortage is over, they will revert back to standard orders further distorting demand estimates.

These factors all contribute to increasing the variability of orders placed within the supply chain. One of the first steps that can be taken to reduce the bullwhip effect is to ensure all stages in the supply chain have access to customer demand information. By centralising the customer demand information and sharing it with all stages, the bullwhip effect can be reduced but it will not be eliminated.

Simchi-Levi et al. (2003) suggest the following methods for coping with the bullwhip effect:

1. Reducing uncertainty by centralising demand information, that is, by providing each stage of the supply chain with complete information on actual customer demand.
2. *Reducing variability.* The bullwhip effect can be diminished by reducing the variability inherent in the customer demand process. This can be achieved through using an 'everyday low pricing' strategy, that is, offering a product at a single consistent price. By eliminating price promotions, a retailer can eliminate many of the dramatic shifts in demand that accompany such promotions.
3. *Lead-time reduction.* Lead time reduction reduces the amount of 'safety stock' estimated to be carried.
4. *Strategic partnerships.* Engaging in any of a number of strategic partnership initiatives can eliminate the bullwhip effect. These initiatives are outlined in the following sections.

We have included an exercise in Appendix 1, based on the 'beer game' model, to explore the magnitude of the 'bullwhip effect'.

Information and integration

Wright and Race (2004) observe that information enables the supply chain to be integrated. Within any supply chain, there are many systems. Managing any one of these systems is complex and involves a series of trade-offs with the need to balance the two objectives of customer satisfaction and resource utilisation. Managing the whole supply chain requires even more complex trade-offs. The complete supply chain needs to be considered as a whole and decisions concerning the whole need to be made. In many supply chains, there is no common owner to coordinate the whole process, each step will be separately owned and controlled and each with an understandable aim to do the best for their operation. Without coordination, the result is local optimisation, and each member of the supply chain tries to optimise their own operation without consideration of the impact of its actions on the other member components in the supply chain. What is desirable is global optimisation, which implies that we identify what is best for the whole system. To do this involves addressing the following two issues:

1. Who will optimise?
2. How will the savings obtained through the coordinated strategy be split between the different supply chain facilities?

These issues can be addressed in various ways.

Strategic alliances

In order to achieve an integrated supply chain, the various members need to work together. The three most important types of supply chain-related strategic alliances are third-party logistics (3PL), retailer-supplier partnerships (RSP) and distributor integration (DI).

Third-party logistics

The use of a third party to take over some or all of a company's logistics responsibilities is now common; 3PL is simply the use of an outside company to perform all or part of the firm's materials management and product distribution function. This might include one or all of the activities of transportation, warehousing, package delivery and information systems; 3PL relationships are certainly more complex than traditional logistics supplier relationships. Modern 3PL arrangements involve long-term commitments and often multiple functions or process management. The aim is to allow organisations to focus on their core competencies and allow specialist organisations to manage non-core activities. However, unless the subcontractors or partners are competent, the danger is that control will be lost. Any subcontracting has to be carefully thought through as once an activity has been subcontracted out, and skilled staff (intellectual capital) have gone, it is hard to rebuild.

Retailer–supplier partnerships

As customer satisfaction becomes more important in gaining a competitive edge, and due to large-scale world-class competition, prices have been driven down and margins have become tighter in retail, it makes sense to try and create cooperative efforts between suppliers and retailers. The objective should be to achieve benefits for all parties and not for one party to try and dominate at another's expense. The types of retailer-supplier partnerships can be viewed on a continuum. At one end is information sharing, in the middle is continuous replenishment enabled by sharing information from point of sale, and at the other end, is a consignment scheme of vendor-managed inventory (VMI).

In a simple quick response strategy, suppliers receive point of sale (POS) data from retailers and use this information to synchronise their production and inventory activities with actual sales at the retailers. In this strategy, the retailer still prepares individual orders, but the POS data is used by the supplier to improve delivery performance and hence reduce supply variability.

In a continuous replenishment strategy, sometimes called rapid replenishment, vendors receive POS data and use this data to prepare shipments at previously agreed-upon intervals to maintain specific levels of inventory.

In a VMI system, the supplier decides on the appropriate inventory levels of each product and the appropriate policies to maintain these levels. The goal of many VMI programmes is to eliminate the need for the retailer to oversee specific orders for replenishment. The ultimate is for the supplier to manage the inventory and only receive payment for it once it has been sold by the retailer, in essence, the retailer is providing an outlet for the supplier!

Distributor integration

Modern information technology has enabled this strategy in which distributors are integrated so that expertise and inventory located at one distributor are available to the others. DI can be used to address both inventory-related and service-related issues. In terms of inventory, DI can be used to create a large pool of inventory across the entire distributor network, thus lowering total inventory costs while raising customer service levels. Similarly, DI can be used to meet the customer's specific needs by directing those requests to the distributor best suited to address them. The downside is that if you were a retailer stocking high-value electronic equipment, why would you want to deplete your stock by supplying a competitor with goods so that they can make a sale? Who is making the profit and who has incurred the financial cost of stock holding and carrying the risk?

Who has the power?

In days gone by in the food supply chain, the power was with the farmers. After the Second World War, farmers in the western countries of Europe, North America and Australia and New Zealand were given government subsidies and grants. Without a doubt, farmers in the main did use subsidies and grants to restructure and adopt labour-saving machines. But today even the wealthy countries in the European Union can no longer afford to support extravagant subsidies to maintain inefficient farming. During the period that farmer power was waning, manufacturing and food processors went through mergers and takeovers. For example, in the United States, four beef processors control over 80% of beef processing. In this system, the farmer becomes a contractor, providing labour and capital but never owning the product as it moves through the system. The major management decision for their farms is not made by the farmers. Professor Lang of City University says it is a similar story with agrochemicals, seven firms account for 90% of worldwide sales. In the grocery industry, the large supermarket chains dictate to the farmers what to sow, when to sow, what fertilisers and chemicals to use, when to harvest and how to pack and set the standards for rejecting or accepting produce. The farmer does the work and takes the risk but has little choice but to accept the terms of the supermarket. The international fast-food giant McDonald's operates in a similar fashion. The upside for the consumer is a consistent standard of quality.

Even though the manufacturers have become giants, it is now accepted that the power is with the retailers, rather than with the manufacturers. In the grocery industry, and also for other retailers of fast-moving consumer goods, large conglomerates such as Walmart (trading as ASDA in the UK) and Tesco are the big spenders. In the UK in 2006, five major supermarket chains accounted for just on 70% of food sales, and over 50% of food in the UK was sold from 1000 huge super or hypermarkets. Cap Gemini Ernst and Young in an extensive market analysis, 'The State of the Art Food Report' in 2003 concluded that in the near future four or five large retail organisations will operate on a worldwide scale.

However, today, the UK's largest supermarket Tesco is in serious trouble and for 2015 posted a loss of £6.4 billion, the biggest loss ever recorded in the UK high street. They announced that they would be closing 200 stores and a distribution centre. Among the reasons given by analysts is that consumer habits have shifted to lower-priced discounters including the German grocers Aldi and Lidl. Another reason is that consumers tend now tend to buy in smaller top-up lots rather than in a large weekly shop. A further growing phenomenon is online purchasing where customers only order what they need rather than become mesmerised by in-store colourful displays and specials. Online shopping now accounts for 15% of all UK retail (including groceries). Whereas previously a Tesco customer might pick up non-food items when in the store, now when buying groceries online, they restrict themselves to what they need in the grocery line rather than buying on impulse.

Add to this that consumers have a growing degree of choice and a greater ability to make comparisons. As a result, their expectations are rising, and their needs are constantly changing. In 1975, items available to consumers (stock-keeping units, SKUs) by supermarkets totalled 14,000, by the end of 2016, the number is estimated to be 300,000! In 2016, it is estimated that in the United States, 15,000 new items will be added to the list, of which only 4000 will survive. The actual number held on the shelves in a US supermarket in 1975 was just below 9000 and in 2015 it had grown to almost 50,000!

Value in this environment is a moving target. Any organisation must be flexible to be able to adapt to these changes. It is very difficult for a single organisation to possess all the capabilities required to keep up. The large retailers can control, or as some say blackmail, the manufacturers and processors. Smaller organisations do not have this clout. They now look for suppliers who can provide the skills and capabilities needed as they require them. Smaller firms form partnerships with appropriately skilled suppliers that last as long as the need exists. As demand changes so do the partnership arrangements.

Retail pricing

Pricing is an important component of retailing. The firm's decision on the price of the product and the pricing strategy impacts the consumer's decision on whether or not to purchase the product. In its particular segment of the supply chain, whether it is B2B or B2C, a business generates its revenue from the sale of its end products or services. The operating income is essentially the difference between sales revenues and the cost of goods sold. Short-term price promotion is often used to increase sales. However, a lower price reduces revenue. On the other hand, a higher price may reduce sales and may or may not increase revenue. The big supermarket chains are often involved in so-called 'price wars'. The optimisation of pricing is a big challenge in retaining. The question is how does pricing affect the supply chain as a whole? Aggressive advertising and 'specials' may result in short-term increases in sales but will result in spikes in demand up the supply chain, resulting in the bullwhip effect. Who gains from a price war? For example, if one gas station reduces the price of petrol, the competition will soon follow suit. Petrol sales will go up, but overall the real need for petrol will not increase. An increase in demand in one week will be followed by reduced sales in the following week. If I fill my tank up with bargain-priced petrol, I will not drive round and round the block to use it up. Overall, my consumption in a two-week period will not change, but the effect on the supply chain can be quite dramatic. To overcome spikes in the supply chain and mitigate the bullwhip effect, Walmart, Lidl and Aldi employ everyday low prices.

The technology of internet usage has increased and developed dramatically, and price comparisons can be done by customers through online access. Consumers are very selective regarding the purchases they make due to their knowledge of the monetary value.

So what are the guidelines?

Retail pricing is broadly based on the following:

*   Manufacturer's recommended retail price (MRRP).
*   Economic theory of price and volume.
*   Cost plus mark-up.
*   Regulatory control.
*   What the competition is doing or threatening to do.

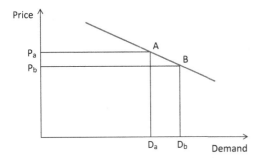

Figure 15.4 Economic theory of pricing

An MRRP is the price that the company that produces a product recommends for sale at retailers. MRRP does not necessarily correspond to the price retailers actually use or to the price customers are willing to pay. Retailers may need to set their prices below MRRP to move inventory, especially for items with low demand or during a sluggish period in the economy.

In the economic model, the price is set to maximise profit and assumes a lower price for higher demand as shown graphically in Figure 15.4. At a lower demand level (Da), price (Pa) is higher than the price (Pb) at a higher demand level (Db).

A retailer may choose to set the cost plus mark up the direct variable cost, the total direct cost or the total cost of sales. As shown in Figure 15.5, the mark-ups at direct costs are higher than the mark-up at the total cost of sales.

In order to control price fixing among retailers, there are some regulatory controls on retail prices in the United States and Europe. For example, the US Federal Trade Commission Act gives the Federal Trade Commission (FTC) the power to pursue companies that may engage in unfair competition or deceptive practices. The EU antitrust rules likewise cover all activities on local markets, not just local companies

Advances in technology

The merging of information and communications technologies has supported the growth in supply chain partnerships. These technologies have enabled extensive connectivity. Today's computer networks, open systems standards and the Internet enable people working in different areas of the supply chain to maintain constant contact. Since information transactions have become so easy, there is less of a need to restrict operations to within traditional organisational boundaries. These new capabilities offer the ability for supply chain partners to share information in real time. This enables the partnering firms to hold lower inventories and incur fewer transaction costs. These lower costs can in turn be passed on to the customer in the form of lower prices and better value. Or alternatively are retained as increased profits!

Organisations are increasingly recognising that great improvements in value can be attained by coordinating the efforts of partners along the supply chain. When firms focus only on their internal operations, they are making decisions in isolation and, as a result, this can lead to the overall performance of the supply chain deteriorating. Firms that work together and share their plans and other information are actually able to improve the overall supply chain performance to their mutual benefit.

• Cost base Selling price(£)	£	Mark-up	%
• Direct variable cost	200	250	500
• Direct semi-variable cost	100		
• Total direct cost	300	70	510
• Indirect cost	100		
• Total cost of sales	400	30	520

Figure 15.5 Cost plus pricing

The Internet and the supply chain

The power of the internet in providing ready information and a quick exchange of information has enabled major changes in business practices. The direct business model employed by industry giants such as Dell Computers and Amazon enables customers to order products over the Internet and thus lets these companies accept orders directly from end users, which allows them to forward products directly to the customer without having to go through a go-between. Apart from parcel delivery, third-party distributors and warehouses are no longer needed. However, the direct business model no longer gives Dell a competitive edge. Customers now prefer to buy their laptops and tablets fully loaded with software off the shelf from a retail store rather than having to go online and order a customised PC and wait for delivery. Dell has recognised this and is now selling its computers through retail stores but has, of course, retained its direct business.

In general, the retail industry was slow to respond to competition from virtual stores and recognise the potential of the Internet. It is, however, now common for 'bricks and mortar' retailers to also have a 'click and mortar' or Internet shopping facility for customers. Unlike the turn of the century dot-com companies, which for the most part did not carry any stock but acted as an online order taker for customers, the large click-and-mortar companies such as Kmart, Target, Tesco, Walmart and Barnes and Noble have distribution and warehousing infrastructure in place. One model is for high volume, fast-moving consumer goods to be stocked in retail stores and online orders supplied from there, and slower-moving products to be stocked centrally for online ordering and supply. A push strategy is used for the high-volume, fast-moving goods, and a pull strategy for low-volume, slow-moving goods.

Likewise, the Internet and the emerging e-business models have produced expectations that many supply chain problems will be resolved merely by using these new technology and business models. While it has promised so much, in reality, expectations have not been achieved. In many cases, the downfall of some of the highest-profile Internet businesses has been attributed to a lack of sound logistics planning.

Nonetheless, in developed countries and progressively in the emerging giant economies of India and China, most people have a computer at home or have access to a computer at work. In the UK, 15% of retail sales in November 2015 were online and the percentage is growing.

Online retailing

Online retailing (sometimes known as e-tail) is a form of electronic commerce that allows consumers to directly buy goods or services from a seller over the Internet using a web browser. Online businesses vary from self-employed entrepreneurs to very large online retailing corporations like Alibaba, Amazon and eBay.

Online retailing is growing at an astonishing rate. Retailers who ignore e-commerce may see their trade lessening as customers continue to shift to ordering products online. However, you need to think carefully and weigh all the advantages and disadvantages.

There are many attractive advantages of the online retailing business model including:

Easy access to market – in many ways, the access to market for entrepreneurs has never been easier. Online marketplaces such as eBay enable anyone to set up an online shop and sell products within minutes.

Reduced overheads – selling online can remove the need for expensive retail premises and customer-facing staff, allowing you to invest in better marketing and customer experience on your website.

Potential for rapid growth – selling on the internet means traditional constraints to retail growth, for example, finding and paying for larger or better premises are not major factors. With a good e-marketing strategy and a plan for a scale-up of order fulfilment systems, you can respond and boost growing sales

Widen your global market – one major advantage over premises-based retailers is the ability to expand your market beyond local customers very quickly. You may discover a strong demand for your products in other countries. You can respond by targeted marketing, offering your website in a different language or perhaps partnering with an overseas company

Customer intelligence – the ability to use online marketing tools to target new customers and website analysis tools to gain insight into your customers' needs.

Customer convenience – the ability to shop without leaving your house. This is very attractive to both young professionals and older 'silver surfers'.

However, there are some distinct disadvantages of online retail businesses. These include:

Website costs – planning, designing, creating, hosting, securing and maintaining a professional e-commerce website is not cheap, especially if you expect large and growing sales volumes.

Infrastructure costs – even if you are not paying the cost of customer-facing premises, you will need to think about the costs of physical space for order delivery, dealing with returns and staffing for these tasks.

Security and fraud – the growth of the online retail market has attracted the attention of sophisticated criminal elements. The reputation of your business could be fatally damaged if you don't invest in the latest security systems to protect your website and transaction processes

Advertising costs – while online marketing can be a very expensive way of getting the right customers to your products, it demands a generous budget – especially if you are competing in a crowded sector or for popular keywords.

The Covid-19 pandemic forever changed online shopping behaviours according to a survey (UNCTAD, 2020) of about 3700 consumers in nine emerging and developed economies. The survey showed that following the pandemic, more than half of the survey's respondents did shop online more frequently. Consumers in emerging economies made the greatest shift to online shopping, according to the survey. In the United States, consumers paid US$32 billion more online for the same amount of goods as compared with the previous two years. In Europe, 67% of consumers used online retailing due to Covid-19.

Customer trust – it can be difficult to establish a trusted brand name, especially without a physical business with a track record and face-to-face interaction between customers and sales staff.

CASE EXAMPLE: ONLINE GROCERY AT OCADO

Ocado was founded in the UK in 2000 by Tim Steiner (present CEO) with two other merchant bankers of Goldman Sachs. Ocado was launched as a concept and started trading as a business in partnership with Waitrose (of John Lewis Group) in January 2002. Ocado offers the freshest high-quality food and a wide range of grocery products online at affordable prices. In 2014, Ocado's sales reached the £1 billion mark and is set to become the leading online European food retailer.

Ocado's own brands include Ocado, Fetch and Sizzle. Other products include own-brand groceries from the Waitrose supermarket chain and also a selection of name-brand groceries and other items, including flowers, toys and magazines A range of Carrefour's products are also sold via Ocado.

The company has a warehouse-based model, operating purely online without any physical shops. It currently has 18 purpose-built warehouse storage and picking centres.

At Ocado, IT is not just a business support function, IT is the business (evidenced by the CEO also being the CTO). IT is integral to Ocado's success from the warehouses equipped with bespoke supply chain systems capable of managing and sorting over

20,500 grocery lines and organising over 100,000 deliveries per week to the point of delivery, In July 2009, Ocado released their first app for the iPhone. The app, called 'Ocado on the Go', allows users to do their grocery shopping without the need of a computer. In April 2010, the company extended the app to Android devices. The Android app has a number of features that the iPhone app does not have, including the ability to control the app using voice activation.

Today, Ocado's services are available to over 16 million households across the UK, and the company has grown rapidly since its inception, with revenues of £1 billion in 2014. The UK grocery market remains a huge opportunity for Ocado, with a total market size of £130 billion, of which only 4% is online so far. The online grocery market size is predicted to grow to £20 billion in 2019. Following the COVID-19 Pandemic, the online grocery and retail market exploded to £170 billion in 2022. Ocado's success to date has been remarkable given the market dynamics in UK groceries and the entrenched grocery competitors like Tesco (revenues of £50 billion), Sainsbury's (revenues of £22 billion) and ASDA (revenues of £15 billion). Ocado struck a deal with Morrisons in 2015 to run the supermarket's belated entry to online sales.

However, there are business challenges too. All major supermarkets have set up their own online retail and delivery services. In November 2008, the John Lewis

Partnership transferred its shareholding of 29% into its staff pension fund and in February 2011, the John Lewis pension fund sold off its entire Ocado shareholding. Waitrose now competes with Ocado online in the southeast of England and the companies' ten-year supply contract has a break clause in 2017, raising concerns that Waitrose could walk away. Ocado has dismissed fears that Waitrose could stop supplying it by saying the John Lewis supermarket chain needs Ocado as much as Ocado needs Waitrose.

There are also environmental challenges. Ocado's Customer Fulfilment Centre (CFC), in Warwickshire employs around 2000 employees. Access to the site is via a dual carriageway so sustainable travel solutions such as walking and cycling are limited, which means the main mode of travel is by car.

Although Tim Steiner, Ocado's CEO, confirmed on 2 February 2016 that it was not in talks with rival Amazon for a takeover, the possibility of a hostile takeover by Amazon or eBay cannot be ruled out.

Summary

Retailing accounts for 6% of the GDP of advanced economies and hence the performance of retail supply chains is vital for advanced economies.

Although business-to-customer e-tail is here to stay, the use of the Internet for business-to-business integration is the real issue for this chapter. Integration of the supply chain players has been made possible with the use of the internet and associated technologies.

The impact of the new technologies on the supply chain provides an interesting development. The Internet and evolving supply chain strategies have seen a shift in transportation and order fulfilment strategies away from case and bulk shipments to single-item and smaller-size shipments and from shipping to a small number of stores to serving highly geographically dispersed customers. This shift has seen the importance of partnerships with parcel industries. It has also increased the importance and complexity of reverse logistics of handling the significant numbers of product returns. One of the big winners in the new developments is the parcel industry. An important advantage for the parcel industry is the existence of an excellent information infrastructure that enables real-time tracking. Those players in this industry who work to modify their own systems in order to integrate them with their customers' supply chains are likely to be successful.

As organisations come to understand the power of the Internet, new models of business are sure to evolve. One thing is certain, supply chains of the future will be managed along the lines of the theoretical ideal we gave at the beginning of this chapter. It is obvious that the big players will take the coordination role. We are of the opinion that is the consumers who will benefit. There will be greater selection, quality will be consistent and grocery items will be fresher. Although prices will not go down, savings in costs throughout the supply chain will keep prices at a reasonable level.

The future looks to be exciting and bright, but not necessarily for the big players!

Discussion questions

1. Describe the 'theoretical model' of a retail supply chain from the 'point of receipt of goods' to the 'point of sale'.

2. Based on the information in the case example of Zara, discuss the success factors of Zara retailing and supply chain practices.
3. What is the 'bullwhip effect'? Explain the factors causing the 'bullwhip effect'. Suggest steps to be taken in supply chain planning to reduce this effect.
4. Discuss how retail pricing can play a vital role in managing revenues in competitive grocery supermarkets. Explain the bases of setting a retail price.
5. What are the factors driving the growth of online retailing? Also, discuss the challenges of online retailing.
6. What is the 'bullwhip effect' in supply chain management? What are the key factors contributing to the 'bullwhip effect' and how would you reduce their impact? Explain how the simulations on the 'beer game' can help assess the impact of forecast errors contributing to the 'bullwhip effect.
7. Based on the information provided in the case example of Ocado, what are the success factors of the Ocado business model? Discuss the potential challenges facing Ocado.

Exercise

Plays-r-us is a retailer of children's toys. The imported *Babydoll* from China costs €3000 per 1000 units. The import duty is 10%. The packaging material costs €500 per 1000 units. The estimated overhead for the projected volume is €1000 per 1000 units. Assuming a 30% mark-up, what should be the selling price for each *Babydoll?*

16 Sustainable green supply chains

Introduction

Organisations are facing increasing challenges to balance business performance with environmental issues and these challenges have created a new area of green supply chain management. A green supply chain refers to the way in which organisational innovations and policies in supply chain management may be considered in the context of a sustainable environment. Industry is a complex web of buying, making, selling and delivering. The opportunities for environmental considerations at each stage of supply chain management provide sustainable environmental measures that lead to savings beneficial to both organisations and individual end consumers. The objectives of green supply chain management are aimed at a win–win strategy. Environmental regulations are also changing the way supply chains are designed and managed. The problem is that the sheer number of regulations, other influences such as changing consumer sentiment and the complexity of global trade make it difficult for companies to decide exactly how they should respond to these pressures.

Not surprisingly, there are instances in recent history where the performance of manufacturing businesses was drastically affected due to negligence in environment and safety standards. A failure in product safety that caused deformed 'thalidomide children' is still haunting the manufacturers. The gas explosion of 1984 in Bhopal, India, which killed over 1000 people, permanently damaged the business of the manufacturers. Food poisoning costs to John Farley and Wests were huge. Environmental pollution by chemical companies in New Jersey resulted in numerous legal battles with consumers and also affected their business performance. And in 2015, efforts by Volkswagen to defeat and deceive emission tests led to a scandal costing an estimated US$5 billion in damages and damage to reputation and future sales that cannot be quantified. On a global scale, industrial pollution is the main contributor to the so-called 'greenhouse' effect and climate change. Suffice to say, climate change is taken very seriously by all governments and ensuing regulations are being enforced.

Greenhouse gases include carbon dioxide, methane CFCs (chlorofluorocarbons) and nitrous oxide. CFCs are produced only in industrial processes. The combustion of fossil fuels (coal, oil and natural gas) is the major source of manufactured carbon emissions. Greenhouse gases allow incoming radiation from the Sun to pass through the atmosphere of the Earth. The Earth absorbs the radiation and reflects it back. When this outgoing radiation meets particles of a greenhouse gas, the radiation is absorbed by the particle, and on a large scale, all greenhouse gases around the Earth form a sort of warm blanket causing global warming. Some scientists believe that increased emissions of greenhouse gases, particularly carbon dioxide, are causing energy to be trapped, increasing the global temperature.

DOI: 10.4324/9781003341352-19

CFCs were used in aerosols, refrigerator coolants and air-conditioners. They were a strong contributor to the greenhouse effect but are relatively easy to regulate because they only result from the manufacture of refrigeration units and aerosols. Methane and carbon dioxide emissions are linked to much larger economic infrastructures and are more difficult to regulate. In 1997, the Kyoto Protocol was drawn up in Kyoto, Japan, to implement the United Nations Framework Convention for Climate Change. It achieved little, however, there have been annual meetings of the parties since 1997. In November 2015, the 11th meeting 'The Paris Climate Change Conference (COP21)' appears to have made considerable progress in getting agreement among the 195 parties attending. It was accepted at the conference that key roles in achieving targets lie with China and the United States. Pope Francis, in support of the conference, published an encyclical calling for action against climate change. France was seen as a model country for delegates because it is one of the few developed countries to decarbonise electricity production and fossil fuel energy while providing a high standard of living; 90% of its electricity is from zero-carbon sources including nuclear, hydroelectric and wind. All members agreed to reduce their carbon output as soon as possible and to do their best to keep global warming to well below 2°C. However, these are promises rather than firm commitments. The stated objectives of the Conference are predicated upon an assumption that industrial nations including China, India, the United States, Brazil, Canada, Russia, Indonesia and Australia (these nations generate more than 50% of the world's greenhouse emissions) will voluntarily take active steps to drive down their emissions.

Whatever actions that are and will be taken, it is clear that no organisation can in the long term hope to avoid legislation and regulations designed to honour the spirit of the 2015 conference in Paris.

Our personal belief is that environment and safety are not just social or political issues, they are vital ingredients contributing to the performance of an organisation. In manufacturing industries, there is much scope for the environment and safety. Accidents do occur and likewise there are many opportunities to prevent accidents. Apart from humanitarian reasons, it is a truism that accidents cost money. Likewise, many businesses and organisations are facing declining reserves of natural resources, increased waste-disposal costs, keener interest in their human rights records and tighter legislation. These rising environmental pressures and social expectations can be turned to commercial advantage if a strategic approach is taken to develop a 'green' supply chain. The strategic approach of a green supply chain involves complex longer-term considerations involving not just industry, but environmental protection as an important international issue. Industrialised countries, including the United States, are spending between 0.5% and 1.5% of their gross national product (GNP) on the control of pollution. It is a big subject and any attempt to make a comprehensive analysis of all the issues is beyond the scope of this book.

Learning objectives

Learning objectives for this chapter are:

1. What is a green supply chain?
2. Green initiatives by manufacturers and suppliers.
3. Green initiatives by governments and non-profit organisations.
4. Green initiatives by retailers.
5. Green initiatives by consumers.
6. Sustainable green thinking.

What is a green supply chain?

A 'green supply chain' according to Walton et al. (1998) refers to buyer companies requiring a certain level of environmental responsibility in core business practices of their suppliers and vendors. Many businesses have internal standards, policies and/or environmental management systems that govern their own environmental performance and efficiency. And it is becoming increasingly common for organisations to advertise their standards in their marketing. But if their suppliers are not aware of, or do not follow these same standards, the buying company is likely to be using products that do not meet their standards, and, in some cases, could be accused of misleading advertising.

A supply chain can be complex, with environmental issues occurring at the second- and third-tier supplier levels.

Green supply chain concepts manage environmental impacts where they occur, ideally before they occur. As shown in Figure 16.1, green supply chains recognise the disproportionate environmental impact of supply chain processes in an organisation and balance the issues arising from both sides to satisfy the stakeholders. The stakeholders in the green supply chain are not just buyers and suppliers, they also include governments, regulatory bodies, non-profit organisations and above all consumers.

Green initiatives by manufacturers and suppliers

It is reasonable to state that manufacturing industries are major players in environmental issues. But when the issues relate to safety, whether for products or workplaces, they apply seriously to both manufacturing and service organisations. Lack of safety in the product or in the workplace will inevitably cost money. Accidents mean lost production time plus time-wasting inspections by government officials and perhaps legal costs, as well as the cost of correcting the situation. It has to be cheaper to do it right the first time!

The Advanced Studies Centre of the Massachusetts Institute of Technology back in 1976 studied the cause and effect of environmental factors on the performance of a wide range of companies from different industrial sectors. It found in all cases that those companies that were most advanced in environmental protection were also the most profitable. On reflection, it is not surprising that an efficient (and profitable) company will be

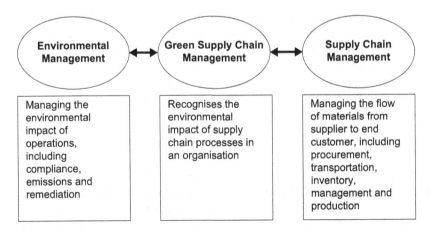

Figure 16.1 Green supply chain concept

safety-conscious and environmentally aware and will be following best practices. It is, however, surprising that the investments in environmental protection by manufacturing companies swing to the political pendulum rather than to business objectives. A report by the US Environment Protection Agency (2000) has concluded that 'a number of leading U.S. companies are providing increasing proof of the link between improved environmental performance and financial gains'. For example, the GM Corporation reduced disposal costs by US$12 million by establishing a reusable-container program with suppliers; Commonwealth Edison saved US$25 million through more-effective resource management. Re-evaluating a company's supply chain – from purchasing, planning and managing the use of materials to shipping and distributing final products – with an emphasis on environmental performance leads to savings. However, environmental performance is too often forgotten by supply chain managers. What are supply chain managers missing? Many managers are unaware that improved environmental performance means lower waste-disposal and training costs, fewer environmental-permitting fees and, often, reduced materials costs. In efforts to green their supply chain, some customers may expect suppliers to meet standards equivalent to their internal standards. Others may request that their suppliers implement an environmental management system (EMS) or become certified to other industry standards. Many environmental standards and models are available, from national ecolabel certifications to international standards. One of the better-known environmental standards is put forth by the International Organization for Standardization (ISO), known as ISO 14001. 'It is becoming more common for companies to include ISO 14001 compliance as a minimum standard in their procurement policies' (Darnall, Jolley and Handfield, 2008).

Both customers and their supply chains stand to gain by collaborating on environmental and efficiency improvements. The benefits of partnering are:

- The supplier knows the product better than the buyer and can maximise efficiencies and minimise associated waste.
- Two or more perspectives (or different expertise areas) are better than one when it comes to designing greener products and processes.
- Working together strengthens the customer-supplier relationship.
- Shared savings and mutual benefits make such efforts even more worthwhile.

Basu and Wright (2005) have established that environmental protection relates to pollution control in two stages. Conventional controls or 'first-generation pollution' controls are applied to pollution in air, water and noise created in the manufacturing process. Such controls are usually regulated by legislation. There is also 'second-generation pollution', which relates to the problems caused by the usage of certain products and chemicals over a long period. The most widespread example of such 'second-generation pollution' is the contamination of land that permeates groundwater.

Causes of pollution

Pollution control engineering has essentially evolved from sanitary engineering and thus the solutions are primarily concerned with effects rather than causes, and with control rather than prevention. The overall ongoing economic impact of pollution has been largely neglected and most of the attention of manufacturing companies has gone to the cost impact of pollution control.

The contamination of land is mostly caused by the disposal of solid wastes by manufacturing industries. With the introduction in the UK of the 'landfill tax', the disposal of solid wastes by incineration will be more cost-effective and environmentally friendly in the future.

The three main gases causing air pollution are carbon dioxide, sulphur dioxide and nitrogen oxides. For many years, the consumption of combustion fossil fuels has been releasing carbon dioxide into the atmosphere faster than it can naturally be absorbed by photosynthesis (provided by trees and plants). As the proportion of CO_2 in the air increases, it absorbs heat and as a result the atmosphere warms up. Sulphur dioxide resulting from the combustion of coal and oil or any sulphur-burning process is another pollutant of air and one of the substances causing 'acid rain'. The damage by acid rain to plants and trees is very evident in parts of Europe. Other acidic gases are the oxides of nitrogen resulting from high-temperature combustion processes in power plants.

Lead is a serious pollutant (neurotoxin) affecting nerves and the brain. The sources of lead include emissions from motor vehicles, lead pipes carrying drinking water, paint and other industrial processes. The Royal Commission on Environmental Pollution recommended in 1983 the benefits of banning the use of lead in petrol. A second pollution-bearing metal is cadmium, which is used industrially in batteries, metal plating and microelectronics. The discharge of cadmium from local industries in the Severn Estuary in the UK severely damaged the local shellfish industry. A third heavy metal is mercury, causing hazards to life even today. In the 1950s, the discharge of industrial effluents with high levels of mercury in a Japanese bay led to deformity and death for villagers who ate fish from the bay.

Another harmful mineral is asbestos, causing painful and fatal diseases such as asbestosis and mesothelioma. Many domestic items such as textured ceilings, ovens and electrical heating equipment in the past contained asbestos. After campaigning by environmental pressure groups, asbestos lagging in power stations and electric sub-stations has been gradually eliminated in the UK.

The noise levels in many 'metal bashing' and packaging industries caused low performance and, more seriously, hearing impairment. Today, there are established preventive and protective measures for noise control.

Cost of pollution

In addition to the long-term immeasurable damage done to vegetation, birds, animals and human beings by air and water pollution, there are many instances of huge compensation bills paid by polluting industries.

The notorious case of mercury poisoning in Japan referred to above led to damages of over US$50 million (1971 value) being awarded to 700 people who were affected and to the estates of 200 people who died.

In 1978, as a result of the wreck of the oil tanker Amoco Cadiz, 200,000 tons of crude oil was discharged into the English Channel. The French Government presented claims amounting to US$2 billion.

In 1992, Cambridge Water Company (UK) was awarded damages of £1 million in compensation for the pollution of land due to tetrachloroethylene by a local leatherworks company.

Benefits of environmental protection

A sound environment protection policy of a company can earn it an extremely marketable environmentally friendly image, leading to higher sales and profitability.

There are also several published examples of 'non-waste technology' where a project of environment control turned out to be a profit earner.

CASE EXAMPLE: DOW CHEMICAL COMPANY

One such example is the Dow Chemical Company's US$7.2 million project for the re-use of cooling water, which produced over 10% return on investment and considerably reduced the pollution of a neighbouring river.

CASE EXAMPLE: 3M COMPANY

The famous 3P programme (Pollution Prevention Pays) of the 3M Company brought about major savings, including US$2 million from the elimination of hydrocarbon wastes from a reactive costing process. When 3M instigated this programme back in 1974, the approach was to capture and control pollution and emissions before they could damage the environment. This approach, although effective, has been changed to a philosophy of prevention rather than containment. The 3P programme now aims to prevent pollution at source by using different materials, changing the process, re-designing the plant and equipment and through recycling waste.

CASE EXAMPLE: SCOTTISH DISTILLERY

Another example is a distillery in Scotland. An effluent treatment project for the control of suspended solids and BOD (biological oxygen demand) produced, with the addition of a drying plant, high-quality cattle feed.

CASE EXAMPLE: DUTCH FLOWER INDUSTRY

About 65% of cut flowers in the world are produced in the Netherlands where land is limited. Mass cultivation in a confined area resulted in fertiliser, herbicide and pesticide contamination.

To correct this problem, growing was shifted to rock wool and water. Fertiliser in the water is recycled through the system to reduce waste. Water-based growth also reduces the risk of installation by weeds and pests, reducing the need for chemical treatments. The new system also greatly reduced variations in growth conditions, greatly improving the predictability of output.

Producers were able to increase output per space and introduce new harvesting methods to reduce costs.

CASE EXAMPLE: TEXAS INSTRUMENTS

Texas Instruments saves US$8 million each year by reducing its transit packaging budget for its semiconductor business through source reduction, recycling and use of reusable packaging systems

---

CASE EXAMPLE: PEPSI

PepsiCo saved US$44 million in 2004 by switching from corrugated to reusable plastic shipping containers for one litre and 20 oz bottles, conserving 98,000 tonnes of corrugated materials.

Environmental strategies

Royston (1979) suggested an eight-point strategy of environmental protection for a manufacturing company.

1. Cut down waste by improving efficiency.
2. Sell waste to someone else.
3. 'Build on' extra to the plant to convert waste into raw materials or products that are valuable to the company or someone else.
4. Work with self-cleansing and dispersing power of the environment to permit maximum discharge of effluent.
5. Negotiate emission standards and subsidies with the authorities and the community.
6. Build a treatment facility needed for residual wastes jointly with another enterprise or the local authority.
7. Build the plant using company staff and know-how.
8. Sell the acquired know-how to others with the same problem.

Green initiatives by governments and non-profit organisations

Environment protection is going in cycles without showing continuous improvement. In the 1970s, the environment was a political hot potato but as we became accustomed to the issues, and without doubt, some issues were overstated (for example, it was widely said in the 1970s that oil would run out by 2000, and, of course, today in 2016 there is a world-wide glut of oil). The scientific evidence of global warming produced by scientists (e.g. of the Royal Society) has seriously created a sense of urgency in governments, including the state governments of the United States, and non-profit organisations worldwide.

One such non-profit organisation in the UK is the National Centre for Business and Sustainability (NCBS), which is committed to advancing sustainable policy solutions and has already shown the way forward through a number of groundbreaking studies. The NCBS is working with a range of businesses and organisations to help integrate the principles of sustainable development into policies, programmes and decision-making processes. The Centre does this by taking a practical approach to sustainability, combining the inspiration of the Co-operative Bank's ethical and ecological policies with a number of practical and applied tools that help put sustainability into a working business context. The NCBS sustainability management services include:

*   Sustainable policy generation.
*   Sustainability appraisals.
*   Measuring and monitoring progress.
*   Sustainability reporting.
*   Sustainability visioning and training.

Political leaders both in government and in opposition are embedding environmental protection and climate change in their political agenda and proposing 'green taxes' to control carbon emissions by industries as well as consumers. A recent UK government-sponsored Stern Review (2006) on 'the economics of the climate change' concluded:

1. There is still time to avoid the worst impacts of climate change if we take strong actions now.
2. Climate change could have very serious impacts on growth and development, and if no action is taken, the global average temperature is likely to rise by 2°C by 2035.
3. The costs of stabilising the climate are significant but manageable (e.g. 1% of global GDP) and delays will be much more costly.
4. Action on climate change is required across all countries and it need not cap the aspirations for growth of rich or poor countries
5. Climate change demands an international response, based on a shared understanding of long-term goals and an agreement on the framework of actions.

The UK government has set up a government-funded non-profit organisation called Envirowise (www.envirowise.gov.uk). Envirowise delivers a valuable government-funded programme of free, confidential advice to UK businesses. This assistance enables companies to increase profitability and reduce environmental impact. On their webpage (March 2016), they claim that since 1994 they have saved in excess of £1.4 billion, in addition to the reduction of landfills and carbon emissions. Their website is well worth a visit to see how they can help any organisation be more efficient by being green.

Countries facing diverse circumstances will use different approaches to make contributions to tackling climate change and these approaches will have both direct and indirect impacts on supply chain management. Key elements of future international frameworks could include emissions trading, technology cooperation, action to reduce deforestation and adaptation of new cleaner technologies in developing countries.

Green initiatives by retailers

Global retail giants Walmart and Carrefour and other supermarkets all over the world are responding to the pressures on packaging waste reduction and other environmental issues of the green supply chain.

The media reports in 2016 are loaded with announcements on 'greening the supply chain' from large retail groups. Walmart, a US company and the world's largest retailer, unveiled its packaging scorecard to major suppliers such as Proctor & Gamble, Unilever and Nestle to cut packaging.

ASDA supermarket, a subsidiary of Walmart in the UK, claimed, as an example, that taking pizzas out of cardboard boxes saved 747 tonnes of cardboard in a year.

'Friends of the Earth', a non-profit organisation in the UK, gave a cautious welcome to Tesco's new environment fund of US$100 million but said the supermarket giant still had a very long way to go if it was serious about greening its operations. Tesco would need to address a number of key areas if it was serious about reducing its environmental impact. These include moving away from car-dependent stores, switching from its global supply chain, radically improving energy efficiency in its stores and cleaning up its supply chains.

Even the airlines, the biggest polluters of CO_2 emissions, have joined the bandwagon. Richard Branson committed the next ten years of profits for Virgin – around US$3 billion – to fighting global warming.

There has been a stronger emphasis on introducing organic and bioproducts. The following case example of 'Carrefour Bio Coffee' illustrates this – by promoting unbranded 500 g/1 kg coffee in bags as 'organic coffee to support fair trading' in 1997, sales increased by 80% in the four years.

CASE EXAMPLE: CARREFOUR BIO COFFEE

Carrefour is a global hypermarket retail chain organisation from France with a turnover of over €100 billion and only second to Walmart, the largest retail company in the world.

The first shipment of coffee beans was delivered in 10 kg sacks to Vitrolles, France, in 1970. The beans were roasted in store and sold in 500 g and 1 kg bags. In April 1997, Carrefour launched the 'organic' coffee brand under the name 'Carrefour Bio' to promote organic products and support fair trading. In 2001, it was decided to establish a 'green supply chain' for 'Carrefour Bio'.

The organic coffee marketed under the name 'Carrefour Bio' is not indexed on the world coffee market. The purchase price is approximately 30% higher than the average price in Mexico. The supplier is contracted to pay a guaranteed minimum price to producers. Producers can obtain up to 60% of the value of the coffee at current international rates; 3000 producers from 37 Mexican communities cultivate coffee using organic methods. Local infrastructure has been introduced to transport people between towns and villages (a two-hour bus ride replacing what was previously a two-day walk). A health scheme has been introduced to provide free medicine and healthcare and a consortium has been set up to buy basic foodstuffs at cost price.

The coffee is cultivated by small farmers working for Uciri cooperative in Mexico using organic methods of farming. Such cultivation helps prevent the land from becoming impoverished. Cultivation is carried out in accordance with French Organic Society standards without the use of organofluorine fertilisers or chemical pesticides for tropical forest conditions. An organic fertiliser comprising sundried hand-picked stoned cherries and animal waste is spread over the plants. This is the only plant treatment used by the farmers.

Cultivation methods are monitored by an organic certification body. An agricultural education centre has also been established catering for organic farming, animal breeding and bio culture.

'Carrefour Bio' coffee project appears to be a win-win initiative for the green supply chain. For Carrefour, sales of the product increased from 29.5 tonnes in 1997 to 54 tonnes in 2001. The fertility of the land has been protected. The average income per family of producers increased from €53 per year in 1985 to €1524 per year in 2000. The local communities benefitted from the infrastructure and facilities for transport, healthcare and education. The consumers are happy with an organic product at an affordable price.

Source: Carrefour Belgium (2002).

Green initiatives by consumers

Consumers have both power and responsibility to enhance the activities and effectiveness of the green supply chain. It is the consumer who pays for the end product or service, and it is the consumer who ultimately suffers or benefits from the impact on the environment. Green initiatives from consumers can be manifested in three ways:

- Make your home green.
- Feedback to retailers.
- Reverse supply chain.

'Make your home green' is becoming a conscious target for many consumers. This is affected in two paths. First, consumers are attempting to minimise 'carbon emissions' by making houses and household appliances more energy efficient and also by moving towards eco-friendly transport. Second, encouraged by local authorities, consumers are making good efforts to the recycling of household waste.

A recent survey in the UK showed that the wasteful packaging from goods bought in the shops accounted for 33% of average household waste. According to a minister in the UK Government, consumers should remove offending or excessive packaging and leave them at the checkout. Under a new reward system of a supermarket chain in the UK, loyalty points are offered in return for not taking away plastic bags. The chain claims that it is giving out 10 million fewer carrier bags a week. Following the introduction of a 5p government levy on each plastic bag, Britain's biggest retailer Tesco reported a 78% drop in the number of single-use carrier bags taken from its stores in England in the first month of charges (*The Telegraph*, 20 March 2016).

A reverse supply chain is a process of getting goods from the customers back to manu-facturers. It's a relatively new trend in supply chain management that focuses on 'green manufacturing' to target recycling, recovery and remanufacturing systems. In these reverse networks, consumers bring products to a retailer or a collection centre. For example, supermarkets in Germany have a bin where customers leave used batteries. Depending on the particular product, it can be refurbished, remanufactured or recycled; making sure the physical flow is efficient. It is estimated that 63 million personal computers were obsolete (worldwide) in 2003 and about ten million electric waste products are dumped per year in Japan. Mobile phones can be returned to the store where the new one is purchased. From there, the phones are resold and re-used in other countries where the technology that is being phased out in developed countries is being introduced. Many other products have the potential for a second use, including computers, auto parts, printer cartridges, refillable containers and a host of other possibilities. In remanufacturing, reverse logistics introduces additional challenges to planning for a closed-loop supply chain. Plan, source, make and delivery of the products are affected by the reverse flow of used products and materials for subsequent consumption in the manufacturing of new products. Reverse logistics play a key role as retail organisations tend to look at their reverse supply chains more closely to enhance customer satisfaction, cost/time efficiencies and supplier performance.

CASE EXAMPLE: XEROX COPIER TAKE-BACK PROGRAMME

Xerox Corporation is an American document management company, which manufactures and sells a range of colour and black-and-white printers, multifunction systems, photocopiers, digital production printing presses and related consulting services and supplies. Xerox is headquartered in Stamford, Connecticut.

In early the 1990s, Xerox launched a new initiative to take back used copiers as a source of materials for new machines. Customers like the programme because they no longer worry about machine disposal.

As a result, 70 to 90% by weight of machines were re-used and 72,000 tonnes were diverted from landfills in 2003. Xerox estimates that 'several millions' were saved per year.

CASE EXAMPLE: GREENING THE BREWING INDUSTRY SUPPLY CHAIN

Throughout the world, organisations are being forced by governments and social pressure, including their direct customers and the final consumers, to consider green environmental issues.

Often those that are calling for direct action are expecting others to take the action. An example of this pressure on producers and suppliers is with Walmart, which in February 2012, claimed that they will cut some 20 million metric tonnes of greenhouse gas emissions from their supply chain before 2016. This equates to removing more than 3.8 million cars from the road. Although this is laudable, on closer examination, it is found that Walmart, themselves not being a producer or manufacturer, is expecting their suppliers to take action. The focus will be on products with the highest embedded carbon such as milk, bread, meat and clothing, and the suppliers of these products are being 'asked', in effect told, to examine the carbon lifecycle of their products from raw materials through to recycling. Costs involved in being energy efficient, such as re-designing packaging and use of organic fertilisers, will be for the supplier to cover and apparently it is expected that any savings made, for example, with cheaper packaging and fewer freight costs, are to be passed on to Walmart.

On the other hand, no matter who is calling for action, energy efficiency must benefit any organisation. A good example is Sierra Nevada Brewery, which, since beginning operations in 1980, has successfully combined a green focus with the production of a quality product. Their approach has three stages.

* Input materials and supplies.
* Processing.
* Waste; re-use, recycling and waste disposal.

Input materials where possible are obtained from 'green' suppliers. This includes malt, yeast, hops, water, CO_2, glass, pallets, cardboard, stretch wrap and office station-ery. Green suppliers are those that are energy efficient, use organic fertilisers and use recyclable materials and materials that are biodegradable. Sierra Nevada has their own CO_2 recovery plant that recovers CO_2 gas from fermentation, purifies the gas and re-uses it in the brewing process. They claim that this creates a quality of CO_2 that is of better quality than can be obtained from commercial suppliers.

For a processing plant in 2005, they installed four 250 kW fuel cells and subse-quently in 2007/2008 they installed the largest private solar power system in the United States. The fuel cells plus the solar system mean they are now self-sufficient for electricity and have a surplus that is sold to the Californian state grid.

Waste management includes operating their own water treatment plant. Organic waste such as grains, yeast and hops are recycled and used as animal feed. They have their own estate for growing hops.

Not only does Sierra Nevada have an excellent reputation, plus awards for being green, they consistently win awards for their lagers, ales, stouts, port and barley wine.

Heineken also is taking proactive green measures. They published plans for the next ten years (2020) to reduce carbon emissions by 40% and water usage down from 4.9 litres per litre of beer to 3.7. This is well behind SABMiller's aim of 3.5 litres of water per litre of beer by 2015 or Anheuser-Busch InBev's even more aggressive aim of 3.5 litres per litre of beer within the next 18 months (by 2012).

An InBev brewery, Budweiser in Georgia (USA), could serve as a benchmark for water per litre of beer. In 2007, following a disastrous three-year drought, regional authorities required industrial users of water to reduce consumption by 10%. Budweiser produces up to eight million barrels of beer per year and thus was a major consumer of water. To reach the target of 10%, the brewery carried out an audit of the water 'footprint' per bottle, which included cleaning, cooling and steam production. By re-using (reclaiming) rinse water for heating and cooling, the net water use in the powerhouse was reduced to zero and overall only 3.1 litres per litre of beer is now used.

SAB Miller has gone further. They considered water usage across the whole supply chain including growing farms. They found in South Africa, due to large-scale irriga-tion, 155 litres of water were being used, per litre of beer, and in the Czech Republic, the ratio was 45:1. Working with growers, they are developing ways of reducing water consumption.

From the above, it can be seen that green issues are not just political or societal issues, they are vital issues for the performance and sustainability of any organisation

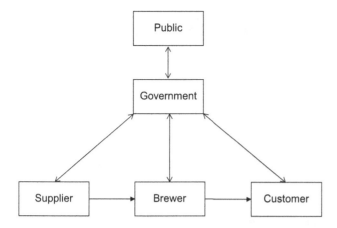

Figure 16.2 Green participants in brewing

(saving water not only reduces costs, it also leads to sustainability and an improved public image).

Internal standards, policies and environmental management are now commonplace. Indeed, many organisations advertise their standards and go out of their way to publish what they are doing 'to save the planet'.

The green supply chain includes the producer, the suppliers to the producer and downstream the customers out to the end user. Other stakeholders and influencers are governments, regulatory bodies and the general public (irrespective of whether they are or are not consumers). Figure 16.2 shows for the brewing industry that:

1. The general public are aware of green issues, but they are not a direct driver for the industry. However, their concerns cannot be ignored, and they are heavily influenced by the media who are quick to publish any adverse green effects or poor practices.
2. Governments, especially Western governments, have taken a strong green stance and in the long term, no producer can hope to avoid legislation, regulations and green audits.
3. Customers, however, in the form of the end consumer, are not key drivers. The consumer might read the label and react positively to words such as 'natural', but most are more interested in consistent quality and taste (and price) rather than 'green' issues.
4. Suppliers are the Achilles' heel. No matter how efficient the brewery is, it is difficult to enforce green thinking and compliance on the various tiers of suppliers, especially remote overseas suppliers.

Once it is accepted that there is a growing public interest, governments cannot be ignored, internal green actions are not only ethically desirable but will reduce costs, the real issue is how to manage the suppliers. This is where problems can arise and lead to bad publicity. Media investigations can uncover a problem with a third-tier supplier and the producer's reputation will be tarnished. An example in another industry illustrates this. The Body Shop (now owned by L'Oréal), the British cosmetics giant that built its reputation on organic-based cosmetics claimed to be sourcing ingredients from companies that protected local farmers. However, in September 2009, it was reported that 90% of palm oil used by the Body Shop was sourced from Daagon Organics in Columbia and that Daagon was a leading member of a consortium that used riot police to evict 123 long-tenured families to grow palm oil plants. It could be argued that the Body Shop acted in good faith and was unaware of the actions being taken by Daagon and the police. The media however showed no mercy, and it was said that the Body Shop had an obligation to audit its suppliers. In short, if a company advertises its standards and then sources from suppliers who do not follow those standards, they are likely to be accused of misleading advertising.

As far back as 1979, Royston provided an eight-point strategy of environmental protection for a manufacturer:

1. Cut down waste by improving efficiency.
2. Sell waste to someone else.
3. Build an extra plant to convert waste into raw materials or products that are valuable to the company or to someone else.
4. Work with state authorities and local communities to agree on conditions for the disposal of final residue.
5. Negotiate emission standards and subsidies with local authorities.
6. Build a treatment plant jointly with another enterprise or the local authority for residual waste.
7. Build the treatment plant using its own staff and know-how.
8. Sell the acquired know-how to others with similar problems.

It is a truism dating back to Frederick Taylor (late 19th century) that if it can't be measured, it can't be managed. With any improvement process, the first stage is to establish the baseline (where are we now), set targets and audit and measure progress. Royston recommended forming a high-level energy and environment committee to set targets for waste avoidance. The committee would:

1. Establish programmes working with shop floor personnel.
2. Identify legislative trends.
3. Predict future waste costs in light of present expenses.
4. Report progress to management.
5. Audit savings.

These recommendations are still relevant. Today, assuming that we have got our own house in order, we recommend including key suppliers and immediate customers in a working group to look at the supply chain to determine where costs can be reduced by the elimination of waste for the benefit of all parties. No matter what our own stance is on climate change, it cannot be denied that the brewing industry is under the spotlight and has to be seen to be taking action. This book advocates that a green approach will save costs, raise the image of a company and overall will be good for business. A win-win scenario.

Sustainable green thinking

The concept of green thinking is not new. Pearce (1992) analysed the relationship with nature and the environmental strategies identified with the Green Movement. Elkington (1994) coined the phrase 'triple bottom line' as a new concept of accounting practice. The triple bottom line or TBL (and also known as 'people, planet, profit') captures an expanded spectrum of values and criteria for measuring organisational success: economic, environmental and social. TBL is not without its critics, and it is now more aligned with corporate social responsibility (CSR). Sustainability or sustainable development was first defined by the Brundtland Commission of the United Nations (1987) as 'the needs of the present without compromising the ability of future generations to meet their own needs'.

With the above background, Basu (2011) developed the 3Es model (efficiency, environment and ethics) as the three dimensions of sustainable green thinking. As shown in Figure 16.3, each aspect includes specific attributes, for example, efficiency relates to lean thinking, energy saving, the green economy and green logistics. Better training, greater awareness and improved communication on green issues characterise the green economy of an organisation. Green logistics refers to buyer companies requiring a certain level of environmental responsibility in the core business practices of their suppliers and vendors. Ethics include issues and processes related to health and safety, fair trading, carbon footprints and CSR. The most important dimension is environment containing pollution control, resources (including energy), conservation, climate change and biodiversity. Climate change relates to the factors (such as CO_2 emission) causing longer-term alterations in weather statistics. Major energy companies like BP (www.BP/suatainability) are focusing on new energy technology and low-carbon energy products in alternative sources, such as wind, solar, biofuels and carbon capture and storage (CCS). The variety of life on Earth and its biological diversity is commonly referred to as 'biodiversity' where each species, no matter how small, has an important role to play.

The primary focus of green thinking is on the environment and its sustainability while efficiency and ethics contribute to the quality and sustainability of the environment. Therefore,

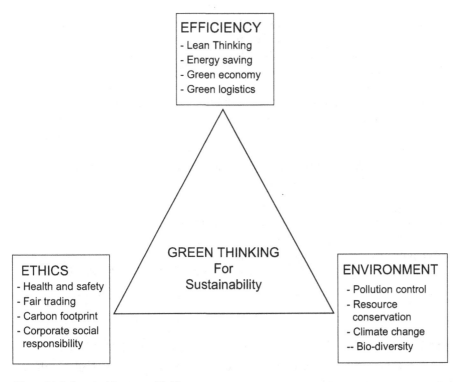

Figure 16.3 Sustainable green thinking concept

the three dimensions and their attributes are interrelated. For example, energy saving and green logistics in efficiency are closely linked to the environment. Likewise, the pillars of fair trading and carbon footprint within ethics are intimately related to the environment.

CASE EXAMPLE: LEADERSHIP IN SUSTAINABILITY BY UNILEVER

Unilever has been the food and beverage super-sector sustainability leader on the Dow Jones Sustainability Index (DJSI) for 16 straight years. Launched in 1999, the Dow Jones Sustainability Indexes are the first global indexes tracking the financial performance of the leading sustainability-driven companies worldwide.

Investors perceive sustainability as a catalyst for enlightened and disciplined management, and thus, DJSI is a crucial business success factor. Highly regarded by influential investors all over the world, the DJSI helps shape the increasingly popular sustainability-driven investment portfolios.

The Unilever Sustainable Living Plan is Unilever's groundbreaking and ambitious roadmap to achieve its growth vision in a way that increases the social value of its brands while simultaneously reducing its environmental impact. Unilever reports its progress in achieving the goals set forth in the USLP and therefore Unilever wanted to ensure that the sustainability data collected and reported by its manufacturing sites was accurate.

As a pilot exercise, ERM (a leading global provider of environmental, health, safety, risk and social consulting services) offered to extend its existing audit to a Unilever facility. This work involved completing a detailed review of the environment, health and safety sustainability data that had been reported, and comparing this data to the situation on-site. As a result, ERM made a series of recommendations that Unilever adopted.

The sustainability-related audit took one day to complete and, following its success, has now become a standard process for all Unilever sites across the world.

ERM's involvement will enable sites to ensure the accuracy of the data collation and reporting. As a long-term partner, ERM has completed 82 audits for Unilever in the last three years.

Integrating ERM's recommendations on sustainability into Unilever's existing audit programme will help Unilever in:

- Reporting against its new sustainability goals.
- Safeguarding the accuracy of EHS data being reported across the Americas.
- Drive performance improvement.
- Leveraging ERM's experienced auditors.

Adapted from www.erm.com (accessed 20 March 2016).

Summary

'The scientific evidence is now overwhelming: climate change is a serious global threat, and it demands an urgent global response', concludes Nicholas Stern (2006).

Note this has been disputed by other scientists but irrespective of what we believe, the pressure is on industry and nations to adopt a green approach to the supply chain. In this chapter, we have attempted to present a balanced view of various initiatives adopted by manufacturers and suppliers, government and non-government organisations (NGOs), retailers and also consumers. Every stakeholder has a role and responsibility in 'greening' the supply chain. We have shown that there are commercial benefits in reducing waste (e.g. excessive packaging). Large retailers like Walmart, Carrefour and Tesco are probably facing disproportionate demands from environmental pressure groups and regulatory bodies but nonetheless are showing visible efforts to respond to these demands. As Saha and Darnton (2005) ask, 'are companies really green or are they pretending to be?'

Continuous education on environmental awareness as a whole can play a major role in raising awareness of green thinking and sustainable development. Global organisations concerned about sustainable development suggest that meeting the needs of the future depends on how well we balance social, economic and environmental objectives or needs (and also the 3Es in Figure 16.3) when making decisions today.

In alignment with the outcomes of COP26, I would propose six key priorities to ensure a sustainable green supply chain and also to support net-zero emissions by 2050.

1. Retrofit houses and buildings with appropriate insulations and green heating systems supported by national government grants.
2. There should be statutory rules that companies should disclose their plans every year for green supply chains and actions being taken for a sustainable environment.
3. Oil and gas companies should invest in targeted R&D and develop technologies that deliver plans minimising the use of fossil fuels.
4. Both the private and public sectors should also invest in continuous research to develop technologies for direct air capture, carbon capture and storage and green hydrogen.
5. There should be the momentum of international and national initiatives for a system of carbon pricing that could lead in time to a levy on carbon emissions.
6. We should continue to invest in renewable energy, electric transport and afforestation.

Discussion questions

1. Explain why it is vital for global organisations to work towards a sustainable green supply chain strategy.
2. What is a green supply chain? Explain why a green supply chain policy can enhance the competitive advantage of a global organisation.
3. By using the case example of Carrefour Bio Coffee, explain the key principles of fair trading.
4. Describe with the help of a diagram of the 3Rs model (Basu, 2011), the key factors contributing to the sustainable green thinking concept.
5. Describe what green initiatives the following key stakeholders of global supply chains should adopt for sustainability:
   Manufacturers and suppliers
   Governments
   NGOs
   Retailers
   Consumers

17 Supply chains in major projects

Introduction

Project management is the discipline of organising and managing resources in such a way that these resources deliver all the work required to complete a project within defined scope, time and cost constraints. A project is a temporary and one-time endeavour undertaken to create a unique product or service. This property of being a temporary and one-time undertaking contrasts with processes or operations, which are permanent or semi-permanent ongoing functional work to create the same product or service repeatedly. The Project Management Institute's 'Body of Knowledge' (PMI, 2008) adds that project management is the most efficient way of introducing unique change.

Because of the one-off unique nature of a project and the repetitive nature of operations, the traditional approach of project management has been consciously different from that of operations management. As supply change management is inextricably linked with operations management, the mindset of project managers usually excludes the principle of supply chain management. The primary objectives of project management are to achieve scope, within time, within budget and manageable risk. All these can be measured and managed. The quality of the delivered project is a further measure, and the measure of quality is often less tangible and more of an opinion or perception. Hence, the objectives of project management, once the scope of the project is established, are identical to those of supply chain management. That is, the right products/materials including correct quantities (in project management terms achieving scope) delivered on time and at an acceptable cost and quality. However, there is a paradigm shift regarding supply chain management when it applies to major projects. Typically, a major project involves several stakeholders working together with controlled resources to deliver a completed project. A major project has many suppliers, contractors and customers: it has procurement and supply, demand planning and scheduling. It usually lasts over several years and has long lead times. Major projects, such as High Speed 1 Channel Tunnel, London Crossrail, the Panama Canal, London 2012 Olympics and Heathrow Terminal 5, to name a few, lasted for several years and were managed like an enterprise. Therefore, we believe that the management of major projects will benefit from adopting some customised supply chain management principles as discussed in this book. One such customisation is the 'building blocks' of a project supply chain.

Learning objectives

Learning objectives for this chapter are:

1. Building blocks of a project supply chain.

DOI: 10.4324/9781003341352-20

2. Are all building blocks suited to all projects?
3. Project supply chain buildings and the project life cycle.

Building blocks of a project supply chain

It is important that a 'total supply chain management approach' is applied and all the building blocks of the supply chain are examined. The synergy that results from the benefits contributed by all elements as a whole far exceeds the aggregate of gains achieved for an individual element. The integrated approach is truly more than the sum of its parts. If one concentrates exclusively on isolated areas, a false impression may be inevitable and inappropriate action taken.

This maxim can be illustrated by the Indian folk tale of four blind men who were confronted with a new phenomenon – an elephant! As none of the men could see what was in front of them, each tried to ascertain the situation in their own way. The first man, by touching its ear, assumed that the elephant was a fan. A second was hit by the elephant's tail and concluded that it was a whip. The third man bumped into a leg and thought it was a column, while the fourth, on holding the trunk, decided that it was an oversized hose. Each man, on the evidence he had, came to a logical conclusion. However, their deductions were the result of looking at only partial data and in fact all had made an erroneous judgement by failing to construe that the total object was an elephant. As with all feedback devices, where a basic message is given, inferences and decisions may be drawn from isolated data that will be false and misleading.

A story in a business context will further underline the limitations of tackling only one part of the whole problem. Following attending a conference, the project director of a multinational company decided that earned value management (EVM) must be the best way forward in a major project. So, he organised his project team, called in experts from a big consulting firm and set up an EVM training programme. The team did an excellent job on two labour-intensive work packages by systematically reviewing earned values, planned values and actual spends at the critical stages of those work packages. As a result, the two enterprises were progressing well and fortunately both were on time and budget. However, it soon transpired that it was very difficult to estimate the planned values and actual spends of many critical work packages governed by procurement schedules. Furthermore, EVM failed to take into account the impact of risks and issues related to quality and safety. Therefore, in isolation, the EVM programmes did not improve the overall performance of project management.

As we mentioned in Chapter 2, our model for total supply chain management comprises six building block configurations, viz:

- Customer focus and stakeholders.
- Resources and time management.
- Procurement and supplier focus.
- Supply and stock management.
- Building and installation.
- Handover and closure.

In addition, there are three cross-functional integrating processes:

- Systems and procedures.
- Regular reviews.
- Quality and performance management.

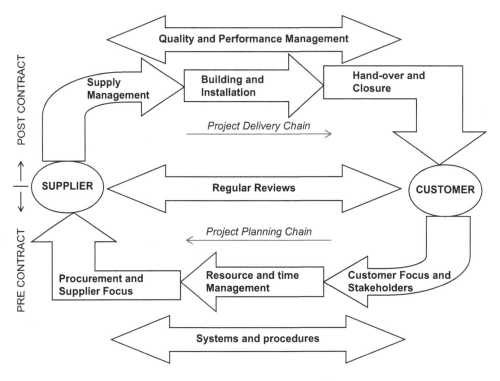

Figure 17.1 Project supply chain building blocks

This model for the customised building blocks of project supply chains (Basu, 2011b) is illustrated in Figure 17.1. Each of the building blocks is briefly described below.

It is also important to point out that there are three streams or categories in Figure 17.1 depending on the affinity of the building blocks (also see Figure 17.5). These are:

1. *Project planning chain*. In this stream, the building blocks are dealing with project planning activities and information flow. The building blocks in this stream are:
    *   Customer focus and stakeholders.
    *   Resources and time management.
    *   Procurement and supplier focus.
2. *Project delivery chain*. Here, the building blocks relate to the project implementation and closure activities and the physical flow of materials on site. The building blocks in this stream are:
    *   Supply management.
    *   Building and installation.
    *   Handover and closure.
3. *Project integration*. At this stage, the building components of project supply chains are acting as the integrators of other building blocks at various stages of the project life cycle. The building components in this stream are:
    *   Systems and procedures.
    *   Regular reviews.
    *   Quality and performance management.

Customer focus and stakeholders

Customers exist both at the start and end of the supply chain. A customer is the person who is paying for the goods or services or is most affected by the outcome of the process. In a project supply chain, a customer could be a sponsor, an investor or an end user. Let's not forget that the demand for a product or service is created by customers.

The basis of all supply chain planning and decisions is underpinned by the forecast of future demand. A supply chain process cannot exist without knowledge and planning for the future. All 'push' processes are executed in anticipation of customer demand, and all 'pull' processes are carried out in response to customer demand. It is a misconception that demand forecast is not required in a pull or just-in-time procedure. Without a forecast of future demand in a pull system, a manager cannot plan the capacity and have the resources required to respond to a customer order. For a traditional push process, a manager arranges the level of production and capacity based on the forecast of future demand. Even in a service industry, where the demand is not discrete, business planning will be unsatisfactory without an estimate of future requirements. In a not-for-profit organisation, demand is unpredictable, but it does have customers and it has a core budget based on demand forecast.

In all instances of a supply chain, the first step is to forecast what the customer exigency will be in the future. It is important to note that is not possible to produce a perfect forecast as there are so many variables affecting future demand, such as past need, promotion and advertising of the product, market share, state of the economy, price discounts, competition and the introduction of new products. Peter Drucker once said, 'The best way to predict the future is to create it'. There are also some recognised characteristics of forecasts, for example, there will always be a forecast error, longer-term predictions are less accurate than short-term estimates and aggregate projections are usually more accurate than individual calculations. In a project supply chain, the importance of demand forecasts cannot be underrated. Without a good forecast or materials, resources and third-party services, the forward planning of resources and procurement schedules would be inadequate and expensive.

It is recognised that a critical determinant of project success is agreeing to the success criteria with key stakeholders before any design or planning activity. In addition to customers, stakeholders comprise many interested parties who will be affected by the outcomes of the project. The demand forecast depends on project deliverables that determine the success criteria by which the success or otherwise of the completed project is judged. Stakeholders, although they may not have a direct pecuniary interest, will also be judging the project, and therefore it is wise to involve them when determining the criteria by which success will be judged. For example, large projects such as building a new motorway will disrupt traffic, require houses and other buildings to be demolished and the progress of the project will be hotly debated in the media by the general public, conservationists and politicians. Therefore, the demand forecast is also dependent on the agreement with key stakeholders with a direct financial interest.

Resources and time management

A primary objective of supply chain management is to optimise supply capacity to fulfil demand in time. Financially, resources will not be infinite. Satisfying customers on time can be crucial, but when delays occur to make up time, an increase in capacity is expensive, be it machines and equipment, warehouse space, transport, stocks of input materials and finished product, and, of course, people. Therefore, a supply chain manager when forecasting must make decisions regarding capacity levels and buffer it to meet the variation in demand and unforeseen delays. In operations management, this can be achieved either by adjusting capacity or production in order to hold output stocks of goods. An organisation may provide excess capacity to satisfy demands for peak periods or set an upper limit of the capacity based on the average demand. This allows them to balance the cost of holding excess inventory on one hand or losing sales on the other. In project management, capacity management means having sufficient resources on hand, which can include stockpiling material, to keep to time schedules and meet milestones.

There are a few options for capacity optimisation open to a manager and there are proven processes to assist them. One such process is aggregate planning where an organisation determines levels of capacity, production and inventory over a planning horizon to maximise the profit. Another established process in operations management is enterprise resource planning (ERP), which has evolved from materials requirement planning (MRP) and manufacturing resource planning (MRPII). ERP is closely linked with sales and operations planning (S&OP) and comprises a series of sequential processes by using a single set of databases, namely, demand planning, rough cut capacity planning, master operations scheduling, materials requirement preparation, detailed capacity planning, purchase scheduling and production scheduling. Number crunching is done using a computer system such as SAP R/3. The success of ERP depends on the structured review process by planners, managers and users. There are ERP systems available that can be tailored for project management.

In project management, critical path scheduling and earned value management are popular tools for assigning resources and time. The planning processes are supported by software such as MS Project and Primavera. However, the application of ERP in major projects is now assisting resources planning and procurement schedules and is interfaced with enterprise project management (EPM) systems.

Procurement and supplier focus

Project procurement is often considered the focal point of a project supply chain and the supply chain manager is usually selected from a procurement background. The procurement activities in projects have two main subdivisions: the buying of materials and placing contracts with suppliers and contractors. Hence, procurement and supplier focus are interconnected. The optimisation of internal capacity can be supplemented by buying in external capacity and resources. As Reid and Sanders (2002: p. 56) say:

> Make or buy is a type of backward integration decision, where the company decides whether to purchase certain materials or tasks or perform the operation itself. Often this is called outsourcing. Many companies routinely out-source certain services, such as janitorial services, repair, security, payroll, or records management.

For the supply chain, the procurement of external capacity and resources could include packaging materials, part built-up assemblies, contracting out utilities and maintenance, hiring contract or casual labour, selecting approved suppliers and outsourcing.

In a typical manufacturing organisation, the cost of bought-in resources and built-up components account for 60 to 90% of the cost of goods sold (COGS). Thus, a powerful way to improve shareholder returns is to address the reduction of purchasing costs. Proper purchasing and supply management can give a network of suppliers capable of delivering service quality. At the same time, this will allow them to beat competitors in addition to securing cost reduction over a period. In a market-driven competitive world, businesses are continuously seeking new suppliers and partners, including outsourcing.

The Internet has provided new challenges and solutions and has enabled extensive connectivity. These capabilities of e-commerce give supply chain partners the facility to share information in real time. It is now recognised that great improvements in value can be attained by coordinating the efforts along the supply chain. These real-time advantages of the Internet are now being achieved in major projects. In short, projects that collaborate and share plans and information are able to improve the overall supply chain performance to their mutual benefit.

The development of a professional service industry has also in recent years increased considerably; however, as observed by Mitchell (1998), purchasing teams appear to have made less effort to reduce costs by outsourcing services. Nonetheless, the importance of service level agreements and supplier partnerships is growing in the global supply chain. A survey by Wade (2003) showed that 31% of the total procurement cost is for bought-in services.

The selection of appropriate or preferred suppliers should involve alternative and complementary attributes between those suppliers and the receiving organisation. Slack et al. (2012) suggest four basic capabilities to make sensible trade-offs:

- Technical capability – the product or service knowledge to deliver sustainable quality.
- Operations capability – the process knowledge to ensure effective supply.
- Financial capability – the financial strength to fund the business.
- Managerial capability – the management talent to develop future business.

It is important to raise the standards of suppliers as well as to learn from them by working in partnership with them. Tightly controlled service level contracts are being replaced by joint service agreements with the free exchange of data and knowledge. Success will depend on mutual trust, a highly developed commercial relationship and an efficient system of data exchange.

The traditional service level agreements (SLAs) where suppliers are penalised for non-conformance of time, cost and specifications are not appropriate for procurement strategy based on partnerships. The traditional procurement thinking should be revisited and there ought to be a move where a client organisation is actively managing the cause of risk or non-conformance and not the effect of that risk. The supply partners are in turn encouraged and incentivised to improve performance and create a competitive advantage for their businesses. This type of progressive partnership approach is illustrated by the so-called 'T5 Agreement' of the London Heathrow Terminal 5 Project by the British Airport Authority (BAA).

CASE EXAMPLE: BAA T5 AGREEMENT

BAA's Terminal 5 programme at Heathrow Airport was one of Europe's largest construction projects, designed to cater for approximately 30 million passengers a year and provide additional terminal and aircraft packing capacity. The facility opened to the public on 30 March 2008 and represented a £4.2 billion investment to BAA.

To achieve the audacious targets in money and programme that they had set themselves, BAA had to consider a novel contracting and procurement strategy. Suppliers signing up to BAA agreements were expected to work in integrated teams and display the behaviours and values akin to partnering. Before embarking on the Terminal 5 (T5) programme of works, BAA looked at a number of UK construction major projects to ascertain the lessons learnt, particularly where they had gone wrong. BAA decided that they had to have an agreement that could cope with an adaptable and dynamic approach, dealing with the uncertainties and embracing integrated teams. So BAA wrote its own bespoke agreement or contract. The same conditions of the contract applied to all key suppliers irrespective of type or usual position as a subcontract.

The key features of the T5 Agreement include:

- BAA as the client organisation held all the risk all of the time during the total life cycle of the project – on time, on budget and to quality.
- This was underpinned by BAA's unique insurance policy against risk. It was not so much about the cost of the BAA policy but the value it released. It did not increase the cost of the project as the insurance covered the supply chain on T5.
- As BAA would underpin all financial risks, contractors did not need to worry that they would be held financially accountable when things went wrong.
- Contractors or suppliers were committed to teamwork in partnership. There was a requirement for a high level of transparency between BAA and its suppliers.
- Contractors worked to predetermined fixed profit levels.
- Profit was the key driver of supplier incentives. By taking away the financial risk, BAA was removing the key commercial constraint and thus suppliers were enabled to focus purely on technical delivery.
- The T5 Agreement was then supported by other documents such as the Commercial Policy, which defined an appropriate commercial tension, and the Delivery Agreement, which was the legal deed and conditions of the contract.

BAA divided the programme into 18 projects ranging in size from £10 million to £200 million. These were then split further into 150 sub-projects and then were divided into circa 1000 work packages. The suppliers were engaged as and when on plans of work or where a supplier's capability was required. From the very start, BAA requested that suppliers work together in completing the projects, even those that are traditionally rivals or lower-tier sub-contractors. At a corporate level, BAA ensured that all suppliers understood that corporate objectives were aligned to achieve a high-quality product within expected costs. BAA also dealt with challenges in encouraging the entire workforce to understand, appreciate and trust the working relationship both between contractors and BAA. They constantly reinforced this message to the workforce.

The T5 project achieved completion complying with targets for time, budget and quality and having generated a teamworking and partnership culture. The T5 Agreement as a whole looks likely to become a template for other major programmes. It now represents a serious alternative procurement route for major programmes of work and project supply chains.

Source: BAA Terminal 5 Project; Basu et al. (2009).

Supply management

Physical inventory – whether equipment or material – must be controlled in projects. Although this is an area of neglect in many undertakings, the good practice of operations in assets and stock management should be applied to projects. Inventory management is generally considered a critical process in operations management, and in accounting terms, inventories are capitalised in projects and thus often overlooked in project management. The importance of inventory management is particularly relevant to major projects with a high level of in-process inventory. Therefore, major projects should benefit from principles of inventory management as applied in operations management.

The purpose of inventories or stocks in operations is to buffer against variations in demand and supply. Inventories usually reside in three stages of a manufacturing process: input stocks (e.g. raw and packaging materials), process stocks (e.g. semi-finished products) and output stocks (e.g. finished products). Wild (2003) introduced the concept of consumed and non-consumed stocks. Consumed articles (such as materials or products) are used by the process or customers and must be replenished in shorter cycles. Non-consumed items (for instance, capital equipment and labour) are repeatedly used by the process and need repair and maintenance and are replaced at longer intervals.

Inventories could be allocated either by design or can accumulate as a result of poor planning and scheduling. Generally, inventory is viewed as having a negative impact on business, incurring the costs of capital (interest paid or interest foregone), storage space, handling, insurance, obsolescence and increased risk of damage and theft. On the other hand, a lack of inventory leads to lost production in the factory and unrealised sales at the end of the supply chain. Holding an inventory of materials and finished products can be seen as an insurance against the uncertainty of supply and as a means to overcome unforeseen variations in demand.

Inventory management is a good indicator of the effectiveness of supply chain management. It is relatively easy to achieve higher levels of customer service by accumulating excessive stocks. It will also obscure short-term operational problems. But this is a costly and risky option in terms of cash flow. Obsolete inventory, be it caused by changes in technology, fashion or due to foodstuffs past their use-by date, clearly has little salvage value. Therefore, it is vital to optimise the inventory level.

In thus optimising inventory levels, two types of stocks are considered: cycle stock and safety stock. First, cycle stock depends on costs associated with ordering, transportation, quantity discount, lead times from suppliers and customer demand. On the other hand, safety stock is the buffer against the variation of demand during the lead time and depends on forecast accuracy, the reliability of suppliers and customer service levels.

Project managers might have a nonchalant attitude towards inventories but not so the accountants. The deliveries from suppliers, whether material or equipment, must be received, inspected and possibly stored before use. The same attention to records and the control of goods from external suppliers should also be applied to internal suppliers.

Building and installation management

In a project supply chain, 'building and installation' is the building block that makes things happen. It is where plans are executed in sites and facilities to produce goods or services for customers. This stage is comparable to operations management in manufacturing industries.

In the building and installation (or production) phase, heavy items of equipment are procured and civil work is undertaken. On completion of this civil work, mechanical, electrical and control facilities are installed. This stage differs dramatically from the previous planning and procurement periods. First, whereas the previous segments are evolutionary in character, the production element is highly mechanistic. The aim is not to develop new technical options but to build as efficiently as possible.

At a construction site, a management team is established to execute and control work physically in the arena. It is a proven practice to delegate the post-contract building and installation action activities to a major contractor or a consortium of contractors. Organisational responsibilities, control systems and communication processes can have a marked effect on the degree of day-to-day control of the project. There are many publications (Meredith and Mantel, 2003) explaining the requirements of the major activities and processes involved in the building and installation phase. These obligations include:

* Kick-off and launch.
* Prepare project management plan.
* Organise facilities and resources.
* Building a team.
* Control requirements.
* Celebrate key milestones.

It is important to also highlight the role of 'project personality' in the production phase of the project. Nichols and Jones (2010) identified two types of 'project personality'. One is the 'silo' personality focusing internally on one element or function of the project. The other is 'system' character thinking holistically of the project outcome. The authors argued that this 'silo' persona is most appropriate for the building phase while holistic thinking and inter-functional teamwork are better suited to all other stages.

The specific role of supply chain management during building and installation includes the supply of resources, equipment and materials underpinned by effective logistics support and contractual or partnering agreement. It is also important to ensure a robust forecasting and review process.

Handover and closure

There is no doubt that supply chain order fulfilment is the Achilles' heel of the e-business economy. At the end of every e-commerce, online trading and virtual supply chain there is a factory, a warehouse and transport. The Internet has elevated the performance of information accessibility, currency transactions and data accuracy, but the real effectiveness of the supply chain from the source to the customer cannot be achieved without the physical efficiency of the supply chain.

In the context of project management, the final handover and closure process determines the success and sustainability of project outcomes. The skill with which the closure is managed has a great deal to do with the quality of life after the project. A successful closure is the destination of the project supply chain. The closure stage of the project may have less impact on technical success or failure, but it has a huge influence on the residual attitudes of the client and end users towards the project.

Systems and procedures

Systems and procedures are essential components to integrate the building block configurations of the total supply chain. There are three major categories of systems and procedures:

* External regulatory and internal quality standards.
* Financial and accounting procedures.
* Information and communication technology.

The activities of a supply chain are affected by both national and international regulatory requirements on packaging, storage, pallets, vehicles, working hours, tariffs and many other issues. In addition, an organisation maintains its own quality standards and service level agreements with its suppliers and partners. The bodies of knowledge and project methodologies such as PMBOK (2008) and PRINCE2 (2009) are powerful guidelines to integrate the building blocks of project supply chains in order to successfully deliver a project.

Another important issue is improving the financial performance of the company. Under pressure to participate in fashionable improvement activities, or to become involved with the newest business wisdom, management may lose sight of the real issue – improving profitability. In response to pressures from stakeholders, there is a risk of overemphasis on short-term financial performance. Consequently, this myopic approach results in over-investment in short-term fixers and underinvestment in longer-term development plans. There is a need for a balanced approach.

The Internet, now taken for granted, has seen the use of technologies to create electronic communication networks within and between organisations and individuals. The implementation of ERP, websites, e-commerce, electronic data interchange and e-mail systems have transformed the process of the exchange of ideas. It has allowed individuals within organisations, and both business-to-business as well as business-to-customer to communicate freely together and to share data in 'real time'. Information technology (IT) has now grown into information and communication technology (ICT). In this ICT domain, we consider two broad areas:

* Information technology and systems.
* e-Business.

There is a visible absence of a dedicated chapter on systems and procedures in the published books on supply chain management, which this volume aims to rectify.

Regular reviews

Regular reviews of the project supply chain are comparable to S&OP in operations management. S&OP is a cross-functional management review process to integrate the activities of the total supply chain. The classical concept of sales and operations planning is rooted in the MRPII process. In basic S&OP, the company operating plan (comprising sales forecast, production plan, inventory plan and shipments) is updated on a regular monthly basis by the senior management of a manufacturing organisation. The virtues, application and training of the S&OP have been promoted by Oliver Wight Associates (see Ling and Goddard, 1988) since the early 1970s.

Project review gatherings are held regularly, and their frequency and participation depend on the type of meeting. Project team meetings by work packages or task groups are generally held every week and led by the team manager. Project progress groups (also known as 'gateway' review meetings) usually take place every month and are led by the project manager. Milestone review meetings are convened at predetermined dates and participated by the project board and the project manager. In addition, ad hoc review groups (e.g. pre-audit, health safety and environment) are also scheduled with specific agendas.

Quality and performance management

Quality and performance management acts both as a driving force of improvement and a fact-based integrating agent to support the planning, operations and review processes. The foundation of performance management is rooted in quality management principles supported by key performance indicators.

There are many different definitions and dimensions of quality to be found in books and academic literature. Basu (2004) defines quality with three dimensions: design quality (specification), process quality (conformance) and organisation quality (sustainability). When an organisation develops and defines its quality strategy, it is important to share a common definition of quality and each department within a company can work towards a common objective. The product quality should contain defined attributes of both numeric specifications and perceived dimensions. The process quality, whether it relates to manufacturing or service operations, should also comprise some defined criteria of acceptable service levels so that the conformity of the output can be validated against these criteria. Perhaps the most important determinant of how we perceive sustainable quality is the functional and holistic role we fulfil within the establishment. It is only when an organisation begins to change its approach to a holistic culture, emphasising a single set of numbers based on transparent measurement with senior management commitment, that the 'organisation quality' germinates.

A good reference line of key performance indicators of a supply chain is the 'balanced scorecard' by Kaplan and Norton (1996). Kaplan and Norton argue that 'a valuation of intangible assets and company capabilities would be especially helpful since, for information age companies, these assets are more critical to success than traditional physical and tangible assets'. The balanced scorecard retains traditional financial measures, customer services and resource utilisation (internal business process) and includes additional measures for learning (people) and growth (innovation). This approach complements measures of past performance with drivers for future development.

Are all building blocks suited to all projects?

The objectives of supply chain management – to balance the demand and supply for the right product or service on time and at an affordable price – remain the same for all businesses. However, it is also true that supply chains serving different markets should be managed in different ways. Both Fisher (1997) and Christopher (2000) have drawn the distinction between 'lean supply chain' and 'agile supply chain'. Agility should not be confused with lean or leanness. 'Lean' is about doing more with less, often with minimum inventory and by placing the emphasis on efficiency. On the other hand, the key characteristics of an agile supply chain include responsiveness and flexibility.

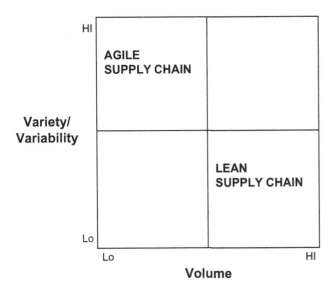

Figure 17.2 Lean and agile supply chain

As shown in Figure 17.2, the approaches for an agile or lean supply chain are determined by volume and variety/variability. An agile supply chain responds quickly to changes in demand whether this is caused by a low volume for high variety products or the unpredictability of demand. By contrast, a lean supply chain works very efficiently when the volume is high and variability is low. The occasions for a purely agile or purely lean supply chain are likely to be infrequent. It is a popular perception, though not always validated, that functional or commodity products need a lean supply chain and innovative and new products require agile supply chain management. As Christopher (2000) points out, there will often be situations for a 'hybrid strategy' where a combination of the two may be appropriate.

Our building blocks of the total supply chain will apply to both lean and agile supply chains but their end objectives require different ways of using these building blocks. In a lean supply chain, the emphasis will be on accurate demand and capacity planning, keeping the inventory low and running the plant efficiently. However, in an agile supply chain, the weight will be given to high service levels by responding rapidly to the end customers. This will require flexibility in process and plant capacity and a higher inventory, usually of semi-finished products, nearer the demand point.

Lean project management principles may have provided some good measures to deal with the uncertainty of project work, but their apparent complexity is pushing project managers towards the lean approaches of supply chain management. This lean thinking attitude to minimising waste in the project supply chain is championed by the Lean Construction Institute (LCI; www.leanconstruction.org). The goal is to build the project while maximising value, minimising waste and pursuing perfection for the benefit of all project stakeholders. This approach has been defined as lean construction. By first focusing on workflow, lean construction unplugs clogs in the project stream and gradually planning, design, construction, delivery and closure of the scheme are better coordinated to deliver maximum value for the project owner. Ballard (2001) has proposed a method of reducing cycle time in home building projects within the context of even flow production. His innovation is the formation of multi-craft teams to overlap activities in each phase of the project and also reduce activity durations through time studies.

CASE EXAMPLE: LEAN PROJECT MANAGEMENT

Morris & Spottiswood is a property solutions business established in 1925 and based in Glasgow, Edinburgh and Manchester. The company provides innovative solutions within clients' property space. This is delivered primarily through partnering relationships with leading retail, financial and public sector organisations.

Morris & Spottiswood ran its first lean project management in 2002/2003. The project's scope was to investigate the annual expenditure of an externally hired plant. Using techniques such as Pareto analysis, value stream mapping, cause and effect and implementation planning, a cross-function team investigated existing processes and established improvements that led to the delivery of short-, medium- and long-term benefits to the business.

The quantifiable savings resulting from lean project management was approximately £200,000 in the first year.

Source: www.morrisandspottiswood.co.uk/.

Major project organisations are showing positive interest in Six Sigma and courses and conferences are on offer for project members. Bechtel was one of the early users of Six Sigma in delivering their multinational projects as the following case example illustrates.

CASE EXAMPLE: SIX SIGMA AT BECHTEL

Founded in 1898, Bechtel is one of the world's premier engineering, construction and project management companies; 40,000 employees are teamed with customers, partners and suppliers on a wide range of projects in nearly 46 countries.

Bechtel has completed more than 22,000 projects in 140 countries, including the Hoover Dam, the Channel Tunnel, Hong Kong International Airport, the reconstruction of Kuwait's oil fields after the Gulf War and the Jubail industrial city.

Bechtel was the first major engineering and construction company to adopt Six Sigma, a data-driven approach to improving efficiency and quality. Although it was originally developed for manufacturing firms, the company was confident that Six Sigma would work in professional services organisations such as Bechtel. Six Sigma has improved every aspect of Bechtel's business, from construction projects to regional offices, saving time and money for both customers and the company.

Six Sigma uses a rigorous set of statistical and analytical tools to produce dramatic improvements in work processes (see Basu and Wright, 2003). Bechtel launched Six Sigma in 2000, when the company was experiencing unprecedented growth – and facing corresponding process challenges. The company has now implemented Six Sigma in its key offices and business units around the world. About half of its employees have had Six Sigma training, and most of its major projects employ its methods from start to finish.

The investment of Bechtel in Six Sigma reached the breakeven point in less than three years, and the overall savings have added substantially to the bottom line, while also benefiting customers. Some examples:

- On a big rail modernisation project in the UK, a Bechtel team used Six Sigma to minimise costly train delays caused by project work and reduced the 'break-in' period for renovated high-speed tracks.
- At a US Department of Defense site in Maryland, Six Sigma helped achieve significant cost savings by streamlining the analysis of neutralised mustard gas at a project to eliminate chemical weapons.
- To speed up the location of new cellular sites in big cities, Bechtel developed a way to let planners use computers to view video surveys of streets and buildings, making it easier to pick the best spots.
- In a mountainous region of Chile, Six Sigma led to more efficient use of equipment in a massive mine expansion, with significant cost savings.
  Six Sigma is the most important initiative for change we have ever undertaken. We're happy to report that it's becoming 'the way we work'

Source: www.bechtel.com (2006).

The introduction of Six Sigma to the High Speed 1 (HS1) project delivered both cost savings and programme benefits. The Six Sigma programme trained 23 Black Belts and around 250 Green Belts and Yellow Belts. A further 100+ senior managers were educated to act as Champions in improvement projects. Over 500 such upgrading schemes were completed, leading to a cost saving/avoidance of at least £40 million. These ventures covered and benefited a wide range of activities across the whole HS1 task, including numerous architectural, civil and railway construction activities. Consequently, this ensured timely third-party methodology approvals, thus facilitating procurement, accelerating drawing reviews and allowing the timely generation of construction record documentation. It is evident that some of the improvement projects, such as the reduction of lead time in methodology approvals and drawing reviews, also applied lean thinking concepts.

The supply chain in the service sector will also need all the building blocks of the total supply chain, although they should be used and managed differently depending on services. For example, in an insurance service industry, the approach to inventory management would be different to that adopted in an automobile manufacturing business. In the service sector, the variation in demand is buffered by managing 'non-consumed' stock (such as people and databases), while in the manufacturing sector, the emphasis is on consumed stock (e.g. materials).

Project supply chain building blocks and project life cycle

The life cycle of a project (Figure 17.3) typically goes through four stages, viz, initiation, design, execution and closure (Turner, 1999). It is important to note, as shown in Figure 17.4, that these four aspects of the project life cycle are also in congruence with the eight processes of PRINCE2 (2009). The nomenclature of each phase of the project

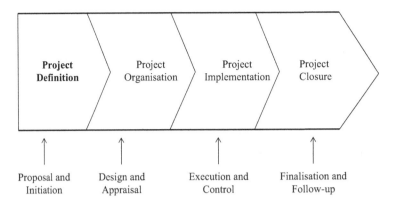

Figure 17.3 Project life cycle

life cycle often varies from Turner's given names in many project applications (e.g. definition, design, implementation and handover) or it may have more stages (e.g. concept,
feasibility, implementation, operation and termination in BS 6079). However, alternative
periods of the project life cycle can be easily aligned to Turner's given names. Hence, the
'building blocks' of the project supply chain are aligned with Turner's project life cycle
as shown in Figure 17.5.

In Figure 17.5, project supply chain building blocks have been presented as an
'open bracelet' against the four stages of the project life cycle. The building blocks
of project planning chains (viz. customer focus and stakeholders, resources and time
management and procurement and supplier focus) align with the first two stages of
the project life cycle (proposal and initiation and design and appraisal). the project
planning chain constitutes 'pre–contract' planning activities managed by the customer
of the project, often referred to as the 'intelligent client' (www.apm.org.uk). The

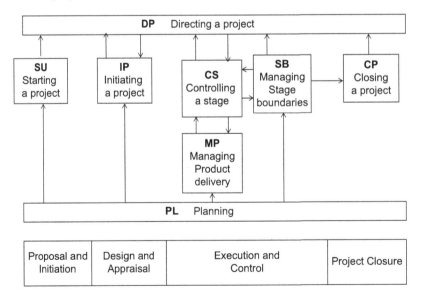

Figure 17.4 PRINCE2 and project life cycle

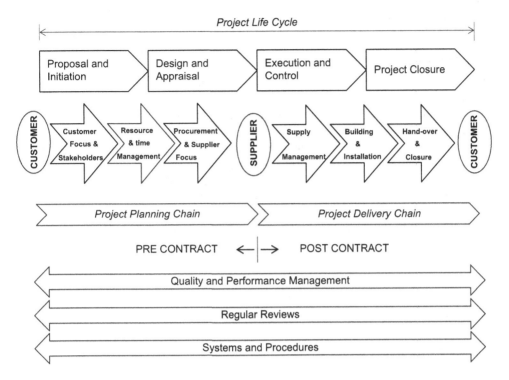

Figure 17.5 Project supply chain building blocks and project life cycle

project delivery chain encompasses 'post-contract' delivery activities managed by a consortium of main suppliers and contractors in collaboration with the customer or client. The integrating functions (systems and procedures, quality and performance management and regular reviews) span across all building blocks of the project supply chain and the four stages of the project life cycle.

Summary

In this chapter, we have explained the characteristics and roles of supply chain building blocks in total supply chain management. The building blocks consist of nine components out of which six are for supply chain configuration (customer focus and stakeholders, resources and time management, procurement and supplier focus, supply management, building and installation and handover and closure). Three components are for supply chain integration (systems and procedures, quality management and regular reviews). These building blocks will be applicable, to a varying degree, to all types and strategies of supply chains regardless of whether they are primarily pull or push processes, agile or lean supply chains or if they are within the construction, manufacturing, technology or service sectors for projects.

In this chapter, we have also aimed to present supply chain management as an interface between operations and projects and this interface works well when a major project with several years duration is managed as an enterprise. However, the concepts, building blocks and processes presented in this chapter should also benefit smaller projects with multiple suppliers and complex requirements of resources.

Discussion questions

1. Explain why the application of supply chain management processes is so important in major projects.
2. What are the building blocks of a project supply chain? How do they compare with the building blocks of an operational supply chain?
3. Who is responsible for managing the project planning chain and who is responsible for managing the project delivery chain?
4. How would you justify the application of Six Sigma and Lean thinking in managing the supply chain of a major project lasting over four years?
5. What are the learning points of the supplier partnership agreement of the Heathrow Terminal 5 project?

18 Quantitative analysis and optimisation in global supply chains

Introduction

Designing and structuring optimum global supply chain networks is a complicated decision-making process. The typical input to such a process is as follows:

- A set of global markets to serve.
- Demand projections for the different products in different markets.
- Information about future macroeconomic conditions.
- Cost of financing.
- Transportation and production costs.

Given the above requirements, companies have to decide at the operations level, a demand forecast, an optimum stock level, production batch sizes and procurement order quantities, and very often consider the availability of products. In addition, at a strategic level, the company has to decide:

- Where to locate factories.
- How to allocate production activities to the various facilities of the network.
- How to manage the distribution of products (e.g. where to locate distribution facilities).

    Proven digital software and integrated systems are available to address these complex issues. In order to reduce the proportion of subjective judgements and understand the rationale of computer solutions, it is important to address and understand the mathematics behind these decision processes. Standard mathematical techniques have been developed in the context of operational research or operations research (Churchman et al., 1968). Additionally, there are many mathematical models that address complex global supply chain requirements and provide solutions (Kouvelis et al., 2001)

In Chapter 5, qualitative methods of demand forecasting, operations planning and stock management in making management decisions for global supply chains were described.

Learning objectives

In this chapter, we aim to address quantitative methods to analyse and understand the complexities of various supply chain management processes with a particular focus on:

- Demand forecasting.
- Inventory management.
- Transportation.
- Location models.

DOI: 10.4324/9781003341352-21

Demand forecasting

We established earlier that demand forecasting is the starting point of supply chain planning. We also observed a trend of larger and larger swings in inventory demand for upstream echelons of the supply chain players in response to small changes downstream in customer demand. These swings are referred to as supply chain dynamics or the 'bullwhip effect'. Uncertainty in demand forecast also leads to unnecessary large holdings of safety stock. The importance of demand forecasting in managing global supply chains cannot be emphasised enough. In demand forecasting, it must be acknowledged that many significant factors influence both the process and accuracy of demand forecasting, including the following:

- Historical demand and trends of existing products.
- Lead time of procuring or replenishing existing products.
- Introduction plan of new products:
    Advertising, promotion and discount plans.
    Market share and relative growth of the product portfolio.
    Competition and market intelligence.
- Global economy and emerging markets.

Chapter 5 primarily concentrated on qualitative forecasting methods that rely on human experience and judgement. Qualitative methods include the regular review of past demand (factor 1) but are heavily tempered by the executive consensus on the other six factors. With a shorter review cycle (such as monthly) qualitative methods is a proven forecasting process when limited historical data is available. When reliable data over a long period is available, quantitative methods are expected to provide a sound basis for demand forecasting. There are two quantitative methods of demand forecasting that are prevalent.

Time series. Time series methods use historical demand. The one independent variable is the time used to analyse trends or seasonal factors that influence the demand data. These methods are relatively simple and are suitable for forecasting demand for established products where the demand pattern does not change significantly from one cycle to the next.

Causal models. Causal models employ many factors other than time when predicting forecast values. These methods assume the correlation and interdependencies of multivariates. For example, product spending or consumer spending power is correlated to demand. Another version of causal models is the simulation of 'what if' scenarios to prepare both medium-term and longer-term demand plans.

Time series demand forecasting

The objective of a time series forecasting method is to predict the systematic component of demand that comprises a level and trend and sometimes also a seasonal factor. Seasonal factor is usually applied as a multiplying factor. Thus, if:

F_t = forecast of demand (systematic component) at period t
L_t = estimate of level at period t
T_t = estimate of trend (increase or decrease) at period t
S_t – estimate of seasonal factor at period t

Then

$$F_t = (L_t + T_t) S_t$$

The level (L_t) and trend (T_t) are estimated by two popular methods, viz. moving average and exponential smoothing. The appropriateness of each method depends on the characteristics of demand and systematic component

Moving average

The moving average method is used when the demand has no observable direction of trend or seasonality. In this method, the level in period t is estimated as the average of demand of the most recent N periods. The forecast (systematic component) is stated as:

$$F_{t+1} = L_t$$

where $L_t = (D_t + D_{t+1} + ... + D_n)/N$

For example, we make the forecast of period 6 at the end of period 5 by taking the average of demands in the previous four periods. The selection of N (the number of periods) depends on the apparent variation of demand

An example of simple moving average is shown in Table 18.1 and graphically illustrated in Figure 18.1.

The calculations are simple as:

For a four-week moving average, $F_5 = (650 + 670 + 710 + 780)/4 = 703$

Similarly, for a six-week moving average, $F_7 = (650 + 670 + 710 + 780 + 850 + 910)/6 = 762$

As illustrated in Figure 18.1, the graph for a six-week average is smoother than that for a four-week average. There are problems with using the simple moving average as a forecasting tool. The moving average is tracking actual data, but it is always lagging behind it.

Table 18.1 Simple moving average

Cycle	Demand	Four-week moving average	Six-week moving average
1	650		
2	670		
3	710		
4	780		
5	850	703	
6	910	753	
7	870	813	762
8	780	853	798
9	890	853	817
10	920	863	847
11	790	865	870
12	840	845	860

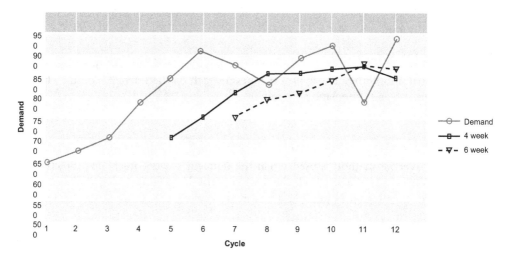

Figure 18.1 Graphs illustrating simple moving average

The moving average will never reach the peaks or valleys of the actual data – it smooths out the data.

Nevertheless, for its simplicity, it is often a popular method. There are some variations of moving average methods such as Weighted moving average and cumulative moving average, but these methods are closer to exponential smoothing methods as described below.

Exponential smoothing

The simple exponential smoothing methods, similar to moving averages, are appropriate when the demand has no observable trend or seasonality.

The formula for simple exponential smoothing method is

$$F_{t+1} = \alpha D_t + (1 - \alpha)F_t$$

where α = the smoothing parameter $0 \leq \alpha \leq 1$

High α such as 0.7 puts weight on recent demand while low α such as 0.1 puts weight on previous periods.

An example of simple exponential smoothing is shown in Table 18.2 and graphically illustrated in Figure 18.2.

Sample calculations are as follows:

For cycle 3, when α = 0.1, forecast = 0.1 × 775 + 0.9 × 820 = 825.50

Similarly for cycle 3, when α = 0.6, forecast = 0.6 × 775 + 0.4 × 820 = 793.00

As illustrated in Figure 18.1, the graph for α = 0.1 is smoother than that for α = 0.6. Values of α close to one have less of a smoothing effect and give greater weight to recent

Table 18.2 Simple exponential smoothing

Cycle	Demand	Forecast $\alpha = 0.1$	Forecast $\alpha = 0.6$
1	820		
2	775	820.00	820.00
3	680	815.50	793.00
4	655	801.95	725.20
5	750	787.26	683.08
6	802	783.53	723.23
7	798	785.38	770.49
8	689	786.64	787.00
9	775	776.88	728.20
10		776.69	756.28

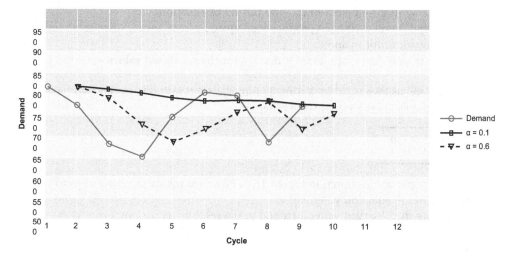

Figure 18.2 Graphs illustrating simple exponential smoothing

changes in the data, while values of α closer to zero have a greater smoothing effect and are less responsive to recent changes. Therefore, the choice of the value of α depends on the user's preference for the smoothing effect of forecasts.

Linear regression

Linear regression analysis is a tool to establish the 'best fit' linear relationship between two variables and is often used to measure the trend in demand forecast data. Two common methods are:

* Method of intercept and slope.
* Method of least square.

In a practical business environment, the team members normally resort to drawing an approximate straight line by employing their visual judgement. Sometimes, they use the 'method of intercept and slope'. Both of these practices are the estimated 'best fit' relationship between two variables. The reliability of such estimates depends on the degree of correlation that exists between the variables.

Regression analysis is used not only to establish the equation of a line but also to provide the basis for the prediction of a variable for a given value of a process parameter. Given a significant co-relation between the two variables, regression analysis is a very useful tool, enabling one to extend and predict the relationship between these variables.

The 'method of intercept and slope' for developing the basic steps is as follows:

1. Consider the equation of $y = mx + c$, where m is the slope, c is the intercept and x and y are the two variables.
2. In the equation of $y = mx + c$, substitute each of the pairs of values for x and y and then add the resulting equations.
3. Form a second similar set of equations, by multiplying through each of the equations of Step 2 by its co-efficient of m. Add this set of equations.
4. Steps 2 and 3 will each have produced an equation in m and c. Solve these simultaneous equations for m and c.
5. Plot the straight line graph for $y = mx + c$ for the calculated values of m and c.

Consider where an investigation was made into the relationship between two quantities y and x and the following values were observed:

y	5	8	9	10
x	1	2	3	4

The values are plotted as shown in Figure 18.3. Now we follow the basic steps to calculate m and c in the equation $y = mx + c$.

Substituting the observed values of x and y, the resulting equations are:

$$5 = m + c$$

$$8 = 2m + c$$

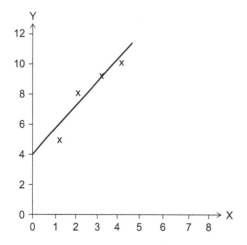

Figure 18.3 Linear regression analysis

$9 = 3m + c$

$10 = 4m + c$

$32 = 10m + 4c$ (18.1)

Multiplying each of the equations by its co-efficient of m, the resulting equations are:

$5 = m + c$

$16 = 4m + 2c$

$27 = 9m + 3c$

$40 = 16m + 4c$

$88 = 30m + 10c$ (18.2)

We then simultaneously solve Equations (18.1) and (18.2) for m and c.
We find that

$m = 1.6$

$c = 4$

Hence $y = 1.6x + 4$

We calculate two pairs of values for x and y to draw a straight line as shown in Figure 18.3.

| y = demand | 4 | 8.8 |
| x = time | 0 | 3 |

In the above example, constant 4 measures the estimate of demand at period $t = 0$ and slope 1.6 measures the rate of change of remand per period.

Holt's model

Holt's model provides a method of predicting demand when there is an observed trend but no seasonality. The demand is assumed to be represented by the following equation:

$D_t = at + b$ (similar to the above regression model $y = mx + c$)

In this case, systematic component = level + trend.
We determine the values of a and b by a regression analysis of demand (D) and time period (t).
At period $t = 0$, our initial level $L_0 = b$, and our initial estimate of trend $T_0 = a$.

In Holt's model, we apply a smoothing constant for level as α where $0 \leq \alpha \leq 1$ and a smoothing constant for trend as β where $0 \leq \beta \leq 1$.

After reviewing the demand for period $t + 1$, the estimates for both level and trend are revised as follows:

$$L_{t+1} = \alpha D_{t+1} + (1 - \alpha)(L_t + T_t)$$

$$T_{t+1} = \beta (L_{t+1} - L_t) + (1 - \beta)T_t$$

It is important to note that the revised estimate of either level or trend is a weighted average of the observed value and the old estimate. Hence Holt's method is also known as double exponential smoothing.

Winter's model

Winter's model provides a method of predicting demand when there is an observed trend and also seasonality.

In this case, systematic component = (level + trend) × seasonal factor.

We obtain trend by a linear regression method. Seasonal factor for a period t is the ratio of the actual demand to the demand without seasonality. We obtain the estimate of the seasonal factor for a given period by averaging seasonal factors for similar periods.

In period t, the forecast for future periods is given by the following equation:

$$F_{t+1} = (L_t + T_t)S_{t+1} \text{ where } S_t \text{ is the estimate of the seasonal factor at period t.}$$

After reviewing the demand for period $t + 1$, the estimates for level, trend and seasonal factor are revised as follows:

$$L_{t+1} = \alpha(D_{t+1}/S_{t+1}) + (1 - \alpha)(L_t + T_t)$$

$$T_{t+1} = \beta(L_{t+1} - L_t) + (1 - \beta)T_t$$

$$S_{t+1} = \gamma(D_{t+1}/L_{t+1}) + (1 - \gamma)S_t$$

where $0 \leq \alpha \leq 1$ and $0 \leq \beta \leq 1$ and $0 \leq \gamma \leq 1$

Forecast error measures

Measures of forecast errors or forecast accuracy are important indicators in supply chain planning. These measures assist the planners in a number of ways including:

- They help to correct forecast estimates.
- Contingency plans account for forecast errors.
- Safety stock levels depend on forecast accuracy.

There is a number of ways forecast errors can be measured.

Bias indicates an average bias whether the forecast is too high (negative bias) or the forecast is too low (negative bias).

Mean absolute deviation (MAD) indicates an average bias in absolute value corrected for signs – how many units the forecast is off from the actual data. For example, if the distance or variation from actual to forecast was for one period plus 4 and for the next period minus 4 (+6 and −4) the absolute deviation for the two periods is 10. Thus, the average or mean is 5 (10/2) The logic being in forecasting it is just as bad being over as it is being under!

Mean absolute percentage error (MAPE) indicates on an average basis, how many percentage points are off from the data.

Mean squared error (MSE) is a forecast error measure that penalises large errors more than small errors

If E_t is the error in period t, there are n periods and D_t is the demand in period t, then

$$\text{Bias} = \Sigma E / n$$

$$\text{MAD} = \Sigma |E| / n$$

$$\text{MAPE} = \Sigma |E| / n \times 100\% / D$$

$$\text{MSE} = \Sigma E^2 / n$$

$$\text{Standard deviation } \sigma = \sqrt{\text{MSE}} = \sqrt{(\Sigma E^2 / n)}$$

Also assuming a random distribution of errors, standard deviation $\sigma = 1.25$ MAD.

Worked-out examples of different measures of forecast error are shown in Table 18.3.

Because of its simplicity and robustness, MAD is the most popular measure of forecast error. It works well with a distribution without mean or variance and it is also related to standard deviation by a factor (e.g. 1.25).

Table 18.3 Examples of forecast error measures

Period	Demand (D)	Forecast	E	Absolute E	Square of E	Abs E/D
1	1600	1650	−50	50	2500	0.0313
2	2200	2010	190	190	36100	0.0864
3	2000	2200	−200	200	40000	0.1000
4	1600	1580	20	20	400	0.0125
5	2500	2480	20	20	400	0.0080
6	3500	3520	−20	20	400	0.0057
7	3300	3310	−10	10	100	0.0030
8	3200	3200	0	0	0	0.0000
9	3900	3850	50	50	2500	0.0128
10	4700	4720	−20	20	400	0.0043
Cumulative			−20	580	82800	0.2639
			Bias = −2			
				MAD = 58		
					MSE = 8280	
						MAPE = 2.64%

Causal forecasting

In causal forecasting, assuming that the variables are closely correlated, our knowledge of the value of one variable (or several variables) enables us to forecast the value of another variable.

In a causal model,

$$y = f(x_1, x_2, \ldots x_n)$$

where f is a forecasting function and $x_1, x_2, \ldots x_i$, is a set of variables. In this representation, the x variables are often called *independent variables*, whereas y is the *dependent variable*.

There are two commonly used methods applied for causal forecasting and these are:

- Multiple regression.
- Structural equation modelling.

In simple regression, $Y = b_0 + b_1 x$.

While in multiple regression, $Y = b_0 + b_1(x_1) + b_2(x_2) + b_3(x_3) + \ldots + b_n(x_n)$. In this method, a variate value (Y) is calculated for each respondent or independent variable.

The objectives of multiple regression, usually carried out by SPSS software, are to

1. Determine if the prediction is statistically significant (< 0.05).
2. Determine the correlation co-efficient (r), positive or negative ($0 < r < 1$).
3. Evaluate the correlation (R^2) between the single dependent variable and the multiple independent variables. (R^2 represents the 'goodness of fit' and is equal to the regression sum of squares (RSS)/total sum of squares (TSS)).
4. Identify the relative importance of each of the multiple independent variables in predicting the single metric dependent variable.

Structural equation modelling

The analysis of causal forecasting is also carried out by structural equation modelling (SEM) based techniques. The advantage that SEM-based techniques have over first-generation techniques (such as multiple regression analysis) is the greater flexibility that a researcher has for the interplay of theory and data. SEM enables the researcher to construct immeasurable variables measured by indicators (also called observed variables) as well as measurement errors. Hence, it overcomes the limitations of first-generation techniques such as multiple regression.

SEM techniques such as LISREL or AMOS estimate the causal relationship between variables by means of co-variance analysis. The assumptions of co-variance-based SEM include normally distributed data, independent observations, random sampling of data and a large sample size to validate testing and inference. An alternative method partial lease squares (PLS) is primarily intended for causal-predictive analysis in situations of high complexity but low theoretical information. Unlike SEM models, PLS models assisted by software (e.g. SmartPLS) do not require alternative models that are equivalent in terms of overall model fit. The underlying procedure of PLS follows a simple or multiple regression process.

Regardless of whichever tool, AMOS or SmartPLS, is chosen, it is essential that a causal model with appropriate constructs is developed that complies with the governing factors of demand forecast. The simple causal model as shown in Figure 18.4 includes two exogenous constructs (viz. customer service and promotion) leading to an endogenous

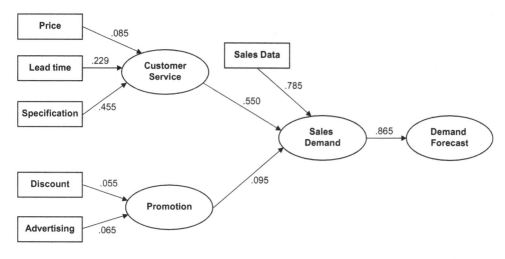

Figure 18.4 A causal forecast model

construct (viz. sales demand). Each construct is supported by relevant indicators providing input data. The outcome of this model is demand forecast.

Paths in the model in Figure 18.4 show the governing factors of demand forecast. Customer service is governed by price, lead time and specification. Promotion is governed by discount and advertising and sales demand is governed by two exogenous constructs (viz. customer service and promotion) and an indicator (sales data). After the data collection for all indicators, the data was validated. The simulation of the model by AMOS produced estimated coefficients for each link as shown in Figure 18.4. When we look at the estimated coefficients, we can see the relative impact of each indicator and construct on the outcome of the demand forecast.

Inventory management

In Chapter 8, we described simple inventory management models for both ROL/ROQ and fixed interval policy. Assumptions were:

- Demand is deterministic at a constant consumption rate.
- Lead time is also deterministic.
- No shortages are permitted.

However, in real-life situations, we have to allow for shortages, lost sales, quantity discounts, variable demands and other constraints. In this chapter, we aim to address these complex conditions

Inventory model with shortages

Figure 18.5 represents graphically the inventory situation where shortages are allowed.
The above situation is defined by the following parameters:

S is the inventory at the beginning of each interval,

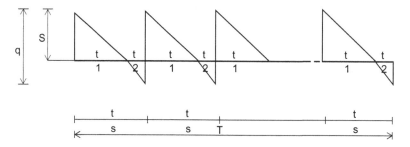

Figure 18.5 Inventory situation with shortages

Q is the inventory including the shortage quantity,
T is the total time period (e.g. one year),
D is the deterministic demand during the period T,
C_1 is the ordering cost per replenishment,
C_2 is the stockholding cost,
C_3 is the cost of shortages,
V is the total expected cost during T,
t_1, t_2, and t_s are time periods as shown in Figure 18.5.

Using a simple similarities of triangles, we observe that:

$$t_1 = (S \times t_s)/q \text{ and } t_2 = (q - S)t_s/q \text{ and } t_s = Tq/D$$

The average inventory cost during $t_1 = S.C_2.t_1/2$
Similarly, average shortage during $t_2 = (q-S)C_3.t_2/2$
Hence, $V = (S.C_2.t_1/2 + (q-S)C_3.t_2/2 + C_1)D/q$
Substituting the values of t_1 and t_2, we get

$$V = (S^2.C_2.t_s/2q + (q-S)^2.C_3.t_s/2q + C_1)D/q$$

And then substituting the value of ts, we get

$$V = S^2C_2.T/2q + (q-S)^2 C_3.T/2q + C_1.D/q \text{ (1)}$$

Proceeding by the use of calculus for Equation (18.1), we get

$$dV/dS = SC_2T/q -(q-S)C_3T/q$$

$$dV/dq = -S^2.C_2.T/2q.q + (4q(q-S) - 2(q-S)^2/4q^2)C_3.T - C_1.D/q^2$$

Solving the equations for S and q, we get

$$q0 = \sqrt{2DC_1/TC_2} \times \sqrt{(C_2+C_3)/C_3} \tag{18.3}$$

$$S0 = \sqrt{2DC_1/TC_2} \times \sqrt{C_3/(C_2+C_3)} \tag{18.4}$$

Example

A manufacturer has to supply 24,000 units of boxes per year to his customers. Inventory holding cost is £0.10 per unit and the ordering cost is £350 per order. If the shortage cost is £0.20 per unit per month, calculate the optimum inventory levels:

- at the beginning of each order cycle and also
- including the shortage quantity.

Substituting in Equations (18.3) and (18.4), we get

$$q0 = \sqrt{2 \times 2400 \times 350/12 \times 0.10} \times \sqrt{(0.10 + 0.20)/0.20} = 4578 \text{ units}$$

$$S0 = \sqrt{s \times 2400 \times 350/12 \times 0.10} \times \sqrt{(0.20/(0.10 + 0.20)} = 3056 \text{ units}$$

Inventory model with quantity discount

In practice, we cannot assume a simple unique cost $c0$ per unit of an item. Purchasing $c0$ may vary according to the discount scheme, e.g.

$$c_0 = p_0 \text{ if } b_0 \leq Q \leq b_1$$

$$c_0 = p_1 \text{ if } b_1 \leq Q \leq b_2$$

and so on as illustrated in Figure 18.6.

If we consider the cost of buying x units, the cost to the supplier per year is given by

$$V = xc_0 + xC_1/Q + C_2.Q/2 \tag{18.5}$$

If we assume the cost of an item depends on the marginal cost per item (B) and a set-up cost (A), then the cost of a lot size (Q) is given by

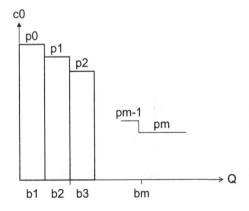

Figure 18.6 An illustration of quantity discounts

$$Q = A + BQ$$

Hence cost per unit $c_0 = A/Q + B$ (18.6)
Substituting the value of c0 from Equation (18.6) in Equation (18.5), we get

$$V = xB + x(C_1 + A)/Q + C_2.Q/2$$

Seeking the minimum for V we differentiate and setting $dV/dQ = 0$, yields the optimum lot size $Q_0 = \sqrt{(2x(C_1 + A)/C_2}$

If c_0 follows the rule illustrated in Figure 18.6, then the minimum cost per year can be expressed by a set of equations as

$$V_i = xp_i + xC_1/Q + C_2Q/2 \text{ where } b_i \le Q \le b_{i+1} \text{ and } I + 0, 1, 2, \dots m$$ (18.7)

The solution is an iterative process by evaluating the optimum lot size of each price and then select the lot size for the total minimum cost.

Safety stock

The concept of safety stock is simple. Its purpose is to prevent stock-outs during the lead time. Stock-outs stem from factors such as fluctuating customer demand (forecast inaccuracy) and variability in lead times for procuring the item and the service level expected by the customer. Figure 18.7 shows the stock profile with the safety stock of a ROL/ROQ system.

Some operations managers use experience-based judgements to set safety stock levels, while others base them on a portion of cycle stock level of say 10 or 20%, for example. Although easy to execute, such techniques generally result in poor performance. A mathematical approach to safety stock is likely to justify the required inventory levels to business leaders by optimising customer service against stock carrying costs. Safety stock determinations are not intended to eliminate stock-outs for all conditions, but they should be aimed at reducing the risk of stock-outs.

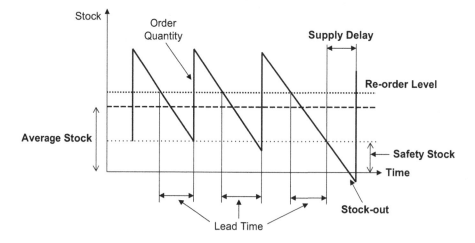

Figure 18.7 Stock profile with safety stock

There are many complex mathematical formulae available for calculating safety stocks depending on the demand rates, variation of demands, lead times and the variation of lead times and the level of customer service. One such formula for safety stock (ss) is:

$$ss = z_\alpha \times \sqrt{E(L)\sigma_D^2 + (E(D))^2 \sigma_L^2} \qquad (18.8)$$

where,

- α is the service level, and Z_α is the inverse of the normal cumulative distribution of α,
- $E(L)$ is the average lead time, and σ_L is the standard deviation of lead time,
- $E(D)$ is the average demand per unit of time (must be consistent with unit of L), and σ_D is the standard deviation of demand (King, 2011).

By applying complex formula, with the assistance of computer programs, operation managers very often come across very high levels of safety stock and these have proven to be impractical. We propose a simplified approach. It is easier to control the variation of lead times by a rigorous procurement policy than the variations of demand. As discussed earlier, there are several external factors influencing the demand forecast that are often beyond the control of planners. The level of customer service can be set for a product depending on its importance in the business plan. Therefore, it is concluded that there are three key factors influencing the safety stock of an item:

- Forecast accuracy (or forecast error).
- Average lead time.
- Level of customer service.

Brown (1982) suggests a simple formula for calculating safety stock (ss) as:
Safety stock (ss) = MAD × safety factor, where MAD represents forecast accuracy and safety factor depends on lead time and service level as shown in Table 18.4.
It is evident from Table 18.4 that safety factor decreases with decreasing service level and increases with the increasing value of lead time.

Table 18.4 Safety factors for given lead times and service levels

Service level	Lead time 1	Lead time 2	Lead time 3	Lead time 4	Lead time 5
99%	2.90	4.10	5.02	5.80	6.48
98%	2.56	3.62	4.43	5.18	5.72
97%	2.35	3.32	4.07	4.70	5.25
96%	2.19	3.09	3.79	4.38	4.90
95%	2.04	2.88	3.53	4.08	4.56
94%	1.94	2.74	3.36	3.88	4.34
93%	1.84	2.60	3.19	3.68	4.11
92%	1.75	2.47	3.03	3.50	3.91
91%	1.68	2.38	2.91	3.36	3.76
90%	1.60	2.26	2.77	3.20	3.58
89%	1.29	1.82	2.23	2.58	2.88

Example

Assume the demand and forecast data of a product is given in Table 18.3. Calculate the safety stock of this product when the lead time is three months and service level is 95%.

MAD from Table 18.3 is 58
Safety factor from Table 18.4 is 3.53
Hence safety stock = MAD × safety factor = 58 × 3.53 = 205

Transportation model and technique

A major concern for distribution planners is in deciding which distribution centres should be supplied by which factory or supplier. Furthermore, the choice could be what form of transport should be used among rail, road, sea or air. The cost of transporting one supply point to a distribution destination varies depending on the location, distance and chosen form of transport. The number of possible choices for transport operation can be very large but the problem can be reduced to a manageable solution by assigning a transport network based on the distance as shown in Figure 18.8. Other rationale (e.g. availability of rail infrastructure) can also be applied in assigning the links in the network.

(NB: S1, S2 and S£ are sources; D1, D2, D3 and D4 are destinations.)

The assignment of routes in Figure 18.8 provides the basis of the 'first feasible solution'. However, any warehouse may be supplied from any factory or from two or three factories, and the planner's requirement is to find a combination that minimises the total cost of transport. Let us investigate the problem with some numbers.

The numbers on the right-hand and bottom margins in Figure 18.9 are respectively, the number of items available at each factory and the number of items required at each warehouse. The numbers inside the table represent the unit costs of transport from the ith factory to the jth warehouse. By using the so-called 'North-West Corner Rule', the assigned quantities of products in the network shown in Figure 18.8 as the first feasible solution is determined as shown in Figure 18.10.

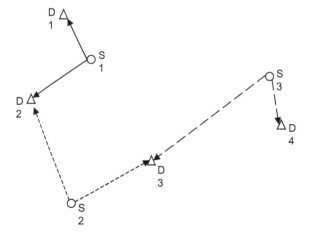

Figure 18.8 A transport network based on the relative distance between the supply and demand points

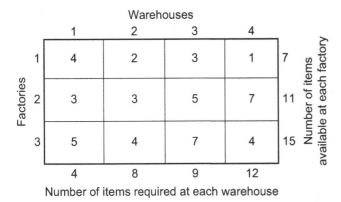

Figure 18.9 Items available from factories and required at warehouses

Figure 18.10 Assigned quantities in the 'first feasible solution'

The total cost associated with the first feasible solution, by taking the quantities from Figure 18.10 and corresponding unit costs from Figure 18.9, is computed as follows:

$$\text{Total cost } V_1 = X_{11}{\times}C_{11} + X_{12}{\times}C_{12} + X_{22}{\times}C_{22} + X_{23}{\times}C_{23} + X_{33}{\times}C_{33} + X_{34}{\times}C_{34}$$

$$= 4{\times}4 + 3{\times}2 + 5{\times}3 + 6{\times}5 + 3{\times}7 + 12{\times}4 = 136$$

Now that one has a feasible programme and has determined the corresponding total cost, how does one know whether or not this solution is optimal? In order to find an optimal solution (i.e. the minimum total cost), it is necessary to evaluate alternative possibilities.

The iterative process of finding the optimum solution by evaluating the opportunity costs associated with the alternative allocation of quantities for transportation can be found in books devoted to operational research (Churchman et al., 1968). When we follow the iterations the optimal total cost of transport is 118.

Location models

The location of optimum global manufacturing and distribution facilities is a complicated decision-making process and often a model-based quantitative approach is applied. The typical input to such a process is a set of markets to serve, a set of products that the company will produce and sell, demand projections for the different markets, information about future mac-roeconomic conditions and costs for transportation and production. Given the above informa-tion, companies have to decide, among other things, where to locate factories, how to allocate production activities to the various facilities of the network and where to locate distribution facilities. There are three main approaches in structuring global facility networks: (1) *focused factories*: where plants may be located in different parts of the world and each specialises in a specific product family. (2) *Process focused*: where individual plants are typically dedicated to performing specific process steps for a variety of different products. (3) *Market focused*: where plants are located at markets that they plan to serve. Most global facility networks that firms use are hybrids of the above approaches. For example, product/process focused networks have plant subnetworks that produce specific product families.

There have been attempts to develop complex mixed integer programming models that capture essential design trade-offs of such networks (Kouvelis et al., 2001). These models provide a framework to analyse the relative importance of each cost and demand parameter but are often inadequate to find an optimal solution. Let us examine the fol-lowing plant location model.

N = number of potential plant locations (i = 1, 2, .. N)
M = number of demand points (j = 1, 2, ... M)
D_j = annual demand from market j
V_i = total capacity of plant i
F_i = fixed cost per year to keep plant i open
C_{ij} = cost of transport from plant i to market j
d_{ij} = quantity shipped from plant i to market j
x_i = 1 if plant i is open and 0 for not open

The objective function of the problem can be expressed as the following mixed integer programming model,

$$Y_{ij} = Min \ \Sigma F_i x_i + \Sigma C_{ij} d_{ij}$$

Subject to

$$\Sigma d_{ij} = D_j \ for \ j = 1, 2, ... M$$

$$\Sigma d_{ij} \le V_i x_i \ for \ i = 1, 2, .. N$$

The above constraints require that the demand in each market is satisfied and each plant can only supply according to its capacity. The objective function aims to minimise the total cost, both fixed and variable, of the network. It is possible to solve the model by using the 'Solver' tool in *Excel* software and the cells in *Excel* spreadsheets identify deci-sion variables and costs. The decision variables should help to analyse the relative impor-tance of variables and minimum cost should identify an acceptable solution.

More complex models may also be developed to analyse country-specific constraints (e.g. government subsidies, local infrastructure, available skills). However, in reality, the location of facilities and global supply chain networks are decided by taking into account both quantitative and qualitative factors for alternative project options. The decision is also governed by strategic factors as discussed in Chapter 19.

Summary

The key learning points of this chapter include:

- Major factors governing demand forecast decisions.
- Techniques of planning demand forecast by time series tools such as moving average, exponential smoothing, linear regression, Holt's model and Winter's model.
- Inventory management with more complex requirements such as shortages and quantity discounts.
- Factors influencing safety stocks and how to estimate them.
- Transportation cost model and how to compute the costs.
- Location models and their practical implication.

We have addressed the learning objectives for students and practitioners of global supply chain decision making. Both students and practitioners should be able to identify the role of mathematical models in demand planning, inventory management and supply chain network design. For the practitioners, circumstances will determine management decisions, however, the quantitative tools outlined should help to reduce the proportion of subjective judgements.

It is better to be approximately right than exactly wrong, but it is important to understand the relative importance of independent and dependent variables in decision making. A mathematical framework of supply chain models should help to formulate a quantitative mindset for students and practitioners.

Discussion questions

1. Identify the key factors that should be taken into account for demand planning in a large department store (e.g. John Lewis).
2. What are the three factors governing forecast accuracy? What information do MAD, MAPE and MSE prove to a demand planner?
3. Explain with examples Holt's method and Winter's model. Discuss the appropriateness of each model.
4. Explain when and why you may consider structural equation modelling (SEM) for forecasting purposes.
5. Consider the supermarket Tesco is deciding on the economic order quantity for Unilever products. What costs should it consider when making the decision?
6. Discuss the effect on the order size if shortages are allowed.
7. Illustrate with an example how you would determine the order size with a volume-based quantity discount.
8. Discuss with examples of how transportation models can be effective in managing global supply chains.

Exercises

9. Determine the cost of storage and ordering per year for the order quantities of (a) 1000, (b) 2000, and (c) 3000 items given the following:

$C1 = £150$
$D = 12,000.year$

Also, storage space is available in increments each sufficient for storing 1000 items. The cost per year for each of these increments is £500 and the fixed cost of storage is £0.50 per year. No safety stock is required.

10. For what range of values of Q is the variable cost per year if it is within 20% of its minimum value?

11. The total annual demand for an item is 200, the ordering cost is £20, and the holding cost per unit per year amounts to 50% of the purchase cost. The cost per unit of the item depends on the total quantity ordered as follows:

Less than 500	£1.21
500–999	£1.00
More than 1000	£0.81

Find the economic lot size and optimal value of cost per year.

12. The cost C1 in £ of ordering and receiving a quantity is given by

Q	C1
0–50	10
51–200	20
Over 200	30

Annual demand is 900, unit cost is £2 and holding costs per unit time are 10% of unit cost. Find the economic lot size and optimal value of cost per year.

13. The demand for an item held by a retailer is 150/week on average. Demand is not seasonal and has not changed from its average for the past two years. From a study of two years' data, it has been found that the standard deviation for weekly demand is 20 items.

The stock holding cost is £0.4/item and the re-order cost is £17/order regardless of quantity. A 90% service level is provided.

Design a fixed interval stock control system and explain and explain any assumption you make.

14. PC World sells 10,000.

15. Toshiba L50 PCs every month. Each PC costs £500 and it has a holding cost of 20%. For what fixed cost per order would an order size of 10,000 units be optimal? Also, for what fixed cost per order for an order size of 2500 units would be optimal?

16. Weekly demand for 2 litres of Persil liquid detergents at a Tesco store is normally distributed with a mean of 3000 and a standard deviation of 1000. The replenishment lead time from Unilever is four weeks. Tesco uses a fixed interval review policy under which it orders Unilever detergent products including Persil every 12 weeks.

What is the average order size for Persil?

How much safety stock of 2 litres of Persil does the Tesco store carry?

17. The total annual demand for an item is 2000, the ordering cost is €20, and the stock holding cost per unit per year amounts to 10% of its purchase cost. The cost per unit of an item is €80.

Find the economic order quantity (EOQ) by using the formulae:

$$EOQ = \sqrt{(2Dc1/c2)} \text{ where D = annual demand}$$

$$c1 = \text{ordering cost per lot}$$
$$c2 = \text{stockholding cost per unit per year}$$

18. A garden centre selling sacks of fertiliser has an average demand of ten sacks per day. The stock is replenished every 15 days.

Assuming that for a level of 95%, safety stock = 1.64 × standard deviation of demand during lead time.

Determine the re-order level of the fertiliser when the standard deviation for 15 days is 11.6.

(Hint: R = Average demand in lead time + safety stock)

19. The Ford Motor Company has an engine plant in England and a car assembly plant in Germany. The assembly plant delivers 1500 completed cars to distributors every year. Engines are transported by trucks to Germany. The transport and shipping cost for each truck is £1000. The ex-works cost of each engine is £1500 and the stock-holding cost for engines in England is 20% per year.

Calculate by using the EOQ formula how many engines should be transported by trucks in each trip.

20. A sports shop in Rio de Janeiro sells football t-shirts to tourists at the rate of 2000 shirts per year. The ordering cost is £20 and the holding cost per unit per year amounts to 50% of its purchase cost. The purchase cost per unit of the t-shirt depends on the total quantity ordered as follows:

Less than 500	*500–999*	*1000 or more*
1.21	1.00	0.81

a)   Find the economic lot size.

b)   Calculate the optimum value of cost per year.

21. The weekly average demand for a Nokia mobile phone handset at a high street store is 300. The demand pattern is normally distributed with a standard deviation of 200. The lead time of supply is two weeks. The store monitors its inventory continuously and tries to maintain a service level target of 95%.

a)   Determine the safety stock of Nokia handsets that the store should carry.

b)   What should be the reorder point?

22. Joyamaya Toys is a family owned business for children's leisure products. The planning office of the company is based at High Wycombe, Buckinghamshire, and the distribution of products including mail orders is carried out from a rented warehouse in Milton Keynes. The turnover of the company in 2002 was £14 million.

The weekly sales forecast of the 'Game Boy' including additional confirmed orders from customers is shown in Table 18.1. The planning office has the following additional demand and supply data:

- Distribution demand: 10 units each in weeks 3 and 6
- Promotion: 15 units in week 4 and 5 units in week 5
- Master production schedule (MPS) lead time is 2 weeks
- The delivery of MPS is due on week 2

Total Demand Manaement

Weeks

	1	2	3	4	5	6	7	8
Sales Forecast	30	25	20	20	20	20	25	30
Customer Orders	10	5	–	–	–			5
Distribution Demand						6		
Promotion								
Total								

Demand/Supply Review										
Weeks										
		1	2	3	4	5	6	7	8
On hand 50	**Forecast Demand**									
	Actual Demand									
	Projected Available	20								
	Available to Promise									
Order Quantity 70	**MPS at receipt**									

Normal actual demand-replace forecast
Abnormal actual demand-don not replace forecast

   a)   By taking into account additional requirements for distribution demand and promotion, complete Table 1 and calculate the demand for the 'Game Boy'.

   b)   By using the total demand from Table 18.1 as forecast demand in Table 18.2 and the given data for MPS, calculate 'Projected available' in Table 18.2.

23. A popular product at Beaconsfield Garden Centre is orchid plants imported from Southeast Asia. These plants are nurtured in temperature and humidity-controlled greenhouses. The monthly sales figures for orchid plants for 2006 are shown in the following table:

Jan	Feb	Mar	Apr	May	Jun	Jul	Aug	Sep	Oct	Nov	Dec
80	70	90	100	115	100	120	110	70	80	60	130

   a)   Forecast the monthly demand for January, February and March 2007 by using simple exponential smoothing with $\alpha = 0.1$.

   b)   Evaluate MAD.

24. A call centre in Bangalore recorded the incoming overseas calls as shown in the following table. This data is to be used for forecasting the staff and investment in facilities.

Year	1998	1999	2000	2001	2002	2003	2004	2005	2006
Call minutes	35	39	44	49	56	63	73	84	96 (millions)

   a)   Plot the data on a scatter diagram and develop a linear regression that best fits these data.

   b)   Is linear regression a good forecasting tool for the call centre? How do you justify your response?

   c)   What is the forecast for overseas calls in 2010?

25. The sales figures for the first 12 weeks of 2006 at Domino Pizza shop are shown below:

Week	Demand	Week	Demand	Week	Demand
1	110	5	98	9	116
2	116	6	122	10	112
3	120	7	100	11	96
4	128	8	106	12	92

   a)   Estimate the forecast for the next four weeks using

       i.   a four-week moving average

ii. exponential smoothing with α = 0.1
b) Evaluate the MAD and MAPE for each method of forecasting
c) Which of the two methods do you consider more appropriate and why?

26. The following table shows the actual sales of a new BMW 320i motor car from a car dealer for 20 successive periods. Calculate the forecast demand by:
a) the simple four-week moving average
b) exponential smoothing (α= 0.2)

   Also compare the difference between actual and moving average with the difference between actual and exponentially smoothed forecast.

Period	Actual sales	Period	Actual sales
1	10	11	10
2	12	12	11
3	12	13	14
4	10	14	12
5	8	15	9
6	10	16	10
7	11	17	13
8	12	18	14
9	9	19	11
19	8	20	10

27. Calculate the linear regression of Y and X and, using the equation Y = mX + C and the data in the following table, calculate Y for the following values of X
a) 130
b) 90

Y	2	5	4	3	5	6	7	6	8	9
X	20	45	30	30	45	65	65	60	70	70

28. Demand '000

	2006	2007	2008	2009	2010
Q1	10	12	15	4	13
Q2	20	24	30	16	28
Q3	20	24	30	25	?
Q4	50	60	45	55	?
FY	100	120	120	100	???

Questions

i. Forecast demand for quarter three (Q3), and quarter four (Q4) 2010 and for the full year.

ii. Suggest reasons as to why demand began to decline in Q4 2008 and whether in your opinion the recovery in demand experienced in Q2 2010 is sustainable.

29. Kapai is a beach resort of low-priced cabin-type accommodation catering to family groups and backpackers. The capacity of Kapai is 120 guests at any one time. The limitation is the number of beds.

   The number of 'guests' per month staying at Kapai for the last four years is shown below.

Forecast the demand for each of the last three months and for the full year of 2017. Show your calculations.

	2013	2014	2015	2016	2017	
Jan	120	120	120	120	60	School holidays
Feb	120	120	120	120	60	School holidays
Mar	50	45	55	45	25	Includes Easter
Apr	5	5	5	6	3	
May	60	55	65	61	30	School holidays
June	4	6	5	6	2	.
July	6	4	5	6	3	
Aug	60	65	55	60	32	School holidays
Sep	6	5	4	6	2	
Oct	4	5	6	5	?	
Nov	5	5	5	5	?	
Dec	60	65	60	60	?	School holidays
Fy	500	500	505	500		

Additional influencing circumstances:

The downturn at the beginning of 2017 has been assumed to be due to:

i.   The weather; an unseasonably wet summer (January and February).

ii.   Increasing cost of transport and petrol.

Increased cost of living (food, rent, mortgages = less disposable income).

30. Silver Fern, the CEO of The Aces High (sportswear manufacturers), has provided sales figures for the last few years and has asked you for an updated forecast of sales and profit through to December 2017

Actual sales by quarter ($'000)

	2013	2014	2015	2016	2017
Jan–Mar	800	660	945	930	940
Apr–Jun	1050	900	1080	1055	1080*
July–Sept	975	865	1040	1005	–?–
Oct–Dec	1085	1075	1135	1115	–?–
Full-year	3900	3500	4200	4105	–?–
Budget	4200	4000	4200	4400	4800
Actual net profit before tax	$390	315	360	310	?

*April –June figures are based on sales invoiced, and goods on order for delivery in June. Silver is comfortable with the figure of $1,080,000 for the April/ June quarter.

Performance statement for the three months ended 31 March 2017.

Full-year budget ($'000)

	Actual Q1 YTD	Budget Q1	FY Budget
Sales per month	940	1200	4800
Cost of sales			
Labour	235	300	1200
Materials used	235	300	1200
Gross profit	470	600	2400
Selling expenses	140	180	720
Head office expense	250	250	1000
Interest	25	5	20
Profit before tax	55	165	660

Relevant information from Position Statement as of 31st March 2017.

Total for 3 months

Accounts receivable	1050
Inventory raw materials	400
Inventory of finished goods (cost of materials plus labour)	600
Fixed assets: Factory buildings and plant	2000
Total assets	4050
Liabilities (bank and creditors)	550
Equity (Shareholders' funds)	3500

31. A furniture company is under pressure from its bank to reduce its debt level. As a consultant, you observe (May 2017) that they have a large number of machines idle and you find that most of the plant is leased and could be returned to the leasing companies given one month's notice. You also note that there is a large stock of raw material and finished stock and how much storage space is used (you think 'no wonder they had to build an extension').

You ask how work is scheduled. It is explained that there are 22 factory workers and that they are all kept fully employed. Work is scheduled up to 12 months in advance and standard times for each element of every job are used. For simplification, they aggregate the standard times up to 20 hours, and each 20 hours of standard time equals a unit of work. For example, a Queen Anne bed takes 1.2 units of work (24 hours of labour).

The next nine months' production schedule is:

(Using June as an example for calculations; June has 22 work days × 8 hours per day × 22 people = 3872 hours. Divided by 20 gives 193.6 available units of work).

	Total available units in months	Units of work scheduled	Demand (for delivery at end of month)
June	193.6	192	140
July	184.8	184	165
Aug	193.6	192	165
Sep	184.6	184	160
Oct	184.6	184	150
Nov	193.6	192	200
Dec	150	150	160
Jan	125	125	70
Feb	176.0	175	200
		1578	1410

June, July and August are definite orders, the balance is based on past experience. February (and March) are always big demand months.

Your quick calculation is that for the next six months they are planning to make enough stock to cater for about seven months' demand. The latest balance sheet as on 31 March shows that the factory has four months of finished goods on hand at the end of March. This is partly explained by a big order delivered in April. Nonetheless, it is estimated that there are three months of finished goods on hand at present. Part of their good reputation is that they always deliver on time and that this is company policy. You find customers usually order some weeks in advance.

The factory manager advises that 12 months ago, a computer package was installed based on an EOQ approach with a reorder point for each item of stock allowing for supply lead times.

The formula used by the system is

EOQ which equals the square root of (2 DA/IC) where:

A = $ cost of placing an order

D = Annual demand in units

I ★ = Carrying cost for holding inventory for a year

C = Unit cost of the item.

★The carrying cost interest rate is 30% p.a., being 20% cost of funds, 5% for obsolescence and 5% for storage. The cost of placing an order is estimated at $10 per order.

The purchasing officer is not certain of the details but says the system is backwards looking and uses the last four years' actual purchases in its calculations 'the computer people said it would work very smoothly because the system would self-adjust'. Before the new system was installed, the factory manager advised he didn't rely on past usage but calculated orders on known future demand. He believes that all stock should turn over at least three times a year 'but now I think about 25% of the stock is just taking up space and gathering dust and you can usually get material locally more or less when needed'.

What are your recommendations?

19 Global supply chain strategy

Introduction

Business strategy involves building capabilities in the longer term by leveraging the core competencies of the organisation to achieve a defined high-level business objective. Some of the characteristics of a business strategy that distinguish a strategy from an operation include:

- Stressing *longer-term* rather than short-term objectives.
- Setting *broad* objectives that *direct* an enterprise towards its overall goal.
- Dealing with *total picture* rather than stressing detail activities.
- *Detached* from day-to-day activities.

Business strategy is also known as corporate strategy. While the business strategy constitutes the overall direction that an organisation wishes to go, the operations strategy constitutes the actual strategic framework of operations to meet a specific operational objective. As shown in Figure 19.1, operations strategy derives from business units.

Supply chain strategy is underpinned by the business unit of supply chain management, but it is also closely related to the strategies of other business units, especially sourcing strategy. Due to closer interdependency, we will consider sourcing strategy as part of supply chain strategy.

Learning objectives

Learning objectives for this chapter are:

1. Why supply chain strategy is important.
2. Developing a supply chain strategy.
3. Capacity strategy.
4. Sourcing strategy.
5. Supplier strategy.
6. Location strategy.
7. Distribution strategy.

Why supply chain strategy is important

So, why is a supply chain strategy so important? Well, one good reason is to operationalise and support your business strategy. At some point, a business strategy must be executed

DOI: 10.4324/9781003341352-22

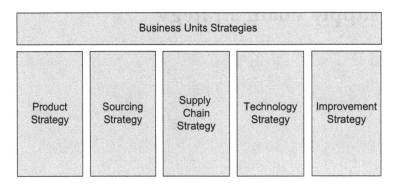

Figure 19.1 Operations strategies of business units.

and typically this is done through the operational components of a company. Supply chain strategy also focuses on driving down operational costs and maximising efficiencies. Another reason that supply chain managers obsess with short-term performance is that by following a set, even if it is a proven process, the opportunities for alternative processes available in the market can be missed. The driving forces of global supply chains are so dynamic that it is vital to think 'out of the box' for future competitiveness. For many enduringly successful enterprises, from Amazon to Walmart, Apple to Zara, changing global supply chain strategies have been central to their success. By providing a clear purpose, the organisation keeps sight of the strategy and is able to devise tactical steps to achieve these goals. Another reason for having a supply chain strategy is to establish how you develop your capability in specific areas of the supply chain 'building blocks' to work with your supply chain partners, including suppliers, distributors, customers and even your customers' customers and suppliers' suppliers to manage your internal operations. As the marketplace becomes more dynamic and competitive, it is critical to reinforce existing relationships and work together. For all these reasons, a well-executed supply chain strategy results in sustainable value creation for the organisation.

As shown in Figure 19.2, we will discuss some key areas of strategies covering the 'building blocks' of global supply chains.

The key areas of supply chain strategies are:

Capacity strategy.
Sourcing strategy.
Location strategy.
Supplier strategy.
Distribution strategy.

Developing a supply chain strategy

Consultants and academics, and most certainly supply chain practitioners, require a proven methodology for developing a strategy. Organisations also seek a simplistic solution to their complex problems. Sometimes, third-party advisers approach an organisation with a multi-factor assessment tool to develop a business strategy akin to a 'solution in search of a problem'. Academic research also appears to encourage causal modelling or

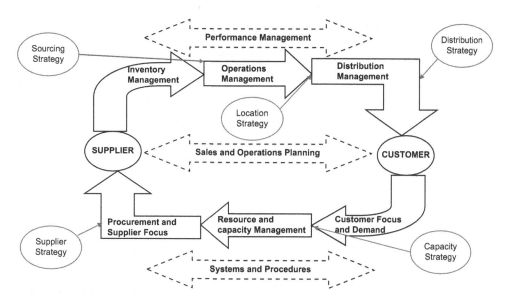

Figure 19.2 Key areas of supply chain strategies

complex mixed integer models to analyse and develop global supply networks. Despite all these mechanistic, one size fits all approaches, we find a mixture of experience with an understanding of alternatives using evidence-based data is the soundest way to develop a strategy.

Essential steps and processes in developing a supply chain strategy like any other aspect of an operations strategy are:

- Understand and align supply chain strategy with corporate business strategy.
- Assess the extended supply chain.
- Select appropriate tools and evaluate options.
- Include a risk analysis.
- Develop an implementation plan.

The first step for a supply chain manager is to clearly understand how the organisation chooses to compete. This is important for the obvious reason of working off the same hymn sheet. For example, if the business strategy is to be a low-cost provider, the supply chain strategy should support this with a lean strategy (just-in-time approach where there is high volume and low variability). On the other hand, if the business focuses on high-margin novel products, the supply strategy should be agile and rapidly responsive (high variability and low volume). At best, supply chain strategy can be the enabler of the business strategy.

The next step is to conduct a detailed, realistic assessment of the capabilities that exist within the organisation and ideally the extended supply chain. Even if you have a good roadmap, you will get lost if you do not know where you are at the start. There are some tools (such as the European Foundation of Quality Management, EFQM) that enable a holistic assessment of the strengths and weaknesses of the extended supply chain.

There are many tools available to analyse supply chain effectiveness and evaluate strategic options including the following:

- SWOT analysis (Strengths, Weaknesses, Opportunities and Threats)
- PESTLE analysis (political economic societal, technology, legal and environmental)
- Operations performance
  - Quality speed dependability flexibility and cost trade-off
  - Balanced scorecard
- Holistic performance
  - *ASK* (Basu and Wright, 2005)
  - EFQM
- Evaluate options
  - Net present value
  - Risk-reward matrix

The explanation and application of the above tools can be found in Basu (2004). *ASK* is software for the holistic analysis of a business based on 200 questions and the details can be found in Basu and Wright (2004).

Any strategy is not worth the paper it is written on unless it can be implemented in practice.

'Making it happen' – the supply chain strategy is essential. The development of an implementation plan should include activities and tasks, a project organisation with roles and responsibilities, a corresponding timeline and performance metrics. The implementation plan should also contain a defined project life cycle of definition, planning implementation and closure.

Capacity strategy

Capacity strategy is the first of the supply chain strategy areas at the start of supply chain building blocks, spanning both customer demand and resources management. For many businesses, capacity strategy may be a contradiction in terms as some managers may consider it as part of day-to-day operations rather than a longer-term strategy. However, if a business does not have strategic decisions for in-house and third-party capacity, resources planning cannot be effective. Capacity decisions are usually considered at three levels:

- Strategic capacity for a planning cycle of years.
- Medium-term capacity for a planning cycle of months.
- Short-term capacity for a planning cycle of weeks.

Strategic capacity decisions or capacity strategy determine decisions on investing in buildings, equipment and technology. As a planner develops a master production schedule (MPS), the schedule is based on the belief that all required materials and capacity needed to meet this schedule will be available. By performing rough cut capacity planning (RCCP) based on the demand forecast prior to the start of production, the planner is able to reconcile the goals of management with the capabilities of available resources. For this, it is essential for the planner to know the capacity strategy of the organisation. As discussed in Chapter 5, there are two types of capacity strategy, viz. maximum capacity strategy and adjustable capacity strategy. These are also known as level capacity strategy and chase demand strategy, respectively.

Capacity strategy depends on several factors of which three factors are the most significant:

1. *Variability of demand.* The first step of capacity strategy or capacity planning is demand forecasting. As discussed in Chapter 5 and Chapter 18, the variability of forecast is shown as trend and seasonality and is measured by a number of metrics including mean absolute deviation (MAD). However, the bottom line is if the demand is manageably predictable then it is easier to set a level capacity strategy, otherwise, we need an adjustable capacity strategy.
2. *Customer service.* The need to provide high customer service (e.g. fire service, ambulances and life-saving medical products) will encourage the provision of excess capacity. When the level of customer service is relatively low (e.g. furniture removal), the capacity could be set at an average level with possible loss of trade.
3. *Stock-holding policy.* A stock-holding policy that provides output stocks enables the fluctuation of demand through the use of physical stocks. This policy allows a relatively stable level of capacity. The safety stock will reflect the variability of demand, lead time and service level to be provided.

Figure 19.3 illustrates a 'decision tree' type of approach to the selection of capacity strategies depending on the above three factors. With reference to Chapter 6, here we show

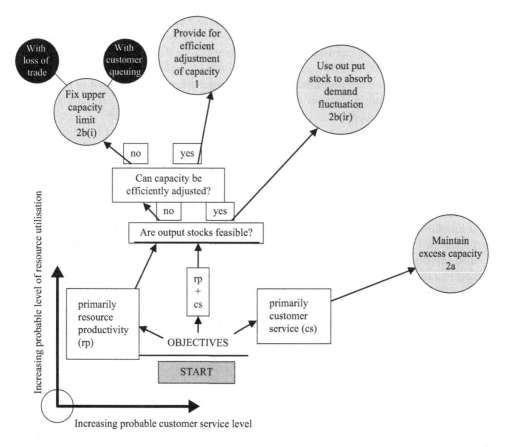

Figure 19.3 A 'decision tree' for capacity strategy

both the 'variation of the adjustment of capacity' (Strategy 1) and three options of 'elimination of need to adjust' (Strategy 2a, 2b(i) and 2b(ii)).

The concept of a 'decision tree' for developing a capacity strategy has also been discussed in Chapter 6. With this approach, demand is manipulated to match the available capacity.

The following case example illustrates a capacity strategy in a growing demand market for a deli restaurant in the United States.

CASE EXAMPLE: CAPACITY STRATEGY FOR MINKIES DELI

Doron Atzmon set up Minkies Deli four years ago as a local deli serving a wide range of tasty, nutritious and healthy products. It has been a great success and he has just opened a butcher across the street from it too. 'People love the food we sell', he explained. 'We offer a wide range of products, sandwiches, salads and hot dishes. If customers want something that's not on the menu, we'll prepare that too! Some people love this and are happy to wait for what they want. However, I think other customers who have less time would be happy with less choice if it means they could get their lunch more quickly'.

The deli currently stocks over 400 different items sourced from 30 local suppliers and Doron constantly travels around the country in search of new and interesting products. 'The products that we sell in the deli are also the ones we use in our sandwiches, salads and hot dishes', he explains. 'All our stock is on display and we simply cook up items that are starting to reach their best before date'.

'For instance, we recently bought some Spanish Calasparra brown rice. It's wonderful stuff, but no one bought it! I ended up cooking it up and selling it in the deli instead. Only having a small storage area means we keep track of everything and only buy what we need'.

'The original idea was to sell great products and serve fresh food to customers eating in the deli', Doron continues. 'However, customers also want to take it away to eat either at home or at work. Although we're easily able to cope with the steady flow of customers during the day, lunchtime is a challenge! Increasingly, people take food away and we get at least two large orders each day from local businesses. As well as myself, there is one other person serving customers during the day and two at lunchtime. These two work well together preparing drinks and serving customers. However, I'm struggling to keep up with demand in the kitchen as everything is made to order. Although the large takeaway orders are great for business, they don't come in until the last minute and mean other customers have to wait while I prepare them. I don't really know what to do as we're unable to expand the physical area and I can't afford to employ any more staff'.

Source: www.minkiesdeli.co.uk (accessed 25 November 2015).

Sourcing strategy

Globalisation has created not only great opportunities for global supply chains but also has introduced a high level of complexity and risks. Globalisation is the process by which the world is becoming increasingly interconnected as a result of massively increased trade and cultural exchange. The biggest companies are no longer national firms but are multinationals with subsidiaries in many countries. Globalisation has given access to a wider market, cost base and skill sets, but it has also made multinationals dependent on the health of local economies.

Supply chains have always involved risk. The romantic-sounding Silk Road, which connected Europe and China with camel caravans, was always highly vulnerable. Although from ancient times to the present day, globalisation has played a major role in expanding the opportunities for many business organisations to be more efficient but it has also created additional risks. Therefore, it is critical to assess not only the cost benefits of an option but also its potential risks. The risks of managing global supply chains are discussed in Chapter 20.

Sourcing strategy is arguably the biggest challenge of global supply chain management. To make it more confusing, there are many names attached to sourcing strategy such as outsourcing, off-shoring, manufacturing outsourcing, business process outsourcing (BPO) and strategic outsourcing. Outsourcing is already seen as a global phenomenon According to Statista, an independent statistics portal, the global market size of outsourced services increased from US$45.6 billion in 2000 to US$104.6 billion in 2014 (see Figure 19.4).

First, let us address the confusing terms of outsourcing and off-shoring. Outsourcing is a generic term, for both manufacturing and services, meaning whether to buy in the product or service from a third party or to carry out the operation in-house. Off-shoring is simply outsourcing from another country. As shown in Figure 19.5, off-shoring is closely related to outsourcing and the objectives are also similar, that is, to reduce the cost of non-strategic processes. Multinational companies also focus on selected operations in their own overseas sites and these are off-shore operations rather than off-shore outsourcing or simply off-shoring.

Next, let us address the distinction between manufacturing outsourcing and business process outsourcing. Manufacturing outsourcing is for producing manufactured products or components by a third party while business process outsourcing is for buying in

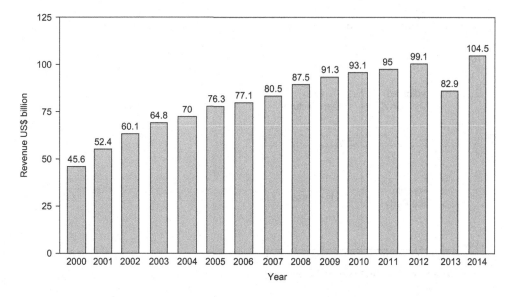

Figure 19.4 Global demand for outsourcing

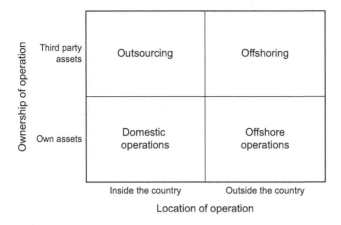

Figure 19.5 Outsourcing and off-shoring

services for information products. There is a common objective of reducing costs for both manufacturing and business process outsourcing. However, there are also differences. Manufacturing outsourcing is in most cases for producing older commodity products, but business process outsourcing is usually for filling in the capability gaps (e.g. in cloud computing and IT infrastructure support). There are also exceptions to the general rule. For example, a service company may outsource low-skill call centre services and a manufacturing company may buy in highly specialised manufactured products such as aero engines.

The decision criteria for manufacturing outsourcing and business process outsourcing are provided respectively in Figures 19.6 and 19.7.

Manufacturing outsourcing strategy (Figure 19.6) is closely linked with both the product life cycle and the Boston Consulting Group (BCG) matrix. As shown in Figure 19.8, at the 'launch' stage of the product life cycle, the BCG portfolio is 'wild cat' and

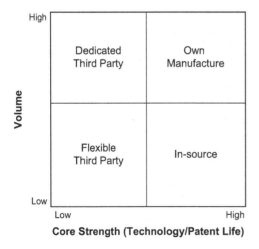

Figure 19.6 Manufacturing outsourcing strategy

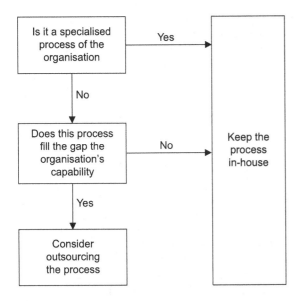

Figure 19.7 Business process outsourcing strategy

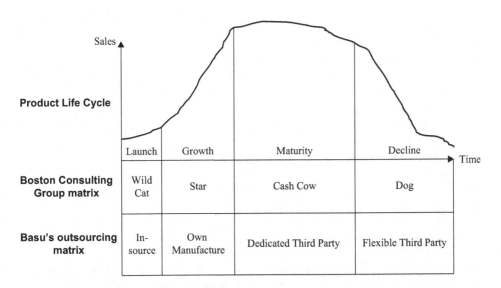

Figure 19.8 The relationship between the product life cycle model, BCG matrix and manufacturing strategy

the manufacturing strategy is 'in-sourcing' or manufacturing with your own existing resources. At the 'growth' stage of the product life cycle, the BCG portfolio suggests a 'star' product and manufacturing strategy is to invest in their own manufacturing capability. When the product is 'matured', it becomes a 'cash cow' in the BCG matrix and the manufacturing strategy is to transfer production to a dedicated third-party partner. At the 'decline' stage of the life cycle, the product becomes a 'dog' in the BCG matrix, losing its competitive advantage and the manufacturing strategy is to continue production with any third party as long as the product has a profit-generating demand.

The following two case examples illustrate strategies for manufacturing outsourcing and business process outsourcing, respectively.

CASE EXAMPLE: MANUFACTURING OUTSOURCING AT HORNBY

Hornby's business is the development and supply of hobby and toy products. The company's two principal brands, Hornby and Scalextric, are distributed through a network of specialist and multiple retailers throughout the UK and overseas. The Hornby decision to outsource its manufacturing to China was taken against a background of difficult trading conditions and low profitability. The primary objective at the time was to achieve cost savings but the real benefit has been to leverage these cost savings to create real value through an improved product and increased sales. Apart from the closure of a manufacturing facility and the shipment of most of the production tooling to China, there would inevitably be a long-term loss of knowledge and skills.

The success of any strategy is based on the robustness of its implementation. In order to achieve Hornby's objectives, it was necessary to invest considerable effort in the operational phases of the programme. This means, if managing the process in-house, releasing a management team to specifically oversee the outsourcing programme. When transferring manufacturing to another country, a key issue for Hornby was to maintain the continuity of supply. Once a current batch of product had been manufactured in the UK, the tooling was collated and shipped to China along with the necessary tooling documentation. The complexity of the process was increased due to the decision two years earlier to outsource die-castings and pressings to UK subcontractors. In hindsight, these processes should have been retained until the outsourcing process was complete.

In engineering terms, liaison with the Far East partners was achieved by frequent visits to China to discuss the manufacturing issues at a product level. The importance of the whole programme however demanded a permanent presence in China to coordinate the project at a local level. The decision was taken to employ a local general manager who would ensure that the programme was adhered to and issues resolved quickly. An administrative presence is still retained in Hong Kong to deal with day-to-day issues and be on hand if circumstances dictate. It is also important with a complex product to have ownership of the quality team. Hornby employs local quality inspectors in China that ensure the product quality standards are maintained.

Culturally, Chinese manufacturers do business in a different way to that of the West and it is important to recognise this cultural difference and work within the boundaries and not impose Western ideas. The key to Hornby's success is the effective combination of the right supplier and in-house product development activities.

In any manufacturing organisation, there is a balance between direct labour costs and the overheads incurred by support activities such as technical resources and supervision. To maintain manufacturing costs, some of this overhead has to be lost. The Hornby scenario was based on outsourcing the majority of manufacturing but retaining a core of employees for logistics operations including product customisation and order processing and despatch. A period of re-training and reallocation of staff followed the completion of the project and skills were utilised in other areas of the business such as shop floor supervision and technical staff being employed in a customer service and repairs capacity.

Questions

1. What are the key factors that influenced Hornby to outsource manufacturing to China?
2. Discuss the implementation issues adopted by Hornby to ensure a successful transfer of facilities, skills and processes to China.

CASE EXAMPLE: BUSINESS PROCESS OUTSOURCING, SAAS IN OXFORD BOOKSTORE, INDIA

Standing regally in the heart of Calcutta's Park Street, the Oxford Bookstore has been a haven for book lovers and intellectuals since the 1920s. A part of Rs 2200 crores (US$35 million) Apeejay Group, the iconic bookstore celebrated 90 years in 2010.

But things weren't always this good. When Subhasish Saha, CTO, Apeejay Group, joined in April 2008, the bookstore's IT infrastructure suffered from serious challenges. Traditionally, the book retailing business has been prone to excess purchases, an overstocking of stock-keeping units and a pile-up of non-moving or slow-moving inventory.

It's a problem that all Indian book retailers without IT systems face, given that India produces over 80,000 new titles a year. Oxford, for example, adds about 50,000 new titles a year to the Rs 2 lakh (US$3200) it already maintains. What made it harder for Oxford was its decentralised approach. This allowed a single title to have multiple codes across each of Oxford's 25-plus stores, making it almost impossible to get a fix on the number of copies it had of a popular title.

If the iconic bookstore was going to meet that target, it needed visibility along its entire supply chain, from its supplier down to its stores – the sort of visibility that an ERP system could provide. The problem was that an SME like the Rs 37 crores (US$0.6 million) Oxford Bookstore didn't have the deep pockets an ERP implementation called for.

'Management was looking for a model that would allow Oxford Bookstore to leverage its full IT potential without large one-time IT capital investments or issues of scalability', says Saha. Theoretically, that's exactly what a SaaS model offers. Some solution providers have tested it with industries like apparel, admittedly, the idea remains unconventional in India – and it had almost never been tried in Indian retail before.

Few providers offered the complete set of services Saha wanted and there was no guarantee that once a deal had been inked, Saha's small account wouldn't get jostled aside by larger ones. At the same time, Oxford's management was apprehensive about using a SaaS model because it had heard about security challenges, and had fears about vendor lock-in.

After more research, Saha decided to outsource the services to a vendor who provided the implementations of SAP IS retail delivered via a SaaS model. Today, the ERP-SaaS project has centralised all Oxford titles across all branches into a single directory controlled by an ERP. Data from here flows to all modules including a store inventory module and the bookstore's points of sale. It also covers the company's payroll and accounting needs, and web tools. The ERP-SaaS project also helped increase footfall. Online sales have jumped a full 100% and revenues have risen by 50%. It's also made other aspects of running a retail business easier, including managing a CRM, a loyalty program and discount schemes. Saha estimates that Oxford will recover the cost of the ERP-SaaS implementation in four years.

Questions

1. What were the problems and challenges facing Oxford Bookstore in April 2008?
2. Discuss the key features of the business case for outsourcing ERP-SaaS in Oxford Bookstore.

Another often-used term is strategic sourcing, which is basically a strategic buying process. We define strategic sourcing as the procurement process of evaluating, selecting and aligning with suppliers or a group of suppliers to achieve operational improvements in the organisation's longer-term procurement objectives. Strategic sourcing should be aligned to the company's longer-term objectives. For example, it does not benefit an organisation to select a supplier for a multiple-year agreement based on its local presence of supply if the organisation is evaluating global outsourcing operations in support of business growth and cost-competitive objectives. The following case example illustrates a strategy for strategic sourcing.

CASE EXAMPLE: STRATEGIC SOURCING AT DIAL CORPORATION

Dial Corporation, the Phoenix-based manufacturer of soaps and detergent products and consumer goods, separated from Viad Corp., its parent company in 1996, and became an independent entity to better focus on its core competencies. Accompanying that change was a restructuring of Dial's corporate functions into a business–unit approach, which included an overhaul of the purchasing function from a decentralised organisation operating at the site level, to a central body headed by a chief procurement officer (CPO). This provided Dial with an opportunity for strategic sourcing strategy in their purchasing function.

Prior to the split of Dial, purchasing managers at each of the Dial sites were responsible for all purchases including detergent raw materials and ancillary services. It was typical for buyers at one facility to buy the same raw material as a buyer at another Dial plant from two different suppliers and at different prices. While a decentralised purchasing structure can have its advantages, it was ineffective in taking advantage of Dial's volume requirements and corporate-wide buying power. Early on, corporate management realised the need for a smaller, more strategic purchasing function featuring a corporate buying group led by a corporate officer. Dial's CPO and senior vice president, Michael H. Hillman explains: 'When we centralized the purchasing function, we combined all of our purchases and developed a strategy in which commodity experts would purchase those items in their area of expertise across all of the business units'.

By simplifying its supply base, working closely with its key suppliers and developing a system for implementing innovative cost-saving ideas, purchasing was able to drive $100 million in total costs from the system in five years from 2001. The fact that top management at Dial saw the need for corporate leadership for its purchasing practices speaks volumes to the importance it places on controlling its costs and generating significant savings through leveraged buying and supply chain management.

Questions

1. What are the driving forces of Dial Corporation in developing a strategic sourcing strategy?
2. What are the benefits achieved by strategic sourcing at Dial Corporation?

Supplier strategy

Supplier strategy is interwoven with the procurement strategy managing global supply chains.

The first step of supplier planning is the determination of the procurement strategy. Consideration is given to types of contracts or partnerships with major suppliers and the various tiers of subcontractors. Primary decisions will be required in the procurement strategy regarding whether all of the major supplies should be procured from a single supplier or if a significant portion should be obtained from multiple suppliers.

In order to develop a supplier strategy, we propose to identify the types of suppliers as follows:

1. *Transactional.* Suppliers who are used for basic requirements on an ongoing basis, but who represent no significant benefits to the organisation. These types of suppliers are chosen for low values of spend for procuring day-to-day supplies. From this perspective, the focus is on meeting internal needs and maximising profits at the expense of the supplier. Transactional suppliers are usually chosen from multiple quotations and controlled by traditional purchase orders.
2. *Transitional.* Suppliers may offer a mixed portfolio of some significant and some basic supply requirements. These suppliers are specialists and are useful for procuring

high-risk items in the short term. This can prove difficult to manage and it is often necessary to force a change in the nature of the engagement so that it is more clearly defined by legally bound service level agreements. A key measure is the number of suppliers moving in and out of this section.

3. *Collaborative.* Suppliers who are highly visible to the organisation and who are used regularly for longer-term medium-risk items of strategic value. The intention here is often to develop the relationship, particularly through senior-level interventions and well-defined strategic contracts. Progress is made through a mix of working on existing issues and developing new collaborative projects. This is supported by broader programme performance and other strategic benefits, such as knowledge sharing.

4. *Partner.* Suppliers who have a significant influence over the sustainable competitiveness of the organisation and who need to be engaged from multiple perspectives for the long term. The partnership is based on a longer-term deal for supplying relatively low-risk but high-volume items. The original equipment manufacturer (OEM) and the supplier both share the risk and benefits. Communication across all levels of both organisations is abundant as a mechanism for protecting the relationship. The customer is particularly careful to respond to supplier needs and provide critical resources when required. The relationship is comparable to the one between the corporate team and the sister companies in a multinational organisation. Key to the success of the whole programme is procurement's ability to manage spend on behalf of the organisation.

In terms of the hierarchy of relationships, the model in Figure 19.9 with two axes of value spend and strategic risks might be representative of what to expect. Although each supplier will appear within a specific band, it is important to acknowledge its relative position to other bands and suppliers. The collaborative suppliers and partner suppliers are also known as preferred suppliers who are usually selected by a rigorous process and tested over many years.

The agreements for transactional and transitional suppliers are bound by traditional service level agreements (SLAs), while more flexible supplier collaborative partnership contracts are appropriate for collaborative and partner suppliers. Collaborative suppliers are supported by a robust risk management plan. The key features of supplier collaborative

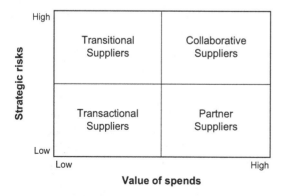

Figure 19.9 Types of suppliers

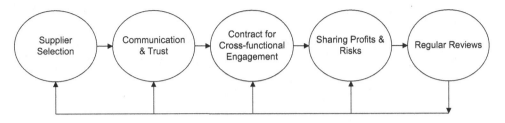

Figure 19.10 Supplier collaborative partnership model.

partnership contracts are supplier selection, mutual trust and sharing of both profits and risks as outlined in a model in Figure 19.10.

Although Volkswagen was seriously involved in an emissions scandal in October 2015 (www.bbc.co.uk/news/business-34324772), it is still an example of good business processes in their global operations. The following case example illustrates their supplier strategy in Brazil.

CASE EXAMPLE: VOLKSWAGEN BRAZIL SUPPLIER PARTNERSHIP

Far back in 1997, Volkswagen (VW) implemented the modular consortium concept of supply chain partnership at its new assembly complex in its Brazilian plant in the Sao Paulo province. In order for this concept to be successful, VW first had to drastically reduce its number of suppliers from 400 to only eight. These suppliers had to go through a rigorous preferred vendor assessment process. Then, these eight suppliers were invited to locate their bases of operations at the VW Brazil plant where they were provided with their own offices and staff. In addition, VW asked them to each invest an additional US$50 million in their respective modules. For agreeing to this investment and sharing of risk, the partners were guaranteed long-term contracts from five to 15 years.

At the facility, seven modules are sequentially integrated with each partner occupying a specific section of the plant and taking full responsibility for the quality control and mounting of complete assemblies for that section of the module. VW approves the final vehicle, and the partners only receive payment on this completely finished product, not on the individual parts as is the normal industry custom. By basically outsourcing the assembly operation, VW not only reduces its assembly labour costs but can focus on logistics, engineering, quality assurance and customer service.

This type of partnership has presented unique challenges for VW and the supplier partners to overcome. A plan of daily meetings, constant communication of all the partners and the integration of 52 information systems providing immediate data access are used to coordinate their many activities. In order to prevent conflicts between the different staff, wages and benefits are the same and all employees wear identical uniforms featuring a VW logo and their firm's logo. Finally, a master craftsperson takes personal responsibility for the vehicles and performs final tests and conducts a pre-delivery functional audit to ensure quality standards and maintain conformity within the production process.

Although implementing the modular consortium has produced many challenges, the benefits are noteworthy. By introducing the modular concept, VW's overall costs are down 15–25% and flexibility has increased due to the small number of suppliers. Also, individual customisation of orders is made quicker through increased communication and easier decision making. Most importantly, gain sharing rewards of reductions in product defects and order fulfilment times and improvements in on-time delivery and product performance have been seen throughout the plant. The success of this venture was made possible through planning, communication and hard work to ensure quality standards – now VW and its supplier partners are reaping the rewards through increased revenues.

The supplier partnership agreement of 1997, with some minor refinements, is still operational in VW Brazil today.

Questions

- What are the terms and conditions for the suppliers in the supplier partnership agreement of VW Brazil?
- Describe, with key bullet points, how the challenges of this partnership agreement were implemented.
- What are the major benefits of this supplier partnership agreement for both VW Brazil and the suppliers?

Location strategy

The location of facilities is also an important strategy in managing global supply chains. There are three types of facilities to consider and these are for manufacturing (e.g. factories), services (e.g. head offices, call centres) and transport (e.g. warehouses). The decision process for each type of facility is slightly different but they share most of the common factors. The decisions for both manufacturing and services are becoming increasingly global while decisions for warehouses are more local or regional. Choosing the location of a manufacturing site may also be dependent on different factors. For example, locating a frozen vegetable processing site is a very different type of decision from locating a new mobile phone handset manufacturing factory. In general, a manufacturing site is likely to be near a major supplier of raw materials and the availability of skilled resources. Warehouse locations are influenced by transport infrastructure and the proximity and density of customer demands. The location of a service centre could be more flexible but accessibility and visibility by customers are to be seriously considered.

In the selection of a facility location, there are seven generic factors that should be considered for comparing the options:

1. Variable and fixed operational costs.
2. Political risks, government rules, attitudes and incentives.
3. Cultural and economic issues.

4. Location of markets.
5. Labour availability, attitudes and productivity.
6. Availability of supplies, communications and energy.
7. Exchange rates and currency risks.

The analysis starts with the primary factor of costs comprising both variable and fixed costs. Variable costs consist of the costs of labour, materials and transport. Fixed costs are associated with the costs of the site, buildings, machinery and equipment and overheads. As shown in Figure 19.11, although fixed and variable costs of four options are primary considerations, the consideration of volume throughput can also influence the selection of a site.

In selecting an off-shore site, the availability of skilled labour and labour rates are important. However, incentives from the government and the political stability and health of its economy can be deciding factors. Location strategy tools (break-even analysis, centre of gravity method, multi-factor rating method, etc.) in such circumstances could only offer guides.

Adapting from Chamania et al. (2010), we have developed the 7Cs of the governing factors of the global location strategy. The 7Cs are:

1. *Cost.* As indicated earlier, costs are both fixed and variable. Included are the costs of buying or leasing land, office equipment, communications, wages, training, taxes and IT infrastructure. Costs are important but companies solely seeking the lowest-cost venue, rather than one that matches the organisation's needs and capabilities, often end up paying more than they anticipate. It is important to investigate the future

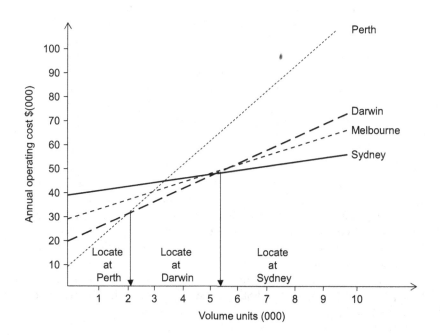

Figure 19.11 Fixed and variable costs and volume considerations for a factory site.

trend in the cost structure of the location. For example, a city (like Jakarta) may have a lower-cost structure at present, but it is showing signs of a rapid rise in operating costs in the future.

2. *Capacity*. Skills capacity is of utmost importance when a company needs to set up a manufacturing site in a short period of time and can use its in-house talent to develop these new employees. Many regions in developing nations that have stellar technical capacity are still relatively inexpensive. China. India, Brazil, Mexico and Eastern Europe offer the engineering skills and infrastructure at competitive costs that are known to be among the best in the world. Many West European automakers, white goods manufacturers and suppliers of advanced components have already implemented advanced manufacturing facilities in so-called emerging economy countries (e.g. 'Electronic City' in Bangalore, India).

3. *Capability*. The longer-term capability of a site is assessed by the presence of specific technical skills and expertise that a company explicitly needs, as well as a sufficiently sophisticated work and operational environment. This category includes such desirable features as nearby universities and R&D centres established by foreign and local companies. In addition, companies that seek high capability should look for the presence of innovation clusters targeted at their line of business. For example, the ecosystem of Silicon Valley can attract multinationals. Similarly, India is dotted with software development clusters and Ireland is fast becoming a haven for medical device companies because of its local technical expertise. Singapore and Finland are attractive locations for innovation centres because of their sustainable capabilities.

4. *Community*. Community in this context refers to the Economic Community, which was a regional organisation that aimed to bring about economic integration between its member states. There are about 40 or so economic communities in the world. However, arguably the most effective of these was the EEC (European Economic Community) which now operates as the EU or European Union. Other active communities include NAFTA (North American Free Trade Association), ASEAN (Association of SE Asian Nations), AEC (African Economic Union) and TPPA (Trans-Pacific Partnership Agreement). It has to be said the deregulation of trade barriers and sharing of resources between the partner countries have accelerated the globalisation process. Global companies are taking these advantages. For example, Nissan invested in a manufacturing site in northern England to gain easier access to the European market. Proctor & Gamble set up factories in Mexico to utilise NAFTA benefits.

5. *Communication*. The ability to seamlessly share information between the new site and company headquarters without cultural and language obstacles. Technical knowledge in most companies is tribal where processes and methods are not documented. In addition, product engineering is often iterative, with multiple cycles among many functions, including design, development, testing, prototyping and manufacturing. 'This makes regular two-way communication between a new engineering location and headquarters critical to ensuring successful integration of the site into the global network as well as critical to the ongoing operations' (Chamania et al., 2010). Compatibility of language thus plays an important role in the site selection process. In spite of the power of the Internet and Skype, the proximity of sites of a common objective is an advantage.

6. *Culture*. Culture in this context covers many facets. The location can attract talent, measured by the accessibility of infrastructure, macroeconomic factors and the

quality of lifestyles. It also includes the level of political stability, government policies supporting R&D, incentives to attract investment and the absence of bureaucratic red tape. By way of illustration, many European companies, such as Volkswagen, Siemens, Faurecia and ABB, have established R&D centres in Eastern Europe, although costs there are higher than in other developing countries. The attraction is primarily cultural: a shared history and time zones close to those at headquarters.

7. *Customer.* Although the above Cs are of the utmost importance, there is another C that should not be overlooked, that is, the customer. To be close to exploding consumer markets, companies often find that opening manufacturing facilities in China and India, for example, is essential. In those cases, even after completing a conventional analysis, companies for which the customer base is crucial may find that this gives them a smaller number of cities to choose from. Whatever the region, in today's globalised environment, more than a few cities will manifest each of the best characteristics to match a company's needs.

Distribution strategy

Distribution strategy is the closest link to customers and therefore the success of any form of supply chain management is often determined by the effectiveness of the distribution strategy and its execution. As a simple example, I buy a book online from Amazon, although I am happy with the convenience of ordering, I shall be unhappy if the book is not delivered in time. I shall blame Amazon for this poor delivery service.

There are two aspects of distribution strategy, one is how you choose the mode of logistics to deliver the products and the other is the strategy of choosing the channels of distribution. We have discussed the strategy of logistics in Chapter 10 under the heading of strategic alliances. We have discussed their four types of distribution alliances: third-party logistics (3PL), retailer supplier partnership (RSP), distribution integration (DI) and customer relationship management (CRM)

In this section, we aim to discuss the strategy of channel management. Product distribution (or place) is one of the four elements of the marketing mix. Distribution of products takes place by means of channels. Channels are sets of interdependent organisations (called intermediaries) involved in making the product available for consumption to the end user or customer. Agents, wholesalers and brokers are intermediaries that act on behalf of the producer but do not take title to the products.

Channel management can be defined as the process by which a producer or supplier directs marketing activity by involving and motivating parties comprising its channel of distribution. There are many functions to be carried out in moving the product from producer to customer. Those functions each require funding and, often, specialist knowledge and expertise. The advantages of using intermediaries as opposed to marketing directly to end users can be argued. Direct delivery reduces the cost of distribution. On the other hand, the use of specialist knowledge and expertise of an intermediary helps to penetrate the market and increase sales. It is important to recognise that in managing global supply chains, particularly for off-shore logistics, the assistance of local agents, underpinned by their knowledge and experience of local markets and regulatory requirements, can prove to be invaluable with an appropriate channel management strategy.

Figure 19.12 shows some commonly used channels of distribution.

With the advancement of digital technology in addition to the traditional P-channels (physical distribution channels), we now also have E-channels (Internet/online distribution

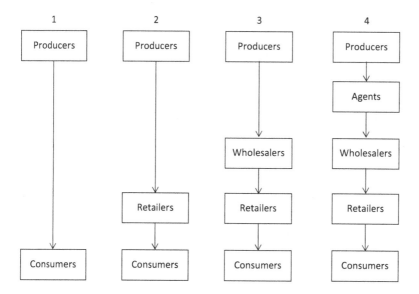

Figure 19.12 Channels of distribution

channels) and M-channels (smart mobile phone/apps distribution channels). Business-to-business (B2B) marketing describes marketing and commerce transactions between businesses, such as between a manufacturer and a wholesaler, or between a wholesaler and a retailer. However good a product or service, it must be distributed to give customers easy access to it. The necessity of distribution can be converted into a competitive advantage by managing channels of distribution.

There are a number of key decision areas influencing the channel management strategy and the appointment of intermediaries. These include the price policy, terms and conditions of sale, territorial rights and the definition of responsibilities. In addition, a choice has to be made between extensive and intensive coverage of the market. It is of utmost importance to develop the terms of engagement with the intermediaries similar to the agreement with a supplier as discussed earlier.

The following case example illustrates how a well-structured channel management agreement between a marketing company and a producer of agricultural products can work for mutual benefits with assigned responsibilities for quality, cost and delivery.

CASE EXAMPLE: CHANNEL MANAGEMENT FOR FRESH PRODUCE

FP Marketing (name changed for reasons of anonymity) is the central marketing organisation for its own and associated growers and is based in the UK, with an annual sales turnover of over €100 million. It coordinates crop production and volumes both in the UK and overseas and supplies consolidated and value-added (packaged) fresh produce to large multiple retailers in the UK, under retailers' own labels; 90% of their business is in supply to UK multiple retailers, the remainder constitutes product that does not meet retailer specifications and is marketed to UK wholesalers or processors. FP Marketing is a category management (CM) supplier to UK multiple retailer chains.

FP Grower (name changed for reasons of anonymity) is a southern Italy based family grower business of some 20 types of fresh produce, most notably tomatoes, and has an annual sales turnover of €10 million. They have 180 ha (80 ha glasshouse and 100 ha open field, in order to manage demand throughout the year). They grow and undertake primary value-adding functions (washing and basic packing in preparation for delivery). Their principal dedicated and 'partner' customer is FP Marketing; 60% of their product goes to intermediaries like FP Marketing and 35% direct to retailers, with the remainder 5% to wholesale markets; 80% of FP Grower's customers are overseas (UK, Austria, Switzerland and Germany). FP Marketing does invest some funds in agronomic development in southern Italy but owns no means of production in the region.

Multiple retail chains will specify quality assurance through the determination of produce from accredited sources. These are normally European baseline production standards, environmental growing conditions and so forth. FP Grower, for example, offers four types of certifications including EUREPGAP and is trialling a limited acreage of organic certified produce. With respect to further utilising quality and production systems as a means of market differentiation, UK retailers have developed their own further standards, additional to or inclusive of baseline accreditation.

FP Grower's motivation is to find a wide market for its produce, while FP Marketing, with its CM-based interaction with retail customers, identifies opportunities for sub-branding by regional identity. In this way, retail customers (through the expertise and packaging operations of FP Marketing) in the UK are keen to differentiate for both UK and overseas (e.g. southern Italy) produce as a means of further value added.

In terms of branding, FP Grower does have a named identity, but as this is mainly used as an identifier on outer cases for wholesale and intermediary customers, brand identity does not appear on packs at the retailer level; and if there is pack identity, it is with the retailer's own label brand. FP Grower's customers collect product (using their own transport arrangements) from them at the farm, which is packed 'on demand' to customers' specifications. As a result, FP Grower does not benefit from the directly attributed brand identity. FP Grower's principal customer, FP Marketing, is responsible for all of the value adding in terms of packaging and on-pack marketing for UK retail customers.

The vertical channel arrangement between FP Grower and FP Marketing does offer FP Grower something that they do not have from other customer sources, and that is a contractual agreement As a result, FP Grower is happy with this arrangement as it provides security of business that is not forthcoming from other customers, who provide regular business but not price stability. This may be a further reason why FP Grower has not developed customer markets dedicated to regional association – these things are more difficult to achieve without further contractual/collaborative agreements. However, FP Grower is looking to expand by exploiting seasonal gaps with UK customers interested in winter production and to add service value through further quality and logistic improvement.

Vertical coordination through a CM-type system does have clear advantages for primary producers like FP Grower and intermediaries like FP Marketing through the consistency of a planned contractual arrangement. As this further develops, this can allow further market differentiation (through, for example, production method or varietal specialisation or emphasis on regional identity). However, control remains firmly in the hands of the multiple retailer customers, whose name and identity value-adding services are conducted in.

FP Marketing does acknowledge that there may be scope for more of these value-adding activities to take place closer to the country and point of production. However, FP Marketing is quick to point out that to supply the retail market outside of Italy, for example, the UK, it would be much harder to replace what they do in terms of providing the consolidation and all of the value-added services that large UK retailers require.

Questions

1. What are the key features of CM? What are the advantages of CM for FP Marketing and FP Grower?
2. Explain how FP Grower manages quality and how FP Marketing benefits from product differentiation.
3. Explain how the branding of fresh produce (e.g. tomatoes) is applied by FP Grower, FP Marketing and the retailer along the supply chain.

Summary

The key learning points of this chapter include:

- Global supply chains provide more opportunities and risks than domestic supply chains due to numerous links interconnecting a wide network of firms. Therefore, it is of vital importance to develop longer-term supply chain capabilities to manage these opportunities and risks to a competitive advantage.
- Supply chain strategies can span all aspects of operations and services, but the most challenging areas of strategic decisions are managing capacity, suppliers, sourcing and location and distribution channels. We have covered all these important areas of strategies.
- We have developed models for sourcing and outsourcing both manufacturing and service operations. It is important to note that Basu's manufacturing strategy model relates very closely to the product life cycle model and the BCG portfolio matrix.
- Depending on the level of strategic risks and revenues, we have classified suppliers into four categories, viz. transactional, transitional, collaborative and partner. In managing global supply chains, carefully drawn supplier engagement agreements, especially for preferred collaborative and partner suppliers, creates a longer-term business advantage.
- The consideration of operating costs alone does not determine a location strategy for a site whether it is for manufacturing, services or physical distribution. We have

developed multiple factors for deciding on a location strategy. These are the 7Cs: cost, capacity, capability, community, communication, culture and customer.

- Direct delivery may reduce cost and improve services in a domestic supply network, but the knowledge and experience of local agents and intermediaries add value and marketing advantage through an appropriately designed distribution channel supported by robust agreements.

Discussion questions

1. What are the characteristics of a supply chain strategy that distinguish a strategy from an operation? Why is a supply chain strategy important?
2. Describe the key areas of supply chain strategies.
3. Explain the essential steps and processes in developing a supply chain strategy.
4. In the capacity strategy case example for Minkies Deli, what is the level of demand in these markets? Assess its impact on capacity.
5. How could Minkies manage demand and capacity in its growing business?
6. Explain how globalisation has affected the factors for a sourcing strategy. What are the specific considerations for an outsourcing strategy as compared to an off-shoring strategy?
7. Discuss the distinctive decision criteria of a manufacturing outsourcing strategy and a business process outsourcing strategy.
8. In the selection of a facility location, what are seven generic factors that should be considered for comparing the options? Compare these with the 7Cs proposed by Chamania et al. (2010).
9. Discuss the advantages of channel management based on strategic decisions. What are the opportunities and challenges of new digital channels?

20 Supply chain risk management

Introduction

If something can go wrong, it will go wrong at the worst possible time.

Supply chain risk management 'is the implementation of strategies to manage both everyday and exceptional risks along the supply chain based on continuous risk assessment with the objective of reducing vulnerability and ensuring continuity' (Wieland and Wallenburg, 2012). In the past, manufacturers such as Henry Ford attempted to own or control the supply chain. For example, Henry Ford owned coal mines, steel mills, railways and river barges to supply his factory. Today, most manufacturers outsource as much as possible and buy in built-up components. Volkswagen is an exception. They employ a largely vertically integrated strategy whereby they manufacture their own components. At the other end of the scale, General Motors (number three behind Toyota) outsource as much as possible and their factories are little more than assembly lines of built-up components. By comparison, in 2015, Volkswagen became the largest auto manufacturer in the world, producing 10.5 million units and employing 590,000 people, whereas General Motors with a centralised strategy produced 9.9 million and employed 220,000. This means that for Volkswagen, the ratio of units per person was 18 and for General Motors 45. At first look, this would seem that GM is 250% more efficient than VW. A look at the reported profit figures for 2015 tells a different story; VW's profit was $US14 billion, and GM's was $US9.7 billion. By making most of the components in-house, VW has better control of the supply chain in terms of design, quality and delivery and thus reduces risks associated with relying on outsourced supply. Toyota follows a blended model, in 2015, they employed 350,000 people and produced 10.2 million units with a ratio of 29 units per person, but with a whopping profit of $US18.1 billion. Toyota is famous for its collaborative approach with suppliers. Toyota will, for example, provide technical expertise to help their suppliers become efficient and suppliers are encouraged to make suggestions about design. General Motors is more at arms' length, they tell suppliers what they want and do not get involved in the day-to-day operation of the supplier.

Leaving the auto industry aside, it is a truism that today, manufacturers, and increasingly service and retail industries, spend most of their budget on buying in goods and services. This allows organisations to get on with what they are good at, euphemistically known as concentrating on core competencies.

The more that is outsourced, the greater the risk.

Risks include:

Failure of a supplier (becomes insolvent and ceases to trade).
Suppliers taken over by your competitor (it is not unknown for an organisation to buy out a competitor's supplier).

DOI: 10.4324/9781003341352-23

Price increases (if a company is dependent on one supplier, the supplier has the power).

Fluctuating and unreliable delivery times.

Variation in quality.

Societal issues (e.g. where the media find a supplier in the supply chain using child labour or cutting-down rainforests).

Loss of security (commercially sensitive product information).

Exchange fluctuations (for overseas suppliers).

Regulatory and compliance (different countries have different codes and codes are likely to change).

Cultural issues and breakdown in communication.

Third-party fraud.

We daresay you can think of other more extreme potential risks including forces of nature such as earthquakes and tsunamis, shipwrecks, strikes, revolutions and even war.

A risk is something that might happen that will have an adverse effect. Risk management requires a structured approach and like sales and operations, planning needs to be a team effort including senior management from all key departments (marketing, sales, manufacturing, operations, purchasing, human resources and finance as a minimum). The risk management team needs to meet on a regular basis to identify risks. From identification, action and contingency plans will be developed to provide a risk management plan. This plan needs to be kept up to date but might need to be promulgated on a need-to-know-only basis. As will be seen below, some of the planned actions will be commercially sensitive and confidentiality will be important.

The first stage in risk management is to determine the potential risks no matter how outlandish (e.g. terrorist attack) these may be. Each identified risk should be rated on a scale of one to five as to the likelihood of the risk actually happening, and second, the magnitude of the effect if it does happen needs to be assessed.

Learning objectives

Learning objectives for this chapter are:

1. Examples of supply chain risks.
2. Managing risks in global supply chains.

Examples of supply chain risks

Change of government in a key supplier's country: 4/5.

Ramification: if there is a change in government the chances are of changes in labour law, the likelihood being 3/5. This would result in a price increase of up to 50%.

Having determined a risk and the effect if the risk actually happens, what can we do?

The ideal would be to avoid or prevent the risk (have a binding contract limiting price increase, find an alternative supplier, or if possible, transfer production in-house).

Key supplier bought out by competitor: 2/5.

If this happens, we will be starved of material and the competitor will be privy to some of our trade secrets. A buyout of our supplier is not likely, but the result would be very serious.

We could buy shares in our supplier or look for an alternative supplier.

Whatever the risk, there will be a range of actions that can be taken. However, as any firefighter will tell you, it is easier to prevent a fire than to put one out. And if a fire does occur, the firefighters who have prepared for contingencies will be more effective than people running around contradicting and blaming each other. No one wants a fire but knowing what to do will ease the situation.

Insurance and buying forward foreign exchange are obvious approaches to recovering losses, but insurance does not bring back the dead or in commercial terms does not bring back lost customers when an organisation fails to perform. If a container of key components is lost, insurance will cover the value of the material lost, but if the factory ceases to produce and delivery dates are not met, what are the overall and ongoing and perhaps unknown costs? It is foolish not to have insurance, but in itself, insurance does not constitute risk management.

When dealing with suppliers, it is incumbent on the purchaser to ensure that the product specification is such that conformance to standards can be measured. Taking a leaf out of Nike's and Toyota's books, it is prudent for the purchaser to be empowered to visit suppliers' facilities and be able to monitor production. Monitoring should not be restricted to meeting product specifications but should include cleanliness, working conditions and fair pay. The approach taken should not be of a policing nature but rather be that of a friendly and helpful collaborator.

When appointing a new supplier, due diligence should be taken as to the financial strength and ownership of the supplier and their reputation in the market for honesty and reliability.

A recent study 'Managing Risk in the Global Supply Chain' (www.globalsupplycha ininstitue.utk.edu; retrieved March 2016) found that none of the 150 companies surveyed used outside expertise in assessing risk in their supply chains, 90% do not quantify risk when outsourcing production, 66% had risk managers in their firms either in legal or compliance, but virtually all ignored supply chain risk, and 100% acknowledged insurance as a highly effective risk mitigation tool 'but it was not on their radar screen nor in their purview'.

These are startling findings. Remember our opening statement to this chapter:
'If something can go wrong, it will go wrong at the worst possible time'.

Potential global supply chain risks

With the general introduction of business risks as described previously, let us now have another look at what all these risks mean for global supply chains. Disruption to supply chains has increased recently, particularly at two levels: (1) threats to oil supply in the Middle East and North Africa at the mouth of the Gulf of Oman and the variation in oil prices; (2) threats to supply lines in general through the random acts of terrorism in capital cities in Europe and the United States. These threats will create extra pressure to simplify production processes through innovation, shortening supply chains through repositioning factories and moving away from a reliance on a single supplier.

The potential sources of supply chain risks are summarised as follows:

External risks:
- Natural disasters.
- Terrorism, war, sabotage cybercrime.
- Political uncertainty.

Internal risks:
- Demand variability.
- Lack of capacity.
- Financial uncertainty.
- Enterprise underperformance.

Supplier risks:
- Regulatory risks.
- Financial losses.
- Upstream supply risk.
- Supplier relationship management.

Distribution risks:
- Infrastructure constraints.
- Warehouse inadequacies.
- Cargo damage or theft.

Managing risks in global supply chains

Having defined risk and identified its major sources, let us examine how to manage supply chain risk with a structured process. There are some simple questions to be addressed in a risk management process, such as:

- When and how do we start?
- How do we know the areas of risk?
- What do we do with them?
- Who should take action?
- How can we learn and improve?

The intuitive questions on risk management including the above can be addressed by a formal process as shown in Figure 20.1, indicating that risk management is structured common sense.

Define and plan

It is important to note that risks only exist with defined objectives. We can start the risk management process by clearly defining which objectives are at risk. It is also important to recognise that the causes and challenges of risks are likely to be different for each process. Hence, it is vital to define the risks clearly and scale the risk process at the outset. The deliverables provided by the define phase may be a single document, such as a risk register defining the objects of risk in a spreadsheet with additional columns allocated to the probability occurrence and the impact on objectives (see Table 20.1). The depth and complexity of the risk process to be applied to the specific task should be decided at the 'Define and Plan' stage of the risk management process.

Identify

The next step is to populate the risk register further and identify the risks with the potential of affecting the objectives. The outcomes could be either a threat or an opportunity. There are different risk identification techniques (e.g. interviews with key stakeholders, SWOT analysis)

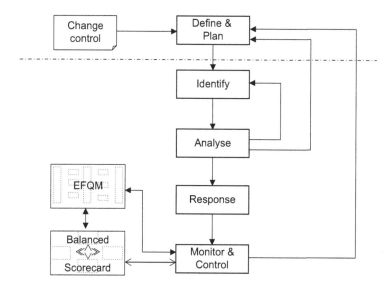

Figure 20.1 A risk management process

and it is good practice to apply more than one technique. The SWOT analysis is carried out by structured brainstorming sessions with leaders of major business units. The interviews with key stakeholders are also critical to capture their perspectives on possible risks that may be experienced by the supply chain. There are other techniques for identifying risks including cause and effect analysis, scenario analysis, flow charts and structured checklists. The success of all these techniques depends on how the risk management team has been formed based on the experience, knowledge and judgement of team members. Each identified risk should be allocated to a risk owner who should be assigned to ensure its successful mitigation. Whenever a change of specification or scope is considered, its risk potential is recognised by document-ing the objects of change in the risk register. That is why risk management is a dynamic and iterative process covering each stage of the project life cycle.

Analyse

A key stage to follow is to analyse the priority of risk objects to identify the worst threats and best rewards. The most popular method is to estimate the probability of occurrence (as a percentage) and the impact (on a scale of one to ten), giving a resultant risk factor (see Table 20.1).

The values of risk factors may also be categorised as:

Above 0.7: Extreme
0.5 to 0.7: High
0.3 to 0.49: Medium
Below 0.3: Low

The allocation of probability and impact scale is subjective depending on how much the con-sequences matter. The assessment of priority by a risk register has its limitation but it also offers

Table 20.1 A typical example of a risk register (based on hypothetical objectives of an NHS Hospital Trust in the UK)

Ref	Start date	Source	Description	Probability (%)	Impact (scale 1–10)	Risk factor	Action	End date
1	1/9/12	Trust Board	Failure to meet waiting list targets	90	8	0.72	Increase theatre capacity	Ongoing
2	1/5/11	ICU	Excess use of agency staff	80	7	0.56	Funding approved to increase staffing	January 2013
3	2/4/10	All wards	Obsolete bed stock	75	7	0.52	Capital bid for replacement	Five-year plan
4	1/1/11	A&E	Non-compliance with clinical standards	70	8	0.56	Report from the clinical risk management committee	February 2012
5	31/10/11	HR	Threat to retaining Investor in People Award	90	5	0.45	Enhanced training programme	February 2013

a structured and systematic document with a single set of data for management review. A more advanced form of a risk register is failure mode and effects analysis (FMEA) (Basu, 2009). FMEA is a systematic and analytical quality planning technique at the product, design, process and service stages assessing what potentially could go wrong and thereby aiding faulty diagnosis. The objective is to classify all possible failures according to their effect measured in terms of severity, occurrence and detection and then find solutions to eliminate or minimise them.

The potential failure modes for each function are listed and then the effects of each failure mode, especially the effects perceived by the use, are described. The causes of each failure mode are then examined and summarised. Current controls to detect a potential failure mode are identified and assessed. The severity of the potential hazard of the failure to personnel or system on a scale of one to ten is then determined. The next step is to estimate the relative likelihood of occurrence of each failure, ranging from highly unlikely (1) to most likely (10). The ease with which the failure may be detected is also estimated on a scale of one to ten. A risk priority number (RPN) for each failure is the product of the numbers estimated in the previous three steps (viz. severity, occurrence and detection). The potential failure modes in descending order of RPN should be the focus of the improvement action to minimise the risk of failure.

Although both the risk register and FMEA use numbers, these analyses are based on subjective perceptions to prioritise risks for further consideration. These are qualitative risk assessment processes considering each risk independently. However, it is often necessary to analyse the combined effect of risks on overall project outcomes. This is where quantitative risk assessment processes can be applied. Monte Carlo simulation (Basu, 2009) is the most popular quantitative approach because of its proven statistical reliability and validity of results and there are software tools to support it. The applications of the Monte Carlo technique in p-risk management are focused on two stages of the project life cycles, viz. feasibility and implementation. At the feasibility stage, the simulation is the perfect tool for evaluating a pro forma of investment opportunities. We know that at the initial stage of a project there is uncertainty regarding input since pro forma is by definition an estimation of performance. We also know that the Monte Carlo technique will calculate answers that accurately reflect the uncertainty of input data. During the implementation stage of a project, the Monte Carlo technique examines the overall uncertainty of project completion times (see Figure 20.2). The technique is also very useful in assessing the probability and consequence of critical risks in a risk register during the implementation of a supply chain project.

Respond

Following the analysis of risks, the next stage is to consider what should be done in response. Arguably, this is the critical stage of the total risk management process. It is where risk management strategies and decisions make a difference. There are many strategies for responses but most of them are the following responses or a combination of them:

- Avoidance
- Deflection
- Reduction
- Acceptance

The purpose of avoidance is to eliminate the root causes of risk, if possible, or change the specification or scope of the objective. This strategy may encourage innovation but very often it affects the quality standards.

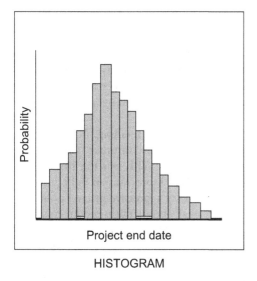
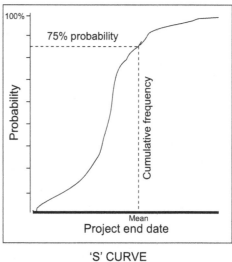

HISTOGRAM   'S' CURVE

Figure 20.2 Output from a Monte Carlo simulation

The strategy of deflection involves another party or supplier to manage the risk. The responsibility risk is transferred usually to a third party with more knowledge and experience to deal with the issue. This strategy is likely to affect the completion time.

The aim of reduction is to reduce the probability and the impact of risk by allocating more appropriate resources. A reduction can also be achieved by changing the scope of the objective. This strategy is similar to avoidance but to a lesser degree.

Acceptance is usually the last resort when other strategies cannot be effectively applied. The response here is to allow contingency in cost with the expectation that the supply chain process or project will be continued without significant change. Some risks, especially related to health and safety, are also safeguarded by appropriate insurance policies.

Monitor and control

As indicated earlier, project risk management is a dynamic process – it is an iterative process with regular reviews and management control. Risk exposure also changes continually. It is a common practice to allocate dedicated resources to document, analyse and monitor risk reports, but the responsibility of implementing risk responses and corrective actions is accountable to the specific team leader of the task where the risk is located. The purpose of a formal review process is to ensure that planned responses are achieved in time and also to develop new responses when appropriate. It is therefore vital that the risk management plan is monitored on a regular (usually monthly) basis to ensure that it is relevant to changing circumstances. The key issues should be resolved, if necessary, at the final stage of the sales and operations planning meeting. It is also a good practice to embed the key performance indicators with the central project performance management systems usually based on a balanced scorecard (Basu, 2009) and EFQM (Basu, 2009).

CASE EXAMPLE:

Carrefour and Fair Trade – minimisation of product and environmental risks

Carrefour is a global hypermarket retail chain with headquarters in France that operates worldwide. Carrefour translated into English means crossroads. In France, there are 1242 Carrefour super and hypermarkets plus 3245 convenience stores and 897 'hard discounters'. Worldwide, Carrefour employs over 500,000 people and sales for 2015 were €86.3 million.

Carrefour is regarded as a pioneer in aspects of grocery retailing. For example, in 1976, Carrefour broke with the classic conventions of consumer marketing when they launched their own brand line 'Produits Libres'. This was the first line of unbranded products in grocery retail. Initially, Produits Libres was an unbranded line of about 50 products with sober packaging and a very aggressive pricing policy. The line was developed in partnership with French small and medium producers. To gain acceptance in the market, Carrefour's set high-quality requirements that were stringently monitored. The launch of Produits Libres was partly done to counter the reluctance of certain national brands to supply their products to hypermarkets. Aware of its important role with respect to consumers, Carrefour introduced precautionary product principles. These innovative initiatives included dating eggs and the banning of genetically modified products from all of their own brand products. In 1991, Carrefour created Carrefour Quality Commitment Lines to guarantee quality, taste and product authenticity while offering attractive prices to consumers and fair pay to producers. Carrefour increased its offer to the market by adding complementary product lines geared towards specific segments in keeping with consumer expectations. Regional specialities were highlighted through the 'Reflets de France' brand (1995) followed by the 'Carrefour Bio' certified organic brand in 1997 and 'Marque n°1', a discount product line offering the lowest prices on the market. Once customers' preference for buying environmentally friendly products became significant, Carrefour began labelling own-branded products to show support for ecosystems: species and crop variety are protected and also sustainable management of the land is ensured. Moreover, emissions are low, and the usage of water is controlled in the sense as not to overuse or pollute it. Finally, the customer is confident that they are buying a product with no or only low chemical treatment. Since the 1990s, Carrefour has also changed its policy with regard to packaging. It became more environmentally friendly based on three main alternations: packaging weight was reduced, all packaging became recyclable and substances presenting a potential environmental risk were removed. Regarding the launch of their own environmental label, consumers could now decide to contribute to sustainability themselves. In addition, they knew that Carrefour was concerned about the environment with respect to packaging and their label. It can be assumed that because of those changes, many environmentally conscious customers are attracted to shop with Carrefour.

Today, Carrefour and Fair Trade are synonymous.

Fair Trade is an organised social movement and market-based approach that aims to help producers in developing countries and promote sustainability. The movement advocates the payment of a fair price to producers as well as establishing social and environmental standards. It focuses in particular on exports from developing countries to developed countries. In 2010, it is estimated that there are approximately 570 producing organisations in 57 countries supplying handicrafts, coffee, cocoa, sugar, tea, bananas, honey, cotton, wine, fresh fruit, chocolate and flowers. Fair Trade's strategic intent is to work with marginalised producers and workers in order to help them move towards economic self-sufficiency and stability. It also aims to allow them to become greater stakeholders in their own organisations, as well as play a wider role in international trade.

The Fair Trade initiatives of Carrefour have their origins in coffee harvesting and production. The first shipment of coffee beans to Carrefour was delivered in 10 kg sacks to Vitrolles, France, in 1970. The beans were roasted in store and sold in 500 g and 1 kg bags. In April 1997, Carrefour launched the 'organic' coffee brand under the name 'Carrefour Bio' to promote organic products and support fair trading. In 2001, it was decided to establish a 'green supply chain' for 'Carrefour Bio'. The organic coffee marketed under the name 'Carrefour Bio' is not indexed on the world coffee market. The purchase price is approximately 30% higher than the average price in Mexico. The supplier is contracted to pay a guaranteed minimum price to producers. Producers can obtain up to 60% of the value of the coffee at current international rates; 3000 producers from 37 Mexican communities cultivate coffee using organic methods. A local infrastructure has been introduced to transport people between towns and villages, an example in one area being a two-hour bus ride rather than what was a two-day walk for the workers. A health scheme has been introduced providing free medicine and healthcare and a consortium has been set up to buy basic foodstuffs at cost price. The coffee is cultivated by small farmers working for Uciri cooperative in Mexico using organic methods of farming. Such cultivation helps prevent the land from becoming impoverished. The cultivation is carried out in accordance with French Organic Society standards without the use of artificial fertilisers or chemical pesticides for tropical forest conditions. Organic fertiliser comprising sundried handpicked stoned cherries and animal waste is spread over the plants. This is the only plant treatment used by the farmers. Cultivation methods are monitored by an organic certification body. An agricultural education centre has also been established catering for organic farming, animal breeding and bio-culture. The 'Carrefour Bio' coffee project appears to be a win–win initiative for a green supply chain. The fertility of the land has been protected. The latest available figures show that the average income per family of producers increased from €53 per year in 1985 to €1524 per year in 2000. The local communities benefit from the infrastructure and facilities for transport, healthcare and education. Consumers are happy with an organic product at an affordable price. For Carrefour, sales for the product increase yearly.

Postscript. Consumption of coffee continues to grow, and the value of the coffee trade makes it the world's second-most valuable commodity after oil, and worldwide there are 25 million coffee growers, most of whom still face immense hardship.

Summary

In this chapter, we have set out to explore why risk management is important in the context of global supply chains and how to manage the causes and effects of risks. We have discovered that risk management also offers opportunities for improved outcomes and thus a very important contributor to supply chain performance. In the context of supply chain processes and projects, because of the uncertainty of their outcomes, the role of risk management is even more significant. We have identified that in addition to the uncertainty of the processes, there are external risks, particularly related to oil production and random acts of terrorism. The generic risk management plan of project management (comprising the stages of define, identify, analyse, respond and monitor, and control) is also applicable to managing risks in global supply chains.

We can summarise the key learning points as follows:

1. Risk is everywhere and we need to find it before it happens.
2. Risk is both a threat and an opportunity.
3. Risk applies to all assets and objectives, at every level and every stage of supply chain processes.
4. Risk can be measured as the expected deviation from the expected value.
5. Risk management is a dynamic process and continuous risk measurement/assessment should lead to better decisions and outcomes.
6. The key to risk management is deciding what risks to hedge, what risks to pass through and what risks to take based on an objective process.
7. To manage risk can generate new shareholder value. The goal is to optimise risk-reward profiles of projects according to stakeholder risk appetite.

Discussion questions

1. What are risks in managing a supply chain? Discuss the additional potential risks caused by globalisation.
2. Describe the major steps in a risk management process suitable for managing a global supply chain.
3. Explain a risk register with an example. Discuss how a risk register compares with FMEA. When is it more appropriate to use FMEA instead of a risk register?
4. Based on the information provided in the case example of Carrefour, explain how Carrefour addressed the potential environmental risks of coffee supply.

Part 4

Integrating supply chain management

21 Systems and procedures

Introduction

We have described the components of supply chain building blocks in Part 2, Chapters 5–10, highlighting the key issues, opportunities and challenges in managing a total supply chain. These features have been further explored with the current trends in Part 3. Now the key question is: how are these building blocks interfaced or integrated to provide the synergy of managing the total supply chain as one unit? The processes in each building block are standardised or formalised by systems and procedures. The effectiveness of systems and procedures can be achieved by using sales and operations planning (S&OP) and performance management processes.

Learning objectives

This chapter considers in the context of supply chain management, the following three cornerstones of systems and procedures:

1. Quality management.
2. Financial management.
3. Information and communication technology.

Quality management

What is quality?

Quality has two levels, a basic level and a higher level. At the basic level, common definitions 'fitness for purpose', 'getting it right first time' and 'right thing, right place, right time' apply. (These definitions have all been so overused that they are almost clichés.) An understanding of what we mean by basic level and higher levels of quality can best be explained by illustration.

Consider a bus service. What as passengers are our basic requirements? First, unless the bus is going more or less where we want to go, we won't catch it. The second requirement is timing – usually we have a timeframe by which we judge a bus service. If we start work at 9 am, unless the bus gets us to the office before 9 am, we won't catch it. Another consideration will be cost. Therefore, the basic requirements in this example would be the route, the time and the cost, and depending on alternatives, we would probably rank them in that order.

DOI: 10.4324/9781003341352-25

A bus service could meet all these requirements (right thing, right place, right time and right cost), but still not be a quality service. If the service was unreliable (sometimes late, sometimes early, sometimes did not keep to the route), then we would not consider it a reliable service. But supposing the bus met all our basic requirements, got us to work on time every time and at a reasonable cost, but it was dirty, the driver was surly, the seats were hard and it leaked exhaust fumes. Then, although it met our basic requirements, there is no way we would describe it as a quality service.

In other words, to meet our perception of quality, there are certain basic requirements that have to be met, and there are certain higher-order requirements that have to be met. In this case, we would expect polite service, a clean bus, reasonably comfortable seating and certainly no exhaust fumes. A truly high-quality service would mean that the bus was spotlessly clean, had carpet on the floor and had piped music as well as all the other attributes. But no matter how comfortable the ride, how cheap the fare, unless the bus is going our way, we shan't be interested in catching it. To have your product described as a quality product, the customer will expect higher-level benefits. These higher-level benefits are what give an organisation a competitive edge, and often the difference costs very little to achieve.

There are many different definitions and dimensions of quality to be found in books and academic literature. We have selected three dimensions of quality from the literature, which are shown below, and we have added a three-dimensional model.

One of the most respected definitions of quality is given by the eight quality dimensions (Table 21.1).

The above dimensions of quality are not mutually exclusive, although they relate primarily to the quality of the product. Neither are they exhaustive. Service quality is perhaps even more difficult to define than product quality. A set of service quality dimensions (see Table 21.2) that is widely cited has been compiled by Parasuraman, Zeithamel and Berry (1985).

Our third authoritative definition of quality shown in Table 21.3 is taken from Wild (2003: p. 644).

The list of quality dimensions by both Garvin and Parasuraman et al. are widely cited and respected. However, one problem with definitions is that if time permits, the reader will find several other useful definitions and dimensions. Wild's definition of design/ process quality does provide a broad framework to develop a company-specific quality strategy.

Table 21.1 Garvin's product quality dimensions

Performance refers to the efficiency (e.g. return on investment) with which the product achieves its intended purpose.
Features are attributes that supplement the product's basic performance, for example, tinted glass windows in a car.
Reliability refers to the capability of the product to perform consistently over its life cycle.
Conformance refers to meeting the specifications of the product, usually defined by numeric values.
Durability is the degree to which a product withstands stress without failure.
Serviceability is used to denote the ease of repair.
Aesthetics are sensory characteristics such as a look, sound, taste and smell.
Perceived quality is based on customer opinion.

Source: Garvin (1988).

Table 21.2 Parasuraman et al.'s service quality dimensions

Tangibles are the physical appearance of the service facility and people.
Service reliability deals with the ability of the service provider to perform dependably.
Responsiveness is the willingness of the service provider to be prompt in delivering the service.
Assurance relates to the ability of the service provider to inspire trust and confidence.
Empathy refers to the ability of the service provider to demonstrate care and individual attention to the
 customer.
Availability is the ability to provide service at the right time and place.
Professionalism encompasses the impartial and ethical characteristics of the service provider.
Timeliness refers to the delivery of service within the agreed lead time.
Completeness addresses the delivery of the order in full.
Pleasantness simply means good manners and politeness.

Source: Parasuraman et al. (1985).

Table 21.3 Wild's definition of quality

The quality of a product or service is the degree to which it satisfies customer requirements. It is
 influenced by:
Design quality: the degree to which the *specification* of the product or service satisfies customers'
 requirements.
Process quality: the degree to which the product or service, which is made available to the customer,
 conforms to specification.

Source: Wild (2003).

Figure 21.1 Three dimensions of quality

Nonetheless, one important dimension of quality is not clearly visible in the above models: the quality of the organisation. This is a fundamental cornerstone of the quality of a holistic process and an essential requirement of an approved quality assessment scheme such as EFQM (European Foundation of Quality Management). Therefore, a three-dimensional model of quality has been developed (Basu, 2004) as shown in diagrammatic form in Figure 21.1.

Table 21.4 Basu's organisation quality dimensions

Top management commitment means that organisational quality cannot exist without the total commitment of the top executive team.

Sales and operations planning is a monthly senior management review process to align strategic objectives with operation tasks.

Single set of numbers provides the common business data for all functions in the company.

Using appropriate tools and techniques relates to the fact that without the effective application of appropriate tools and techniques, the speed of improvement will not be assured.

Performance management includes the selection, measurement, monitoring and application of key performance indicators.

Knowledge management includes education, training and development of employees, sharing of best practice and communication media.

Teamwork culture requires that teamwork should be practised in cross-functional teams to encourage a borderless organisation.

Self-assessment enables a regular health check of all aspects of the organisation against a checklist or accepted assessment process such as EFQM.

Source: Basu (2004).

When an organisation develops and defines its quality strategy, it is important to share a common definition of quality and each department within a company can work towards a common objective. The product quality should contain defined attributes of both numeric specifications and perceived dimensions. The process quality, whether it relates to manufacturing or service operations, should also contain some defined criteria of acceptable service level so that the conformity of the output can be validated against these criteria. Perhaps the most important determinant of how we perceive sustainable quality is the functional and holistic role that we as individuals have within the organisation. Organisation quality can only germinate when the approach is holistic, and a single set of numbers based on transparent measurement is emphasised with senior management commitment. We have compiled a set of key organisation quality dimensions shown in Table 21.4

Hierarchy of quality

With the subject of quality, like many management subjects such as marketing and strategic management, a number of technical terms have evolved. In some cases, rather than helping us to understand the underlying concepts or techniques, technical terms tend to add a further complication to our understanding. Often, the terms used are given different connotations by different people, the meanings become blurred, and terms become interchangeable. In this section, we discuss the various ways in which quality can be managed. We also discuss the strengths and weaknesses of each method. For these reasons, we have developed a hierarchy of methods of quality management. Our hierarchy approximates the evolution of quality management from simple testing to a full total quality management (TQM) system.

Quality by inspection

Traditionally, in manufacturing, the concept of quality was conformance to certain dimensions and specifications, the cliché being 'fitness for purpose'. Quality control was achieved by inspection and supervision. Inspection is the most basic approach to quality. The aim being for an inspector to detect, and if sufficiently serious to reject before despatch if a product deviates from a set standard. Inspection will at least provide the customer with an acceptable product. Quality inspection is an expensive method of achieving a basic level of quality. It requires the employment of people to check on the operators. Inspection and supervision do not add value to a product but do add to the cost!

The stage of production where the inspection takes place is important. If the only inspection is at the end of the production line, then, if deviations from the standard are discovered at this late stage, the cost of reworking could well double the cost of the item. If a deviation from the standard is not detected, the final inspector is the customer, by which time it is too late. If the product is found to be below standard by the customer, the manufacturer has the problem of putting it right. Putting it right could include the cost of scrapping the unit and giving the client a new one, or in extreme cases, a total product recall with all the costs and losses of consumer confidence that this entails.

Quality inspection at a more advanced level includes checking and testing at various stages of production so that errors can be detected early, and remedial action taken before the next stage of the process takes place. At a still higher level of inspection, materials are inspected on receipt and then probably tested again before being drawn from the store. Of course, all these tests and checks take time and cost money. The cost is easy to quantify when the checks are carried out by people whose prime job is to test and check the work of others.

We contend that when people know everything they do is subject to testing and checking, then the onus is no longer on them to get the job right first time and they come to rely on the inspector. We believe that the inspector or supervisor will be conditioned to find a percentage of errors, after all, that is the main reason for employing inspectors. This attitude will be reinforced further by an error percentage being built into the standard costs. Thus, a level of error becomes accepted and is built into the cost of the product.

The costs of relying on inspection by people other than the operator are therefore twofold:

1. A level of error becomes accepted as standard and is included in the price.
2. Inspectors do not add value to the product. Inspectors are an added cost.

The next stage above quality inspection can be designated as quality control.

Quality control

With quality control, the aim is not only to monitor the quality at various stages of the process but to identify and eliminate causes of unsatisfactory quality so that they don't happen again. Whereas inspection is an 'after-the-fact' approach, quality control is aimed at preventing mistakes. With quality control, you would expect to find in place drawings, raw material testing, intermediate process testing, some self-inspection by workers, keeping of records of failure and some feedback to supervisors and operators of errors and percentage of errors. The end aims are to reduce waste by eliminating errors and to make sure that the production reaches a specified level of quality before shipment to the customer.

Quality assurance

Quality assurance includes all the steps taken under quality control and quality inspection. It includes, where appropriate, the setting of standards with documentation for dimensions, tolerances, machine settings, raw material grades, operating temperatures and any other safety quality or standard that might be desirable. Quality assurance would also include the documentation of the method of checking against the specified standards. Quality assurance generally includes third-party approval from a recognised authority such as the International Organization for Standardization (ISO). However, ISO accreditation in itself does not suggest that a high level of quality has been reached. The only assurance that ISO accreditation gives is that the organisation does have a defined level of quality and a defined procedure that is consistently being met. With quality assurance, one would expect to move from the detection of errors to correction of process to prevent errors. One would also expect a comprehensive quality manual, recording of failures to achieve quality standards and costs, use of statistical process control (SPC) and the audit of quality systems.

Total quality management

The fourth and highest level in our hierarchy of quality is total quality management. The lower levels of quality inspection, quality control and quality assurance are aimed at achieving an agreed consistent level of quality, first by testing and inspection, then by rigid conformance to standards and procedures, and finally by efforts to eliminate causes of errors so that the defined accepted level of quality will be achieved. This is a cold and sterile approach to quality. It implies that once a sufficient level of quality has been achieved, then apart from maintaining that level which in itself might be hard work, little more needs to be done. This is often the Western approach to quality and has its roots in Taylorism (see Taylor, 1947). Taylor believed in finding the 'best method' by scientific means and then establishing this method as the standard. This approach is top-down, the bosses determine the level of quality to be achieved, and then the bosses decide on the best method to achieve the desired level of quality. Control methods of inspection and supervision are then set in place to ensure that the required level of quality is maintained. This does not mean that management is not taking into account what the customer wants or is ignoring what the competition is doing. It just means that they, as managers, believe they know what is best and how it can be achieved. To this end, supervision and inspection become an important method of achieving the aim with little input expected from the workers.

Total quality management is on a different plane. Total quality management does, of course, include all the previous levels of setting standards and the means of measuring conformance to standards. In doing this, SPC will be used, systems will be documented and accurate and timely feedback on results will be given. With TQM, ISO accreditation might be sought, but an organisation that truly has embraced TQM will not need the ISO stamp of approval.

Any organisation aspiring to TQM will have a vision of quality that goes far beyond mere conformity with a standard. TQM requires a culture whereby every member of the organisation believes that not one day should go by without the organisation in some way improving the quality of its goods and services. The vision of TQM must begin with the chief executive. If the chief executive has a passion for quality and continuous improvement, and if this passion can be transmitted down through the organisation, then, paradoxically, the ongoing driving force will be from the bottom up.

Generally, it is the lower-paid members of the organisation who will physically make the product or provide the service, and it is the sum of the efforts that each individual puts into their part of the finished product that will determine the overall quality of the finished article. Likewise, generally, it is the lower-paid staff members, such as shop assistants, telephone operators and van drivers who are the contact point with the customer and the wider public. They, too, have a huge part to play in how the customer perceives an organisation. It is on the lower level that an organisation must rely on for the continuing daily level of quality. Quality, once the culture of quality has become ingrained, will be driven from the bottom up, rather than achieved by direction or control from the top. Management will naturally have to continue to be responsible for planning and providing the resources to enable the workers to do the job. But, unless the factory operators, the telephone operators, the cleaning staff, the sales assistants, the junior accounts clerk and the van drivers are fully committed to quality, TQM will never happen.

TQM, however, goes beyond the staff of the organisation – it goes outside the organisation and involves suppliers, customers and the general public.

Once a relationship has been built with a supplier, that supplier is no longer treated with suspicion, or in some cases, almost as an adversary. Instead of trying to get the best deal possible out of the supplier, the supplier becomes a member of the team. The supplier becomes involved in the day-to-day problems and concerns of the organisation and is expected to assist, help and advice. The supplier becomes part of the planning team. Price and discounts will no longer be the crucial issues, delivery of the correct materials at the right time will be the real issues, and suppliers will be judged accordingly. Once a supplier proves reliable, the checking and testing of inward goods will become less crucial. Ideally, the level of trust will be such that the raw materials can be delivered directly to the operator's workplace rather than to a central store.

Consider the difference to your organisation if the raw materials were always there on time, were of the right quantity and quality and were delivered to the operator's workplace and not to a store; each operator knew the standards and got the job right first time every time and so on right down the line. Then the organisation would not need anyone involved in checking anyone else's work. Supervisors and middle management would no longer be policing each step of a job.

At the end of the process is the customer. TQM organisations are very customer conscious. As the supplier is regarded as part of the team so too is the customer. This is more than just wishy-washy slogans such as 'the customer is always right'. This means really getting alongside the customer and finding out exactly what they want. The ultimate is that the customer, like the supplier, becomes part of the process.

CASE EXAMPLE: TOYOTA CUSTOMER DEMAND SYSTEM

An example of the way the world is moving can be found with Toyota, where the aim is to produce a car within 72 hours of the order being placed by a customer. The customer orders online, usually in a Toyota dealers showroom, a new vehicle and specifies ('customises') from a limited range size of engine, colour, sound system and so on. The customer's order goes directly online to the factory and updates the production schedule and goes further upstream to the suppliers of the factory to provide the necessary components directly to the relevant workstations in the factory. Taiichi Ohno, the 'father' of the Toyota Production System is quoted as saying 'we are looking at the time line from the moment the customer gives us an order to the point where we receive the cash. And we are reducing the time line by removing the non-value wastes'.

What does this mean? It means no more raw material stockpiling, no more stocks of finished goods (materials flow like water into the factory, through the factory and down to the customer), reduction in needs for capital, storage space and insurance and it means that the customer is getting what she or he prefers (such as colour, upholstery, sound system, engine size and countless other options). Obviously, a system such as the Toyota process does not, and cannot, make allowances for mistakes. A system such as this relies on good planning by management, quality designed into the product, well-trained workers who are empowered to work as a team, suppliers who are trusted to supply when required and who are also part of the team, an integrated computer system and, as Taiichi Ohno said, the elimination of non-value wastes.

We are now looking at a totally new type of organisation: the old bureaucratic style of management, with the associated rules relating to the span of control, appraisal systems and incentive schemes, is simply no longer appropriate. Instead, organisations have to be designed around the process. For example, instead of having a centralised purchasing department, why could not the operator, or a group of operators on the shop floor, phone or e-mail the daily order directly to the supplier (and for the materials to be delivered directly to the workstation rather than to the store). If each group of operators around a process were working as a team, why would a large central human resources department be needed? The operating team itself would not need a supervisor. Maybe a team leader would be necessary to hurry management along and ensure that management planning was sensible. The aim here is not for the front-line operators to be working harder but for them to take control and accept responsibility for their operation. It does not mean fewer people turning out more, but it does mean the elimination of several levels of management, and it does get rid of the matrix of responsibility for human resources and other 'service' or staff departments as shown on the old-fashioned organisation charts. With fewer levels of management, communication becomes less confused and responsibilities (and areas of mistakes) become much more obvious.

For TQM to work, a company has to go through a total revolution. Many people, especially middle managers, have to be won over. Workers, too, have to want to accept responsibility. TQM will mean a change of culture.

The cost of TQM can be measured in monetary terms. The emphasis will be on prevention rather than detection; thus, the cost of supervision and inspection will go down. Prevention costs will go up because of the training and action-orientated efforts. But the real benefits will be gained by a significant reduction in failures – both internal (e.g. scrap, rework, downtime) and external (handling of complaints, servicing costs, loss of goodwill). The total operating cost will reduce over time (say three to five years) as shown in Figure 21.2.

The adoption of a standard such as ISO 9001 Quality Assurance (for further details see www.iso.org) rather than streamlining an organisation might actually serve to increase the need for audits and supervision. ISO to this extent can therefore be seen to be contrary to the philosophy of TQM. With TQM, staff members are encouraged to do their own

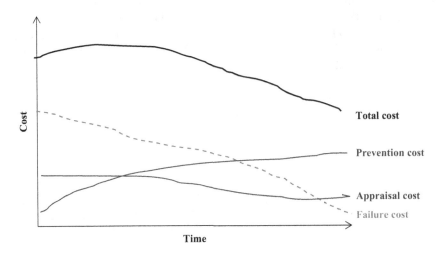

Figure 21.2 Cost of quality

checking and be responsible for getting it right the first time and the need for supervision becomes almost superfluous. With ISO, the standard method will likely be set by management edict and, once set in place, the bureaucracy of agreeing and recording improvements may stultify creative improvements.

ISO tends to be driven from the top down and relies on documentation, checks and tests to achieve a standard, somewhat bland, level of quality assurance. TQM on the other hand, once established, relies on bottom-up initiatives to keep the impetus of continual improvement. However, as the Deming method of TQM does advocate a stable system from which to advance improvements, the adoption of the ISO approach will mean that there will be a standard and stable system. To this extent, ISO will prove a useful base for any organisation from which to launch TQM.

As shown in Figure 21.3, ISO can be depicted as a wedge that prevents quality from slipping backwards, but the hypothetical danger is it can also be the wedge that impedes progress.

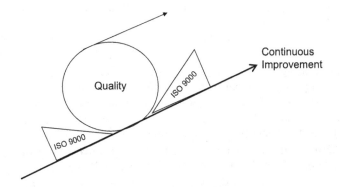

Figure 21.3 The wedge

Notwithstanding the benefits of obtaining a standard stable system through ISO procedures, it must be queried why a true quality company would need ISO. If the customer or potential customer is NOT insisting on ISO accreditation, then the time and effort (and the effort expended will be a non-recoverable cost) make the value of ISO to an organisation highly questionable.

Gaining ISO accreditation is a long and expensive business. Internally, it requires much time and effort, and most organisations underestimate the time and effort involved. Generally, recording the systems alone will require the full-time efforts of at least one person.

TQM to FIT SIGMA

> Today, depending on whom you listen to, Six Sigma is either a revolution slashing trillions of dollars from corporate inefficiency, or it's the most maddening management fad yet devised to keep front-line workers too busy collecting data to do their jobs.
>
> (*USA Today*, 21 July 1998)

It has been almost 20 years since the above statement was made. During this time, the 'Six Sigma revolution' has created a huge impact in the field of operational excellence, yet conflicting views are still prevalent.

Let us evaluate the arguments for both sides. On a positive note, the success of 'Six Sigma' in General Electric under the leadership of Jack Welch is undisputed. In the GE company report of 2000, their CEO was unstinting in his phrase: 'Six Sigma has galvanised our company with an intensity the likes of which I have never seen in my 40 years of GE'. Even financial analysts and investment bankers compliment the success of Six Sigma in GE. An analyst at Morgan Stanley, Dean Witter, recently estimated that GE's gross annual benefit from Six Sigma could reach 5% of sales and that share value might increase by between 10 and 15%.

However, the situation is more complex than such predictions would suggest. In spite of the demonstrated benefits of many improvement techniques such as total quality management, business process re-engineering and Six Sigma, most attempts by companies to use them have ended in failure (Easton and Jarrell (1998). Sterman et al. (1999) conclude that companies have found it extremely difficult to sustain even initially successful process improvement initiatives. Yet more puzzling is the fact that successful improvement programmes have sometimes led to declining business performance causing layoffs and low employee morale. Motorola, the originator of Six Sigma, announced in 1998 that its second-quarter profit was almost non-existent and that consequently it was cutting 15,000 of its 150,000 jobs!

To counter heavyweight enthusiasts like Jack Welch (GE) and Larry Bossidy (Allied Signal), there are sharp critics of Six Sigma. According to critics, Six Sigma is not new, critics say that it is really statistical process control in new clothing. Others dismiss it as another transitory management fad that will soon pass. And it is true that some consultants oversell the expected benefits. It is usually claimed in the United States that training one Six Sigma Black Belt will save US$250,000 per project and according to a leading Six Sigma consultant, Martin Wurtzel, this is not achievable. He says from many years of experience savings range from US$100,000 to US$200,000 per Black Belt deployment depending on the project selected. As for any business project, selection, resources and management are necessary to achieve desired results (Wurtzel, 2016).

It is evident that like any good product, 'Six Sigma' should also have a finite life cycle. In addition, business managers can be forgiven if they are often confused by the grey areas of distinction between quality initiatives such as TQM, Six Sigma and Lean Sigma.

Against this background, let us examine the evolution of total quality improvement processes (or in a broader sense operational excellence) from ad-hoc improvement to TQM to Six Sigma to Lean Sigma. Building on the success factors of these processes, the key question is: how do we sustain the results? We have named this sustainable process FIT SIGMA™ (see Basu and Wright, 2003; Basu, 2011).

What is FIT SIGMA? First, take the key ingredient of quality, then add accuracy in the order of no more than 3.4 defects in 1,000,000. Now implement this across your business with an intensive education and training programme. The result is Six Sigma. Now let's look at Lean Enterprise, an updated version of classical industrial engineering. It focuses on delivered value from a customer's perspective and strives to eliminate all non-value-added activities ('waste') for each product or service along a value chain. The integration of the complementary approaches of Six Sigma and Lean Enterprise is known as Lean Sigma. FIT SIGMA is the next wave. If Lean Sigma provides agility and efficiency, then FIT SIGMA allows sustainable fitness. In addition, the control of variation from the mean (small sigma 'σ') in the Six Sigma process is transformed to company-wide integration (capital sigma 'Σ') in the FIT SIGMA process. Furthermore, the philosophy of FIT SIGMA should ensure that it is indeed fit for the organisation.

Compare getting a company fit to getting yourself fit. When you go to a gym for the first time, the trainer will assess your level of fitness and your reason for wanting to become fit (getting fit to run a marathon would require a different set of exercises and diet than that required by a professional tennis player). No matter what sport, getting fit does not only mean losing weight, but it will also include building-up muscle. This is where many companies go wrong, they see Six Sigma as a means of reducing fat from the system, usually by getting rid of people including middle management. They don't realise getting fit will include adding resources where required. Six Sigma is not about saving costs, it is about making the best use of resources, not just losing 'fat' but building up strength.

Financial management

Historically, the relationship between financial management and operations management has been like oil and water, 'them and us'. The 'quality movement' of the 1980s appeared to have encouraged some operations managers to move away from involvement in costs and measurements. Some operations managers, both in the manufacturing and service sectors, took the stance that cost and measurement were 'internally focused', the concern of the 'bean counters', whereas the quality movement was externally customer focused. But, in fact, this was not what the quality gurus such as Deming, Juran, Crosby, Feigenbaum and Peters were saying. Their message was that measurement is important in achieving quality. For a start, without a scorecard of some type, it is not possible to determine if improvements are being made.

Traditionally, accountants have seen themselves as the conduit through which quantitative information flows to management. Accountants work on historical data of what has happened, and their reports cover arbitrarily set periods of time, with little allowance that business activities do not stop on 30 June or 31 December (or whatever other arbitrary date has been designated as the time to take a snapshot of the financial position of the business). From a conventional point of view, and from the point of view of stakeholders, such as shareholders and bank managers, there has to be a way of measuring the performance of an organisation and currently there is no better method than accounting reports. It follows therefore that for accountants to do their job of reporting to meet the conventional requirements, information will be required from the manufacturing arm of the business. This cannot be disputed. Therefore, if information is being provided, then it is useful to try and use that information to improve the productivity of the organisation.

In response to pressures from stakeholders, there is a risk of overemphasis on short-term financial performance. Consequently, this myopic approach results in over-investment in short-term fixers and under-investment in longer-term development plans. Furthermore, the emphasis on short-term results can cause organisations to reduce costs in general across the board without any effective analysis of value-creating activities.

It makes sense, therefore, that financial factors are integrated with operations and that operations managers focus on the cost of manufactured goods. Improved quality, delivery and flexibility should eventually improve the profit margin, but the impact of any operations cost is straight to the accountants' 'bottom line'. After all, operation is responsible for an ex-works cost or ex-facilities cost, which accounts for a significant part of the cost of sales. There are indications that there has been a gradual shift in operations towards financial management, probably influenced by the following factors.

The growth of the 'share owning' population has generated a new breed of consumers who are interested in the financial performance of a company. This has required financial management to become conscious of external requirements.

With the increase in external sourcing and third-party operations, the cost base and its control in manufacturing and services have been sharpened.

The economic recession in the late 1980s, and 20 years later the global financial crisis of 2008, forced many manufacturing and service industries to adopt restructuring and cost-reduction initiatives.

The well-publicised balanced scorecard shows the role of the financial perspective, as one of the four perspectives, has to be accepted by operations managers that 'financial measures are valuable in summarising the readily measurable economic consequences of actions already taken' (Kaplan and Norton (1996). It is therefore important for any company to focus on the key issues of financial management in order to enhance competitiveness through operations cost advantages. These issues include achieving business objectives, understanding strategic cost factors and cost-effectiveness.

Achieving financial objectives

We do not intend to delve into the sophisticated world of financial management involving the method of financing, tax implications, currency movements and so on. However, as indicated earlier, it is important that key financial parameters and objectives of the business should be understood and incorporated into manufacturing objectives. Key financial concepts are:

Sales value. The total turnover of the business in money terms.

Net profit. The money made by the business after charging out all costs. This can be expressed before tax or after tax.

Capital employed. Total investment tied up in the business comprising shareholder funds. With the double-entry system of accounting, shareholders' funds, or capital, will always equal the total of all the assets less all the liabilities.

Working capital.: Working capital refers to the funds available and is the difference between current assets (debtors, inventory, bank balances and cash) less current liabilities (creditors, short-term loans and the current portion of long-term loans).

Cash flow. Cash-flow statements show where and how the working capital has increased or decreased.

There are only four basic sources for an increase in working capital and likewise only four basic uses to explain a decrease in working capital, namely:

- Increase in working capital:
    Profits from operations.
    Sale of fixed assets.
    Long-term borrowing.
    Increase of shareholders' funds through the issue of shares.
- Decrease in working capital
    Losses from operations.
    Purchase of fixed assets.
    Repayment of long-term loans.
    Distribution of profits to shareholders (dividends).

The key financial indices influencing the financial objectives of a business are:

Trading margin = Net profit/Sales value × 100

Asset turn = Sales value/Capital employed

Return on investment (ROI) = Net profit/Capital employed × 100

Balanced sheet ratios

Balanced sheet ratios are the cornerstones of financial accounting and are concerned with the longer term and external requirements of creditors, shareholders, prospective investors, inspector of taxes and persons outside the management as well as with the internal requirements of the management.

Operating ratios

The operating ratios are in the domain of management accounting for tactical management and these ratios can be classed as follows.

1. *Sales to capital.* This ratio measures the efficiency of the use of capital. The higher sales per pound of capital the more effectively is capital being employed.

2. *Cost of sales to stock and sales to debtors.* These ratios help to assess whether stock is too high or debtors are taking too long to pay. Our example above shows that it would take 11 months at the current rate of sales to sell all the stocks. Similarly, the debtors are taking on average four months to pay. Whether these examples show a poor situation depends on the business and its terms of trade; at face value, they would certainly seem to be excessive.

3. *Return on investment and return on sales.* These ratios are widely used as measures of efficiency and performance evaluation. In addition, wide use is made of ROI to assess the validity of new projects. Most companies set a minimum return on investment rate that must be exceeded before a new project can proceed.

In spite of some criticism, ROI has continued to be the most important single index of the financial objective of a manufacturing business. Value-based management methodology is favoured by many companies today. One such performance measure is Economic Value Added (EVA), which is a trademark of Stern Stewart & Co. EVA accounts for the cost of doing business by deriving a capital charge. A positive EVA rating indicates that the company has created value. Often firms become so focused on earnings that they lose sight of the cost of generating those earnings in the first place. EVA has become a popular tool to which the executive's bonus may be linked. It is important to note that ROI and EVA are closely related as shown by the equation:

EVA = (ROI – WACC) × TCE, where WACC is the weighted average cost of capital and TCE is the total capital employed.

Hamel and Prahalad (1994) attacked managers obsessed with denominators (capital employed). The right approach to manufacturing is to identify high leverage points of both increasing profits and reducing capital employed. Low-cost manufacturing is a desirable manufacturing objective as long as the investment decisions are geared to longer-term requirements and the measures do not affect the specified standards of quality, delivery and safety. The measures indicated in the ROI improvement tree (Figure 21.4) have been covered in other sections of the book, but it is useful to focus on a total picture of cost advantages so that the inter-relationship between different elements and their relative weight can be visualised.

In special cases, simulation of cost modelling is justifiable.

The financial objectives of a business, especially in the manufacturing sector, include increasing asset turn, improving profit margin and improving ROI, but these three indices may appear to be conflicting, as shown in Figure 21.5. For a given ROI, profit margin goes down with increased asset turn and vice versa. However, when analysed more closely by managing the improvement of both numerator and denominator (i.e. operations improvement and asset management), the company performance can move to a higher ROI curve and retain improvements in both profit margin and asset turn.

Understanding strategic cost factors

There are a number of strategic factors affecting financial management that drive the business strategy of an organisation in both manufacturing and service sectors. We shall review three areas:

• Revenue growth by volume and product mix.
• Asset utilisation and investment.
• Cost-effectiveness.

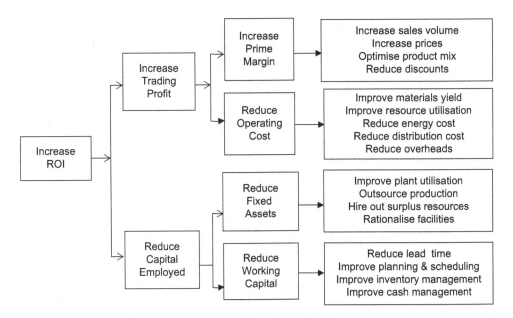

Figure 21.4 Company profitability: tree of improvement

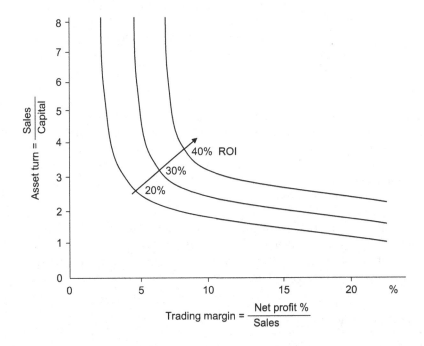

Figure 21.5 Capital assets productivity

Volume and mix

Costs are determined by volume (including variety and variations) and investment policy. These are strategic in a sense that they relate to the way the company may decide to react to the competition and developments in the marketplace.

Volume, in general, is good for business as the higher volume reduces the overhead or fixed cost per unit of production. However, the advantage of 'economies of scale' should not be pushed beyond the natural capacity of a site as the unit cost could go up due to constraints in site capacity and services. As variety increases, the unit cost of manufacturing may also increase due to technology cost, lower utilisation of plant and increased overhead/infrastructure. With flexible manufacturing, variety is essential to be competitive in segmented markets. Manufacturing should in these cases accommodate variety by incorporating higher flexibility of plant and operations. Variation is another determinant of product cost. If there are unstable variations in sales demand, supplier lead time and plant performance, then the planning effectiveness will go down and buffers in stock, capacity and resources will be necessary.

Asset utilisation

It is important that formal investment appraisal procedures and investment policies are in place. However, the rate of discounted cash flow (DCF) yield should vary according to the type of investment as indicated in Table 21.5.

Evaluation should include all tangible benefits and intangible benefits. Table 21.5 is indicative only to demonstrate the relative importance of investments. The actual limit of DCF yield is set by each company depending on financing charges, depreciation rate for a capital asset and the life cycle of the product.

Cost-effectiveness

Cost cutting or cost reduction exercises, if they are panic driven, or a 'chairman's 5% reduction target' will only give short-term results and will cause imbalances and disruptions in operations. Other legitimate concerns will be the negative effect on quality, innovation and customer service. And although direct factory labour might account for only 5 to 15% of the total ex-works cost (see Figure 21.6), overwhelming emphasis usually is given to the reduction of labour cost. New and Mayer (1986) state:

> In the past, whole work study departments were maintained to control the direct labour content of unit cost. Yet there were many plants that spent twice as much on purchased materials as on direct labour that do not even attempt to measure purchasing performance realistically. The real business focus should be to improve

Table 21.5 Discounted cash flow yields

Cost reduction projects	10–25%
Capacity expansion	
Replacement	20–25%
Strategic	15–20%
New technology	10–15%
Environment and safety	0–15%

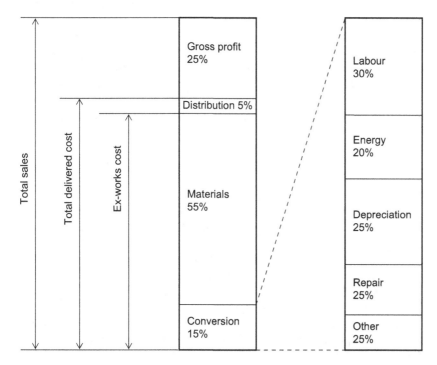

Figure 21.6 An example of cost structure

continuously and to be capable of competing in the future. Although strategy and innovation are important, the hard fact is that unless there is a positive operational cash flow the business cannot plan for the future. Therefore it is vital to have cost improvement even in a profitable company, but the approach must be cost effectiveness, not cost cutting.

The key principles of a cost-effectiveness programme are identified in the following section.

Ensure a continuous training programme to instil classical work-study or industrial engineering principles in all employees. 'Green Belt' training programmes should be considered even if the organisation is not following a pure Six Sigma programme.

Understand the strategic drivers of cost, that is, volume/capacity, variety and variation and their impact on the marketplace and competition.

Evaluate the effect of any company saving measures on quality, safety and customer service.

Identify the leverage of cost structure and set priorities of effort and 'go for gold'. But as a rough guide, the amount of effort allocated to manufacturing cost reduction should be proportional to the rest of the costs of the company.

The programme should be company-wide, although manufacturing is the key player.

The principles of value engineering should be applied in identifying and emphasising operations where no value is added.

Cost-effectiveness is a continuous process for all manufacturing businesses, but some businesses may require a quick and significant change in their cost structure. Study teams should then be formed to carry out ad-hoc exercises, such as big-scale value analysis, restructuring or site rationalisation (including plant closure).

Value analysis is a technique used to examine each element of a process to find a cheaper material or better method with the aim of maintaining or enhancing the value of the product in performance terms and at the same time reducing the cost. Big-scale value analysis (BSVA) uses a value analysis technique but in addition examines the total delivered cost (see Figure 21.6) of the business and has a short time scale (usually less than one year) with emphasis on company-wide implementation. The cost model in Figure 21.6 is a typical example of a fast-moving consumer good (FMCG) business and obviously the proportion of cost elements would vary depending on the product.

Accounting systems

It is vital that the company has a reliable accounting system in place to provide fast and accurate cost information. The minimum requirements should be standard costing and budgetary control.

Some companies are moving towards activity-based costing (ABC), particularly for supply chain management. The accurate cost information provided by ABC can give a company a competitive advantage. However, the experience of Western companies, according to De Meyer and Ferdows (1990), suggests that the implementation of activity-based costing has not been successful, perhaps due to the historical inertia of standard costing. Any half-baked implementation could be more harmful than useful.

Information and communication technology

This section is aimed to complement Chapter 13.

The focus of information technology within organisations has shifted dramatically over the last 40 years from improving the efficiency of business processes within organisations to improving the effectiveness of the value chain reaching suppliers, customers and consumers. During the 1960s and 1970s, businesses focused on the use of mainframes to process large quantities of data. In the 1980 and early 1990s, organisations focused on using personal desktop computers to improve personal efficiencies. The last decade with the revolution of the Internet has seen the use of technologies to create electronic communication networks within and between organisations and individuals. The implementation of enterprise resource planning (ERP), websites, e-commerce and e-mail systems during the past 20 years have allowed individuals within organisations to communicate together and share data. Information technology (IT) has now grown into information and communication technology (ICT). In this ICT foundation stone. we consider two broad areas:

- Information technology and systems
- e-Business

Information technology and systems

IT is rapidly changing and becoming more powerful. It is a continuing source of competitive advantages for manufacturers and the supply chain if used correctly. By 2000, the personal computer (PC) on the desk of an average operations manager even then had more computing power than the average £100 million a year manufacturing plant had in 1990. This IT revolution was available to everyone and how a company puts it to work determines to a great extent their competitiveness in the global market.

The rapid growth of information technology created problems and challenges. Many senior managers of companies lacked any detailed understanding of the complexity of technology. They either follow the fashion (e.g. 'no one was fired for choosing IBM') or they are discouraged by the cost of technology, or from a lack of evidence of savings in a new field. When executives read about all the clever things seemingly low-cost computer technology can do, they feel frustrated when the systems experts say, 'It will take three years to develop the software'. Most senior managers also feel lost in a blizzard of buzzwords and are conscious of well-published failures. For example, the UK National Health System electronic care records project 2002–2011 was discontinued after £2.3 billion were spent, described by members of parliament as one of the worst and most expensive contracting fiascos ever, and the US Air Force Enterprise Resource Planning project 2005–2012 was cancelled at a cost of US$1.1 billion, and in Denmark 2007–2012, da:Polsag, police case file management was cancelled after DKK500 million expenditure. The list of costly failure is endless.

Yet another issue is the implementation of systems to the benefit of the users. When a company looks for an IT solution to a problem without re-engineering the process, refining the existing database or training the end users, the application is doomed to fail. Real disasters can be very expensive. For example, the US$60 million Master Trust accounting system for Bank of America had to be scrapped because it could not keep accurate accounts.

Figure 21.7 shows a framework of IT strategy comprising three levels of hardware strategy, software strategy and implementation strategy.

IT hardware strategy

Hardware requires auditing with a refresh cycle of ideally three years but no more than five years. Chief information officers (CIOs) have the ongoing challenge of having sufficient IT capability to respond to new business needs and balance the cost of capital spending with operating efficiency and at the same time to be mindful of risk. The rapid growth in data storage has placed pressure on CIOs and has tempted them to keep old storage hardware. Keeping older and not always reliable unsupported hardware can be costly and risky. Using hardware until it breaks down or the supporting application is no longer available might save capital expenditure in the short term but could prove disastrous in

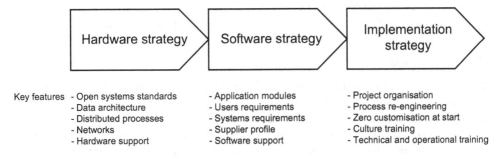

Figure 21.7 Information technology strategy

the longer term. Across a supply chain, there will be significant differences in the way organisations run their operations and in the applications that are used. New hardware is quicker, uses less power, requires less maintenance, is more reliable and reduces labour (helpdesks, fixing and maintenance).

A well-managed refresh audit will ensure the correct trade-offs between capital expenditure and lowering maintenance and power costs, as well as identifying actual and expected needs.

A well-designed refresh policy delivers both operational and financial requirements.

Operational:
Reduces risk of incidents/outages.
Reduces the duration of outages.
Reduces IT infrastructure complexity.
Adds new capabilities/functionality by using new hardware.
Reduces security issues by replacing unsupported hardware.
Financial:
Reduces capital expense and operating expense.
Increases the transparency of the IT budget and spend to business users.
Improves visibility into future infrastructure investments.
Centralises the funding of refresh investments.

The hardware strategy should also include the capability of local hardware support both by suppliers and the company's own staff. The support capability may influence the selection of hardware. A sensible strategy is to go with the market leaders who are setting the de facto standards.

ERP systems are supply chain IT systems that exchange information across all functions of an organisation or enterprise and can be extended across the supply chain to gain integration and sharing of information. There are several modules of an ERP system that can be installed either stand-alone or in interaction with other modules. Some of the key modules are finance, purchasing, master production scheduling, materials management, sales and distribution, supplier management and human resources. ERP systems clearly hold major advantages over 'legacy systems' in functionality, scope and flexibility of applications.

The shift of supply chain IT software systems from the old 'legacy' to ERP systems has also created a major shift of the hardware technology platform from mainframes to client/server platforms. In a client/server architecture, each computer or process on the network is either a client or a server. Servers are powerful computers or processes dedicated to managing disk drives (file servers), printers (print servers) or network traffic (network servers). Clients are PCs or workstations on which users run applications.

IT software strategy

At the early stage of information technology, applications software was limited to financial and commercial areas. Now a company is faced with a bewildering array of software ranging from design/process engineering to manufacturing, supply chain and administration. Versions of specific software and systems technology will continue to change. Therefore, it is vital that a manufacturing company formulates a software strategy through careful planning.

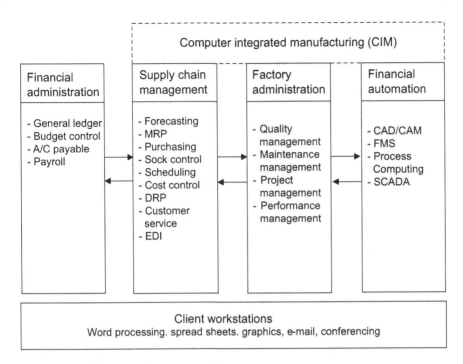

Figure 21.8 Application software modules

The first step is to identify the areas of application depending on the activities size and priorities of the company. Figure 21.8 shows a framework of application software in five key areas, namely financial administration, supply chain management, factory administration and 'client' workstation. The traditional computing modules of accounts and payroll are in financial management. The biggest area of application is in supply chain management starting from sales forecasting to customer service and electronic data interchange (EDI). At the factory shop floor, there are two application areas, namely factory administration – comprising management information systems – and factory automation – comprising design, process engineering and automation of equipment. The software for client workstations is PC based. During the late 1980s, many manufacturing companies searched for one turnkey package and invested in what is known as computer-integrated manufacturing (CIM) with limited success. If a company follows an 'open systems' policy for hardware and relational database, then different proprietary software packages stand a better chance of being interfaced and database information can be shared in a client-server environment. Probably the most significant advantage is in the enterprise view of a business that ERP systems allow.

The software policy should include standard packages for the company in specific areas of application. The selection of software should conform to the key criteria of user requirements, systems requirements, supplier profile and software support. The earlier examples of applications software were relatively inflexible, and the approach was 'systematise the customer' rather than 'customise the system'. Many disillusioned customers attempted to build their own software and burnt their fingers in the process. In the present climate, the software tools have become flexible, the IT technology is advancing

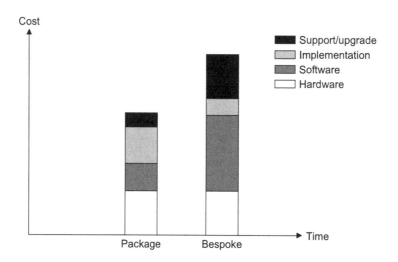

Figure 21.9 Software development strategy

rapidly, competitive expert support is provided by specialist software houses and thus it is prudent to buy appropriate software rather than develop your own (see Figure 21.9). The software should conform to open systems requirements and the supplier should be both reputable and locally available for support. The company should also build up its own IT support staff, especially a 'user support' service.

There is a major conflict in developing a software strategy between a 'best of breed' approach and a 'single integrator' approach. In a 'best of breed' approach, the best functionality solution for each individual function is chosen and companies attempt to integrate different types of systems. Although the company is likely getting the best solutions in each area, the problems of integration often offset the advantages of the best solutions. ERP providers offer flexible modules that allow a single integrated framework of different functions of a supply chain stage. A single integrator approach also offers the advantage of technical support and maintenance contract with a single source supplier.

Implementation strategy

The success of an IT strategy depends on well-managed implementation as much as it does on the selection of appropriate hardware and software.

Similar to a company-wide programme such as TQM, the implementation must have top management commitment. This should be reflected in setting up a project team comprising members from all users (marketing, logistics, manufacturing, accounts) and business systems. The project manager is usually chosen from the main user group. For example, if the application software is for supply chain management, then the project manager should ideally have a logistics background.

The project team should receive both technical training and operational training (functionality of the software). The project manager then prepares a clearly stated action plan with target dates and resources for key activities. The plan must include review points and steering by the members of the board.

It is essential that the existing procedures and processes are thoroughly and systematically reviewed. There are various tools for analysing the flow and requirements of the existing systems. Statistical process control (SPC) techniques are widely used. Nowadays, some companies are using computer-aided software engineering (CASE) tools to analyse the structure, database and flows of the existing process and comparing them with the proposed software for implementation. With the success of the business process re-engineering (BPR) approach of Hammer and Champy (1993), some companies are using an IT application as a catalyst and applying the principles of BPR to re-engineer the total business processes of the company. The approach should depend on the depth and breadth of the application systems, but there is no doubt that the existing systems must be reviewed and refined when implementing a new system.

One important rule is that the user should not try to customise the system at the outset. Often after acquiring experience with the new system, the user may find that the need and nature of customisation could be different. However, it is necessary that a 'prototype' is tested for a new system using the company's own data.

After the training of the project team, the training programmes should be extended to all potential users of the system. The training features should contain both cultural education to establish acceptance by everyone concerned and operational training to understand the functionality and operations of the new system. Training documents are designed specifically for the users' needs. The next stage is the data input and 'dry run' of the new system in parallel with the existing system before the system goes live. There are benefits of forming a users' group for exchanging experience with users drawn from within and outside the company.

e–Business

It would appear, from today's press, that all business problems can be solved by e-business while, at the same time, they blame all business failures and any economic downturn on e-business as well! Given the volume of news items, it may appear that defining 'e-business' is to state the obvious. Or is it?

The distinctions between e-commerce, e-marketplace and e-business are poorly interpreted. For example, the most popular perception of e-business is online shopping. However, it should be noted that in 2015 in the UK, 25% of retail sales were made online.

Let us clarify some items. e-Commerce is the transactional electronic exchange for the buying and selling of goods and services.

The 'e-marketplace' is the online intermediary for electronic transactions between buyers, sellers and brokers. This is also referred to as the digital marketplace, portals or hubs.

Early opportunities were observed in the enabling infrastructures and Internet-based networks (Internet, Intranet and Extranet), replacing existing telephone, fax and EDI networks. The early success of e-procurement vendors (e.g. Commerce One, Ariba, Info Bank) was well received. The old suppliers suffered many problems, including that of authorisation with no conformity of systems between business partners. It was like having different telephone systems for each of the people to whom you speak. This has been transformed by Trading Portals that interconnect the contents of different suppliers and making them usable by all buyers.

In a report by Basu (2003), the complex web and infrastructure of e-business applications have been simplified as shown in Figure 21.10 to illustrate the 'building blocks'.

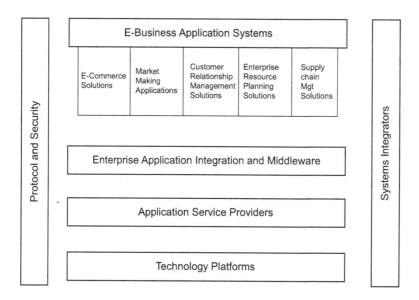

Figure 21.10 e–Business building blocks

There are five key types of e-business application systems that enable businesses to trade and conduct electronic transactions or communications. These are:

- e–Commerce solutions for both sell-side and buy-side applications.
- Market-making applications that enable multiple buyers and sellers to collaborate and trade.
- CRM solutions to facilitate improved business partnerships with customers.
- ERP solutions for site-based planning and execution of operations.
- Supply chain management solutions for optimising the demand and supply in the total supply network including the suppliers.

In order to support the interfacing and integration of application systems, there are technology building blocks. These include enterprise application integration (EAI), middleware applications, application service providers (ASPs) and technology platforms.

e-Commerce solutions

The buy-side applications of e-commerce, initially targeted at larger buyers, enable companies to levy across new or existing vendors. Solutions are increasingly aiming at integrating ERP systems with the organisation's own suppliers and customers. The new application developers are utilising the opportunities created by the lack of integration of ERP systems with other Internet systems and outside companies.

Initially, the buy-side application vendors (including Commerce One and Ariba) were driven by pure-play solutions for the purchase of MRO (maintenance, repairs and operations) or indirect goods. The huge potential of e–procurement offered by 'pure companies' has been recognised and seized by established ERP vendors such as SAP and Oracle, and software vendors like Netscape and Datastream.

The buy-side vendors, whether pure-play or not, are focusing on packaged buy-side application suites and looking to move into the direct procurement area. This requires a greater degree of understanding of business processes in specific industries and rigorous validation of the data processing.

The sell-side application vendors are looking to provide services for content management and transaction processing. Hence, there are some subcategories of software within this group. These include cataloguing, profiling, configurations and payment technologies. As a result, this sector is highly fragmented.

Market-making applications

There are broadly two types of market-making applications. The first allows businesses to buy or sell by online auctions or bidding. Buyers place an open order to purchase an item and the sellers have the opportunity to bid. The second mechanism is the exchange or two-way auction platform containing a high-speed bid/ask bartering process.

ERP applications

Internet technology has certainly enhanced the collaborative business culture by enabling online transparent information and transactions. The company-centric enterprise application vendors including SAP and Oracle (J D Edwards Enterprise One) have extended into supply chain management and customer relationship management.

Customer relationships management solutions

It is fair to state that most businesses regard the retention of customers as an important goal and therefore the criteria of customer relationships management (CRM) are not new for most enterprises. However, the collaborative Internet-based network has enhanced the need for customer intimacy and personalisation. A number of software solutions have been developed to provide some powerful holistic functionalities including:

* Customer databases for knowing and understanding customer characteristics.
* Managing the relationship with key business partners (e.g. customers).
* Providing value-added services to retain customer loyalty.
* Transparency and real-time acceptability of information for both customers and suppliers.
* Optimising cross-selling opportunities.

Supply chain management solutions

There are now few companies that do not recognise that the Internet has a profound effect on supply chain performance. The key issues of the e-supply chain have been covered in more detail in Chapter 13. Applications that fall into this category are essentially decision-support software packages for optimising multiple levels of demand and supply in the global supply chain.

The collaborative planning forecasting and replenishment (CPFR) for key stakeholders of the total supply chain has emerged and is discussed in Chapter 12. In CPFR, data and process model standards are developed for collaboration between suppliers and an enterprise with proscribed methods for planning (agreement between the trading partners to conduct business in a certain way); forecasting (agreed-to methods, technology and timing for sales, promotions and order forecasting); and replenishment (order generation and order fulfilment). These solutions consider the constraints of transportation, supply capacity and inventory requirements. The ultimate objective is order fulfilment within the time and cost acceptable to customers.

The early leading vendors in the market, for example, i2 now part of IBM and Manugistics (acquired by JDA Software in 2006), have been surpassed by SAP and Oracles J D Edwards Enterprise One

EAI and middleware

The benefits of using an e-business solution increase in direct proportion to the degree of integration between the customer and the marketplace. It is impractical to make any attempt to change the software and platform of the acquired customer to those of the acquirer. Therefore, the effectiveness of handling real-time transactions in an e-business environment will depend on the technology 'building blocks' enabling the integration and interfaces of all parameters.

The key set of 'building blocks' is EAI and middleware applications that bring together the information the exchange needs from disparate internal systems. This is often referred to as 'back-end integration' and can account for up to 75% of the costs of going online.

Application service providers

'An ASP is an agent or broker who assembles functionality needed by enterprises or SMEs and packages it with outsourced maintenance and other services' (Durlacher, 1999).

The growth of ASP solutions started with packaged services provided by e-commerce application software vendors (e.g. Ariba, Commerce One, Broadvision). The penetration of the market came from the ASP's ability to take responsibility for system development and maintenance while avoiding the overhead of expensive IT staff. This means that smaller firms are being offered fully managed and large organisations are receiving part-managed ASP services.

Technology platforms

Technology companies are forming strong partnerships or alliances to provide end-to-end technology solutions, especially to SMEs.

Protocol and security

Protocol and security are the key building blocks of data transmissions and data security. The Internet uses a special language or protocol to ensure the safe arrival of data at its intended destination. This language has two parts:

* Transmission Control Protocol (TCP)
* Internet Protocol (IP)

TCP divides the data into small 'packets' adding information that allows the receiving computer to assure undamaged transmission. IP puts end 'address labels' on each packet.

HTML or hypertext markup language is the TCP and XML or extensible markup language allows the dynamic logging of text in documents. This enables internal systems at the customer and the marketplace to send machine-readable messages to each other. XML is hailed as the 'lingua franca' for data transfer in the cyber realm. The flexible formats of XML offer a transition from EDI fixed formats to self-identifying data.

System integrators

The final piece of the e-business 'building block' is the art and science of pulling together all elements of an e-business project and making it work. The lower end of the market for SMEs and start-up companies has been addressed by ASPs working together with hardware vendors,

However, in a multi-functional, multi-site large application business, it is necessary to redesign the way they work in terms of both processes and culture in order to gain sustainable benefits from e-business. This requires not only the integration of IT systems between businesses but also process improvement and continuous education. There is a gap between software functionality and the existing business process. Furthermore, the number of users in an e-business project is many times more than those expert users of an ERP application. Thus, the challenge of the shift of culture is much greater in implementing the business.

New opportunities

As discussed in Chapter 4 and Chapter 13, there are many new opportunities for applying new technologies in managing global supply chains. One of the key benefits of cloud computing is the opportunity to replace up-front capital infrastructure expenses with low variable costs that scale with your business. Companies no longer need to plan for and procure servers and other IT infrastructure weeks or months in advance. As part of cloud computing, small and medium-sized enterprises (SMEs) can afford to invest in licensed and expensive ERP systems (also called 'on-demand software') on a so-called SaaS (Software as a Service) platform.

Artificial intelligence (AI) is the simulation of human intelligence processes by computer systems. AI research has been divided into subfields such as particular goals (e.g. 'robotics') and the use of specialised tools ('machine learning'). Specific applications of AI include expert systems, natural language processing (NLP), speech recognition and machine vision.

AI programming concentrates on three cognitive skills: learning, reasoning and self-correction. Learning processes of AI programming focus on acquiring data and creating rules or algorithms to provide computing devices with step-by-step instructions for how to complete a specific task. Machine learning (ML), a fundamental concept of AI research, is the study of computer algorithms that improve automatically through experience. Reasoning processes of programming focus on choosing the right algorithm to reach the desired outcome. Finally, self-correction processes of programming are designed to continually fine-tune algorithms and ensure they provide the most accurate results possible.

AI is relevant to any intellectual task and advanced robotics. Modern AI applications are too numerous to list here; however, some high-profile examples include autonomous vehicles (such as drones and self-driving cars), medical diagnosis, creating art (e.g. poetry), proving mathematical theorems, playing games (such as chess), search engines (for instance, Google), online assistants (such as Siri), image recognition in photographs, spam filtering, the prediction of judicial decisions and the forecasting of demands, to name a few.

Since the introduction of the iPhone by Apple Inc. in June 2007, the iPhone iOS has dominated the mobile market, but Google Android has now demonstrably overtaken iPhone in terms of market share. In addition to the social media revolution, mobile technology and its 'apps' have encroached upon and indeed come to dominate our daily lives. Mobile and wireless devices are also enabling organisations to conduct business more effectively. Mobile applications can be used to support e-commerce with customers and suppliers, and to conduct e-business within and across organisational boundaries. There are two broad choices involved in deploying a system to mobile users, such as creating custom native apps targeted at major mobile platforms or developing a web application optimised for mobile access.

The Internet of Things (IoT) describes the network of physical objects connecting and exchanging data with other devices and systems over the Internet. IoT technology is generally related to smart homes including security devices and home appliances that can be controlled by smartphones. The IoT can also be used in industries and healthcare systems. There are however some concerns regarding IoT, especially in the areas of security and privacy.

A significant disruption in digital technology has been created by blockchain technology, which is popularly used as a generic term that most people associate with cryptocurrency (e.g. bitcoin). However, arguably, it is more useful as distributed ledger technology, also known as 'trustware', because it replaces interpersonal trust with technological verification. This new form of technological trust can reduce the capacity of operators to behave opportunistically, enhance input verification and ensure transparency and traceability during transaction time.

Summary

This chapter has covered quality management, financial management and information technology. We are not suggesting that we have written a complete accounting textbook or the definitive work on information technology. Far from it.

With quality management, we have however gone into greater depth. Quality management is not a discipline restricted to one body of knowledge or expertise. Quality management is for everyone in the company to know and understand in detail.

We have shown quality management has three dimensions – design quality, process quality and organisation quality. Furthermore, quality is basically what the customer wants and it operates on two levels – basic requirements of specification, time and cost and higher-level requirements covering after-delivery service and customer focus issues. We accept quality has a price but the cost of not performing can be unknown and is probably unknowable.

We also discussed a hierarchy of quality methods ranging from inspection at the end of the process, to no inspection by supervisors and the reliance on suppliers, and each worker in the process to get it right first time, every time. For such a bold approach to be viable – for example, no supervisors, no inspectors – workers must be empowered. But more than that, they must want to be empowered, and managers must believe and trust. For most companies, this is a desirable goal but probably not something to be attempted overnight!

We also covered ISO certification. We believe that many people see ISO as a goal in itself. We say ISO certification may be a step on the way to TQM, but it is only a small and expensive step. We suggest that a true TQM company does not need certification.

With financial management, we introduced key concepts and ratios. Unless the factory manager understands these ratios, they will always be at the mercy of the accountants. The ratios are explained simply and illustrated with easily understood examples. If you have some accounting knowledge, don't skip this section, take five minutes to work through the examples and consider how they apply to your organisation.

Some time is spent on ROI and some time on cost-cutting. Both these areas are of particular concern to the factory manager. ROI can be used to prevent you from getting much-needed equipment. Cost-cutting, if applied 5% across the board, will inevitably hit the factory the hardest. Other sections probably do have some slack or spare capacity but does your factory? It is important that the factory manager understands ROI and that the factory manager can defend themself against ill-judged cost-cutting exercises.

For information technology, we have taken a more general approach. This section is equally applicable to all functions of the organisation. The key issue in any new IT system is knowing what you want, going with a system with local support and initially making do with off-the-shelf software. We have not discussed uninterrupted power supply, disaster recovery, the need to back-up files and so on. All these issues are nuts and bolts and should be second nature to your IT manager. This section was not written for the professional IT manager. It was written to give the average manager an understanding of the strategy of IT implementation. We have also addressed the opportunities and challenges emerging from e-business technologies and powerful software solutions such as SAP.

During the last ten years, we have experienced the growth of e-business applications and enabling infrastructures that have rapidly increased productivity by streamlining existing business processes. We have also seen over the last few years some dramatic failures of e-commerce companies.

The time has come to take a fresh look at Internet technology. We need to see the Internet as a powerful enabling technology that can be used in almost any business and part of almost any strategy. The key question now is not whether to deploy Internet technology, but how to deploy it.

With a good understanding of the scope of systems and procedures and new opportunities of digital technology discussed in this chapter, supply chain managers should be better equipped to integrate the building blocks of supply chains to provide, improve and sustain supply chain performance.

Discussion questions

1. What are three building blocks that integrate the processes in other building blocks of supply chain management? Explain why they are integrators.
2. What are the three dimensions of quality in supply chain management? Describe the key components of organisation quality.
3. Describe the hierarchy of quality and explain how quality assurance could lead to TQM.
4. Discuss the key components of the cost of quality model. Which component is more difficult to measure and why?
5. How do you distinguish TQM and Six Sigma? Describe the evolution of TQM to FIT SIGMA.

6. Explain why achieving financial objectives is also important in measuring the performance of supply chain management. Suggest three key financial indicators.

7. Discuss the key steps to implement a successful cost-effectiveness programme. Comment on the appropriateness of a Six Sigma or FIT SIGMA programme.

8. Discuss the implementation strategy of digital transformation in the global supply chain of a multinational organisation.

9. Explain the distinctive features of the three dimensions of quality: product, process and organisation. Discuss and distinguish between the dimensions of quality as presented by Garvin and Parasuraman.

10. Identify from the customer's viewpoint those dimensions of quality in supply chain management that could be important for the following products/services:
    a) QE2 Cruise
    b) Medical centre
    c) Supermarket service
    d) Rolex watch
    e) Package holiday
    f) Ford Motor Company
    g) Norwich Union Insurance Company
    h) Advertising of a Nokia mobile phone

11. How would you distinguish between inspection, quality control, quality assurance and TQM?
    What are the appropriate areas or stages of application for each scheme in supply chain management?
    What does 'total' mean in TQM?

12. What are the features and philosophies common to both TQM and Six Sigma?
    Explain the new features, if any, in a Six Sigma programme.
    What are the additional features of Lean Sigma and FIT SIGMA?

13. Explain the various elements of the 'cost of poor quality'.
    Why is it that some quality-related costs, after the delivery of goods, are more significant to the supplier?
    List the key elements of the internal and external failure costs in your organisation.

14. What are the major software systems to manage total supply chain management? Discuss how the shifts in technology platforms have increased the effectiveness of supply chain software systems.

15. Discuss the relative advantages of a 'best of breed approach' and a 'single integrator approach' to implement supply chain ICT systems. What type of industries would be most likely to select which approach and why?

16. What are the critical success factors of implementing an ERP system in an FMCG multinational company? Recommend the key steps of implementation.

17. Discuss the new opportunities of applying digital technology in managing global supply chains.

22 Sales and operations planning

Introduction

Alongside systems and procedures (Chapter 21) and performance management (Chapter 23), sales and operations planning (S&OP) is an integrator of the building blocks of total supply chain management. Systems and procedures provide the tools, performance management offers the metrics and sales and operations planning delivers the processes to make it happen. With S&OP, the general manager and their staff can operate their supply chain more effectively, set attainable objectives with a single set of data for all departments, communicate approved sales and operations plans over a planning horizon, measure performance and achieve target results. The data from the business plan is converted into sales, inventory and production plans with formal discussions and agreement of each department at appropriate stages. All key managers and staff are involved in the process but not at the same meeting. Thus, S&OP provides both effective control over a company's operation spanning all the building blocks of the total supply chain and acceptance of staff in all departments. S&OP and its hybrids are also known by other names in different organisations, such as sales inventory and operations planning (SIOP), senior management reviews (SMR), integrated business management (IBM) and collaborative planning forecasting and replenishment (CPFR).

Learning objectives

In this chapter, we cover the characteristics, applications and benefits of S&OP under the following headings:

Background to S&OP.
Definition.
Key steps of S&OP.
S&OP in service organisations.
Collaborate planning forecasting and replenishment.
Global S&OP.
Shift in performance criteria.
Benefits of S&OP.

Background to S&OP

The classical concept of S&OP is rooted in the manufacturing resource planning (MRPII) process. In the basic S&OP, the company operating plan (comprising sales forecast,

DOI: 10.4324/9781003341352-26

production plan, inventory plan and shipments) is updated on a regular monthly basis by the senior management of a manufacturing organisation. The virtues, application and training of the S&OP have been promoted by Oliver Wight Associates (see Ling and Goddard, 1988) since the early 1970s.

Every organisation usually has some form of regular planning meeting in which the financial and business plans are reviewed and often some marketing and operational targets are discussed by a group of managers. These monthly meetings tend to deal with short-term problems and opportunities and usually decisions are made by the subjective judgements of an influential senior manager. In many companies, what passes for S&OP is often little more than a monthly review of the performance of the master production schedule. Many software providers also take the view that it is best done as an extension of the existing product-level planning process. In our experience, both of these approaches fail to achieve the very real business benefits that an effective S&OP process can deliver. S&OP should be treated as a formal planning and execution process and not as a set of planning meetings. Whether the business processes are forecast-driven MRPII processes or order-driven pull or just-in-time processes, the role of S&OP is equally important. Furthermore, there must be a process within S&OP that breaks down the aggregate plan into detailed plans.

In recent years, the pace of change in technology and marketplace dynamics has been so rapid that the traditional methodology of monitoring the actual performance against predetermined budgets set at the beginning of the year may no longer be valid. Fundamentally, businesses are managed on current conditions and up-to-date assumptions. There is also a vital need to establish an effective communication link, both horizontally across functional divisions and vertically across the management hierarchy to share common data and decision processes. Thus, S&OP has moved beyond the operations planning at the aggregate level to a multifunctional senior management review process.

For the S&OP process to work, the decision-making group, usually the executive board, need to be provided with quantitative information as well as qualitative information over a planning horizon of around two years. Moreover, if the purpose is to find the best option, or indeed the least worst, the decision-making group need to be presented with alternatives that explore the relative costs, benefits and risks of different courses of action. The future is harder to predict for the medium term than the immediate short-term future. Irrespective of medium or short term, forecasting is as much an art as a science and it is usually necessary to explore several possible scenarios, assigning to each a degree of risk and probability.

Definition

The traditional S&OP is a senior management review process of establishing the operational plan and other key activities of the business to best satisfy the current levels of sales forecasts according to the delivery capacity of the business.

Ling and Goddard (1988) summarise a 'capsule description of the process':

> It starts with the sales and marketing departments comparing actual demand to the sales plan, assessing the marketplace potential and projecting future demand. The updated demand plan is then communicated to the manufacturing, engineering and finance departments, which offer to support it. Any difficulties in supporting the sales plan are worked out … with a formal meeting chaired by the general manager.

Dick Ling, almost the founding father of S&OP, defines S&OP as a process, rather than a system, and says it is 'The process that enables a company to integrate its planning within the total company'. The outcome of the process is the updated operation plan over 18 months or two years (the 'planning horizon') with a firm commitment for at least one month.

The process is data-driven. A report for each product family is prepared for the planning horizon and it is usually divided into five sections containing 'a single set of numbers' for the sales plan, production plan, inventory, backlog and shipment.

Key steps in S&OP in manufacturing organisations

In developing the key steps of the S&OP process, two key challenges should be addressed at the outset. They are the simplification of the process and the accuracy of demand forecasts.

Simplification

Most businesses are complex and generate a mass of data at the operational level in terms of the number of stock-keeping units (SKUs), materials and resources used. For example, the financial manager wants the numbers in dollars, the marketing manager expects numbers in SKUs, the manufacturing manager likes to plan by tonnage while the logistics manager prefers the numbers to be in terms of cases or pallets. A model that attempts to flex each one of these becomes too unwieldy. Projecting out two or more years at this level of detail for each unit is not a problem for the computer; we now have access to more than enough computing power to do this. The difficulty is in analysing, understanding and evaluating the mass of output that such an approach generates. Companies that have tried doing it this way have found it virtually impossible to interpret the results. Therefore, we need a single set of numbers to be understandable and usable by all departments of the supply chain.

Forecast accuracy

The nature of the S&OP means that it needs a planning horizon that stretches well beyond the master production scheduling (MPS), usually between 18 months and two years but sometimes more depending on the nature of the business. Because of the rate at which forecast accuracy deteriorates with time, any forecast produced at the SKU level becomes unusable as the accuracy is simply too low to be of any use.

These potential problems are overcome by:

- Grouping demand together into families, so that aggregating the variations in each homogeneous family reduces the forecast error.
- Identifying the small number of critical resources, whether labour, equipment, material or plant must be dealt with separately.
- Selecting a single unit of data for demand, production and inventory with an acceptable conversion factor to help interpretation by respective departments.

S&OP has become an established company-wide business planning process in the Oliver Wight MRPII methodology (Wallace, 1990). To understand the key steps of S&OP in a manufacturing organisation, it is also important to understand MRPII methodology.

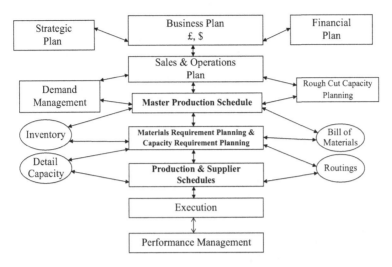

Figure 22.1 Manufacturing resource planning

Materials requirement planning (MRP) is the set of techniques that use bills of material, inventory on hand and order data, and the production schedule or plan to calculate quantities and timing of materials. Such a plan is incomplete if it doesn't take into account whether manufacturing resources (e.g. plant, people, energy, space) will be available at the desired time. MRPII arose from an appreciation of the need to time and phase materials with resource availability to achieve a given output date. Manufacturing resource planning is an integrated computer-based system. A computer-based approach is essential due to the amount of data required. Various software systems are available, each based on the same principles. MRPII is depicted in Figure 22.1.

With manufacturing resource planning, the planning process arises from the innovation of new products and the strategic marketing plan. Starting with this information, a business plan is constructed to determine and communicate estimates of the sales volume of each product range. The business plan should be developed at least once a year and during the year periodic updates will be required.

From the business plan, an operations plan is formulated that covers the materials and other resources needed to translate the business plan into reality. It follows that to keep the operations plan in line with updates to the business plan, regular communication is required between the various functions involved. This updating process is best achieved by face-to-face meetings that we recommend should take place at least once a month and always with all parties present at the one time. There is a very real danger of misunderstandings and ambiguities if meetings are not face-to-face and if all concerned are not present at the same time. Meetings need not be long drawn-out affairs. From experience, we believe that any planning meeting that takes longer than an hour is wasting time. The key managers at these meetings will be from sales, operations and planning. The issues that will be agreed upon will include time and availability of resources, and conflicting requirements and priorities will be resolved. Above all, demand is the crucial issue, and as future demand can never be certain, there should be a formal mechanism of forecasting using the best combination of historical models, past results from promotions, data from customers and market intelligence. Likewise, the inventory data system has to be up to date and accurate with details of raw materials on hand, goods on order, lead times and finished goods on hand.

Only with up-to-date information, and with the continuous review and management of information, can an organisation hope to achieve a balance of resources and stocks of inventory to meet planned service levels. The master planning and production scheduling process therefore have to be continuously monitored and updated to ensure that this occurs.

The master production plan or master schedule is at the heart of MRP where both the timing and quantity of orders are determined by offsetting from the current stock the demand during the lead time to meet the master production plan.

The next stage is to follow a rough-cut capacity planning process to assess to what extent the capacity of manufacturing facilities could meet the master schedule. The feedback loop at this level tests the master plan against problem areas such as known bottlenecks and other critical resource areas. Often, as this is a short- to medium-term approach, action has to be taken to make the best use of existing resources rather than to add extra long-term resources. The company should decide which alternative to follow if the existing resources are not adequate, for example, review the schedule, increase resources, work extra shifts, delay maintenance, outsource to third parties and so on. With computer systems, it is relatively straightforward to simulate using 'what if' scenarios to evaluate alternative courses of action.

Having established that the resources are sufficient, or having adjusted the plan to fit the resources, then the next step is the detailed materials requirements planning and the detailed capacity requirements planning for day-to-day operations. This stage includes the production of detailed bills of materials for each product or batch of products. With the revised master schedule for each product and SKU, and bills of material for each SKU, the materials required for each item of raw materials (RM) and packaging materials (PM) are then matched with the current inventory levels to derive the additional procurement requirements. The requirements are modified, if required, after comparing with the detailed capacity planning process. The execution of the planning process then commences with the final production scheduling and purchasing (supply planning) processes.

We have outlined a generic description of the manufacturing resource planning process. There are of course variations – more significantly between batch production processes and continuous production processes and between so-called 'push' or 'pull' demand systems. With the 'push' system, stocks of materials and of finished goods are used to ensure maximum plant capacity utilisation by having level production. The 'pull' system is driven by customer orders and just-in-time principles that can result in some under-utilisation of capacity. It is said that just-in-time requires greater flexibility and reliability of plant plus a multi-skilled workforce. In its simplistic form, just-in-time is reactive (demand pull), whereas MRPII can be described as proactive. MRPII looks forward and determines what will be needed to achieve a desired output date. Internally, MRPII is a push system – inventory is driven through the process by the schedule. Thus, customer requirements are linked to the resources and materials necessary to precisely meet a just-in-time delivery date. From a customer's point of view, it could be argued that as long as the goods arrive on time and meet the specifications, the system used by the manufacturer is irrelevant!

The process has been developed and applied primarily for manufacturing organisations. The key members of all departments, such as R&D, marketing, sales, logistics, purchasing, human resources, finance and production, participate in the process but not at the same meeting. S&OP addresses the operations plan that deals with sales, production, inventory and backlog and thus is it expressed in units of measurement such as tonnes, pieces and so on, rather than dollars or euros. The operation plan is reconciled with the business plans or budgets, which are expressed in terms of money.

The S&OP or senior management review process has been proven to be a key contributor to sustaining the performance level achieved through a TQM or Six Sigma programme (Basu and Wright, 2003: p. 97). The S&OP agenda, in addition to its main focus of establishing the operation plan, contains the reviews related to performance and key initiatives. This provides an effective platform for senior managers of all functions to assess the current performance and steer the future direction of the business.

Key steps

With the above backdrop, we can now describe the key steps of the S&OP process.

The diagram in Figure 22.2 shows the five steps in the S&OP process that will usually be present, and this process can be adapted to a specific organisation's requirement.

New product review (Step 1). Many companies follow parallel projects related to new products in R&D, marketing and operations. The purpose of this review process in Step 1 is to review the different objectives of various departments at the beginning of the month and resolve new product-related assumptions and issues. The issues raised will impact on the demand plan and the supply chain at a later stage of the process.

Demand review (Step 2). Demand planning is more of a consensus art than a forecasting science. Demand may change from month to month depending on market intelligence, customer confidence, exchange rates, promotions, product availability and many other internal and external factors. This review at the end of the first week of the month, between marketing, sales, IT and logistics, establishes agreement and accountability for the latest demand plan identifying changes and issues arising.

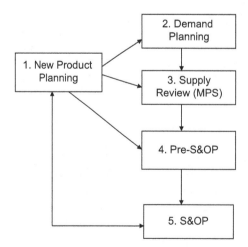

Figure 22.2 Five steps of the S&OP process

Table 22.1 Agenda for S&OP meeting

Performance review	20% of meeting time
• Customer service	
• Actual sales vs plan	
• Actual production vs plan	
• Actual inventory vs plan	
• Financial performance	
• Critical root-cause analysis	
• Balanced scorecard (selected KPIs)	
Forward plan	80% of meeting time
• Sales plan	
• New product introduction	
• Production plan	
• Inventory plan	
• Backlog and backorders	
• Pre-S&OP issues	
• Financial projections	

Supply review (Step 3). In the current climate of increasing outsourcing and supply partnerships, the capacity of supply is highly variable and there is a need to ensure the availability and optimisation of supply every month. This review, usually on the second week of the month, between logistics, purchasing and production, establishes production and procurement plans and raises capacity, inventory and scheduling issues.

Reconciliation review (Step 4). Issues would have been identified in previous reviews of new products, demand and supply. The reconciliation step goes beyond the balancing of numbers to assess the business advantage and risk for each area of conflict. This review looks at issues from the business point of view rather than departmental objectives. This is also known as the pre-S&OP review and its aim is to minimise issues for the final S&OP stage.

Senior management review (Step 5). Senior managers or board members, with an MD or CEO as Chair, will approve the plan that will provide clear visibility for a single set of numbers driving the total business forward. The agenda (see Table 22.1) includes the review of key performance indicators, business trends of operational and financial performance, issues arising from previous reviews and corporate initiatives. This is a powerful forum to adjust business direction and priorities. This is also known as the S&OP review.

In each process step, the reviews must address a planning horizon of 18–24 months in order to make a decision for both operational and strategic objectives. As shown in the example below, the demand forecasts of product groups are reconciled with respective inventory projections to establish the master production schedule over the planning horizon. There may be a perceived view that S&OP is a process of aggregate/volume planning for the supply chain. However, it is also a top-level forum to provide a link between business plan and strategy. It is emphasised that even though these five steps are usually executed in the order presented above, it is best to view S&OP as an iterative process since a well-executed S&OP process leads to iterative improvements over time.

SALES AND OPERATIONS PLANNING: EXAMPLE

Table 22.2 shows a worked-out example of a product pack: Aquatic 500 is the unit of packs. The report is divided into four sections:

- Sales
- Stock
- QA release
- Production

In addition, it contains some useful data, such as production batch size (180), lead time (two months) and stock target (three months). The columns to the left of the line 'Today' show historical data and to the right is the information for the planning horizon in the future.

The data for the sales budget are taken from the annual business plan. 'Latest forecast' represents what the sales and marketing teams are projecting based on the latest information. This data is updated every month. The stock target for each month is based on the sales forecast for the next three months, as the target is three months' stock cover. Due to a technical problem, production was suspended for six months and is resumed from this month. Therefore, a backlog of orders or negative stock (−1194) has been built up in the current month.

The projected stock is calculated by using the formula:

Stock this month = Stock last months   Sales + Delivery

For example, the projected stock for October =

−2094 − 500 + 3600 = 1006

It is important to note that planned production should be in multiples of the batch size, that is, 180 and the volume is available after two months' lead time.

A key feature of S&OP emerging from the above five steps is that S&OP is not only a driver in an MRPII system, but it also acts as an integrator of all building blocks of the supply chain and all functional departments of the organisation. As shown in Figure 22.3, S&OP spans all departments and key departmental plans at the aggregate level are embedded in S&OP. An updated aggregate new product plan is reconciled with the total sales demand plan. These are then communicated by appropriate review meetings to manufacturing and finance departments, which offer ways to support them by reconciling them with an aggregate finance plan and a supply plan.

It is also important to note that meetings to manage five key steps (viz. new product planning, demand planning, supply review, pre-S&OP and S&OP) support the MRPII processes as shown in Figure 22.4. For example, the demand management process is supported by new product planning meetings and demand planning meetings. Supply review meeting supports and establishes MPS and subsidiary manufacturing processes are supported by weekly and daily meetings.

As shown in Figure 22.5, the key S&OP meetings in five steps are conducted each month in successive weeks and are supported by other important business meetings on

Table 22.2 S&OP forecast of Aquatic 500

Product:
Toothpaste
Pack: Aquatic 500

Unit: Packs

Lead time: 2 months
Stock target: 3 months
Supply: Source

Shelf life: 3 years

Product batch size: 180

Month	−6 Feb	−5 Mar	−4 Apr	−3 May	−2 Jun	−1 Jul	1 Aug	2 Sep	3 Oct	4 Nov	5 Dec	6 Jan	7 Feb	8 Mar	9 Apr	10 May	11 Jun	12 Jul
Sales																		
Budget	500	500	500	525	600	600	600	550	550	525	525	525	525	525	525			
Forecast	500	400	459	400	500	400	500	400	500	400	500	500	500	500	500			
Actual																		
Stock																		
Target	1250	1350	1300	1400	1300	1400	1300	1400	1400	1500	1500	1500	1000	500	0			
Projected	956	556	106	−294	−794	−1194	−1694	−2094	1006	606	1906	1406	1806	1306	806			
Actual																		
QA release																		
Planned	0	0	0	0	0	0	0	0	3600	0	1800	0	900	0	0			
Actual																		
PRODUCTION																		
Planned	0	0	0	0	0	0	3600	0	1800	0	900	0	0	0	0			
Actual																		

Year to date

Sales budget 3225
Sales forecast 2650

Actual sales
Forecast performance
Stock performance

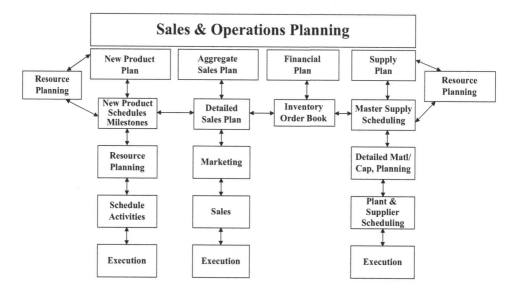

Figure 22.3 Span of sales and operations planning

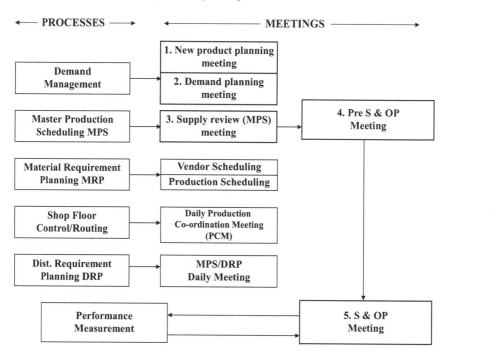

Figure 22.4 S&OP processes and meetings

Annual

Strategic Review

Quarterly

Business Review
Monthly

New Product Planning Meeting	1st Week
Demand Planning Meeting	1st Week
Supply Review (MPS) Meeting	2nd Week
Pre - S & OP Meeting	3rd Week
S & O Meeting	4th Week

Weekly

Vendor Scheduling
Production Scheduling

Daily

Production Co-ordination Meeting
MPS/DRP Meeting

Figure 22.5 S&OP planning cycles and meetings

annual, quarterly, weekly and daily schedules. The visibility of these meetings must not be construed as an indication of 'too many meetings' of talking shops. On the contrary, these are aimed at cascading the communication process across the organisation to arrive at rapid decisions based on quantitative data understandable and usable by all stakeholders.

CASE EXAMPLE: S&OP ENSURES SUSTAINABLE PERFORMANCE AT GSK TURKEY

GlaxoSmithKline Turkey (GSK Turkey, previously known as GlaxoWellcome Turkey) was awarded MRPII 'Class A' certification in 1999 by business education consultants Oliver Wight Europe.

GSK Turkey launched a programme (known as EKIP) in January 1998 to improve company-wide communications and sustain a robust business planning process using MRPII 'best practice' principles.

Since September 1998, the company has improved and sustained a customer service level of 97% and an inventory turnover of around 5.0. The sales turnover in 1998 increased by 20% in real terms in spite of some supply shortfall from the corporate network in the first half and the adverse economic and political conditions of Turkey. GSK Turkey has been recognised as a major business in the pharmaceutical giant GSK Group and the business plan for 1999 was aiming at a turnover of US$110 million.

As part of the MRP II Class A programme, GSK Turkey installed an S&OP process that was underpinned by a set of business planning meetings at various levels. In spite of the GW and SB merger and the corporate Lean Sigma initiative, the S&OP process has been continued by the company every month.

The vigour of the S&OP process, which is championed by the managing director, has helped the company to sustain and improve the business benefits and communication culture especially when they were challenged by a number of initiatives in hand, including:

- Transfer of office.
- Rationalisation of factory and warehouse.
- Corporate Lean Sigma programme.
- Merger of GlaxoWellcome and Smith Kline Beecham.

Source: Basu and Wright (2004).

S&OP programmes have saved manufacturing companies millions in supply chain costs and improved inter-departmental coordination with no loss to customer service. A recent report by Booz Allen Hamilton (2006) quoted the following examples of improvements by S&OP:

A global commodity manufacturer saved $120 million from operational improvement initiatives and reduced inventory by $100 million, largely as a result of S & OP work.

A North American durable goods manufacturer reduced its inventories by 30 percent saving $300 million.

A European cosmetics manufacturer reduced its working capital needs by more than 15 percent, while improving its promotion planning.

S&OP in service organisations

With appropriate adjustments for the units of the products, the S&OP process can also be applied to service industries. This will encourage the managers in non-manufacturing sectors to review the demand, capacity, inventory and scheduling and enhance the synergy of different functions.

Many service organisations already have existing processes that are designed to support the medium- to longer-term decision-making activities that are required to turn the long-term business plan into reality. In many cases, these revolve around the capital spend authorisation process, the associated justifications and approvals, and the subsequent development and implementation of specific projects.

In many cases, these work well, but it reflects a situation where the integration between the business plan, the operational plan and the projects that will deliver future capability is at best informal. Mostly it resides in the minds of the main players, the executive team. A service organisation, such as a bank or insurance company should have a distinct marketing and sales function and an operation function. Service companies without a formal S&OP process are experiencing a lack of integration between marketing and operations, particularly in terms of timing and customer demand. This has adversely affected their ability to meet increasing customer demand in the operational horizon.

S&OP, properly established, provides a level of integration between short-term operational plans and long-term business plans that helps to address this problem. It is not a complete solution in that it enables the uncertainty to be explored and at least it informs the decision-making process and allows alternative courses of action to be compared.

There are five major factors why companies undertake an S&OP process supported by an ERP system:

- Integrate financial information.
- Integrate customer order information and demand plan.
- Standardise and speed-up supply processes.
- Reduce inventory.
- Standardise HR information.

It is true that ERP is basically a second-generation MRPII system that is predominantly in manufacturing organisations. However, if we consider the above five reasons from the standpoint of a service organisation, we see that all factors, arguably with the exception of 'reduce inventory', are applicable to justify an ERP system. More importantly, if the ERP process is considered rather than the software, it is evident that the interaction between all functions with a 'single set of numbers' is equally important for an effective service enterprise.

The second and third factors of applying ERP relate to resource planning. Every service company has customers, demands, in-house resources and suppliers, and therefore, requires resource planning to deliver effective customer service. We call this operations resource planning (ORP) as illustrated in Figure 22.6.

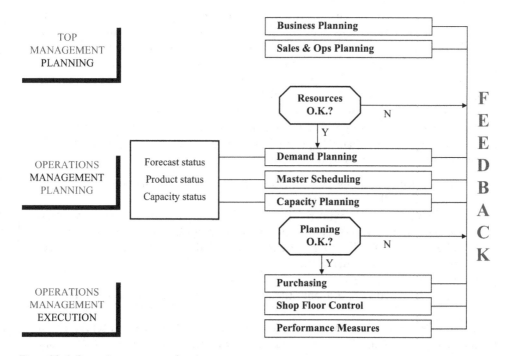

Figure 22.6 Operations resource planning

It is evident from Figure 22.6 that although ORP is not as detailed as MPRII, the key steps of the process are similar. From the business plan, a sales and operations plan that covers key products and resources is needed to deliver the business plan. The monthly sales and operations planning meeting by senior managers approves the master operations plan. The operations team will review the product portfolio, supplier status and capacity of resources and ensure that purchase orders are raised to procure appropriate resources or services from suppliers. If the capacity of owned resources is adequate, then an internal control document for the customer order is processed. But a partnership with customers and suppliers can and will achieve very obvious benefits to all. As a result of such a radical change, each of the service providers, the supplier and the customer, achieve benefits in:

- Lower operating costs.
- Improved service levels.
- A greater certainty of a continued relationship.

The boundaries between companies will blur as they view themselves as part of an ecosystem, supply chain, or value chain.

Hasso Platner, co-founder and vice chairman, SAP

CASE EXAMPLE: S&OP IN FINANCIAL SERVICES

The S&OP principles were turned into practice for the securities division of a diversified financial services company that operates in more than 40 locations worldwide. This division was serving brokerage clients employing about 3000 staff performing more than 600,000 transactions per month.

Before management started using some of the S&OP principles, the service philosophy of their operations department appeared to be 'Give everything to everybody, as best as we can'. In line with this unspoken philosophy, a sprawling system had developed as operations tried to serve a variety of different customers with no regard for their individual needs. Further complicating the issue was poor coordination between the sales force in the field and the operations teams in parts of the business. The result was wildly inefficient, with services delivered in ways that turned out to be several times more expensive than necessary.

To create a more sustained operation, management adopted the key S&OP principles, particularly applicable to their business, including:

- Set service and supply policies (e.g. what should be the maximum time that a customer is allowed to queue).
- Tighten forecasts by regularly reviewing the factors that drive demand volatility (e.g. promotion and pricing) and using forecast tools.
- Use analytical models to guide executives in balancing the trade-offs between resources and customer service.
- Communicate across functions through formal review meetings.
- Track key metrics (e.g. agent utilisation and number of processing errors).

The results were significant. Costs decreased by 15%. Processes and services were also changed dramatically, not only in terms of efficiency (e.g. lead times) but also in terms of effectiveness. The time taken to open new accounts was reduced by up to 60%, document reject rates also improved from 30 to 10% and the accuracy of response improved across all channels by over 10%.

Source: Booz Allen Hamilton (2006).

Collaborative planning forecasting and replenishment

CPFR is the latest in a series of concepts and initiatives that have emerged, developed, evolved and sometimes died in the name of a 'new concept' of supply chain management. A number of programmes and methods make up the current replenishment soup that has existed in industry over the past two decades including MRPII, enterprise resource planning (ERP), efficient consumer response (ECR), just-in-time (JIT), vendor-managed inventory (VMI), distribution resources planning (DRP) and jointly managed inventory (JMI) to name a few. CPFR falls into the last category as it truly is a well-developed and tested method of jointly managing inventory and replenishment throughout the supply chain process.

CPFR is often closely associated with the e-supply chain (also see Chapter 13) in which the CPFR process is supported by an ERP system (such as SAP R/3) and electronic linking of customer and supplier data using Internet technologies. The support of technology enables the adoption of collaborative planning and scheduling with critical suppliers and customers allowing effective sharing of forecasts and order status. The real-time access to data has enabled trading partners to have visibility into one another's critical demand, order forecasts and promotional forecasts through a systematic process of shared brand and category plans. This sharing is enabled by technology through the review of exceptions and the resolution of issues can only be effective when CPFR is embedded into the S&OP process. The S&OP meetings of the original equipment manufacturer (OEM) should include key suppliers and business partners linked virtually through a teleconference or video conference network. Under CPFR in its pure form, both trading partners develop a joint business plan for the specific product group that also includes a promotion calendar. The retailer and manufacturer also agree on a joint sales forecast. The joint sales forecast can drive production scheduling and distribution planning. Any changes from any of these forecasts are defined as exceptions. These exceptions will generate collaborative actions in joint S&OP meetings to re-align planning for the channel.

The origin of CPFR is attributed to a working group formed in 1995 between Walmart stores and Warner-Lambert Company to pilot test a new model for collaboration on the forecasting and replenishment of Listerine in stores. There have been many reports on the benefits of CPFR. After seven years, a study by the Grocery Manufacturers of America (GMA; 2002) showed that two-thirds of the survey correspondents said some CPFR activities are in place at some level in their companies. The survey also reported that among the experienced users of CPFR, 67% achieved a 1 to 10% improvement in forecast accuracy and 56% reported a decrease in inventory and an improvement of service levels by up to 10%. While most GMA member companies entered CPFR partnerships with downstream wholesalers and retailers, only 6% of companies were piloting with an upstream partner (suppliers of production materials, warehouse space, etc.). AMR Research (2001) reported on the range of results actually achieved by early adopters of

CPFR, which included 10% to 40% reduction of inventory levels for both the manufacturer and retailer.

CASE EXAMPLE: CPFR IN WHIRLPOOL

> Five years ago, sales people at Whirlpool said the company's supply chain staff were 'sales disablers'. Now, Whirlpool excels at getting the right product to the right place at the right time – while keeping inventory low. What made the difference?
>
> VP Global Supply Chain, Whirlpool

One of the key factors in the turnaround of Whirlpool's supply chain was the rollout of a new S & OP process. Whirlpool Corporation is a global manufacturer and marketer of major home appliances, with annual sales of over US$21 billion in 2015, 100,000 employees and more than 70 manufacturing and technology research centres around the globe. With the head office based in Michigan, the company markets Whirlpool, Maytag, KitchenAid, Brastemp, Jenn-Air, Bauknecht, Indesit and Consul, and is now the largest home appliance manufacturer in the world.

The old planning environment of Whirlpool was inadequate and planning tools did not go far beyond Excel spreadsheets. With the introduction of the S&OP process, the company now has the ability to pull together the long-term and short-term plans of marketing, sales, finance, logistics and manufacturing and produce forecasts that all participants could base their operation plans on.

The next step of Whirlpool was to push its forecasting capability in the global supply chain further by implementing CPFR. With CPFR, the company can use i2 software supported by a web-based network to share their forecasts with trading partners (such as Walmart and Sears) and collaborate on the exceptions. Within 30 days of the launch of CPFR, the forecast accuracy error was cut from 100% to 45%. To put it into perspective, a one-point improvement in forecast accuracy across the board reduced the total finished goods position of the company by several million dollars.

It is worth noting that Whirlpool Corporation is the principal supporter of Habitat for Humanity, a non-profit organisation dedicated to building low-cost affordable housing and has donated 73,000 appliances to this cause.

Updated from Slone (2004).

Global S&OP

The pure-play S&OP principles have been well established and their vital role in supply chain management cannot be faulted. However, in recent years, multinational organisations with global operations have realised that the changes to both their business and the global supply chain environment have shaped the legacy S&OP processes to a new level of global planning. To remain competitive, these leading organisations now have updated their site or country-centric processes to develop and implement a global S&OP process.

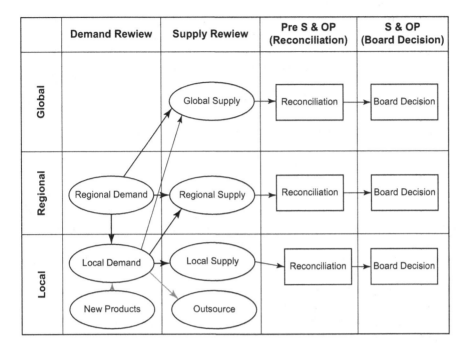

	Demand Rewiew	Supply Rewiew	Pre S & OP (Reconciliation)	S & OP (Board Decision)
Global		Global Supply	Reconciliation	Board Decision
Regional	Regional Demand	Regional Supply	Reconciliation	Board Decision
Local	Local Demand / New Products	Local Supply / Outsource	Reconciliation	Board Decision

Figure 22.7 Global S&OP model

As shown in Figure 22.7 as a typical global S&OP model, the fundamental steps within the local S&OP remain the same in global S&OP but they now have to span the collaborative nature of each process and deal with new requirements including the following.

Demand reviews. The demand from the sales region may differ from the capacity of the supply plants in the same region. Therefore, the demand review of a region includes the aggregate demand forecast of the countries in that region. The regional demand review follows the local reviews of that region, and each local review also takes into account the impact of new products and external factors.

Supply reviews. The review of local supply capacity follows the traditional S&OP principles of rough-cast capacity planning (RCCP) of critical plants and materials and also the outsourcing contracts or partnerships. The shortfall of capacity or the surplus capacity, as the case may be, is then aggregated with the needs of other sites in the region. For the sourcing of the most critical items, the capacity of the global network is compared

Reconciling. The reconciliation of demand and supply goes hand in hand with the local adjustments and regional allocations to optimise the loading of factories across the supply network. The reconciliation by traditional pre-S&OP processes is carried out in stages, such as first local, then regional and finally global pre-S&OP.

Executive decisions. S&OP processes at the board level are structured to resolve the tension between local sales units and regional or global supply units (e.g. high service levels in Europe vs lower operational costs in Africa). In addition to resolving the issues arising from the local pre-S&OP meeting, executive decisions of global S&OP processes are essential to balance the objectives of regional business models.

Communications. Sales units may be in a different country or continent from the supplying factory. No longer are the same individuals present in all meetings, so the use of formalised narratives and communications is vital. The enabling tools for communication include CPFR information systems, ERP data, emails and Skype.

Case example: Global S&OP at a multination food and drinks organisation

A multinational food and drinks business formed through several years of mergers and acquisitions was faced with a supply problem when unanticipated demand from the BRIC (Brazil, Russia, India and China) economies resulted in significant supply issues causing poor customer service and increased costs. A root-cause analysis found that the old country-centric S&OP processes were no longer fit for purpose within the new global demands. Consultants worked with the organisation through a number of distinct project phases:

- Conceptual design: aligning stakeholders to the S&OP Model.
- Detailed design: expanding the global S&OP model into process activities, assigning which activities were supported by what technology, defining the roles that under-took activities, defining KPIs and designing the meeting packs. Developing a range of educational material to take the design out into the business.
- Systems integration: ensuring common business processes in all sites and integrating the CPFR information system with the ERP systems of each site.
- Pilot phase: testing the design in the live business and refining the process, technology and people elements of the design.
- Implementation: supporting the client's team as they develop competence as global S&OP practitioners to become self-sustaining.

Consultants' sector knowledge and the use of traditional S&OP processes accelerated the joint team's work to complete the whole design within six months. The approach builds commitment from the first day of the programme in a joint team to deliver key workshops, engagement events, conference room pilots, communication material and executive steering groups. Rapid delivery of the design and the pilot built momentum within the client's senior executives to support and champion S&OP. This was critical to maintaining progress through the longest phase of the global roll-out. The approach also leveraged those who were converted to 'sell' to their peers in future waves of implementation, creating truly effective bottom-up, top-down engagement. The new global process brought the right information to the fingertips of the key decision makers, helped break down the old functional silos and ensured that the decisions made optimised value to the entire business. Early successes were created when country-level sales and marketing entities started to break out of a 'silo' mindset and worked proactively to close gaps over several months rather than last-minute 'buying of volume'.

Adapted from Capgemini (2009).

Shift in performance criteria

A little more than a decade ago, companies were urged to attain so-called 'world-class' performance within their enterprise. The departments within companies were striving for islands of excellence and then with a succession of operational excellence initiatives (e.g. TQM, BPR, MRPII, and Six Sigma) the 'walls' between departments were gradually demolished. Organisations started to become customer focused with established performance metrics in all areas of the business (e.g. 'balanced scorecard'). However, it is fair to say that both the business model and the performance metrics were site-centric or at best confined within the company or enterprise. Although the need for externally focused performance metrics from the perspective of a customer or an external supplier was identified, unfortunately, in most companies, metrics were not identified, or if identified not implemented beyond mere lip service.

With web-based technologies now accelerating, it is becoming imperative to rethink the selection and implementation of external metrics. This shift is not only in the measurement criteria but also in the mindset of business practices. Collaboration requires a capacity to 'work in association, sometimes, with an enemy' and does not achieve its business success at the competitor's expense. Figure 23.2 (see Chapter 23), adapted from Basu (2001), summarises some specific areas where performance criteria have shifted along with changes from an enterprise-centric business to a collaborative supply chain.

In order to utilise the advantages of collaboration, the buy-in and commitment of employees to the new mindset is essential. However, to make the process a reality, it is also imperative to review and redesign new performance management systems.

Traditional methods of measuring a company's performance by financial indices alone have virtually disappeared from large organisations. Nonetheless, many performance management systems are still internally focused and spend more time on direct productivity and asset utilisation measures than others.

There is evidence (Kaplan and Norton, 2000) that the balanced scorecard (BSC) approach of Kaplan and Norton has made a significant impact on performance management results. Many companies benefited from applying selected metrics in the four perspectives of the BSC, viz.

- Financial
- Customer
- Internal processes
- Learning and growth

This fundamental approach has proven to be sound where strategy is aligned with operation and external factors are shaping internal processes. But there are still implementation challenges to be tackled including

- Too many measures lead to number games.
- Few measures fit all organisations.
- Lack of clarity and common definition of metrics.
- Continuous change of requirements.

According to Howard et al. (2000), many performance management systems are 'receiving a failing grade' and about half of these measurement systems are still too inwardly focused. They seem to concentrate on past performance but offer little insight into how companies are likely to perform in the future. As a result, many companies are missing competitive opportunities.

The collaborative culture of the integrated supply chain has triggered the emergence of new measures, particularly in five key areas.

1. *External focus.* The perception of performance is what and when delivered to the customer and not how efficiently the product is made. Customers are demanding

order fulfilment (not just online transaction efficiency) with end-to-end visibility of demand and supply.

2. *Power to the consumer.* Consumers now wish to exercise a global choice of suppliers with data for comparative performance rather than supplier specifications. It has become important to provide access to instant information.

3. *Value-based competition.* There is evidently more emphasis on the speed and quality of service than cost or quality. In addition, the competitive advantage is now the delivery time and customer relationship management (CRM).

4. *Network performance.* World-class manufacturing at the factory level is not sufficient. Presently, success depends on a unit performing as an integral part of the network. The gradual increase in outsourcing is creating more dependence on network performance.

5. *Intellectual capital.* The sustainable success of a company has now shifted to the intellectual property and people culture of the company rather than its physical assets.

The impact of new measures on the collaborative supply chain is contributed less by the new metrics and significantly more by the way they are managed. For example, one new metric is the direct feedback from customers via automatic reply cards in the Internet or CRM systems. However, this new data does not add any value unless appropriate actions are taken with a significant paradigm shift from 'measurement' to 'management'. A six-step cycle is recommended in order to implement and sustain the benefits of a performance management system with new measures.

Benefits of S&OP

The quantifiable benefits of S & OP and CPFR in increasing customer service and sales and reducing inventory levels have been well reported and some of these have been shown earlier. Intangible benefits are perhaps more significant because S&OP, properly established, provides a level of integration between the short-term operational plans and the long-term business plans, allowing multifunctional managers and trading partners to simultaneously evaluate risks and opportunities. Although S&OP may not provide a complete solution, it highlights uncertainties for investigation. If uncertainties cannot be removed, at least information for the decision-making process is provided and alternative courses of action can be compared.

Some of the major intangible benefits of S&OP are:

1. S&OP provides a practical up-to-date review of the operational plan of an organisation while meeting the business objectives of profitability, productivity and customer service.

2. It provides more timely and informed decision making with more accurate budgets, leading to reduced emergency and contingency costs on capital projects.

3. It allows an excellent forum for senior managers of all functions to synergistically work to a common objective and integrate the building blocks of supply chain management. The 'finger-pointing' culture is thus eliminated.

4. It is data-driven and based on a 'single set of numbers' for all departments and thus helps to reconcile disputes and planning issues.

5. It can play an effective role in sustaining the high level of performance achieved by a TQM or Six Sigma-related programme.

Summary

In this chapter, we have described the need for a company-wide, data-driven process, such as S&OP, led by the top management to integrate all the building blocks of the supply chain to ensure sustainable customer service at an appropriate cost and quality of products or services. The process includes a single set of data over a planning horizon of around two years for all functions, such as marketing, purchasing, manufacturing, logistics and finance. There is a clear distinction between the S&OP process and an S&OP meeting. The process involves data preparation and then reviews in a series of meetings in progressive steps (e.g. new products planning, demand planning, supply review, pre-S&OP and S&OP). An S&OP meeting is part of the S&OP process.

Although its origin is in MRPII, an adapted version of S&OP can be, and has been, applied in service organisations to achieve remarkable benefits in the supply chain. A service organisation is likely to have a business plan, a sales forecast, a capacity plan for resources and above all customers and suppliers, thus, an appropriate S&OP process is possible.

The extended supply chain supported by an e-supply chain network and CPFR systems can only be effective if the S&OP process of the OEMs also includes key suppliers and customers. The visibility and instant access of supply chain data and targets by stakeholders will only be more productive when the plans and their exceptions are reviewed and agreed as part of the S&OP process.

Beginning the S&OP process requires a significant effort from all departments in managing initial education, self-assessment, data preparation and scheduling meetings. The initial meetings are likely to expose two problem areas. First, the format, timing and accuracy of data will take a few cycles to become stable. Second, managers will be defensive when the performance targets in their departments are not achieved. Over time, data accuracy will improve and the finger-pointing and excuses will gradually disappear. It is therefore sensible to start the monthly cycle meetings at an early scheduled date than waiting for data to improve. Whenever a forum is operated in a positive manner with top management leadership, continuous improvement will follow.

The well-established four- or five-step S&OP model is at the core of supply chain integration and improvements, but it should be adapted to suit the specific requirements of global organisations. A global S&OP model such as the one presented in Figure 22.7 is essential to enable today's global businesses to have the competitive edge needed to succeed in today's hugely challenging globalised environment.

Discussion questions

1. What is the definition of S&OP? Discuss the background of S&OP.
2. Explain why a properly administered S&OP process is essential for the success of supply chain management.
3. Describe the key steps of an S&OP process in a manufacturing company.
4. Discuss how you would implement S&OP in a service organisation. How does it differ from the S&OP of a manufacturing organisation?
5. A manufacturer of disk brake components has a full order book and adequate manufacturing capacity. However, customer service is unsatisfactory as shown by the average order fill efficiency for the current year of only 82%.

Explain how the S&OP technique can set up a process to improve the order fill efficiency.

6. On the basis of your analysis of the total supply chain case study, critically review to what extent the company in Turkey fulfilled the best practices of supply chain building blocks with particular reference to:
   - Systems and procedure.
   - Sales and operation planning.
   - Performance management.
   - Lean and agile supply chains.
   - Green supply chain.

7. Describe the key steps to be followed in a successful global S&OP process. What are the additional requirements in a global S&OP as compared with a country-based S&OP?

23 Global supply chain performance management

Introduction

Fast ongoing changes in globalised business environments have introduced fresh challenges, risks and opportunities to manufacturing companies. In a global supply chain survey conducted in 2013 (PwC, 2013), one key finding was 'companies that acknowledge supply chain as a strategic asset achieve 70% higher performance'. Performance management of the entire supply chain and its processes is essential when developing the supply chain. Performance measurement metrics provide information for internal needs and external stakeholders' purposes as well as enabling continuous improvement of performance.

It is generally considered that performance measurement for a supply chain is difficult to assess over the whole supply chain, but each component of the chain should be able to measure with some confidence the performance of its section of the supply chain. This chapter says that it is possible to devise a set of measurements that can be used to determine in one sense the efficiency of the chain as a whole, and in another sense, provide measurements of performance at each level designed to foster internal efficiency, which, in turn, will improve the performance of the overall chain. This chapter is presented in three sections. The first section of this chapter deals with how performance is measured at the organisational level, the second section considers the supply chain as a process and the third section considers various approaches to implementing improvements and methods to maintain benefits.

Learning objectives

Learning objectives for this chapter are:

1. Measures of performance.
2. Supply chain as a process.
3. Making it happen.

Measures of performance

Basic operational objectives

In operations management (see Chapter 8), the twin objectives of an operation are customer service and resource utilisation, and there are many methods of measuring the performance of both of these objectives. From the customer's perspective, customer service is measured in basic terms of specification, cost and time. The measures are centred on:

- Specification. Did the product or service meet specifications?
- Cost. How much did it cost relative to other suppliers?

DOI: 10.4324/9781003341352-27

- Time. Was delivery on time and/or how long did we have to wait for our order or request to be addressed?

From the supplier of the product or service, the specification, cost and time are measured but from a different perspective:

- Specification. How well do we meet the standards of customer specification that have been set by us?
- Cost. That is what we can afford to give and what we are prepared to give.
    Is our price right, i.e. are we too cheap or too expensive? And can we increase the price without losing sales?
- Time. What is our percentage for on-time delivery and how long do we keep the customer waiting before we serve them or answer their queries? Are customer queues too long? And are we losing business?

Thus, although the customer and supplier both measure performance in terms of specification, cost and time, the reasons and therefore the approach to measurement will be significantly different.

Indeed, in some cases, suppliers do not truly know what their customers really want or how their customers are measuring performance. Not all organisations have a system of feedback from customers as to customer service, the argument being that as long as we are making sales and increasing our market share, and providing that customer complaints are minimal, why bother? Needless to say, this is NOT our stance.

Our approach is customer service is the driver for an efficient supply chain.

Resource utilisation

Resource utilisation is measured by the operations manager in terms of efficient use of in terms of time and cost. Resources consist of the following

People
Equipment and machines
Vehicles
Space
Materials
Inventory (input material and components, work in progress, output stocks)
Information technology

Within the organisation, there will be a myriad of specific measures and areas of measurement. For a good deal of the 19th and 20th centuries, generally, accountants were seen to be the conduits of information for performance measurement. The importance of financial reports and measurements contained in reports cannot be denied. Financial measures are listed in Table 23.1.

For all of the above, the emphasis is on sales revenue and profit, and according to Wild (2003), all are affected by supply and demand and are dependent on the efficiency of the operation. We add that the operation in turn is dependent on the performance of the supply chain.

Operations managers, although mindful of financial measures, also have their own set of measures. These can be categorised as utilisation measures and performance measures,

Table 23.1 Financial measures

Return/capital employed
Return on assets
Net asset turnover
Profit/sales
Sales/capital employed
Sales/fixed assets
Sales/Stock
Stock turnover
Sales/Employee
Profits/employee
Current ratio
Gross profit
Cost of sales
Debtor days
Creditor days
Cash flow
Sales per square metre
Gearing

as shown in examples of performance metrics in Table 23.2. These are examples only and not comprehensive. It will be observed that the measures used by operations are not in conflict with those used by the accountants but are more at the tactical day-to-day level. The accountants tend to look at results as a measure of what has happened and whether plans and targets (budgets) have been achieved. Operations managers are also vitally interested in results but use measurement to influence and control to achieve the desired results.

Investor measurement

A critical performance measurement is made by investors (and the share market). Failure to provide a satisfactory return on investment will lead to a drop in share price, higher funding rates and closer scrutiny by investors. When an organisation is under pressure to reassure the investors, and the share market, pressure will be applied to cut back on costs and to shed people. An example is Ford Motors, which announced, following a very poor financial result, that it was closing 16 factories and 30,000 people were to be made redundant in 2008. This was meant to be the last big restructuring but in 2013 three further plants were closed in Germany, and now in 2016, the group has said it will be shedding hundreds of jobs in the UK and Germany as part of a programme to save US$200 million. This is after reporting a profit for the first time in four years for the European operation. Jim Farley head of Ford's European, Middle East and African business is reported as saying, 'We are absolutely committed to accelerating our transformation, taking the necessary actions to create a vibrant business that is solidly profitable in both good times and in down cycles'. The share price in April 2008 was US$6.70 and had dropped to US$3.25 by April 2009. The price rose to US$12.63 in April 2010 and reached a peak of US$16.13 in April 2014, now in April 2016, it dropped to US$12.80 from $14.00 in January

Self-centred measurement

All of the above performance measures are at one level of the supply chain, be it first-, second- or third-tier suppliers of materials, manufacturer, processor, distributor, warehousing

Table 23.2 Utilisation measures and performance measures

Operations utilisation measures	
Plant and machinery	Output/throughput per hour
	Usage %
	Capacity % used
	Space occupied
	Downtime (repairs, service/maintenance)
	Machine cost (capital cost/depreciation or lease cost)
	Set up time
	Overall equipment effectiveness (OEE)
People	Output/ throughput per hour
	Capacity % used
	Idle or ineffective time
	Absenteeism
	Accidents/illness
	Labour cost content
Materials	Yield %
	Waste/scrap %
	Rework
	Rectification
	Recalls
	Material cost
Performance: Areas to be measured	
Location	Transport costs
Layout	Movement and throughput
	Space utilisation
Work methods	Value added per hour
	Accident rates
	Industrial disputes
	People required numbers and skill levels
	Employee turnover
Capacity management	Capacity available measured in possible output
	Capacity % achieved
Scheduling	On-time deliveries or % of late deliveries
	Value/amount of work in progress
	Customer queue time
Materials management	Supplier performance
	Stock turn, days of stock held
	Capital tied up in stock
	Stock shortages; late deliveries of input materials leading to disruptions and delays
	Lead times (input and output)
	Late delivery to customers
	Customer queues
	Obsolescent stock (past used by date, out of fashion, outdated technology).
Quality	Reject rates
	Returns from customers
	Warranty claims
	Customer complaints
	Reworks
	Rectification and recalls

(Continued)

Table 23.2 (Continued)

	Performance penalties
	Quality system costs
	Product tests/laboratory costs

(It is also important to observe the 'cost of quality' model (Basu, 2009) where there are four main components, viz. design cost, appraisal cost, internal failure cost and external failure cost.)

Maintenance	Downtime
	Cost of own maintenance staff and utilisation of staff
	Operating hours between breakdowns per machine
	Life cycle of machines
	Cost as % of current asset value

The marketing department also has measures that include:

- Market share
- Orders on hand
- Order lead time
- Repeat business
- Number of complaints
- Warranty claims
- New product development and launch
- Time to market
- Conversion of leads to sales.

or retailer. Obviously, the immediate upstream provider and the immediate downstream customer will have an impact on the performance of a supply chain component and in turn each member will be judging the performance of its immediate upstream suppliers. However, the purpose of all the measures listed above, be they financial, operational, marketing or by investors is to achieve internal efficiency and ultimately to achieve an acceptable return on investment.

In the simplified supply chain shown in Figure 23.1, one component of the chain, the manufacturer, measures the performance of itself, and of its immediate customer and its immediate supplier. In this example, the measurement is seen as being two way, but frequently, measurement is self-centred and little effort is made to measure performance

3rd Tier

2nd Tier

1st Tier Supplier →

← MANUFACTURER →

← Distributor

Warehouse

Retailer

End User

Figure 23.1 Simplified supply chain

from the supplier or customers perspective, let alone try to measure performance for the whole supply chain!

From self-centred to supply chain centred

By now it will be clear that we view the supply chain in its entirety. The strength of the supply chain movement has been to encourage managers to think outside the box, and to recognise that organisations are not an island unto themselves. Organisations are interdependent on other organisations up and down the supply chain and need to recognise financial as well as logistical limitations and advantages of inter-company, including international, transactions. Some organisations have achieved integration of their supply chain to an advanced level from a position of dominance and power. Organisations such as Toyota and others who follow a lean 'just-in-time' approach in manufacturing and organisations such as Walmart in the United States and Tesco in the UK and McDonald's worldwide have been able to control the performance of their supply chain to meet their objectives.

The lean production methods of Toyota require internally a flexible workforce, single minute exchange of dies (SMED), small batches, elimination of non-value-adding activities, scheduling to balance the line and to reduce queues, simple easily understood control measures and feedback, and minimal stock holding (workflows like water). Continuous improvement (Kaizen) is so engrained in the culture at Toyota, staff are not aware of any other way of thinking! Being internally efficient is crucial to a lean system, but no lean system is possible without the cooperation of suppliers and customers. Toyota does not dictate to customers, but certainly enforces controls and standards on suppliers out to several tiers of their supply chain. Toyota requires and insists on quick response, delivery on time and delivery exactly to specification with up to 16 deliveries (hourly) required per day from immediate suppliers. Performance of all of this requires shared values, standards, targets and measures. Toyota does not neglect customer satisfaction. From the customer aspect, performance is measured in two ways: from internally set standards of product quality, on-time delivery and service and externally from feedback from customers. Despite all this, Toyota is not perfect and is prepared to publicly admit so.

Following recalls of over one million vehicles in Japan and 400,000 sports utility vehicles in the United States in 2006, Katsuaki Watanabe, the Toyota president, told a news conference, 'the world class quality we have built is our life line There will be no growth without an improvement in quality. This is the biggest task that this management must undertake'. It was advised that a new division dedicated to gathering user information on quality problems more quickly should be set up. However, despite these fine sentiments, Toyota has continued to be plagued with quality issues, the latest at the time of writing being a recall of 320,000 vehicles for improperly programmed airbags.

The Tesco, Walmart and McDonald's approach is to manage the supply chain right back to when the seed goes into the ground. They do not themselves plant or harvest the seed, but they tell the farmer when to plant, what variety, what fertilisers and type of pesticide to use, when to harvest and so on right down the supply chain through processing and distribution until the product reaches their retail outlets. Performance at each stage of the supply chain must comply with their standards and measurements. Customers at supermarkets benefit from a wide range and choice of products, standardised quality of products and prices are lower than any independent trader could hope to achieve.

Shift of criteria

A little more than a decade ago, companies were urged to attain so-called 'world-class' performance within the enterprise. The departments within a company were striving for islands of excellence and then with a succession of operational excellence initiatives (e.g. TQM, BPR, MRPII and Six Sigma), the fences between departmental turf were gradually demolished. The organisations started to become customer focused and established performance metrics in all areas of the business (e.g. 'balanced scorecard') began to emerge. However, it is fair to say that both the business model and the performance metrics were site-centric or at most were confined within the company or enterprise. The need for externally focused performance metrics from the perspective of a customer or an external supplier was identified. Unfortunately, in most companies, in practice, these metrics were not implemented beyond mere lip service.

However, with web-based technologies now accelerating the collaborative supply chain, it is becoming imperative to rethink the selection and implementation of external metrics. This shift is not only in the measurement criteria but also in the mindset of business practices. Collaboration requires a capacity to 'work in association, sometimes, with an enemy' and does not achieve its business success at the competitor's expense. Figure 23.2, adapted from Basu (2003), summarises some specific areas where performance criteria have shifted along with changes from the enterprise-centric business to the collaborative supply chain.

In order to utilise the advantages of collaboration, the buy-in and commitment of employees to the new mindset is essential. However, to make the process a reality, it is also imperative to review and redesign the new performance management systems.

Agile supply chains

All of the above examples are agile supply chains, and each is dominated by a key player. The characteristics of an agile supply chain are quick customer response at each level of the chain, flexibility, scheduling triggered by customer demand, open and real-time information flow, simultaneous new product development, and as Morgan (2004) says,

ENTERPRISE	INTEGRATED SUPPLY CHAIN
❑ Autonomous and adversarial	❑ Networked and collaborative
❑ Opaque to the outside world	❑ Transparent to customers and partners
❑ Internally focused site centric	❑ Externally focused market centric
❑ Strategically long-term	❑ Strategically agile
❑ Hierarchical and information hoarding	❑ Knowledge creating and sharing
❑ Technologically constrained	❑ Web enabled
❑ Enterprise excellence	❑ Network Excellence

Figure 23.2 Shift of criteria

pipeline cost improvements. If agile is to be achieved, measurement and control, or at the least monitoring of performance, is necessary.

Morgan (2004) also injects a dose of reality. He says that:

> very small organisations do not have the time, resources or information to undertake the analyses required for optimisation activities. Medium sized enterprises may have the information as their management systems develop, but can lack the skills to interpret and apply it.

While we agree with Morgan, we add that no matter how efficient and well-intentioned a small or even a medium-sized enterprise is, it is not likely that they can get a Walmart or a McDonald's to dance to their tune.

Supply chain as a process

Perfect order, perfect supply chain

A perfect order begins with raising the product order, EDI, correct transaction codes, all items available, correct picking of items, transport available, paperwork complete and correct, delivery at the right temperature, arrives on time, is undamaged, invoices correct and payment made on time. Outside of Toyota and some other world-class companies, 100% perfect delivery is rare. If we accepted that 95% performance is good, then in a supply chain of six levels each performing at 95%, the end result is 73.5% efficiency. If 98% efficiency is achieved at each level, then efficiency is 88.6%. For Toyota, anything less than Six Sigma at each level is not acceptable. Six Sigma equates to 99.9996.6% or 3.4 errors per million opportunities, in effect, zero defects. However, Toyota does not expect Six Sigma to be achieved for every activity. Likewise, nor do we, our approach is FIT SIGMA. With the FIT SIGMA philosophy (Basu, 2011), it is not necessary to achieve Six Sigma for every activity, some activities are not critical, while others are. The approach is to understand which activities are critical, determine the level of performance of these activities, strengthen those that are weak and build on those that are strong. FIT SIGMA is explained in greater detail later in this chapter.

Process-based approach

There are two ways of measurement, one is to measure activities, and the other is to identify and measure processes. The process-based approach concentrates on the process rather than activities. A complete supply chain is a process. The very name supply chain indicates one entity managed as a whole and not a series of self-centred entities managed independently. The desired end result of the process for a supply chain is to satisfy the customer with the delivery of a perfect order.

In a simplified supply chain, the process to satisfy a perfect order is:

Supplier
　→ Inward logistics
　　→ Factory
　　　→ Outward logistics
　　　　→ Warehouse
　　　　　→ Retailer
　　　　　　→ End user

From supplier through all the levels of the supply chain out to the end user is the process.

Each component in the overall process will have to carry out a set of activities, and as shown earlier in this chapter, each component will have a set of measurable standards.

These financial, operational and marketing performance measures, although inward-looking if taken with a determination to correct and improve, will lead to an efficient use of resources and will facilitate customer satisfaction. As explained, the achievement of high standards of performance relies to a large extent on demand and supply. Thus, many of the standards and measurements for performance can without much effort be related to the viewpoint of the immediate supplier and the immediate customer. If each component takes a customer-centric view, a perfect order will achieve:

- *Specification.* Customer specification will be 100%.
- *Price.* The price will be better than or at least comparable to the competition.
- *Time.* Delivery will be in full and on time.

Sounds familiar? Refer back to the opening paragraphs of this chapter. If each component is achieving the delivery of a perfect order, then the process as a whole, that is, the complete supply chain process, can be said to be performing to the customer's satisfaction, as indeed it appears to do for customers of Walmart, Tesco, McDonald's and Toyota. Bearing in mind each component is a customer of another component, and each component will be getting its desired level of service in the form of a perfect order from upstream. To achieve this desired state, it follows that each component internally will be continuously improving its own efficiency in the use of resources.

Chan and Qi (2003) have developed a scoreboard-type approach for process-based measurement of the supply chain. The dashboard consists of seven elements: cost, time, capacity, capability, productivity, utilisation and outcome.

- *Cost – inventory carrying costs.* Inventory management accounts for a mass of total materials handling costs. Effective management should achieve lower costs. Hence, inventory-carrying costs deserve much attention in assessing performance of inventory management. Inventory capital cost, storage space cost and risk cost are the three key parts of inventory carrying costs.
- *Time – flow rate.* Inventory flow rate is based on the ratio of the inventory level (in terms of stock units or value) to the average inventory cycle time. Flow rate is an indicator of cycle time of inventory within the warehouse. The faster inventory flows through the warehouse, the lower investment in inventory and the improved investment in inventory returns.
- *Effectiveness – inventory accuracy.* This concerns inventory record errors when physically cycle counting and checking at regular intervals. Maintaining high inventory accuracy is critical, not only for financial controls, but also for the effectiveness of subsequent materials requirement planning and order delivery. Inventory accuracy indicates the effectiveness of both physical inventory management and documentation management.
- *Availability – inventory availability.* Availability is one of the most important performances from the customer's viewpoint. Inventory availability indicates the customer service level and is largely concerned with customer satisfaction. The two often-used measures are order fill rate (order availability) and stock-out rate (stock unit availability). The former is based on the percentage of demand order filled from stock in total. The latter refers to the rate of stock-outs and the duration of stock-outs.

- *Productivity – inventory productivity.* For the inventory management process, which consumes a great number of inputs – labour, facilities, capital, space and energy – assessing its productivity is indispensable traditionally. The total productivity, multi-factor productivity and partial factor productivity, all need to be measured.
- *Utilisation.* Most of the resources, which inventory management process consumes, deserve attention in utilisation. Besides the utilisation of labour, facilities and capital, there are two more: working inventory rate and stock unit utilisation. The former is based on the percentage of working inventory in the total inventory held. It indicates the effectiveness of inventory-holding strategies. The latter refers to storage space utilisation, which indicates the effectiveness of storage policies.

Chan and Qi (2003: p. 187) add that 'metrics are selectively adopted according to the management and measurement emphasis'.

So far in this chapter, we have shown that traditional measurements, be they financial, operational marketing or from the investor's perspective are self-centred and based on specific activities. Although some effort will be made by most companies to measure immediate customer satisfaction, it is difficult for organisations to measure the performance of the supply chain. Indeed, if an organisation is not in a dominant position in the supply chain, there is little chance that it can influence the performance of the supply chain in its entirety. However, the supply chain taken as a process can be measured. We provided a dashboard of measurements. If each member of the supply chain is measuring its own internal activities with the express aim of continuous improvement and is delivering a perfect order to its customers, it follows that the supply chain as a whole will be customer-centric. The result being that the entire process of the supply chain will be geared towards delivering perfect orders to the end user. Each player in the supply chain will benefit by being leaner and more profitable.

The premise being that if each component is internally efficient and determined to deliver perfect orders, beginning with the original supplier flowing down through each component of the chain out to the end user, then the entire chain will be efficient and each player will benefit.

Making it happen

The first section of this chapter dealt with how performance is measured at organisational level, the second section considered the supply chain as a process and a process-based measurement, the third section considers how an organisation can self-evaluate and become efficient.

Theory of constraints

The theory of constraints (TOC) is a management philosophy developed by Goldratt (1992). The theory is that the output of an organisation is limited (constrained) by internal resources, market factors and policy. Resource constraint means not enough resources to meet demand, market constraints mean capacity is more than the market demands and a policy constraint (i.e. a policy of no overtime) can limit output. TOC tries to improve system performance by focusing and eliminating constraints. In service operations, where it is often difficult to quantify the capacity constraint, TOC can be very useful. For companies that employ skilled workers and for many service organisations, the constraint is often the time of one or a few key employees. The key steps in this process are:

1 *Identify.* The first step in applying TOC is to identify the constraining factor (bottleneck department or section).
2 *Exploit.* Determine the throughput per unit of the constraining factor (by department or section of a department).
3 *Subordinate.* Prevent the resources needed from waiting in a queue elsewhere (i.e. backing up at a non-constrained resource).
4 *Elevate.* If the constraint still exists, find ways to increase the capacity of the constraining section.
5 Go back to Step 1.

Implementation of TOC, although simple in principle, is often difficult because it may require a complete change in the way an organisation operates. For example, TOC requires a shift from cost-based decision making to decision making based on continuous improvement.

As discussed earlier in this chapter, a company's performance is measured in financial terms. Quarterly or annual financial reports create an immediate impact on the share value of the company and consequently senior managers are driven to improve the share price. Thus, the traditional accounting model of balance sheets and profit and loss performance statements are still used to judge the success of management and the organisation. By their very nature, these are backwards-looking historical documents. Thus, although we operate in an age where information is close to being real time, performance is still judged on past results.

Kaplan and Norton (1996) argued that 'a valuation of intangible assets and company capabilities would be especially helpful since, for information age companies, these assets are more critical to success than traditional physical and tangible assets'. They created 'the balanced scorecard', which retains traditional financial measures, customer services and resource utilisation (internal business process), and also includes additional measures for learning (people) and growth (innovation). This approach complements measures of past performance with drivers for future development.

The balanced scorecard

The concept of the balanced scorecard was first introduced by Kaplan and Norton in an article in the *Harvard Business Review* in 1992, 'The Balanced Scorecard – Measures That Drive Performance'. This generated considerable interest for senior business managers and led to the next round of development of the scorecard. The focus was shifted from short-term measurement towards generating growth, learning and value-added services to customers. This methodology was then published by Kaplan and Norton in a number of articles in the *Harvard Business Review* and culminated in their 1996 book 'The Balanced Scorecard'. Many companies are now using the balanced scorecard as the central organising framework for important decision processes. The evolution of this technique has gradually transformed the performance measurement process into a strategic management system. The balanced scorecard (BSC) is a conceptual framework for translating an

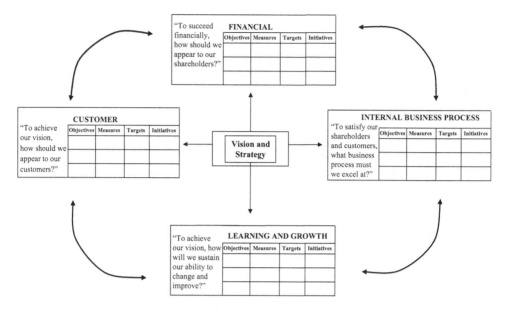

Figure 23.3 Balanced scorecard

organisation's strategic objectives into a set of performance indicators distributed among four perspectives (see Figure 23.3):

- Financial
- Customer
- Internal business processes
- Learning and growth

The indicators are aimed to measure an organisation's progress towards achieving its vision as well as the long-term drivers of success. Through the BSC, an organisation monitors both its current performance (e.g. internal processes, finance, customer satisfaction) and its effort to improve and sustain performance (e.g. innovation and employee development). It is also balanced in terms of internal efficiency and external effectiveness. Later, David Norton (1999) extended the elements of the overall scorecard to six, these being:

- Return on investment
- Budget
- Shareholder value
- Customer
- People
- Quality

Targets (scores) are formulated for each element, communicated and consensus achieved, executed and results are evaluated with corrective action taken so that the targets (scores) are achieved. Norton says that it is important that all elements are linked and not considered in isolation. The BSC has been applied successfully in several organisations around the world. It is evident that the key performance indicators of both manufacturing and service organisations, as we have described earlier, can be incorporated into a properly designed BSC. The scorecard, with some customised changes, provides a management tool for senior executives primarily to focus on strategies and longer-term objectives. The organisations could vary from a large multinational business to a non-profit-making public service unit. The scorecard is sometimes named the 'Executive Dashboard'. The key performance indicators (KPI) are reported as:

Current actual
Target
Year-to-date average
Variance to YTD target

When the actual performance value is on or above target then the value is shown as green. If the actual is below the target, but within a given tolerance, then the colour becomes amber. It is depicted in red when the value is below the tolerance limit of the target. Another area of application is to assess the performance at the tactical operation level. Usually, the top-level indicators (also known as 'vital flow') are designed in such a way that they can be cascaded to 'component' measures and the root causes can be analysed. Basu (2002) emphasised the impact of new measures on the collaborative supply chain. The Internet-enabled supply chain or e-supply chain has extended the linear flow of the supply chain to collaborative management supported by supplier partnerships. This has triggered the emergence of new measures, especially in five areas:

- External focus.
- Power to the consumer.
- Value-based competition and customer relationship management.
- Network performance and supplier partnership.
- Intellectual capacity.

The design features and application requirements of the BSC can be adapted to the collaborative culture of the integrated supply chain (see Chapter 13).

Total operations solutions.

'Total Operations Solutions' (Basu and Wright, 2005) enables self-assessment against 20 defined areas (called 'foundation stones') to identify areas of improvement for achieving the full potential of the business. The business is built from these foundation stones up and consists of the 'six pillars' of total solutions. The pillars are:

- Marketing and innovation
- Supply chain management
- Environment and safety
- Facilities
- Procedures
- People

Self-assessment is done through 200 questions, ten for each foundation stone. Although the checklist is aimed at manufacturing operations, it can be adapted easily to service operations. From scores for each foundation stone, current performance gaps are determined. Examples of the questions used are shown in Table 23.3. Note two of these questions were given in Chapter 5 and are marked with an asterisk.

A software called *ASK 2.0* (see Appendix 3) is available containing guidelines for scoring each of the 200 questions of 20 foundation stones supporting six pillars. This software enables a holistic self-assessment and health check of all operations of the business

With total operations solutions, larger projects are also assessed based on an organisation's strategic goals and requirements. The viability of the project is then established based on certain quantifiable criteria including ROI (return on investment) and strategic

Table 23.3 Sample assessment questions

	Poor			Excellent	
	0.1	0.2	0.3	0.4	0.5
How good is your integrated point-of-sale system					
*How effective is the inclusion of key suppliers in the planning process?					
*How effective are you in the sharing of common coding and databases with					
suppliers and customers using the Internet or electronic data interchange?					
How effective have you been in the co-development of new products?					
How effective are you in sharing risks and cost savings with your suppliers?					
How good are you at meeting delivery as determined by customers?					
How well do you work with suppliers to improve each other's processes?					
How satisfactory is your post-delivery performance in terms of invoice accuracy?					
How well do you record and seek causes for the return of goods and/or customer complaints?					
How well is the cost of non-conformance to quality standards communicated					
to staff (cost of rework, scrap, replacement, overtime, lost business)?					
How cost-efficient is your distribution operation when distribution cost is expressed as a percentage of sales?					
(Over 8% is poor, less than 1% is excellent.)					
How easy is it for customers to contact the right person in your organisation					
when they want to place an order or need knowledge of your product?					

goals. With total operations solutions, before any improvement project is commenced, five factors are considered.

1. What is the project's value to the business in terms of overall financial performance? This factor can be applied by monitoring the savings on a monthly basis.
2. What resources will be required? How much will they cost? The timescale of the project is also included in this factor.
3. What metrics will be used to monitor the performance of specific large projects? Examples are DPMO (defects per million opportunities) and RTY (rolled throughput yield).
4. What will the impact be on the external market? It will be important to monitor customer service and sales revenue to ensure that there is no erosion due to key people's commitment to the project.
5. That the project does not take on a life of its own and that it continues to align with the overall mission and strategy of the business.

A recurring challenge for companies who have invested significant time and resources in implementing proven improvement plans such as total operations solutions or Six Sigma is how to ensure sustainable performance beyond the duration of a one-off corporate exercise. The annual review of the change programme during the budget planning is ineffective because 12 months is a long time in a competitive marketplace. In order to steer the benefits of the programme and the business objectives to a sustainable future, the senior managers who are in the driving seats must have a clear view of both the front screen and the rearview mirrors and they must look at them as frequently as possible to decide on their direction and optimum speed. In recent years, the pace of change in technology and the marketplace dynamics have been so rapid that the traditional methodology of monitoring actual performance against predetermined budgets set at the beginning of the year may no longer be valid. It is fundamental that businesses are managed based on current conditions and up-to-date assumptions; there is also a vital need to establish an effective communication link, both horizontally across functional divisions and vertically across the management hierarchy, to share common data and decision processes. A solution to these continuous review requirements recommended in total operations solutions is sales and operations planning (S&OP) as described in Chapter 22.

Self-assessment and certification

In order to maintain a wave of interest in the quality programme and also to market the competitive advantage of quality, many companies dedicated the effort to the pursuit of an approved accreditation such as ISO or an award such as the Malcolm Baldridge Award (in the United States) and derivatives of the Baldridge Award in other countries. The certification and awards have had a chequered history. After a peak in the early 1990s, the Baldridge Awards gradually lost their impact in the United States and companies (e.g. GE, Johnson & Johnson) started developing their own customised quality assessment process. Encouraged by the customer demand for the ISO stamp of approval, there was a rush for ISO 9000 certification in the 1990s, but companies became disillusioned by the auditors ensuring compliance with current procedures without necessarily improving standards. A number of consultancy companies attempted to introduce their own awards to progress an improvement programme (e.g. Class 'A' by Oliver Wight).

European Foundation of Quality Management

The European Foundation of Quality Management (EFQM) award is derived from the Malcolm Baldridge National Quality Award. There are similar accolades available in other countries, such as the Canadian Excellence Award and the Australian Quality Award. The EFQM Award was established in 1991. It is supported by the European Union and the countries in the EU have their own support unit (e.g. British Quality Foundation in the UK). The EFQM model provides a set of checklist questionnaires under nine categories, each containing maximum points. They are:

* Leadership: 100 points
* People management: 90 points
* Policy and strategy: 80 points
* Resources: 90 points
* Processes: 140 points
* People satisfaction: 90 points
* Customer satisfaction: 200 points
* Impact on society: 60 points
* Business results: 150 points
      Total: 1000 points

The scoring of each sub-criterion is guided by the RADAR logic that consists of four elements:

* Results
* Approach
* Deployment
* Assessment and review

As shown in Figure 23.4, the first five categories (leadership to processes) are 'enablers' and the remaining four categories are 'performance' related.

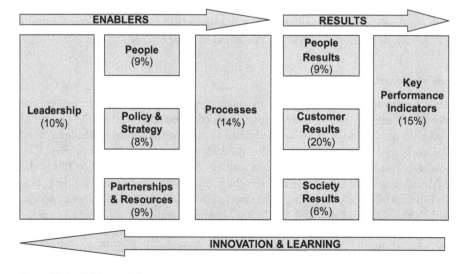

Figure 23.4 EFQM model

The EFQM excellence model is intended to assist business managers in better understanding best practices and supporting them in quality management programmes. The EFQM currently has 19 national partner organisations in Europe and the British Quality Foundation is such an organisation in the UK. Over 20,000 companies, including 60% of the top 25 companies in Europe, are members of the EFQM.

The model has been used for several purposes, of which the four main ones are given below:

1. *Self-assessment.* The holistic and structural framework of the model helps to identify the strengths and areas for improvement in any organisation and then to develop focused improvements.
2. *Benchmarking.* Undertaking the assessment of defined criteria against the model, the performance of an organisation is compared with that of others.
3. *Excellence awards.* A company with a robust quality programme can apply for a European Quality Award to demonstrate excellence in all nine criteria of the model. Although only one EQA is made each year for company, public sector and SME (small and medium enterprise), several EQAs are awarded to companies who demonstrate superiority according to the EFQM excellence model.
4. *Strategy formulation.* The criteria and sub-criteria of the model have been used by many companies to formulate their business strategy.

FIT SIGMA (Basu, 2011)

Six Sigma is a whole system approach to the improvement of quality and customer service to improve the bottom line. Like all total quality programmes, Six Sigma takes a whole systems approach and requires a culture whereby everyone at all levels has a passion for continuous improvement with the ultimate aim of achieving perfection. Six Sigma sets a performance level that equates to 3.4 errors per million opportunities. FIT SIGMA recognises that not every organisation needs the intensive and expensive 'all or nothing' investment required to achieve Six Sigma. With FIT SIGMA, we identify key areas where zero defects are essential and areas where zero defects are possible, but we also recognise that there are areas where zero defects are not essential or practical. We say rather than the organisation having to strive to fit a mathematical formula that Six Sigma should be adapted to meet the needs of the organisation. The programme comprises the following features:

1. Establish the policy of external certification such as EFQM or customised self-assessment such as total operations solutions.
2. Develop or confirm the checklist of assessment.
3. Train internal assessors in the common company assessment process (one assessor for every 500 employees as a rough guide). The assessors should also carry out normal line or functional duties.
4. Train experts (Six Sigma-trained Black Belts) and department managers in the self-assessment checklist and process.
5. Carry out quarterly self-assessments by departmental managers.
6. Ensure six-monthly (at the initial stage) and annual (at the later stage) assessments by the internal assessors.
7. Analyse gaps and implement measures to minimise the gap.

8   Consider corporate awards, depending on the performance attained.
9   Review the checklist with the change of business every two years.
10   Consider external accreditation ONLY if it adds value to the business.

The above methodology is applicable to all types of business, both manufacturing and service, and all sizes of operations, whether large, medium or small. A larger organisation is likely to have its own resources to develop and maintain the process; a smaller organisation may require the assistance of external consultants to develop the process.

Signature of quality

Signature of quality is another approach and is illustrated with the following case example.

Case example: Janssen-Cilag applies 'signature of quality' for continuous self-improvementJanssen-Cilag is the pharmaceutical arm of the American Johnson & Johnson Group of companies with their European head office based in High Wycombe, UK. Janssen-Cilag is among the top ten pharmaceutical companies in the world.

The company markets prescription medicines for a range of therapeutic areas of gastroenterology, fungal infections, women's health, mental health and neurology.

The commitment of the company to the values and standards laid out in 'Our Credo' drives management to strive continually for excellence in a number of overlapping areas. Based upon the principles of the Baldridge Award, the quality management team of Janssen-Cilag developed a self-assessment process known as 'Signature of Quality (SoQ)'. The process is supported by a checklist on a carefully constructed questionnaire in five interdependent areas:

- Customer focus
- Innovation
- Personnel and organisational leadership
- Exploitation of enabling technology
- Environment and safety

SoQ is managed as a global process from the US office and each site is encouraged to prepare and submit a comprehensive quality report meeting the requirements. The assessment is carried out by specially trained quality auditors and a site may receive an SoQ Award based on the results of the assessment.

SoQ has been reported to be successful in Janssen-Cilag as a tool for performing a regular 'health check' and as a foundation for improvement.

Case from Basu and Wright (2003).

Knowledge management

Our final comment in the chapter is that knowledge once gained is too important to lose. The key principles of knowledge management are:

1. Systematically capture knowledge from proven 'good practices'.
2. Select examples of best practice that provide added value to the business.
3. Inculcate knowledge between all functions.

It is essential to establish a learning organisation culture. Unless staff at all levels are sharing in knowledge, and truly believe that the business can benefit from shared knowledge, the gathering of knowledge will have achieved little. If an organisation believes that they already know what the best practice is and are satisfied with incremental improvement, it will be left behind. History shows that knowledge progresses in leaps and bounds. The development of a learning culture does not just happen, words are not enough. The support structure required to develop a knowledge-sharing culture needs the following:

- A champion as a focal point to coordinate the process.
- Regular 'best practice' forums to promote learning, sharing and networking.
- Internal and external benchmarking using one of the approaches detailed above.
- Continuous communication through websites, newsletters, etc.

The development of a learning organisation culture does not happen overnight. It takes time and requires support. Our experience is that time and money spent in knowledge management is an investment in the most valuable resource of competitive advantage – people.

Supply Chain Operations Reference

The supply chain operations reference (SCOR) model has been developed by the Supply Chain Council to describe the business activities associated with all phases of satisfying a customer's demand. The model itself contains several sections and is organised around the five primary management processes of plan, source, make, deliver and return. By describing supply chains using these process building blocks, the model can be used to describe supply chains that are very simple or very complex using a common set of definitions. As a result, disparate industries can be linked to describe the depth and breadth of virtually any supply chain. The model has been able to successfully describe and provide a basis for supply chain improvement for global projects as well as site-specific projects.

The SCOR model contains five levels of analysis:

Level 1: Process type

The top level of the SCOR plan defines the five fundamental perspectives of plan, source, make, deliver and return.

- Plan: planning of demand and supply balance.
- Source: process to source product or service.
- Make: process to make materials into products.
- Deliver: process to provide product or service.
- Return: process for purchasing to return material or for distribution to receive rejected products.

Level 2: Process categories

The second level of SCOR is the configuration of process categories. For example, the manufacturer under the Make section could select a strategy of 'making to stock' or 'making to order'.

Level 3: Process elements

In the third level of SCOR, every process is divided into detailed process elements. For example, the 'source to stock' category is divided into five elements, namely, scheduling material, receiving material, checking material, stocking and payment.

Level 4: Implementation

The fourth level is implementation between partners of the supply chain. Since January 2007, organisations using SCOR have had access to benchmark metrics.

Level 5: Performance metrics

There are over 250 SCOR metrics that are organised in a hierarchical (and codified) structure from organisation level 1 to process level 2 to diagnostic level 3. The metrics are categorised into five performance attributes: reliability, responsiveness, agility, costs and asset management efficiency. The first three attributes are considered customer-focused; the latter two are internally focused. Evidently, there are too many SCOR metrics, albeit categorised, causing a significant challenge for a company to select, define and prioritise the specific requirements for each attribute. We recommend SCOR as a reference backdrop but not as a prescriptive process.

For further information on the SCOR model, see www.supply-chain.org.

Capability Maturity Model Integration

According to Wikipedia, the United States Air Force funded a study at the Carnegie-Mellon Software Engineering Institute to create a model for the military to use as an objective evaluation of software subcontractors. The result was the capability maturity model (CMM), which has been superseded by the more comprehensive capability maturity model integration (CMMI).

The CMM can be used, especially in large IT projects, to assess an organisation against a scale of five process maturity levels. Each level ranks the organisation according to its standardisation of processes in the subject area being assessed. The five levels of maturity are:

Level 1: Initial

At maturity level 1, processes are usually ad hoc and the organisation usually does not provide a stable environment. Success in these organisations depends on the competence of the people in the organisation and not on the use of proven processes.

Level 1 software project success depends on having high-quality people.

Level 2: Repeatable

At maturity level 2, software development successes are repeatable. The processes may not repeat for all the projects in the organisation. The organisation may use some basic project management to track costs and schedules.

Basic project management processes are established to track cost, schedule and functionality. The minimum process discipline is in place to repeat earlier successes on projects with similar applications and scope. There is still a significant risk of exceeding cost and time estimates.

Level 3: Defined

The organisation's set of standard processes, which is the basis for level 3, is established and improved over time. These standard processes are used to establish consistency across the organisation. Projects establish their defined processes by the organisation's set of standard processes according to tailoring guidelines.

A critical distinction between level 2 and level 3 is the scope of standards, process descriptions and procedures. At level 2, the standards, process descriptions and procedures may be quite different in each specific instance of the process. At level 3, the standards, process descriptions and procedures for a project are tailored from the organisation's set of standard processes to suit a particular project or organisational unit.

Level 4: Managed

Using precise measurements, management can effectively control the software development effort. In particular, management can identify ways to adjust and adapt the process to particular projects without measurable losses of quality or deviations from specifications. Organisations at this level set quantitative quality goals for both software process and software maintenance.

A critical distinction between maturity level 3 and maturity level 4 is the predictability of process performance. At maturity level 4, the performance of processes is controlled using statistical and other quantitative techniques and is quantitatively predictable. At maturity level 3, processes are only qualitatively predictable.

Level 5: Optimising

Maturity level 5 focuses on continually improving process performance through both incremental and innovative technological improvements. Quantitative process-improvement objectives for the organisation are established, continually revised to reflect changing business objectives, and used as criteria in managing process improvement. The effects of deployed process improvements are measured and evaluated against the quantitative process-improvement objectives. Both the defined processes and the organisation's set of standard processes are targets of measurable improvement activities.

A critical distinction between maturity level 4 and maturity level 5 is the type of process variation addressed. At maturity level 4, processes are concerned with addressing special causes of process variation and providing statistical predictability of the results. At maturity level 5, processes are concerned with addressing common causes of process variation and changing the process to improve process performance to achieve the established quantitative process-improvement objectives.

Benchmarking

According to Karlof and Ostblom (1994), benchmarking is a continuous and systematic process for comparing your own efficiency in terms of productivity, quality and best practices with those companies and organisations that represent excellence.

Dale (2007) suggests three main types of formal benchmarking:

- Internal benchmarking
- Competitive benchmarking
- Functional benchmarking

Internal benchmarking involves benchmarking between the same group of companies so that best practices are shared across the corporate business.

Competitive benchmarking relates to a comparison with direct competitors to gather data on 'best in class' performance and practices.

Functional benchmarking is a comparison of a specific process in different industries to obtain information on 'best in school' performance and practices.

Internal benchmarking is the easiest one of the three to carry out while competitive benchmarking is often the most difficult one to put into place. Organisations are usually keen to share data in functional benchmarking when there is no direct threat of competition.

A benchmarking process seeks to provide knowledge in a number of areas including:

1. What are the potential opportunities for improvement in our products or processes?
2. Who are the 'best in class' industry leaders in our competitive market?
3. How is our performance compared with those of industry leaders?

The above three objectives could be provided respectively by internal, competitive and functional benchmarking. The application areas usually depend on the type of benchmarking.

Internal benchmarking is widely used by a multinational business with a number of subsidiaries in different countries or a national business that operates with some kind of branch structure of divisions. In such cases, the business contains a number of similar operations that can be compared. GlaxoSmithKline uses internal benchmarking to compare key performance indicators and to identify potential cost savings in its business. The Foods Division of Unilever has used internal benchmarking to compare best-proven practices for each of its major manufacturing sites.

Establishing a benchmarking partnership with other competitors can be mutually beneficial to both parties for the purpose of positioning the company in the market. External consultants and industry associations often play a key role to set up and conduct benchmarking on competitive issues and opportunities such as e-commerce, purchasing commodity-type materials and customer-perceived quality.

The object of functional benchmarking is to identify the best practice wherever it may be found. The purpose is to benchmark a part of the business that displays a logical similarity, even in different industries. For example, a battery manufacturing company may want to benchmark its standard of direct delivery with Dell Computers, an organisation of acknowledged excellence in this area. Similarly, a pharmaceutical company may compare their production line changeover practices with Toyota Motors in Japan.

Summary

This chapter has addressed the various measures of performance including hard and soft measures and the selection of appropriate measures should depend on the specific supply

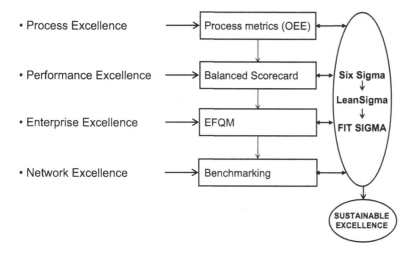

Figure 23.5 In search of excellence

chain of the organisation. The supply chain performance is also shown to be a process of integrating the building blocks and stakeholders of the total supply chain, and if each member of the process is efficient and dedicated to passing on a perfect delivery, the process as a whole will be efficient. It is accepted that few players in a supply chain can dominate or control another player. However, each player can strive to become more efficient in their activities. To become efficient, it is first necessary to know our existing level of performance and to identify gaps in performance. Various approaches for self-analysis were explained and illustrated. Analysis is the first step, improvement (getting fit) is the next and staying fit is the final stage. This chapter shows how FIT SIGMA can be used to maintain fitness. We concluded with a section on the importance of knowledge management.

The performance measurement metrics have to be designed separately for each company and supply chain. The performance measurement system should be based on the strategy, value drivers and important goals of the companies and the whole supply chain. There are several different approaches for global supply chain performance measurement. We suggest, as shown in Figure 23.5, the approach for supply chain excellence should be at the appropriate level of the global organisation.

Discussion questions

1. Discuss the basic operational objectives of supply chain performance management.
2. Explain the shift of criteria in managing global supply chains as compared with managing local supply chains.
3. Why is a balanced scorecard called balanced? Explain the four perspectives of the balanced scorecard suggested by Kaplan and Norton.
4. Discuss the key steps to implement a balanced scorecard in a global manufacturing company. Suggest high-level KPIs covering four perspectives.
5. Discuss the six pillars of measuring total operations solutions. Explain why the 20 foundation stones of six pillars are vital for a 'holistic health check' of an organisation.

6. Discuss the components of EFQM and explain how EFQM can be applied in an organisation for both self-assessment and an EFQN award.

7. What is SCOR? Describe its five levels of application. Discuss the advantages and disadvantages of applying SCOR to measure supply chain performance.

8. A major European logistics business employing over 10,000 staff and operating in ten countries wishes to implement a performance management system based on the principles of the balanced scorecard. What are the key performance indicators (not more than ten) that you would recommend? Outline the key steps for implementing the Balanced Scorecard.

9. The EFQM Excellence model enables an organisation to carry out periodic self-assessments and review its business processes and results. Show how you would use the model and methodology in:
   a) Continuous self-assessment in a multi-site manufacturing company.
   b) Establishing best practices in a government department
   c) Monitoring the progress of a Six Sigma programme in a multinational organisation containing both manufacturing and service operations.

10. A privatised national carrier implemented ISO 9000:2000 in selected departments. The management of the organisation is considering the next step to roll out EFQM in all departments. Explain how you would implement the transition and roll out.

11. You are a management consultant with particular expertise in the continuous improvement of all types of business. Recommend the appropriate tools for improving the performance of the following operations:
   a) A small insurance company.
   b) The production line of a medium-sized manufacturing company.
   c) A large multinational pharmaceutical company.
   d) A high street bank.

24 Case study examples

Introduction

In the preceding three chapters, we aimed to establish how systems and procedures (Chapter 21), sales and operations planning (Chapter 22) and performance management (Chapter 23) act as integrators of the building blocks of total supply chain management. In this chapter, we illustrate the interdependency of the building blocks with two case studies. The first case study is based on the experience of a pharmaceutical company in dealing with all aspects of supply chain management by applying appropriate good practices relevant to each building block. The second case study is a variation of the well-known beer game (Senge, 1990) to illustrate how the stakeholders (e.g. factory, warehouse, distributor and retailer) are dependent on the forecasts, processes and inventories of one another. The third case study is on Dyson. The fourth case study illustrates the application of Six Sigma to improve the processes and supply chain effectiveness in a major climate change initiative for a large solar energy installation in California.

Case study 1. Total supply chain case study

Background

A multinational pharmaceutical company in Turkey (hereinafter referred to as 'the company') was awarded MRPII 'Class A' certification in 1999 by business education consultants Oliver Wight Europe. The application of sustainable behavioural and performance metrics was applied to monitor and facilitate the attainment of MRPII to Class A status.

As part of the MRP II Class A programme, GSK Turkey installed a sales & operations planning (S&OP) process that is underpinned by a set of business planning meetings at various levels. The company went through major changes following the 'Class A' award, including the global merger with another multinational pharmaceutical company and the corporate lean sigma programme. In spite of these seismic changes, the S&OP process has been continued by the company every month.

The rigour of the S&OP process, which is championed by the managing director, has helped the company to sustain and improve the business benefits and communication culture, especially when they were challenged by a number of local initiatives in hand, including:

- Transfer of the head office.
- Rationalisation of factory and warehouse.
- New product introduction.
- Mobile network for the sales force.

DOI: 10.4324/9781003341352-28

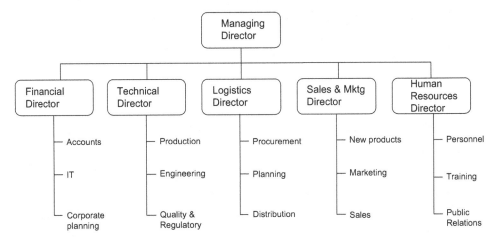

Figure 24.1 Company organisation chart

The organisational structure of the company in general remained the same with some changes in personnel after the merger (see Figure 24.1).

Project scenario

However, the situation was quite different with the company in the late 1990s. During the growth period of a blockbuster drug, a manufacturing plant was installed in 1984 at Gebze, an industrial town approximately 80 km from the head office in Istanbul. The Gebze factory gradually expanded to accommodate manufacturing and secondary packing facilities for antibiotics and tertiary packaging of imported corporate products for the local market. By the beginning of 1997, the Gebze factory was producing nearly 25% of the company turnover of over US$100 million. A distribution warehouse was built in 1992 at the Gebze site and this was managed by the logistics department of the company. With the assistance of a local software consulting firm, the IT department implemented the financial module and limited planning modules of an ERP system called *MFG-Pro*. Although the company was enjoying a period of growth both the internal communication and external customer service were not satisfactory. Some of the problems and challenges were as follows:

*   The customer order fill was only around 85%, while the stock cover was over six months.
*   The communication and interpersonal relationship between the head office (Istanbul) and the factory (Gebze) was poor.
*   The distribution warehouse appeared to require additional storage capacity and modernisation.
*   Although an ERP system (*MFG-Pro*) was operational, it was not effective because of poor data accuracy and a lack of understanding of the functionality.
*   The company depended heavily on the supply from Corporate Export (based in Ware, England), which could not assess the priority of the company in Turkey.

- The corporate global supply chain programme (which required Y2K-enabled 'legacy' or new systems) demanded considerable resources from the company in Turkey.

The challenges were compounded by an audit report by the US Food and Drug Administration (FDA). During an audit of the computer systems of a European factory supplying to the US market, the FDA issued a warning (Form 483) regarding the batch validation of the MRP (materials requirement) system of the factory. The corporate quality division mandated that all sites with links to the US market must conform to the validation policy for MRP systems while other sites (such as Gebze) were recommended to follow the policy.

Following a request from the logistics director of the company in Turkey, the corporate Business Excellence Group from Stockley Park, UK, visited Turkey, and carried out a feasibility study and put forward the following recommendations in September 1997:

1. Changes:
   - Implement a company-wide sales & operations planning process (see Figure 24.2) supported by appropriate training
   - Re-engineer the manufacturing resource planning (MRPII) process according to company requirements.
   - Update *MFG-Pro* planning modules to comply with re-engineered MRPII requirements and validation guidelines.
   - Install a performance management process to work towards MRPII Class A standards.
2. Time scale:
   - *MFG-Pro* will have to be Y2K enabled by the end of 1999.
   - The work on Business Process Excellence and MRPII processes is expected to take 18 months leading to MRPII Class A

Figure 24.2 Project organisation

3. Cost:
   - US$50,000 will be available from a corporate fund to ensure the validation of Y2K compliance of *MFG-Pro*.
   - The training, consulting and other costs for the Business Process Excellence project are expected to be self-financing and supported by the company in Turkey

Project launch

The company in Turkey launched a programme (known as EKIP) in January 1998 to improve company-wide communications and sustain a robust business planning process using MRPII 'best practice' principles.

The logistics director was involved in an MRPII Class A project when he was previously working in Bristol Myer Squibs and was appointed as the project manager for EKIP. He invited two consultants from Oliver Wight (OW) Group, who are known to be specialists in MRPII processes to run a two-day training workshop for managers. The OW consultants advised the following:

- Set up a project team with specific task groups for S&OP, demand management, production planning, *MFG-Pro* update, quality and validation, performance management and training and communication.
- To achieve MRPII Class A, the company should fulfil performance criteria (e.g. order fill 95%, BOM accuracy 99%, MPS performance 95%, supplier delivery performance 95%, inventory record accuracy 99%), the MRPII process integrated with the software *MFG-Pro* and a sustainable S&OP process.

The logistics director decided that after the OW training workshop, the company will do everything themselves except the software support from a local consulting firm to update *MFG-Pro*.

Corporate review

The supply chain problem escalated, and the logistics director had to spend more time troubleshooting day-to-day operations. In three months, there was little progress with the EKIP except for some Y2 K-related systems specifications for *MFG-Pro* and the formation of task groups. The relations between the logistics team at the head office and the production team at Gebze deteriorated further.

A key member of the Corporate Manufacturing and Supply Strategy Group from England reviewed the status of Project EKIP and recommended a full-time project manager, a revised organisation and a road map to Class A for GW Turkey. The logistics director continued as part of the steering team and continued to be a key player in the success of the project.

Implementation

Following the recommendations of the corporate review, the first task was to appoint a full-time project manager. After considering candidates from production, engineering, logistics, IT, finance and sister companies, a management accountant was chosen to lead the project. The primary criteria of selection included project management experience, business knowledge and leadership qualities. With some guidance from the corporate Business Excellence Group, a project definition report was prepared as summarised below:

PROJECT EKIP

Project definition report

Purpose

To install a performance management process to work towards MRPII Class A standards.

To update the ERP system (*MFG-Pro*) to comply with validation guidelines, Y2K compliance and re-engineered MRPII requirements.

Scope

The project will include:

- Re-engineering of MRPII process according to company requirements.
- A company-wide S&OP process supported by appropriate training.
- Updating of *MFG-Pro* to comply with FDA validation, Y2K and re-engineered planning modules.
- Development of a balanced scorecard.

Excluded from the scope of work are:

- Rationalisation of factory and warehouse.
- Transfer of head office.
- Corporate global supply chain project.
- Y2K compliance of other legacy systems.

Objectives

The project will be executed with minimum disruption to existing business.

MFG-Pro will be updated and Y2K enabled by the end of 1999.

The S&OP process will be operational by September 1998.

MRPII Class A award will be targeted by April 1999.

The employees will receive sustainable training and education to support the process in the longer run.

Product breakdown

The product breakdown structure of Project EKIP comprised:

- S&OP process
- Demand management
- Master production schedule and capacity planning
- Bill of materials and procurement
- Manufacturing and distribution
- Quality management, risk/change control and process validation
- Balanced scorecard
- Education, training and communication
- *MFG-Pro* systems

Life Cycle

Project EKIP comprises two streams of project life cycle:

Business process excellence

*   Definition
    Project definition report
    Initial education
    Project launch
*   Organisation
    Project organisation structure
    Project plan
    Training
*   Implementation
    S&OP meetings
    MRPII re-engineering
    Balanced scorecard
    MFG-Pro interface
    Education and communication
*   Closure
    MRPII Class A audit
    Award ceremony

ERP Systems

*   Definition
    Systems functionality
    Regulatory requirements
    Y2K requirements
*   Organisation
    Systems design
    Systems customisation
    User training
    MRPII business process interface
*   Implementation
    Conference room piloting
    Systems cut-over
    Validation
*   Closure
    Handover
    Operational manual
    Systems support

Execution Strategy

External support

*   *MFG-Pro* development by a local software company.
*   S&OP initial training by Oliver Wight.

- Y2K modification by a local software company.
- Two audits and Class A awards by Oliver Wight.

Corporate Support
- Part of steering team
- Business process training
- Balanced scorecard development
- Validation guidelines

Local Support
- All other activities
- Project management
- Steering team, project team and task teams

The project organisation (see Figure 24.2) comprised a steering team headed by a 'torch bearer' (managing director) and project team led by the project manager and a supporting task team. The project team consisted of the project manager and leaders from each task team. The steering team members were mostly the company board members and the project manager and the business excellence director from the centre. Steering team members also act as 'mentors' of task teams according to their functional responsibilities. The progress of the project was reviewed every week by the project team and every four to six weeks by the steering team. The project deliverables were accomplished in time including the Y2K deadline and the development of a balanced scorecard. The critical success factors were the total commitment of the top management, continuous education of task teams, robust communication with stakeholders and a good interface between the business requirements and software (*MFG-Pro*).

Ongoing process and sustainability

The achievement of MRPII Class A did set the foundation for continuously improving and sustaining supply chain performance. The key drivers of this process were S&OP meetings supported by balanced scorecard and business planning cycle. The company also retained a core team from the project for continuous training of employees and cost-effectiveness projects. When the lean sigma initiative from the centre was rolled out to the company in Turkey, both the core team and the company culture were ready for it. Selected members of the staff were trained as 'Black Belts' (called Experts) and 'Green Belts' (called Advocates) and many projects were identified and implemented. Lean sigma pushed the performance boundaries achieved by Class A and, for example, 95% customer service level was aiming high towards 'perfect orders' with service level of at least 99%. During the consolidation of the merger process, there was a temporary lull in lean sigma activities for about three months and after the re-organisation of the programme team, the second wave of training and new projects was launched.

The projects in lean sigma also included the concept of lean and agile supply chains. The company in Turkey was designated as the supply hub for specific therapeutic product groups for the Middle East and North African market. One such product group is Cephalosporin (antibiotics). The countries in the region had different secondary and tertiary packs and also leaflets in their respective languages. The secondary pack sizes were standardised depending on the dose form and lean manufacturing principles were applied and semi-finished products were produced to stock according to the regulatory shelf life of products. The finished products were scheduled as per confirmed orders from each country of the region and appropriate tertiary packaging and leaflets in country languages were assembled as per order. The average lead time was reduced from 120 days to 27 days.

In the light of FDA recommendations, SAP R/3 replaced *MFG-Pro* software after two years and the global supply chain system driven by 'Manugistics' was linked with the ERP system of SAP R/3. The company in Turkey was able to participate in the CPFR process with Corporate Manufacturing and Supply in Brentford (UK) and other manufacturing sites in the global supply chain network. The company also established EDI links with a number of key local suppliers. Some key local suppliers were also sometimes included in S&OP meetings by invitation.

The company is also working with corporate R&D to incorporate environmental, health and safety considerations into the design of new products through environmental health and safety (EHS) staff participation in and support for new product teams, and through the use of the Eco-design Toolkit. EHS involvement in the new product teams also provides a unique opportunity to influence supply chain decisions and highlight systemic EHS issues early in the product development process. The Eco-design Toolkit is available on the corporate intranet and includes a green chemistry and technology guide, a materials guide and a green packaging guide. The company also provides oversight and audit of EHS issues with the support of experts from the centre for critical suppliers and contract manufacturers of materials that are used exclusively by the company.

Terminology

BOM	Bill of materials
CPFR	Collaborative planning forecasting and replenishment
EHS	Environment health and safety
ERP	Enterprise resource planning
FDA	Food and Drug Administration
MPS	Master production schedule
MRPI	Manufacturing resource planning
OW	Oliver Wight
Y2K	Year 2000

Questions for total supply chain case study

1. Following the slow start of Project EKIP, your team has been asked to visit Turkey three months after the project launch to review the status of the project and develop your project organisation. You could consider the following:
   a) Project organisation chart.
      * Steering team
      * Project team
      * Project manager
      * Task teams
   b) Who should be the project manager?

    c)   What are the task teams and their deliverables?

    d)   Outline a time plan in a Gantt chart.

    e)   Roles of external and internal consultants.

2. What are the critical success factors of Project EKIP? Discuss how the success of the EKIP project helped the company in Turkey to improve and sustain supply chain performance.

3. On the basis of your analysis of the total supply chain case study, critically review to what extent the company in Turkey fulfilled the best practices of supply chain building blocks with particular reference to:

- Systems and procedure
- Sales and operation planning
- Performance management
- Lean and agile supply chains
- Green supply chain

More questions for total supply chains:

> 1. What are the key requirements of a quality management plan for Project EKIP leading to a successful implementation of *MFG-Pro* and MRPII Class A?
> 2. What are the additional regulatory requirements for GlaxoWellcome?
> 3. Discuss how MRPII Class A may ensure a regular review of holistic self-assessment.

Case study 2. Beer game

The beer game is a role-playing simulation developed at MIT in the 1960s to clarify the advantages of taking an integrated approach to managing the supply chain; it particularly demonstrates the value of sharing information across the various supply chain components. This simulation was further illustrated in the concepts of systems thinking and integrated learning organisations in Senge's 'Fifth Discipline' (1990).

    Essentially, the beer game is a simplified supply chain consisting of a single retailer, a single wholesaler that supplies the retailer, a single distributor that supplies the wholesaler and a single factory with unlimited raw materials that supplies the distributor. Each component in the supply chain has unlimited storage capacity, and there is a fixed supply lead time and order delay time between each component. In the beer game, each player manages one of the supply chain components. Each week, the retailer observes external demand, fills that demand, if possible, records backorders to be filled and places an order with the wholesaler. Each of the other components also observes the demand, fills the demand, if possible, records the backorder situation and places an order, or in the case of the factory, schedules production. As a result of a change in external demand, the whole supply chain has to react to this change. Order processing and filling delays are built into the simulation, which causes the delay in the system. As a result, the players tend to over-order, especially when in a backlog situation. As a result, the system appears to experience widely oscillating demand that is amplified as we move further up the supply chain. Thus, inventory and backorder levels usually vary dramatically from week to week during the game. At the end, players instinctively blame the other players for causing the situation. What they don't accept is that the system itself was capable of reacting in a way that they did not expect. In effect, the beer game demonstrates the phenomenon known as the 'bullwhip' effect.

There are various versions and hybrids of the beer game in the public domain. Our aim in this case study is to demonstrate with the aid of a simple distribution operation (Charlie's warehouse), how the systems dynamics of the supply chain behave in a controlled environment.

Charlie was driving home after a stimulating MBA workshop. The lecturer had begun a session on supply chain management by saying that 'the dynamic nature of the supply chain is evident in the changing nature of the structure of the supply chain and in the day-to-day activities of the players. In a typical supply chain, each participant can create disturbances, either independently or in response to actions taken elsewhere within the supply chain. These disturbances frequently create a chain reaction'. To demonstrate this latter phenomenon, the lecturer introduced the workshop members to the 'beer game'. In the game, the members were assigned roles and participated in a simulation of a simple production and distribution system.

There is no real beer in the beer game, and it does not promote drinking, though it generally leads to some robust exchanges between participants. The lecturer observed 'What is interesting about the beer game is that it has been played so many times, yet the patterns of behaviour generated in the game are remarkably similar'.

Charlie pondered on what he had learnt from the analysis and discussion at the end of the game and considered how he could apply this new-found knowledge to his own operation.

Charlie's operation

Charlie is the operations manager of a wholesaler that supplies 50-plus retailers. The products stocked come under the heading of personal hygiene. There is a range of 220 products (line items). Products are received from several distributors and, in some cases, directly from the manufacturer. There are three main distributors (accounting for 80% of the product lines and about 78% of the demand). There are 20 other distributors plus two factories that supply direct to Charlie. The major distributors are in competition with each other as their products are very similar and, in some cases, the only perceptible difference is the brand name. Two of the distributors are sourced from the one factory, Busby and Co.

There is no seasonal demand by consumers, in fact, retailers have advised Charlie that consumer demand is almost constant, that is, there is no particular day or month in which demand for any of the products is markedly higher or lower than any other day or month. Although Charlie accepts what the retailers say, nonetheless, he has never been able to understand why the size of orders from retailers fluctuate to the extent that they do. Over a 12-month period, the total demand is 52,000, which Charlie would have expected would give an average demand of 1000 per week, but in reality, for some weeks, retailer's orders can be as high as 4000 (and this high demand might last for two or even three weeks), and in other weeks, the demand is almost nothing. Charlie tries to keep sufficient stock on hand so that he can satisfy a retailer's order within two days. There is a two-week lead time from the larger distributors, but from the two direct supply factories and some of the smaller distributors, the lead time can be up to four weeks.

Charlie uses a computerised spreadsheet and records on a daily basis the amount of stock on hand for each line item, the amount received and the date, the amount ordered and the date of order, the amount issued and the amount of any backorders. From this information, the computer automatically

- Calculates the average past lead time to replenish stock for each line item,
- The average demand calculated from the last four weeks' demand, and
- E-mails an order to the distributors and the two direct supply factories.

The computer allows one week of 'safety' stock in its calculation of the amount ordered. For example, one of the largest distributors is XTRA. XTRA is very reliable and when an order is placed, they will generally supply within two weeks. Thus, the computer calculates that for an XTRA product, when the stock level drops to the computer's calculation of three weeks' demand, the computer will automatically trigger an order on XTRA after deducting any stock already on order. The assumption being that the stock will be received from XTRA within two weeks and thus the stock level will not drop below the safety level of one week's demand. Similar calculations are made for automatic ordering on all the other distributors and on the two factories that supply directly to Charlie.

A problem occurred three months ago when one of the larger distributors POISE Limited announced a price rise. The retailers learnt of the impending price rise before Charlie did, and there was some panic ordering by many of the retailers. As a result, Charlie ran out of stock for almost one-third of the line items. POISE Limited took six weeks to deliver new stock. By then, most of the retailers wanted to cancel their backorders.

Due to the fluctuations in order size, Charlie finds he has either too much stock or not sufficient stock to meet the desired two-day turnaround of orders. Seldom does he have the desired level of stock for all line items; some will be badly overstocked and there will be stock-outs for other items. Another problem is people. Charlie has eight warehouse staff. Some days they have little to do, and at other times, he has to ask them to work overtime. Staff turnover is high, and new staff make mistakes. There is also some degree of stock 'shrinkage' and Charlie suspects this is due to theft by staff.

Amos the accountant has advised Charlie that bank interest rates have increased and that the landlord is asking for a 15% rent increase. The accountant has calculated that if Charlie can reduce stock holding by 10% that it will be possible to sublet part of the warehouse and thus reduce overhead costs. The accountant also suggests that Charlie could reduce the number of staff he employs and suggests that the two-day delivery target to the retailers could be changed to five days, Amos adds that 'you are paying too much in overtime'.

Charlie decides to do some calculations. His figures are shown below.

CHARLIE'S WAREHOUSE

Distributor

XTRA	POISE	JANES	OTHERS	TOTAL
Annual demand (units)				
14,000	12,500	15,100	10,400	52,000

Average delivery lead time
(5-day work week)

| 10 days | 15 days | 12 days | 13 days | 12.4 days |

Stock on hand (units)
(as at **today**)

| 1200 | 100 | 1900 | 1600 | 4800 |

Total desired maximum stockholding =
5 days 'safety' plus 12.4 days re-order =   17.4 days
Total desired minimum stockholding =   5 days
Desired average stockholding =   11.2 days

Questions for the beer game

1. Consider and suggest reasons for the fluctuations in demand for Charlie's warehouse.
2. Charlie is a customer of the distributors. Consider how Charlie would measure their performance. Compare Charlie's service requirements to the service he aims to give to his customers, the retailers.

Charlie is only one component of the supply chain. Consider how using shared electronic information could benefit the major members of this supply chain. In your answer, consider the benefits and dangers of sharing information with other components of a supply chain, bearing in mind that some components are serious competitors.

Case Study 3: Dyson vacuum cleaners (adapted from Marsh 2005)

It is impossible to separate the very British Dyson vacuum cleaner from its very British inventor. Together, they are synonymous with innovation, as well as legal battles against established rivals like Electrolux, Bosch-Siemens, Miele, Whirlpool and Hoover (Maytag and Candy SpA).

James Dyson was born in Norfolk in 1947. He studied furniture design and interior design at the Royal College of Art from 1966 to 1970 and his first product, the Sea Truck, was launched while he was still a student.

Early development

Dyson's foray into developing vacuum cleaner technology happened by chance. In 1978, while renovating his 300-year-old country house, Dyson became frustrated with the poor performance of his conventional vacuum cleaner. Whenever he went to use it, there was a disappointing level of suction. One day, he decided to take the machine apart in order to find out what was wrong with the design. He noted that the appliance worked by drawing air through the bag to create suction, but when even a fine layer of dust got inside, it clogged its pores, stopping the airflow and inhibiting suction. In his usual style of seeking solutions from unexpected sources, Dyson noticed how a nearby sawmill used a cyclone – a 30-foot-high cone that spun dust out of the air by centrifugal force – to expel waste. He reasoned that a vacuum cleaner could separate dust by cyclonic action using the same principle. This would spin dust out of the airstream that would, in turn, eliminate the need for both a bag and filter. James Dyson set out to replicate the cyclonic system he had observed working successfully at the sawmill and to apply it to a domestic context.

Over the next eight years, Dyson tried to license his dual cyclone concept to established vacuum manufacturers, only to be turned down. At least two of these initial contacts forced him to file patent infringement lawsuits, which he won in out-of-court and in-court settlements. Finally, in 1985, a small company in Japan contacted him out of the blue after seeing a picture of his vacuum cleaner in a magazine. Mortgaged to the hilt and on the brink of bankruptcy, Dyson took the cheapest flight to Tokyo to negotiate a deal. The result was the G Force vacuum cleaner, priced at US$2000, which became the ultimate domestic appliance status symbol in Japan. In June 1993, using money from the Japanese licence, Dyson opened a research centre and factory in Malmesbury, Wiltshire. Here he developed the Dyson Dual Cyclone and within two years it was the fastest-selling vacuum cleaner in the UK.

Dyson went on to develop the Root 8 Cyclone, which removes more dust by using eight cyclones instead of two. In 2000, he launched the Contrarotator washing machine, which uses two drums spinning in opposite directions and is said to wash faster and with better results than traditional washing machines. In 2005, the company's sales reached £470 million, roughly two-thirds of which came from outside the UK, while pre-tax profit for the year was £103 million, up 32% on 2004. Almost all the sales come from vacuum cleaners – a product through which Dyson has built large sales in the United States, Japan and Australia.

Initially, Dyson was nearly bankrupted by the legal costs of establishing and protecting his patent. His journey has been a remarkable one, from a frustrated product user to a man whose innovation is as eponymous as the Hoover. It took him more than 14 years to get his first product into a shop – this can be seen on display in the Science Museum, London. Other Dyson products can be viewed in the Victoria & Albert Museum, the San Francisco Museum of Modern Art and the Georges Pompidou Centre in Paris.

Marketing

Dyson believes the most effective marketing tool is word of mouth, and today the company claims 70% of its vacuum cleaners are sold on personal recommendation. An enthusiastic self-publicist, Dyson believes that if you make something, you should sell it yourself, so he often appears in his own advertisements. He also holds true to his no-nonsense, factual manner. When a Belgian court banned Dyson from denigrating old-style vacuum cleaner bags, he was pictured wearing his trademark blue shirt and holding a Dyson vacuum cleaner in a press advertisement that had the word 'bag' blacked out several times. A note at the bottom said: 'Sorry, but the Belgian courts won't let you know what everyone has a right to know'.

Dyson has sometimes shunned advertising altogether. For example, in 1996–1997 the company spent its marketing budget sponsoring Sir Ranulph Fiennes' solo expedition to Antarctica and gave £1.5 million to the charity Breakthrough Breast Cancer. As rivals started to manufacture their own bagless cleaners, Dyson knew he would have to advertise more aggressively and in 2000 he appointed an advertising agency to promote the business. The marketing strategy, however, remains loyal to Dyson's original principles, with an emphasis on information and education rather than brand-building. Moreover, it seems to be working, as one in every three vacuum cleaners bought in Britain today is a Dyson.

The use of vacuum cleaners is largely related to national preferences for carpets rather than floor tiles. In many warm countries, floor tiles are more usual instead of carpets, and these can be swept rather than vacuumed. In regions where houses are predominantly carpeted, such as in Northern Europe, Eastern Europe and North America, the number of households owning vacuum cleaners is high. In 2005, approximately 95% of households owned vacuum cleaners in Belgium, Germany, Japan, the Netherlands, Sweden, the United States and the UK. Indeed, many Belgian households possess more than one vacuum cleaner, as traditional versions are often complemented with hand-held cleaners or cleanettes. In parts of Eastern Europe, it is also common to carpet walls, which provides additional demand for vacuum cleaners. However, few products are sold in China and India. Vacuum cleaners have only been available in China for ten years, but ownership has not become widespread. In India, many of the rural population do not have the means for such appliances and the power supply is erratic.

Latest developments

In recent years, one of the most significant developments in the market has been that of bagless technology. Dyson UK pioneered its dual cyclone technology back in 1993 and its technology is protected by patent; however, other manufacturers were quick to develop their own bagless versions. In the United States, bagless vacuum cleaners increased their market share from just 2.6% in 1998 to over 20% in 2005.

Dyson has decided to move most of its vacuum cleaner production from the UK to the Far East (Malaysia). Although Dyson is still a leading vacuum cleaner brand, it is beginning to lose out to cheaper machines that have developed their own bagless technology.

The dilemma Dyson faces is between dropping its own prices or reinforcing the power and quality of its brand. The loyalty of Dyson's customers has dropped off and the company's market share in the UK by volume has also decreased.

Besides vacuum cleaners, Dyson is also trying to make headway in washing machines, an industry with global annual sales of £15 billion and with big competitors including Whirlpool of the United States and Japan's Matsushita. Dyson gained success in vacuum cleaners through high price and stylish machines that featured a new way of sucking up dirt without a bag, which appealed to consumers' desire to try something new. Then, in 2000, Dyson unveiled a novel type of washing machine – called the 'Contrarotator' because it featured two drums spinning in opposite directions. Despite this innovation, the design faced a manufacturing challenge. Most industry analysts say that the complexity of manufacturing washing machines, which feature a host of sophisticated mechanisms including pumps and motors that have to work reliably, is a lot higher than for the relatively simple design of a vacuum cleaner. Dyson's washing machine is very expensive, retailing at more than £500, or twice the price of a standard washing machine sold in the UK. And whether consumers will pay significantly extra for a new design – even if its performance is better – is open to question.

Questions for Dyson

1. In spite of his talent for invention, James Dyson nearly went bankrupt until rescued by a Japanese company. What are the key learning points from the development of the Dyson Dual Cyclone vacuum cleaner?

2. Until now Dyson has concentrated its efforts in the UK, the United States, Japan and Australia. In your opinion, which new international and emerging markets should be allocated more marketing resources in order to develop them into global markets?

3. In order to develop, produce and distribute Dyson products in the global market, suggest an action plan, taking into account global supply chain management principles, to roll out the products and services.

Case study 4: Six Sigma Ivanpah Solar Electric Generating System

The Ivanpah Solar Electric Generating System in California was the first mega project in the United States to combat the consequences of climate change or global warming created by fossil fuels. On October 27, 2010, the then Governor of California, Arnold Schwarzenegger, himself a proponent of green energy, and other dignitaries gathered in the Mojave Desert to break the ground for the construction.

The Ivanpah Solar Electric Generating System in California is the largest solar energy facility in the world and was a joint venture of Bechtel and BrightSource. Bechtel was founded in California and is now headquartered in Virginia. It is the largest project management and construction company in the United States. It is the first global project management organisation that has used Six Sigma to deliver many major projects to customers. BrightSource Energy is also based in California and designs, develops and deploys solar thermal technology to produce high-value electricity for power markets worldwide.

Ivanpah was considered an appropriate venture for applying Six Sigma because the scheme had a budget of £2.4 billion over several years and Ivanpah had a lot of repetitive operations. The project was operationally challenging, requiring the design, construction and installation of around 173,500 large heliostats. A heliostat is a device that includes a mirror, usually a plane mirror, which turns to keep reflecting sunlight towards a predetermined target.

In this project, each heliostat is the size of a garage door and consists of two mirrors mounted on a post that tracks the sun throughout the day to direct sunlight to boilers or solar receiver steam generators (SRSG). The sunlight heats the water inside the boilers to create superheated steam, which then generates electricity. The delivery of over 173,500 heliostats requires a complex assembly process with components sourced from different specialist suppliers.

Bechtel's project team joined with engineering and construction experts from BrightSource to form a Six Sigma group and all colleagues went through the Black Belt and Green Belt training programme together. The team identified six areas for process improvements by using Six Sigma: supply chain management, material handling, heliostat assembly, field transportation, heliostat installation and tower erection. In each of these spheres, especially in heliostat assembly, the team found new or more efficient ways of achieving results. For example, by using Six Sigma, tool group members managed to redesign a stable process that would enable craftsmen to assemble 500 heliostats per day. The Six Sigma philosophy of 'continuous improvement' also carried over to the daily work of craftsmen.

All the processes involved in the heliostats including transportation had to be developed from scratch. The kind of project complexity and supply chain requirements embedded in the Ivanpah project was a good fit for the Six Sigma approach. Bechtel used Six Sigma tools and processes to address the design, procurement and construction challenges of heliostats. The result was the development of new procedures that helped to meet sustainable performance goals and execute the project successfully. Six Sigma methodology was also instrumental in ensuring teamwork among project group members while simultaneously building trust and credibility with stakeholders.

The Six Sigma philosophy of 'continuous improvement' also carried over into their daily work. Craft would have competitions to see which teams could insert the most pylons or build and install the most heliostats in a day according to project specifications. These competitions created a tremendous sense of team spirit and pride in their work. Craft participation in the Six Sigma process was critical and led to discretionary effort that strengthened customer satisfaction throughout the build.

The additional input of Green Six Sigma will ensure the sustainability of the process and also sustainable environmental standards. The sustainability of the processes will be achieved by embedding sustaining processes, such as performance management, knowledge management, self-assessment and senior management reviews. The sustainable environmental standards will be achieved by Green Six Sigma tools, such as Material Flow Analysis, Carbon Foot Print Tool and Circular Economy.

Questions for the solar energy project

1. What are the driving forces for a £2.4 billion mega project such as the Ivanpah Solar Electric Generating System in California?
2. Why was Six Sigma applied to improve the processes and supply chain effectiveness of the project?
3. Discuss how Green Six Sigma could add additional value to the outcomes of the project.

References

Alicke, K., Karlsson, P. and Hoberg, K. (2016), 'Big data and the Supply Chain: The big supply chain analytics landscape', *McKinsey Quarterly*, February 2016, Seattle.

Alicke, K, Barriball, E, Foster, T, Mauhourat, E and Trautwein, V (2022), *Tacking the Pulse of Shifting Supply Chains*, McKinsey Global Publishing, Seattle

Amann, W. and Ionescu-Somers, A. (2006), '*Hindustan Lever: Leaping a Millenium*', Class Discussion Paper, Henley Management College, Oxfordshire

AMR Research (2001), *Beyond CPFR: Collaboration Comes of Age* Association of Management, Yonkers, NY.

Association of Project Management (2004), *Body of Knowledge*, Fourth Edition, Association of Project Managers, High Wycombe, UK

Ballard, G. (2001), 'Cycle time reduction in home building', The Proceedings of the 9th Annual Conference of the International Group for Lean Construction, Singapore, August 2001

Barnatt, C. (2001), 'The second digital revolution', *Journal of General Management*, Vol.27, No.2, pp. 1–16

Barsodi, R. (1929), *The Distribution Age*, Arno Press, New York

Basu, R. (2001), 'The new criteria of performance measurement', *Measuring Business Excellence*, MCB Press, Vol.5, No.4, 2001, pp. 7–12

Basu, R. (2002), *Measuring eBusiness in the Pharmaceutical Sector*, London, Reuters

Basu, R. (2004), *Implementing Quality*, Thomson, London

Basu, R. (2009), *Implementing Six Sigma and Lean*, Elsevier, Oxford

Basu, R. and Wright, J.N. (2003), *Quality Beyond Six Sigma*, Butterworth Heinemann, Oxford.

Basu, R. and Wright, J.N. (2004), *Total Operations Solutions*, Butterworth Heinemann, Oxford.

Basu, R. (2001), *Six Sigma to Fit Sigma*, IE Solutions, Atlanta, July 2001.

Basu, R., and Wright, J.N. (2005), *Total Operations Solutions*, Elsevier, Oxford

Basu, R. (2003), *Measuring e-Business*, Reuters, London

Basu, R. (2011a), *FIT SIGMA: A Lean Approach to Building Sustainable Quality Beyond Six Sigma*, John Wiley & Sons, Chichester, UK

Basu, R. (2011b), *Managing Project Supply Chains*, Gower Publishing, UK (now Routledge, UK)

Basu, R. (2012), *Managing Quality in Projects*, Gower Publishing, UK (now Routledge, UK)

Basu, R. and Wright, J.N. (1997), *Total Manufacturing Solutions*, Butterworth Heinemann

Basu, R. (2022), *Green Six Sigma: A Lean Approach to Sustainable Climate Change Initiatives*, John Willey & Sons, Chichester

Basu, R, Little, C and Millard, C (2009), 'Case study: A fresh approach of balanced scorecard in the heathrow terminal 5 project', *Measuring Business Excellence*, Vl.13, No.4, pp. 22–33.

BBC News 12 January 2003

Blackstone, J.H. (2013), *APICS Dictionary*, Chicago, IL

Booz Allen Hamilton (2006), (M Sanderson, P Doshi and C K Szymanowska), *Lessons from the Shop Floor: Applying Sales & Operations Planning to Financial Services*

Breggren, C (1993), *The Volvo Experience*, MacMillan Press, Basingstoke, UK

Bruntland Commission on Environment and Development (1987), *Our Common Future Report*, United Nations, New York

Burke, R. (2004), *Project Management*, John Wiley & Sons, Hoboken

Capgemini (2005), *Trends in Project Performance Improvement*, Capgemini Netherlands, Utrecht, Summer 2005

Capgemini (2009), 'Global Sales & Operations Planning', www.capgemini.com/resources/global_sales_and_operation_planning

Capgemini (2011), *Digital Transformation of Supply Chains*, Capgemini Consulting, London

Capgemini Ernst and Young (2003), *'The State of the Art in Food' Report*. USA

CAPS Research (2003), *Managing Your Service Spend in Today's Services Economy*, CAPS Research, Tempe, AZ

Catherwood and Van Kirk (1992), Center For Advanced Purchasing Studies (CAPS), Arizona, USA

Chamania, A, Mehra, H and Sehgal, V (2010), 'Five Factors of Finding the Right Site', *Strategy and Business, Issue* 61, pp. 11–17

Chan, F.T.S. and Qi, H.J. (2003), 'An Innovative Performance Measurement Method for Supply Chain Management', *Supply Chain Management: An International Journal*, Vol. 8, No.3–4, pp. 209–23.

China Technews (2007), www.chinatechnews.com retrieved April 2007

Chopra, S. and Meindl, P (2016). *Supply Chain Management: Strategy, Planning and Operations*, Prentice Hall

Christian Salvesen, UK (2002), for further information www.salvesen.com/business/central

Christopher, M. (1992), *Logistics and Supply Chain Management*, Pitman Publishing

Christopher, M. (2000), 'The Agile Supply Chain', *Industrial Marketing Management*, Vol. 29, pp. 37–44.

Churchman, C.W., Ackoff, R.L. and Arnoff, E.L. (1968), *Introduction to Operations Research*, J. Wiley & Sons, New York

Council of Supply Chain Management Professionals (2015), *26th Annual State of Logistics Report*, CSCMP, Illinois

Cremer, D.D. and Kasparov, G. (2021), 'AI Should Augment Human Intelligence, Not Replace It', *Harvard Business Review* Website, 18 March, 2021

Cunnane, C. (2018), *The Impact of Economic Nationalism on Global Supply Chains*, Logistics Viewpoints, Dedham, Massachusetts

Darnell, N., Jolley, J and Handfield, R. (2008), 'Environment Management Systems and Green Supply Chain Management: Complements for Sustainability?', *Business Strategy and Environment*, No. 15, 2006.

Dale, BG (2007), *Managing Quality*, Prentice Hall, New York

Dawson, C. (2000), 'Managing the Project Life Cycle', Chapter 23 in *Handbook of Project Management*, Gower, Gower, Farnham, Surrey, 2004

De Meyer, A. and Ferdows, K. (1990), *Removing the Barriers in Manufacturing*, INSEAD, Fontainebleau, France.

Durlacher Research Ltd (1999), *Business to Business e-Commerce*, Durlacher Research Ltd, London

Easton, G.S and Jarrell, S.L (1998), 'The Effects of Total Quality Management on Corporate Performance: An Empirical Investigation. *Journal of Business*, Vol 71, No. 2, pp. 253–307.

FAO (2022), 'The State of Food Security and Nutrition in the World 2021', *Food and Agricultural Organisation of United Nations, Rome*

FDA (2004), '*Combating Counterfeiting Drugs*', Food and Drug Administration, Maryland, USA, February 2004

Fearon, H.E. and Bales, W.A. (1995), *Purchasing of Nontraditional Goods and Services*, Centre for Advanced Purchasing Studies, Tempe, AZ

Fisher, M.L. (1997), 'What Is the Right Supply Chain for Your Product?' *Harvard Business Review*, March-April, pp. 105–116.

Fisher, M.L., Raman, A., and McClelland, A.S. (2000), 'Rocket Science Retailing is Almost Here, Are You Ready?' *Harvard Business Review*, July–August 2000, pp. 115–124

Fitzgerald, M., Kruschwitz, N., Bonnet, D. and Welch, M. (2013), 'Embracing Digital Technology: A New Strategic Imperative', *MIT Sloan Management Review*, October 2013

Food and Agriculture Organization (2002), '*The State of Food and Agriculture*', FAO Information Division, Rome

Ford, D., Gadde, L-E., Hakansson, H., and Snehota, I. (2003), *Managing Business Relationships*, John Wiley & Sons

Foster, C., and Frieden, J. (2017), 'Europeans Have Lost Faith in Their Governments and Institutions. Why? We Did the Research.' *The Washington Post* [Washington, DC], 22 Sept. 2017, Politics sec.

Gack, G. (2006), *How does Six Sigma relate to the Project Management Body of Knowledge (PMBoK)?* http://software.isixsigma.com retrieved 30 November, 2006

Gartner (2021), '*Innovation Insight for Cloud-Native Application Protection Platforms*' *Gartner Report (by Neil MacDonald and Charlie Winckless), August 25, 2021*, Gartner Corporation, Stamford

Garvin, D. (1988), *Managing Quality: The Strategic and Competitive Edge*, Free Press

Gasos and Thorben (2003)

Gerstner, L. (2002), *Who Says Elephants Can't Dance?: Leading a Great Enterprise through Dramatic Change*, Collins

Getz, D. (2005), *Event Management and Event Tourism*, Cognizant Communication Corporation

Goldratt, E.M. (1999), *The Theory of Constraints*, North River Press

Goldratt, E.M. (1992), *The Goal*, North River Press

Gravin, D (1984), 'What Does Product Quality Really Mean?', *Sloan Management Review*, 25(2)

Grocery Manufacturers of America (2002), *CPFR Baseline Study – Manufacturer Profile*, GMA Report, Washington DC

Grönroos, C. (2000), *Service Management and Marketing, A Customer Relationship Management Approach*, Wiley, New York

The Guardian (2021), *Brexit One Year on: So How's It Going*, 25 December 2021

Gummesson, E. (2001), *Total Relationship Marketing*, Butterworth Heinemann, Oxford

Hamel, G. and Prahalad, E.K. (1994), 'Competing for the Future', *Harvard Business Review*, Jul–Aug, 72, No. 4.

Hammer, M. and Champy, J. (1993), *Reengineering the Corporation*. Harper Collins.

Harris, J. (2022), 'It's been Devastating', *The Guardian*, 3 August, 2022

Hartman (1991), *Implementing the Balanced Scorecard*, Harvard Business School Publishing, Boston (2000)

Hayes, R.H. and Wheelwright, S.C. (1985), *Restoring our Competitive Edge- Competing Through Manufacturing*, John Wiley and Sons, New York

Helleiner, E (2021). 'The Diversity of Economic Nationalism', *New Political Economy*, Vol.26, No.2, pp. 229–238

Howard, T., Hitchcock, L. and Dumarest, L. (2000), *Grading the Corporate Report Card Executive Agenda*, Vol.3, No.1, AT Kearney, Chicago

Hughes, J., Ralf, M. and Michels, W. (1998), *Transform Your Supply Chain: Releasing Value in Business*, Thompson Business Press, London.

Hutchins, J.M. and Sutherland, J.W. (2008), 'An Exploration of the Measures of Social Sustainability and Their Application in Supply Chain Decisions', *Journal of Cleaner Production*, Vol. 16, pp. 1688–1698

IBM Global Services (April 2004), IBM Corporation, Somers

IBM Global Services (2006), *Business Impact of Outsourcing: A Fact-based Analysis*, IBM Corporation, Somers

Industrial Marketing and Purchasing Group (2007), www.impgroup.org

International Monetary Fund (2005), *World Economic Outlook*, April 2015

Jones, D.T. and Clarke, P. (2002), 'Creating a customer driven supply chain', *ECR Journal*, Vol.2, No.2, pp. 1–11. 2002

Kaplan, R.S. and Norton, D.P. (1996), *Balanced Scorecard*, Harvard Business School Press, Boston

Kaplan, R.S. and Norton, D.P. (2000), 'Putting Balanced Scorecard to Work', *Harvard Business Review*, September-October, 2000

Karlof, B and Ostblom, S (1994), *Benchmarking: A Signpost to Excellence and Productivity*, J Wiley & Sons, Chichester, UK

Kilpatrick, J. (2022), 'Supply Chain Implications of the Russia-Ukraine Conflict', *Deloitte Insight*, March 2022.

Khanna, T. and Palepu, K.G., (2006), 'Emerging Giants: Building World-Class Companies in Developing Countries', *Harvard Business Review*, October 2006

Knowledge Storm (2006), www.knowlwdgestorm.com, retrieved July 2006

King, P.L. (2011), 'Crack the Code', *APICS*, Vol. 20, No.4, pp. 33–36

Kouvelis, F and Niederhoff (2007), *On the Globalisation and Operations and Supply Chain Strategies*, Soringer, New York.

Kulkarni, P. (2005), *The Marine Seafood Export Supply Chain in India*

Kulkarni, S (2001), *Beyond the Bricks – Organisations Look to Create Extended Supply Chains over the Internet*, White Paper, Wipro Technologies, India

Kouvelis, P. and Resenblatt, M.J. (2001), *A Mathematical Programming Model to Global Supply Chain Management: Conceptual Approach and Managerial Insights*, Washington University, St Louis

IMP (2007), *Industrial Marketing and Purchasing Group, About IMP*, www.impgroup.org

International Institute of Sustainable Development, Canada, December 2005

Kupila, M. (2003), 'Putting the Human Back in Humanitarian', International meeting in Good Humanitarian Donorship. Stockholm, June 2003

Lang, T. (2003), Battle of the Food Change Guardian Unlimited, www.guardian.co.uk/food/focus/story, retrieved June 2006

Lieberthal, K. and Lieberthal, G. (2003), 'The Great Transition', *Harvard Business Review*, October 2003

Liker, J (2004), *The Toyota Way*, McGraw Hill, New York

Ling, R.C. and Goddard, W.E. (1988), *Orchestrating Success*, J Wiley & Sons, New York

Logistics Today, Cleveland, 8 September 2006

Lombard, A.J. (2015), *Supply Chain Management Support by Implementing an Effective MRPII System*, unpublished MBA Dissertation, Henley Business School, UK

Lukka, A and Viskari, K. (2004), Proceedings Supply Chain World Conference, Chicago

Lynch, R.L and Cross K.F. (1991), '*Measure Up!: Yardsticks for Continuous Improvement*' Blackwell Publishers, NJ, USA

Lyson, K. and Farrington, B. (2006), '*Purchasing and Supply Chain Management*' Financial Times/Prentice Hall

Mao, H. and Gorg, H. (2020), 'Friends Like this: The Impact of the US–China Trade War on Global Value Chains', *The World Economy*, Vol.43, No.7, pp. 1776–1791.

MCA (2002), *Strategic Outsourcing*, Management Consultants Association, London

McDonalds India (2007), www.Mcdonaldsindia.com retrieved April 2007

Melnyk, S.A., and Swink, M. (2002), '*Supply Chain Structure and Strategy*', McGraw-Hill, Irwin.

Meredith, JR and Mantel, SJ (2003), *Project Management*, J Wiley & Sons, New York

MGI (2017), *Artificial Intelligence: The Next Digital Frontier?*, McKinsey Global Institute, University of Pennsylvania, Philadelphia, USA

Minnesota Pollution Control (2007), www.pca.state.mn.us

Mitchell, V.W. (1998), 'Buy-phase and buy-class Effects on Organisational Risk Perception and Reduction in Purchasing Professional Services', *Journal of Business & Industrial Marketing*, Vol.13, No.6, pp. 461

Morgan, C. (2004), 'Structure, speed and salience: performance measurement in the supply chain', *Business process Management Journal*, Vol.10, No.5, pp. 522–36

NASSCOM (2016), India Leadership Forum, Hotel Grand Hyatt, Mumbai, 10–12 February, 2016

National Retail Federation USA (2010), *National 2010Retail Security Survey*, Washington, DC.

Naylor, J.B, Mohamed M. N and Berry, D. (1999), 'Leagility: Integrating the Lean and Agile Manufacturing Paradigms in the Total Supply Chain', *International Journal of Production Economics*, Vol. 62, No. 1, pp. 101–118.

Negroponte, N. (1995), *Being Digital*, Random House, New York

New, C.C. and Mayer, A. (1986), *Managing Manufacturing Operations in the UK*. British Institute of Management.

The New York Times (2012), 'Ikea Admits Forced Labor Was Used in 1980s', *The New York Times*, November 16, 2012

Nichols, M. and Jones, S. (2010), 'Genesis of Project Personality', Major Projects Association 28th Annual Conference, Bucks, UK, 23–24 September 2010

NHS Purchasing and Supply Agency (2004), *The Agency's Role in Delivering eProcurement in the NHS*, February 2004, pages 2–4.

Nishi, D (2006), *Finding the Needle in the Haystack*, Chain Store Age, New York

Norton, D.P. (1999), 'The Balanced Scorecard: Translating Strategy into Action' in Proceedings Institute for International Resource, Auckland New Zealand, also see www.bscol.com. "The Balanced Scorecard Collaborative".

O'Brien, W. (2001), 'Enabling Technologies for Project Supply Chain Collaboration', in NSF/ICIS Infrastructure and Information Technology Workshop, Arlington, VA, June 2001

O'Toole and Mikolaitis (2002), *Corporate Event Project Management*, Wiley, New York

Oakland, J.S. (1992), *Total Quality Management*, Butterworth-Heinemann, Oxford

Ohno, T. (1998), *Toyota Production System: Beyond Large Scale Production*, Productivity Press, Cambridge

Oliver, M. (2006), '*Applying Commercial Supply Chain Management Techniques to Humanitarian Organisations*' MBA Dissertation, Henley Management College

Oliver Wight (2007), www.oliverwight.com

Orwell, G. (2018), '*Notes on Nationalism*', Penguin Modern, London. (the first issue was published in the British magazine *Polemic* in October 1945)

Parasuraman, A., Zeithamel, V., and Berry, L. (1985). 'A Conceptual Model of Service Quality', *Journal of Marketing*, Vol.49, No.Fall, pp. 41–50.

Pearce, I. (1992), 'Thinking Green', *Environmental Management and Health*, Vol.3, No.2, pp. 6–12

Pharro, R. (2000), 'Processes and Procedures', Chapter 6 in *Handbook of Project Management*, Gower, 2004

Pinch, L. (2005), 'Lean Construction', *Construction Executive*, November 2005

Plunkett, J.W. (2007), '*Plunkett's Retail Industry Almanac 2008*', books.google.co.uk

Project Management Institute (PMI), *Body of Knowledge* (2008)

Porter, M.E. (1985), *Competitive Strategy*, Free Press, New York

PRINCE2 (2009), Office of Government Commerce, London

Pryke, S. and Smyth, H. (2006), '*The Management of Complex Projects: A Relationship Approach*', Blackwell Publishing, Blackwell, NJ, USA.

Purchasing Management Association of Canada, Toronto, Ontario M5G1Z3

PwC (2013), *Global Supply Chain Survey*, Price Waterhouse Coopers Report, London

Raji, I.O and Rossi, T (2019), 'Exploring Industry 4.0 technologies as drivers of Lean and Agile Supply Chain Strategies', *Proceedings of the International Conference on Industrial Engineering and Operations Management*, Toronto, October 23-25, 2019.

Reid, R.D and Sanders, N.R (2002), 'Operations Management' *John Wiley and Sons Retail e-Business*, April 2001.

Royston, M.G. (1979), *Pollution Prevention Pays'*, Pergamon Press, Pergamon, Oxford

Saha, M., and Darnton, G.,(2005), Green Companies or Green Con-panies?, *Business and Society Review*, June 2005

Sayle, A.J. (1991), Meeting ISO 9000 in a TQM World, AJSL, UK.

Schonberger, R (2003), *World Class Manufacturing*, Free Press, Cambridge.

Schmenner, R.W. (1993), '*Operations Management*', New York, McMillan.

Scott, C., and Westbrook, R. (1991), 'New Strategic Tools for Supply Chain Management', *International Journal of Physical Distribution & Logistics Management*, Feb 1991 Vol.21, No.1

Scottish Enterprise: Glasgow (2006)

Senge, P (1990), *The Fifth Discipline: The Art and Practice of the Learning Organisation*, Century, London

SGS Maine Pointe (2022), *Five Ways 3D Printing Will Have a Massive Impact on the Supply Chain and Drive Competitive Advantage*, www.mainepointe.com, retrieved August 2022

Shingo, S. (1988), *A Revolution in Manufacturing, The SMED System*. Productivity Press, New York.

Shirose, K. (1992), *TPM for Workshop Leaders*, Productivity Press

Silver, J.R. (2004), *Professional Event Co-ordination*, John Wiley and Sons, Chichester

Simchi-Levi, D. Kaminsky, P. and Simchi-Levi, E. (2003), *Designing and Managing the Supply Chain*, 2nd ed., London, McGraw-Hill.

Skinner, B.F. (1969), *Contingencies of Re-inforcement*, Century-Crofts, Appleton

Skinner, S. (2001), *Mastering a Basic Tenet of Lean Manufacturing – Five S*, Manufacturing News, USA, 8(11), June

Slack, N. and Lewis, M. (2002), *Operations Strategy*, Financial Times/Prentice Hall, London

Slack, N., Chambers, S., Johnston, R., and Betts, A. (2012), *Operations and Process Management*, FT Prentice Hall, London.

Slone, R.E. (2004), 'Leading a Supply Chain Turnaround', *Harvard Business Review*, October 2004

Smith, J. (2001), *Benchmark for Extranet and Online Communities*, Benton Foundation, Washington, DC

Smyth, H. (2004), 'Competencies for Improving Construction Performance Theories and Practice for Developing Capacity', *Journal of International Construction Management*, April, 2004.

Statistica (2015), www.statista.com/statistics/189788/global-outsourcing-market-size/ [accessed June, 2022]

Statistica (2022), 'Covid-19 Deaths Worldwide as of May 9, 2022, by Country', Statistica Inc., New York

Statistica (2022b), 'United Kingdom: Distribution of the Workforce Across Economic Sectors from 2009 to 2019', Published by Statistica, February 2022

Sterman, J.D., Keating, E.K., Olivia, R., Repenning, N.P., and Rockart, S. (1999), 'Overcoming the Improvement Paradox', *European Management Journal*, Vol.17, No.2, pp. 120–134.

Stern, N. (2006), *Stern Review: The Economics of Climate Change*, HM Treasury, 2006, ISBN-10: 0521700809.

Stratford, D. and Tiura, D. (2003), 'Keeping the Savings You Thought You Were Getting in Services Sourcing', in 88th Annual International Supply Management Conference Proceedings, The Institute for Supply Management, Tempe, AZ, 2003

Supply Chain Council (2007), www.supply-chain.org/

Supply Chain Planning UK Ltd (2007), www.scp-uk.co.uk

Simci-Levi, D, Kaminsky, P and Simchi-Levi, P, (2003), *Designing and Managing the Supply Chain*, McGraw-Hill, London

Suri, R. (1998), 'Quick Response Manufacturing: A Companywide Approach to Reducing Lead Times' *Productivity Press*, New York

Sutton, J. (2004), '*The Auto-component Supply Chain in China and India: A Benchmark Study*', The Toyota Centre, London School of Economics and Political Science, February 2004

Swank, C.K. (2003), 'The Lean Service Machine', *Harvard Business Review*, October 2003, pp. 123–129.

Taichi Ohno (1988), 'The Toyota Production System: Beyond Large Scale Production', *Productivity Press*.

Taiichi Ohno (1973), *Toyota Style Production System*. Toyota Education Department, Japan

Taiichi, O. (1988), *Toyota Production System*. Productivity Press.

Taylor, D. (1997), '*Global Cases in Logistics and Supply Chain Management*' Thomson Learning, London

Taylor, F.W. (1947), *The Principles of Scientific Management*. Harper & Brothers

The Guardian (2006), Too Much Packaging? Dump it at Checkout, *The Guardian*, 14 November 2006

The Institute for Supply Management (2004)

The Purchasing Management Association of Canada (2007), 'Code of Values and Ethics', *Times of India*, Sept. 6, 2006 'The Dream''

Treacy, M. and Weisma, F. (1993), 'Customer Intimacy and Other Value Discipline', *Harvard Business Review*, January-February 1993

Tum, J., Norton, P. and Wright, J.N. (2005), '*Management of Events Operations*' Elsevier, Oxford.

Turner, R., ed. (1995), *The Commercial Project Manager*, McGraw Hill

Turner, R. (1999), *The Handbook of Project Based Management*, McGraw-Hill, London

Turner, R. (2000), *Projects and Project Management*, Chapter 4 in *Handbook of Project Management*, Gower, 2004

UK Government Office of Science (2014), *The Internet of Things: Making the Most of the Second Industrial Revolution*, Crown Publications, London.

UKICE (2022), 'Post-Brexit Imports, Supply Chains, and the Effect on Consumer Prices', *UK in a Changing Europe (UKICE)*, 27 April, 2022, Kings College, London

UNCTAD (2020), 'Covid-19 and E-commerce', United Nations Conference on Trade and Commerce, Geneva

Unilever (1994), 'Leading Manufacturing Practices', *Unilever Research & Engineering Division*, Brazil Unilever

Unilever (2004), *Unilever Tangos to Sinfonia in Latin America*, Application Development Trend Articles

Unilever Research (2000), *100 Years of Innovation: The Story of Unilever Research Port Sunlight*, URL Port Sunlight, UK.

US Environmental Protection Agency (2000), *Lean and Green Supply Chain*, EPA 742-R-00-001, January 2000

US EPA (2019), '*Global Greenhouse Emission Data*', United States Environment Protection Agency, Washington, DC

Wade, S.D. (2003), Managing Your "Services Spend" in *Today's Services Waking up to the Retail · Revolution, The Times of India*, 2006, September 6, p. 3.

Walker and Guest (1952), *The Man on the Assembly Line.*

Wallace, TE (1990), *MRPII: Making It Happen*, J Wiley & Sons, Chichester, UK

Waller, D.L. (2002), *Operation Management: A Supply Chain Approach*, Thomson, 2002

Waller, M. (2005), 'Hurricane Katrina Showed Importance of Logistics and Supply Chain Management', *Supply & Demand Chain Executive*, October 10, 2005.

Walmart (2015), Walmart Logistics, retrieved December 2015, www.corporate.walmart.com/our-story/our-business

Walton, S., Handfield, R. and Melnyk, S. (1998), The Green Supply Chain: Integrating Suppliers and Environmental Management Process, *The International Journal of Supply Chain Management*, Vol.34, pp. 22, 1998

Watanabe, Katsuaki (2006), Reuters, Aug 3, 2006.

Wheelwright, S.C., and Hayes, R.H. (1985), *Restoring our Competitive Edge- Competing Through Manufacturing*, John Wiley and Sons

Wieland, A. and Wallenburg, C.M. (2012), 'Dealing with Supply Chain Risks: Linking Risk Management Practices and Strategies to Performance', *International Journal of Physical Distribution and Logistics Management*, Vol.42, No.10, pp. 887–905

Wild, R. (2003), *Operations Management*, Thomson, London

Williams, R. (2014), 'How Supply Chains Have Become a Global Battleground', *The Guardian*, 20 May, 2014

World Bank (2022), '*War in the Region*', Office of the Chief Economist, World Bank, Washington, DC

Womack, J. and Jones, D. (2003), *Lean Thinking*, Touchstone Books, London

Womack, J. and Jones, D. (1998), *Lean Thinking*, Touchstone Books, London

Womack, J., Jones, D., and Roos, D (1990), *The Machine That Changed The World*, Rawson and Associates, New York.

World Bank (2022). *World Development Report 2022*, World Bank, Washington, DC.

Worthen, B. (2005), 'Supply Chain: How Wal-Mart Beat Feds to New Orleans'*CIO Magazine*, November 1, 2005

Wright, J Nevan and Race, P. (2004), '*The Management of Service Operations*' Thomson Learning, London

Wright, J. Nevan (1999), *The Management of Service Operations*, Cassell, London

Wright, J. Nevan (2012), *Operation and Supply Chain Service*, Victoria Cengage Learning, Melbourne

Wurtzel, M. (2016). 'Reasons for Six Sigma deployment failures', www.bpminstitute, retrieved March 2016

Yusuf, Y.Y., Gunasekaran, A., Adeleye, E.O., and Sivayoganathan, K (2003), 'Agile supply chain capabilities: Determinants of competitive objectives', *European Journal of Operational Research*, Vol. 159, No.2, pp. 379–392.

Zeng, M. and Williamson, P.J. (2007). 'The Hidden Dragon', *Harvard Business Review*, March, 31 2007.

Xu, Z., Elomri, A., Kerbache, L. and El Omri, A. (2020). 'Impacts of COVID-19 on global supply chains: Facts and perspectives', *IEEE Engineering Management Review*, vol. 48, no. 3, pp. 153–166

www.covisint.com, retrieved October 2007

www.consumerreports.org, retrieved January 2016

www,yStats.com, Research Report 8 March 2016, retrieved April, 2016

www.aerospace-technology.com/projects, retrieved 10 December, 2006

www.bechtel.com (2006), retrieved November, 2006

www.EffectiveInventory.com, retrieved November, 2006

www.mcdonaldindia.com, retrieved October 2007

www.chinatechnews.com, retrieved April 2007

www.bms.com, retrieved November 2006

www.hermesabrasives.com

www.Supplychainopz.com

www.TradeGecko.com

www.envirowise.gov.uk

www.erm.com, accessed 20 March 2016

www.morrisandspottiswood.co.uk

www.bechtel.com, retrieved April 2016

www.apm.org.uk

www.minkiesdeli.co.uk, accessed 25 November 2015

www.bbc.co.uk/news/business-34324772

www.globalsupplychaininstitue.utk.edu, retrieved March 2016

www.bpminstitute, retrieved March 2016

www.capgemini.com/resources/global_sales_and_operation_planning

Appendix 1

Bullwhip effect supply chain game

Background

A national foods company in the UK has three focused factories. One in Dundee, producing preservatives, one in Leeds, producing individually bagged potato crisps, and one in Birmingham making chocolate biscuits. The company has a limited variety of products, but a high volume of sales throughout the UK. The distribution network consists of three regional distribution centres (RDCs) based in Carlisle, Leister and Bristol, and also 22 local warehouses distributed evenly throughout the county. The flow of the supply chain comprises customer to retailers (supermarkets), to local warehouses, to RDCs and then to factories, depending on the product. Cycle one starts with a customer order, and opening and closing stocks for each supplier are 100 units each. In cycles two, three, four, five and six, the customer places an order with 105 units in each cycle.

Rules

You are invited to take part in the six cycles of order supply from the factory to the customers, with the following assumptions:

1. The Closing Stock of cycle one is the Opening Stock of cycle two, as the Closing Stock of cycle two is the Opening Stock of cycle three and so on.
2. The quantity of an incoming order to a supplier equals the Closing Stock of that supplier (a supplier being retailer, warehouse, RDC and factory).
3. Order out equals twice the Closing Stock minus the Opening Stock of that particular supplier.
4. A customer will place an order and each subsequent supplier will determine the Opening Stock, Closing Stock and Replenishment Order for the next stage.

You will be provided with cards for placing orders and keeping stocks at each stage.
  Let's play!

Locations of factories and RDCs

Appendix 2

Supply chain game results

	Customer	Retailer		Local warehouse		RDC		Factory	
	Demand	Order	Stock	Order	Stock	Order	Stock	Order	Stock
Cycle 1	100	100	O 100	100	O 100	100	O 100	100	O 100
			C 100		C 100		C 100		C 100
Cycle 2	105	110	O 100	120	O 100	140	O 100	180	O 100
			C 105		C 110		C 120		C 140
Cycle 3	105	105	O 105	100	O 110	80	O 120	20	O 140
			C 105		C 105		C 100		C 80
Cycle 4	105	105	O 105	105	O 105	110	O 100	140	O 80
			C 105		C 105		C 105		C 110
Cycle 5	105	105	O 105	105	O 105	105	O 105	100	O 110
			C 105		C 105		C 105		C 105
Cycle 6	105	105	O 105	105	O 105	105	O 105	105	O 105
			C 105		C 105		C 105		C 105

Note: O, opening; C, closing.

Appendix 3
ASK 2.0

The Advanced Self-assessment Kit (ASK) 2.0 interactive software provides a truly practical way of assessing, monitoring and improving business performance. This invaluable and user-friendly tool can be used by managers, in both manufacturing and service sectors, for regular business assessment and also by individuals of class-based groups as part of regular training.

The software contains guidelines for scoring each of the 200 questions of 20 foundation stones supporting six pillars.

Total Business Solutions
- Pillars and Foundation Stones

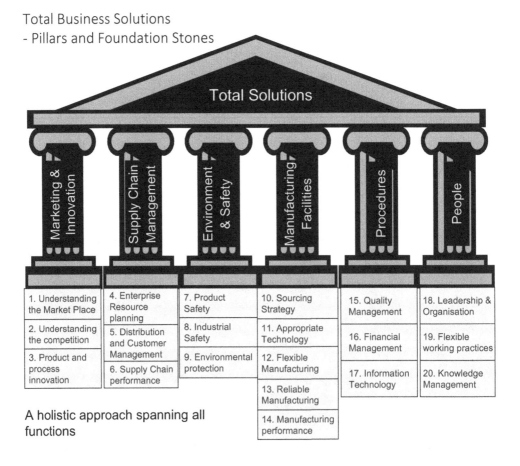

1. Understanding the Market Place	4. Enterprise Resource planning	7. Product Safety	10. Sourcing Strategy	15. Quality Management	18. Leadership & Organisation
2. Understanding the competition	5. Distribution and Customer Management	8. Industrial Safety	11. Appropriate Technology	16. Financial Management	19. Flexible working practices
3. Product and process innovation	6. Supply Chain performance	9. Environmental protection	12. Flexible Manufacturing	17. Information Technology	20. Knowledge Management
			13. Reliable Manufacturing		
			14. Manufacturing performance		

A holistic approach spanning all functions

Assessments are scored and a series of visual graphs are used to identify positioning in comparison with the ideal and previous assessments. The user can vary the setting of target scores and/or weighting of each of the 20 foundation stones as appropriate. An advanced version of the software enables the user to change or align questions to company requirements.

The ASK 2.0 software (CD + manual) for all versions of Windows is available at £149.00 from Performance Excellence Ltd (basurn@aol.com).

Appendix 4

Glossary

3D printing (also known as additive manufacturing) is the construction of a three-dimensional object or a prototype from a CAD model or a digital 3D model.

Activity network diagram is a network analysis technique to allow a team to find the most efficient path and realistic schedule of a project by graphically showing the completion time and sequence of each task.

Additive manufacturing. See 3D printing.

AI. Artificial intelligence demonstrated by technology as opposed to natural intelligence displayed by living creatures.

Balanced scorecard. Introduced by R Kaplan and D Norton in the early 1990s, a balanced scorecard is a concept for measuring a company's activities in terms of its vision and strategies to give managers a comprehensive view of the performance of a business. Typically, it comprises simple tables broken into four sections of 'perspectives' labelled 'financial', 'customer', 'internal business processes' and 'learning and growth'.

Bar chart. A bar chart, also known as a Gantt chart, indicates scheduling activities. Horizontal bars show the various activities with the length of the bar proportional to the duration of a particular activity.

Benchmarking is rating an organisation's products, processes and performances with other organisations in the same or another business. The objective is to identify the gaps with competitors and the areas for improvement.

Best practice. Best practice refers to any organisation that performs as well or better than the competition in quality, timeliness, flexibility and innovation. Best practice should lead to world-class performance.

Big data analytics. Big data analytics involve complex applications with predictive models and what-if analysis by analytics systems.

Black belts are experts in Six Sigma methods and tools. Tools include statistical analysis. Black belts are project leaders for Six Sigma initiatives and they also train other staff members in Six Sigma techniques.

Blockchain. It is a type of database of information structured in a table format to allow for easier searching for specific information.

BPR. Business process re-engineering has been described as a manifesto for revolution. The approach is similar to taking a clean piece of paper and starting all over by identifying what is really needed to make the mission of the organisation happen.

Brainstorming. A free-wheeling group session for generating ideas. Typically, a group meeting of about seven people will be presented with a problem. Each member will be encouraged to make suggestions without fear of criticism. One suggestion will lead to another. All suggestions, no matter how seemingly fanciful, are recorded and subsequently analysed.

Brexit. **(Britain exit)** was the withdrawal of the United Kingdom from the European Union on 31 January 2020. The UK is the only sovereign country to have left the EU.

Capacity planning. Capacity planning specifies the level of resources (e.g. facilities, fleets, equipment, systems hardware and labour force size) that best supports the enterprise's competitive strategy for production.

Carbon footprint. A carbon footprint is the total set of greenhouse gas (GHG) emissions caused by an organisation, event or product. For simplicity of reporting, it is often expressed in terms of the amount of carbon dioxide, or its equivalent of other GHGs, emitted. A carbon footprint can be measured by undertaking a GHG emissions assessment of an individual, organisation or country.

Carbon offset is the process of reducing the net carbon emissions of an individual or organisation, either by their own actions or through arrangements with a carbon-offset provider.

Cause and effect diagram. The cause and effect, fishbone or Ishikawa diagram was developed by Kaoru Ishikawa. The premise is that generally when a problem occurs the effect is very obvious and the temptation is to treat the effect. With the Ishikawa approach, the causes of the effect are sought. Once the cause is known and eliminated, the effect will not be seen again.

CIM. Computer-integrated manufacturing.

Circular economy. It aims for a world without waste by recycling and reusing. It is also an important tenet of Green Six Sigma.

Cloud computing. On-demand availability of computer system resources, especially data storage and computing power.

CMMI. Capability maturity model integration (CMMI) is a process improvement approach that provides organisations with the essential elements of effective processes. It was developed by the SEI (Software Engineering Institute) at Carnegie Mellon University in Pittsburgh.

Collaborative planning forecasting and replenishment (CPFR). Data and process model standards are developed for collaboration between suppliers and an enterprise with proscribed methods for planning (agreement between the trading partners to conduct business in a certain way), forecasting (agreed-to methods, technology and timing for sales, promotions and order forecasting) and replenishment (order generation and order fulfilment).

Continuous improvement is always looking for ways to improve a process or a product, but not necessarily making radical step changes. If the basic idea is sound, then building on it will improve quality. In Japan, this is known as Kaizen.

COPQ. The cost of poor quality (COPQ) is made up of costs arising from internal failures, external failures, appraisal, prevention and lost opportunity costs. In other words, all the costs that arise from non-conformance to a standard. Chapter 3 discusses COPQ in some detail.

Corporate governance is the system of rules and processes by which a business is directed and controlled.

Corporate social responsibility is a form of business self-regulation by engaging in or supporting ethically oriented business practices.

CRM. Customer relationship management (CRM) is the development of the database and strategies necessary to have the maximum client relationships in terms of quality, cost, reliability and responsiveness.

CRP. Capacity requirement planning (CRP) is a computerised technique to predict resource requirements of all available workstations (also see RCCP). RCCP balances workloads at a high level, and CRP will then fine-tune the workload balance.

CTQs. In Six Sigma, CTQs are referred to as critical to quality. This simply means the identification of factors that are critical for the achievement of a level of quality.

Cycle time is the elapsed time between two successive operations or the time required to complete an operation.

Demand forecast. The prediction, projection or estimation of expected demand over a specified future time period.

Distribution channels. The selling channels are supported by an enterprise. These may include retail sales, distribution partner (e.g. wholesale) sales, original equipment manufacturer (OEM) sales, Internet exchange or marketplace sales and Internet auction or reverse auction sales.

Distribution requirements planning (DRP). Process for determining inventory requirements in a multiple plant/warehouse environment. DRP may be used for both distribution and manufacturing. In manufacturing, DRP will work directly with MRP. DRP may also be defined as distribution resource planning, which also includes determining labour, equipment and warehouse space requirements.

DMAIC is the cycle of define, measure, analyse, improve and control, see Chapter Nine for detailed discussion.

E-business. Electronic-business is more than the transfer of information using information technology. E-business is the complex mix of processes, applications and organisational structures.

EDI. Electronic data exchange.

EFQM. The European Foundation for Quality Management is derived from the American Malcolm Baldridge Quality award. It is an award for organisations that achieve world-class performance as judged by independent auditors against a checklist. The checklist is detailed and extensive and covers leadership, people management, policy and strategy, partnerships and resource, processes, people satisfaction, customer satisfaction., impact on society and business results.

Enterprise Resource Planning (ERP) is the extension of MRPII systems to the management of complete business functions including finance and human resources.

EU. European Union

Fishbone diagram. See Cause and effect diagram.

FIT SIGMA, also see TQM, Six Sigma and Lean Sigma. Fit Sigma incorporates all the advantages and tools of TQM, Six Sigma and Lean Sigma. The aim is to get an organisation healthy (fit) by using appropriate tools for the size and nature of the business (fitness for purpose) and to sustain a level of fitness. Fit Sigma is a holistic approach.

Flow process chart. A flow process chart sets out the sequence of the flow of a product or a procedure by recording all the activities in a process. The chart can be used to identify steps in the process, value-adding activities and non-value-adding activities.

Forecasting process. A forecasting process provides a mechanism for soliciting participation from individuals who have knowledge of future events and compiling it into a consistent format to develop a forecast. The forecasting process concentrates on defining how information will be gathered and reconciled into a consistent picture of the future. In cases where a statistical forecast is used, the process will also define how much weight should be given to the mathematical models versus input from participants to develop the final consensus forecast.

Gantt chart,   see Bar chart.

Globalisation   is the process of integration among people, organisations and governments. It has shaped the world over the past 50 or so years, from the revolution in information technology and logistics and trade deals to diminishing national and geopolitical boundaries.

Green belts   are staff trained to be Six Sigma project leaders, they work under the guidance of black belts (see black belts).

Greening the supply chain   refers to buyer companies requiring a certain level of environmental responsibility in core business practices of their suppliers and vendors.

Green Six Sigma   is an adaptation of Six Sigma for climate change initiatives. One key feature of Green Six Sigma is the extension of DMAIC to DMAICS where S contains tools and processes for sustainability.

Industry 4.0   relates to the fourth industrial revolution. It conceptualises rapid change to technology, industries and processes in the 21st century primarily due to the digital revolution.

Inventory management.   The process of ensuring the availability of products through inventory administration activities such as demand planning, stock optimisation and monitoring the age of the product.

IoT.   The Internet of Things describes a network of physical objects connected by sensors to the Internet.

IPCC.   Intergovernmental Panel on Climate Change is the most effective body of international scientists to monitor climate change activities.

IPMVP.   International Performance Measurement and Verification Protocol.

Input process output (IPO) diagram.   All operations or processes have inputs and outputs. The process is the conversion of inputs into outputs. Analysis of inputs should be made to determine factors that influence the process, for example, input materials from suppliers meeting specifications, delivery on time and so on.

Ishikawa.   See Cause and effect diagram.

ISO 9000.   To gain ISO 9000 accreditation, an organisation has to demonstrate to an accredited auditor that they have a well-documented standard and consistent process in place that achieves a defined level of quality or performance. ISO accreditation will give a customer confidence that the product or service provided will meet certain specified standards of performance and that the product or service will always be consistent with the documented standards.

Just in time (JIT)   was initially a manufacturing approach where materials are ordered to arrive just when required in the process, no output or buffer stocks are held, and the finished product is delivered directly to the customer. Lean Sigma incorporates the principles of JIT and now relates to the supply chain from the supplier and the supplier's supplier through the process to the customer and the customer's customer.

Kaizen.   Kaizen is a Japanese word derived from a philosophy of gradual day-by-day betterment of life and spiritual enlightenment. This approach has been adopted in industry and means gradual and unending improvement in efficiency and/or customer satisfaction. The philosophy is doing little things better so as to achieve a long-term objective.

Kanban.   Kanban is the Japanese word for card. The basic Kanban system is to use cards to trigger movements of materials between operations in production so that a customer order flows through the system. Computer systems eliminate the need for cards, but the principle is the same. As a job flows through the factory, completion of one stage of production triggers the next so that there is no idle time, or queues, between operations. Any one job can be tracked to determine the stage of production. A 'Kanban' is raised for each customer order. The Kanban system enables production to be in batches of one.

Key performance indicators   (KPIs) include measurements of performance such as asset utilisation, customer satisfaction, the cycle time from order to delivery, inventory turnover, operations costs, productivity and financial results (return on assets and return on investment).

Kyoto Protocol.   The Kyoto Protocol was adopted in Kyoto in December 1997 by 192 countries. It extends the 1992 UNFCCC objective to reduce greenhouse gas emissions based on the scientific consensus of global warming.

Lean Sigma.   Also see Just in time (JIT). Lean was initially a manufacturing approach where materials are ordered to arrive just when required in the process, no output or buffer stocks are held, and the finished product is delivered directly to the customer. Lean Sigma incorporates the principles of Six Sigma and is related to the supply chain from supplier and supplier's supplier through the process to the customer and the customer's customer.

Master production schedule.   The master production schedule (also commonly referred to as the MPS) is effectively the plan that the company has developed for production, staffing, inventory and so on. MPS translates your business plan, including forecasted demand, into a production plan using planned orders in a true multi-level optional component scheduling environment. Using MPS helps you avoid shortages, costly expediting, last-minute scheduling and inefficient allocation of resources.

Materials requirement planning (MRP).   MRP is a dependent demand system that calculates materials requirements and production plans to satisfy known and forecast sales orders. MRP helps calculate volume and timing requirements to meet an estimate of future demand. There are three major types of computer-based MRP systems: MRP I, 'Closed loop' MRP and MRP II.

The Monte Carlo technique   is a simulation process. It uses random numbers as an approach to model the waiting times and queue lengths and to examine the overall uncertainty in projects.

MRP (II).   Manufacturing resource planning is an integrated computer-based procedure for dealing with all of the planning and scheduling activities for manufacturing and includes procedures for stock re-order, purchasing, inventory records, cost accounting and plant maintenance.

Mudas.   Muda is the Japanese for waste or non-value adding. The seven activities that are considered are excess production, waiting, conveyance, motion, process, inventory and defects. For further details, see Chapter 1.

Overall equipment effectiveness(OEE)   is the real output of a machine. It is given by the ratio of the good output and the maximum output of the machine for the time it is planned to operate.

Pareto.   Wilfredo Pareto was a 19th-century Italian economist who observed that 80% of the wealth was held by 20% of the population. The same phenomenon can often be found in quality problems. This is also known as the 80/20 rule.

Paris Climate Agreement.   The Paris Climate Agreement (also known as the Paris Accord) is an international treaty on the climate crisis. Its stated aim is to radically reduce global carbon emissions and restrict the rise of the Earth's temperature to less than 2°C. This treaty was signed by all 189 participating countries in Paris in December 2015 at COP 21.

PDCA. The plan-do-check-act cycle was developed by Dr W. E. Deming. It refers to: planning the change and setting standards; doing – making the change happen; checking that what is happening is what was intended (standards are being met); and act – taking action to correct back to the standard.

PESTLE. Political, economic, social, technical, legal and environmental is an analytical tool for assessing the impact of external contexts on a project or a major operation and also the impact of a project on its external contexts. There are several possible contexts.

PMBOK. Project Management Body of Knowledge (PMBOK) is essentially a collection of good project management principles, techniques and guidelines that help to manage projects.

Poka Yoke. Refers to making each step of production mistake-free. This is known as mistake proofing. Poka Yoke was developed by Shingo (also see SMED) and has two main steps, (1) preventing the occurrence of a defect and (2) detecting the defect.

Project. A project is a unique item of work for which there is a financial budget and a defined schedule.

Project charter. A project charter is a working document for defining the terms of reference of each Six Sigma project. The charter can make a successful project by specifying necessary resources and boundaries that will in turn ensure success.

Project management involves the planning, scheduling, budgeting and control of a project using an integrated team of workers and specialists.

Process mapping. Process mapping is a tool to represent a process with a diagram containing a series of linked tasks or activities that produce an output.

PRINCE2. **PR**ojects **IN** **C**ontrolled **E**nvironments is a defined methodology with roles and responsibilities and deliverables. It is the UK's project management methodology.

QFD. Quality function deployment is a systematic approach to determining customer needs and designing the product or service so that it meets the customers' needs first time and every time.

Quality circles. Quality circles are teams of staff who are volunteers. The team selects issues or areas to investigate for improvement. To work properly, teams have to be trained, first in how to work as a team (group dynamics) and then in problem-solving techniques.

Resource utilisation and customer service (RU/CS) analysis is a simple tool to establish the relative importance of the key parameters of both resource utilisation and customer service and identify their conflicts.

Rough cut capacity planning (RCCP). The RCCP process considers only the critical work centres (bottlenecks, highly utilised resources, etc.) and attempts to balance longer-term workloads and demand at a high level.

SCOR. The Supply Chain Operations Reference (SCOR) model is a process reference model that has been developed and endorsed by the Supply Chain Council as the cross-industry standard diagnostic tool for supply chain management.

S&OP. Sales and operations planning is derived from MRP and includes new product planning. Demand planning and supply review provide weekly and daily manufacturing schedules and financial information. Also see MRP(II). San OP is further explained in Chapter 6, see Figure 6.10.

SCM.   Supply chain management.

SIPOC   is a high-level map of a process to view how a company goes about satisfying a particular customer requirement in the overall supply chain. SIPOC stands for supplier, input, process, output and customer.

Single minute exchange of dies (SMED).   This was developed for the Japanese automobile industry by Shigeo Shingo in the 1980s and involves the reduction of changeover of production by intensive work study to determine in-process and out-process activities and then systematically improving the planning, tooling and operations of the changeover process. Shingo believed in looking for simple solutions rather than relying on technology.

Six Sigma.   Six Sigma is a quality system that in effect aims for zero defects. Six Sigma in statistical terms means six deviations from the arithmetic mean. This equates to 99.99966% of the total population or 3.4 defects per million opportunities.

Social sustainability   is about identifying and managing business impacts, both positive and negative, on people.

Strengths, weaknesses, opportunities and threats (SWOT)   is a tool for analysing an organisation's competitive position in relation to its competitors.

Total productive maintenance (TPM)   requires factory management to improve asset utilisation by the systematic study and elimination of major obstacles – known as the 'six big losses' – to efficiency. The 'six big losses' in manufacturing are breakdown, set up and adjustment, minor stoppages, reduced speed, quality defects and start up and shut down.

TPS.   Toyota Production System.

TQM.   Total quality management is not a system – it is a philosophy embracing the total culture of an organisation. TQM goes far beyond conformance to a standard – it requires a culture where every member of the organisation believes that not a single day should go by without the organisation in some way improving its efficiency and/ or improving customer satisfaction.

Value analysis   is very often a practice in purchasing and is the evaluation of the expected performance of a product relative to its price.

Value chain,   also known as Porter's value chain. According to Michael Porter, the competitive advantage of a company can be assessed only by seeing the company as a total system. This 'total system' comprises both primary and secondary activities.

Value stream mapping (VSM)   is a visual illustration of all activities required to bring a product through the main flow, from raw material to the stage of reaching the customer.

Vendor-managed inventory (VMI).   In the VMI process, the vendor assumes responsibility for managing the replenishment of stock. Rather than a customer submitting orders, the vendor will replenish stock as needed. This process is sometimes referred to as supplier-managed inventory (SMI) or co-managed inventory.

World class.   World class is the term used to describe any organisation that is making rapid and continuous improvements in performance and is considered to be using 'best practice' to achieve world-class standards.

Zero defects.   Philip Crosby made this term popular in the late-1970s. The approach is right thing, right time, right place and every time. The assumption is that it is cheaper to do things right the first time.

Index

Printed in the United States
by Baker & Taylor Publisher Services